AGRICULTURAL ECONOMICS

SECOND EDITION

H. Evan Drummond
University of Florida

John W. Goodwin
Oklahoma Panhandle State University

Upper Saddle River, New Jersey 07458

Library of Congress Cataloging-in-Publication Data

Drummond, H. Evan (Harold Evan), 1943-
Agricultural economics/H. Evan Drummond, John W. Goodwin.—2nd ed. p. cm.
Includes bibliographical references and index.
ISBN 0-13-047452-5
1. Agriculture—Economic aspects. 2. Agriculture—Economic aspects—United States. I.
Goodwin, John W. II. Title.
HD1433 .D78 2004
338.1—dc21
2002034571

Editor-in-Chief: Stephen Helba
Executive Editor: Debbie Yarnell
Associate Editor: Kimberly Yehle
Managing Editor: Mary Carnis
Production Editor: Janet Kiefer, Carlisle Publishers Services
Production Liaison: Janice Stangel
Director of Manufacturing and Production: Bruce Johnson
Manufacturing Buyer: Cathleen Petersen
Creative Director: Cheryl Asherman
Cover Design Coordinator: Miguel Ortiz
Marketing Manager: Jimmy Stephens
Cover Design: Marianne Frasco
Cover Image: Photo courtesy of Thomas Wright, used by permission of the Institute of Food and Agricultural Sciences of the University of Florida
Interior Design: Carlisle Communications, Ltd.
Composition: Carlisle Communications, Ltd.
Printing and Binding: Courier Westford

Prentice-Hall International (UK) Limited, *London*
Prentice-Hall of Australia Pty. Limited, *Sydney*
Prentice-Hall Canada Inc., *Toronto*
Prentice-Hall Hispanoamericana, S.A., *Mexico*
Prentice-Hall of India Private Limited, *New Delhi*
Prentice-Hall of Japan, Inc., *Tokyo*
Prentice-Hall Singapore Pte. Ltd.
Editora Prentice-Hall do Brasil, Ltda., *Rio de Janeiro*

The photo on the cover is a cornicopia.

1 0 9 8 7 6 5 4 3 2
ISBN 0-13-047452-5

CONTENTS

CHAPTER 5

Money and Financial Intermediaries 84

CHAPTER 6

Monetary Policy 99

CHAPTER 7

The Circular Flow of Income 115

CHAPTER 8

Fiscal Policy 139

CHAPTER 9

International Trade   160

CHAPTER 10

Agricultural Policy   194

CHAPTER 11

The Firm as a Production Unit   206

CHAPTER 12

Costs and Optimal Output Levels   219

CHAPTER 13

Firm Supply and the Market   250

CHAPTER 14

Imperfect Competition and Government Regulation   258

CHAPTER 15

The Theory of Consumer Behavior   278

CHAPTER 16

The Concept of Elasticity   301

PREFACE

*T*his text is designed for a one-semester (or two-quarter sequence) introductory course in agricultural and environmental economics. Many texts view agricultural economics in a rather narrow context of the profit-maximizing farm business. We prefer a broad view of the food system that emphasizes linkages between and among financial institutions, the macroeconomy, world markets, government programs, farms, agribusinesses, food marketing, and the environment. The objective of this text is to cover many topics lightly rather than any one or two topics in depth. The text is designed to allow a maximum of "skipping around" rather than requiring a strict sequential ordering of the chapters.

Economics is about decision making. It deals with how decisions are made under varied conditions and situations. It also deals with the evaluation or implications of alternative decisions for a given situation. Since decisions are a fact of everyday life, economics is with us in most of what we do. Even monks in a monastery who sell fruitcakes to support their spiritual endeavors make economic decisions when they decide what ingredients to buy and what price to ask for their product.

You, the college student, are surrounded by economic decisions as you pursue academic success at the institution of your choice. Several of the economic decisions you must make will be discussed briefly to introduce you to six economic concepts that will recur throughout this book. These concepts form the foundation of how economists approach decision making.

SUPPLY AND DEMAND

There is probably no better known (and more poorly understood) concept in economics than supply and demand. Supply and demand are the central nervous system of the economic organ: they are the key to price determination. One decision that each college or university student must make is, What am I going to major in? The specific answer to that question depends upon the criterion used by the individual student to make a choice.

A student who bases his or her choice of a major on potential income is certainly into the use of supply and demand. In today's market we all know that computer engineers earn more than high school teachers. Why is that? It is a simple matter of supply and demand in the determination of the price for computer engineers and for high school teachers. In Chapter 3 the basic foundations of supply and demand will be examined in detail.

OPPORTUNITY COST

A second fundamental concept of economics is the concept of opportunity cost. Whenever a resource is employed in one activity, that means it can't be used in another. Something must be given up to do something else. The value of what is forgone is the opportunity cost of doing something else.

A relevant economic question that each college student should ask is, What does it cost for me to attend the university? Most students will think of "costs" as tuition, residence hall fees, meals, and the like. From the economist's point of view, probably the single biggest cost (if you are in a public university) is the opportunity cost of the student's own time. By attending college you are forgoing the income you would earn flipping burgers at the Burger Barn. Full-time pay at minimum wage (which is probably what you would make as a high school graduate) is about $12,000 a year. Therefore, $12,000 is your annual opportunity cost of attending the university.[1]

DIMINISHING RETURNS

A basic concept in economics is that as you add more and more of something while holding everything else constant, the additional benefit from each additional unit eventually begins to decline. That is, the benefits increase at a decreasing rate. This we call diminishing returns.

In the context of the university student this is illustrated by asking a familiar question: How much should I study for the next test? Initially, you might think the answer is "as much as possible," but closer examination will show that after some point the additional benefit associated with each additional hour of study will begin to decline and eventually fall so low that you are probably better off to get some sleep rather than pulling an all-nighter.

Diminishing returns are something we find in all kinds of economic activity. Eating, sleeping, fertilizing house plants, and exercising all exhibit diminishing returns—eventually.

MARGINALITY

The discussion of diminishing returns unwittingly introduced you to the concept of marginality. The margin in economic terms refers to the "next additional" unit. So in the above example, when we spoke of "an additional hour of study," we could equally have said "a marginal hour of study." In most economic analyses it is what happens on the margin that dictates decision making.

A question many postsecondary students ask is, Should I get a 2-year associate's degree or a 4-year bachelor's degree? The economist would evaluate this question by asking what the marginal costs and marginal returns are for the extra 2 years. That is, assume you have the 2-year associate's degree, and then base your

---

[1]One reason so few students pursue a Ph.D. degree is that the opportunity cost of doing so is very high. Ph.D. candidates already have a Master's degree and could easily be earning $20,000 to $40,000 per year for the 3 or 4 years spent studying for the Ph.D. In other words, the opportunity cost of seeking a Ph.D. easily exceeds $100,000. That's quite an investment.

decision on the costs and returns of the additional or marginal 2 years to earn the bachelor's degree.

The economic theory of the firm is based on marginal revenues and marginal costs. The economic theory of the consumer is based on marginal utility and marginal cost. The investment decision of 2 more years of higher education is based on the marginal returns and marginal costs (including opportunity costs) of that investment. In pollution control, the decision about more abatement depends on marginal benefits and marginal costs. In other words, it is safe to say that in economics all the action is on the margin.

COSTS AND RETURNS

As previously illustrated, most of economics deals with the trade-off between costs and returns. Measuring the costs and returns associated with some economic activities can be a little tricky. Identifying the costs associated with most economic activities is usually fairly straightforward once the concept of opportunity cost has been mastered.

The nature of economic returns to an economic activity is a little less cut and dried. We use different terms to refer to returns in different situations, but nonetheless they are all returns. In the theory of the firm we call returns "revenue." In the theory of the consumer we call returns "utility." In investment analysis we call returns "returns." And finally in resource and environmental economics we call returns "benefits." Estimating returns often involves making a number of assumptions about the timing of the returns, the duration of the returns, and the value of the returns.

For example, what is the return to a bachelor's degree? The main return is that a B.S. graduate earns more than a high school graduate. The salary difference between the two at the present time at different age levels is easy to measure. But will those salary differences still be the same when you reach those age levels? If we assume that they will remain the same, then we can easily calculate the lifetime earnings difference attributed to the B.S. degree. But there are probably other important returns to education that can't be measured as easily, such as the pleasure one receives from being a college student, and the networking initiated during the college experience.

What is critical is that we evaluate alternatives by comparing the costs and returns of a marginal decision. That is what economics is all about.

EXTERNALITIES

Finally, economists talk about economic activities in terms of transactions. A typical transaction involves a seller and a buyer making a trade. A college student attending the university to increase his or her earning power is an economic transaction.

Frequently, the parties to a transaction do not bear all the economic costs of that transaction and/or do not receive all the economic returns of that transaction. When that happens, we call the costs not borne or the returns not captured externalities of the transaction.

The economics of attending college is full of externalities. On the cost side, much of the cost of attending is not borne by the student but by state government and/or the university foundation through gifts and grants. On the returns side, society captures some returns because a college graduate will presumably be a better citizen and will be less likely to become a burden on society as a prison inmate. These are benefits society receives from your education that you do not directly capture. Hence they are externalities.

A FINAL WORD

Economics is frequently called "the dismal science." It is our fervent hope that your study of economics and the reading of this book will not be a dismal experience. In fact, we hope it will be an enlightening and enjoyable one. In an effort to keep a potentially ponderous text somewhat light, we occasionally poke fun at one target or another. Rest assured, our intention is to amuse and not to offend. If you feel offended by anything in this text or have any other comments about the text, please drop us an e-mail at *evd@ufl.edu.*

We would like to thank the following reviewers for their valuable input: Joey Mehlhorn, Middle Tennessee State University; C. Matthew Rendleman, Southern Illinois University; and Bryan Schurle, Kansas State University. In addition, we'd also like to thank the reviewers from the first edition: Delmy Calderon-Salin, Texas A&M University-Kingsville; Bert Greenwalt, Arkansas State University; Robert N. Shulstad, University of Georgia; Larry Eichmeier, North Iowa Area Community College; and Kenneth Pippin, Arkansas Technical University.

H. Evan Drummond
John W. Goodwin

The Food Industry

*I*n an earlier time, farmer Brown entered his pig pen and hollered "soo-e" to call his steeds to dinner. On college campuses today a similar call of "pizza" can usually attract an immediate crowd of students. Food is one of the great universals in our lives and one of the things that brings us together. The industrial complex that produces, processes, and distributes that food is one of the largest industries in the world. It is estimated that approximately 23 percent of all jobs in the United States are related to some aspect of the food industry, even though farmers represent only 2 percent of the population. In many developing countries, more than half of the labor force is engaged in agriculture. There can be little doubt that on a global basis the **food industry** is the largest industry in terms of people employed and value of product. In a later chapter we will talk about that industry in the developing world. For now, we will talk about the food industry in the United States and the rest of the developed world.

Food industry all firms, large and small, engaged in the production, processing, and/or distribution of food, fiber, and other agricultural products.

MAJOR SECTORS—AN OVERVIEW

There is a universal myth that Mom (or Grandma) prepares the Thanksgiving feast, and it is a wonderful myth that is sure to endure. The reality is that someone other than Mom produced the feed that was fed to the turkey in Minnesota or North Carolina, and that someone else converted that turkey on the hoof to the Butterball® that Mom bought at the store, and that someone else delivered that turkey to Mom's favorite supermarket in faraway Deming, New Mexico. Each "someone" is part of the food industry that prepared the Thanksgiving feast—Mom (or Grandma) was little more than the final actor on the stage when the curtain came down.

The food industry (other than Mom or Grandma) can be divided into four major sectors: farm service, producers, processors, and marketers. For every $100 spent at the supermarket, the farm service sector accounts for about $13 while the production sector (i.e., farmers) accounts for about $8. The remaining $79 goes to processors of agricultural commodities and the marketing system that brings food to your table.

Farm Service Sector

As shown in Figure 1–1 the **farm service sector** provides the producer with the inputs he or she buys, such as feed, fertilizer, fuel, equipment, and chemicals. Many of the firms in the farm service sector are household names such as John Deere, DuPont, and Monsanto. These are large, multinational corporations with a network of local sales representatives. There are also a variety of small, local service companies in any rural community that serve the diverse needs of local farmers for irrigation equipment, farm structures, and so on.

Farm service sector those firms that produce and distribute the goods and services that farmers (producers) buy as a part of their business activities.

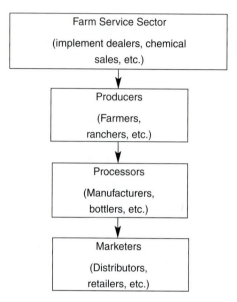

FIGURE 1–1   The Food Industry

The farm service sector is not limited to the sellers of goods. There are also numerous firms that provide farmers with services such as banking, accounting, insurance, legal advice, and agronomic consulting. As farming becomes increasingly complex, farmers are pressed to rely heavily on providers of farm services. It is a fast-growing and highly localized sector of the food industry.

Producers

Producers sector
those firms engaged in the production of raw food, fiber, and other agricultural products.

The **producers sector** includes all of those firms engaged in the biological processes associated with the production of food and fiber. Farmers, ranchers, grove owners, and nursery owners are examples of producers. As shown in Figure 1–1, producers buy from the farm service sector and sell to the processor sector. The unique thing about producers is the link, often a nostalgic link, to the biological processes of producing raw food products. While the link to mother nature is appealing, we will see shortly that most producers are rapidly becoming little more than food factories.

Processors

Processors sector
those firms that convert raw agricultural products into food products in the form that the consumer eventually buys.

The **processors sector** creates value by converting raw agricultural commodities into those products that the consumer wants. Processors change the form of food and create value in the process. Processors can be divided into two groups—the processors of **commodities** (such as flour milling which turns wheat into flour), and the processors of **food products** (such as the bread baker who turns flour into bread). Frequently, one company will engage in both activities, such as Hershey, which processes cocoa beans and manufactures chocolate bars, or ConAgra Foods, which processes soybeans into soybean oil and produces margarine under the Blue Bonnet®, Fleischmann's®, and Parkay® brands. Incidentally, ConAgra Foods also processes turkeys under the Butterball® brand name, and sells soybean oil directly under the Wesson® brand.

Marketers

The **marketers sector** also creates value in the food industry by changing the time and place of food. Wheat is harvested in Kansas in June. The consumer wants a hamburger bun in Rhode Island in December. The distribution system that ties the producer and consumer together is the marketing system. It brings the consumer what she wants, where she wants it, and when she wants it. The absolutely incredible thing about the marketing system is that you can almost always get what you want, when and where you want it. The food marketing system is so effective and efficient that most of us take it for granted. Only when the system is disrupted by a hurricane or a massive snow storm do we remember how flawlessly and easily the food distribution system usually operates.

MAJOR SECTORS—TRENDS AND ISSUES

The food industry, like any other major industry, is in a continuous dynamic of change and adjustment. In the remainder of this chapter we will highlight some of the trends and issues in each sector. The issues and trends in the farm service sector and the processing sector are virtually identical, so we will not specifically deal with the farm service sector.

Producers and Farm Structure

In a Jeffersonian view of the nation, farmers were the bedrock of democracy. In the reality of today, farmers constitute less than 2 percent of the population, and only one-twelfth of the farms really produce the food we eat. Characterizing the attributes of the American farms and farmers is known as the study of **farm structure.** That is, what do farms in the United States look like today?

　　If there is one lesson to be learned from the study of farm structure in the United States, it is that there is no such thing as an "average" farm. As is the case in many situations, averages cover up more than they reveal.

Number of Farms

There are roughly 2 million farms in the United States. The United States Department of Agriculture (USDA) defines a **farm** as any establishment that produces (or should have produced) at least $1,000 of farm products each year.[1] Thus, an individual who sells a couple of fattened cattle is considered to be a farmer.

　　Since there are roughly 290 million Americans, the average American farmer feeds himself and 145 other Americans. Agricultural exports account for

Commodities raw agricultural products that have not been processed. Wheat, cattle, and raw milk are examples.

Food products food and agricultural commodities that have been processed into the form where they are ready for sale to the consumer.

Marketers sector that set of firms that distributes food products from processors to the final consumer when and where the consumer wants it. That consumer may be a retail shopper or someone eating at an away from home dining facility.

Farm structure the study and analysis of farm characteristics such as the physical and economic size of farms, ownership of farms, and characteristics of the farm manager and his or her family.

Farm defined by the U.S. Department of Agriculture as any establishment that has (or should have had) at least $1,000 of sales of agricultural products during the year.

---

[1] Farm pr1oducts include food, fiber, turfgrass, ornamentals, flowers, and a variety of other specialty crops. Excluded are seafood and forestry.

an additional 50 or so mouths to feed, so the average American farmer actually feeds approximately 200 people. Thus, our food chain, viewed as an inverted pyramid from producer to consumer, has a very narrow base.

Ownership

There is a myth, frequently propagated by the popular press, that farming is being taken over by large, corporate farms. The other side of this coin is that the family farmer—owner and operator—is disappearing. To some extent, in limited cases, the myth has some validity, but in the broad scheme of things it is little more than a myth.

Of the 2 million farms in the United States, more than 90 percent are sole proprietorships, meaning that the farm operator is self-employed.[2] Family corporations and partnerships account for most of the remaining 10 percent of farms. Non-family corporations only account for 1 percent, or approximately 20,000, of all farms. The self-employed family farmer is still very much a part of our social fabric.

Farm Types

Typology a system developed by the USDA that classifies farms based on economic size and characteristics of the farm operator.

Recently the USDA has started classifying farms into a **typology** based on the characteristics of the farm operator and the value of farm sales. In creating this typology, one of the critical questions asked of farm operators is "What is your primary occupation?" About 14 percent or nearly 300,000 farmers responded "retired." An astounding 40 percent of farm operators listed their primary occupation as a non-farm occupation. That is, they are just hobby farmers who work off the farm and maintain the farm as part of their lifestyle. As a group, these hobby farms operated at an economic loss. Retirement and hobby farms sure aren't producing what the rest of us eat.

Another 38 percent of farm operators listed their primary occupation as farming, but had gross sales of less than $250,000. Assuming a profit rate of 3 percent of sales, a farm with sales of $250,000 would only generate $7,500 of profit—hardly enough to support a farm family. In addition, most of these farms had sales of less than $100,000. These economically non-viable farmers aren't the folks who are producing much of what the rest of us eat, either.

That leaves 8 percent, or about 160,000, of farms that are large, economically viable farms that produce most of the food and fiber in the food industry. In fact, these few farms produce about two-thirds of the sales of all farms.

So, what is the typical American farm like? In terms of numbers, most farms are either retirement homes or hobby farms. The trend among these "farms" is increasing numbers and smaller farm units—it is a way of life rather than an economic unit. In terms of food production, there are about 160,000 farms that produce most of what we eat. Almost all of these farms are family farms, with only about 20,000 large, non-family farms. And the clear trend among these food producers is toward fewer, larger farm units. Also, these large farms are becoming increasingly specialized in what they produce, legitimizing the term "food factories."

---

[2] Data for this and the next section are drawn from *Structural and Financial Characteristics of U.S. Farms: 2001 Family Farm Report*, Robert A. Hoppe, editor, Economic Research Service, USDA, Agriculture Information Bulletin #768, May 2001.

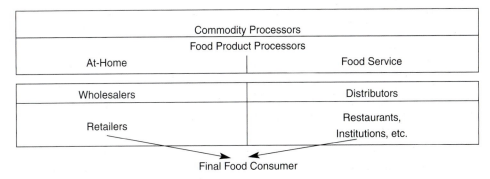

FIGURE 1–2   Detail of the Processors and Marketers Sectors

Processors—Extending the Reach

Food processors are those companies that turn raw agricultural commodities into food and/or food ingredients. As shown in Figure 1–2, the processing sector can be divided into those firms that primarily process commodities and those that process food products. Food product processors can be further divided into those that produce for the retail food consumer and those that produce for **food service** providers. Today roughly one-half of all spending on food is for food eaten away from home—it is this market that the food service processors serve.

Commodity Processors

Commodity processors buy raw agricultural commodities from producers or from storage facilities called **assemblers.** The raw commodities are then shipped to a large industrial processing plant where they are converted into food ingredients that can be used by food product processors. For example, soybean processors buy raw soybeans from the farmer and process those beans into soybean oil and soybean meal. The oil is used by food processors to make margarine, cooking oil, mayonnaise, and a variety of other products. The meal is primarily used as an ingredient by feed producers in the farm service sector. For the most part, commodity processors are companies that most of us have never heard of. Some of the leading commodity processors are Staley, Cargill, CPC (formerly Corn Products Company), and Archer Daniel Midland (ADM). In fact, ADM is the world's largest processor of corn, oilseeds, and cocoa. ADM is also the country's largest processor of wheat. Nonetheless, you have never seen a bag of ADM flour on the supermarket shelf because ADM only sells in bulk to food processing companies.

Food Product Processors

Food product processors buy food ingredients and combine them to produce the food we buy in the store or eat at a restaurant. Because many food product processors sell food under their own brand names, many of these companies are very common household names such as Campbell's, Heinz, Hershey's, and Nabisco. Many common food brands are produced by processors that produce under a variety of brand names. For instance, Jell-O® and Kool-Aid® are produced by Kraft;

Food service that segment of the food industry that processes for and distributes to the away from home market for food.

Assemblers those firms that buy raw agricultural commodities directly from farmers (producers) in small quantities and sell to processors in larger quantities.

and Reese's® peanut butter candies and JollyRancher® candies are produced by Hershey Foods.

A good example of a food product processor is the Coca-Cola Company. It buys high fructose corn sweetener from a commodity processor such as ADM and other ingredients from other processors and combines them using their secret formula to produce Coke® in cans and bottles for the retail market and in bulk for the food service industry. Following the diagram in Figure 1–2, Coca-Cola also plays the role of wholesaler and distributor in the marketing sector. So, Coca-Cola spans both the last half of the processing sector and the first half of the marketing sector.

Concentration in Processing

Concentration the dominance of an industry by a few firms, usually measured by the percent of the total market owned by the largest four (or any other number) firms.

A current concern, and one that has generated several legislative proposals at the national level, is the degree of industrial **concentration** in some of the food processing sectors. Concentration is an economic concept that refers to the degree to which a small number of firms control a large share of the market. The most common method for measuring concentration is the percent of the total market accounted for by the four (or any other number) largest producers. For instance, in the United States 87 percent of breakfast cereal is produced by the four largest producers, and virtually all baby food is produced by the three largest processors.

By far the greatest concern about concentration among agricultural processors is in the meat packing business. About 85 percent of all beef is processed (i.e., slaughtered) by four companies that have been rapidly buying out smaller competitors as the industry consolidates. Moreover, the largest poultry producer, Tyson Foods, recently bought the second-largest beef processor. In other words, concentration and consolidation is crossing species lines that have previously separated processors. Some cattle producers have called for federal legislation that would prevent any further consolidation.

Market power the ability of a firm or group of firms to control price and/or quantity traded in a market because of the dominance of the firm(s) in the market.

Is concentration bad? Processors say that by consolidating into fewer, larger processors they are able to cut costs which benefits consumers. Opponents argue that concentration provides the processors with unusual **market power** that allows them to buy from farmers who have little market power at prices that border on exploitation. For example, it is becoming common for meat packers (i.e., processors) to force producers to sign secret contracts such that no one knows what price other cattle producers are receiving or what price other packers are paying.

Globalization

Globalization the expansion of firms across national boundaries.

In most instances, food processors tend to be on the forefront of **globalization** because the demand for processing technologies is truly global. We all need food to survive. Among the commodity processors, most of the successful processors are very internationalized with processing facilities all over the globe. To fail to behave globally in the commodity processing business is a recipe for corporate failure.

In food products processing, the drive to globalization has not been as strong, as consumers in each country have different tastes and preferences. While a soybean is a soybean in every country, the final food product may be soy protein meal in one country, tofu in another, and a nice steak in a third. There are three truly global food product processing companies: Coca-Cola, Unilever, and Nestlé, which is the largest processor of food products in the world. While most Americans only associate Nestlé with chocolate bars and hot cocoa mix, Nestle also appears in this country under brand names such as Nescafé®, Taster's Choice®, Perrier®, Friskies®, Alpo®, Mighty Dog®, Baby Ruth®, Butterfinger®, PowerBar®, and Carnation®. On a global basis, their strong suit is in the infant formula market. Many food product processing companies are making a big push to globalize, realizing that growth of the domestic food market in the United States is basically stagnant, while the growth of the processed food market in many developing countries is exploding. This is an emerging challenge for domestic stand-outs like the Campbell Soup Company, H. J. Heinz, and Hershey Foods.

Marketers

Marketers are the companies that tie the final food consumer to the processor. Their job is to make certain that whatever the consumer wants is there when and where the consumer wants it. As shown in Figure 1–2, the traditional retail marketing system is quite distinct from the food service distribution system.

Wholesale–Retail Marketers

As noted earlier, about one-half of expenditures on food is for food to be prepared at home. Notwithstanding the bucolic appeal of farmers' markets and roadside vendors, most food purchased for home consumption is purchased at a retail supermarket. Traditionally, most retail stores purchased food from wholesalers, who purchased food in bulk from processors and sold it in smaller batches to retailers. Many retailers, particularly the smaller ones, still use this system. However, many of the larger chains combine the wholesale and retail functions into a single firm, thereby reducing transaction costs.

The largest food retailer in the United States in terms of sales volume is Kroger. It sells about $50 billion of food per year through 2,300 retail outlets, many of which carry the Kroger name.[3] Like most retail chains (Wal-Mart is a notable exception), Kroger has grown by acquiring small local chains and adding the small chains to the Kroger distribution system. Many of these stores still bear their local name, such as Ralphs, King Soopers, City Market, Dillons, Smith's, Fry's, QFC, Kessel, Cala Bell, Owen's, JayC, Fred Meyer, Hilander, Gerbes, Pay Less, Food4Less, and Foods Co. In addition, Kroger runs convenience stores under the Turkey Hill, Kwik Shop, Loaf 'N Jug, Quik Stop, and Tom Thumb names. Like most larger retail chains, Kroger is not only into wholesaling but also food product processing with 42 manufacturing plants producing some 3,000 products that are sold through the Kroger chain.

This illustrates one of the dominant trends in the food system—**vertical integration.** This refers to combining several steps in the food system chain into a single firm. Examples of vertical integration, such as Kroger, abound in the food system. Tyson Foods is an example of a company that is in the farm service sector, producing its own chicken feed; the production sector, hiring farmers to raise the birds; and the processing sector. Con-Agra is both a commodity processor and a food products processor. Smithfield Farms is both a producer and processor of pork products. Vertical integration allows the firm to coordinate different stages in the food system through management, whereas without integration

Vertical integration the combination of different businesses at different stages of the production/marketing sequence under a single management.

---

[3] Total food expenditures in the United States are about $800 billion. About half of that, or $400 billion, is through retail outlets, so Kroger commands about one out of eight retail food dollars.

that coordination is accomplished through the ebb and flow of markets and market prices. So, with vertical integration as a dominant trend, we are seeing a rise in the role of management and a decline in the role of markets in the food system.

Food Service System

About half of our food expenditures are for "away from home" food. This includes food consumed at restaurants, cafeterias, and other for-hire eating establishments; as well as institutional food provided by entities such as prisons, schools, the military, and college campuses. Food delivered by the food service distributors is either delivered in bulk (a gallon of catsup for the military mess) or in individual portions (a cordon bleu ready to be microwaved by a restaurant).

To keep the verbiage simple, we will hereafter refer to all providers of away from home meals as "restaurants." Most restaurants get most of the food they serve from **food service distributors.** This is a specialized part of the food marketing chain. Unlike food retailers that wait for customers to come to them, food service distributors go to the customer, usually with daily delivery available. These distributors maintain large warehouses of food produced by food service processors and distribute it to restaurants as it is needed.

One of the largest food service distributors is Sysco, with annual sales in excess of $20 billion. Most of what Sysco sells to restaurants are products produced by food service processors; but not unlike Kroger, Sysco has vertically integrated backward into the food service processing sector and now sells both its own products and those of other food service processors.

Some restaurants, like McDonald's, have vertically integrated by providing their own food service distribution network. In this case, the restaurant chain buys in bulk from food service processors and then distributes that food to individual stores in the chain using their own trucks. As with all vertical integration, this gives management more control over a broader range of the marketing chain.

Food service distributors those firms that distribute food products from food processors to away from home dining facilities.

Summary

The food industry consists of literally millions of firms working in one or more of four distinct sectors: the farm service sector, the producers sector, the processors sector, and the marketers sector. While the activities performed in each of the four sectors are distinct, many firms in the food industry have vertically integrated across sector boundaries.

In the farm service sector we find firms that produce inputs and/or services that are purchased by producers. These include feed manufacturers, implement dealers, chemical companies, lawyers, bankers, and farm consultants. The common thread of all firms in the farm service sector is that their primary consumer is the producer (farmer, rancher, and so on).

Producers refer to all who produce and harvest our food, fiber, and other agricultural commodities. Farmers, ranchers, nursery operators, vineyard and orchard operators, grove owners, and others are included in the producers sector. Most farms in the United States produce very little because producing food and fiber is not the primary objective of the owners of most farm units. Most farms are recreational or retirement activities. About 8 percent of all farm units—those with sales in excess of $250,000 per year—produce most of our food and fiber.

Processors buy raw agricultural commodities from producers and sell finished food products to the marketers sector. Some processors are commodity processors. These firms buy, store, and transport raw agricultural commodities and then convert those commodities into food ingredients. Food product processors buy these ingredients and use them to produce the food products we eat. Some firms are commodity processors only, others are food product processors only, and still others do both. An important public policy issue facing processors is concern about the level of concentration in food processing and the effects of that concentration on both producers and consumers.

Marketer firms buy food products from processors in bulk, store them, transport them, and distribute them to consumers in small, convenient lots. One marketer chain serves the needs of the retail food customer while another serves the needs of the food service sector.

Throughout the food system examples of vertical integration are found. Most of the bigger, faster-growing firms in the food sector tend to be vertically integrated. With vertical integration comes market power and market coordination—both of which raise questions about the impact of vertical integration on the final consumer.

KEY TERMS

Assemblers

Commodities

Concentration

Farm

Farm service sector

Farm structure

Food industry

Food products

Food service

Food service distributors

Globalization

Market power

Marketers sector

Processors sector

Producers sector

Typology

Vertical integration

PROBLEMS AND DISCUSSION QUESTIONS

1. Identify the four sectors in the food industry. For firms in each of the four sectors, identify what they buy and what they sell. From what firms do they buy inputs, and to what firms do they sell their outputs?

2. An important part of the farm service sector is the Cooperative Extension Service, which has an office in virtually every county of the United States. Contact the local office of your Cooperative Extension Service or visit the website of your state office of Cooperative Extension Service to determine what this publicly funded agency does. Who are the clientele and what are the services provided?

3. What proportion of all farm units in the United States is economically viable with sales of at least $250,000 per year?

4. Discuss the following proposition and its implications: most farm owners are more interested in a rural way of life than in food production.

5. Archer Daniels Midland is not only the largest commodity processor in the United States, but it is also unique in that it has virtually no vertical

integration in either direction. Get a profile of this interesting company by visiting them at **admworld.com.**

6. ConAgra Foods is an example of a large commodity processor that has a high level of vertical integration. It is a food processor as well as a commodity processor and produces for both the consumer market and the food service market. Visit **conagra.com** to profile this major agricultural processor.

7. Kraft Foods is the largest food processor in the United States. While the Kraft name is usually associated with cheese, it produces a variety of food products under a large number of brand names. List the domestic brands used by Kraft. You can prepare your list from their website at **kraft.com.**

8. What is vertical integration? What are the advantages of vertical integration? What are the concerns about vertical integration?

9. What is concentration in the processor sector and why is it considered to be a threat to producers?

10. Identify the major beef packers (i.e., commodity processors) in the United States and the share of the market held by each.

11. What is globalization?

12. At almost any highly visible international meeting there are groups of protesters who are against globalization. One of the largest, most visible protest groups is Greenpeace. Visit their U.S. website at **greenpeaceusa.org** to learn why they oppose globalization. What are their arguments against globalization?

13. Food retailing tends to be a regional phenomenon. What are the leading food retailers in your region? Are these retailers part of a larger chain such as Kroger or Albertson's?

14. During the 1990s Wal-Mart went from no food retailing to being the third largest food retailer in the United States. Has Wal-Mart, with its Superstores, arrived in your community as a food retailer? Meet with the store manager of a local supermarket and ask what the impact of Wal-Mart will be, or has been, for food retailing in your community.

15. What food service distributor serves your student union? Get on the Internet or visit with a sales representative to learn more about this food service distributor. The director of your student union can help you with this task.

Introduction to Agricultural Economics

*A*s the name rightly implies, agricultural economics is that part of economics that surveys agriculture in its many facets and forms. The agricultural economist is concerned with the entire food and fiber system, from the inputs used in production all the way through the production, processing, distribution, and consumption chain.

The food and fiber system is related to almost every facet of our economy and our environment. As a result, the study of agricultural economics necessarily encompasses a great deal more than just the activities of the farmer or rancher. Since the food and fiber system is an important part of our natural environment, some agricultural economists deal with issues of resource conservation, pollution control, and water management. Others study the agribusiness sector as purchasers, processors, and distributors of food and fiber products.

As these examples illustrate, the scope of agricultural economics is very broad and quite diverse. The common thread is that each deals with one of the many facets of the food system described in the previous chapter.

AGRICULTURAL ECONOMICS

Economics is a social science. The objective of any scientific inquiry is to observe and describe a particular range of phenomena, to organize those observations into recognizable patterns, and, where sufficient regularity warrants, to formulate "laws." It is these laws that gives the scientist a basis on which to make predictions. The social scientist must deal with the laws of human nature, and since humans are not consistent in their behavior, the laws of the social scientist are necessarily less reliable and more open to exception than those of the physical or biological scientist. Nevertheless, the economic behavior of most persons is generally consistent and, therefore, to some degree predictable.

Economics is that particular social science that deals with the allocation of scarce resources among an unlimited number of competing alternative uses. Economists use the word "resources" to describe anything tangible: wheat, barbed wire, hamburgers, water, labor, clean air, and recreation facilities. Every resource is relatively *scarce,* meaning that the availability of every resource is insufficient to satisfy all of its potential users. Scarcity creates the need for a system to *allocate* the available resource among some of those potential users. **Agricultural economics** is the social science that deals with the allocation of scarce resources among those competing alternative uses found in the production, processing, distribution, and consumption of food and fiber.

Economics the social science that deals with the allocation of scarce resources among an unlimited number of competing alternative uses.

Agricultural economics the social science that deals with the allocation of scarce resources among those competing alternative uses found in the production, processing, distribution, and consumption of food and fiber.

BASIS FOR ECONOMICS

The study of economics rests on three foundations: *self-interest, scarcity,* and *choice.* Without scarcity, there would be no need for an allocation system. Before the industrial revolution there was no scarcity of clean air. It was consumed in unlimited quantities at a zero price with no choices to be made about who was to get it and how much of it they should get. Such is not the case today. Clean air is now quite costly. We pay for it with each dollar we spend on pollution control. We also pay an even dearer price—the damage to our health that pollution causes. Both of these costs are evidence of the scarcity of air, and both indicate the need for an allocation system.

Choice is important because without choices there is no decision to be made. As previously stated, economics is about decision making and allocation. Without choices there would be no need for economics. A supermarket is the epitome of choice. With approximately 30,000 different bar codes in one store the consumer is given choices of goods, brands, sizes, and flavors. Because of these choices our lives are enriched.

In addition to scarcity and choice, there is a third equally important driving force of economics: self-interest. Self-interest is what drives the consumer to seek more "stuff" at a lower price. It is self-interest that drives the producer to produce as efficiently as possible. It is what encourages the trucker to ship produce from one region to another. All economic activity is driven by self-interest. It is the fuel that drives the engine.

BASIC ECONOMIC DECISIONS

Every economic system must resolve five basic issues:

1. *What* to produce. Should we use our abundant corn crop to produce meat or alcohol fuel?
2. *How* to produce it. Should tomatoes be grown in greenhouses in Minneapolis for the central Minnesota market, or should they be produced in the fields of south Florida and shipped to Minnesota? Should those tomatoes be produced using chemical insecticides, or should they be grown without chemicals?
3. *How much* to produce. As contrary as it may sound, you will learn in a later chapter that one of the biggest problems in agriculture in the United States is a tendency to overproduce. How much is enough?
4. *When* to produce. Should a stand of timber be cut today and used for pulp, or should it be left growing for several more years until it reaches a diameter sufficient to serve as saw timber?
5. *For whom* to produce. Should this year's production of sirloin steaks be equally distributed among everyone in the society, or should some potential consumers be excluded from the market because of financial limitations?

ECONOMIC SYSTEMS

The basic questions of what, how, how much, when, and for whom must be answered in each society: they simply cannot be avoided. The institutional and political systems of a society determine the manner in which these decisions will be made. At one extreme of possible allocation mechanisms lies the free market or **price system.** In this system, each individual producer and consumer, restricted only by financial resources, is free to choose what, how, how much, and when to produce or consume. The financial resources of each consumer resolves the "for whom" question. At the other extreme is the **command system** in which all decisions with respect to what, how, how much, when, and for whom are made by a central planning agency or other administrative individual such as an absolute dictator or tribal chief.

An advantage of the price system is that it provides the consumer with sovereignty and freedom in making economic decisions. In addition, the price system is a very **efficient**[1] mechanism for making most of the what, how, how much, and when decisions. But, the price system has shortcomings even its most ardent supporters recognize. First, when it comes to making the "for whom" decision, the price system is far from egalitarian. In a price system, the old adage that the rich get richer and the poor get poorer has some validity. Second, there are a number of resources that a price system cannot efficiently allocate. These goods, frequently called public goods or nonmarket goods, include education, national defense, and fire protection.

The advantages of a command system are that it is very effective in allocating public goods and it can be quite egalitarian in making the "for whom" decision. The disadvantages of a pure command allocation system are the loss of individual freedom to make economic decisions and the inherent inefficiencies of central planning agencies.

The political institutions of the United States fully embrace a price system for allocating resources, but with some adjustments to correct for the difficulties noted above. To address the "for whom" question for goods that are considered to be necessary for all citizens, we have a number of programs designed to transfer economic power from the relatively rich to the relatively poor. Examples include the progressive income tax system, Medicare, public education, food stamps, and the Social Security system. The institutional fabric of the United States includes a pure command allocation system for some public goods such as national defense, and a mixed price/command system for other goods such as higher education.

LEVELS OF ECONOMIC ACTIVITY

There is a great deal of similarity between a wood screw and a common nail: both may be used to fasten two pieces of wood together, and both are longer than they are wide. While both a hammer and a screwdriver can be used to insert either into a piece of wood, only one tool is best suited for each of the wood fastening devices. Economics is not unlike wood fastening devices: just as a hammer should be chosen to drive a nail, the appropriate economic tool must be chosen to fit the particular economic problem being analyzed. Much of the economic misinformation that appears daily in the press, and with alarming frequency on the tongues of aspirants to public office, is a consequence of using an inappropriate economic tool for the particular economic problem being discussed.

---

[1] "Efficiency" is a word that economists use to describe the relationship between the effectiveness of achieving some goal and the cost of achieving that goal. The price system is efficient when compared with the command system because the cost of running the price system is nil compared with the inevitable bureaucracy associated with a command system.

Price system   an allocative system in which economic choices are based on prices.

Command system an allocative system in which economic choices are made by some central administrative unit.

Efficiency   a general economic concept used in a variety of situations measuring output per unit of input. The higher the ratio, the more efficient the process.

Economics can be divided into three parts: microeconomics, market economics, and macroeconomics. The important distinction among the three is the level of aggregation of the analysis. As will be demonstrated later, what is valid logic when dealing with the economics of the individual may not necessarily be valid when dealing with the economics of a group or an entire society. Thus, as the level of aggregation changes, the economic tools must also be changed. An ordinary screwdriver may serve the needs of the home owner well, but it would be totally inappropriate for the production worker on an assembly line who is expected to drive thousands of screws a day. Again, the level of aggregation is critical.

Microeconomics

Microeconomics of production the economics of the individual producer or firm making management decisions.

Microeconomics deals with the economics of individual producers and consumers. The **microeconomics of production** examines the economics of the individual producer or firm as that firm acquires resources and combines them in the production process to earn as much profit as possible. The production management decisions that affect the profit of the firm include which inputs to purchase, what production technique to use, which product to produce, how much of each product to produce, and when to produce them. Obviously, the firm manager, whether farmer or rancher or owner of a donut shop, is deeply involved in the "what," "how," "how much," and "when" allocation decisions. In the study of production microeconomics we will develop a set of management rules detailing how the rational firm manager should resolve production management decisions to maximize the profit that the firm is able to earn from a given set of productive resources.

The microeconomics of production, like all branches of economics, is not without controversy. In fact, some pundits claim that the only common thread among all economists is a strong proclivity to argue. For many, that's exactly why economics is exciting and fun. The production microeconomics that is developed later in this text is known among economists as the neoclassical theory of the firm. From the point of view of this theory, the firm is seen as being completely subservient to the market, and the firm manager is seen as being interested only in profit maximization.

The most consistent critic of neoclassical microeconomic theory is John Kenneth Galbraith, who, in his many works, has argued that this theory is appropriate only for what he calls the "entrepreneurial sector" of the economy. This sector of the economy is composed of small individual firms, such as the family farm or ranch, the local florist, the barber shop, and the local mortician. According to Galbraith, the entrepreneurial sector accounts for approximately one-half of all production in the United States. The other half of all goods and services produced comes from what Galbraith calls the "corporate sector." This sector is composed of a relatively few firms—perhaps one or two thousand compared with the millions that together constitute the entrepreneurial sector (there are approximately 2 million farms alone). Galbraith argues that in the corporate sector "the initiative in deciding what is to be produced comes not from the sovereign consumer who, through the market, issues the instructions that bend the productive mechanism to his ultimate will. Rather it comes from the great producing organization which reaches forward to control the markets that it is presumed to serve and, beyond, to bend the customer to its needs."[2] The firms in the corporate sector are able to control markets through the

---

[2] Exerpt from *The New Industrial State* by John Kenneth Galbraith. Copyright © 1967, 1971, 1978 by John Kenneth Galbraith. Reprinted by permission of Houghton Mifflin Company. All rights reserved.

use of planning, specializing, and organizing within the technostructure that controls the corporations. The technostructure or management of the firm is concerned not so much about the profits of the firm as it is about its own continued and improved existence. Finally, Galbraith argues that because of the size of the firms in the corporate sector and because of their command of technology, they are able to use the power of government to achieve their own objectives. The rise of the military-industrial complex is the most visible example of this process.

Galbraith's basic argument is that while we have the vastly different entrepreneurial and corporate production sectors, we have only one microeconomic theory to describe the behavior of both. He argues that since the basic assumptions upon which neoclassical microeconomic theory rests are obviously inconsistent with the observed behavior of firms in the corporate sector, neoclassical microeconomic theory is neither capable of nor appropriate for analyzing the behavior of firms in the corporate sector of the economy of the United States. Most economists would not take issue with this point, even if they find themselves in violent disagreement with Galbraith's alternative to neoclassical microeconomics.

For production agriculture, the neoclassical model is undoubtedly appropriate since most agricultural commodities are produced by the millions of farms and ranches that easily fall into the entrepreneurial sector. However, agricultural economists should question whether the neoclassical theory is a valid tool for analyzing such large agricultural processors as Kraft, Kellogg's, or Campbell's. Some of these very large and dominant agricultural processors may be closer to Galbraith's model of the "Industrial State" than to the neoclassical model presented in this text. But in either case, the neoclassical model is a good jumping off point to develop an understanding of the principles of production management.

After this long digression into the theoretical underpinnings of production microeconomics, we return to the other branch of microeconomics—the **microeconomics of consumption.** The consumer is faced with the economic problem of deciding what to purchase given the limited resources (i.e., money and time) available. The role of scarcity, choice, and self-interest in making consumption decisions is clearly and poignantly expressed by the face of a young child clutching a few precious coins in a store full of candy. The individual consumer must make a number of consumption decisions on a daily basis. Many of these decisions are not the products of conscious deliberation; instead, they tend to be habitual or impulsive. The consumer must decide what to buy and what not to buy. Should I buy pork or beef for supper tomorrow? Or should I buy neither so that I will have enough money to buy a hot new CD? An examination of the economics of these decisions will enable us to develop some general rules of behavior suggesting how consumers will react to changes in relative prices or incomes. The consumer must also decide when to consume. Should I go into debt today to buy a new Corvette, or should I continue to save so that I can buy the 'vette later without going into debt? After all, the old Geo will do almost everything a new Corvette will do.

Each consumer faces the inevitability of scarcity in the form of a limited budget. Given this scarcity, each consumer in a price allocation system uses his or her sovereignty to resolve the "for whom" allocative decision. The "for whom" consumption decisions that a price system entails may be modified by subsidized school breakfast and lunch programs, food stamps, and other government programs.

Microeconomics of consumption the economics of the individual consumer making decisions about the allocation of the family budget.

Market Economics

Market an interaction between potential buyers and potential sellers.

Markets[3] are the primary price determination mechanism found in the institutional framework of most countries. To the economist, a **market** is established whenever potential buyers and potential sellers interact to establish prices and exchange goods. A market should be distinguished from a marketplace. The latter refers to a physical location, while a market refers to the interaction of buyers and sellers irrespective of their physical location. Auctions on the Internet provide a vivid example of the difference between a market and a marketplace.

Price takers potential buyers and potential sellers in a perfectly competitive market who face a "take it or leave it" decision at the prevailing market price.

Market economics encompasses the study of the dealings in a particular commodity by all of its potential buyers and potential sellers taken as a group. In the neoclassical model, each participant in a market is a **price taker,** yet the collective decisions of all participants in a market determine the price that all take. As a price taker, the only decision each producer or consumer can make is a choice of whether or not to buy or sell at the market price. As the number of yes votes changes, so too will the price. In this manner, each individual takes the market price, but all individuals together determine or make the market price.

Marketing the study of the creation of value that occurs as a good moves from producer to consumer.

In the economics of markets we study how value is created as a commodity moves from producer to consumer. Four changes occur in the **marketing** of a good: time, place, form, and possession. It is a complex and interesting system that converts the Minnesota farmer's August wheat harvest into a New York banker's toast on a cold, snowy January morning. The *form* of the wheat must be changed to that of bread; the *place* of the wheat moves from Minnesota to New York; the *time* of the wheat shifts from the August harvest to the chills of January; and the *possession* of the wheat cum bread changes from the farmer to the banker. To follow the wheat through its long and tortuous journey is to study the economics of agricultural marketing.

Agribusiness firms engaged in farm service marketing, agricultural production, food processing, food distribution, and consumption.

In traditional societies most of the functional changes required in agricultural marketing are performed by middlemen. In the contemporary agricultural system of the United States, most of these functions are performed by extremely sophisticated business firms that specialize in performing certain functions or in marketing specific products. These specialized firms have become known collectively as **agribusiness.** The study of the management, financing, and marketing decisions of agribusinesses is a specialized branch of agricultural economics that deals with the economics of Galbraith's corporate sector.[4]

Macroeconomics

Macroeconomics considers the entire economics system, usually at the national or international level. Its focus of concern is with how the total economic system operates, and how various policies and institutions affect the vitality of the economic system. Issues—such as the unemployment rate, the rate of inflation, the balance of payments, and the federal deficit—form the material part of macroeconomics. The economic system's performance at the macro level is crucially important to the agricultural producer or consumer because the "micro" management decisions

---

[3] Most authors include market economics as a part of microeconomics. We prefer to deal with microeconomics (the economics of individual units) and market economics (the economics of the interaction between producing and consuming units) as separate topics.

[4] For example, in *Principles of Agribusiness Management* (Waveland Press, 1993), Beierlein, Schneeberger, and Osburn identify the four functions of management: planning, organizing, controlling, and directing. These tasks are a far cry from the neoclassic price taker.

each must make are predicated on the existing "macro" economic situation. For example, if the rate of inflation changes rapidly, firm managers must be able to perceive how that change might affect their operations and then be prepared to make any and all appropriate adjustments.

Macroeconomics is that branch of economics that stares back at each of us as we watch the television news or read the daily paper. It deals with the impact of public policies such as food stamps, pesticide controls, or agricultural price supports on each sector of the economy individually and on the entire economy collectively.

The macroeconomist also deals with international issues. For the agricultural sector of the United States, an international perspective is becoming increasingly important for at least three reasons:

1. The foreign buyer is one of the most important buyers of U.S. crop production. An estimated 40 percent of U.S. cropland is used to produce food and fiber that is eventually exported to another country.
2. Imports, particularly petroleum, are very important in the cost structure of U.S. farmers, food processors, and distributors.
3. We share a humanitarian concern for that segment of the world's population that lives in hunger. In addition, there is an element of self-interest involved, for we must realize that hunger, like ideas or beliefs, frequently lies at the heart of significant social revolutions and wars.

In an earlier era international trade was hampered by transportation delays and communication difficulties. Today those hindrances have all but disappeared. This has led to the "globalization" of agricultural trade and agribusiness. As one author put it, we are all living in a highly interdependent fashion on "spaceship earth."

BASIC SKILLS OF THE AGRICULTURAL ECONOMIST

The study of agricultural economics provides the student with an opportunity to explore phenomena common to everyday life from the perspective of an analytical scientist. Just as artists or novelists try to explore human behavior through their chosen media, economists observe the behavior of man as an economic creature and try to develop rules for behavior that will help every participant in economic society achieve their goals. Thus, the role of the economist is to devise rules for making decisions in an ever-changing, uncertain economic environment. These rules can be used to make production, consumption, marketing, and financial decisions. By studying the logic of these managerial rules, the student can learn how to adjust managerial decisions to the changing environment in which our economic activity occurs. Since most readers of this book are neophytes to the study of economics, it is important that you be forewarned about some of the pitfalls that have devoured many of those who preceded you through the logical maze called agricultural economics.

As with all sciences, economics is a way of thinking—a well-defined logical system designed to improve our understanding of the behavior observed in society. While it is the subject matter of economics that sets it apart from other social sciences, there are also several aspects of the economist's way of thinking that are somewhat unique. Some of the more important of these deserve a bit of explanation.

Economic Models

Since economics is a social science concerned with the behavior of individuals within their society, it is impossible for economists to explain, much less predict, all behavior. Different people act differently. But, as a general rule, most people will act in similar and, therefore, predictable ways. An expected pattern of economic behavior is called an **economic model.** It is the basic building block in the logic of the economist.

Economic model a conceptualization, based on assumptions, of how economic activity occurs.

A model will usually include some assumptions about human behavior as well as a number of other assumptions about the institutional environment in which a particular form of human behavior, economic activity, will take place. Once a model has been developed, the economist uses the model in an attempt to describe the appropriate economic behavior that will lead to the eventual achievement of some goal. That is, an economic model is a set of logical premises from which can be deduced the appropriate behavior pattern that will lead to the attainment of an explicit goal.

A frequently used economic model is the "perfectly competitive firm." This model includes a number of assumptions about the firm and about the environment in which it operates. For instance, the assumption is made that the firm is so small relative to the market that its actions will not affect the market. There is also an assumption that the firm manager attempts to maximize profits given a particular resource endowment. For the case of a typical farm firm, these assumptions seem to be realistic. Once the model of the perfectly competitive firm is developed, it is a straightforward process to logically deduce the rules of managerial behavior that will achieve profit maximization.

An obvious question that must be asked is whether the economist's model is consistent with reality. Are the assumptions valid? If the assumptions aren't valid, then the results may not be appropriate. Frequently, the economist finds that the assumptions of a particular model do not represent reality with a mirror-like accuracy, but do at least provide a close approximation of the situation being studied. In this case the economist takes the basic model as a starting point and asks what changes need to be made to make the model better fit the situation. The deductive process is then repeated to arrive at an answer to the specific situation being studied.

At best, economic models approximate reality in a manner that enhances our ability to conceptualize and simplify the real world we are examining. Even though the assumptions of a model are frequently violated, models do provide the economist with an internally consistent mechanism for conceptualizing problems, and they force the economist to reason in a systematic, deductive manner.

Ceteris Paribus

Ceteris paribus a shorthand way of saying "let one economic variable (the cause) change and see how another economic variable (the effect) changes, assuming that everything else remains unchanged."

Ceteris paribus is a Latin phrase that roughly translates to "everything else being equal." Since it is generally assumed that any economic principle is valid only when all other external factors remain the same, the *ceteris paribus* assumption is frequently invoked. As a kind of scientific shorthand, the economist will frequently end the statement of a proposition with the phrase "*ceteris paribus*" rather than saying "this proposition is predicated on the assumption that all other factors remain constant." This allows the examination of a cause-effect relationship between two factors, knowing that other factors are not involved in the relationship being examined. This use of the *ceteris paribus* assumption gives economics much of the logical rigor required in a scientific inquiry.

Opportunity Cost

One of the more powerful concepts in economics is the concept of **opportunity cost.** All economic resources have value. Sometimes that value is determined in a marketplace where the user of a resource pays the prevailing price for the use of the resource. On other occasions, resources are used that have economic value, but those resources are not purchased in the open market. In this latter case, economists use the principle of opportunity cost to determine the economic value of a resource even though there is no manifest market value of that resource.

> **Opportunity cost** a measure of how much of an earning opportunity is foregone by using a resource in its current employment. Used by economists to establish an economic value for those resources that do not have an expressed market value.

To see how this works, let's look at an example of Dusty, who owns a small farming operation. Among other things, Dusty's farm produces a corn crop. An economist, Dr. Marge E. Nall from the state university, wants to determine the cost of producing corn. The costs associated with many of the resources used to produce corn are very easy to identify and measure. "How much fertilizer did you buy, and what did it cost?" Dr. Nall wants to know. The costs associated with fuel, seeds, fertilizer, and most other purchased inputs are easy to determine because the value or price of those resources has been determined in the markets for fuel, seeds, and fertilizer.

> **CAUTION** *A common mistake students of economics make is to confuse "price" and "cost." Price refers to a per unit concept. What is the price per gallon of gasoline, for example. Cost refers to a total concept of price times quantity purchased. What did it cost to fill up your car?*

But Dr. Nall realizes that there are other resources used in the production of corn that are not purchased in the marketplace but nonetheless contribute economic value to the enterprise. Two examples will suffice—Dusty's own labor and Dusty's land. Both of these have economic value because if either were absent, there would be no corn crop. But how do we determine the economic value of each?

This is where opportunity cost comes into play. Opportunity cost is the economic value of a resource in its highest value alternative use. That is, if a resource (such as Dusty's labor) is being used in one economic activity, then that resource has given up the opportunity of being used in another economic activity. What are the earnings foregone in that other activity? That is the opportunity cost of the resource. It is important to note that unlike the cost of fertilizer, opportunity costs cannot be measured directly; they can only be estimated indirectly.

Let's return to our example of Dusty's labor. Certainly that labor has economic value that should be accounted for by Dr. Nall in estimating the costs of producing corn. She recognizes that rather than measuring the cost of Dusty's labor, she is going to have to estimate the opportunity cost of his labor. Dusty provides both management and manual labor to the corn enterprise, but he does not pay himself for that labor.

But Dusty's neighbor, Imma Rose, is an absentee landowner who hires a full-time farm manager to run her operation. If Dusty were not managing his own farm, he could be managing Imma's: that is his highest earning opportunity or alternative use of his time. So, whatever Imma pays her farm manager is Dusty's opportunity cost.

There still remains the question of the economic value of Dusty's land. Certainly the value of the land should be part of Dr. Nall's estimation of the cost of producing corn. If Dusty were not farming corn on that land, what would be the next highest value of the land? Well, if Dusty didn't farm it, he could rent it out. What is the prevailing rental rate in the area for corn land? That is easy to determine, and that is the opportunity cost of Dusty's land in his corn crop.

The study of economics is all about economic values—costs and returns. When available, we use market prices to determine economic value. When market prices are not available, we use the concept of opportunity cost to estimate those values.

Diminishing Returns

Diminishing returns as additional units of an economic variable are used, the additional impact of that variable will eventually increase at a decreasing rate.

In the economics of both production and consumption, the concept of **diminishing returns** is central to the process of economizing. The basic idea of diminishing returns is that as you increase the amount of something, *ceteris paribus* (that is, holding the amounts of everything else constant), the additional "bang for the buck" will eventually increase at a decreasing rate—diminishing returns.

Two examples will suffice. In consumption the idea of diminishing returns is expressed in the "law of diminishing marginal utility." Marginal utility refers to the additional utility or satisfaction associated with one additional unit of a good being consumed, *ceteris paribus*.

Operationally what this law says is that the amount of total utility gained from consuming a good eventually increases at a decreasing rate assuming the consumption of everything else remains constant. That is, the additional or marginal utility associated with a fourth slice of pizza is less than the additional utility associated with the third. And the additional utility gained by the fifth slice will be less than that gained from the fourth. This is an example of diminishing returns in consumption.

On the production side the concept of diminishing returns is embodied in the "law of diminishing marginal product." This law states that if you add additional units of an input to fixed amounts of other inputs, the additional production from each additional input will eventually decrease.

In practice, if you add additional units of fertilizer to a fixed amount of land, eventually the response per unit of fertilizer will begin to increase at a decreasing rate. That is, if farmer Jones increases nitrogen per acre from 300 pounds/acre to 400 pounds/acre, he notes that output grows by 25 bushels/acre. If he increases from 400 pounds/acre to 500 pounds/acre, the growth in output will be only 20 bushels/acre. Output is increasing at a decreasing rate.

The concept of diminishing returns applies to both production and consumption. This does not preclude the possibility of increasing returns over some range of production or consumption. But eventually, diminishing returns will set in and ultimately become negative. In the case of consumption, the additional utility of that first beer may be quite high, but eventually and inevitably the additional returns from each additional beer will diminish and finally turn negative (with predictable consequences). Likewise, too much fertilizer can actually burn the crop, creating negative returns.

Marginality

As indicated earlier, economics is a science. This implies a certain element of rigor and a contribution to the orderly evaluation of our economic behavior. Perhaps one of the greatest contributions of economics is the concept of marginality.

In economics the term **marginal** refers to an additional or an incremental unit of something. Most economic analyses deal not with the total value of production or consumption but instead with the marginal value of production or consumption, for it is on the margin where economic decisions are made.

As previously shown, as the consumer consumes additional units of a good, *ceteris paribus*, the additional satisfaction or utility obtained by each unit decreases. At any given level of consumption the economist focuses on the economics of the marginal or additional unit. The relevant economic question of the consumer should be, Is the marginal utility associated with one additional unit greater than the marginal cost of acquiring that unit? Regardless of the current level of satisfaction or utility, if the marginal utility is greater than the marginal cost, then the consumer can increase total utility by consuming the marginal unit.

The same basic principle applies to production as well. We know that as additional units of fertilizer are applied to a given amount of land, *ceteris paribus*, the incremental or marginal returns to that fertilizer decline. This is illustrated in Figure 2–1, showing declining marginal returns (*MR*) as the amount of fertilizer is increased, *ceteris paribus*.

The marginal cost (*MC*) of obtaining additional units of fertilizer is a constant equal to the price per unit of fertilizer—$15 in this example. At any level of fertilizer use, be it 5 units or 25, the additional cost of acquiring one more unit of fertilizer is always $15.

Economizing occurs on the margin. Let us suppose that the farmer in Figure 2–1 is currently using Q_1 units of fertilizer. What are the economics of adding a very small amount of incremental or additional fertilizer at this point? If additional fertilizer is used, it will add $20 to returns and only add $15 to costs. The farmer's profits at this marginal point will therefore increase by $5 per acre. What are the farmer's total profits? We don't know. But we do know that given a choice between profits of x and $x + 5$, the economically rational farmer will prefer $x + 5$.

At output level Q_3, the marginal return from a small addition of fertilizer is $10 while the marginal cost is $15. Clearly, the farmer's profit would decrease by $5/acre if additional fertilizer were used. In fact, at this marginal point, removing one unit of fertilizer from production would have the effect of decreasing marginal returns by $10 and decreasing marginal costs by $15. Since costs fall more than returns, profit must increase by $5/acre.

At Q_1 it is possible to increase profits by using *more* fertilizer; at Q_3 it is possible to increase profits by using *less* fertilizer. At Q_2, profits are maximized because a marginal shift in either direction would result in a decrease of profits. Q_2 is the profit maximizing amount of fertilizer to be used.

Using marginal analyses we are able to determine economic optimizing behavior. By ignoring total costs or returns and concentrating only on marginal costs and returns, we are able to focus on the economizing process. From the economist's perspective, everything happens on the margin.

Logical Fallacies

Since almost everybody (with the possible exception of young children prior to the arrival of the tooth fairy) is a participant in economic society, we all become "experts" at economics. Economists probably suffer the criticisms of more "armchair quarterbacks" than any pro football coach. Unfortunately most amateur economists start with good intentions but end with bad economics. One reason that many erstwhile economists go astray is that they fall into any one of four logical traps that have been known to snare large numbers of agricultural economics students and an occasional professor as well.

The Correlation–Causation Fallacy

Correlation and causation
correlation means that two variables are related to one another but not necessarily in a cause–effect manner. Causation means that there is a cause–effect relation between the two variables. Causation implies correlation; correlation does not imply causation.

Correlation refers to two events that share some sort of mutual relationship in a regular, predictable fashion. **Causation** refers to two events in which there is a cause-and-effect relationship between the two. Therefore, when two events have a causal relationship, they also have a correlation. For instance, the rotation of the moon about the earth causes tides. Consequently, there is a predictable correlation between tides and the moon. The fallacy is to assume that if two events are correlated, then they must be related in some sort of causative manner.

Frequently, events that are correlated behave in a mutual relationship because they are both related in a causative fashion to some third event. Some ancients thought that thunder shook the rain out of the clouds. They reasoned that thunder caused rain. While thunder and rain are often associated with one another (that is, correlated), we now know that thunder does not cause rain. Instead, both rain and thunder are caused by the movement of air masses, and hence they frequently occur together.

Fallacy of Composition

This fallacy may be described as that in which what is true of a part is therefore asserted to be true of the whole. Perhaps the most famous example of a fallacy of composition in economics was the statement by Charles Wilson. A former General Motors executive who served as President Dwight Eisenhower's Secretary of Defense, Wilson asserted that "what's good for General Motors is good for America."[5]

In many situations it is perfectly valid to reason that what is true for the individual must also be true for the group. Adam Smith, the father of economics as a science, wrote that "what is prudence in the conduct of every private family, can scarcely be folly in that of a great kingdom." The main thesis of his seminal work titled *An Inquiry into the Nature and Causes of the Wealth of Nations* was

---

[5] While this statement is widely attributed to Secretary Wilson, official Senate transcripts contend that he said "What's good for the country is good for General Motors and vice versa."

that each individual acting in his or her own self-interest would also act in a manner that would benefit society as a whole. And, in general, this is still true today. As we will show later, the farmer who attempts to maximize profits also provides food to the consumer at the lowest possible price. That is, if each farmer freely attempts to do what is in his or her best interest, both farmers and consumers will benefit.

But there are instances where individual self-interest may not be in the best interest of the group. These are the cases where the fallacy of composition appears. A few quick examples will illustrate this point. A spectator at a football game can improve his view of the game by standing. By so doing he is better off, but society as a whole is worse off because he destroys the view of many. In making the fallacy of composition the spectator would declare: "If I stand up I can see better. Thus, if everyone stood up everyone could see better."

Perhaps the most common fallacy of composition in economics concerns the operation of the federal government. Many people reason that since it is prudent for a typical family to spend no more than it earns, the same must be true for the government. As will be shown in a later chapter, it is frequently in the best interests of society for the government to spend more than it takes in, running a budget deficit and enlarging the federal debt.

The Post–Hoc Fallacy

In Latin this fallacy is described as "*post hoc, ergo propter hoc.*" As a service to those few who don't read Latin, this translates to "after this, therefore because of this." The basic fallacy here is the belief that because one event precedes another, the first is the cause of the second. The proud rooster, convinced that his crowing causes the sun to rise, is guilty of this fallacy.

A careful pundit might note that after George W. Bush became president, the U.S. economy went into the first recession since when his father was president. While the statement is accurate, the implication that the recession was caused by the younger Bush is incorrect. In fact, the seeds of the 2001 recession were sown well before Mr. Bush took the oath of office. In anatomy it is relatively easy to distinguish between the tail and the dog, but in the logical framework of economics it is much more difficult. This difficulty gives rise to the "post hoc" fallacy.

The Zero–Sum Game Fallacy

This fallacy is common in economics and is easily stated: if someone gains, someone else must lose. This fallacy is at the heart of the nearly universal suspicion that both producers and consumers are repeatedly exploited by "middlemen." The fallacy is often expressed by the question, Who got the better part of the deal? Let's examine this fallacy more fully.

The basis of economics is exchange. Usually a good or service is exchanged for money. The farmer sells his wheat to an elevator and buys his fertilizer from a supply store. As with most of us, the farmer thinks the price he receives as a seller is "too low," and the price he pays as a buyer is "too high." If all buyers feel prices are too high and all sellers feel prices are too low, it is a wonder that economic transactions are ever consummated. The skeptic would claim that in a transaction the buyer and seller both emerge equally worse off. To the contrary, both are better off, for each has acquired something he wanted more than what he had. If they hadn't, then they never would have traded in the first place. A completed economic transaction, assuming there was no coercion, is a win–win situation rather than a win–lose situation as this fallacy suggests.

When the farmer buys his fertilizer, he is implicitly saying that he places a greater value on the fertilizer than he does on the money he exchanges for it. Thus, when he has the fertilizer, he has increased the total amount of value he commands. The same is true of the seller, but to him the value of the money is greater than that of the fertilizer. As a result of the exchange, the perceived value controlled by each is increased even though both will complain about the price of the transaction.

The zero-sum game fallacy maintains that value is available only in some finite quantity and that, like matter in physics, it can be neither created nor destroyed. Nothing could be further from the truth. Value can be created and it can be destroyed. As long as economic transactions are conducted with neither coercion nor constraint, an increase in the value held by one participant does not necessarily have to be the result of a decrease in the value held by the other. Usually, both should be better off.

FACTS, BELIEFS, AND VALUES

Economics, particularly in its policy applications, inevitably must deal with the value system of individuals and society. Therefore, it is important to distinguish between facts, beliefs, and values.[6] Facts are what we *know to be the case.* There is usually agreement among people concerning the validity of facts, but where agreement does not exist, there does exist an accepted objective method designed to test, and thus settle, any disputes over validity. Beliefs are what we *think to be the case.* There is frequently disagreement about the validity of beliefs. One person may believe that today's unemployment rate is higher than it was 10 years ago, but doesn't know for sure. Values are what we think *should be the case.* Values serve as the basis for making policy choices. Total agreement about values is never anticipated, so in every eco-political system there must be some procedure for determining which values shall dominate. In our institutional system, the political process is the primary mechanism for converting a socially affirmed set of values into policies and programs. Quite frequently, well-intentioned people confuse their personal values with economic fact. The result of this is the reduction of economics from a social science to a useless polemic—an event that frequently occurs in any year that is exactly divisible by four.

WORDS

CAUTION   *The medical profession uses a language that few of us can understand. Veterinarians are no different. The language they use is powerful because it is unequivocal. There is complete, uniform agreement on the meaning of each phrase, such that communication among medical doctors can be precise, exact, and efficient. Unfortunately for the student of economics, there is no similarity between medicine and economics. Beware of this difficulty!*

---

[6] In a previous section we talked about economic value in exchange. In this section we are discussing value in its philosophical sense.

As a social scientist, the agricultural economist studies the behavior of man as both producer and consumer. For the most part, the words the economist uses to describe that behavior and environment are taken from everyday language. The failure of economics to develop its own unequivocal nomenclature leads to two serious difficulties, both of which make the study of economics more excruciatingly painful than it should otherwise be:

1. There is frequent disagreement among economists on the exact meaning of specific words. And, to make matters worse, most economists frequently use these words without providing the reader with a rigorous definition of exactly what is perceived as the correct definition. Examples of words in this category are "profit," "capital," and "resources."
2. Many of the words whose definition is generally accepted by economists are also used by noneconomists in a very different way. As a result, the student begins the study of economics thinking he or she already knows with certainty what words such as "demand," "savings," and "rent" mean, only to discover that to economists these words mean something entirely different.

The authors can offer the student no quick cures for these interpretive problems, nor can they promise to be completely immune from this dreaded malady themselves, for it seems to afflict all economists. The best we can do is to give you fair warning and to encourage you to think in terms of the words that have special meaning for the economist when you seem to be falling into a logical contradiction, or when you encounter an idea that seems to make no sense at all. It may be that not being well versed in the terminology of economics is at the root of your difficulties. The successful student of economics will master and embrace the vocabulary of economics. To help you in this endeavor, definitions are provided in the margins throughout the text, and a glossary is provided at the back of the book.

SUMMARY

Agricultural economics is a social science that deals with the allocation of scarce resources among those competing alternative uses found in the production, processing, distribution, and consumption of food and fiber. The three key foundations of economics are self-interest, scarcity, and choice. Every economic system must make five allocative decisions: what to produce, how to produce it, how much to produce, when to produce, and for whom to produce. Economic decisions can be made using the price system, the command system, or some combination of the two.

Microeconomics deals with the decision making of the individual producer or consumer. Market economics deals with the collective economic behaviors of all potential producers and consumers of a single good. Macroeconomics deals with economic activity at the aggregate level and is concerned with such issues as inflation, unemployment, international trade, and the like.

Economists use several tools that are fairly unique. Economic models are a set of logical premises from which can be deduced appropriate behavioral criteria that will lead to the attainment of some explicit goal. Economists analyze the impact of changes in one economic variable on another economic variable, assuming that everything else remains constant. This is called the *ceteris paribus* assumption. When the economic value of a resource is not revealed in the marketplace, we can estimate its value using the concept of opportunity cost—its value in its highest paying alternative use. Most economic activity exhibits diminishing returns, which means that increases in the activity eventually occur at a decreasing rate. Economic decision making occurs at the level of the marginal, or additional, unit. If marginal benefits exceed marginal costs, then the marginal unit should be added to the total.

There are a number of logical fallacies that can distort economic reasoning. Just because two economic variables are correlated to one another does not imply that one causes the other. What is true for an individual may not be true for the group. Just because one event happened after another event does not imply that the first caused the second. Most economic transactions are win–win situations in which both parties are made better off. If one party is better off, that does not imply that the other party must be worse off.

Words are one of the greater impediments to a clear understanding of economics. Economists sometimes use words that can take on different meanings in different situations. In addition, economists use common words to define specific economic concepts. Success in economics requires the student to adopt the vocabulary of economics.

KEY TERMS

Agribusiness
Agricultural economics
Ceteris paribus
Command system
Correlation and causation
Diminishing returns
Economic model
Economics
Efficiency

Marginal
Market
Marketing
Microeconomics of consumption
Microeconomics of production
Opportunity cost
Price system
Price takers

PROBLEMS AND DISCUSSION QUESTIONS

1. What are the five allocative decisions that must be made within each economic system?
2. Discuss the advantages and disadvantages of the price system of allocation compared to a command system.
3. Give an example drawn from the life of a college student of each of the following types of logical fallacies: fallacy of composition, correlation–causation fallacy, post–hoc fallacy, and the zero–sum game fallacy.
4. Give an example of an economic question that would be answered by an analysis at the microeconomic level, at the market level, and at the macroeconomic level.
5. Economic transactions that involve no coercion are win–win situations. Why?
6. Using the concept of *ceteris paribus,* describe an illustration of diminishing returns in the consumption of pizza.
7. Explain the concept of marginality.

APPENDIX

EXPRESSING RELATIONSHIPS

CAUTION   *If you look closely at almost every standard economics textbook, you will find an appendix to a preliminary chapter that has a title similar to the above. Why? Do the authors copy one another or is it all part of sinister plot? Neither!*

Those of us who have taught a number of students over the years have learned that often those students who are not doing well on the tests are not having difficulty with the economics, per se, but instead are having trouble understanding some of the common tools of economists. At the introductory level, the tools most frequently used by economists are charts and graphs. The purpose of this section is to provide some assistance for those who might have difficulty using these common tools.

Relationships

Economics is the study of relationships—relationships between income and consumption, between advertising expenditures and consumer behavior, and between costs and returns. A relationship simply means that as one item changes some other item changes—either in association (correlation) or as a consequence (causation). Economics is the study of systematic relationships in our economic lives. As a result, how we describe these relationships is central to the study of economics.

Basically, there are four distinct methods used by economists to describe relationships:

- With the spoken or written word
- With a chart, table, or schedule
- With a graph
- Mathematically

Each alternative has certain advantages and disadvantages. The four methods are listed in order from the least specific to the most specific and from the easiest to understand to the most difficult to comprehend. Most introductory economics books (this one included) struggle to compromise these advantages and disadvantages by concentrating on the middle ground of charts and graphs.

To illustrate these four approaches to describing relationships, let's look at a well known relationship—that between the Fahrenheit and the Celsius temperature scales.

1. With Spoken or Written Words

The Fahrenheit scale and the Celsius scale are both measures of temperature. In the Celsius scale water freezes at 0° and boils at 100°. The same values on the Fahrenheit

FIGURE 2–2 Chart of
temperature scales.

	Celsius	Fahrenheit
Absolute zero	−273°	−460°
Crossover point	−40°	−40°
Freezing point	0°	32°
Body temperature	37°	98.6°
Boiling point	100°	212°

scale are 32° and 212°. A 1° change on the Celsius scale is equivalent to a 1.8° change on the Fahrenheit scale.

2. *Charts, Tables, or Schedules*

Figure 2–2 illustrates the relationship between the Fahrenheit and Celsius temperature scales using a chart, table, or schedule. A chart is simply a listing of some possible equivalencies on the two scales. The critical points at which water changes from a solid state to liquid and from a liquid to a gas are highlighted.

The advantage of a chart is that a greater quantity of information can be presented in a more abbreviated form than is possible with a verbal description. The disadvantage is that information is provided for only specific portions of the relationship. For instance, what is normal room temperature? Imagine the shock of a Texan visiting relatives in Toronto when they tell her to turn the air conditioner thermostat down to 22°![7]

3. *Graphs*

A graph of the relationship between Celsius and Fahrenheit is shown in Figure 2–3. The advantages of a graph are that it presents a quick, easily perceived expression of the fundamental relationship and it presents information over the entire range of the relationship rather than just at a few points on the relationship.

When working with a chart, our eyes tend to read from top to bottom, so the first thing we read is the column headings. This tells us what relationship is contained in the chart—which variables are included. To read a graph properly, the same basic information is needed. Usually the relationship being graphed is indicated by the labels on the two axes. Most graphs show the relationship between two variables—one on the horizontal axis and the other on the vertical axis. The line drawn on the graph illustrates the relationship between the two variables. In Figure 2-3 the graph shows two important aspects of the relationship between Celsius and Fahrenheit. First, since the line is a straight line, the relationship between the two scales is *linear* or constant. That means a given change in one variable will always produce the same change in the other whether the level of the temperature is high or low. Second, since the line is upward sloping, the relationship is a *direct* relationship, meaning that an increase in one variable is associated with an increase in the other. An upward-sloping graph always describes a direct relationship.

---

[7] Unlike their neighbors to the south, Canadians (and most of the rest of the world) use the Celsius scale. A normal room temperature is 22° in Celsius which is equal to 72° Fahrenheit.

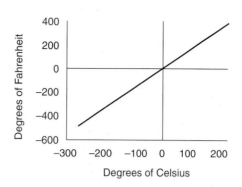

FIGURE 2–3 Graph of the relationship between Fahrenheit and Celsius temperature scales.

A downward-sloping line indicates that there is an *inverse* relationship between the two variables being graphed. In an inverse relationship, an increase in the value of one variable is associated with a decrease in the value of the other variable. A perfectly vertical or horizontal line indicates that there is no relationship between the two variables: a change in the value of one generates no change in the value of the other.

4. Math

Finally, the relationship between Celsius and Fahrenheit can be described easily using the language of mathematics. The advantage of math is that it is totally inclusive; that is, all possible values are expressed, and it is very compact. The language of mathematics is quite precise so there is little chance of misunderstanding. The difficulty with math is that you have to know the rules of math to use the language, and it is difficult to describe many nonlinear relationships accurately. In the language of math the relationship between Celsius (C) and Fahrenheit (F) is

$$C = (5/9)*(F - 32) \text{ or } F = (9/5)*C + 32$$

Unfortunately, much of the mathematics that is appropriate to describe economic relationships requires the use of calculus, so most introductory economics texts don't use math. Instead, charts and graphs get a good workout.

Reading Graphs

As previously indicated, the first things to check out on a graph are the axis labels. If you don't know which variables you are dealing with, then any knowledge of the relationship is meaningless. *Failure to read the axes is probably the most common mistake in reading graphs.* A picture may well be worth a thousand words, but if you don't know what's in the picture you'd better stick to the thousand words.

The second key to reading graphs effectively is to identify the nature of the relationship between the two variables. The relationship between two variables can be direct, inverse, or complex. The latter is a relationship that has both direct and inverse segments. Also, relationships can be linear or nonlinear. Figure 2–4 gives several examples. The left panel is the direct linear relationship examined previously. In the center panel is a well known economic relationship called an Engle's Curve. This illustrates a bit of common sense: the higher a person's income, the lower the proportion of that income spent on food. After one's income level is

FIGURE 2–4
Examples of
relationships expressed
with graphs.

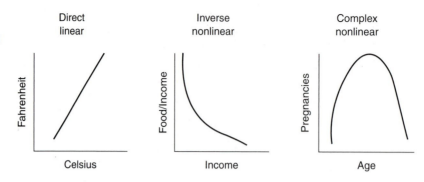

sufficient to acquire an adequate diet, the amount of food consumed will not change significantly with increases in income, but the composition of the diet may change to higher-priced foods. This is a nonlinear, inverse relationship.

The right panel of Figure 2–4 is an example of a complex relationship driven by the laws of biology. The number of pregnancies (measured in pregnancies per 1,000 women of the age group) increases from puberty to about the age of 25, and then it begins to taper off. This complex relationship is, of course, nonlinear. During the past few decades this particular curve has been getting flatter (i.e., fewer women pregnant per 1,000), and its peak has been moving to the right (i.e., women are wait-ing longer to enter the childbearing years). Both of these phenomena are partially driven by the economics of the contemporary American family, but that is another story for another day. What is important is that graphs can also be used to make

Comparative statics
a before–after
comparison to
determine the impact
of some action.

before–after comparisons. Economists call such comparisons **comparative statics** since two static situations are compared. A hypothetical (and greatly exaggerated) comparative static illustration of the above phenomenon is shown in Figure 2–5.

Another important aspect of a graph is the **rate of change** of one variable to a unit change in the other. The rate of change of the variable on the vertical axis is mea-sured by the steepness of the curve. The steeper or more vertical the line, the greater

Rate of change the
amount of change in
one variable caused
by or associated with
a unit change in
another variable.

the rate of change of the variable on the vertical axis to a unit change of the variable on the horizontal axis. For an upward-sloping curve the rate of change is positive, and for an inverse or downward-sloping curve the rate of change is negative.

The apparent rate of change of a graph can be influenced by how the two axes are scaled. If they both have the same scale, then the steepness of the curve is an accurate measure of the rate of change of the variable; but if different scales are used for the two axes, then distortion is possible. For instance, in Figure 2–6 the up-per panel is a copy of the relationship shown earlier. The axes on this graph were scaled automatically by the chart-drawing software to fill up the available space

FIGURE 2–5
Comparative static
evaluation of changes
in hypothetical child-
bearing patterns.

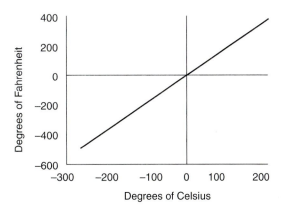

FIGURE 2–6 Scaling of axes can affect graph.

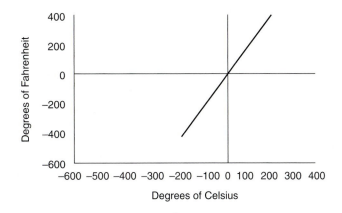

with the available data. In the lower panel the same relationship is drawn on axes that are scaled differently. The change in the apparent relationship is obvious. This is a clear example of the power of a clever graph maker to generate a graph that shows what the maker wants to show rather than what the data actually show. Every U.S. President, politician, and minister building a new church keeps at least one such graph maker busy at all times.

Slope of a Line

An extremely important characteristic of a graph is the slope of the line or curve at any point on the graph. The **slope** of a line or curve is a measure of the rate of change of the relationship. The rate of change of linear relationships (such as the temperature scales) is constant. For nonlinear relationships, the slope changes as movement along the curve is made. Figure 2–7 shows a portion of the temperature scale graph that has been greatly magnified so that you can see the change from one temperature level to the next. The specific values of the two scales are shown to the left of the chart. As you can see from the chart, if you want to turn the air conditioner down to room temperature of about 72° F, you should crank it down to about 22° C. As can be seen in Figure 2–7, a 1° change in Celsius is associated with a 1.8° change in Fahrenheit. Since this relationship is a direct relationship, increases in Celsius are always associated with increases in Fahrenheit and decreases in Celsius are always associated with decreases in Fahrenheit.

Slope at any point on a curve, slope is equal to the ratio of rise (vertical change) to run (horizontal change); and it is equal to the rate of change of the relationship at that point.

FIGURE 2–7 Close-up of the Celsius-Fahrenheit relationship.

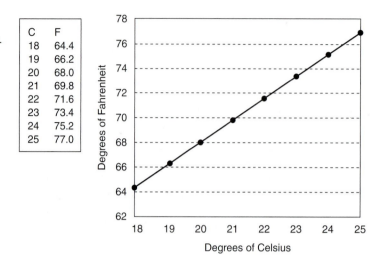

C	F
18	64.4
19	66.2
20	68.0
21	69.8
22	71.6
23	73.4
24	75.2
25	77.0

FIGURE 2–8 Determining the slope of a line.

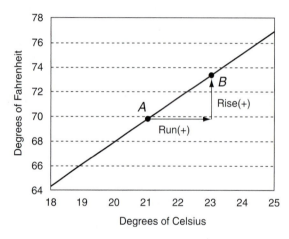

The slope of the line in Figure 2–7 measures the amount of change in Fahrenheit for a 1-degree change in Celsius. The slope of a line is always its *rise* over *run:*

$$\text{Slope} = \frac{\text{rise}}{\text{run}}$$

As you move between any two points on a line, the rise is the amount of vertical change and the run is the amount of horizontal change. For example, in Figure 2–8 movement from point *A* to point *B* involves an increase of 2° (from 21° to 23°) on the Celsius scale (horizontal movement or run) and an increase of 3.6 (from 69.8° to 73.4°) on the Fahrenheit scale (vertical movement or rise). Therefore, the slope between the points *A* and *B* is

$$\text{Slope} = \frac{\text{rise}}{\text{run}} = \frac{+3.6}{+2.0} = +1.8$$

A movement on Figure 2–8 from point *B* to point *A* would result in a negative rise and a negative run. Consequently, the slope would again be a positive 1.8. The general rule is that slope between any two points on a curve is not dependent on the direction of movement between the points.

Since the relationship between Celsius and Fahrenheit is linear, the slope is the same between any two points on the curve. The ratio of rise to run always gives the amount of rise per unit of run, or the amount of change in the variable measured on the vertical axis per unit change of the variable measured on the horizontal axis.

The relationship between Celsius and Fahrenheit is a direct relationship, meaning that an increase in one is associated with an increase in the other. Therefore, the slope of a direct relationship is always positive.

For an inverse relationship, an increase in one variable is associated with a decrease in the other. An inverse relationship is graphed as a downward-sloping line, and the slope is negative because the signs of the rise and run are opposite. This is illustrated in Figure 2–9 which shows the hypothetical relationship between the price per unit of hamburgers and the quantity of hamburgers purchased per unit of time. As common sense would suggest, if the price of hamburgers increases from $1.00 per burger to $1.50, the quantity of burgers purchased per week will decrease—from 6 to 4 in Figure 2–9. This is shown as a movement from point B in Figure 2–9 to point A. Movement from B to A involves a positive rise and a negative run. Hence the slope between B and A (and all other points on the line) is negative. Likewise, movement from A to B would involve a negative rise and a positive run, also resulting in a negative slope. As in the case of positive slopes, the larger the absolute value of the slope, the steeper the line. Very low slope values are associated with relatively flat or nearly horizontal lines.

Slope of a Curve

The slope of a curve can be measured over an arc of the curve or at a single point on the curve. Figure 2–10 illustrates the arc method of determining the slope of a curve. Between points A and B a straight line can be drawn, and the slope of that line is measured the same as for any other line as the rise over the run. The slope of this line is a measure of the "average" slope of the curve between points A and B. As you can imagine, as the distance between A and B grows smaller and smaller, the accuracy of the arc measurement increases.

In most cases, the measure of the slope of an arc of a curve is not an adequate measure of the slope of the line. A more accurate measurement is the slope of a curve at a point on that curve. The slope at a point is measured as the slope of a tangent line at that point on the curve. In Figure 2–11 the measurement of the point slope at points A and B is illustrated. At both points a line has been drawn tangent to the curve. The slope of this tangent line is the slope of the curve at that point.

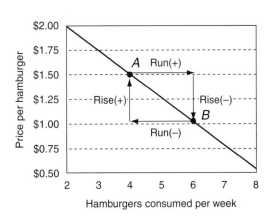

FIGURE 2–9 Slope of a negatively sloped line.

FIGURE 2–10
Measuring slope
across an arc of a
curve.

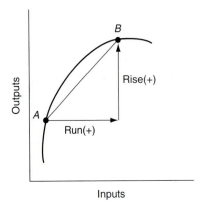

FIGURE 2–11
Measuring slope at a
point on a curve.

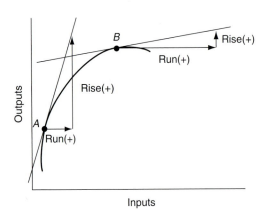

Clearly the slope at point *A* is much greater than at point *B*. Since the slope is the rate of change, the fact that the slope is greater at *A* indicates that output at *A* is increasing at a much faster rate than at *B*. That is, a unit increase in input at *A* will produce a larger increase in output than would occur for the same unit increase in input at *B*.

The curve in Figure 2–11 is drawn with fairly high or steep slopes at low levels of input and fairly low or flat slopes at higher input levels. Since slope measures the rate of change of output, we can say that output is increasing at a decreasing rate.

Special Cases

Two special cases of slope are illustrated in Figure 2–12. In panel A the slope of a tangent to the curve at the point drawn is infinite—all rise and no run. The slope of a vertical line is infinity. Panels B and C illustrate curves that have a slope of zero

FIGURE 2–12 Slopes
of infinity and zero.

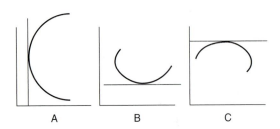

at the point of tangency. In these two cases the rise is zero over an infinite run, hence the slope is zero. In both cases, as movement is made along the curve, the slope becomes less and less steep as the point of zero slope is approached. After than point, the previous slope is reversed (from positive to negative or vice versa) and the slope begins to increase. It is a fundamental concept of math that when the slope of a curve is equal to zero, that point on the curve is either a maximum point (Panel C) or a minimum point (Panel B). As a result, slopes equal to zero take on particular interest in many cases.

Recall that the slope of a curve is equal to the rate of change of the curve. Therefore, when the rate of change of a function is equal to zero, that function will usually either be at a maximum or minimum value[8]. Since a lot of economics has to do with maximizing and minimizing behavior, points at which slopes of curves are zero take on added significance.

KEY TERMS

Comparative Statics
Rate of Change
Slope

---

[8] The exception to this general rule is known in mathematics as a local extrema or a saddle point. Imagine in your mind's eye a three-dimensional saddle. Now draw a line through the middle of the saddle from the horse's neck to the rump. This U-shaped line reaches a minimum in the seat of the saddle. But that is a minimum in one direction only, for if the line drawer moves from this local minimum to the left or right, the line will be lower than at the saddle point. In two-dimensional space, draw an S-shaped line along a 45° line. At the first bend of the curve a local maximum will be reached where the slope of a tangent is zero, but soon after the curve will exceed that local maximum. These are exceptions to the general rule that when the slope of a curve is zero, it is either a maximum or minimum point on that curve.

Introduction to Market Price Determination

*T*here is probably no branch of economics that is more widely known yet more widely misunderstood than the mystery of how prices are determined through the interaction of demand and supply. That the economics of market price determination is a mystery to many politicians is repeatedly demonstrated to the great embarrassment of the economists in their constituencies. That it remains a mystery to many students of economics is a frequent cause of a declining grade point average. The process of establishing a market price was so mysterious to early writers that Adam Smith observed that markets seem to be "led by an invisible hand." Vladimir Lenin, certainly no fan of free markets (nor of spiritual belief), noted that markets were like a car that "is steered by something illegal, something unlawful, something that comes from God knows where." As we shall see, Adam Smith's invisible hand and Lenin's wayward car are really nothing more than individual self-interest manifesting itself in a free market.

MARKETS

Market an interaction between potential buyers and potential sellers.

The interaction of potential buyers and potential sellers establishes a **market.** It is important to distinguish between a marketplace and a market. The former is a physical facility where buyers and sellers can come together. A market—the interaction between potential buyers and potential sellers of a good or service—can occur at any number of locations, or simply over the Internet. Frequently a regional or national market is composed of numerous smaller interrelated markets. For example, the national corn market in the United States is composed of several markets trading corn in a variety of forms; it is influenced by foreign markets for corn as well as foreign and domestic markets for other grains. When we talk about any market, it is important to specify the temporal and spatial dimensions of that market. The market for corn in October in Mason City, Iowa, is composed of grain elevators willing to buy corn and farmers willing to sell their recent harvest. The market for corn in Chicago in April is composed of grain traders (such as the elevator operators in Mason City) as sellers and industrial users or exporters as buyers. These two markets are distinct but highly interrelated. The markets for shelled corn and cornmeal are also distinct yet interrelated. What is important to appreciate now is that the forces which determine market price are identical in every market. It is this process of price determination in a free market that will be the central theme of this chapter.

Perfect competition a market in which there are so many buyers and so many sellers that no one of them can influence the market by his or her actions.

For the time being, we will examine the operation of markets in a **perfect competition** or free market model. In a later chapter, this assumption will be relaxed when we examine the effects of imperfect competition and monopolies. It is assumed in the perfectly competitive model that there are so many buyers and so many sellers that each is insignificant relative to the market. As a consequence, no buyer or seller can influence the price in the market by his or her actions. Both buyers and sellers are **price takers.** The only decision the buyers and sellers make is whether or not to trade at the price given to them by the market. The shopper at a typical supermarket is an example of a price taker—a buyer so insignificant relative to the total size of the market that her buying decisions cannot influence price levels.[1] The typical farmer selling steer calves at an auction is also a price taker because he is such a small seller relative to the size of the national market that any decision by him alone to withdraw from the auction would have no perceptible impact on the general price level for steers on that day.

Price takers potential buyers and potential sellers in a perfectly competitive market who face a "take it or leave it" situation at the prevailing market price.

DEMAND AND SUPPLY

Before getting further into the system of price determination, the concepts of demand and supply need to be examined. If these are fully mastered, the remainder of market economics will be a relatively easy ride.

CAUTION   *The economist's concept of demand and of supply is probably different from your existing concept. So read carefully and master these two fundamentals.*

Demand

The concept of demand will be examined in depth in a later chapter. For the time being, let's define **demand** as the quantities of a good that buyers are willing to purchase at a series of alternative prices, in a given market, during a given period of time, *ceteris paribus.* The most important aspect of this definition is that demand is a *relationship* between quantities and prices. At different *prices*, different *quantities* will be demanded. Demand is a series of these possible price-quantity combinations. Demand refers to the desires or intentions of buyers rather than their actual purchases. Demand shows how much buyers are *willing* to purchase at various prices, *ceteris paribus,* whether or not those prices are actually observed in the market.

The impact of the time and place dimensions in the definition of demand is of obvious importance. The world is replete with examples of how the willingness of consumers to purchase certain commodities changes with time and place. The demand for turkeys is certainly much different around the end of November than it is the rest of the year, and you find few stores with snow shovels on the shelf in Florida.

Demand   the quantities of a good that buyers are willing to purchase at a series of alternative prices, in a given market, during a given period of time, *ceteris paribus.*

REVIEW   *Demand:*

- *Is a relationship, not a quantity*
- *Describes consumers' desires, not their actions*
- *Assumes that everything else besides the price and quantity of the good under consideration remains the same (i.e., demand is defined* ceteris paribus*)*
- *Is defined for a given place and a given time period*

---

[1] A challenge for those who wish to demonstrate the powerlessness of an individual in a competitive market: next time you are at the supermarket try bargaining with the manager over the price of ground beef or chicken. Just see how much power you have.

FIGURE 3–1
Demand schedule for ground beef at retail outlets in the New York City metropolitan area, typical week.

Price per Pound ($/lb)	Quantity Demanded (Million lb/Week)
$1.00	15.0
1.25	13.9
1.50	12.5
1.75	10.9
2.00	9.0
2.25	6.9
2.50	4.5
2.75	1.9

Quantity demanded how much of a good or service a buyer is willing to purchase at a single, specified price, in a given market, at a given time, *ceteris paribus.*

Demand schedule a schedule identifying specific price-quantity combinations that exist in a demand relationship.

Demand is a two-dimensional concept—the two dimensions being price and quantity. The relationship between these two dimensions is *demand.* The **quantity demanded** is a one-dimensional concept that refers to how much of a good or service a buyer is willing to purchase at a single, specified price, in a given market, at a given time, *ceteris paribus.* It is very important to distinguish between the two related but different concepts of demand and quantity demanded.

As suggested in the previous chapter, the demand relationship can be described in words, with a schedule, as a graph, or as an equation. The relationship is the same regardless of the method used to illustrate it. A hypothetical **demand schedule** is shown in Figure 3–1. This schedule shows the relationship between prices for ground beef and the quantities demanded in the New York City metropolitan area during a typical week. As we might expect, when the price of ground beef increases, the quantity that consumers would be willing to purchase is reduced. The reasons for this inverse relationship are several. They will be examined in detail at a later point in this book. Suffice it to say at this point that as ground beef gets more expensive, *ceteris paribus,* consumers will react by either switching from ground beef to some other meat or giving up meat altogether for one or two meals per week. Notice that for a change in price, the *quantity demanded* changes, but the *demand* relationship remains unchanged.

Because it is so frequently misunderstood, the last point merits restatement. Demand refers to the price–quantity relationship illustrated in the demand schedule. A change in price causes a jump to a different point on the schedule, but it does not change the schedule itself. So, a change in price does not cause a change in demand, but it does cause a change in the quantity demanded. Demand is a relationship, but not a point on that relationship. Quantity demanded is not a relationship, but a point on that relationship.

As with all demand schedules, the one shown in Figure 3–1 is defined under the *ceteris paribus* assumption that everything else (other than the price and the quantity demanded of ground beef) remains constant. From a practical point of view, this means that our demand relationship shows how consumers would react to different prices for ground beef, assuming that the prices for chicken, pork, and other cuts of beef all remained the same. If the price of ground beef increases while that of chicken remains constant, then the *relative price* of ground beef to chicken has increased. In this case, it is only natural to expect the quantity demanded of beef to decrease.

Demand curve a two-dimensional graph illustrating a demand relationship.

The information contained in the demand schedule shown in Figure 3–1 can easily be converted into a **demand curve**—a common two-dimensional graph such as that shown in Figure 3–2. Remember that a graph can be used to show the rela-

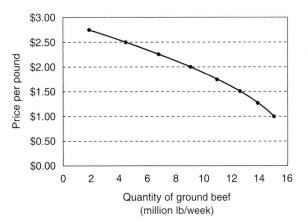

FIGURE 3–2
Demand curve for ground beef at retail outlets in the New York City metropolitan area, typical week.

tionship between two variables. In this case the two variables are the price and the quantity demanded of ground beef. The vertical axis measures different prices per pound of ground beef, while the horizontal axis shows different quantities demanded per week. Each price–quantity combination contained in the schedule of Figure 3–1 is transferred to the two-dimensional graph in Figure 3–2 and marked with a small dot at the appropriate set of coordinates. The first dot on the left is at a price of $2.75 per pound, and the quantity consumed at this price is 1.9 million pounds.[2] Once a dot is entered for each price-quantity demanded combination shown on the demand schedule in Figure 3–1, the dots can be connected by a smooth line to produce a *demand curve.*

The advantage of a demand curve is that it provides a visual presentation of the demand relationship and it allows for easy interpolation of prices between those listed in a demand schedule. For instance, using the demand curve in Figure 3–2, we can see that at a price of $1.60, approximately 12 million pounds of ground beef would be the quantity demanded.

Supply

The concept of supply will be developed in depth in a later chapter. For the time being, however, we will define **supply** as the quantities of a good that sellers are willing to offer at a series of alternative prices, in a given market, during a given period of time, *ceteris paribus.* Notice that this definition is identical with that of demand, except that supply is a relationship between *prices* and *quantities* that sellers are willing to offer. Supply describes a relationship, not a quantity.

As is the case with demand, it is important to distinguish between supply and the quantity supplied. The **quantity supplied** is a one-dimensional concept that refers to how much of a good or service a seller is willing to offer at a single, specified price, in a given market, at a given time, *ceteris paribus.* It is very important to distinguish between the two related but different concepts of supply and quantity supplied.

Figure 3–3 and 3–4 show a **supply schedule** and a **supply curve** for ground beef in the New York City metropolitan area. As we would expect, when the price of ground beef increases, sellers willingly offer greater quantities for sale. This direct

Supply the quantities of a good that sellers are willing to offer at a series of alternative prices, in a given market, during a given period of time, *ceteris paribus.*

Quantity supplied how much of a good or service a seller is willing to offer at a single, specified price, in a given market, at a given time, *ceteris paribus.*

Supply schedule a schedule identifying specific price-quantity combinations that exist in a supply relationship.

Supply curve a two-dimensional graph illustrating a supply relationship.

---

[2] The dot farthest to the left of Figure 3–2 corresponds to the last line of the demand schedule in Figure 3–1. Each line of the demand schedule in Figure 3–1 corresponds to a dot on the curve in Figure 3–2.

FIGURE 3–3 Supply schedule for ground beef at retail outlets in the New York City metropolitan area, typical week.

Price per Pound ($/lb)	Quantity Supplied (Million lb/Week)
$1.00	0.5
1.25	1.6
1.50	3.0
1.75	4.6
2.00	6.5
2.25	8.6
2.50	11.0
2.75	13.6

FIGURE 3–4 Supply curve for ground beef at retail outlets in the New York City metropolitan area, typical week.

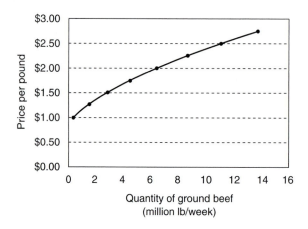

relationship between prices and quantities supplied is expected for several reasons. If prices are relatively low, some suppliers might be induced to sell their ground beef in another market, such as Boston or Pittsburgh. For this reason, as the price of ground beef in New York falls, *ceteris paribus,* the quantity of ground beef that will be offered in New York will also decline. A second reason why a direct relationship between prices and the quantities supplied can be expected is because suppliers will react to relatively low prices by building up their inventories of ground beef, thus reducing the quantity supplied at the low prices. Conversely, if suppliers feel the price of ground beef is relatively high, they will draw down inventories causing the quantity supplied to increase.

As in the case of demand, the time and space dimensions are an important part of the concept of supply. It takes a year to significantly increase the output of grain crops. Several years are required to expand beef production, and beef slaughter over the intervening period must be reduced to accomplish the expansion.

The supply curve in Figure 3–4 was derived from the supply schedule in Figure 3–3 in exactly the same manner as the demand curve was derived from a demand schedule. Note that the axes are labeled in exactly the same manner as for a demand curve since the two variables being graphed are exactly the same—price per unit and pounds of ground beef per week. The upward slope of the supply curve shows a positive relationship between prices and the quantity supplied.

CAUTION   *Movement along a supply (demand) curve causes a change in the quantity supplied (quantity demanded), but it does not change the supply (demand) relationship.*

PRICE DETERMINATION

The interaction of demand and supply is fundamental to the process of price determination and market clearing. So long as a perfectly competitive market is allowed to operate with no external controls and no regulations on trading, the market price will adjust so as to clear the market of goods by equating the quantity demanded with the quantity supplied. This is illustrated in Figure 3–5, which shows the combined schedules of demand and supply of ground beef in New York City. Remember that both supply and demand refer to the *willingness* or *intentions* of sellers and buyers in the market, not to actual transactions. At a price of $2.15, the intentions of buyers are consistent with those of sellers. At this price, the quantity willingly demanded is equal to the quantity willingly supplied and the market is cleared. In this market a price of $2.15 is the **equilibrium price.** In Figure 3–6 the same supply and demand relationships are shown as a graph with the equilibrium

Equilibrium price
that price at which the quantity supplied in a market is equal to the quantity demanded.

Price per Pound ($/lb)	Quantity Demanded (Million lb/Week)	Quantity Supplied (Million lb/Week)	Market Condition
$1.00	15.0	0.5	Shortage
$1.25	13.9	1.6	Shortage
$1.50	12.5	3.0	Shortage
$1.75	10.9	4.6	Shortage
$2.00	9.0	6.5	Shortage
$2.15	**7.75**	**7.75**	**Equilibrium**
$2.25	6.9	8.6	Surplus
$2.50	4.5	11.0	Surplus
$2.75	1.9	13.6	Surplus

FIGURE 3–5   Market schedules for ground beef at retail outlets in the New York City metropolitan area, typical week.

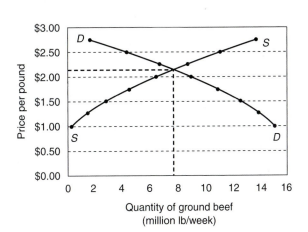

FIGURE 3–6   Market curves for ground beef at retail outlets in the New York City metropolitan area, typical week.

point being the point at which the two curves cross, identifying the one unique price at which the quantity willingly supplied is equal to the quantity willingly demanded. This is the market clearing or equilibrium price.[3]

For free and competitive markets, the market price will always move toward the equilibrium price until a stable equilibrium that just clears the market is attained. At any price other than $2.15, either a surplus or a shortage will develop in the market, which, in turn, will put pressure on the price of the product to move back toward the equilibrium price. For instance, at a price of $2.75/pound retailers in New York would be willing to offer 13.6 million pounds of ground beef for sale during a typical week. However, consumers desire to purchase only 1.9 million pounds *at that price*. There is a difference of 11.7 million pounds of ground beef between what sellers are willing to sell and what buyers are willing to buy at a price of $2.75 per pound. As the week draws to a close, what would butchers do? Obviously, each butcher would want to get rid of the excess ground beef that had not been sold during the week: he either sells it or smells it. So, here sits a butcher in his shop with a lot of ground beef that is about to rot. What would he do? He would lower his price to encourage consumers to eat more ground beef and to encourage consumers to buy from his shop rather than from his competitors. Of course, all of his competitors would have the same idea at approximately the same time, so the average or typical price in the market would move in a downward direction. This illustrates the basic principle that in a free market the existence of a surplus creates a downward pressure on market price. Therefore, if for some reason the market price is above the equilibrium or market clearing level, there are automatic forces (an invisible hand perhaps) that will tend to push the market price lower. Notice that the butcher lowers his price voluntarily in order to protect his own self-interest. No central planning agency is needed here—just self-interest!

The same sort of automatic adjustment mechanism takes place if the market price should wander below the equilibrium price level. In this case a shortage will develop and consumers, each acting in his or her own self-interest, will bid against one another for the limited quantity available. Butchers will be encouraged to raise prices as signs of shortages—such as declining inventories, customer lines, and panic buying—appear. Thus, a market price that is below the equilibrium price will cause a shortage, inducing market prices to rise as long as the market is not constrained by any type of external regulation. This phenomenon is also shown in Figure 3–7, where prices below the equilibrium level cause shortages to occur as the quantity consumers *want* to consume is greater than the quantity retailers *want* to provide. When these intentions or wants are inconsistent, there will automatically develop pressures to correct the errant price. These pressures are created by the perceived self-interests of buyers and sellers as they interact in a market.

As shown in Figure 3–7, at a price of $1.75/pound the quantity being taken off the market (quantity demanded) is greater than the quantity coming onto the market (quantity supplied). So at that price inventories are being depleted. As sell-

---

[3] The astute reader will note that the demand and supply schedules in Figure 3–1 and Figure 3–3 did not contain information for a price of $2.15. Since this is the equilibrium price for this market, it has been added to Figure 3–5.

For the mathematically inclined, the demand function used throughout this chapter is $Q_d = 17 - 2P^2$ where Q_d is the quantity demanded at alternative prices P. The supply function is $Q_s = 2P^2 - 1.5$. At market equilibrium the quantity demanded is equal to the quantity supplied. So, set $Q_d = Q_s$ and solve for P. You should get $2.15. Plug this price back into the supply and demand functions and you should get 7.75 million pounds in each case.

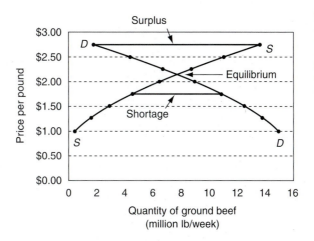

FIGURE 3–7 Surplus and shortage in the market for ground beef at retail outlets in the New York City metropolitan area, typical week.

ers see their inventories being drawn down, it is only natural that they would increase the price because they perceive that the market could bear a higher price. A pressure for price to move back toward an equilibrium is thus ensured.

The important point here is that large numbers of buyers and sellers, each acting out of self-interest, will automatically drive prices to their equilibrium levels. Price determination in a price allocation system is an automatic, self-correcting process.

CHANGES IN SUPPLY AND DEMAND

A market can be likened to a pond in which the water always returns to its own level after being disturbed. If a stone is thrown into a pond, the water will be disturbed temporarily, but with time the water will return once again to a stable equilibrium with a smooth surface. This equilibrium will remain stable until disturbed again by some external force. In the same manner, if the price in a market changes because of some force that is external to the market, there will be some initial disruption, but the forces of the market will automatically correct for that disruption as rapidly as possible. When the market price is pushed to the level of a new equilibrium price, a stable equilibrium will again prevail until such time as some force external to the market again causes a change in the equilibrium price. Some disturbances to a stable pond will cause the equilibrium level of the pond to change. For instance, if a large boulder is thrown into a small pond, it will disturb the equilibrium situation of the water and cause the new equilibrium level to be higher than the previous level. A **demand/supply shift** due to an external disturbance (i.e., a change in a *ceteris paribus* condition) will cause the same thing to happen in a market. There will be an initial disequilibrium because the new equilibrium price (like the level of the pond) will be either higher or lower than the previous market price. This initial disequilibrium will result in a surplus or shortage that will generate pressures on the market price to move to a new level where a stable equilibrium can again be attained.

An example of a demand curve shift is shown in Figures 3–8 and 3–9. In these figures, the demand for ground beef in New York City used in previous examples is repeated. Now assume that one of the *ceteris paribus* conditions for the demand relationships shown in the previous figures was that the price of chicken was $0.80 per pound. That is, the demand schedules we have examined

Demand/supply shift a change in the demand/supply relationship caused by a change in one of the *ceteris paribus* conditions.

Price per Pound ($/lb)	Quantity Demanded (Million lb/Week)	Quantity Demanded (Million lb/Week)	Quantity Supplied (Million lb/Week)
	Chicken $0.80/lb	Chicken $0.60/lb	
$1.00	15.0	13.9	0.5
1.25	13.9	12.1	1.6
1.50	12.5	10.0	3.0
1.75	10.9	7.4	4.6
1.90	9.8	5.7	5.7
2.00	9.0	4.5	6.5
2.15	7.75	2.0	7.75
2.25	6.9	1.2	8.6
2.50	4.5	*	11.0
2.75	1.9	*	13.6

*The function used turned negative at these high prices. No market exists at these prices.

FIGURE 3–8   Market schedules for ground beef at retail outlets in the New York City metropolitan area, typical week.

FIGURE 3–9   Market curves for ground beef at retail outlets in the New York City metropolitan area, typical week.

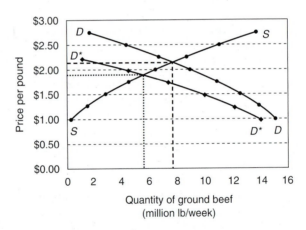

previously showed how much ground beef consumers were willing to buy at alternative prices for ground beef, assuming that the price of chicken remained constant at $0.80 per pound. The data in the center column of Figure 3–8 show what would happen to the demand for ground beef if the price of chicken were to fall to $0.60 per pound, *ceteris paribus*. It is easy to imagine how most consumers would react to the price change for chicken: instead of eating chicken for one meal per week, the typical family might have two meals of chicken. Consumers would substitute the now cheaper chicken for ground beef in the diet. Therefore, the quantity of ground beef demanded at each and every price for ground beef would likely decline. The price decline for chicken encourages consumers to substitute chicken for ground beef, causing an inward shift of the ground beef demand curve to D^*D^* in Figure 3–9. As a result of the inward shift of the ground beef demand curve, consumers demand a lesser quantity of beef at every price for beef.[4]

At the old equilibrium price of $2.15 there is now market disequilibrium. Suppliers are still willing to supply 7.75 million pounds per week at $2.15, but consumers are no longer willing to consume that much ground beef at that price. Since many consumers switched to the now cheaper chicken, they will purchase only 2 million pounds of ground beef at $2.15,[5] so a surplus of ground beef on the New York market will develop. The existence of the surplus will automatically force retail outlets to lower ground beef prices until a new equilibrium price is found. In this example, the new equilibrium in the market for ground beef will be established at a price of approximately $1.90 with about 5.7 million pounds per week being the market clearing quantity traded. So we see that the final effect of a decline in the price of chicken on the ground beef market is to cause the equilibrium price and the quantity traded of ground beef to decline as a result of a shift in the demand relationship for ground beef.

Let's briefly review what occurred in the previous example. The ground beef market was in equilibrium at a price of $2.15. Then a change in one of the *ceteris paribus* conditions caused a shift of the entire ground beef demand curve. This, in turn, caused the equilibrium price of ground beef to decline to a new equilibrium level at $1.90. It is important to realize that the decline in the price of ground beef is the result of a change in the *ceteris paribus* conditions. This is an illustration of a very simple (but important) principle of economics that market prices are the *result* of the interaction of supply and demand, rather than the cause of supply and demand. A frequent mistake of the beginning student of agricultural economics is to think that the price of ground beef will determine the supply and demand of ground beef in a given market. To the contrary, it is supply and demand that determine price. An equilibrium price will not change unless there is a shift in either the supply or demand for the product, and supply and demand shift only if there is a change in the *ceteris paribus* conditions. Thus, the direction of causality for price determination in a free, competitive market will always be as shown in Figure 3–10.

The direction of causality will never be reversed. As shown in Figure 3–11, markets are the dog, and price is the tail. Just as the tail always follows the dog, prices always follow the market. And just as the tail never pushes the dog, product price changes never cause a change in the supply or demand of that product. Things can get a little tricky here, so make sure you have it clear in your mind that a change in the price of chicken, *ceteris paribus*, will *cause* a shift in the demand for beef. A change in the price of beef is the *result* of a shift in the demand or supply of beef; it is never the cause of it.

---

[4] As indicated earlier, words are the bane of economics (and students of economics). Your authors see the demand shift in Figure 3–9 as an "inward" shift. Some economists see this as a "downward" shift, while others see this as a "shift to the left." This is a case where it is very likely that the phrases used by your instructor may well be different than those used in this text.

[5] To find this value on Figure 3–9 trace the dotted line from the previous equilibrium horizontally to the intersection with the new, shifted demand curve (D^*D^*). Then read down to the horizontal axis to see the quantity consumers are willing to consume at a price of $2.15/pound on the newly shifted demand curve.

FIGURE 3–10
Direction of causation
in market adjustments.

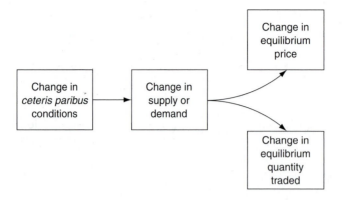

FIGURE 3–11
Relationship between
markets and prices.

> **CAUTION** *While it is a basic premise of market economics that prices are determined by supply and demand, the confused student will usually ask, "But if the price of ground beef falls, won't the demand for ground beef rise?" The answer is an emphatic no! The student has made two serious mistakes. First, the student has confused "demand" and "quantity demanded"; second, the student has confused correlation with causation. What has actually happened is that as a result of the shift in the demand (a two-dimensional relationship) for ground beef, the equilibrium price and quantity traded in equilibrium decline. Notice that both price and quantity traded decline simultaneously as a result of the demand curve shift. Thus, price and quantity demanded are not causally related, but instead are linked together like Siamese twins: when one moves, the other is certain to move as well. Since both price and quantity traded change simultaneously, it is relatively easy, but most incorrect, to infer causality. To do so is to fall into the logical trap we discussed earlier—the correlation-causation fallacy. Beware of making this logical error!*

One final warning for the beginning student of market price determination: in 99.9 percent of the cases, a change in a given *ceteris paribus* condition will cause a shift in either the supply curve or the demand curve, but not both. In our ground beef example, the supply relationship is not dependent on the price of chicken, but the demand relationship is. Notice that even though the supply of ground beef does not change when the price of chicken falls, the market clearing (i.e., equilibrium) quantity supplied of ground beef will change because a change in the price of chicken causes the ground beef demand curve to shift, which will, in turn, cause the market clearing quantity traded to decline.

The basic principles of market economics will be used throughout the remainder of this book. In later chapters, a more thorough understanding of the fundamentals of supply and demand will be developed emphasizing the *ceteris paribus* conditions that are important shifters of supply and demand. With these tools it will be possible to anticipate how changes that are external to a given market will affect that market. It is very important that the agricultural producer be able to evaluate how changes in the economic environment will affect his or her operations. This is the essence of management—how to adjust to changing conditions. Economics allows the manager to systematically anticipate change. The use of simple, but powerful, market equilibrium analysis is usually the starting point for these evaluations. Later chapters will explain how the economist not only predicts the direction of change but also estimates how much a market price or quantity traded will change as a result of some external change.

CONCEPT OF ELASTICITY

Supply and demand are relationships between prices and quantities. This simple statement is one of the fundamental lessons of any course in economics. These relationships are the basic notions of economics. They describe the behavior of producers and consumers, respectively. In later chapters we will intensively study the economic behavior of each as they pursue their own self-interests.

As pointed out earlier, words are very important in understanding economics. One of those important words is "**elasticity.**" This is an economic concept that refers to *price responsiveness.* Either supply or demand may be characterized as being "elastic" or "inelastic." These terms are relative rather than absolute and are used primarily for comparative purposes.

Supply or demand that is elastic is very price responsive—that is, a relatively small change in price will bring about a relatively large response in either quantity supplied or quantity demanded. At the other end of the spectrum, a supply or demand relationship that is inelastic is not at all price responsive—that is, a relatively large change in price will bring about only a small change in the quantity supplied or quantity demanded.

Figure 3–12 gives examples of elastic and inelastic supply and demand relationships.[6] What is important at this point in time is to remember that *in*elastic means *non*responsive. The classic example of a good for which demand is very *in*elastic is *in*sulin. Very large price changes for this good will bring about small (if any) changes in the quantity demanded. By comparison, the demand for Texaco gasoline is very elastic because a one- or two-penny change in the price of Texaco, *ceteris paribus* (i.e., the price of Shell and Exxon remaining the same), will bring about a large change in the quantity demanded of Texaco gasoline.

This concept of price responsiveness will be fully explored in a later chapter and used throughout this text. Just remember that *in*sulin is *in*elastic.

Elasticity a measure of how responsive the quantity demanded by consumers or the quantity supplied by producers is to a change in the equilibrium price.

---

[6] The diagrams in Figure 3–12 are designed to make a point about elasticity and price responsiveness. Any well-trained economist knows that as one moves along a straight line supply or demand curve, the elasticity changes. At this point in time, rejoice that you are not concerned about this technicality, but that you do understand what elastic and inelastic mean.

FIGURE 3–12
Examples of elasticity.

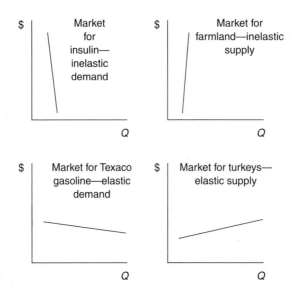

SUMMARY

A market exists when potential buyers and potential sellers of a commodity interact. The interaction may be face-to-face, on the phone, or on the Internet. Demand (supply) is a relationship between the quantities of a good buyers (sellers) are willing to buy (sell) at a series of alternative prices, in a given market, during a given period of time, *ceteris paribus*. Quantity demanded (supplied) is the amount of a commodity a buyer (seller) is willing to buy (sell) at a specified price. Supply and demand relationships may be described by either a schedule or a graph. Movements along a demand (supply) curve will change the quantity demanded (supplied) but will not change demand (supply).

Equilibrium prices in a market are determined by the interaction of supply and demand. An equilibrium price is one at which the quantity supplied is equal to the quantity demanded. At prices above (below) the equilibrium price a surplus (shortage) will develop and drive the price back to the equilibrium level.

A change in either the supply or demand relationship is called a shift. A shift will occur only when one of the *ceteris paribus* conditions external to the market changes. A shift of supply or demand will usually result in a change in the equilibrium price and the equilibrium quantity traded. Changes in the price of a product are a result of a shift in the supply or demand of the product: they are not a cause of a shift in supply or demand.

Elasticity is a measure of price responsiveness. The concept of elasticity may be applied to both supply and demand. Goods that are not responsive to price changes are termed inelastic, while those that are price responsive are called elastic.

KEY TERMS

Demand
Demand curve
Demand schedule
Demand/supply shift
Elasticity
Equilibrium price
Market

Perfect competition
Price takers
Quantity demanded
Quantity supplied
Supply
Supply curve
Supply schedule

PROBLEMS AND DISCUSSION QUESTIONS

1. Clearly distinguish between demand and quantity demanded.
2. A demand schedule for rice is shown below.
   a. At a price of $4.00, what is the quantity demanded?
   b. If the price increases to $5.00, what happens to the quantity demanded?
   c. If the price again increases to $6.00, what happens to demand? [Hint: the correct answer is nothing]

   DEMAND FOR RICE

Price per Unit	Quantity Purchased
$3.00	78 units
4.00	56
5.00	43
6.00	30
7.00	15

3. The following four events are noted in a marketplace:
   a. The price of chicken goes up.
   b. The price of beef goes up.
   c. The demand for chicken shifts.
   d. The quantity consumed of chicken increases.

   Diagram the order of causation of these four events using arrows and numbers such as

   $1 \rightarrow 2 \rightarrow 3 \rightarrow 4$ or $\quad 1 \rightarrow 2 \begin{array}{l} \nearrow 3 \\ \searrow 4 \end{array}$

4. A grocer notes that last week he sold 4,000 heads of lettuce at $0.59 per head. This week he sold only 3,500 at $0.49 per head. Was this change due to a supply shift or a demand shift? Draw a supply-demand diagram to illustrate your answer.

5. Indicate whether the demand for the following goods is elastic or inelastic (Hint: remember to think about price changes for each item, *ceteris paribus*):

   Health care

   Gasoline

   Food

   Folger's coffee

   Cigarettes (assuming that smoking is addictive)

   Marlboro cigarettes

   Tomato soup

   Milk

6. What single characteristic of the above goods seems to separate the inelastic goods from the elastic goods?

7. Draw a supply-demand diagram illustrating the impact of a drought in the corn belt on the market for corn. Be certain you clearly label the axes and identify the change caused by the drought.

Financial Markets

*A*gribusiness is *big* business. The food industry is the second largest in the United States. Only the medical industry accounts for a larger share of personal consumption expenditures. One of the challenges facing any firm is how to finance operations. This chapter is about how firms (large and small, in agribusiness or in other sectors) obtain funds to finance their operations and how the financial markets that provide these funds operate. As with any market, in financial markets the forces of supply and demand interact to establish a market clearing price. Financial markets are a good market to study because the forces that shift supply and demand are usually very visible and highly predictable. And information on prices is readily available on a daily basis in most newspapers or almost instantaneously on the Internet.

The primary role of financial markets in our economy is to convert savings into investments. **Financial institutions,** those businesses that make this conversion, "buy" and "sell" funds in just the same way J.C. Penney buys and sells underwear. Think of your local bank. It is an example of a financial institution. It buys deposits and sells loans to borrowers. In so doing, the bank converts savings into investment. It is important to understand that "savings" to the economist has a much broader meaning than the lay interpretation. To the economist **savings** includes payments to pension funds, premiums on insurance policies, and any other form of consumption foregone. For different kinds of savings, there are different financial intermediaries. But, collectively they are all part of the same market for financial funds. It is to that market we now turn.

> **Financial institutions** businesses that convert savings into investments. They buy and sell financial funds and in so doing create a market for funds. Also called "financial intermediaries."

> **Savings** that part of income that is not used for consumption. Some saving is involuntary, such as required payments into a retirement account.

HOW FIRMS OBTAIN FUNDS

Other than differences in scale, there is little financial difference between the choices facing farmer Jones as he expands his operation and those facing Wal-Mart in building a new Sam's store.

Let's suppose Joe Jones currently farms 600 acres. His neighbor, Bert Smith, is getting old and wants to sell his 400-acre operation for $1,500 per acre, or $600,000. Joe wants to buy Bert's adjacent farm to expand his operation to 1,000 acres. How does he do it? Basically, there are three alternatives:

- Joe can use his savings of previous profits he has earned from his 600 acres.
- Joe can go to the bank or some other financial institution (such as an insurance company) and borrow the funds necessary to buy Bert's land.
- Joe can offer to make Bert a partner in the larger farm with a promise to split future profits on a 60/40, or any other mutually agreeable, basis. This can be done either through a partnership or by forming a corporation and giving Bert 40 percent of the stock ownership of the new corporation.

Retained earnings
profits of a business
firm that are retained
by the firm rather than
paid out to the owners
of the firm. Retained
earnings can be used
by the firm to make
additional investments
in new plant and
equipment.

Bonds   legal
agreement between
lender and borrower
when business firms
borrow from the
public.

Stock   claim of
partial ownership of a
business firm.

Interest rate   the
price of money.
Financial institutions
buy money at one
interest rate and sell it
to potential borrowers
at a higher interest rate,
thereby earning a profit
on the transaction.

Wall Street   a
common reference to
financial markets in
general. Wall Street, in
New York City, is the
location of the New
York Stock Exchange
and many other major
financial institutions.

Corporation   a legal
entity that is formed to
own and operate a
business.

Charter   a legal
document, similar to a
constitution, that
establishes a corpora-
tion and lays out the
rules that will govern
the corporation.
Charters are submitted
to and approved by
the secretary of state
in the state in which
the corporation is
legally established.

When Wal-Mart (now the second or third largest food retailer in the country) wants to expand, it basically faces the same three alternatives that Joe faces:

- It can use previous profits, called **retained earnings,** to finance an expansion.
- It can borrow the funds necessary from the financial markets by issuing **bonds** to investors.
- It can sell ownership shares of the company by issuing additional shares of **stock,** which it sells to the public.

Financial markets include myriad institutions that facilitate the process of moving money from potential savers to potential borrowers. The primary institutions in the financial markets are banks, insurance companies, mutual funds, brokers,[1] and pension funds. Together these institutions collect billions in savings on a daily basis and invest these savings by making loans to potential borrowers. In essence, these financial intermediaries buy and sell funds, creating a market for funds or a market for money. The forces of supply and demand create a market clearing price for money that we call the **interest rate.**

The primary instruments used by potential borrowers to obtain funds on financial markets are stocks and bonds. Stocks are shares of part ownership in a firm (the third alternative in both previous cases). Bonds are promissory notes issued by the borrower of funds to the lender of funds promising to pay interest on the funds during the period of the loan and promising to repay the borrowed funds at the end of a specified period (the second alternative in both previous cases). We first turn to the market for stocks. Later in the chapter we will examine the market for bonds.

STOCK

The stock market is a part of daily life in our society. One item that is included in every evening news broadcast, every single business day, is a report on the stock market. Was "the market" up, or was it down? Since many Americans have a significant portion of their savings invested directly in the stock market or invested indirectly by a pension or retirement fund, what happens to stock prices on any given day is of more than passing interest. People who buy and sell stock do so for only the purest of motives—self-interest.

Not unlike the automobile business, there is a market for new stocks and a market for used or previously issued stock. Most of the trading on **Wall Street** is trading of previously issued shares of stock that are passed on from owner to owner. To understand the role of stocks in the capital formation process we will turn first to the largely unknown market for new stocks and then turn to the more familiar market for previously issued stock.

Newly Issued Stock

A **corporation** is a legal entity that is formed to own and operate a business. The legal document creating the corporation is known as the **charter.** The charter au-

---

[1] We refer here to a broad range of financial services companies such as Merrill Lynch, Citigroup, and others.

thorizes the corporation to issue **shares of stock** (or part ownership) up to some maximum number of shares. Usually for a fairly new corporation, millions of shares will be authorized in the charter, but only a few thousand will actually be sold to and held by individuals. The rest of the authorized, but not yet issued, shares are held by the corporation. These shares are one source of additional funds if the corporation wants to expand its operations.

The owner of each share of stock is an equal co-owner of the corporation. Each share entitles the owner of that share to one vote in the business of the corporation. Each year the shareholders elect a **board of directors** to run the company on their behalf. The board of directors is responsible for hiring and firing the managers of the corporation and for making important strategic decisions. If shareholders are collectively unhappy about how the corporation is being managed, they can vote to elect a different board of directors.

A company that offers to sell shares of its stock to the public must do so under strict guidelines imposed by an agency of the federal government known as the **Securities and Exchange Commission** (SEC).[2] Among the requirements of the SEC is a ban on advertising the offering and the required publication of an extensive document giving detailed information about the financial situation of the firm and the firm's intended use of the funds to be raised. This document is called a **prospectus.**

Usually when a company offers additional shares of stock for sale (or makes an initial offering), an announcement (not an advertisement) is placed in major financial publications such as *The Wall Street Journal* (*WSJ*). These announcements, because of their bleak appearance to avoid being "advertisements," are known as **tombstones.** A typical tombstone is shown in Figure 4–1. In this example, Gator Internet Technologies (GIT) is offering to sell 4 million shares to the public at a fixed price of $15.00 per share. Simple arithmetic suggests that this offering will generate gross sales of $60 million if all shares are sold.

Notice the disclaimer at the top of this tombstone stating that this is an announcement and not an "offer to sell."[3] At the end is a statement concerning the availability of the prospectus. The SEC requires that a potential buyer of the offering receive (but not necessarily read) a copy of the prospectus before actually buying the stock. In the lower left-hand corner of the tombstone is the date of issue—April 1, 2002. Usually tombstones appear a day or two after the shares are actually sold, further emphasizing that this is an "announcement" rather than an "advertisement."

The bottom half of the tombstone lists the **underwriters** of this public offering. The underwriters are the "deal makers" or investment bankers who serve as retailers of GIT's new stock. If you want to buy some of these new shares of GIT, you must buy them from one of the underwriters listed on the tombstone. The **lead underwriter** is always listed at the top and frequently in larger type than the other underwriters. The lead underwriter is the financial firm that has taken responsibility for establishing the size of the offering and the offer price with GIT and then finding other underwriters to participate in the offering.

This tombstone is an announcement that the underwriters listed have already bought all 4 million shares of GIT at an undisclosed wholesale price (the usual

---

Shares of stock
one share of stock means one unit of ownership of the corporation. If 4,000 shares of stock have been sold by the corporation to the public (i.e., individuals, pension funds, and the like), then the owner of one share owns one four-thousandth of the corporation. If the corporation issues (i.e., sells to the public) 1,000 additional shares, then the holder of one share owns one five-thousandth of the corporation. This is known as dilution. The terms "stock," "share," and "share of stock" are used interchangeably.

Board of directors
a group of individuals elected by shareholders to manage a corporation on behalf of the shareholders. The board hires and fires the management of the company and makes broad policy decisions.

Securities and Exchange Commission   a federal regulatory agency that enforces laws to protect investors from fraud in the sale of stock by corporations and in the trading of stock by brokers and others.

---

[2] The strict guidelines are designed to protect the consumer from sellers of stock who misrepresent the company issuing the stock. Unfortunately, rules and regulations can't prevent predators from engaging in illegal activities. As with all laws, their value lies only in establishing expected behavior and punishing those caught in violation of those expectations.

[3] The SEC prohibits advertising of a new issue and making an offer to sell without a prospectus.

This announcement is neither an offer to sell nor a solicitation of an offer to buy any of these Securities. The offer is made only by Prospectus. Copies of the Prospectus may be obtained in any State from only such of the underwriters as may legally offer these Securities in compliance with the securities laws of such State.

Gator
Internet
Technologies

4,000,000 Shares

Common Stock

Price $15 Per Share

Brown, Black, & Blue

Alvarez & Jones   Sam Hill & Co.   Rip & Tide

Harper & Bacon

April 1, 2002

FIGURE 4–1   Announcement of a new stock issue.

Prospectus a document corporations must provide to prospective buyers of the stock of the company. The prospectus gives a detailed account of the corporation's current financial and legal status, and discusses the intentions of the corporation with regard to the use of the funds raised by selling stock.

Tombstone an announcement in the newspaper that a corporation is selling shares of its stock to the public.

Underwriters financial firms that buy newly issued stock from corporations in large lots (i.e., wholesale) and sell it to the public in smaller blocks (i.e., retail). The underwriters collect the difference between the wholesale price and the retail price. They also bear the risk that some of the stock may not sell at retail.

Lead underwriter usually no one underwriter wants to assume all the risk of a new issue, so a consortium of underwriters is created to share the risks of a new issue. The lead underwriter creates the consortium and deals with the corporation on behalf of the other underwriters.

underwriters' fee is 7 percent) and that they are ready to sell all shares at retail ($15.00), profiting from the mark-up on each share sold. In this arrangement, all risks associated with the success or failure of a public offering are shifted from GIT to the underwriters. GIT gets $13.95 per share (assuming the usual 7 percent fee) or a total of $55.8 million from the underwriters regardless of what happens with the public offering. For their efforts, the underwriters will get $4.2 million if the issue sells out at $15.00 per share.

Most new stock is issued by corporations that already have previously issued stock trading on the market. In these cases, pricing the new issues is fairly easy because the market has already placed a known value on the stock of the company. However, if the company has no previously issued stock that is being traded, then determining the value of the new issue is more problematic. These situations are called **initial public offerings,** or IPOs.

The lead underwriter plays a very crucial role in an IPO. GIT obviously wants to sell its stock at the highest price possible. The lead underwriter wants to price the stock at a low enough price so there is little risk of the offering not being **fully subscribed,** that is, not selling out. If a new issue is not fully subscribed, then the underwriters are stuck with the stock. The lead underwriter negotiates with GIT on behalf of the other underwriters to determine a mutually agreeable offering price.

The underwriters are required by the SEC to sell this new stock only at the offering price for the period of the offer—usually several months. If the day after the offer some adverse news hits GIT, it is possible that the underwriters are going to be offering to sell shares at $15 while the public is willing to pay no more than $9. In this case, the underwriters are stuck with a lot of overpriced stock, and they will suffer a loss when they are finally allowed to sell off their inventory below the offering price. Obviously the underwriters accept a very great risk in search of a relatively small profit that will be forthcoming if the offering is fully subscribed. In addition, if the shares of GIT move up to $20 on the open market, the underwriters must still sell their inventory at the offer price of $15. In this case, they will sell out in a hurry as smart investors buy from the underwriters at $15 and sell on the open market at $20. This process of buying and selling on different markets to take advantage of a price difference between the two markets is known as **arbitrage.**

At the end of the offering process, GIT has raised $55.8 million that it can use to build a new plant or otherwise expand the business, the underwriters have either made a bundle or lost a bundle, and there are 4 million new shares of ownership of GIT in existence. The previous owners of GIT (those who held privately issued shares of the company) are obviously concerned about the value of their shares of ownership being **diluted** by the additional shares issued. This is a valid concern if the additional shares were sold to reduce debt or cover expenses. But if the funds raised from the sale of additional shares were used to buy additional assets, then holders of existing shares find that they have a slightly smaller share of a larger pie with the net result being little change of ownership value.

Previously Issued Stock

When Sue bought 100 shares of GIT's new offering, she paid $1,500 to GIT's underwriters.[4] In this transaction, part of the ownership of GIT is transferred from GIT to Sue. If, in several months time, Sue decides she wants a new refrigerator rather than part ownership of GIT, she is free to sell that part ownership to any willing buyer. She calls her friend Sam and offers to sell him the 100 shares for $1,200.[5] Sensing a good deal, Sam exchanges his $1,200 for Sue's 100 shares. Sam is now part owner of GIT. When Sue sells her shares to Sam, what does GIT receive? Absolutely nothing. The only time a firm receives any funds from stock sales is when the firm issues new or additional shares. Thereafter, those shares trade hands from owner to owner with no additional benefit to the issuing corporation.[6]

In reality, Sue was lucky to find Sam. In order to expand the market for its shares, most corporations seek to have those shares listed on an established stock **exchange.** When a company has its shares listed, then potential buyers and sellers of shares in that company have a common "meeting place," greatly facilitating the

---

[4] When a customer buys a new issue stock from a broker, no commission is paid by the customer since the issuing company has already paid the broker underwriting fees.

[5] This assumes the market price of GIT has fallen to $12 per share from the offer price of $15 per share.

[6] While the transfer of shares from holder to holder provides the issuer no additional funds, the obligations of the issuer to the holder to distribute profits and the like are transferred. Corporations usually hire banks to serve as transfer agents to keep track of their obligations to their shareholders.

Initial public offering a new stock offering by a corporation that has not previously offered stock to the public. No market price has been established for a company issuing an IPO.

Fully subscribed a new stock offering that is sold out.

Arbitrage the practice of simultaneously buying and selling a single product on two different markets to profit from the price differential between the two markets.

Dilution reducing the value of previously issued shares by issuing new shares. Assumes the value of the company does not grow as rapidly as the number of shares does.

Exchange financial intermediaries that provide a physical marketplace where potential buyers and sellers of stock can meet. Each exchange "lists" or agrees to trade shares of specific companies. If a potential seller of shares of XYZ wanted to find potential buyers, the most likely place to look is at an exchange that lists XYZ. Corporations can have their shares listed on multiple exchanges.

buying and selling of their stock. In the very early days, one such meeting place was along Wall Street in downtown New York City.[7] After a while the traders moved indoors and started listing offers to buy and sell on large boards. In time, the New York Stock Exchange was formed, and it has been known ever since as the "big board."

Today there are three major stock exchanges in the United States—the New York Stock Exchange, the American Stock Exchange, and the Nasdaq Stock Market (previously called "over-the-counter").[8] In general, bigger and more established companies trade on the New York Stock Exchange. The Nasdaq Stock Market tends to specialize in smaller, newer (and hence more speculative) stocks. While there are minor technical differences in the way the three exchanges operate, the general process at each is the same. There are also smaller regional stock markets in several major cities around the country.

In the early days, an individual wanting to buy or sell stock in a company would physically present himself at Wall Street to make an offer and bargain with other prospective buyers/sellers. When buyers and sellers were few in number, this worked fine. However, as with most things, times have changed. On a typical day the big board will trade as many as 1.2 billion shares of stock in 3,500 different companies. If all those buyers and sellers were standing around on Wall Street today, they would constitute quite a crowd. Instead, potential buyers and sellers are brought into the exchange electronically through a national system of **brokers.**[9] Brokers take orders from individual buyers/sellers and convey those orders to floor representatives at the exchange. If the traders on the floor of the exchange are able to match buy and sell orders, then a trade takes place. For the services of a broker, you pay a **commission** that is usually figured as a percentage of the size of the trade.

Many individual investors have started bypassing the traditional broker-floor representative system by contacting a floor representative directly over the Internet. Since the costs associated with a virtual broker are less than those of a real human broker, the commissions charged by Internet brokers are a fraction of those in the traditional system.

Large institutional investors (pension funds, and so on) usually place their buy/sell orders directly through the New York offices of major brokerage firms or directly through their own floor representatives on the exchanges. Since floor representatives also work on a commission basis, their primary concern is that the buy/sell orders of the investors are executed. One role of the floor representative is to take an order to sell 1,000 shares from a pension fund and distribute that among 10 offers to buy 100 shares each from individual investors. Neither side knows who was on the other side of the transaction, as brokers on each side deal individually with their own client and then the brokers clear the transaction through the exchange.

Brokers individuals licensed to carry buy/sell orders of individuals to the different exchanges.

Commission service fee paid to brokers for each trade executed.

Market order instruction to a broker to buy or sell stock at the best price currently possible. That is, make the trade at whatever price is prevailing at the time.

---

[7] In the early days a wooden stockade was constructed along the north side of the small town of New York to keep pirates and Indians out of the community. The location of that early wall became known as Wall Street.

[8] In 1982 the National Association of Security Dealers Automated Quotation (NASDAQ) system was introduced. It formed an electronic network that tied many dealers trading in small stocks together. That network eventually became the Nasdaq Stock Market. In late 1998 the corporations that own the American Stock Exchange and the Nasdaq Stock Market merged into a single corporate entity. It is anticipated that in time the two markets will also merge.

[9] The first brokers were wine merchants who bought wine by the cask and tapped or "broke" the cask to sell smaller quantities to the individual consumer.

There are several ways you can place an order with a broker (human or virtual). The most common for heavily traded stocks is a **market order.** This is an instruction to buy/sell your stock at the going price when the order reaches the floor of the exchange (almost instantaneously today). The broker can tell you what the present **bid** and **ask** prices are for your stock. A "bid" price is the highest currently existing offer to buy, and the "ask" price is the lowest current offer to sell. Usually these two prices are no more than five or ten cents apart.[10] In this case, if you submit a market order to buy, it will probably be executed at the ask price. The alternative to a market order is a **limit order.** A limit order instructs the broker to buy at no more than some specified price or to sell at no less than a specified price. If the market never reaches the specified price, then the order is never executed. Limit orders can be placed as **day orders,** meaning that at the end of the day the order is canceled, or as **good 'til canceled (GTC),** meaning the order stands until it is either executed or canceled. A final kind of order is a **stop loss order.** This order instructs the broker to sell at the market if the price of the stock falls below a specified level. For instance, suppose Maria buys XYZ at $33 per share. She is willing to take no more risk than a loss of $3 per share, so she places a stop loss order at $30. Should the price of XYZ move down to $30, the broker automatically triggers a sell order. There is no guarantee that Maria is going to get $30. If the price is falling rapidly, the next trade may be at $28 or even lower. But in any case, a stop loss order should prevent Maria from waking up the next morning and finding XYZ at $16.

Stock Price Determinants

What determines the price of a stock on an exchange? Quite simply, the same law of supply and demand that determines the price of a used car. The total number of shares issued by a company is a constant at any given point in time and changes only when the company issues additional shares.[11] The price at which shares of the company trade on any given day is the result of willing buyers and willing sellers finding a mutually agreeable price. Trade occurs only when both parties are satisfied. The forces affecting the supply and demand of a company's stock are partially tangible and partially psychological. Stock market analysts who rely on the tangible factors are known as **fundamental analysts.**

The first tangible factor that influences a stock's price is the underlying value of the company. The **book value** of a stock is what a share of stock would be worth if the company were immediately liquidated (i.e., the property of the company were sold) and each shareholder received a proportionate share of the proceeds.

Bid   the highest current offer to buy a stock.

Ask   the lowest current offer to sell a stock.

Limit order instruction to a broker to buy at no more than some specified price or to sell at no less than a specified price.

Day orders   a limit order that is canceled at the end of the day if not executed.

Good 'til canceled (GTC)   a limit order that stands until it is either executed or canceled.

Stop loss order instruction to a broker to sell a stock if the price of the stock falls below a specified level.

Fundamental analysts   stock market analysts who rely on tangible information about the company to estimate the value of the stock of the company.

Book value   the per-share value of the corporation issuing the stock. That is, if the company were liquidated, what the per-share value of the proceeds would be.

---

[10] Today stock prices are quoted in dollars and cents per share. Until recently, stock prices were quoted in eighths of a dollar. Early Spanish coins had marks on them dividing the round coin into eight "pie slice" pieces. To make change, a merchant would tear off one or more of the pieces. They became known as "pieces of eight," and a coinage system based on eighths instead of tenths was created. The British copied the Spanish system and brought it to colonial America. One unfortunate relic of our British heritage is that stock prices were, until recently, quoted in eighths or sixteenths of a dollar, where each sixteenth is 6 1/4 cents. A "point" refers to one dollar. It is common to say "XYZ was up half a point," meaning that the price increased by $0.50 a share. Prices of low-priced shares (less than $5.00/share) were quoted in thirty-seconds of a dollar. Incidentally, it was Thomas Jefferson who proposed and designed our current decimal system of coinage in the United States.

[11] Or if the company buys back some of the shares held by the public. This occurs when the directors of the company feel that the market price of the company's shares is well below the underlying value of the company. In this case, the company uses its profits to buy back shares, thereby increasing the value of the shares of the remaining holders.

Value investors
investors who buy
stock in companies
that have share prices
close to or below the
book value of the
company.

Some investors, known as **value investors,** invest in companies that have share prices close to or below the book value of the company. Their assumption is that these stocks have little downside risk of the price falling even further and great upside potential for an increase in price when other investors realize how cheap the stock is relative to its book value.[12]

Earnings   profits of
the corporation.
Earnings are usually
reported on an
earnings per share
(EPS) basis. The
higher the EPS of a
stock, *ceteris paribus*,
the higher the price of
the stock.

A second tangible factor that influences the price of a stock is the level of profits of the company. In the world of stocks, a company's profits are called **earnings.** Since a part owner of a company holds claim to a share of the earnings of that company, it stands to reason that the greater the earnings, the higher the price for the stock; and the faster those earnings are growing, the higher the price of the stock.

A third tangible factor affecting the price of a stock is the stock's **dividend.** A company can do either of two things with its earnings. It can reinvest those earnings in the company (this is called retained earnings), or it can pay the earnings out to shareholders in the form of a dividend payment. Most large, established companies regularly pay shareholders a quarterly dividend, or distribution of profits. In general, the greater the dividend per share, the higher the price of the stock. For many investors, holding stock is an alternative to simply depositing money in a bank savings account. For these investors, the size and stability of the dividend are very important. These investors are known as **income investors.**

Dividend   a distribution of the corpora-
tion's earnings to the
owners of the
corporation—the
shareholders. Each
share of stock receives
the same dividend.

The psychological factors that affect stock prices deal with expectations—expectations about the future earnings of the company, about the future dividends of the company, and about the company in general. In recent years Home Depot has been a rapidly expanding retailer with sales and earnings per share growing each year. As a consequence, the price of shares of Home Depot has also grown rapidly. In contrast, the expectations about another retailer—Sears—are that it is a mature company with little chance to grow significantly. Sears, and other traditional department stores, have continuously lost sales in recent years to specialty retailers such as Banana Republic and Circuit City. Since expectations about Sears' future are not bright, the price of its stock has been falling in recent years.

Income investors
investors who buy
stocks that pay high
dividends relative to
the price of the stock.

A second psychological factor affecting stock prices is the general expectation about the future of the economy rather than any one individual company. If the expectation is that a recession is looming in the future, then stock prices will fall in general (the "market" will go down). If there is an expectation that the next President is going to cut defense spending, then stocks of defense-related industries will fall.

Technical analysts
market speculators
who don't care about
why a stock is moving
up or down, just that it
is moving.

Finally, the market for stocks has a certain "herd" mentality. There are a number of stock market speculators, known as **technical analysts,** who don't care about why a stock is moving up or down, just that it is moving. If it is moving up, then get on for the ride; if it is moving down, get out. The prophecies of these analysts tend to become self-fulfilling. That is, if several technical analysts decide that XYZ is moving up, they will start buying it, and as a result, the price will move up. Even more analysts see this and also buy XYZ. Buying begets buying, and the potential for a stampede develops. From Dutch bulbs to Enron, all such bubbles have eventually burst leaving the last buyers as the biggest losers.

---

[12] Frequently the book value, according to the accounts of the company, is much greater than the market value of the company if it were in fact liquidated. For example, Eastern Air Lines continued to carry its airplanes on its accounting statements at cost minus depreciation. In reality, when they went belly-up, the owners of Eastern found that the planes had no value because nobody would buy the aged fleet. In fact, the owners had to pay to have the planes stored on the Arizona desert.

52 Weeks

Hi	Lo	Stock	Sym	Div	Yld%	PE	Vol	Hi	Lo	Clse	Chg
16.30	9.70	GtrAu	GAI		—	14	2456	15.20	14.95	14.95	-0.45
n14.85	22.65	GtrInt	GIT		—	28	457	21.15	20.85	21.15	+0.30
8.45	6.25	GtrTvl	GTV	0.16	2.3	9	1645	7.10	6.90	7.00	-0.05
5.45	2.15	GtrZo	GZO		—	—	234	2.30	2.20	2.20	-0.10

FIGURE 4–2 Typical stock quotations.

Reading Stock Reports

Most daily newspapers and Internet portals include several pages of stock prices from one or more of the exchanges. Most major newspapers such as *The New York Times* and *The Wall Street Journal* carry fairly complete data about trading the previous day. Most websites carry current data delayed 15 or 20 minutes. These sources all contain much the same information. A typical portion of a daily listing is shown in Figure 4–2, including the listing for Gator Internet Technologies.

The name of the company is given under the column titled "Stock." Because of space limitations, the name is frequently abbreviated. The first line, "GtrAu" may be a company named Gator Automotive or Gator Automatic Sprinklers. On the second line you find our old friend Gator Internet Technologies (GIT). To the right of the stock's name is the symbol or abbreviation given to that particular stock. The symbol for GIT is GIT. Brokers' orders are based on these symbols rather than names. Most symbols make some sense, but others don't.[13] These symbols are what you see on a "ticker" that runs across your TV screen reporting stock trades.

The two columns to the left of the name of the company record the highest and lowest prices for the stock during the past 52 weeks. GIT has traded between roughly $14.85 and $22.65 per share over the past year and is now trading at about $21—near the top of its 52 week range. Notice the small "n" to the far left for GIT. This means that the stock was newly issued during the past 52 weeks and that the range shown, therefore, is not for 52 weeks but instead from the time of issue to the present.

The three columns to the right of the stock's symbol contain technical information about the stock that is used by analysts to determine what kinds of investment objectives each issue might fulfill. The first column is the amount of dividends per share paid by the company to shareholders during the past 12 months. Of the stocks shown, only Gator Travel (GTV) is currently paying dividends. During the past 12 months it paid $0.16 to the holders of each share of stock. Notice that this is a report of past experience and is no guarantee of future performance. But usually, when a company is paying a dividend, the board of directors does everything possible to continue paying

---

[13] Note that GIT's symbol is GIT. This seems logical. Less clear is why the symbol for U.S. Steel is X. Around the turn of the century U.S. Steel was one of the most heavily traded stocks, so it was given a short, easy-to-remember symbol in an effort to speed up the ticker tape, which records all trades. At that time, Xerox did not exist and Exxon was part of Standard Oil. Most stock symbols are either three or four letters long. There is great prestige in having a single letter symbol. Recently when Chrysler and Daimler-Benz merged to create Daimler-Chrysler, the "C" symbol that Chrysler had used for nearly a century became available. An all-out battle erupted between Citigroup (result of a merger between Citibank and Traveler's Insurance) and Coca-Cola, both wanting to change their symbols to the coveted "C." At the end of the battle, the score was New York 1, Atlanta 0. The symbol for Coca-Cola is still "KO."

Dividend yield the amount of dividends paid per share during the past 12 months expressed as a percentage of the current price of the stock.

Price-earnings ratio the current price per share of the stock divided by the earnings (profits) per share during the past 12 months.

at least the same amount, because dividend cuts usually cause a sharp drop in the price of the stock. You will notice that GIT paid no dividends, so this column is blank.

The second of the three technical columns is the **dividend yield.** Yield is simply the indicated dividend (from the previous column) expressed as a percentage of the current price of the stock. The yield on Gator Travel is 2.3 percent. This yield should be compared with the rate of return on a savings account for a retiree who needs a steady income stream. Since GIT has paid no dividend, its dividend yield is zero, and this column is left blank.

The third column of technical information contains the **price-earnings ratio** (frequently called the P-E ratio). The P-E ratio is calculated as follows:

$$\text{P-E ratio} = \frac{\text{current market price per share of the stock}}{\text{earnings per share in last 12 months}}$$

The P-E ratio tells the investor how much must be paid to claim a dollar of earnings in the company. This measure allows the investor to compare two stocks relative to their earnings regardless of the amount of the earnings per share or the price of the stock. In the case of GIT, the investor must pay $28 for each $1 of earnings, which should be compared with other stocks shown. Since the current price of GIT is around $21 and the P-E ratio is 28, we can use the formula above to determine that the earnings of GIT last year were about $0.75 per share.

In general, investors are willing to pay more for a dollar of current earnings in a rapidly growing company than in a slow growth company, because of the expectation that in several years the level of earnings in the rapidly growing company will increase. Conversely, a company that is fairly stable or mature will probably have a fairly low P-E ratio, reflecting expectations about the future of the company's earnings. Usually, the higher the P-E ratio, the higher the risk and the greater the potential reward of holding the stock. Note that the P-E ratio for some stocks, like Gator Zone (GZO), is not listed. This means that earnings during the past 12 months earnings have been zero or negative.

The next column shows the number of shares of the stock that were traded on the exchange that day.[14] Most stock transactions are made in what are known as **round lots** of 100 shares. The volume listed is the number of round lots traded. For example, GIT shows a volume of 457, meaning that 45,700 shares of GIT were traded on that day. Trades in quantities of less than 100 shares are called **odd lots** and usually involve an additional commission per share.

The next three columns refer to the prices at which the stock traded during the day. Of the many trades that may have occurred during the day, what are shown are the highest price, the lowest price, and the price of the last or closing trade. If the close is near the high, then it is safe to assume that the price pressure during the day was upward. Conversely, if the low and the close are about the same, then pressure during the day was downward.

The final column is "Chg"—the change from the previous close to today's close. GIT's change of + $0.30 with a close of $21.15 means that the previous day's close was $20.85.

Round lots stock transactions involving 100 shares or multiples of 100 shares of stock.

Odd lots stock transactions involving less than 100 shares. The sale of 123 shares would involve one round lot and an odd lot of 23. Commission charges are higher for odd lots than for round lots.

---

[14] There is no law or requirement that shares of a stock listed on an exchange must be traded only on that exchange. In fact, some stocks are listed on more than one exchange. In most cases, off-exchange trading is small in comparison with the volume on the exchange.

Many newspapers with small financial sections publish only the closing price and the change. Most active traders on stock markets shun the closing price in favor of the high when prices are rising and low when they are falling.

Stock Splits

Some small investors tend to shy away from buying stocks with "high" prices.[15] A stock price above $100 per share seems to create a psychological barrier that discourages some investors. In many cases, if the price of a company's stock gets up to the $100 range, the company's board of directors may call for a **stock split** giving each holder of 1 share 1, 2, or 3 additional shares. If the split is a 2 for 1, then the number of shares held doubles and the price of each share is halved.

On rare occasions when the price of a stock is deemed to be too low, a company will call for a reverse split of 1 for 2, or 1 for 4. In a 1 for 2 reverse split, the number of shares outstanding is halved and the price per share is doubled. For all stock splits, value is neither created nor destroyed.

Classes of Stock

Most stock that is issued by companies is **common stock.** The GIT offering in Figure 4–1 is for common stock. Common stock gives the holder part ownership of the company, a vote on corporate affairs including election of the directors, and little else. On some occasions companies will raise additional funding by selling **preferred stock.** As its name implies, holders of preferred stock have preferential rights over the holders of common stock. There are two main differences between common and preferred stock. First, if the company is forced to liquidate (i.e., goes bankrupt), the holders of preferred stock receive compensation before the holders of common stock. Second, unlike common stocks, preferred stocks promise a certain level of annual dividend. The preferred dividend must be paid from earnings before any dividends can be paid to the holders of common stock.

With these advantages, you might wonder why anyone would ever buy common stock instead of preferred. The answer is quite simple: the guaranteed dividend is quite attractive if the firm is not growing, but for a growing firm it is quite likely that in a few years' time the common dividend will grow while the preferred dividend stays at its guaranteed level. Hence, while the common stock has potential for appreciation (i.e., for the price of the stock to increase), the preferred stock has little potential for appreciation. Also, holders of most preferred stock have no voting rights. Shares of preferred stock are shown in stock listings with a small "pf" following the company name.

Finally, some companies (General Motors is a good example) issue different classes of common stock, with each class having its own dividend, ownership rights, and price. Not long after the legendary Howard Hughes died, General Motors bought the Hughes Aerospace company. To finance the purchase, GM issued a new class of stock known as GM-H stock. The finances of GM the automaker and

Stock split action by the board of directors to give shareholders more shares for each share held. The purpose of a stock split is to reduce the price per share in the belief that many investors shun the stock of companies with high stock prices.

Common stock a class of stock that gives shareholders full voting rights in the business of the corporation. Dividends on common stock are at the discretion of the board of directors. Usually the common shareholder is at the end of the line in terms of claimants for the earnings of the corporation, or for assets in the case of bankruptcy.

Preferred stock a class of stock in which a fixed annual dividend is promised if the corporation has earnings from which to pay that dividend. All preferred dividends must be paid before any common dividends can be paid.

---

[15] There is no financial justification for this psychological reality. One share of a $200/share stock is worth just as much as 100 shares of a $2/share stock. However, Berkshire Hathaway, with a stock price in the $80,000 per share range, is out of the reach of most mortals. A round lot would cost a cool $8 million.

Income stock   a stock for which the main attraction is the size and stability of its dividend.

Growth stock
stock of a company with high expectations of future growth. These stocks are purchased in the hope of capital appreciation.

Blue chips   stocks of the biggest, most financially sound companies. These are companies that are expected to be around 10 years from now.

Secondary stocks
stocks of smaller, less financially certain companies. There is a higher degree of bankruptcy risk in secondary stocks than in blue chips.

Low-cap stocks
stocks with low market capitalization or market value as determined by the number of shares of the stock outstanding times the price per share.

Penny stocks
literally, stocks that can be purchased for just a few pennies. Most are either in bankruptcy proceedings or in highly speculative ventures.

GM-Hughes are kept separate such that the price of GM stock is determined by conditions in the auto market and the price of GM-H is determined by how things are going in the defense industry.

Types of Stocks

Like most businesses, the business of Wall Street has its own lingo. Here are a few of the typical expressions that commonly appear in the financial press to describe the stock of different companies:

An **income stock** is one that is primarily purchased (and priced) based on the size, stability, and/or growth of its dividend. Investors buy income stocks as an alternative to putting savings into a bank account or certificates of deposit. In most cases, the prices of income stocks tend to be fairly steady with little chance of a significant appreciation or depreciation of capital.[16]

By comparison, a **growth stock** is one investors buy in the hopes of substantial capital appreciation. Many growth stocks pay little or no dividend and are bought not for current return but in the hopes of future glory. Stocks of many drug companies are classic growth stocks.

Blue chips are stocks of the biggest, soundest companies. In most years the blue chips are profitable, but every once in a while a blue chip will experience difficulty and suffer a loss. In any case, blue chips are expected to be around 10 years from now. Does anyone doubt the continued, successful existence of Coca-Cola or Disney?

Secondary stocks are stocks of established companies that are smaller and with a future less certain than blue chips. While Wal-Mart is a blue chip, stocks of some smaller specialty retailers like The Gap would be considered as secondary stocks.

Low-cap stocks are stocks of companies with a small capitalization or market value. These are the myriad of little minnows all seeking whale status. Investing in low-cap stocks has a much higher risk than buying blue chips, but the potential reward is also much greater.[17]

Penny stocks are stocks of companies that have virtually no value, and hence the shares can be purchased for just a few pennies. Usually these companies are in bankruptcy or in wildly speculative ventures such as diamond mining in the Arctic. Most of the major exchanges will not list penny stocks and delist companies that fall into penny stock status.

Market Indicators

If you are the part owner of XYZ corporation, then the price of XYZ's stock is of great importance. Should the price of XYZ fall, you will naturally be interested to know if it fell along with most other stocks or if it fell while most others went up. To answer this question, a variety of stock indices have been developed in an effort to describe what happened to the average or typical stock during a trading day.

---

[16] Income stocks tend to trade a lot like bonds with the price of the income stock varying inversely with the market rate of interest. Consequently, capital gain or loss is possible with income stocks if interest rates change substantially. Catastrophic events can also hit "secure" income stocks. When Three Mile Island melted down, the stock of its parent company, American Electric Power, lost about half its value in one day.

[17] The lucky investor who bought 100 shares of the IPO of Wal-Mart would be worth about $16 million today.

52 Week					
Hi	Lo	Index	Close	Change	%Chg.
1280	957	Standard & Poor's 500	1246	+19	+1.54
611	477	New York Stock Exchange Composite	591	+8	+1.41
9643	7540	Dow Jones Industrial Average	9467	+191	+2.06
2510	1419	NASDAQ Stock Market Composite	2293	+28	+1.22
753	564	Amex Composite	698	+4	+0.59
665	4944	Russell 1000	648	+9	+1.46
11724	8620	Wilshire 5000	11368	+150	+1.34

FIGURE 4–3 Stock market indexes.

As shown in Figure 4–3, there are a variety of indexes, each of which is built a little differently than the others in the search for the "perfect" index. The two most common indexes are the **Dow Jones Industrial Average** (DJIA) and the **Standard & Poor's 500.** Some indices (such as DJIA) emphasize only manufacturing/service companies; while others emphasize utilities, or transportation companies, or low-cap, or mid-cap, or whatever else. Most measure prices on one exchange only; but the Value-Line, Russell, and Wilshire attempt to measure all stocks on all exchanges. Recently the DJIA added two stocks (Microsoft and Intel) from the Nasdaq exchange to what had previously been an index of stocks exclusively from the New York Stock Exchange.

Since the DJIA is what you hear about on most newscasts, it will be the focus of the remaining discussion. In 1884 Charles Dow calculated the average price of 11 stocks and started printing that average in a newsletter he had founded. In 1889, he and his partner, Eddie Jones, started a daily newspaper they called *The Wall Street Journal (WSJ)*. Dow continued to work with his average by adding companies and deleting them until finally he was satisfied. In 1896 he published his industrial average price in the *WSJ* and called it the Dow Jones Industrial Average. Over time the "average" (really an index) has changed significantly, but the basic concept is unchanged. And the ownership is also unchanged: the Dow Jones Averages are copyrighted by Dow Jones & Co., which continues to publish the *WSJ*.

The DJIA is an index number based on the sum of the prices of 30 blue chip stocks, which are identified in the box on the graph in Figure 4–4. The 30 components don't change frequently, but in the recent years the editors of the *WSJ* (who are solely responsible for deciding how the index is calculated) have added Microsoft, Intel, American Express, McDonald's, and Disney in an effort to include some service and technology-orientated blue chips along with the traditional smokestack companies. While it is easy to think of the DJIA as the sum of 30 stock prices, in reality it is not. Stock splits and the removal of a $30 stock to be replaced with a $70 stock have necessitated the development of an adjustment factor called the "divisor." When one of these events occurs, the divisor is changed to keep the DJIA constant. The closing DJIA in Figure 4–3 was 9467—a number that has no particular meaning except in comparison with what that number was yesterday or last year. For the particular day shown, the DJIA was 191 points higher than yesterday, which represents a 2.06 percent increase from day to day. So if you had $1,000 invested in these 30 stocks, the value of your investment would have increased by about $20 on this day.

The chart in Figure 4–4 gives a graphical representation of what has happened to the DJIA over the past 2 weeks. Each vertical bar represents the range from the daily high to the daily low of the DJIA index. A tick on the bar indicates

Dow Jones Industrial Average an index of the prices of 30 blue chip stocks.

Standard & Poor's 500 an index of the prices of the 500 stocks with the highest market value.

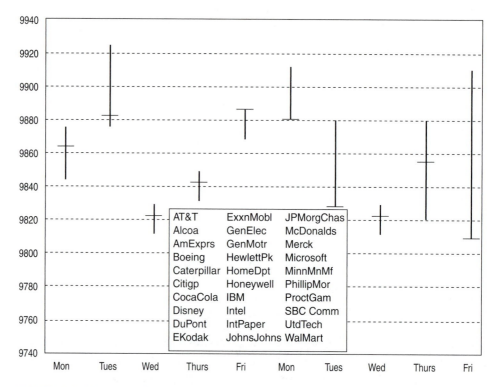

	AT&T	ExxnMobl	JPMorgChas
	Alcoa	GenElec	McDonalds
	AmExprs	GenMotr	Merck
	Boeing	HewlettPk	Microsoft
	Caterpillar	HomeDpt	MinnMnMf
	Citigp	Honeywell	PhillipMor
	CocaCola	IBM	ProctGam
	Disney	Intel	SBC Comm
	DuPont	IntPaper	UtdTech
	EKodak	JohnsJohns	WalMart

FIGURE 4–4 Hypothetical Dow Jones Industrial Average.

where the close occurred. During the second Friday shown, stocks moved up from the Thursday close to more than 9900 and dropped to close at about 9810. Strong breaks in the graph (such as the first Wednesday) indicate that some major news event between Tuesday's close and Wednesday's opening significantly changed investors' expectations causing a dramatic price break.

Investors and Speculators

Investor buyer of stock with a long-run objective of capital appreciation and/or dividends.

Investors are individuals with long-run objectives who seek a maximum return on their savings. **Speculators** have short-term objectives of buying low and selling high. Investors provide the bulk of the funds that come into the stock market, but speculators provide the liquidity or trading action that ensures stock prices will change in an orderly fashion. If speculators think the price of a particular stock is "too low," they will buy the stock, thereby driving its price up. If it becomes "too high," they will sell, thereby driving the price down. It is the liquidity provided by the speculators that makes financial markets operate efficiently.

Speculator buyer/seller of stock with short-run objectives of making a quick profit by buying low and selling high.

Summary—What Makes Stock Prices Go Up and Down?

The prevailing market price for a particular stock on any given day is determined by the forces of supply (potential sellers) and demand (potential buyers). Price changes are driven by forces that affect the entire market, the market segment in which the stock trades, and the individual company that the stock represents.

The Market as a Whole

The whole market tends to react in virtual unison to a variety of macroeconomic stimuli. These broad market movements are measured by market indices such as the DJIA. Movements of the whole market are based on both realized macroeconomic events and expectations of what may happen in the future. Some of the macroeconomic forces that can drive a market up, *ceteris paribus,* include:

- Lower interest rates
- Lower taxes
- Higher profits
- Increased government spending
- Increased employment
- A weaker or falling dollar on foreign exchange markets
- Lower inflation

Each of these is perceived as being "good" for U.S. businesses and therefore good for shares of ownership in U.S. businesses. A reverse trend in any of these macroeconomic indicators would have the effect of driving stock prices down.

Speculators attempt to anticipate macroeconomic news that will affect the market in predictable ways. For instance, the Department of Commerce issues its monthly employment report on a given day each month. A speculator, expecting a report indicating higher employment levels, would buy stocks the day before the report is issued and then sell the day of the report as stock prices move up in response to the report. The successful speculator is one who can anticipate correctly more often than not. If the Department of Commerce report shows employment was down sharply, the speculator will find that he or she has bought high and sold low—not a very profitable proposition.

Market Segments

Stock prices of companies in similar industries tend to vary according to any financial news that will differentially affect that particular group. For instance, utilities (primarily electric companies) are very sensitive to interest rates (because of their heavy borrowing needs to build plants) and energy prices. The September 11, 2001 terrorist attacks led to substantial market segment adjustments. The shares of airlines and other tourism stocks fell sharply. Prices of stocks in the airport scanning business jumped wildly while those of companies in the defense industry rose significantly. Proposals for the government to regulate prices of pharmaceuticals for the elderly predictably pushed the prices of drug stocks down.

The Individual Company

Within groups, stocks trade on the basis of both the reality and the expectation of earnings and dividends of the individual company relative to the performance of similar companies. A quick guide to comparing otherwise similar companies is the price-earnings ratio. For instance, in early 2002 the P-E ratio for Microsoft was 56, and for IBM it was 25. If you were given a choice between putting your retirement funds in either company, which would you chose? Those choices create demand for the stock and influence the price of the stock. Simply put, investors are willing to pay more for a dollar's worth of Microsoft's current earnings than for IBM. Microsoft is perceived by investors as having brighter prospects than IBM for future growth, and hence for appreciation of share value.

BONDS

Bonds, unlike stocks, are infrequently held by individual investors in the United States. Part of the reason for this phenomenon is that few investors really understand bonds, while many think they understand stocks.[18] Even though few individuals hold bonds directly, most Americans own lots of bonds indirectly through institutional holdings by pension funds, insurance companies, and so on.

To understand what bonds are, we will begin with a relationship that most of us understand and then make an analogy to bonds. Assume a simple world of companies and individuals interacting in the market for rental cars. Individuals wish to "buy" rental car services, and companies wish to "sell" rental car services. Buyers and sellers interact in this market to determine an equilibrium price that the buyer agrees to pay and the seller agrees to accept. To consummate the deal, they draw up a rental agreement that specifies two major points:

- The buyer agrees to return the car at the end of the rental period in the same shape as it was accepted at the beginning of the rental period.
- The buyer agrees to pay a rental fee for the period of time the car is kept.

The fine print of the rental agreement spells out all of the legal obligations of each party to the other. Once the terms of the contract are completed (i.e., the car is returned and the rent paid), the contract is terminated and no further obligations on either party exist.

A bond is strictly analogous to the rental agreement in the above example. However, in the case of a bond, what is being rented is cash instead of cars, and the company is renting it from the public (individual or pension fund and the like). Whenever a company borrows money from an individual, the company gives the individual a bond (a promissory note or rental agreement) that specifies two major items:

- The rental price, or how much the company will pay the individual per period of time for the use of the money
- A specific date upon which the company will return the money in the same condition (i.e., amount) it was received

The fine print of the bond spells out the obligations of each party to the other while the bond (or rental agreement) is in effect. As soon as the company returns the original cash borrowed and pays all agreed upon rental fees, the contract is terminated and the bond is extinguished.

---

[18] This is an interesting phenomenon, for most of the variation in bond prices is clearly understood while those of stocks is not. Apparently individuals prefer to invest in instruments driven by psychological expectations (stocks) rather than those driven by tangible economic forces (bonds).

This announcement is neither an offer to sell nor a solicitation of an offer to buy any of these Securities. The offer is made only by Prospectus. Copies of the Prospectus may be obtained in any State from only such of the underwriters as may legally offer these Securities in compliance with the securities laws of such State.

$100,000,000

MOO U.
TECHNOLOGY
TRANSFER

7.5% SUBORDINATED BONDS

DUE APRIL 1, 2022

Insured by *MBIA*

WHITE, GREEN, & ORR

Alvarez & Jones   Sam Hill & Co.   Rip & Tide

Harper & Bacon

April 1, 2002

Characteristics of Bonds

Companies issue or **float** bonds for the same reason they issue stock—to raise money. In the case of stock, they sell perpetual part ownership of the company. In the case of bonds, they become indebted to lenders for a finite period of time. There are a variety of factors that will determine whether a company finances expansion and operations by selling bonds instead of stock, but we won't get into them at this point.[19]

When a company sells bonds to the public, it is borrowing from the public. The process of selling bonds is very similar to that of selling stocks. Figure 4–5 is a typical tombstone for a new bond issue. In this case, the Moo U. Technology Transfer (MUTT) wants to borrow or raise $100 million. In this example, the White, Green, & Orr company was the lead underwriter. The two important characteristics of the

Float slang term for selling or issuing bonds.

---

[19] The criteria for making such decisions is what courses taught by the Finance Department are all about. This decision in a large company is made by the chief financial officer, or CFO.

bonds being offered are shown just below the company title: the annual rental fee and the date when original cash will be returned. Using the tombstone in Figure 4–5 as an example, let's look at some bond terminology.

Face Value

Face value   the amount borrowed when a bond is issued: always $1,000.

The **face value** of a bond is how much cash was borrowed for this bond. Just like a rental car contract specifies what car is rented, a bond specifies how much was borrowed. In virtually all cases the face value of a bond is $1,000.[20] As in the case of stocks, bonds are usually traded in "round lots" of 100 bonds with a combined face value of $100,000.[21] The first important principle of bonds is that over the lifetime of a bond, *the face value of a bond never changes*.[22] Because the face value of virtually all bonds is $1,000, it is not even stated in the tombstone in Figure 4–5: it is understood by convention.

Coupon Rate

Coupon rate   the annual interest payment promised by the bond issuer expressed as a percentage of the face value. A bond with a 6 percent coupon rate promises to pay $60 per year.

Coupon payment the annual interest payment promised by the bond issuer, expressed in dollar amounts.

The **coupon rate** is the annual rental fee that the borrower agrees to pay to the lender.[23] By tradition, this annual fee is expressed as a percentage rate rather than in dollar terms. The coupon rate is the percentage of the face value the borrowing company agrees to pay to the lender each year the contract (i.e., bond) is in force. In Figure 4–5 the coupon rate is 7.5 percent, which means Moo U. agrees to pay 7.5 percent of $1,000, or $75 (the **coupon payment**), each year to the holder of the bond while the bond is in force. A second important principle of bonds is that over the life of the bond *the coupon rate never changes*.[24]

Maturity Date

Maturity date   the date when a bond issuer promises to return the face value to the bondholder.

An important characteristic of a bond is the **maturity date** when the borrowing company promises to return the face value (what was borrowed) to the holder of the bond. At that time the contract is terminated and the bond is extinguished. In Figure 4–5, the maturity date is 2022, indicating that these are "20-year bonds." The maturity date of a bond is part of the original contract between borrower and lender. Most bonds include fine print that allows the issuer of the bond to **call** the bonds prematurely. If the bond is called, the lender will usually receive a premium above the face value as specified in the terms of the bond.

Call   redeem a bond prior to the maturity date specified on the face of the bond. Most bonds are callable at a premium over the face value.

---

[20] In the remainder of this chapter it is assumed that all bonds have face values of $1,000.

[21] Nonetheless, the "wee" folks of the world can easily buy a single $1,000 bond through any broker. However, the commissions on a single bond can be quite high relative to the potential earnings from the bond.

[22] Again, use the analogy to a rental car agreement: you can't rent a Lincoln and return a Yugo.

[23] The term "coupon" is handed down from a common practice in the bond market a century ago. When a new bond was issued, there were a number of paper coupons on the edge of the bond that were dated. When the date on a coupon arrived, the bond owner would take the bond to a bank and the bank would "clip the coupon" and pay the bond owner the indicated amount.

[24] Let's return again to the rental car contract analogy: When you return the car, the rental agency can't say, "Oh, we raised our rates while you had the car; therefore you owe us more." Once set, the rental rate remains constant over the length of the contract. In reality there are a few bonds that feature variable coupon rates, but they will be ignored for the purposes of clarity and simplicity.

From the perspective of the prospective bond buyer (i.e., the lender), the bond in Figure 4–5 is an offer by Moo U. to pay $75 a year from the issue date in 2002 to the maturity date in 2022 and then return the original $1,000 borrowed. By the end of 20 years, the lender (i.e. bondholder) will have received total interest payments of $1,500 from Moo U.

Classes of Bonds

If you read the tombstone for Moo U. carefully, you will see that what is being "announced" is a subordinated bond. That is, payment on this bond is **subordinate** to some other debt instruments of Moo U. The debt of a company is usually arranged in a well defined "pecking order" of who gets paid off first if the company is liquidated in bankruptcy. Normally bonds are in front of preferred stock, and both are in front of common stockholders. Some bonds are subordinated bonds, meaning that they are further back in the preference order in case of liquidation or inability to pay the interest due.

Subordinate a bond that has a lower priority than other (nonsubordinate) bonds in the distribution of proceeds in case of bankruptcy.

Sometimes financial instruments that have all the characteristics of bonds are called **notes** or **bills.** Notes refer to either debt that is highly subordinated in the debt structure of the corporation or debt that is of an intermediate term with a maturity of 1 to 10 years. Bills usually refer to short-term debt with maturities of less than 1 year. Whether an instrument is called a bond, a note, or a bill, they all behave in exactly the same fashion.

Notes a class of bonds that is subordinate to some other debt instruments of the issuer, or is an intermediate-term bond.

There is one other characteristic of the Moo U. bonds that is of interest. The bond is insured by a company called MBIA. In case of financial problems at Moo U., the insurer would become liable for payment of the interest and return of the face value at maturity. Moo U. has clearly decided that the cost of the insurance is less than the cost of the extra coupon payments that would have been necessary on an uninsured bond.

Bills very short-term bonds with maturities usually less than 1 year.

Original Price of the Bond

In most instances, as in the case of the Moo U. bonds in Figure 4–5, the original price of the bond is not listed and is therefore assumed to be equal to the face value of $1,000. In some instances, bonds are priced above or below the face value. In these cases, the price of the bond is expressed as a percentage of its face value.[25]

Trading of Bonds

Should an individual buy this Moo U. bond? That depends on what the alternatives are. If certificates of deposit at the local bank return 5 percent per year and this bond returns 7.5 percent, then maybe the bond is more attractive than the CD. As in all cases of investing, it depends.

---

[25] The most common reason for pricing a bond above or below "par" (face value) is to fine-tune the effective interest rate paid on the bond. Suppose Moo U. and White, Green, & Orr (the lead underwriter) agreed that they would float the issue at a 7.45 percent interest rate. Since, by tradition, coupon rates are usually expressed in eighths or single digit decimals, the only alternatives are 7.4 percent or 7.5 percent. Moo U. can "create" a 7.45 percent yield by setting the coupon rate at 7.5 percent and the price of the bond at $1,006.71, or at 100.67 percent. Since the buyer of the bond has to pay slightly more than $1,000 for each of the 7.5 percent bonds, the effective yield falls slightly below 7.5 percent to 7.45 percent.

Alas, the analogy between bonds and car rental agreements must come to an end. One thing that a bondholder can do that a car rental agreement holder can't do is sell the agreement to a third party. The bond (the promissory note in legal terms) is a promise by the issuing company to pay the holder of the bond the annual interest payment and to return the original face value to the holder at maturity. However, the holder of a bond does not have to be the original lender. That individual is free to sell the bond at any time, to any one, at any price. The market on which previously issued bonds are bought and sold is known as the "**bond market.**" While some bonds are traded on exchange floors in a manner similar to stocks, most bond trading is done "off the floor" via electronic networks that connect institutional investors, brokerage houses, and bond trading firms. While trading in bonds is just as intense as trading in stocks, it is further removed from the public view and less reported in the public press.

While the face value, coupon rate, and maturity of a bond never[26] change, the **price of a bond** can change dramatically over its lifetime. For the Moo U. bond in Figure 4–5, the initial offering price is set by the underwriters at 100 percent (or $1,000). The underwriters are obligated to hold to that price during the offering period. After the initial offer, the price of the bond is free to move up or down as the market may dictate.

Current (or Effective) Yield

The **current yield** of a bond is the coupon payment promised divided by the current market price of the bond expressed as a percentage. If the market price of the Moo U. bond fell to $900, then the current yield would increase to 8.33 percent.[27] Notice what happened in this example: as the price of the bond went down, the current yield went up. This is a third important principle of bonds: *over time the price of a bond and its current yield vary inversely.*

Market Rate of Interest

At any point in time, the interaction of potential borrowers and potential lenders establishes a prevailing **market rate of interest.**[28] The coupon rate offered on a new bond will depend on the prevailing market rate of interest, length of maturity of the bond, and the perceived risk of the issuer. When a bond is newly issued, it is issued at the current risk- and term-adjusted market rate of interest. If the coupon rate of a new issue is greater than the market rate, then the company issuing the bond is paying more interest than is necessary to sell the bonds. If the coupon rate of a new issue is below the current prevailing market rate, then no potential buyers will be found. This leads to a fourth basic principle of bonds: *the coupon rate on newly issued bonds is equal to the current market rate of interest at the time of issue (adjusted for term and risk).*[29]

Bond market
market on which previously issued bonds are bought and sold.

Price of a bond
the price at which a previously issued bond trades on the bond market. The price of a bond may be more than face value (above par) or less than face value (below par) depending on the forces of supply and demand for that particular bond.

Current yield the coupon payment promised by a bond divided by the current market price of the bond expressed as a percentage.

Market rate of interest the prevailing risk- and term-adjusted interest rate at the present time. When bonds are issued, they will be issued at a coupon rate equal to the market rate of interest at the time of issue. Over time the market rate of interest rises and falls as financial markets adjust.

---

[26] "Never" is too strong a word because there are exceptions, but for the purposes of clarity, we will assume these exceptions don't exist.

[27] The annual coupon payments is $75 regardless of the price of the bond. Hence, the current yield would be calculated as $75/$900 = 0.0833, or 8.33 percent. Note the similarities between the dividend yield for stocks and the current yield for bonds.

[28] The Federal Reserve Board controls the monetary policy of the United States and thus has a great influence on the market rate of interest.

[29] Usually, longer-term bonds (those with the furthest maturity date) will have higher coupon rates because the lender has to wait longer to get the face value back. Companies with higher risks of default will always have to offer higher coupon rates.

Bond Prices

Over time, the market rate of interest rises and falls in reaction to macroeconomic conditions at home and in world financial markets. In our increasingly globalized economy, the forces affecting domestic interest rates are often beyond the control of domestic fiscal and monetary policy. In the early 1980s interest rates were very high because the inflation rate was high. U.S. Treasury long-term rates were in the 13 percent range. Today, long-term Treasury rates are around 4–5 percent. The changing of these rates over time has significant implications for the bond market.

Now let's take a look at the market today for a long-term bond issued in the early 1980s with a coupon rate of 13 percent. Remember that the coupon rate never changes over the life of the bond. Suppose the holder of the 13 percent bond decides he wants to sell it to the highest bidder in today's market. Moo U. is currently trying to sell a bond that promises to pay $75 per year, and the holder of the 13 percent bond is trying to sell a bond that promises to pay $130 per year. Which of the two bonds would you rather have? Obviously, the one that pays more. So potential bond buyers would bid up the price of the 13 percent bond. As the price of the 13 percent bond is bid up, what happens to its current yield? It will fall because of the inverse relationship between bond prices and current yields. And, in fact, the price of the 13 percent bond will get bid up to the point where the current yield on that bond is no different from the current market rate (adjusted for term and risk). Competition among bond buyers and sellers will drive bond prices to the point where current yields of old and new bonds are both equal to the current market rate of interest. This leads us to the fifth basic principle of bonds: *the price of a previously issued bond will rise or fall in order to drive the current yield of the bond to the level of the current market rate of interest (adjusted for term and risk).*

Since the current yield of a bond and the price of the bond vary inversely, any increase in the market rate of interest will cause prices of previously issued bonds to fall. Conversely, if the market rate of interest falls, the prices of previously issued bonds will increase.[30] The extent to which changes in the market rate of interest are connected with bond prices depends on the length of the remaining life of the bond. The longer the remaining life span of the bond, the closer the link between changes in market rates and changes in bond prices[31]

As an example of the structure of bond market prices, consider the prices in Figure 4–6 for two U.S. Treasury issues on the same day the Moo U. bond was issued. There are two important things to notice in these bond prices. First, the difference between the current yields of the two Treasury issues and the Moo U. issue is about 1.85 percent: this is the risk premium associated with the insured bonds of Moo U. over the Treasury issues, which are assumed to be the safest bonds possible since they are guaranteed by the same fellows who get to print money legally. Second, notice that both Treasury issues mature in the same year but that they have different coupon rates. The bond market has bid up the price of the 8.87 percent

---

[30] The market rate of interest fell continuously during the 1983–1993 period. This meant that bond buyers not only received interest payments from their bonds but also received capital gains as the value of their bonds increased. For speculators in the bond market this was a time to clean up without being too sophisticated. After all, if prices only move in one direction, it is pretty easy to make money. But as with all bubbles, this one also eventually burst carrying with it the most overextended speculators. The most visible calamity was Orange County, California.

[31] For the holder of a long bond, the receipt of the annual interest payments now is of much greater interest than the receipt of the $1,000 face value some 20 or 30 years from now.

Issuer	Coupon Rate	Maturity Date	Current Price	Current Yield
Moo U. TT	7.50%	2022	$1,000	7.50%
U.S. Treasury	8.87	2022	1,386	5.64
U.S. Treasury	8.12	2022	1,299	5.64

FIGURE 4–6   Market prices of bonds on April 1, 2002.

Bonds	Current Yield	Vol.	Close	Net Change
Monsanto 6s15	5.0	24	120 1/8	+3/8
MooUTT 7.5s22	8.3	12	90 5/8	–1/4
NoGo 6.2s15	—	22	20 1/4	—
Novell 7¾ 10	cv	45	125 3/4	+1/2
Novartis zr25	—	13	70 5/8	+7/8

FIGURE 4–7   New York Stock Exchange bond quotations, March, 13, 2003.

bond substantially higher than the 8.12 percent bond such that current yields on both are exactly the same. So bond *prices* adjust (since coupon rates don't) in a manner to bring *current yields* on all similar bonds into parity.

Bond Price Quotations

Figure 4–7 shows a typical newspaper publication of bond prices for bonds traded on the New York bond market. Among the corporate bonds traded, the first column describes the bond in terms of the name of the issuing company, the coupon rate, and the maturity date. For example, the second bond listed is as follows:

MooUTT 7.5s22

Translation: this is a bond issued by Moo U. Technology Transfer with a coupon rate of 7.50 percent. The "s" is simply a meaningless separator to clearly distinguish between the coupon rate and the maturity date. The bond matures in 2022 (the 20 is implicit).

The next column gives the current yield of 8.3 percent. The "Volume" column lists the actual number of bonds traded that day. "Close" is the closing or last price at which the bond was traded. As we noted previously, bond prices are quoted in percent of face value. Thus, the price of this bond is listed at 90 5/8 or 90.625 percent of face value, or $906.25 per bond. Note that the quotations in Figure 4–7 are for a date nearly 1 year after the Moo U. bonds were initially issued. During that year, the market rate of interest has increased by about 0.8 percentage points, causing the market price of the bonds to fall below the original face value. When a bond trades at a price above its face value, it is said to trade at a **premium or above par.** At a price less than face value it is trading at a **discount or below par.** The final column is the change in price from the previous close.

Some bonds are listed with a current yield of "cv," and others have a coupon rate of "zr." These are convertible bonds and zero coupon bonds. Both will be dis-

Premium or above par   bonds with a current market price above face value.

Discount or below par   bonds with a current market price below face value.

Rate	Maturity	Bid	Ask	Change	Yld to Mat
9¼	Feb 16	134:28	135:02	–21	5.94
7¼	May 16	113:26	113:30	–19	5.94
3⅞	Aug 16i	96:13	96:14	–15	4.08
7½	Nov 16	116:19	116:23	–18	5.96
8¾	May 17	130:19	130:25	–20	5.96

FIGURE 4–8 U.S. Treasury bond quotations.

cussed later. Some bonds show no current yield: these are bonds that are not currently paying the promised coupon payment for one reason or another. These bonds are collectively known as **junk bonds** and are highly speculative bonds best traded only by the very knowledgeable.

Junk bonds bonds issued by companies with extremely high levels of risk and/or bonds on which the issuer has ceased making coupon payments.

Figure 4–8 shows part of the listing of U.S. Treasury issues. These tables are a little different from the New York bond market quotations. First, since every bond listed is issued by the U.S. Treasury, the name of the issuer is omitted. The bonds are listed chronologically in order of maturity from the shortest (closest to maturity) to the longest. The left-most column gives the coupon rate. The next column gives the maturity date. The next two columns are midafternoon bid (highest offer to buy) and ask (lowest offer to sell) prices. These prices are always quoted in 1/32's of a dollar, where a quote such as 101:16 means 101 percent plus 16/32 percent for a total of 101.5 percent of face value, or $1,015 per bond. The "Change" column reports changes from the previous day's quote in thirty-seconds. The "Yld to Mat" is the yield to maturity based on the reported ask price.[32]

Note that as bond maturities get longer, the yield to maturity goes higher. This is to compensate for the greater risk of inflation inherent in longer bonds. Renewed inflation between now and the maturity date would have the effect of reducing the real (i.e., inflation adjusted) value of the return of face value at maturity. The astute reader may note that one bond has a yield to maturity that is much lower than adjacent bonds. The little "i" on the maturity date identifies this bond as one of a new class of inflation adjusted bonds the Treasury recently introduced. For these bonds the face value of the bond is adjusted annually by the official rate of inflation. Since these bonds have no inflation risk, the current yields on them are substantially lower than for traditional fixed-face value bonds.

Treasury bonds and notes are considered to be the safest bonds available in the market. In addition, most Treasury issues are not callable (see below), and the interest earned is exempt from state and local taxes. For these reasons, yields on Treasuries are usually well below those of bonds from the corporate sector.

Other Bond Features

What has been described so far are basic bonds issued by corporations or the U.S. Treasury. There are lots of other wrinkles in the bond market. Here are a few of them.

---

[32] "Yield to maturity" is a more sophisticated calculation than the current yield. Consider the case of a 13.75 percent Treasury that matures in 5 years. That issue is currently trading at approximately $1,400. That gives the issue a current yield of 9.8 percent. The astute observer will say, "Yeah, but the buyer of this bond is paying $1,400 for something that will return $1,000 in 5 years." Right! The holder of this bond stands to lose an average of $80 per year in capital losses. Using a very complex formula, yield to maturity accounts for the combined gains from interest paid and losses from capital depreciation. The yield to maturity of this particular bond is 5.3 percent. This is an extreme case to illustrate the difference between yield to maturity and current yield.

State and Local Government Bonds

States, counties, cities, school districts, state university system housing authorities, and countless other governmental agencies also float bonds. The unique feature of state and local government bonds is that all interest earned from them is exempt from federal income taxes. As a result, the yield on these bonds is usually much lower than on comparable taxable Treasuries.

Federal Agency Bonds

In the past three decades one of the favorite strategies for funding federal programs has been to create a quasi-federal agency and let it float its own bonds to pay for its program. These are known by a variety of names such as Ginnie Mae, Sallie Mae, Freddie Mac, and Farmer Mac. While these are not issues of the U.S. Treasury,[33] they are issues of federally chartered agencies. Consequently, most investors think of them as federal issues and accept low interest rates just barely above rates on Treasury issues.

Foreign Bonds

As the financial world shrinks rapidly, it is becoming increasingly common to find bonds offered for sale in the United States that are denominated in the currency of another country. These bonds include the normal risks associated with any other bond plus the risk of exchange rate fluctuations. Because of the higher risk, the current yields on these bonds is usually above those of dollar denominated bonds.

Yankee Bonds

These are bonds issued by foreign corporations or governments that are denominated in U.S. dollars. In this case, the issuer accepts the exchange rate risk.

Floating Rate Bonds

These bonds are the exception to the rule that coupon rates never change. These bonds have a coupon rate that is recalculated periodically according to a specific formula located in the fine print of the bond. They are primarily used to finance floating rate mortgages.

Zero-Coupon Bonds

As their name implies, these are bonds that have a coupon rate of zero. That is, they pay no interest for the life of the bond. At maturity, they return the face value. When "zeros" are initially sold, they sell at a deep discount to the face value. A typical zero might initially sell for $250 per bond. In 10 years the investor would receive $1,000 with the annual interest accruing implicitly rather than explicitly. These are very popular bonds for people wanting to save for their children's college expenses. Unfortunately, zeros have some unpleasant tax implications that should be thoroughly understood by any potential buyer.

---

[33] Since they are not part of the Treasury financing, they are not part of the national debt. This explains the political popularity of agency financing: you can have a new program with no impact on the federal debt.

Convertible Bonds

These bonds are a hybrid between bonds and stocks. Convertibles are originally sold as a bond (usually with a relatively low interest rate) but with the added provision that the holder of the bond may exchange the bond at any time for a specified number of shares of stock of the issuing company. These instruments offer the security of a bond combined with the capital appreciation potential of a stock. If the price of the stock increases enough, then the holder of the bond would exchange the bond for the stock and sell the stock for a gain.

Callable Bonds

Most bonds are callable—a provision in the fine print that allows the issuing entity to redeem ("call in") a bond before its maturity date under clearly defined rules. Call provisions are included in bonds because the issuer of a bond, particularly a long-bond, doesn't want to get stuck with high interest bonds for a long period of time should interest rates fall.[34] Typically, call provisions for a long-bond may be something like the following: at 20 years to maturity the bond can be redeemed at 110 percent of face value, at 10 years to maturity it can be redeemed at 105 percent, and so on. The effect of a call provision on a callable bond is to put an upper limit on the price of the bond when interest rates fall. If a bond is "called" or redeemed, the holder of the bond has no choice but to give it up at the specified call price. Only bonds that are noncallable have unlimited upward price potential. Most treasuries are noncallable.

MUTUAL FUNDS

Mutual funds are investment companies operating under strict guidelines of the Securities and Exchange Commission—a federal agency. Mutual funds are for-profit management companies that accept cash from private investors and then buy stocks, bonds, and other investment instruments on behalf of the investors. Professional investment advisers hired by the fund make all the investment decisions consistent with the investment objectives and restrictions as stated in the prospectus (offering document).

Mutual funds were created in 1924 by legislation designed to control some of the abuses that had occurred in what were previously known as investment pools or trusts. The popularity of mutual funds as an investment alternative for the small investor dates to the early 1970s, when the concept of a "**family of funds**" under the umbrella of a single fund manager emerged.

Today the industry contains numerous fund managers (Fidelity, Merrill Lynch, and Vanguard are the largest), each of whom manages a family of 10 to 50 different funds—each with specific, unique investment objectives. In some fund families, several funds share the same investment advisers. In others each fund has a unique investment adviser. In some funds it is difficult to distinguish between the

> **Mutual fund** a professionally managed investment company that accepts funds from investors and invests those funds on behalf of the investors.

> **Family of funds** several different mutual funds with different investment objectives managed by a single manager.

---

[34] This is the same phenomenon that is causing home owners today to refinance their home mortgages. When they bought their homes, the prevailing rates may have been as high as 12 percent on 30-year mortgages. Today, the same mortgage can be purchased for 8 percent. The difference over the life of the mortgages is frequently as much as $100,000. So, what do the holders of 12 percent mortgages do? They pay off the 12 percent mortgage and then buy an 8 percent mortgage to replace it. Corporations do the same thing for the same reasons.

manager and the adviser, while in others the management and the adviser are clearly distinct entities. In the latter case, if the performance of the adviser is substandard, the manager will hire a different one.

Usually an investor in a particular family of funds can shift investments from one fund to another at no cost. This provides the investor with flexibility when the investment objectives of the investor change.

How a Mutual Fund Works

Portfolio a listing of the items currently held by a mutual fund on behalf of the investors.

When an investor sends money to a mutual fund to be invested, the fund manager assigns to the investor a number of shares of the mutual fund proportional to the amount of money invested. In this way, the investor becomes the owner of shares of the mutual fund. The mutual fund uses the investor's money to buy a **portfolio** (i.e., collection) of stocks, bonds, and cash equivalents (very short-term investments) consistent with the investment objectives of the particular fund. At the end of every business day, the mutual fund manager calculates the market value of all stocks, bonds, and cash held in the fund's portfolio.[35] The total value of the portfolio is then divided by the number of fund shares outstanding. The result is the average value of the portfolio per share of the fund, or **net asset value** (NAV). For the individual investor in the fund, the value of his or her holdings on any given day is equal to the number of fund shares owned times the NAV of the fund. If prices of the items in the portfolio go up, *ceteris paribus,* then the NAV of the fund goes up. In a typical fund the individual investor may buy or sell shares of the fund on any given day. All transactions occur at the end of the day based on the NAV for that day.

Net asset value the current value of a mutual fund's portfolio divided by the number of shares of the mutual fund issued. NAV is the value of the assets held by the mutual fund per share of the fund.

As an illustration, let's suppose you have $1,000 you want to invest and a friend has told you about this really neat fund called Gator Fund. From an ad in *Business Week* magazine you learn that Gator Fund is managed by the Lake Creatures fund group. You call Lake Creatures' toll-free number and request information on Gator Fund. A few days later your mailbox is blessed with several items: a slick brochure extolling Gator Fund, another brochure that describes the family of funds managed by Lake Creatures, an absolutely dull prospectus for Gator Fund (printed on the cheapest paper possible), and an application to open an account in Gator Fund. You glance at the slick brochures, toss out the prospectus, and attach your $1,000 check to the application form, returning it in a postage-paid envelope.[36]

Open-end fund a mutual fund that will issue additional shares of the fund whenever additional investment funds are received. The number of shares of the fund is unlimited.

Several days later you will receive in the mail a confirmation of your initial transaction. Your confirmation will give the date on which you purchased shares in the fund and indicate that on that date the NAV was $14.23. Therefore, you now own 70.274 shares of Gator Fund.[37] Gator Fund is what is known as an **open-end fund,** which means that each time an investor sends additional money, the fund creates additional shares based on the NAV that day. In an open-end fund there is no limit on the number of shares that may be created or issued. Notice what has

---

[35] This calculation is simply the closing price of each stock held times the number of shares held. Do this for each stock in the portfolio, and the total is the value of the portfolio or total assets of the fund.

[36] Some mutual fund managers have stores in large cities where you can buy shares of the funds, but most transactions of mutual funds are done by mail.

[37] $1,000/$14.23 = 70.274. Most funds calculate shares held to three decimal points. In most cases this confirmation is the only evidence you have of ownership of shares in Gator Fund. If you desire something more tangible, you can request that a certificate for whole shares be issued. The certificate greatly complicates the eventual sale of shares, so most investors forego certificates.

happened to the fund as a result of your purchase. Assets of the fund increased by $1,000, and shares outstanding increased by 70.274. Since both assets and shares increase by the same proportion, the NAV of all other investors is unaffected.

If 6 months later you decide you want to get out of Gator Fund because the NAV has increased to $17.68, then you simply notify the fund manager that you want to sell all shares. Normally your instructions will be followed on the day received. Gator Fund will buy back your shares at the current NAV and mail you a check in the amount of $1,242.44.[38] On the day you sell your shares back to the fund manager, the assets of the fund decrease by $1,242.44 and the shares outstanding fall by 70.274. As a consequence, there is no change in the NAV for all other shareholders.

Managers and Advisors

Every mutual fund has a manager. The manager is responsible for conducting all business of the firm. A board of directors oversees the manager. The board is elected on the basis of one share, one vote by the shareholders of the fund. The manager has three major responsibilities:

- The manager must choose the investment adviser.
- The manager does all the bookkeeping and paying of bills for the adviser and the fund.
- The manager must, by law, be willing to buy shares of the fund from the shareholders at NAV (i.e., to allow the shareholders to convert shares back to cash at the NAV).

If the shareholders think the manager is doing a rotten job, they can elect a board of directors that promises to clean out the old management and put in a new team. When a challenge to existing management occurs, it is called a **proxy battle** because both management candidates will solicit votes from the shareholders by proxy.[39]

The investment advisor is hired by the fund manager to make investment decisions consistent with the investment objectives and restrictions of the fund. These objectives and restrictions are clearly identified in the prospectus and can be changed only by a majority vote of all fund shareholders. Some funds allow the adviser to pursue very risky investment strategies, while other funds prohibit them. Usually investment advisers are hired on an incentive contract that pays them a percentage of the fund's earnings: the more they earn for you, the more they earn for themselves.

And who pays the piper? Both the manager and the adviser are paid fees as set out in the prospectus. Also, the expenses of the manager are paid by the fund. So part of what the manager and adviser earn as investment returns goes to support them. One criterion for comparing different funds is the **total expense ratio**— the expenses per share of the fund (and adviser) divided by the net asset value of

Proxy battle a battle for the control of the board of directors of a mutual fund. Each fund shareholder can vote his or her shares for either candidate by giving that candidate a proxy to vote the shares. Both candidates seek proxies from each shareholder.

Total expense ratio all per-share expenses of a mutual fund's manager and adviser expressed as a percentage of the NAV of the fund.

---

[38] $17.68 × 70.274 = $1,242.44. The only case in which your sell instructions will not be carried out on the day received is if the financial markets were closed for some reason. This can happen as a result of power outages, computer failure, or world events that create so much uncertainty and instability that exchange directors decide to halt trading until the situation is stabilized. For instance, this happened the Friday afternoon President John Kennedy was assassinated. By the following Monday morning the country was calm and the markets reopened.

[39] A proxy is a legal process in which a shareholder of a mutual fund or a corporation can assign the voting rights associated with shares owned to another party, who promises to vote the shares in a specific fashion.

the fund, expressed as a percentage.[40] The expense ratio of funds varies from less than 0.50 percent to as much as 2.00 percent per annum. A high expense ratio means that less of what the fund earns is available for distribution to investors in the fund.

Types of Funds

Most fund managers today manage a *family of funds* with each separate fund appealing to specific or unique investment objectives of the potential investor. The table in Figure 4–9 shows the types of funds identified by a fund rating company— Lipper & Co. As shown in the figure, some funds have very narrow objectives while others attempt to broadly represent all of a market (GI) or all markets (BL).

A stock fund is one that invests almost exclusively in stocks. Some stock funds are sector funds that invest in only one sector of the economy such as gold, health care, or biotechnology. Others invest only in large corporations or in small corporations or in companies that are currently paying dividends. Some funds invest only in stocks of particular countries or regions of the world.

Bond funds invest primarily in bonds. Some are very conservative and invest only in Treasuries, others invest overseas, some invest exclusively in tax-exempt bonds, and some invest in high yield or junk bonds.

A very common type of fund today is the **money market fund.** These are mutual funds that invest strictly in short-term certificates of deposit and other near-cash instruments. Money market funds strive to keep the NAV equal to $1 every day. Hence, the number of shares held is equal to the number of dollars invested in the fund. Over the past two decades money market funds have been very safe and they have offered much higher returns and greater flexibility than banks. Most money market funds allow you to write drafts (they work just like checks) against your fund balance in a minimum amount of $500. In effect, owning shares in a money market fund is like having a checking account that pays you interest on your balance.

Money market fund
mutual funds that invest exclusively in very short-term, near-cash instruments. The fund managers maintain the net asset value of the fund at $1 by varying the interest rate paid to investors. Checks can be written as a means of redeeming shares.

How to Read Mutual Fund Quotations

Figure 4–10 shows a small portion of a typical mutual fund listing in the financial press. The funds are listed alphabetically by fund family name where applicable. The family names are in bold print, left-justified, with each fund within the family indented.

Cappiello-Rushmore is an example of a family of funds: this particular family (as illustrated here) is rather small with only three members. The first fund is called Emerging Growth, which means the fund invests in stocks of small companies that may become major growth stocks in the future. The second fund is called Growth, which suggests it invests in stocks of companies that are considered growth stocks in areas such as the Internet and biotechnology. The third fund is Utility Income, which invests exclusively in utility stocks that pay substantial dividends.

To the right of each fund name is the abbreviation of the investment objective corresponding to the list in Figure 4–9. Next is a column headed "NAV," which is the net asset value of the fund at the close of the market.

---

[40] The total expense ratio of each fund may be found in a special mutual fund summary that appears in *The Wall Street Journal* the first of each month; in financial magazines such as *Forbes, Barron's,* and *Business Week;* and in the prospectus of each fund.

Category	Abrv	Description
		Stock Funds
Capital Appreciation	CP	Seeks rapid capital growth, often through high portfolio turnover
Growth	GR	Invests in companies expecting higher than average revenue and earnings growth
Growth & Income	GI	Seeks price and dividend growth. Includes S&P 500 index funds
Equity Income	EI	Tends to favor stocks with the highest dividends
Small Cap	SC	Stocks of lesser-known, small companies
Mid Cap	MC	Stocks of middle-sized companies
Sector	SE	Stocks of only one sector of the economy
Global Stock	GL	Stocks of all countries including the United States
International Stock	IL	Stocks of all countries except the United States
European	EU	European markets or operations concentrated there
Latin America	LT	Latin American markets or operations there
Pacific Region	PR	Japanese, Chinese, and other Pacific countries
Emerging Markets	EM	Stocks of developing countries such as Turkey, Brazil, and Mexico
Science & Technology	TK	Science and telecommunications stocks
Health & Biotechnology	HB	Health care, medicine, and biotechnology
Natural Resources	NR	Natural resource stocks
Gold	AU	Gold mines, gold coins, or bullion
Utility	UT	Stocks of electric, gas, water, and other utilities
		Taxable Bond Funds
Short Term	SB	Short-term investment grade corporate debt
Short Term US	SG	Short-term Treasuries and other federal debt
Intermediate	IB	Investment grade corporate debt up to 10 years
Intermediate US	IG	Treasuries and other federal debt up to 10 years
Long Term	AB	Investment grade corporate debt more than 10 years
Long Term US	LG	Treasuries and other federal debt more than 10 years
General	GT	Can invest in any type of bonds
High Yield	HC	Invests in high-yield, high-risk bonds
Mortgage	MG	Invests in mortgages & Ginnie Mae
World	WB	Bonds of any country
		Nontaxable Bond Funds
Short Term	SM	Short term state and local government debt
Intermediate	IM	State & Local debt up to 10 years
General	GM	Any mix of state & local debt
Single State	SS	Invests in issues from one state only
High Yield	HM	Bonds with low credit quality and high yield
Insured	NM	Only buys bonds that are insured
		Stock and Bond Funds
Balanced	BL	Both stocks and bonds with primary objective of conserving capital
Stock/Bond Blend	MP	Multipurpose funds that invest in both stocks and bonds

FIGURE 4–9 Mutual fund objectives.

Family & Fund	Obj.	NAV	Load %	Exp. Ratio
California Trust				
CA Tx-Fr Inc	SS	12.38	No	0.61
Equity Income	EI	13.63	No	0.78
S&P Midcap	MC	18.08	No	0.40
Calvert Group				
Income	AB	17.08	3.75	1.43
Intl Eq	IL	21.89	4.75	1.86
New Vision	SC	13.49	4.75	1.82
Cappiello-Rushmore				
Emerg Gro	SC	11.92	No	1.50
Growth	GR	19.17	No	1.50
Util Inc	UT	12.16	No	1.05

FIGURE 4–10   Mutual fund quotations.

Load or no-load funds   some mutual funds charge an initial sales commission when an investor buys shares. This commission is known as a front-end "load," and such funds are called "load funds." Mutual funds that do not charge any initial fee are called "no-load funds."

The last two columns are very important and deserve some special attention. The first shows the maximum initial charge. All mutual funds are either **load or no-load funds.** "Load" in the mutual fund industry refers to a sales charge or commission paid by the buyer of fund shares. The logic of charging an initial load is that new investors should pay management costs up front so that the management expense on existing investors in the fund can be minimized. Today, many funds charge loads in excess of 5 percent. In contrast, a no-load fund charges no up-front fee to new investors. In this case, the purchase price (or offer price) is always equal to the NAV. The burden of paying management fees falls equally on new and existing investors. In Figure 4–10, the Calvert Group family of funds all charge a load, while the other two families shown are no-load funds.

Most studies have found little difference between long-term net returns on load and no-load funds. However, for investors who want to swap funds frequently, there is no doubt that no-load funds are preferred. For example, suppose you had invested $1,000 in the Calvert Group's New Vision fund one year ago. With a 4.75 percent load, New Vision would have taken $47.50 off the top as a load and invested the remaining $952.50 in the New Vision fund. If New Vision earned a 6 percent return in the first year (after expenses), you would have shares at the end of the year worth $1009.65—not much of a return on your original $1,000 investment.

The final column is the expense ratio for the fund. This is all fund expenses per share as a percent of the NAV. The higher the expense ratio, the more you are paying for fund management. Some funds work hard to keep expenses low, claiming that the investor benefits from low management costs. Others argue that good management costs money and that good management will more than pay for itself with higher returns. A fairly new phenomenon are so-called **index funds,** in which the investment adviser simply tries to adjust the portfolio to mimic some index like the Standard & Poor's 500. Since the investment adviser is neither analyzing nor evaluating individual stocks, the costs of advising are minimized. In effect, the investment adviser is little more than a desktop PC that constantly adjusts the portfolio to replicate the index. The total expense ratio on some index funds is below 0.20. In an index fund you will never beat the market, which is what active invest-

Index funds   mutual funds that adjust the portfolio to mimic a market index such as the Standard & Poor's 500 in order to minimize the expense of an investment adviser.

ment advisers attempt to do, but you also won't be bled to death with fund expenses.[41] As always, it depends.

Closed-End Funds

Most mutual funds are *open-end funds* as previously described. The distinguishing characteristic of an open-end fund is that as additional dollars are received by the fund manager, additional shares of the fund are created with no limit on how many shares can be created.

An alternative type of fund is the **closed-end fund.** These funds are much more like shares of stock in an investment company because the number of shares issued is fixed. The fund manager neither buys nor sells (except initially) shares of the fund. Shares of closed-end funds are traded on stock exchanges and, in most instances, trade at a substantial discount to the NAV of the portfolio.

Poor liquidity and the expense of a broker to buy or sell shares are two disadvantages of closed-end funds. One advantage to a closed-end fund is that the manager has no advertising expenses (since the shares are already sold) and greatly reduced bookkeeping responsibilities. Another advantage is that the fund manager is focused exclusively on earning a good return rather than seeking new investors.

> **Closed-end funds**
> a mutual fund with a finite number of shares such that when one investor buys shares another must sell. Shares of the mutual fund basically trade like shares of stock in a corporation and may sell above or below the NAV of the fund.

SUMMARY

Firms, companies, and corporations need financial funds to finance continuing operations and/or to expand existing operations. There are basically two ways a company can generate additional funds: it can sell part of itself, or it can borrow the funds. The first alternative involves the sale of stock in the company, and the second involves the sale of bonds issued by the company.

Shares of stock are certificates of part ownership of the company. A shareholder owns a proportionate part of the company that issued the shares. The company sells shares of stock to the public in order to raise funds. Once a share of stock is sold to the public, it may be traded from one person to the next. Whoever holds a share of stock is entitled to vote at the annual meeting of the company and to share in the profits of the company.

Individuals buy stock for two reasons: to share in the profits of the company, as they are returned to shareholders in the form of dividend payments, and to earn capital gains as the company grows, thereby increasing the value of shares of the company.

Most stock is traded on exchanges or markets where the supply and demand of shares determine the price of a share. From day to day the price of a share may vary depending on what happens to the market in general, to the market sector in which the company competes, and/or to the particular company.

Bonds are promissory notes (i.e., contracts) issued to lenders when a company borrows money from the public. A bond makes two promises to the bondholder: the company will pay a fixed amount of interest annually to the bondholder, and at maturity the company will return the amount borrowed to the

---

[41] According to *Business Week* (February 22, 1999, p. 127), over the past 5 years fewer than 5 percent of actively managed stock mutual funds have had returns that exceeded the returns on the Standard and Poor's 500 index. Investors in index funds say, "If you can't beat 'em, join 'em."

bondholder. The coupon rate determines the amount of the fixed annual payment, and it does not change over the life of a bond.

Once a bond has been issued by a company, the bond may be traded from one person to the next. Previously issued bonds are bought and sold on the bond market. As with most markets, the price of a previously issued bond depends on supply and demand. Factors that influence the price of bonds on the bond market include the market rate of interest at the time the bond is traded, the perceived risk associated with the bond, and the time to maturity of the bond. In general, bond prices increase as the market rate of interest decreases.

Mutual funds are investment companies that buy stocks and/or bonds on behalf of investors in the fund. The fund manager usually hires an investment adviser, who makes the actual investment decisions. If the value of the stocks/bonds in the fund's portfolio goes up, then the value of shares in the fund will go up. The fund manager is required to redeem shares of the fund for cash at the current net asset value of the shares if so requested by a fund shareholder.

KEY TERMS

Arbitrage
Ask
Bid
Bills
Blue chips
Board of directors
Bond market
Bonds
Book value
Brokers
Call
Charter
Closed-end funds
Commission
Common stock
Corporation
Coupon payment
Coupon rate
Current yield
Day orders
Dilution
Discount or below par
Dividend
Dividend yield
Dow Jones Industrial Average
Earnings
Exchange
Face value
Family of funds
Financial institutions

Float
Fully subscribed
Fundamental analysts
Good 'til canceled (GTC)
Growth stock
Income investors
Income stock
Index funds
Initial public offering
Interest rate
Investors
Junk bonds
Lead underwriter
Limit order
Load or no-load funds
Low-cap stocks
Market order
Market rate of interest
Maturity date
Money market fund
Mutual fund
Net asset value
Notes
Odd lots
Open-end fund
Penny stocks
Portfolio
Preferred stock
Premium or above par
Price of a bond

Price-earnings ratio
Prospectus
Proxy battle
Retained earnings
Round lots
Savings
Secondary stocks
Securities and Exchange Commission
Shares of stock
Speculators
Standard & Poor's 500
Stock

Stock split
Stop loss order
Subordinate
Technical analysts
Tombstone
Total expense ratio
Underwriters
Value investors
Wall Street

PROBLEMS AND DISCUSSION QUESTIONS

1. Stock of XYZ Corp. is listed daily in the financial press. Three columns of the listing for XYZ on a recent day are shown below:

Div	Yld %	PE
1.20	4.3	12

a. What was the closing price of XYZ on this day?

b. What are the earnings per share of XYZ for the past 12 months?

2. The current stock price of the Turtle Computer Company is $20 per share. A year ago the price of the stock was $30. During the past 12 months the stock has paid dividends of $2.00 per share from earnings of $4.00 per share.

a. What is the current dividend yield?

b. What is the current P-E ratio?

3. The price of a Treasury bond is listed as 119:8. How much would an investor have to pay for this bond?

4. How is the Dow Jones Industrial Average calculated?

5. How much interest per year (in dollars) would the holder of a typical bond with the following characteristics receive?

Current yield	8.3%
Coupon rate	8%
Price	96

6. The issuer of a bond makes two fundamental promises to the buyer of a bond. What are they?

7. What are the advantages of owning a stock mutual fund as opposed to directly owning stock?

8. What are the three factors that influence the market price of a bond at a particular time?

9. How is the net asset value of a mutual fund calculated?

Money and Financial Intermediaries

Most things have value. Scarcity creates value. From a rare Rembrandt to the lowly pig, things have value. Our labor has value to our employer. A diamond has value to the soon-to-be-wed. Because things have value, man invented money to measure and exchange those values. The existence of money naturally led to money changers, and they eventually evolved into the financial institutions we have today.

While each of us readily recognizes the importance of money in our personal lives, we may not understand the importance of money to the welfare of the macroeconomy. As we will see, too much money in the economy can lead to inflation and too little money can lead to recession. It is to these topics that we now turn.

WHAT IS MONEY?

Money anything that is generally accepted and commonly used as a means of payment.

Our economy operates because of money. Money commands the resources that are basic to economic growth. **Money** is anything that is generally accepted and commonly used as a means of payment.

Many items have been used as money throughout history, and some of these are still in use today. For example, some nomadic groups in Africa still use cattle as money. The forty-niners of the gold rush days used gold dust. The American Indians used beadwork (wampum) and tobacco. Tobacco was again used as money in Europe during and immediately following World War II. The price of the items that American occupation troops wished to buy was often denominated in cigarettes. A pack of Marlboro cigarettes can get a cab in Moscow[1] faster than any ruble can. The Chinese at one time used stone wheels; as a result they needed a wheelbarrow rather than a pocketbook. Many metals have been used in various societies. Regardless of the items used as money, they are all regarded as a means of payment. Within the complex economies of the industrialized countries, money plays three critical roles.

Money as a Medium of Exchange

In societies without money, the exchange of goods must be accomplished through barter. Under a barter system, one good is traded directly for another. A modern economy, based on specialization and the division of labor, could not operate under a system of barter. The use of money as a medium of exchange provides an alternative to barter. We sell our cattle for dollars and cents and then pay dollars and cents to buy a tractor. Money allows us to exchange the value of the cattle for the value of the tractor. It is the oil that lubricates the economic machine.

---

[1] Moscow, Russia, not Moscow, Idaho.

In order for money to serve as a medium of exchange in an effective and efficient manner, it must have several qualities:

- It must be generally acceptable.
- It must have a high value relative to its bulk and weight.
- It must be easily divisible into small parts.
- It must be difficult to counterfeit.

The absence of any one of these qualities would prevent any type of certificate or coin from functioning effectively as a medium of exchange. If it were not generally acceptable, no exchange could take place. Consider, for example, a trip that you may have made into Mexico or Canada. American dollars are generally acceptable in both of these nations and can be exchanged for goods with little difficulty. But any change received is typically in the local currency. If you should happen to bring back a pocket full of Mexican pesos, how satisfactory are they as a medium of exchange at the corner drugstore in Boise? Most of us have seen foreign coins and currency, but few of us are willing to accept them in exchange for goods and services. Thus, any foreign currency you hold is an interesting curiosity, but because it lacks acceptability, it is considerably less than satisfactory as a medium of exchange.[2]

If money did not have high value relative to its bulk and weight, carrying money for purposes of buying one's needs would be more trouble than it is worth. The ancient Chinese use of stone wheels discouraged exchange. The ancient Spartans' use of iron was intended to focus the public attention on the importance of defense rather than on the accumulation of monetary wealth. During times of war, Spartan money was converted to armaments.

If money were not readily divisible, the only transactions that could be consummated would be those that were in exact multiples of the monetary unit. For example, if our smallest monetary unit were a thousand-dollar bill, we would be forced to use barter for purchases of less than $1,000 and for those between $1,000 and $2,000. Conversely, if the economy is afflicted by inflation—that is, if the monetary unit buys less than it bought in some previous period—some monetary units may go out of existence and other new units may be created. In our own system, the less than totally successful reintroduction of the two-dollar bill in the 1970s and the dollar coin in the late 1970s was the result of inflation having drastically reduced the number of items that could be purchased for a dollar or less. Again, the results appear to be less than successful.[3] In 2000 the U.S. Mint tried again with the introduction of the Sacagawea dollar coin.

If money were easy to counterfeit, no money would be generally acceptable. Improvements in scanners and color printers have endangered the integrity of our money in the United States. In order to avoid this situation, the U.S. Treasury has developed the new off-center, large picture bills with many features of microprinting that are difficult to duplicate.

---

[2] As a graduate student in a small Indiana town, one of the authors was told by a bank clerk that they did not accept foreign currency for deposit. What strange thing was he trying to deposit? An income tax refund check issued by the State of New Mexico! Unbeknownst to this teller, most of what is New Mexico today was taken (purchased under duress) from Mexico in the 1840s. Apparently news of this had not yet reached Indiana.

[3] Canada, learning from the errors committed by its neighbor to the south with the Susan B. Anthony dollar coin, introduced a dollar coin in the early 1990s with a loon on the obverse. Today dollar bills have been replaced by the very popular "loonies." In 1997 Canada introduced a two-dollar coin: these are known affectionately as "toonies."

Money as a Store of Wealth

A second function of money is to serve as a store of wealth. With barter, you must trade one good for another at the same time. With money, however, you can sell goods today and retain the money until you need some other good. Thus, you have a claim to physical goods or wealth when you have money. Money itself has no **intrinsic value,**[4] except for what it will buy. Without monetary status, dollar bills would probably be worth about as much as a mail-order catalog.

For money to serve as a satisfactory store of wealth, it must remain fairly constant in value. That is, a dollar must buy about the same amount and quality of goods today as it bought yesterday. In other words, there must be an absence of rampant inflation, or, at least, the rate of inflation must be fairly constant and low enough to avoid significant losses of purchasing power during the time money is held as a store of wealth. When inflation is a serious problem in an economy, people often avoid using money as a store of wealth, trading it for precious metals, diamonds or other tangible goods that they hope will not lose intrinsic value, or, at least, will lose that value more slowly than the money whose value is being quickly eroded by inflation.[5]

> **Intrinsic value**   the market value of the material from which money is made. Gold coins have intrinsic value, while a common dime has little.

Money as a Basis for Keeping Records

A third function of money is to provide a basis for accounting. When you write a check, no coin or currency changes hands. Your check is simply an instruction to the banking system to transfer a specified amount of money from your bank account to that of someone else. The entire transaction has occurred in the records of the banking system and has not involved actual coins or currency in any way. Still, your ordinary business has been conducted by way of the monetary unit of account.

In recent years, the monetary unit of account has become increasingly important in the American economy. The increased use of credit cards, automatic payroll deposits and e-banking mean that more and more of our business is being done without actual money but instead with a monetary unit of account.

---

[4] In our early history coins were made of gold and silver, so the intrinsic value of the coin was its exchange value. The first greenbacks were issued by the Lincoln administration to pay for the Union's expenses in the Civil War (or the War for Southern Independence, since there was nothing "civil" about it). The status of these greenbacks as legal tender became a significant political issue after the war with their value in gold falling as low as $0.73. Finally in 1875 Congress passed the Resumption Act, which stipulated that greenbacks could be exchanged for gold dollars on request. Some diehards who felt all currency should be "hard" currency formed the Greenback Party, which ran presidential candidates in three elections on a platform of eliminating greenbacks. The strongest support for the Greenback Party came from agrarian interests in the newly opening west. The convertibility of greenbacks into gold was ended by President Nixon in 1972, so today there is absolutely no intrinsic value in a greenback.

[5] In the early 1990s, inflation in Brazil was running in excess of 100 percent per *month*, meaning that what cost 10 pesos at the beginning of the month would cost 20 at the end of the month and 40,960 at the end of a year. In such conditions workers would rush to the store to spend their entire paycheck on the day it was received, as stores were marking up prices on a daily basis.

WHAT BACKS MONEY?

Currency is the foundation of our money. Those familiar green sheets of paper provide each of us with the power to acquire tangible goods and services to satisfy our insatiable desires. Yet as we mentioned earlier, currency today has no intrinsic value. Then what gives currency value?

Legal Tender

U.S. currency is **fiat** money. On each piece of U.S. currency you will find the following statement to the left of the portrait: "This note is legal tender for all debts, public and private." This is the fiat, or statement, that greenbacks are hereby declared by the government to be **legal tender** within the laws of the United States. Specifically, "legal tender" means that if an individual or firm refuses to accept greenbacks as payment of money due, then that individual cannot charge interest on the outstanding debt and cannot sue for nonpayment. So the first reason currency has value is that the law says you must accept it.

Currency also has value because of its universal acceptance. It is basically a matter of mutual trust that you accept greenbacks from your employer or parents with the complete expectation that any firm you choose to visit will gladly accept the greenbacks as payment for goods or services. This universal acceptance—mandated as it is by fiat—creates value in exchange where there is no intrinsic value.

Fiat a legal decree by government.

Legal tender a statement by the government that you must accept dollar currency to pay individual debts. Anyone not accepting dollars as a means of payment has no legal recourse to recover the unpaid debt.

Money and Prices

Currency is accepted as a store of value so long as there is reasonable expectation that the currency will be able to purchase about as much at a future point in time as it can presently purchase. If the **purchasing power** of our currency is falling, then the currency will not be a good store of value and individuals will seek to convert currency into tangible goods in the hope that those goods will retain their purchasing power. Of course what causes the purchasing power of currency to fall is **inflation** in the price of goods. So long as the purchasing power of currency is fairly stable, consumers will be willing to hold that currency from day to day until such time as the currency is converted into a physical good or service.

Most of us have seen pictures of German peasants after World War I carrying money around in wheelbarrows. Prices were rising so fast during this period that the purchasing power of the money was virtually wiped out. This is an example of **hyperinflation.** During a period of hyperinflation people lose all faith in the value of the currency and its role as a store of value is diminished.

Purchasing power value of money expressed in terms of units of goods that money can command.

Inflation a decrease in the purchasing power of a currency.

Hyperinflation a vicious inflationary environment in which prices of goods increase daily and there is panic buying of goods in an effort to avoid holding money.

THE MONEY "SUPPLY"

Daily newspapers frequently carry stories indicating that last month the money supply grew rapidly or fell sharply. What happens to the **money supply** is important news because many economists believe that it is the primary throttle and brake of economic activity. If their belief is essentially accurate, then by regulating

Money supply quantity of money in the economy at a given point in time.

the money supply it is possible to regulate the growth and health of the economy. The importance of the money supply in national economic policy will be examined in the next chapter. But first, we need to find out what the money supply is.

The money "supply" is a misnomer. Remember, supply is a two-dimensional relationship between prices for a good or service and the quantities that will be offered by producers at each price. However, what is popularly called the money supply is not a price-quantity supply relationship; instead, it is a one-dimensional measure of the total amount of money in circulation at any given moment. Although it would be more accurate to say "quantity of money supplied," we will continue to use the commonly accepted phrase "money supply" to mean the quantity of money in an economy at any given point in time.

> **CAUTION**   *The "money supply" is really the quantity supplied of money at any given point in time. The use of the term "money supply" is so pervasive, it is used here to mean the quantity of money in circulation at a point in time.*

M1

You might think it would be a relatively easy matter to measure the size of the money supply. Certainly the U.S. Mint keeps records of how much money it has printed and minted. That much is easy. But remember that money is anything that is generally accepted and commonly used as a means of payment. Certainly coins and currency meet these criteria, and therefore constitute part of the money supply. For most of us, the word "money" is synonymous with coins and currency. But, according to our definition, money is anything that is generally accepted and commonly used. Therefore, we must also include checking account balances as a part of the money supply.

Since checks are generally accepted (except in college towns at the end of the semester) and commonly used as a form of payment, they too are part of the money supply. Technically, balances in checking accounts are called **demand deposits** since you are expected to make deposits with the bank prior to asking the bank to transfer funds to another account. The check you write represents nothing more than your instruction (i.e., demand) that your deposits be transferred.

Finally, what we know as traveler's checks also fit our definition of money. So, for our purposes, the money supply is the sum of all coins, currency, demand deposits, and traveler's checks in existence at any given time. This narrow definition of the components of the money supply is known technically as **M1.**

Near-Monies

There are many other forms of financial assets that are classified as "**near-money**" or "quasi-money." Although not generally considered to be part of the money supply, they can be readily transformed into money. **Time deposits** (savings accounts), shares of money market mutual funds, and certificates of deposit are examples of near-money. Notice that few of these near-monies are commonly used as a means of payment. Instead, they must first be converted into money for eventual payment.

In 2002, the total money supply in the U.S. economy, as measured by M1, amounted to slightly more than $1,180 billion, and the quantity of near-monies was nearly three times greater. The sum of M1 plus near-monies is known as M2. As shown in Figure 5–1, the M1 money supply is approximately one-half demand

Demand deposits balances in checking accounts with commercial banks.

M1 the narrowest measure of the money supply, includes currency, demand deposits, and traveler's checks.

Near-money financial assets not included in M1 that can be easily and quickly converted into cash.

Time deposits account balances in savings accounts.

	($ Billions)	
Currency	$587	
Demand deposits	587	
Traveler's checks	8	
Total (M1)	$1,182	$1,182
Time deposits		2,345
Money market mutual funds		984
Other quasi-money items		954
Total (M2)		$5,465

Note: Data are seasonally adjusted for January 2002.
Source: **http://www.federalreserve.gov/releases/H6/Current**

FIGURE 5–1 Money and near-money in the U.S. economy, 2002.

deposits and one-half coin and currency in circulation. The money supply of "only" $1,180 billion supports an economy many times greater in dollar volume since the quantity of money circulates not once but many times through the economy to finance the total number of transactions in any year. The speed with which money is turned over is called the **velocity** of money. In recent years, the velocity of money has been increasing as electronic transfer of funds, e-banking, and other sophisticated technologies have been introduced into the banking system. With electronic transfer, funds move instantaneously; whereas with the traditional method of physically transporting checks, money was frequently tied up in transit, or "floating," between the time each check was written and when it cleared the deposit against which it was written.

Velocity the number of times the average dollar turns over during a period of time. The money supply times velocity is equal to the gross domestic product (GDP).

Credit and Debit Cards

Although credit cards are a commonly used form of payment, they are not part of the money supply. A credit card is just what its name implies—a card that gives the holder credit or a loan in the amount of the purchase. But the card itself is not evidence of money or any deposit anywhere. It is merely evidence that the issuer of the card thinks (and devoutly hopes) the holder of the card has sufficient funds to cover the cost of whatever is charged against the account. That credit is not money is a lesson too often learned the hard way by those consumers who find it convenient to charge what they cannot afford.

Debit cards are nothing more than modern checks. Rather than writing a check, you simply swipe your card in the slot. Rather than signing your name on the check, you simply enter your PIN number. In either case, the result is the same: funds are transferred from your deposits with the bank to someone else's account. A debit card is a claim against your demand deposits, and those deposits are a part of the money supply.

FINANCIAL MARKETS

Money, like any other commodity, is bought and sold on a daily basis. As with corn, pearls, or gold, the object is to buy cheap and sell dear. Sometimes buyers buy in one market and sell in another where the price is slightly higher. Or the buyer may repackage the commodity and sell it at a higher price. The generic term for all firms engaged in financial markets is **financial intermediaries.** These include insurance companies, pension funds, credit unions, loan agencies, savings banks, commercial banks, and merchant banks. All of these are financial intermediaries that in one form or another are buying and selling money. The markets created by financial intermediaries are tightly interconnected such that changes in one usually result in changes or adjustments in all. As an example of one of these financial markets we will examine the commercial banking system.

The Commercial Banking System

Banks[6] and other financial intermediaries borrow money from depositors at one price (interest paid), then turn around and lend it to borrowers at a higher price (interest charged). The difference between the interest paid to the depositor and that charged the borrower should be sufficient to cover the costs of the bank and to provide a reasonable profit, thereby encouraging the bank to stay around for another year.

Fractional Reserve System

Banks in the United States today are closely regulated by the Federal Deposit Insurance Corporation, the Federal Reserve Board, and the Comptroller of the Currency. One of the regulations with which all banks must live is the requirement that they loan out only a fraction of each dollar deposited such that the bank has some reserves from which withdrawals can be made. These reserves are known as **required reserves.** The portion of deposits that are not required reserves are known as **loanable funds** since these are funds that the bank can lend out.

The reserves that banks are required to hold (currently about 15 percent of deposits for large banks) may be held in either of two forms. The first is good old fashioned cash in the vault—the stuff you expect the bank to have when you show up requesting it. The second form of required reserves is the commercial bank's deposits with the Federal Reserve System (these deposits will be explained further in the next chapter). By law, each bank must close the books at the end of the day with sufficient required reserves. Banks that are short of reserves at the end of the day must borrow reserves from someone else, which can be quite costly. Since bankers have no way of accurately predicting how much will be deposited and withdrawn during each day, the task of managing required reserves is challenging.

Figures 5–2 and 5–3 show highly simplified balance sheets for two different banks. In both cases a 20 percent required reserve ratio is assumed to keep the math simple. Both banks have deposits of $200 and must have reserves in vault cash or in deposits with the Federal Reserve of $40 at the end of the day. Therefore, both banks have $160 of loanable funds. Figure 5–2 shows the ideal situation from the vantage point of the banker. This bank has loaned out all of the $160 the bank is authorized to loan. Every penny is working. This banker would be anxiously looking for more deposits so more loans could be made. While the situation in Figure 5–2

Financial intermediaries those businesses that in one form or another are involved in the buying and selling of money.

Required reserves that portion of commercial bank deposits that the bank must hold in reserve (i.e., not loan out) against possible withdrawals.

Loanable funds that portion of commercial bank deposits that do not have to be held as required reserves and can be lent out.

---

[6] Henceforth the term "banks" will refer to commercial banks—those banks that provide check writing and other services to the general public.

Assets		Liabilities	
Assets		**Liabilities**	
Reserves		Demand Deposits	$200
Required	$40		
Excess	$0		
Loans	$160		
Total	$200	Total	$200

FIGURE 5–2 Balance sheet for a typical bank—Fully loaned out.

Assets		Liabilities	
Assets		**Liabilities**	
Reserves		Demand Deposits	$200
Required	$40		
Excess	$30		
Loans	$130		
Total	$200	Total	$200

FIGURE 5–3 Balance sheet for a typical bank—Not fully loaned out.

is ideal from a profit perspective, it is also very precarious because if someone withdrew $10 at the end of the day, the banker would have to come up with $2 more of required reserves. Unfortunately, you can't call in loans at the end of the day.[7]

Figure 5–3 shows a bank that is not fully loaned out. This bank has loans of only $130, leaving it with $30 of **excess reserves.** Both banks have the same resources, but this bank has not fully employed its resources. The earnings forgone on the $30 of excess reserves is substantial. This banker is anxiously seeking additional loan customers. And, of course, the way you can get more customers into your store is to lower your price (i.e., interest rate) just a little below that of your fully loaned out competitor.

Excess reserves bank reserves in excess of the amount of required reserves.

Therefore, the banker walks a very fine tightrope. If the banker falls off either side of the rope, the consequences are costly. If the banker ends the day with excess reserves, then earnings are forgone, which can be costly. However, if the banker ends the day with insufficient required reserves, then additional reserves must be borrowed, which can also be quite costly. How well that tightrope is walked is a measure of the effectiveness of the bank manager. Clearly, how the loanable funds held by a bank are managed is crucial to its financial success. It is to the market for these loanable funds that we now turn.

Supply of Loanable Funds

Banks buy and sell money. The flow of loanable funds into the banking system is the result of three basic motives: safety, convenience, and avarice.

For reasons of safety, most people prefer to deposit money in the bank rather than leaving large collections of currency sitting around the house. Convenience is the second reason people have demand deposits. Being able to pay bills by writing checks is certainly more convenient than presenting yourself before the phone, cable, and water companies every month.

---

[7] To add some relevance to this example, assume that Figure 5–2 is in millions of dollars. While the banker would be tempted to lift $2.00 from the coffee fund to balance the books, that probably wouldn't work for $2 million.

For the most part, deposits made for reasons of safety and convenience are not very sensitive to the price of money or, as it is more commonly called, the interest rate. The third reason people place deposits in banks is avarice—a perfectly respectable human emotion. Avarice results in deposits, typically in savings accounts or certificates of deposit, that are made in hope of earning an attractive return. For these deposits, the quantity offered for deposit will increase as the price (interest rate) increases. Rising interest rates will encourage potential savers to put more money into savings accounts or to purchase certificates of deposit. Should interest rates decline, however, savers will then find it more profitable to withdraw funds in order to employ them in the stock market or in some other more attractive alternative. As a consequence of the positive correlation between interest rates and savings deposits, the supply curve of loanable funds shown in Figure 5–4 slopes upward.

Demand for Loanable Funds

The demand for loanable funds includes the demand by consumers for money to purchase goods and services, and that of businesses to build plant and equipment. The quantity of loanable funds demanded by consumers is inversely related to the interest rate. At relatively low interest rates, consumers (who always want more rather than less) are given an incentive to borrow money to buy that new beauty from Detroit or to move into the larger house the most recent addition to the family has necessitated. But when interest rates are relatively high, consumers find that it may be in their best interest to squeeze one more year out of the old wreck, or that Junior and Sis will just have to share the upstairs bedroom for a few more years.

Businesses may borrow money to purchase new plant and equipment. These purchases are called **investment.** There are many alternative investments that business firms can make—some profitable, some not. The investment decisions a firm makes will be affected by the rate of interest, or price, charged for the money it borrows to finance its expenditures. If the rate of interest is quite low, the number of investments expected to be profitable would be relatively large as low costs increase the likelihood of a return that exceeds expenses. But if the interest rate is

Investment the purchase of plant and equipment by business firms.

FIGURE 5–4 Market for loanable funds.

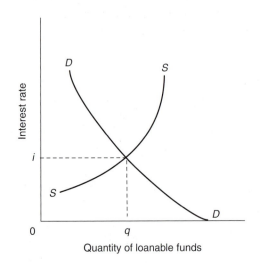

relatively high, the number of investment alternatives expected to be profitable will decrease and the number of loans made will also decrease. Therefore, the demand for loans is a downward-sloping demand curve as shown in Figure 5–4 .

> **CAUTION** *Investment is one of those very dangerous words in economics because it takes on different meanings in different contexts, and because it is a very common word that has certain connotations to the noneconomist. For the economist, when dealing with the macroeconomy, investment has the specific meaning of new plant and equipment purchases by business firms.*

Market Equilibrium

The supply and demand of loanable funds interact to determine an equilibrium price for money. This is shown as interest rate *i* in Figure 5–4. At this interest rate, the quantity of deposits just equals the quantity of money that potential borrowers wish to borrow. Through the normal course of competition, all banks should arrive at approximately equal interest rates that would prevail until such time as a shift in either the demand or supply would cause a change in the interest rate.

The situation of a single interest rate for both savers and borrowers as shown in Figure 5–4 is a substantial oversimplification. In reality, banks "buy" money at one interest rate and "sell" it at a higher interest rate.[8] The difference between the two rates should cover the banks' expenses and compensate for the fact that part of what the bank borrows must remain idle as required reserves. Nonetheless, the concept of interest rate determination illustrated in Figure 5–4 is valid.

Financial Failures

Banks, like any other commercial venture, occasionally go bankrupt when the value of all liabilities (deposits) is greater than all assets (loans and other investments). In any given year a score or two of commercial banks in the United States fail. While it is not uncommon for individual banks to fail, we have had two situations in the past century when the entire banking system failed. It is to these two episodes that we now turn.

Bank Failures in the 1930s

In normal times, the intermediary role of banks is performed with the greatest of tranquillity. But in bad times some depositors may become concerned that the loans made by the bank will not be repaid and demand that their deposits be returned. This concern was not uncommon in the U.S. banking system in the early 1930s. In the 4 years from 1930 through 1933, there were approximately 8,800 bank failures, with most of them occurring in rural areas. In each case of failure, depositors lost all, or at least a part, of what had been deposited with the bank for "safe keeping."

---

[8] An astute reader might suggest that banks don't buy demand deposits, and in fact the customer frequently has to pay the bank for the right to have a checking account. This is true, but banks are still buying those deposits by providing a service. Those customers who don't deposit enough for the bank to earn the cost of that service are charged a fee for the service. For larger depositors (minimum balance of $1,000, for instance), there is no charge for checking accounts. For even larger depositors (in excess of $10,000, for instance), banks will pay a low interest rate on the deposits.

The reasons for the collapse of the rural banking system during this period are not difficult to find. Depositors were given two basic assurances that they would be able to withdraw their deposits:

- The Federal Reserve System (the national central bank) required that banks hold a portion of all deposits in vault cash such that demand deposits could always be met.
- Most outstanding loans were secured by collateral pledged as a security that the loan would be repaid.

However, as it turned out in the early 1930s, neither of these safeguards provided sufficient security for depositors in rural banks. In the first place, the Federal Reserve required minimum cash reserves of only 7 percent on demand deposits and 3 percent on time deposits in rural banks. So, for the rural bank, at most only 7 cents for every dollar deposited needed to remain available as vault cash to cover withdrawals. The rest could be lent out. Since it is in a bank's best interest to lend out as much of its deposits as possible, most rural banks didn't have much cash on hand to pay off depositors should they want their deposits back. Second, most of the loans by rural banks were made to farmers, who used their equity in land as collateral. Unfortunately, in the late 1920s and the early 1930s a combination of bad weather and low prices caused many farmers to suffer significant losses. With no income available to repay loans from the banks, many farmers were forced to sell the farm to pay off the debt. With many farmers being forced to sell land at the same time, the obvious occurred in the market for land: the bottom fell out. The more banks foreclosed on loans collateralized by agricultural land, the less they got for the land.

Astute depositors could see what was happening to the value of the land that was supporting the assets of the banks, and they moved quickly to withdraw their deposits for cash. The more people withdrew their deposits from the rural banks, the faster the remaining depositors rushed to the bank to make sure they would get their deposit out before the bank ran out of money. A rush on a rural bank usually turned into panic as soon as the bank closed its doors, for closed doors signified that all available cash had been withdrawn by a relatively small proportion of all depositors.

Bank panics led to the closing of more than 4,000 rural banks in 1933 alone. By then it had become painfully clear that insufficient reserve requirements and deposit collateral were the two main causes of the bank panics. To solve the first problem, in 1933 Congress authorized the Federal Reserve Board to increase the reserve requirements for rural banks from 7 to 14 percent on demand deposits, and from 3 to 6 percent on time deposits.

The second problem of providing secure collateral for depositors was solved with the formation in 1933 of the Federal Deposit Insurance Corporation (FDIC), an insurance company that insures, up to certain limits, all deposits in participating banks. The banks must pay annual premiums to the FDIC for the insurance protection it affords. Originally established with U.S. Treasury funds that have been long since repaid, the FDIC today operates much in the manner of a private insurance company. There is one big difference, however: if, at any time, the reserves of the FDIC are not sufficient to pay off all claims, it can borrow additional reserves from the U.S. Treasury. So, the ultimate collateral of FDIC insured bank deposits is the U.S. Treasury. Therefore, the collateral the FDIC can provide is a good bit safer than the value of the agricultural land of neighboring farmers.

The combined effect of increased reserves requirements and the formation of the FDIC brought the banking system some desperately needed stability by the end of 1933. Although the depression continued for several more years, bank panics became a thing of the past.

Savings and Loan Failures in the 1980s

There is little doubt that in financial circles the decade of the 1980s will be remembered (none too fondly) as the decade of the debacle of the savings and loan (S&L) industry. The final cost to the taxpayers of this wild, financial frenzy was $550 billion, or approximately $2,200 for every man, woman, and child in the United States. Approximately one-tenth of our current national debt may be attributed to the S&L debacle of the 1980s. The magnitude of the losses staggers the imagination.[9]

After the crises in the financial markets of the 1930s, Congress passed a number of banking laws subjecting financial intermediaries to stringent government regulations. Each type of financial intermediary was limited as to what kind of loans it could make and what kind of deposits it could accept. S&Ls could accept only time deposits—almost exclusively from small individual savers. Maximum interest rates that could be paid on deposits were set by the government—5 percent for banks and 5 1/4 percent for S&Ls. The S&L industry was given an almost exclusive monopoly in the residential mortgage market and was forced to stick almost exclusively to that market. Within this cozy cocoon of regulations the life of a savings and loan manager was pretty easy. Buy money at 5 1/4 percent, sell it at 8 percent, and get home by 4 P.M.

From a technical point of view, what was important about the regulations on the S&L industry was that they were forced to rely on savings accounts for their source of loanable funds and to use those funds almost exclusively for long-term home mortgages. One of the fundamental rules of banking is that the sources and uses of funds should have similar terms or expected lives. Since mortgages are by definition a long-term commitment of funds, it was important that the source of funds also have an expected long term, and time deposits fit this need nicely. Under the regulations, S&Ls were forced to have both long-term sources and long-term uses. In essence, the regulations prevented S&L directors from engaging in what would be considered inappropriate banking practices.

The early 1980s were the dawning of the age of Reaganomics. One tenet of Reaganomics was the need to deregulate American businesses so that they could compete and innovate. Among the industries that were deregulated in the early 1980s were trucking, airlines, railroads, and the financial markets. The rules and regulations that had made S&Ls cozy were suddenly removed, and chaos erupted on financial markets as banks and other kinds of financial intermediaries got into the residential mortgage business and S&Ls got into checking accounts and certificates of deposit.[10] The clear lines between different kinds of financial institutions became blurred, and everybody was trying to get into everyone else's business.

[9] The estimated losses are roughly equal to what was spent on defense in 2 years.
[10] Certificates of deposit as we know them today did not exist prior to deregulation.

Suddenly, with deregulation, savers in S&Ls found that they could withdraw their money and place it in other recently deregulated financial intermediaries at much higher rates of interest. The typical S&L could either watch its deposit base erode or match the competition. But in matching the competition, the S&Ls put themselves in a situation where they were earning 8 percent on long-term mortgages and paying savers 10 percent on deposits. You can't expect to buy money for 10 percent, sell it for 8 percent, and stay in business very long.

In 1980 a grand total of three S&Ls failed. In the late 1980s and early 1990s more than 1,000 of the 3,000 S&Ls that had existed in 1987 failed. It is estimated by the government agency that eventually straightened this mess out that approximately 40 percent of those failures involved some sort of criminal activity.[11]

Banks in the New Millennium

By the turn of the century the S&L crisis was a thing of the past. There can be little doubt that the "trigger" that set off the S&L crisis was the deregulation of the financial industry in the early 1980s. Two new waves of deregulation are sweeping across the landscape of the banking industry in the United States. We can only hope that the consequences of these deregulations will not be as deleterious as the previous deregulations.

The first deregulation concerns interstate banking. Nearly 70 years ago federal legislation prohibited bank holding companies (the corporations that own banks) from owning banks with branches in more than one state.[12] The Riegle-Neal Interstate Banking and Branching Efficiency Act of 1994 eliminates that prohibition. This law allows bank holding companies to acquire banks in any state, and it strikes down state laws that prohibit interstate banks. As of June 1, 1997, commercial banks were able to open branches (as opposed to banks) across state lines. This allowed aggressive banks to spread out of their state of incorporation—usually by consolidating with an existing state bank. In a short 2-week period, NationsBank of North Carolina acquired Barnett Banks of Florida and then was itself gobbled up by BankAmerica of California, which became the first coast-to-coast bank.

Most observers of the banking industry expect that the Riegle-Neal Act will result in a significant consolidation in the banking business with several big interstate banks dominating the industry within several years. The remaining banks may be so large relative to the total economy that the failure of a single bank could seriously disrupt the entire economic system. Only time will tell what will happen in the commercial bank business as a result of this deregulation.

The second major deregulation facing the banking industry was the repeal in 1999 of portions of the Glass-Steagall Act of 1933. The main thrust of Glass-Steagall (which also created the Federal Deposit Insurance Corporation) was to separate the investment business from the banking business. The intent was to get

---

[11] The investigation that eventually led to the impeachment of President Bill Clinton initially began as an investigation of possible fraud in the Whitewater land deal, which led to the collapse of an S&L owned by close friends of the Clintons.

[12] Under previous laws, a bank could have branches in only one state. Many states had reciprocal laws with one another that allowed bank holding companies in one state to own banks in more than one state. But each of those jointly owned banks could only branch in their state of incorporation.

banks out of unregulated investment businesses that were inherently speculative so there would be less chance of banks going under. Prior to Glass-Steagall there was no clear line between banking and investing. Banks were free to accept deposits and use those deposits to buy stocks or real estate.[13] Glass-Steagall built a very high, substantial wall between commercial banks and any kind of investment activity. The investment business went to firms like Merrill Lynch and E.F. Hutton. Investment firms were prohibited from banking, and banks were prohibited from investment services.

That barrier has fallen. Banks, insurance companies, and investment companies can now enter one another's markets. Consolidation of financial services is inevitable as companies seek to provide "one stop" total financial services. The first step in this consolidation was the creation of Citigroup through the merger of Citicorp (banking) and Travelers (insurance). Similar megamergers continue as this industry consolidates and redefines itself.

Since the debacle of the Great Depression we have learned that public faith in the banking system is essential to the economic well-being of our commercial society. The generations that have grown up since the Depression accept the notion of a solvent banking system as a fact of life—something that "just is." Both of the deregulations previously mentioned could potentially destabilize the commercial banking industry. If commercial banks were to go through an experience similar to that of the S&Ls in the 1980s, it would have significant negative implications for our economy. This new era of bank deregulation will require a high level of vigilance by bank regulators and more careful shopping for banking services by the consumer. In this new environment, "rock solid" can turn into gravel very quickly.

SUMMARY

Money is anything that is generally accepted and commonly used as a means of payment. Money has three roles: as a medium of exchange, as a store of value, and as a unit of account. Currency in the United States is legal tender, which means the government says you must accept it for payment.

The purchasing power of money is measured in terms of how many physical goods can be acquired with a unit of money. A decrease in the purchasing power of money is call inflation. When a currency collapses, hyperinflation will occur.

The money "supply" is the total quantity of money in circulation at any point in time. The narrowest measure of the money supply, M1, includes currency, demand deposits (balances on checking accounts), and traveler's checks. Near-monies are financial balances that can readily and easily be converted into cash.

Banks are stores that buy and sell money. A portion of all deposits at banks must be held by the bank as required reserves. The rest can be lent out. The supply of and demand for these loanable funds establish the price of money or the interest rate.

---

[13] There are today in the United States a few specialized banks known as investment banks or merchant banks that accept customers' funds (they are not deposits in a legal sense) and invest the funds on behalf of the customer in a variety of investment alternatives such as stocks, bonds, real estate, and the like. Most investment banks have minimum accounts of $1 million. Investment banks are prohibited from engaging in the activities we normally associate with commercial banks, such as checking accounts and so forth.

The panics that struck the banking system in the early 1930s resulted in significant New Deal legislation creating the Federal Deposit Insurance Corporation and implementing a variety of bank regulations. Deregulation of banks in the early 1980s caused the collapse of the savings and loan industry in the late 1980s. The impact of more recent deregulations has yet to be determined.

KEY TERMS

Demand deposits
Excess reserves
Fiat
Financial intermediaries
Hyperinflation
Inflation
Intrinsic value
Investment
Legal tender

Loanable funds
M1
Money
Money supply
Near-money
Purchasing power
Required reserves
Time deposits
Velocity

PROBLEMS AND DISCUSSION QUESTIONS

1. What is money?
2. What are the components of M1? M2?
3. What three important roles does money play in our economy?
4. What is the relationship between the purchasing power of money and inflation?
5. What are the characteristics of money that are essential for it to serve as a medium of exchange?
6. Money has no intrinsic value. What does that mean?
7. Money is legal tender. What does that mean?
8. What is the definition of interest rate?
9. What is the relationship between loanable funds and required reserves?
10. What were the causes and consequences of the bank panics of the early 1930s?
11. What are the two significant banking deregulations that were passed in the 1990s?

Monetary Policy

*I*n the previous chapter we examined the market for money. We found that in this rather unusual market, the interaction of supply and demand of loanable funds determines at what price and in what quantity financial intermediaries will make loans. As with any free market, the market price and the quantity actually traded are the effects, not the causes, of demand and supply.

The supply of loanable funds and the demand for them at an individual bank strongly influences the microeconomic management decisions of both lenders and borrowers. These individual decisions are repeated millions of times daily throughout the macroeconomy. The aggregation of these millions of microeconomic decisions will, to some extent, determine the vigor and direction of the macroeconomy. When macroeconomic changes occur, microeconomic adjustments are frequently necessary. The essence of management is the adjustment of the microeconomic firm to macroeconomic changes. For instance, when macroeconomic forces cause interest rates to rise, some farmers may decide to forgo buying a new tractor this year. Instead, they will wait until next year in the hope that they will be able to borrow the money to buy the tractor at a lower interest rate, thus reducing the total cost of the purchase.

In this chapter we will examine the macroeconomic forces that determine interest rates and the general level of economic activity. You might question whether interest rates are all that important for agriculture. The undeniable answer is an unequivocal and resounding *yes!* As evidence for this claim, we should point out that in 2001 American farmers paid $14.6 billion in interest—a figure that exceeds what was paid for fuels and property taxes combined. We rest our case.

In the previous chapter, a model of the monetary, or financial, side of the economy was completely developed. The interest rate and the level of loan activity are jointly determined in the market for loanable funds. Changes in the quantity of loans made are caused by shifts in the demand or supply of money. In this chapter we will see how the **Federal Reserve System** (an independent agency of the federal government) can directly cause the supply of money to shift. Frequently, changes in the money market are nothing more than reflections of Federal Reserve Board[1] policy. Deliberate changes in the money supply in an effort to affect the macroeconomy are called **monetary policy.**

The "what," "how," and "why" of monetary policy at the macroeconomic level will be the focus of this chapter. But before proceeding with that discussion, one caveat should be offered: economists hotly debate the extent to which changes in the money supply determine the short-run level and rate of growth of economic activity. There is, however, general agreement among most economists that the

Federal Reserve System an independent federal agency of 12 regional Federal Reserve Banks that serve as banks for commercial banks.

Monetary policy deliberate changes in the rate of growth of the quantity of money in the economy in an effort to achieve macroeconomic objectives.

---

[1] Usually called "the Fed."

long-run money supply and major economic issues such as inflation, economic growth, and full employment are all tied together in some fashion. In this chapter we will try to develop a basic conceptual understanding of the relationship between money and macroeconomic activity. Once these relationships are understood, we can evaluate the policy instruments available to control the money supply and hence economic activity.

THE MONEY SUPPLY AND ECONOMIC ACTIVITY

An economy perceived by the voters at election time as being healthy is a definite political asset for the incumbent, while one that is perceived as being rather anemic is a political albatross that will frequently carry its bearer into the choppy, cold waters of defeat and subsequent early retirement. In our brief history eight sitting presidents who have sought reelection have been defeated. The last four (Hoover, Ford, Carter, and Bush) all lost because of voter dissatisfaction with the economy. During Bill Clinton's 1992 campaign against the first President George Bush, a sign in the Clinton headquarters became quite famous. It read: "It's the economy, stupid!"

Objectives of Macroeconomic Policy

Given the political cost of an unhealthy economy, it would seem realistic to expect that any president would conduct macroeconomic policy in a manner considered acceptable to the voters. Certainly all presidents would like to do just that, not only for the welfare of the people but also to ensure continued residence in the White House. Unfortunately, it is much easier to espouse economic policy success than it is to actually achieve it. To understand why, we need to take a look at the three primary **objectives of macroeconomic policy:** stable prices, full employment, and economic growth.[2]

Objectives of macro-economic policy
(1) stable prices, (2) full employment, (3) economic growth.

Stable Prices

Almost nobody benefits from inflation; hence, there is strong political support for economic policies that ensure relatively stable prices.[3] Inflation is anathema to those who live on fixed incomes, for they see the cost of everything they purchase increase with no commensurate increase in their ability to acquire goods and services. For these people, inflation is equivalent to a decline in their standard of living. Numerous studies have also shown that farmers are adversely affected by unstable prices because the efficiency of price as an allocative mechanism is compromised when prices are unstable. In an inflationary environment, how is an increase in price to be interpreted by a farmer? Do higher corn prices mean there is a shortage on the market, or does it simply mean that the market is well adjusted but the price of corn increased along with everything else? The point is, in our system

---

[2] Some secondary objectives such as the international trade balance and a balanced budget, are not considered here.

[3] The only true "winners" from inflation are those who have accumulated a large amount of debt used to acquire tangible goods such as farmland, houses and cars. With a high rate of inflation (assuming all prices rise in the same proportion), the real value of the debt falls—that is, it takes fewer hours of work to pay off the debt—and the real value of the assets increases at the same rate as inflation. Since the largest debtor around these days is the federal government, it stands to gain from inflation. That's a scary thought.

of price allocation, prices are used to send signals between producers and consumers. If those signals are subject to misinterpretation because of inflation, then the efficiency of the system will be compromised.

Full Employment

An economy that does not fully use the resources available to it is obviously underproducing. More goods and services could be produced if only the idle resources were brought into production. But since the decision to employ resources is made by millions of producing units throughout the economy, it frequently turns out that there are more people willing to work at prevailing wages than there are jobs to be filled. Unemployment also results from labor skill obsolescence. A TV repairman who was a whiz at fixing the old vacuum tube sets of the 1950s may very well be unemployed today if he did not follow the trend and learn how to repair transistorized sets. Whatever the cause, unemployment should be minimized since it wastes resources, it causes social and psychological problems, and it creates unhappy voters.

Economic Growth

Economic growth is synonymous with prosperity, something everyone wants. We all live in the hope that the goods and services available to the next generation will be superior in both quantity and quality. To achieve the ever-elusive "American Dream" requires sustained growth of the American economy. Much of the history of our country has been a history of economic growth. Initially, that growth was fostered by the exploitation of seemingly endless expanses of highly productive land. The formula for achieving growth was simple during the eighteenth and nineteenth centuries: expand the resource base and the economy will expand. Economic growth during the last half of the nineteenth century required additional personnel to run the factories the industrial revolution was creating. Again resource base expansion was the key to economic growth. The massive European immigrations of the 1880s and 1890s were essential to the industrial growth that followed. More recent economic growth in the United States has been technology-based. In this era, we have relied on an expanding intellectual resource base as the source of our growth. We have learned how to use existing resources more efficiently through technological advances. Whatever the source of economic growth, it is certainly one of the three objectives of a successful macroeconomic policy.

How Monetary Policy May Affect These Objectives

The rate of growth of the money supply is an important consideration in achieving each of these three policy goals. Using the model introduced in the last chapter, we see that increases in the money supply (outward shifts of the supply curve of loanable funds) will cause the level of loan activity to increase. As more loans are made to build new plant and equipment, construct new houses, or purchase new tractors, the level of employment and rate of economic growth are stimulated. For example, assume that through government policy the money supply is expanding rapidly. As the supply of loanable funds shifts outward, interest rates will fall and the volume of loans will increase. From the viewpoint of the corn farmer in Indiana, the lower interest rates encourage him to purchase that new tractor he has been looking at but really didn't think he could afford. Since lower interest rates mean lower monthly payments, he buys the tractor. Many of his neighbors do like-wise. As a consequence, the John Deere tractor company must hire an entire new swing shift to produce all of the tractors that farmers want to buy. With lower in-terest rates and a strong market for tractors, John Deere will decide that it should expand its existing manufacturing plant or perhaps open a new plant at another location. Construction workers will be needed to build the plant, and more steel-workers will be needed to produce the steel needed for the additional tractors and new factory. The same sort of thing will happen in the housing, automobile, and other sectors of the economy. In short, a rapid expansion of the money supply re-sults in lower interest rates, which stimulate the economy, causing rapid economic growth and additional employment.

This little scenario shows that merely expanding the money supply achieves the macroeconomic policy objectives of full employment and economic growth. But what about the third objective of stable prices? Here success may not come as easily. In fact, a rapid increase in the money supply may cause inflation.[4] Let's see why.

As previously shown, an increase in the money supply will cause an outward shift in the demand for tractors, houses, automobiles, and just about everything else. If we add up the demand for all of these items, we have what is called **aggregate demand.** This is nothing more than the total quantity of goods and ser-vices that will be purchased by society at each and every price level. Since an in-crease in the money supply will cause the quantity demanded of just about everything to increase at existing prices, we say that the aggregate demand has shifted outward. Remember that an outward shift of a demand curve means that a greater *quantity* will be purchased at each and every *price*. As shown in Figure 6–1, the aggregate demand curve is the total quantity of goods and services that will be demanded within the entire economy during a given period of time at each and every price level. An **aggregate supply** curve is also shown. It indicates how much will be willingly produced within the economy at every price level.

As a result of an increase in the money supply, the aggregate demand curve shifts outward to $D'D'$, causing an increase from Q_1 to Q_2 in the equilibrium quan-tity of goods and services traded. The additional production (Q_1 to Q_2) causes the employment and growth effects of an increase in the money supply we traced ear-lier. But at the same time the increased demand causes the general price level to in-crease from P_1 to P_2. An increase in the general price level for all goods and services is what is known as inflation.

Since an increase in the money supply causes an outward shift of the aggre-gate demand curve, it may cause inflation to worsen at the same time employment and growth improve. What's the poor politician to do? To achieve the policy goal of lower unemployment, the battle against inflation must be compromised. This is exactly what happened in the United States in the late 1960s when President Lyn-don Johnson decided to simultaneously pursue a war in Southeast Asia and his do-mestic Great Society programs. Tax revenues of the federal government were not sufficient to finance both guns and butter, so the Treasury did the obvious: it cre-ated more money to finance both. The additional money in the economy shifted the aggregate demand outward causing production to increase and employment to

---

Aggregate demand
the total quantity of goods and services that will be purchased at alternative price levels.

Aggregate supply
the total quantity of goods and services that will be produced at alternative price levels.

---

[4] Many economists, Milton Friedman being the most notable among them, claim that an increase in the money supply *will* cause inflation. We prefer a more conservative approach in saying it *may* cause inflation.

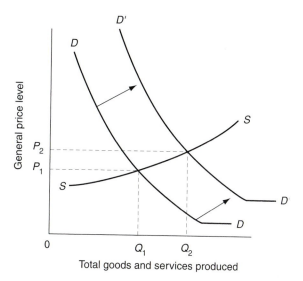

FIGURE 6–1 Effect
on the macroeconomy
of an increase in the
money supply.

General price level

P_2

P_1

0   Q_1 Q_2

Total goods and services produced

rise. Unfortunately, inflation was an inevitable, but undesirable, consequence of the rapidly expanding economy. Pity the poor president. Faced with an unpopular war and a rapidly inflating economy, President Johnson decided it was better to not stand for reelection rather than face defeat (which many considered certain).[5]

In the early 1970s, it became obvious to the political leaders of the nation that a majority of the American people considered inflation to be the number one economic problem confronting the nation. Hence, it became politically expedient to combat inflation. To do this, we just put the money machine into reverse: reduce the rate of growth of the money supply and inflation should eventually be eliminated. When the money supply is reduced, this causes an inward shift of the supply of loanable funds, resulting in rising interest rates and a reduced quantity of loans. Sales of homes and automobiles will decline because of the higher interest rates, as will plant expansions and general business investments. In other words, the aggregate demand within the economy will shift inward, causing the quantity of goods and services produced to decline and the price level to decline (illustrated as a move from $D'D'$ to DD in Figure 6–1). As the price level declines, inflation is reduced and the political objective is achieved. There is, unfortunately, a high political cost to fighting inflation by reducing the rate of growth of the money supply: unemployment will increase, and the rate of economic growth will decline or even become negative. In the latter event, we have what is termed an **economic recession.** This is certainly a steep political price to pay for curing inflation.

As it turned out, none of the Presidents of the 1970s had the political will to drive the economy into the necessary recession to exorcise inflation. As a result, the decade of the 1970s was a period of increasing inflation, reaching a peak of 13.3 percent in 1979. In October, 1979 (the last year of the Carter administration) the Federal Reserve, under the direction of Paul Volker, announced that it was going to adopt a **tight monetary policy** restraining the growth of the money supply until inflation was virtually eliminated. Since it takes time for changes in policy to affect the economy in the expected fashion, there was still raging inflation a year later when the presidential elections were held. Promising to eliminate inflation, Ronald Reagan defeated President Jimmy Carter in a substantial landslide.

Economic recession
period of time when
the real (i.e., inflation
adjusted) economic
growth is negative.

Tight monetary policy
a policy of slow growth
of the money supply
designed to restrain
the economy and
prevent or reduce
inflation.

[5] A decision that Presidents Ford, Carter, and the first Bush no doubt wish they had made.

Year	% Unemployed	% Change Growth	Inflation Rate
1979	5.8	2.5	13.3
1982	9.5	−2.2	3.8

FIGURE 6–2   Macroeconomic Indicators, 1979 and 1982.

With a clear mandate from the public and with the inflation-fighting monetary policies already implemented, President Reagan sat back and strapped himself in for the wild ride that became known as "Reagan's recession." It turned out to be the worst recession since the depression in the 1930s. The results of this premeditated, deliberate recession are illustrated in Figure 6–2. The medicine was harsh, but the results were favorable. The inflation rate fell from over 13 percent to about 4 percent, so the primary policy objective was achieved. But the price was high: the economy went from a 2.5 percent rate of economic growth to a negative 2.2 percent. With the faltering economy unemployment reached 9.5 percent—the highest it had been since 1941. Over this period the number of unemployed in the United States increased by approximately 4.5 million persons!

The Reagan recession was particularly hard on U.S. farmers. The 1970s had been good for U.S. agriculture with high product prices and expanding foreign markets driven by a relatively cheap dollar. As a result, many farmers expanded rapidly in the 1970s, accumulating substantial debt. The recession turned all the factors around as product prices fell dramatically and interest rates soared. Between higher costs, high debt, and lower product prices the American farmer got squeezed. Farm bankruptcies were common features of the evening news on television. By 1982 there were 31,000 fewer farms than had existed in 1979.

But, as shown in Figure 6–2, the bitter medicine performed its desired task.[6] The fundamental policy change that the Federal Reserve Board adopted in October 1979 was to focus on preventing inflation by restraining the growth of the money supply and letting the rest of the economy adjust to that primary objective. That policy has remained in place to this day with annual inflation rates in the 2 to 5 percent range.

The actual relationship between changes in the money supply and each of the three macroeconomic policy objectives is illustrated with the historical data presented in Figure 6–3. Since the effects of changes in the money supply are not transmitted instantaneously through the economy, Figure 6–3 shows the unemployment rates and economic growth 1 year after the change in the growth rate of the money supply. The change in price levels, the inflation rate, is shown 2 years after the rate of change of the money supply. This reflects the fact that it frequently takes longer for the price change impacts of monetary policy to be felt than the initial employment effects. In fact, it is the change in the level of economic activity that causes the change in prices, so we would expect prices to lag behind employment and growth.

In considering the data in Figure 6–3, focus on the pattern of change, not on the actual magnitude of any specific year's data. If graphed, the growth rate of the money supply (as measured by the percentage change in M1) would have a

---

[6] And it did it early enough in President Ronald Reagan's first term that most of the hurt was over by the time he had to stand for reelection in 1984. Campaigning as the savior who slew a decade of inflation, he was easily reelected with Democratic candidate Walter Mondale carrying only his home state of Minnesota and the District of Columbia.

Year	% Change in M1 (t)	% Unemployed (t + 1)	% Change Growth (t + 1)	Inflation Rate (t + 2)
1986	13.59	6.2	3.1	4.14
1987	11.61	5.5	3.9	4.82
1988	4.27	5.3	2.5	5.40
1989	0.99	5.5	1.2	4.21
1990	3.64	6.7	−0.7	3.01
1991	5.93	7.4	2.6	2.99
1992	12.33	6.8	2.9	2.56

FIGURE 6–3   Recent monetary policy and its consequences.

U-shaped pattern over this 6–year period: It starts high, then falls to a low, then rises again. The rate of economic growth follows exactly the same pattern, decreasing as the rate of growth of the money supply fell and increasing as it rose again. The slow rate of growth of the money supply in 1989–1990 had the desired effect of getting the inflation rate down several years later, but at the expense of a mild recession in 1991 (remember the growth data are lagged 1 year). In January 1991, with the Gulf War success, it appeared to most observers that the first President George Bush would be unbeatable in the 1992 elections. But the 1991 recession took its toll, and yet another sitting president discovered how fickle the American voter is when it comes to the economy.

The bitter monetary pill of 1989–1990 worked to perfection. In the following decade inflation was low, employment was high, and economic growth was robust—much to the delight of the Clinton administration. By the end of 2000, however, the party was over and the economy started to slow down. In an effort to avoid or mitigate a possible recession, the Fed poured money into the commercial banking system, dropping short-term interest rates from 6.5 percent to 1.75 percent.

The foregoing discussion should lead to several conclusions:

- Changes in the rate of growth of the money supply affect unemployment, economic growth, and inflation in a predictable, but not always consistent, manner.
- While a causal relationship exists between monetary policy and the macroeconomic objectives, the magnitude of the changes is not precisely related in a functional manner. In fact, as we will see later, there are other types of economic policies that also affect the three macroeconomic policy objectives. These policies may either mitigate or accentuate the impact of monetary policy.
- There are some definite time lags between a change in monetary policy and the consequent changes in unemployment, economic growth, and inflation. The lag appears to be about 2 years for inflation and 1 year for employment and growth.

Monetary policy is certainly important to the agricultural sector. A tight monetary policy always hurts the farmer because high interest rates will increase costs while unemployment and recession will reduce the demand for farm products. Now that we have seen how monetary policy can affect the economy, let's examine how monetary policy is implemented by the Federal Reserve Board.

IMPLEMENTING MONETARY POLICY

Federal Reserve System

Central bank a special bank created by the government to serve as a bank for commercial banks and for the national treasury.

Every country has a **central bank,** which serves as a bank for commercial banks and for the national treasury. In the United States, the central bank is known as the Federal Reserve Bank or the "Fed."[7] The Fed's primary responsibility is to accept deposits from, and make loans to, commercial banks. Simply stated, it is a "bank for banks." The most visible activity of the Fed is clearing checks drawn against one bank but deposited in another. A system of nearly 40 Federal Reserve Banks and branches throughout the country handles this task on behalf of the commercial banking industry. To understand how the nationwide check clearing system works, let's see what happens when a farmer writes a check for $10 against his account in a rural Iowa bank to pay for a mail-order book from Dallas. The book dealer will deposit the check at her Dallas commercial bank. Upon deposit, the bank will (in most cases) credit the account of the book dealer for the amount on the check. From the point of view of the bookseller, her assets (command of funds) have increased by $10. From the point of view of the bank, its liabilities (obligations to depositors) have increased by $10. In order to offset this liability, the Dallas commercial bank will deposit the check with the Dallas branch of the Federal Reserve System and have its account with that branch of the Fed credited for the amount of the check. Now the Dallas commercial bank is in a neutral position: liabilities (to the book dealer) and assets (with the Fed) have both increased by $10. The Dallas Fed will then send the check to the Chicago branch of the Federal Reserve System, which will credit the account of the Dallas Fed for the amount of the check. Now the Dallas Fed is in a neutral position on its balance sheet: it has a $10 liability for the Dallas commercial bank's deposit and a $10 asset in the form of a credit from the Chicago Fed. Finally, the check will move from the Chicago Fed to the Iowa commercial bank, which is located within the Chicago Fed's district. The Chicago Fed will debit the Iowa commercial bank for the amount of the check. This clears the balance sheet of the Chicago Fed by creating equal changes in both assets and liabilities. Finally, the Iowa bank will debit the account of the farmer who wrote the check in the first place. The Iowa bank sees two changes in its accounts: its deposits (assets) with the Chicago Fed have declined by $10, and its liabilities (obligations to the farmer) have decreased by $10. The Fed has served as the financial intermediary between the two commercial banks by crediting and debiting the commercial banks' accounts held with the Federal Reserve System.

Although check clearing is an important responsibility of the Federal Reserve System, it is minor when compared with the Fed's role in controlling the monetary policy of the country. The policies of the Fed determine whether the money supply expands at a rapid or a slow rate. As we have seen, the eventual impacts of these policy decisions directly affect the achievement of the three macroeconomic policy objectives. In order to understand how the Fed implements monetary policies, we first need to examine how the commercial banking system can "create" money.

---

[7] You can learn more about the Fed at its website: **www.federalreserve.gov**.

Money Creation

As we saw earlier, the commercial banking system in the United States is a **fractional reserve system.** In this system, banks[8] lend most of the money that is deposited, keeping only a small fraction in reserve either as vault cash or as deposits with Federal Reserve Banks. These reserves are required to ensure that the bank has sufficient funds available to honor a normal level of withdrawals. The reserve requirements for commercial banks are established by the Federal Reserve Board within broad limits set by Congress. In recent years, the reserve requirements for demand deposits have been 3 percent for the smaller banks and 10 percent for the larger banks.

Since having the ability to create money satisfies almost everyone's childhood fantasies, let's see how the commercial banking system does it. Suppose some **"new" money** came into the commercial banking system. By new money we mean money that has not been deposited anywhere else within the domestic commercial banking system. Examples of new money would include cash that someone had kept in the cookie jar for a number of years that is suddenly deposited in a bank, a foreigner holding dollars who deposits them in an American account, or additional deposits by a Federal Reserve Bank in a commercial bank that does not replace existing deposits. As shown in Figure 6–4, let's suppose that new money worth $1,000.00 is deposited in Bank A and that the reserve requirement for all banks is 12 1/2 percent. Since Bank A's deposits have increased by $1,000, the required reserves of the bank will increase by $125.00 (12 1/2 percent of $1,000). Hence, the free reserves (loanable funds) of Bank A will increase by $875.00 ($1,000 minus $125.00). Bank A will then make every effort to loan out the new free reserves so that the bank can earn some interest. Suppose the bank loans the $875.00 to Ms. Black, who promptly uses the cash to buy a car from Mr. Green. Mr. Green will take the cash received for his old wreck and deposit it in his checking account at his bank, which we will call Bank B.

As a result of Mr. Green's deposit of $875.00, the required reserves of Bank B increase by $109.38 (12 1/2 percent of $875.00) and free reserves increase by $765.62 ($875.00 minus $109.38). Bank B turns around and lends the $765.62 to Ms. Fox, who uses the money to buy a garden tractor from Mr. Katz, who deposits the money in Bank C. The required and free reserves of Bank C will increase by $95.70 and $669.92, respectively. As shown in Figure 6–4 this process will continue throughout the banking system with each bank receiving a new deposit equal to the previous deposit minus the 12 1/2 percent required reserve. By the time this process reaches Bank J (the tenth bank), the initial deposit of $1,000 of new money has generated total deposits in the 10 banks of $5,895.50. How can this be? No single bank has done anything improper, but taken collectively all the banks have facilitated the creation of $4,895.50 over and above the original deposit. Money, in the form of demand deposits, has been created.

If the creation process passes through 25 banks, the total deposits generated by and including the original $1,000 will be $7,715.97. Assuming that the process continues ad infinitum, the total deposits created within the banking system will be $8,000.00. The total required reserves against all of these deposits will be $1,000. Therefore, the total loanable funds created by the initial deposits of $1,000 of new money is $7,000. The amount of total deposits that will be created by the injection

Fractional reserve system commercial banking system in which the government requires banks to hold a portion of all deposits as reserves in the form of vault cash or deposits in the central bank.

"New" money money that comes into the commercial banking system from outside the system that adds to the total amount of deposits in the system.

---

[8] References to "banks" should always be interpreted as "commercial banks," as distinct from Federal Reserve Banks.

	Initial Deposit	Required Reserve	Loanable Funds
Bank A	$1,000.00	$125.00	$875.00
Bank B	875.00	109.38	765.62
Bank C	765.62	95.70	669.92
Bank D	669.92	83.74	586.19
Bank E	586.19	73.27	512.92
Bank F	512.92	64.11	448.81
Bank G	448.81	56.10	392.71
Bank H	392.71	49.08	343.63
Bank I	343.63	42.95	300.68
Bank J	300.68	37.58	263.10
After 10 loops	5,895.50	736.92	5,158.48
After 25 loops	7,715.97	964.50	6,751.47
After ∞ loops	8,000.00	1,000.00	7,000.00

FIGURE 6–4 Example of money creation assuming 12 1/2 percent required reserve ratio.

of some new money into the commercial banking system is equal to the amount of the new money deposited divided by the required reserve ratio. In our example, the total deposits created are equal to $1,000 ÷ 0.125 = $8,000. The amount of new required reserves created will always be equal to the amount of new money that entered the commercial banking system in the initial deposit. Therefore, the amount of new loans generated is equal to the new deposits created ($8,000) minus the amount of new required reserves ($1,000), or $7,000 in the example in Figure 6–4.

The process of money creation through the commercial banking system is very important because it means that the Federal Reserve Board can make rather substantial changes in the total money supply (which includes demand deposits) whenever it injects some new money into the system.[9] Let's turn now to see how the Fed can use the money creation (or money reduction) process to achieve its monetary policy objectives.

Instruments of Monetary Policy

As we have seen, the three broad objectives of macroeconomic policy of stable prices, low unemployment, and rapid economic growth are affected by the rate of growth in the money supply. The **Federal Reserve Board of Governors** attempts to adjust the money supply growth rate through several different policy instruments in order to achieve these three goals or at least to balance the three in some acceptable manner.

The responsibility for the conduct of monetary policy is held exclusively by the Federal Reserve Board of Governors. The Board is composed of seven members, each serving a 14-year term with one member's term expiring every 2 years. Two members serve 4-year terms as chairman and vice chairman. Members of the Board are nominated by the president and confirmed by the Senate. The current chairman of the Board, Dr. Alan Greenspan, is somewhat unique in that he was initially nominated as chairman by President Ronald Reagan, then renominated for a

Federal Reserve Board of Governors
seven-member committee that determines policies and procedures to be followed by the Federal Reserve Banks.

---

[9] The money process also works in reverse. If the Fed pulls money out of the system, the impact on the commercial bank system will also be amplified.

second 4-year term by the first President George Bush, and then renominated for a third and fourth term as chairman by President Bill Clinton. He continues to serve under the second President George Bush, as he has clearly shown the ability to conduct monetary policy beyond political partisanship.[10]

Since the members of the Board are appointed for rather long terms, the Board tends to be relatively independent of political forces. Neither Congress nor the president can direct the Board to pursue a particular monetary policy. Nor can the Board be held accountable to Congress or the president for its actions. Since the chairman of the Board is designated by the president, the chairman is usually rather partisan, but once appointed to a 4-year term as chairman, he or she cannot be removed from that position at the will of the president. Consequently, the Board is usually sensitive to the political implications of its monetary policy but is not driven by political expediency to the same extent as members of Congress and the president.

The Federal Reserve Board implements monetary policy through three policy instruments: the reserve requirement ratio, the discount rate, and open market operations. By making adjustments in each of these, the Board is able to influence the money creation process and thereby bring about shifts in the supply of loanable funds within the commercial banking system. As the supply of loanable funds changes, the macroeconomic performance of the economy will change. We have already seen how this happens, so now let's take a look at how the Fed implements monetary policy.

Reserve Requirement Ratio

The reserve requirement ratio determines the magnitude of new deposits that will be created by a given infusion of new money into the commercial banking system. In the example we previously gave, an infusion of $1,000 of new money caused the total deposits to increase by $8,000 because the reserve requirement was assumed to be equal to 12 1/2 percent. If the Fed wished to pursue a **loose monetary policy** to stimulate the economy, it would reduce the reserve requirement ratio. With a lower reserve requirement, each bank in the system would be able to expand its level of lending activity from its given deposit base. Also, with a lower reserve requirement, any new money coming into the system would support the creation of a larger total deposit base. For example, with a reserve requirement of 10 percent, $1,000 of new money would lead to the creation of additional deposits of $10,000 and additional loanable funds of $9,000.

Since the commercial banking system is very sensitive to the reserve requirement ratio, it is not frequently used as a monetary policy instrument. When it is used, the changes are of very slight magnitudes so as not to totally disrupt the banking system. Obviously, if the reserve requirement were to increase by several percentage points overnight, each commercial bank would have to call in some loans to generate the additional reserves that would now be required. While such a change would certainly cause the money supply to fall, it would cause such a disruption in financial markets that it could be counterproductive.

Loose monetary policy policy of accelerating the rate of growth of the money supply to stimulate the economy, causing faster economic growth and lower unemployment.

---

[10] During his service to Presidents Reagan and the first Bush, Dr. Greenspan's management of the Board and its monetary policy was generally well regarded. As previously shown, he engineered a mild recession in the early nineties (it probably cost President Bush his reelection) that is credited with creating the low inflationary environment of the 1990s. It was not at all without mention in the financial press that during President Clinton's first State of the Union address, none other than Alan Greenspan was seated beside the First Lady in the gallery of the House.

Discount Rate

Every bank is required by law to have vault cash and deposits with the Federal Reserve Banks equal to the required reserve at the close of each banking day. Since banks cannot accurately predict what the level of deposits and vault cash will be at the end of each day, they frequently find themselves in technical violation of the reserve requirement regulation. If that is the case, the bank must borrow some money for overnight deposit with the Federal Reserve Bank. Frequently one bank with excess reserves will lend money to another bank with deficient reserves. These overnight loans are arranged between bankers at a negotiated interest rate called the **federal funds rate.** This interest rate is a closely watched indicator of the amount of loanable funds in the banking system.

Federal funds rate
interest rate charged on an overnight loan of reserves between commercial banks.

For most of us, the idea of lending money overnight sounds like a long run for a short slide. But within the commercial banking system it can be rather significant. Recently commercial banks had deposits of about $530 billion against which the required reserve was about $43 billion. Suppose that only 1 percent of the required reserve was deficient on a given day such that some banks (in aggregate) had to borrow $430 million at a 5 percent annual interest rate. The interest payment for one night would be about $60,000. On an annualized basis this amounts to interest payments among banks of approximately $21 million—which is a lot of money, even to bankers.

Since it is in the best interests of each bank to keep free reserves down to a zero level (that is, to lend out all deposits that can be legally lent out), it is not uncommon to encounter a situation in which the entire banking community shows an aggregate net deficit of required reserves. In this case, the delinquent banks can borrow the required reserves from the Federal Reserve Banks at an interest rate that is called the **discount rate.** This interest rate is fixed by the Federal Reserve Board as a part of its monetary policy. By adjusting the discount rate, the Fed can affect bankers' behavior, and thus engage in monetary policy.

Discount rate
interest rate charged when commercial banks borrow additional reserves from the Federal Reserve Bank.

Suppose the Fed wished to pursue a tight monetary policy. It should increase the discount rate to discourage commercial banks from borrowing from the Fed to cover shortages in their required reserves. This would have the effect of increasing the required reserves that banks hold, *ceteris paribus*, thereby reducing the funds lent out. As the level of loan activity decreased, the objectives of a tight monetary policy would be realized.

Conversely, if the Fed wished to pursue a stimulative or loose monetary policy, it would reduce the discount rate. Suppose, for example, that banks are earning an average of 4 percent on their outstanding loans and that the discount rate is 6 percent. This gives banks a very clear signal that if they have to borrow from the Fed, it will cost more to borrow than the bank can earn on the loans. But if the discount rate were reduced to 3 percent, then the banks would do everything they could to make sure that every possible dollar of deposits was lent out at 4 percent, because even if the bank inadvertently violated the reserve requirement, it could always borrow the deficit from the Fed at 3 percent to cover the shortages. Since the discount rate at 3 percent is less than the 4 percent banks can earn on loans, the bank will still earn a net interest of 1 percent even if it is forced to borrow from the Fed. Hence, a low discount rate relative to market interest rates encourages banks to expand loans, which, in turn, stimulates the economy.

The discount rate is used frequently by the Federal Reserve Board to fulfill monetary policy objectives. Usually changes in the discount rate are considered to be indicators of the general direction of the monetary policy of the Fed. When the discount rate is changed the Fed usually announces a new "target" for the federal funds rate as well. While the federal funds rate is a market rate that fluctuates daily, the Fed, by its actions, can influence the market to move toward the stipulated target rate. Typically, the discount rate will be changed no more than five or six times a year. It certainly is not used to fine-tune monetary policy. That is the role of open market operations.

Open Market Operations

We have seen that the Federal Reserve Banks are really just "bankers' banks." Deposits made by commercial banks at Federal Reserve Banks can be used by the Fed to acquire interest-earning assets such as bonds. The interest income earned is used to pay the expenses of the Federal Reserve System. A substantial majority of the interest-earning assets of the Federal Reserve Banks are debt obligations of the U.S. Treasury, which the Fed has purchased on the "**open market.**" The open market is the public bond market centered on Wall Street where individuals, commercial banks, insurance companies, and others freely trade debt obligations of the U.S. Treasury and other issuers of debt such as corporations and other governmental agencies. Transactions on the open market are typically made through commercial brokers, just as corporate stocks are traded on the New York Stock Exchange through a system of brokers. On any given day, the Federal Reserve Banks will simultaneously buy and sell millions of dollars worth of Treasury obligations on the open market. Through these sales and purchases, the Federal Reserve Banks can directly influence the money supply.

Open market the public, or open, market on which all kinds of bonds are traded.

Frequently the U.S. Treasury finds that Congress has authorized spending levels that are greater than taxes and other revenue sources. In these cases, the U.S. Treasury must increase the national debt by selling additional debt instruments to the highest bidders (those willing to accept the lowest interest rates). When the Treasury sells this debt to the public, it issues bills, notes, and bonds as evidence of who should receive the interest paid by the Treasury. Once issued, these Treasury debt obligations are freely traded on the open or bond market. While the Federal Reserve Banks rarely buy Treasury debt issues directly from the Treasury, they are one of the biggest traders on the open market.

Soon after its founding, the Fed began buying Treasury obligations as a means to finance its operations, but over time, the Board began to realize that its purchases and sales of Treasury obligations in the open market had a very significant effect on the money supply. The reason why should now be plain to see. First, remember that the "money supply" refers to total currency and demand deposits held by the public or deposited in the commercial banking system. Money held by the Federal Reserve Banks is *not* part of the money supply because it cannot be used by the private sector for economic transactions. Given this bit of information, we can now see how the open market purchase and sales of Treasury debt by Federal Reserve Banks can influence the money supply.

Suppose the Fed buys a Treasury bond in the open market. The seller of the bond may be a private investor, a commercial bank, a pension fund, or an insurance company. In any case, when the Fed buys the bond, it is taking a piece of paper (the bond) out of private hands and replacing it with money. Suppose the Fed buys a bond from Mr. Smith, where both the Fed and Mr. Smith are working through their respective brokers. When Mr. Smith's broker says she has found a buyer for his bond, Mr. Smith goes to his bank and removes a piece of paper (the bond) from his safety deposit box. This action certainly has no effect whatsoever on the deposits of the bank. On the following day, Mr. Smith will return to his bank to deposit the proceeds from selling the bond. Bingo! Commercial bank deposits have increased as a result of the Fed buying a bond. So far as the commercial banking system is concerned, this is "new" money because there were no offsetting withdrawals elsewhere in the commercial banking system. When this new money is injected into the commercial banking system, it will be multiplied several times over by the process of money creation. So, by simply buying bonds on the open market the Fed can cause the money supply to increase.

Similarly, if the Fed wished to pursue a tight monetary policy in order to reduce the growth of the money supply, it would sell Treasury obligations on the open market. By selling bonds the Fed is absorbing money from the public and replacing it with paper bonds. As the money is absorbed, bank deposits decline, which creates a reduction of total deposits throughout the system many times greater than the initial sale because the principle of money creation also works in reverse.

Federal Open Market Committee
committee composed of all members of the Federal Reserve Board of Governors and five presidents of regional Federal Reserve Banks who meet periodically to establish the open market policy of the Fed.

Open market operations are conducted by the Fed on a daily and even hourly basis. The basic policy objectives of the open market operations are delineated by a **Federal Open Market Committee** (FOMC), which is composed of the seven members of the Federal Reserve Board and five presidents of the regional Federal Reserve Banks.[11] This committee periodically meets in secret to specify targets of the Fed's open market operations. These objectives are usually stated in terms of a desired rate of growth of the money supply or a target level of the federal funds rate. By being either a net buyer or a net seller of Treasury obligations on the open market, the Fed can cause the supply of loanable funds in the commercial banking system to shift inward or outward.

If bond speculators knew if the FOMC was moving to be a net buyer or net seller of bonds, they could anticipate the Fed and claim substantial speculative profits. To avoid this, the FOMC operates under a strong cloak of secrecy. On a daily basis the Fed trades with numerous bond brokers so that on any given day the Fed may appear to be a buyer to one broker and a seller to another.[12]

SUMMARY OF MONETARY POLICY

The chain of events that are collectively known as monetary policy is now in place. Since the chain has many links, it is worth summarizing them again. It begins with the selective wisdom of the 12 voting members of the Federal Open Market Committee. As they meet eight times a year, the FOMC may decide to tighten or loosen monetary policy or to leave well enough alone for the near future. If the FOMC should decide to tighten, that means they want to slow the economy down. They do this by selling bonds on the open market, which extracts money (in the form of bank reserves) from the commercial banking system. The money creation process (or reduction process, in this case) amplifies the action of the FOMC.

---

[11] The president of the New York Federal Reserve Bank (which conducts all international transactions for the entire system) is a permanent member of the FOMC. The other four seats rotate among the other eleven presidents on a regional basis.

[12] A few years ago several of these bond brokers were found to be colluding (i.e., sharing information) with one another. Those firms are no longer doing business with the Fed.

As money is extracted from the banking system, fewer loans will be made and interest rates will go up. Fewer loans translate into fewer houses being built and fewer cars being bought: the level of economic activity will be restrained. By reducing aggregate demand, pressures on inflation are relieved and price stability is maintained.

If the FOMC wanted to pursue a loose monetary policy to stimulate the economy, they would become buyers of bonds, which would put more reserves into the banks and create more economic activity. The Fed could also lower the discount rate and/or the required reserve ratio in an effort to stimulate the economy.

Monetary policy is one of two basic policies that can be pursued in an effort to achieve stated economic goals. The second alternative is called fiscal policy. Fiscal policy deals with the impact on economic activity of the government as a collector of taxes and as a purchaser of goods and services. In order to understand how fiscal policy can affect the economy it is important to develop a clear understanding of how the macroeconomy of most industrialized countries operates. It is to that task that we now turn.

SUMMARY

Macroeconomic policy seeks to achieve three often contradictory objectives: stable prices, full employment, and economic growth. Monetary policy seeks to achieve these objectives by regulating the rate of growth of the money "supply." An increase in the amount of money in the commercial banking system will encourage banks to make more loans, which will stimulate aggregate demand in the economy.

The Federal Reserve System is composed of 12 regional Federal Reserve Banks that serve as banks for commercial banks. The Federal Reserve Board of Governors and the Federal Open Market Committee have the power to regulate the money supply by adjusting the required reserve ratio, the discount rate, and open market operations.

Most observers attribute the severe recession of the early 1980s to actions by the Fed to halt inflation. They also attribute the unprecedented growth, low unemployment, and low inflation of the 1990s to the policies of the Federal Reserve Board. In 2001 the Fed aggressively lowered the discount rate in an effort to avoid a looming recession and to mitigate the economic impact of the September 11, 2001, terrorist attacks.

KEY TERMS

Aggregate demand
Aggregate supply
Central bank
Discount rate
Economic recession
Federal funds rate
Federal Open Market Committee
Federal Reserve Board of Governors

Federal Reserve System
Fractional reserve system
Loose monetary policy
Monetary policy
"New" money
Objectives of macroeconomic policy
Open market
Tight monetary policy

PROBLEMS AND DISCUSSION QUESTIONS

1. Assume the following:

Long-term interest rates	8%
Discount rate	5%
Marginal propensity to consume	60%
Required reserve ratio	20%
Short-term interest rates	6%

   If the Fed bought $10,000 of bonds on the open market, *ceteris paribus*, what is the theoretical maximum impact of that purchase on:

   a. Deposits in the commercial banking system?

   b. New loans by the commercial banking system?

2. The Fed has three policy tools available to it. Identify these three tools, and indicate how the Fed should change each in order to adopt a looser (more stimulative) monetary policy.

    Buy

3. The three key indicators of the success of macroeconomic policy are the rate of economic growth (measured by the rate of change of the gross domestic product), the rate of inflation (measured by the rate of change of the consumer price index), and employment (measured by the unemployment rate).

   a. Go to the economics briefing room of the White House (**www.whitehouse.gov**) to see the most recent values of these three indicators.

   b. Over the past two years, what is the trend of each of the indicators?

4. What is the current policy of the Federal Open Market Committee? You can find this at **www.federalreserve.gov**. Go to the FOMC calendar, and look at the end of the most recent minutes of the FOMC. (Note: FOMC minutes are not released until several weeks after the meeting.)

   tight

5. Why do most economists feel that high rates of inflation are not good for the economy?

   causes ↑ interest Rates   slows economy

The Circular Flow of Income

S ome people are genuinely amazed to discover that the relationship between the money supply and economic activity is not as consistent as economists suggest. The expected relationships must necessarily be defined in a *ceteris paribus* manner. Unfortunately, monetary policy cannot be implemented in a static, stable macroeconomic environment. The real world refuses to conform obediently to the simplistic monetary model. The macroeconomy is always in a state of flux, so the monetary policy maker must design policies that are targeted at anticipated economic problems rather than any immediate symptoms. If the policy maker guesses wrong, he or she will be forced to eat crow—a very common practice in the real world of economics and, frequently, politics.

Monetary policy is one of two broad policy options available to political leaders who would like to simultaneously achieve the major macroeconomic policy objectives of high employment, rapid economic growth, and stable prices. The second policy option is **fiscal policy,** which deals with the behavior of governments as purchasers of goods and services and as collectors of taxes. As the behavior of governments changes, so will the economy. Like it or not, governments constitute such a large portion of the total economy that changes in government spending and/or taxing can have a powerful effect on the economy. In recent years, approximately one-fifth of all final goods and services were purchased by governments.[1] Perhaps a better indicator of the importance of governments in our economy is the proportion of the total economy that is taken by taxes. In the United States, about 25 percent of personal income is paid to governments in the form or one tax or another.[2] About four-fifths of this is collected by the federal government alone.[3] Hence, by purposefully changing its taxing and spending behavior, the federal government can significantly influence the aggregate level of economic activity.

Prior to the 1930s, the study of fiscal policy emphasized the revenue, or tax collection, side of government finance. For the most part, the tax system was

Fiscal policy the purposeful use of government taxing or spending authority in an effort to influence economic activity.

---

[1] Two things must be noted at this point. First, note the "s" at the end of the word "governments." We are talking here about all public bodies, from the mosquito control district to the federal government. In terms of spending on final goods and services, the aggregate of other governments exceeds the federal government. Second, the federal government is a much larger part of our economy than this figure would suggest, because much of what the federal government does is to redistribute or transfer income from taxpayers to recipients. Programs such as Social Security, Medicare and Aid for Families and Dependent Children are transfer programs that do not show up on the books as purchases of final goods and services.

[2] Japan's tax burden is slightly higher than that of the United States. In most other industrialized countries the percentage is much higher—reaching above 40 percent in Canada, Germany, France and several other countries. (*Source: Business Week,* Jan. 23, 1995, p.30.)

[3] The impact of the federal government is greater on the tax side than on the expenditure side because a significant portion of the taxes collected by the federal government are given to state and local governments as federal grants.

viewed as a necessary evil existing for the purpose of collecting sufficient revenue to keep the federal budget balanced. It was realized that different forms of taxation could affect the economy in different ways, but the task of controlling or regulating the business cycle was left entirely to the monetary authorities. But times change, and in the mid-1930s fiscal policy was recognized as an important alternative to monetary policy for regulating the business cycle in order to maintain the macroeconomic health of the nation. There are two basic reasons that fiscal policy rose to prominence at this time:

- The Great Depression of the 1930s created a need for some new policy alternatives. While it is still hotly debated whether the monetary policies of the early 1930s were appropriate, there is no doubt that they were failing to halt the vicious downward spiral in which the U.S. economy found itself. Something new was needed.

- In late 1935 John Maynard Keynes finished his seminal work, *The General Theory of Employment, Interest and Money,* which developed the basic tenets of contemporary fiscal policy—usually referred to as "**Keynesian policy.**" The power and force of the Keynesian "revolution" cut across the lines of economics, politics, and social philosophy. Keynes' contributions to macroeconomic policy were twofold: the federal government *could* influence the level of economic activity through its fiscal (i.e., spending and taxing) policies; and the federal government *should* intervene in the macroeconomy since, unlike the free market, it is not necessarily self-correcting. It is the second contention that has generated most of the debate over the past seven decades concerning the relative merits of Keynesian economics.

Keynesian policy
fiscal policy, suggested by John Maynard Keynes, of using federal government budget surpluses and deficits to stabilize the macroeconomy during periods of disequilibrium.

In order to appreciate Keynesian fiscal policy, it is necessary to have a general idea of how the contemporary macroeconomic system works. Because its operation is extremely complex and intricate, economists have been known to devote years to its study, only to realize that they have only scraped the surface. In this chapter we will develop a very simple model of this complex system to explain both how it operates and how it can be managed through fiscal policy. We will use a very simple version of the circular flow of income model, realizing that what we lose in specificity, we will gain in conceptual clarity.[4]

STOCKS, FLOWS AND FINAL GOODS

When viewed from the broadest perspective, the economy may be seen conceptually as a continual process of two interdependent activities: production and consumption. Production is the process of combining **factors of production** (often called "resources" or "inputs") into products. These factors of production may be broken into four broad categories:

Factors of production
goods, services, and resources used in the production process to produce goods and services.

- Land—the services of mother nature including air, water, soil, and the like.
- Labor—services of a human nature.

---

[4] Many texts approach the basic macroeconomic model using systems of equations. That approach is avoided here in the belief that mathematical equalities frequently mask conceptual understanding.

- Capital—the services rendered by physical entities such as tractors, fences, computers and telephones. Capital, best defined as "the produced means of production," is one of those dangerous words whose meaning may change depending on context. Here we are talking about *physical capital,* which is used during the production process. This should not be confused with *financial capital,* which is evidence of the ability to acquire factors of production.
- Management—the skill of combining land, labor, and capital in the most effective manner possible to produce the desired product.

Two or more factors of production are involved in the production of all goods and services. For instance, the production of grain requires land (soil, water, sunshine), labor (the farmer's time), and capital (seed, fertilizer, tractor, time, and so forth). The farm manager combines these factors of production as efficiently as possible in an effort to gain a profit. The provision of a simple service such as a man's haircut also involves the combination of land, labor, capital, and management. Land is necessary for the barber shop itself; labor is contributed by the barber; capital is present in the form of the barber's chair, clippers, and scissors; and management is necessary to determine work hours, hire assistants, procure supplies, and finally set a price. All of these factors of production are brought together by the manager into a single production process to generate the ultimate product—a haircut at a price that will attract customers and provide sufficient remuneration to keep the barber in business.

Stocks and Flows

Production requires the **flow,** or use, of factors during the production process. The flow of land, labor, and capital is drawn from the existing stock of natural resources, population, and capital stock. Flow is the amount of a factor of production that is used up during a production process. Hence, flows refer to use rates per unit of time and are usually expressed in units such as hours of labor or depreciation per year. **Stock** is the amount of a factor of production available or in existence at any moment. These concepts are illustrated in Figure 7–1. The sand in the upper

Flow   use of a factor of production during the production process.

Stock   amount of the factor of production available at a point in time.

FIGURE 7–1
Relationship between stocks and flows.

Depleting stock

Flow

Accumulating stock

portion of the hourglass represents the available stock of sand, a portion of which flows through the neck of the glass. Once the stock is completely depleted, it can be replaced by simply turning the entire glass over. This is a **renewable resource.** Many resources such as coal or petroleum are **nonrenewable resources,** the stock of which cannot be replaced once all of the resource has been used up in the production process.

National Wealth

Our national **wealth** is the aggregate value or worth of all stocks of production resources. It is a measure of our national ability to produce. While it is impossible to measure precisely the national wealth of the United States, an estimate of the wealth owned by households is presented in Figure 7–2. This estimate excludes the value of human capital (the labor force and its embodied education) and the value of our abundant natural resources because it is difficult if not impossible to place a monetary value on these resources. The level of national production during any given period of time is dependent on the size of the national wealth and the rate at which that stock is being used up. By investing in our economic system, we have continually increased the national wealth in the United States over most periods of time. Investment occurs when the rate of production is greater than the rate of consumption, with the difference being added to the national wealth. In times of war we find that the rate of consumption flow is greatly increased to meet the immediate demands of war, causing a depletion of national wealth.

Consumption

Consumption is the process of using up something that has been produced. There are two broad classes of goods: intermediate and final. **Intermediate goods** are products that become inputs in the production of yet another product in a more advanced form. Examples of intermediate goods include wheat, flour, iron ore, and steel. These intermediate products are used to produce bread and automobiles, which are final goods because they will be consumed or used up to generate satisfaction or utility for the final consumer.

Renewable resource a factor of production that can itself be produced, such as pulp for paper or human capital.

Nonrenewable resource a factor of production that is available in a finite quantity, such as coal or petroleum.

Wealth total value of the stock of factors of production at a point in time.

Consumption using up something that has been produced.

Intermediate goods goods that will be used in some further production process rather than being consumed.

FIGURE 7–2
Household wealth, 2001 (trillions of dollars).

Tangible wealth			
Real estate	13.2		
Consumer durables	2.9		
Subtotal		16.2	
Financial wealth			
Deposits	4.8		
Corporate equities	5.5		
Mutual funds	2.5		
Pension funds	8.3		
Other	9.3		
Subtotal		30.4	
Total wealth			46.6

Note: Details in this figure might not add to totals due to rounding.
Source: Board of Governors of the Federal Reserve System, *Flow of Funds Accounts of the United States,* Third Quarter, 2001, Table B.100.

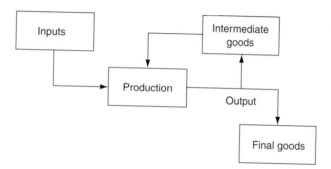

FIGURE 7–3 Final and intermediate goods.

Final goods and services are those goods and services that are ultimately consumed or used up. A loaf of bread, an apple, and a hamburger are examples of final goods. Final goods also include goods that become a part of the production stock of the country. Examples here include a tool die or a carpenter's hammer. As shown in Figure 7–3, a great deal of all production reenters the production process as intermediate goods, while only a small proportion of total production becomes final goods or services.

The dividing line between intermediate and final goods is not always distinct. In some instances, an automobile may be an intermediate good, not a final good. For instance; from the point of view of a traveling salesperson, a car is definitely a factor of production rather than a final consumption good. For a typical farmer a pickup truck is an intermediate good when it is being used to haul feed, but is a final good when it hauls the weekly groceries. Likewise, a bicycle is a final good in most instances, but if an enterprising young newspaper delivery person uses a bicycle to distribute the *Daily Blab,* then the bicycle is definitely an intermediate good used in the production of newspaper delivery services. It is not worthwhile to dwell on the gray areas between final and intermediate goods, for in most cases it will be quite clear which goods are which. And even when it is not so clear, it really isn't very important to the basic principles of the circular flow of income.

Final goods goods that are consumed or that become a part of the capital stock.

THE CIRCULAR FLOW

The Physical Flow

We are now ready to develop the basic **circular flow model.** Think of a simple world in which there are only producers and consumers. Many of the producers manufacture intermediate goods that return to the production process. Final goods eventually emerge from the production process and flow to the final consumer as shown in the upper portion of Figure 7–4. The circular flow is completed when the factors of production, which are owned by the final consumers, flow to producers. These factors of production are combined with previously produced intermediate goods in a continual process that eventually results in final goods and services. Without factors of production, it would be impossible to produce final goods and services since they are really nothing more than transformed land, labor, capital, and management.

In Figure 7–4 we have a flow of goods and services in the upper portion and a flow of factors of production in the lower portion. Hours of labor and acres of land are converted into pounds of beef and quarts of orange juice during the production

Circular flow model a macroeconomic model that emphasizes the continuous flow of goods and services through the production and consumption processes.

FIGURE 7–4 The physical circular flow.

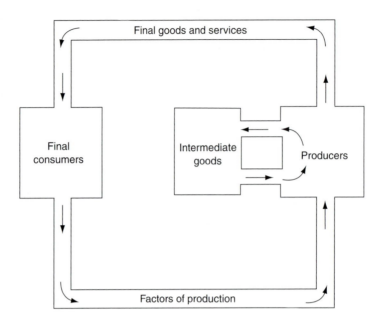

FIGURE 7–5 Roles of producers and consumers in the physical circular flow.

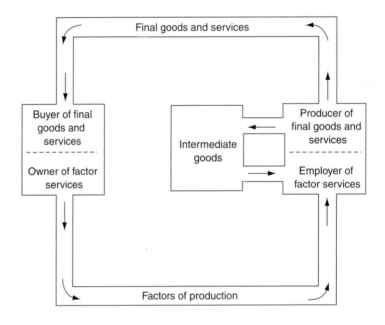

process. The block labeled "producers" is merely a pictorial device that symbolizes the continual process in which land, labor, and capital are combined, recombined, and then converted into final goods and services.

Both the producer and the final consumer play two roles within the economy (Figure 7–5). The producer is both (1) the purchaser of factor services and (2) the seller of final goods and services. The final consumer is both (1) the buyer of final goods and services and (2) the seller of factor services owned. For both the final consumer and the producer, if one side of the flow either prospers or declines, the other side must likewise prosper or decline. With this, we see a demonstration of the circularity of the system. The final consumer provides his services as a coal

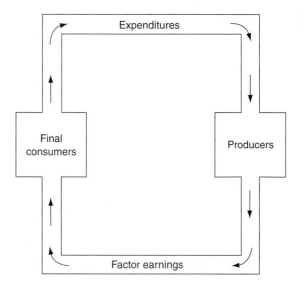

FIGURE 7–6 The economic circular flow.

miner. That coal enters the production process to emerge later embodied in the steel used in a new garden tractor that the miner buys. The circle is complete: the miner is the final purchaser of the factor services he provided. The consumer provides factor services so that he or she will be able to acquire final goods and services. The producer acquires factor services so that final goods and services can be produced.

The Economic Flow

We have seen how physical factors of production are converted into final goods and services. We can view the same process from an economic perspective by observing how money flows around the system. As the upper portion of Figure 7–6 shows, payments by final consumers to producers for final goods and services are called expenditures. (*Note:* for purposes of clarity, the production of intermediate goods is not shown on this and subsequent illustrations.) In the lower portion, where we deal with factors of production, there is a payment from producers to owners of factors of production called factor earnings. Expenditures and earnings are the monetary counterparts of the physical flows shown in Figure 7–4. Note that it is the factor earnings of the coal miner that allow him to purchase a new garden tractor. In this case, the payment made by the producer to the consumer for his labor services is used by the consumer to make expenditures for final goods and services.

   Once again we see a circular flow. Either side of the economy (product side or factor side) is dependent upon the other for its continued livelihood. The circularity of the economic system thus described emphasizes the important interdependence that exists among producers and consumers. They are like the two faces of a coin: each side is equal in value to the other. While the value of the coin may well increase or decrease, the values of the two faces will always remain equal.

The Basic Principle

Figure 7–4 and Figure 7–6 may be combined to show the full economy in both its physical and economic dimensions. In Figure 7–7 the economic flows of earnings and expenditures circle through the system in a clockwise direction. At the same

FIGURE 7–7 The economic and physical circular flows combined.

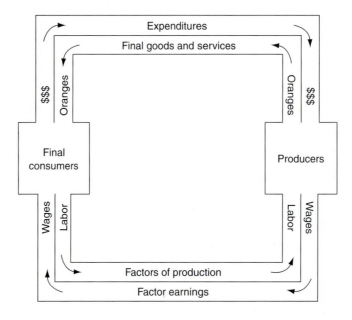

time, the physical flows of final goods and services and factors of production rotate in the opposite or counterclockwise direction. While at first the two flows may appear to be independent of one another, on closer scrutiny you will see that both the physical flow and the economic flow describe the two sides of a single transaction. For instance, if an orange is the physical flow from the producers to the final consumers, there will be an opposite flow of expenditures made for the purchase of the orange from final consumers to producers. This leads us to the **basic principle of the circular flow** of income: *for every physical flow there is an equal but opposite economic flow.*

That the flows are opposite should be obvious. Final goods and services flow in one direction and expenditures for those goods and services flow in the other. With one hand we gladly accept the goods and services that we, as final consumers, purchase, and with the other hand we push the payment for those goods and services across the counter. The exchange of physical goods and services for economic expenditures is the essence of our typical daily transactions. On the other side of the system, factors of production are exchanged for earnings. Once again, the economic and physical flows are clearly moving in opposite directions, reflecting the two sides of a transaction involving inputs. On either side of the system, the economic flows cannot occur unless the physical flows surge through the system, and vice versa. This simple tenet is frequently expressed by labor union leaders as "no pay, no work." The fact that the economic system is a closed circle (as shown in Figure 7–7) is illustrated by the predictable response of management: "no work, no pay."

Now we should ask what creates the equality between the physical and economic flows. Consider the example illustrated in Figure 7–8. Here we have a final consumer of oranges and an orange producer. They have agreed to exchange one dozen oranges for $1.25. The physical good (oranges) flows from the producer to the consumer, while the economic value ($1.25) flows from the final consumer to the producer. If the transaction is consummated, then both have agreed that the terms of trade as measured in dollars per dozen of oranges are acceptable. This

Basic principle of the circular flow for every physical flow there is an equal but opposite economic flow.

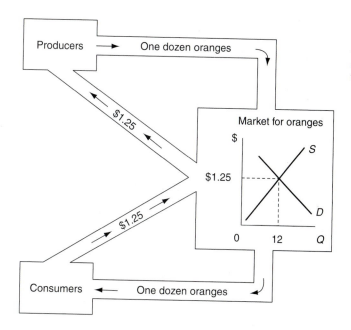

FIGURE 7–8 For every physical flow there is an equal but opposite economic flow.

equivalence between physical value and economic value has been established through the free interaction between buyer and seller in a market. The market that brings buyer and seller together to determine mutually acceptable terms of trade is shown as a "black box" in Figure 7–8. If either participant in this market felt that the terms of trade did not establish an equivalence between physical and economic values, then the transaction would not occur. Therefore, in the absence of any coercion, a free market will always establish an equivalence of value between the physical and economic flows.

Since the only flows that do occur are those that are mutually agreeable, it must follow that all flows represent an equivalence between physical and economic value from the point of view of those producers and consumers making transactions. The cattle rancher who sold his feeder cattle at $35 per hundredweight may not be pleased with the price he received, but he freely accepted the dictates of the market for feeder cattle on that day. For that producer on that day, an equal but opposite flow occurred: feeder cattle flowed out and money flowed in. Remember that a market has two dimensions: prices and quantities. Within our current context, these two dimensions are the economic flow (prices) and the physical flow (quantities). The role of the market is to create an equivalence between prices and quantities that will be mutually agreeable to the two sides of the market.

The role of markets in the circular flow of income is displayed in Figure 7–9. Here we see markets on both sides of the economic system. **Product markets** determine the price and quantity of final goods and services that will reach final customers, while the factor market determines the price and quantity of factors of production that are used in the production process. The arrows indicate what producers and final consumers offer to each market. For the product market, producers offer a physical flow in the form of goods and services, while consumers offer an economic flow of expenditures. Once the product market finds a mutually agreeable price, the physical goods flow to the consumer while the economic flow reaches the producer. The market stands between these two flows operating like a control gate making sure that the opposite flows maintain a balance of equality.

Product markets
markets on which final goods and services are traded.

FIGURE 7–9 The role
of markets in the
circular flow.

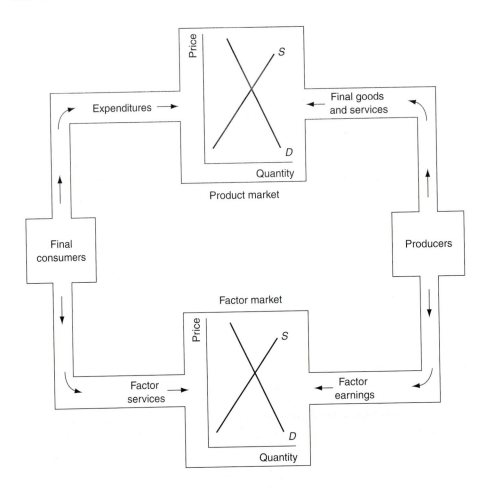

The situation is just reversed for the **factor market.** Here the physical flow originates with the final consumer, who offers factor services for possible employment. The producers, however, offer an economic flow of factor earnings to the factor market to entice the factors of production into employment. Once the factor market establishes a mutually agreeable price for factor services, the producer will receive the physical factor services desired, and if the particular factor of production that is being traded in this market is labor, then this factor market will simultaneously determine the level of employment and the wage rate. Shifts in either the supply side (final consumers) or the demand side (producers) will cause the equilibrium wage and/or employment level to change.

Factor markets
markets on which
factors of production
are traded.

GROSS DOMESTIC PRODUCT AND NATIONAL INCOME

The Gross Domestic Product

The circular flow of income is a continuous, dynamic process in which factors of production are converted into final goods and services. The system illustrated in Figure 7–9 can be thought of as a giant hydraulic system in which the fluid circulates

FIGURE 7–10 The measurement of gross domestic product and national income.

round-and-round propelled by consumers' and producers' pursuit of self-interest. As the flow of water in a home is measured with a water meter out in the front yard to determine how much water has passed through the system, the flow of economic activity through the system in Figure 7–9 is measured to get an idea of the level of economic activity. The most common measure of the magnitude of the economic flow is the **gross domestic product** (GDP). This is a measure of the total expenditures for *final* goods and services within a given time period (usually a year). The concept of GDP is illustrated in Figure 7–10. We have placed a meter in the expenditure flow to measure the rate of flow through the system during a period of time. The total amount of expenditures measured during a year will be an accurate measure of the economic value of all final goods and services produced during the year.

Gross domestic product (GDP) total expenditures on final goods and services during a period of time.

The gross domestic product is measured by economists in the U.S. Department of Commerce and reported in the press on a quarterly basis. The annualized rate of growth of these quarterly estimates is closely watched as an indicator of the health of the economy. If the rate of growth is negative, then the economy is said to be in a recession. A positive growth rate indicates that more jobs are being created and more "stuff"[5] is being produced. Since more stuff is better than less stuff, a growing GDP is desired.

National Income

A similar concept is used to measure the total value of all factor payments during a period of time. This is called **national income,** which is a measure of all payments during a year for the services of land, labor, and capital. If the economy is functioning

National income total value of all factor payments during a period of time.

---

[5] "Stuff" is a highly technical term used by economists to refer to final goods and services.

properly, the total flow through the national income meter during a given period of time should be conceptually equal to that measured by the GDP meter. In reality, there are many minor adjustments in the measurements that cause the two meters to register slightly different results, but for our purposes we will assume that the two flows are conceptually equal.[6]

Measurement Difficulties

There are a multitude of problems that exist in the measurement of GDP and national income. Many economists have made a lifetime career of trying to improve our measurement techniques such that our accounts better reflect the true flow of expenditures and earnings through the economic system. In the United States an entire Bureau of the Department of Commerce works full-time trying to measure the circular flow of income in sufficient detail to provide an accurate view of our macroeconomic performance over time. Unfortunately, the measurement of GDP and national income is fraught with conceptual and empirical difficulties. After mentioning just two of these difficulties we will proceed to enhance our simple model of the circular flow of income, recognizing that our conceptual model ignores some real-world complications.[7]

The first problem is that both GDP and national income are measured at market, determined prices. To the extent that market prices are not a fair estimate of social value, the GDP misrepresents the actual value of the expenditure flows. For instance, what is the appropriate value of cancer research or our national defense? Since both consume factors of production during the year and both produce a final service, we must include these activities in our measurement of the GDP, but at what value? In the absence of any market to determine the value of such economic activities, they are usually included in the GDP at their cost of production as a best estimate of their market value. A related problem is that the GDP may not be a valid measure of the well-being of a given population. Consider the case of a poor country where much of the drinking water is drawn from contaminated pools. A project to develop simple tube wells for drinking water may greatly increase the well-being of the people of the country while changing the GDP by only a small amount. These problems occur when there is a divergence between "value" and "cost of production," and there is no market in which that value can be fairly determined.

A second difficulty in the measurement of GDP and national income is that some economic activity is not included because the good produced is not traded on any market. The most common example of this problem is the traditional housewife. If a mother chooses not to work so she can care for her small children and clean the house, she produces absolutely nothing from the point of view of the GDP—an accounting convenience that can unquestionably infuriate a lot of hard working housewives. However, should this mother decide to hire child care and a

---

[6] The official measurement of GDP and national income deviates from the simple conceptual approach we use here. The official measure of national income excludes some types of receipts used by consumers to purchase final goods and services. Consequently, national income (as measured empirically) is always less than GDP. Nonetheless, we will consider them to be conceptually equal.

[7] The reader should carefully consider the difference between real-world complications and real-world contradictions. Our circular flow model is a conceptual abstraction of the complexity of the real world. An appropriate model should reduce this complexity to a level that can be easily comprehended by ignoring some of the relatively unimportant complications that exist in the real world. But in no case should the process of abstraction, which is necessary in the development of a workable conceptual model, introduce contradictions.

	Then	Now
One gallon of gas		
Price	$0.33	$1.20
Units/hour	2.6	4.3
Six-pack of beer (cheap)		
Price	$0.90	$2.50
Units/hour	0.9	2.1
One pound hamburger		
Price	$0.50	$1.65
Units/hour	1.7	3.1

FIGURE 7–11
Purchasing power of the dollar.

cleaning service, then her expenditures for both services would be part of the GDP since they are market transactions. In other words, if you do it yourself, the value of the work is not included in the GDP since no outright expenditure was made; but, if you hire someone else to do it for you, it is included in the GDP.

The Price Level and GDP

One of the important roles of money is to serve as an accounting unit. By valuing everything in the same monetary units we are literally able to compare apples and oranges based on their relative prices. When viewed in cross section or at a point in time, prices tell us whether oranges are more highly valued than apples or vice versa. Across time, however, prices are not a good measure of relative value because the purchasing power of the dollar has changed over time. Since the measuring stick itself is changing over time, the results from measurements taken at two points in time cannot be compared directly. For example, in 1977 the average price of apples was 10.6 cents a pound. In 1998 the same pound of apples fetched 11.6 cents. These are what are known as **nominal prices** that measure prices in terms of the dollar measuring stick in use at the time. A reasonable question is whether the price of apples in 1998 was greater than in 1977. Certainly the nominal price was higher, but one might ask if the inflation adjusted, or **real price,** was greater.

Inflation-adjusted or real prices account for the change in the purchasing power of the dollar from one time period to the next. Purchasing power measures the value of the dollar in terms of what that dollar can acquire. For instance, as an undergraduate student assistant many years ago one coauthor earned $0.85/hour.[8] Today student assistants are paid $5.15/hour. Are today's students better paid? Let's see using the idea of purchasing power.

Figure 7–11 shows the prices of three essential goods with approximate prices both then and now. For each good, the number of items that could be purchased with 1 hour's worth of pay is also shown. For instance, back then an hour's worth of work would buy only 2.6 gallons of gas, while today's student assistant is being paid the equivalent of 4.3 gallons per hour. For each of the three representative goods, the real price today is lower than it was back then. The goods are cheaper in the sense that it takes less work to purchase each of them. Viewed from a different angle, we can say that the purchasing power of students today is greater than it was back then.

Nominal prices prices observed at any point in time measured in dollars of that time.

Real price price of a good adjusted for inflation.

---

[8] This is what the junior half of the coauthors of this text earned in the early 1960s. The more senior coauthor earned only $0.45 when he was an undergraduate assistant.

FIGURE 7–12
Constructing a price
index.

	Units in the Market Basket	Cost to Acquire	
		Then	Now
Gasoline	10	$3.30	$12.00
Beer	2	$1.80	$5.00
Hamburger	5	$2.50	$8.25
Total		$7.60	25.25
Index		100.00	332.24

Number (then = 100)

Price Indexes

One of the realities that Figure 7–11 illustrates is that over time the prices of goods do not change proportionately. The price of gas has increased by a factor of four, while hamburger only tripled. This leads to the search for the average or typical good that can be used as the ultimate benchmark against which to measure price changes over time. Since no single average good exists, what is normally done is to construct a market basket of goods that reflects the consumption patterns of the average consumer. Based on price changes of this market basket of goods, it is possible to construct an index number corresponding to the nominal cost of the market basket at any point in time.

This process is illustrated in Figure 7–12. The Department of Commerce has determined that the typical market basket of the typical consumer consists of 10 gallons of gas, 2 six-packs of beer, and 5 pounds of hamburger. Using the prices from Figure 7–11, we can calculate the cost of the market basket in both time periods. "Then" is chosen arbitrarily as the "base" year and is given an index number value of 100, meaning that the basket cost 100 percent of $7.60 back "then." The "now" index number is 332.24, meaning that the cost of the basket now is 332.24 percent of the cost then. That is, prices are 3.32 times higher now than they were then based on this hypothetical market basket.

An index such as that in Figure 7–12 is known as a **price index** or an index of prices. There are numerous price indexes that are used to measure different price changes over time, but the most common is the consumer price index (CPI) calculated by the Department of Commerce. The CPI is based on a market basket of approximately 300 goods that are supposed to reflect the spending pattern of a typical urban family. The CPI is calculated on a monthly basis using a procedure not unlike that illustrated in Figure 7–12. The rate of change of the CPI over time is a common measure of the rate of **inflation,** which is the most common measure of the change in the purchasing power of the dollar. During periods of inflation the CPI index will increase, meaning the purchasing power of the dollar has decreased.

The CPI for 2 recent years was:

| 1997 | 160.5 |
| 1998 | 163.0 |

Price index an index number expressing the nominal cost of a market basket of goods at one point in time relative to the nominal cost of the same basket of goods at another point in time.

Inflation a decrease, in the purchasing power of a currency.

Since the CPI increased by 1.56 percent[9] from 1997 to 1998, we say that the rate of inflation for 1997 was 1.56 percent.

Every 15 years or so the Department of Commerce modifies the "market basket" to reflect changes in consumer patterns. The last such revision was based on consumption patterns in the early 1980s and consequently excludes common items like software, computer disks, air bags, CDs, and disposable diapers with elastic bands.

Real and Nominal GDP

Price indexes, as a measure of the purchasing power of the dollar over time, can be used to adjust annual measurements of the GDP to a constant dollar. Calculating the nominal or actual dollar value of GDP year after year is like measuring the height of a growing child with a measuring stick that is constantly changing. In order to accurately measure the child's real growth we have to use the same measuring stick year after year. By converting nominal estimates of GDP to real, or inflation-adjusted, estimates we are able to measure true changes in the level of economic activity.

Gross domestic product is a measure of the total expenditures on all final goods and services. Expenditure is equal to price times quantity. Over time both price and quantity change. The use of a price index to calculate the real GDP eliminates the effect of price changes and allows us to focus on the change in the physical quantity of goods and services produced.

The process of converting nominal GDP (or anything else) to real GDP is quite simple:

$$\text{Real GDP} = \frac{\text{nominal GDP}}{\text{price index}} \cdot 100$$

This procedure will convert the nominal GDP data to the purchasing power of the base year used in the construction of the price index.

For example, in Figure 7–13 the real and nominal GDP are the same in 1996 because that is the base year of the price index used.[10] In years prior to 1996 the real GDP (measured in purchasing power of 1996) is greater than the nominal GDP. For those years after 1996, the real GDP is less than the nominal GDP as the GDP figures are lowered to account for the effects of inflation of prices rather than increases of output.

Figure 7–13 illustrates the danger of working with nominal data. At first blush it would appear that during the Reagan–Bush era (1980–1992) the GDP more than doubled (from $2,796 billion to $6,319 billion.) However, the real GDP increased by only 40 percent during the 12-year period. Almost three-fourths of the apparent increase was accounted for, not by increased production in the economy, but instead by increased prices or decreased purchasing power.

---

[9] Rate of change is always measured as change over the base. Percentage rate of change is change over the base times 100. In this case the change (163.0–160.5) is 2.5 and the base (or original value) is 160.5. Dividing 2.5/160.5 gives 0.0156, which multiplied by 100 yields a percentage change of 1.56 percent.

[10] The price index used in Figure 7–13 is not the consumer price index. It is a GDP deflator using a "chain" market basket that changes over time.

FIGURE 7–13
Nominal and real GDP.

Year	Nominal GDP ($billions)	Price Index 1996 = 100	Real GDP ($billions)
1980	2,796	57.04	4,901
1981	3,131	62.36	5,021
1982	3,259	66.25	4,919
1983	3,535	68.88	5,132
1984	3,933	71.44	5,505
1985	4,213	73.69	5,717
1986	4,453	75.31	5,912
1987	4,743	77.58	6,113
1988	5,108	80.21	6,368
1989	5,489	83.27	6,592
1990	5,803	86.51	6,708
1991	5,986	89.66	6,676
1992	6,319	91.84	6,880
1993	6,642	94.05	7,063
1994	7,054	96.01	7,348
1995	7,401	98.10	7,544
1996	7,813	100.00	7,813
1997	8,318	101.95	8,160
1998	8,782	103.20	8,509
1999	9,269	104.65	8,857
2000	9,873	107.03	9,224

Source: Economic Report of the President, 2002, tables B1 and B2.

Real GDP Per Capita as a Measure of Welfare

Price indexes are used to convert nominal GDP into real or constant dollar values to remove the effects of price inflation. Another common adjustment is to divide the GDP by the size of the population to obtain GDP per capita. This is a measure of how much "stuff" is available to the average consumer (if such a critter exists). Real GDP per capita is frequently used to make international comparisons of the well-being or welfare of the residents of different countries. Clearly the residents of a country such as the United States with a per capita GDP of approximately $30,000 are materially better off than the residents of Angola, where the per capita GDP is estimated at $800. That is, while the average American gets about $30,000 worth of stuff in a year, the average Angolan gets only $800 of stuff.

Limitations

As indicated earlier, the use of GDP as an indicator of economic welfare is full of serious limitations, but it is still better than nothing. Without going into too much detail, there are two additional limitations that need to be mentioned.

First, the use of GDP per capita does not reveal the nature of the income distribution. For instance, the per capita GDP of oil-rich Qatar is $16,700, which is comparable to many European countries. However, what you really have in

Qatar is a handful of multimillionaire sheiks, who profit from the oil exports, and a mass of very poor peasants and nomads. Adding them together and taking an average does not present an accurate picture of what life is like for the typical citizen in Qatar.

Second, a lot of economic activity in poorer countries never enters the cash economy and therefore is never counted in the GDP. As indicated earlier, the valuable work of a housewife/mother is not counted in our GDP. Likewise, the economic value of a subsistence farmer in a poor country is not counted since the fruits of his labor are never traded in a market. As a consequence, much economic activity in poor countries never gets measured, making the poor country appear to be poorer than it actually is.

THE CIRCULAR FLOW BY ECONOMIC SECTOR

The model of the circular flow of income depicted in Figure 7–9 is too simple for the reader to be able to glean any information of real substance. To more accurately understand how the various components or sectors of the economy interact, we need to divide the circular flow into its component parts. As a general rule, economists deal with four economic sectors: households, business firms, governments, and the foreign sector. Each of these four sectors receives earnings and makes expenditures.

Households

This sector includes all of us as individual consumers of final goods and services. Receipts or earnings by the household sector are called **personal income.** Personal income is equal to gross income received by all persons minus personal contributions to social insurance programs (such as Social Security) and payment of personal taxes. Basically, personal income includes wages and salaries received, proprietors' income from farm and non-farm businesses, rental income of landlords, dividend and interest income of individuals, and transfer payments received. Transfer payments are those payments made to individuals for which no productive activity was rendered, such as Social Security payments, unemployment benefits, veterans' benefits, and welfare payments.

Personal income earnings in the household sector.

Expenditures by households are called **personal consumption expenditures.** These include payments made by individuals for all final goods, durable and nondurable, and for services. Examples of durables would be automobiles and washing machines, nondurables would include food and clothing, and services would include haircuts and restaurants.

Personal consumption expenditures expenditures by the household sector.

Business Firms

This sector comprises the economic activity of all firms other than those owned and operated by a proprietor. To give an illustration, the typical family farm or ranch is considered a part of the household sector and that farm's earnings are part of personal income, while a corporate farm whose ownership and operation are not that of a sole proprietor is considered to be a business firm. The dividing line between the two in agriculture is somewhat indistinct, but of little importance. The earnings of business firms in our circular flow of income model are called **retained earnings.** Retained earnings are the firm's final profit, or what remains after all dividends, interest, taxes, and other costs of operation have been paid. Basically, the retained earnings are what the firm has available for reinvestment in the growth of the businesses, depreciation allowances for capital consumption, and inventory adjustments.

Expenditures by business firms are called gross private domestic investment, or **investment** for short. Investment is the total gross purchase of final goods and services by business firms either to replace worn-out equipment or to add to the existing stock of capital as the firm grows. Both retained earnings and investment are defined in "gross" terms. Retained earnings include normal depreciation of capital; investment includes replacement equipment. The amount of investment is a critical determinant of economic growth and vitality. The greater the level of investment, the larger the number of workers employed in the construction or manufacture of final physical capital. If investment is greater than that needed solely to replace existing equipment, it means that firms will be expanding production, thus creating additional jobs and additional output.

Governments

We now come to one of the most interesting sectors of the economy—governments. Notice the very important "s" at the end of this sector's name. While most of us tend to think of government as the federal government, we will soon see that state and local governments actually play a larger collective role in the purchase of final goods and services than the federal government. This sector includes all governments, from special districts for irrigation, schools, and fire protection right up through city, county and state governments. Government earnings are **taxes;** expenditures are simply called **government expenditures.** In calculating both earnings and expenditures, all transfers between different governmental units must be excluded, so we measure only the actual purchase of final goods and services, and actual net tax collections. As shown in Figure 7–14, total or gross expenditures by the federal government are 50 percent greater than that of all state and local government units. But when we look at the purchase of final goods and services by governments, the state and local governments are more important than the federal government. The explanation for this apparent paradox is that many of the expen-

FIGURE 7–14
Receipts and
expenditures of
governments, 2000.

	Total	Federal	State and Local
		($ billions)	
Total expenditures	$3,018	$1,828	$1,190
(−) Transfer payments	1,050	779	271
(−) Grants to S&L governments	246	246	
(−) Net interest paid	262	263	− 1
(−) Subsidies	38	47	− 9
(=) Purchases of final goods and services	1,423	494	929
Total receipts	3,270	2,047	1,223
Surplus (+) or deficit (−)	252	219	33

Note: Detail in this figure might not add to totals due to rounding.
Source: Economic Report of the President, 2002, tables B-84 and B-85.

ditures by the federal government are transfer payments to individuals or grants to other governmental units. Hence, in terms of gross expenditures and receipts, the size of the federal government relative to all other state and local governments is quite large. But from the point of view of the gross domestic product, the federal government turns out to be something of a mouse dressed in an elephant suit.

The Foreign Sector

The foreign sector includes all transactions that involve both an American household or firm and a foreign household or firm. On the earnings side, we must adjust the national income of the United States to include income received by Americans from foreign sources and to exclude income received by foreigners from American sources. For example, if an American owns shares of stock in Sony Corporation that pay her $10 in dividends during the year, that must be included in the national income or earnings of the United States. Conversely, if a Japanese investor owns shares of IBM stock, the dividends paid to the foreign investor are not part of the domestic earnings in the United States and should not be included in the U.S. circular flow of income. If we add to the circular flow of income from foreign sources and subtract payments to foreign sources, the net result is called net foreign earnings.

On the expenditure side, similar adjustments must be made for foreign purchases of American goods and services, and for American purchases of foreign goods and services. When a foreigner purchases a good or service from an American, that becomes a final sale so far as the domestic economy is concerned. Such export sales are part of the gross domestic product because domestic factors of production were used in the manufacture of the good or service. Imports, however, represent the purchase of final goods and services from foreigners and are not part of the domestic product. Therefore, we must add exports and subtract imports from our domestic accounts to arrive at net foreign expenditures.

The Total System

A detailed view of the circular flow of income is now emerging as shown in Figure 7–15. Producers have been divided into four sectors as have final consumers. The system remains circular in the aggregate with total expenditures (GDP) equal to total earnings (national income). But individual sectors frequently earn more than is spent, or vice versa. As shown in Figure 7–16, in 2000 the firms and foreign sectors each spent substantially more than they earned, resulting in dissavings in each sector. The household and governments sectors earned more than they spent with savings of nearly $1.85 trillion in 2000.[11] Some of this household "savings" is not what we typically think of as savings (bank deposits, and so on). Savings (or the difference between earnings and expenditures) also include payments on insurance premiums, pension funds, and other forms of systematic savings that accumulate over our lifetime.

---

[11] The difference between spending and earnings of the governments sector of the GDP accounts is not directly related to the national debt, which is a financial accounting concept. In the GDP accounts we consider the behavior of governments only as a purchaser of final goods and services. As shown in Figure 7–14, a great deal of government spending is excluded from GDP.

FIGURE 7–15 The circular flow of income by economic sector.

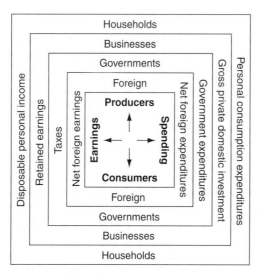

FIGURE 7–16 GDP by sector, 2000.

	Expenditures	($ billions)	New Saving
Households	6,728	8,319	1,591
Firms	1,767	876	− 891
Governments	1,741	1,992	251
Net foreign	− 364	− 1,314	− 950
GDP	9,873	9,873	0

Note: Detail in this figure might not add to totals due to rounding.
Source: Economic Report of the President, 2002.

The important point illustrated in Figure 7–16 is that while the circular flow is a closed system in the aggregate, there is a good deal of intersector transfer going on from the saving sectors to the dissaving sectors. As we shall see, it is the smooth, frictionless flow among the sectors that is the key to economic prosperity.

THE ROLE OF FINANCIAL INTERMEDIARIES

Our examination of the circular flow of income has now taken us back to where we started—financial markets. Viewed from the perspective of the circular flow of income, the aggregate savings of the household and government sectors in 2000 were equal to the dissavings of the other two sectors. That is, the market for loanable funds was cleared in 2000 with the quantity of loans demanded by firms and foreigners of $1,842 billion and the quantity of loanable funds supplied by the household and governments sectors of $1,842 billion. The price of saving and borrowing (the interest rate) continually adjusted to market conditions in 2000, thus establishing an equilibrium between savers and dissavers (borrowers).

It should be clear that the intersectorial redistribution of earnings and expenditures in the circular flow of income is achieved through the use of financial intermediaries such as banks, savings and loan associations, mortgage companies, pension funds, finance companies, and other participants in the "money market." Without these intermediaries, it would be difficult for the relatively large borrow-

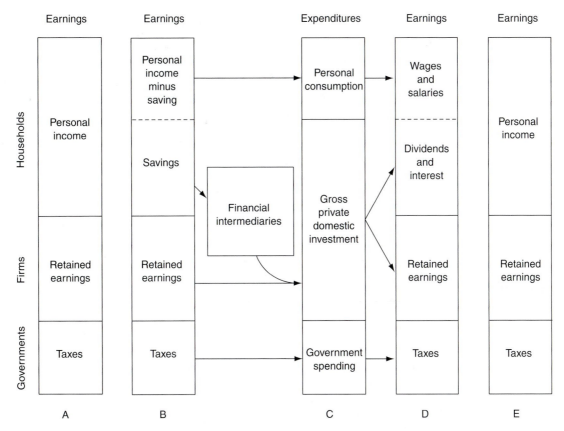

FIGURE 7–17 Role
of financial intermediaries.

ing demands of a relatively small number of business firms to be met by the relatively small savings of a large number of savers.

A typical example of a financial intermediary is an insurance company. Every month insurance companies receive millions of dollars from households in the form of premium payments. These premiums are then invested by the insurance company in the form of large loans to business firms to build a new plant or establish a new shopping center. The insurance company is nothing more than a conduit through which savings flow from households to the other sectors.

A simplified view of the redistributive role of financial intermediaries is shown in Figure 7–17. Several simplifying assumptions have been made in this figure. First, we assume that there is no foreign sector, since that sector is relatively small. Second, we make the heroic assumption that government earnings (taxes) are equal to government expenditures. With these simplifications, all savings occur in the household sector and all dissaving will be in the business firm sector. In Figure 7–17, the height of each column represents either total earnings or total expenditures within the economy during some period of time. Figure 7–17 should be read from left to right, with movement from column to column representing rotation around the circular flow of income.

In column A the total earnings flow of the economy is broken down into its three component parts: personal income, retained earnings, and taxes. Column B also shows earnings but emphasizes that a portion of the earnings of households will be saved through financial intermediaries rather than being used for the purchase of final goods and services. In column C we have used the basic principle of the circular flow of money to turn earnings by sector into expenditures by sector. The financial intermediaries convert household savings into investment by business firms such that households spend less than they earn while businesses spend more than they earn. The expenditures in column C are converted back to earnings in column D. Here it is emphasized that since households helped finance the investments made by business firms, they should expect to receive a portion of the earnings generated by those investments. The payment by business firms for the use of household savings is made in the form of either interest payments or dividends. These payments by firms to households become part of the total earnings of households as shown in column E. Note that column E is identical with column A: the circular flow of income has made a full circle, and the distribution of earnings is unchanged.[12]

The situation illustrated in Figure 7–17 represents an equilibrium in the circular flow of income in which earnings equal expenditures, which equals earnings. This illustrates the classical view of the macroeconomy as an economy in equilibrium. According to the classical view, equilibrium in the macroeconomy was the normal situation just like equilibrium in markets was the normal situation. And as with markets, occasional external shocks to the macroeconomy would require adjustments to the new situation. So, in the classical view, events like inflation, recession, and unemployment were seen as signs of adjustment to a new equilibrium in the economy.

Equilibrium in the macroeconomy is, of course, an ideal situation, but it demonstrates the important role of financial intermediaries in our macroeconomy. In the next chapter we will examine what happens when the financial intermediaries do not perform their essential role in the economy and explore some policy alternatives that are available to remedy this situation.

SUMMARY

The circular flow of income is an economic model of the macroeconomy. There are two sectors: firms as producers and households as consumers. In production, factors of production are combined to make final and intermediate goods and services. Intermediate products are those that will be used as an input in some further production process. Final products are those that will be consumed or become a part of the capital stock.

Households buy final goods and services from firms and sell factors of production to firms. This creates a circular flow of physical items. Payment for the final goods and services is called expenditures, and they flow from households to firms. Payment for factors of production is called factor earnings, and they flow from firms to households. This creates an economic circular flow of money or payments.

The physical and economic flows are equal but opposite. The equality between the two flows is established in the product market in the case of final goods, and in the factor market in the case of factors of production. If the value of the physical and economic flows were not equal, the transaction in the market would not take place. The existence of markets ensures the equality.

---

[12] The situation depicted in Figure 7–17 is that of a static economy. Note that the total earnings in column A are exactly equal to the total earnings in column E, even though we have gone through an economic cycle. In reality, the size of the economy and the intersectorial distribution of earnings will change over time as the total earnings of households, firms, and governments either increase or decrease.

The total value of all final goods and services that flow through the product market is called gross domestic product (GDP). The total value of all factors of production that flow through the factor market is called national income. On a conceptual level, gross domestic product should be equal to national income.

Economic growth is measured by a change in GDP. But GDP measured in nominal or current dollars measures both the change in the quantity of goods produced and the change in the price of those goods. In order to eliminate the price change effect, nominal measurements must be converted to real measures using a price index.

The circular flow model can be expanded by breaking the economy into four sectors: households, firms, governments, and foreign. Each sector has earnings, and each sector buys final goods and services. Usually the household sector spends less than it earns, resulting in savings. At the same time firms usually spend more than they earn, resulting in dissaving or investment. It is the role of financial intermediaries to convert savings into investment.

KEY TERMS

Basic principle of the circular flow
Circular flow model
Consumption
Factor markets
Factors of production
Final goods
Fiscal policy
Flow
Government expenditures
Gross domestic product (GDP)
Inflation
Intermediate goods
Investment
Keynesian policy

National Income
Nominal prices
Nonrenewable resource
Personal consumption expenditures
Personal income
Price index
Product markets
Real price
Renewable resource
Retained earnings
Stock
Taxes
Wealth

PROBLEMS AND DISCUSSION QUESTIONS

1. Within the context of the circular flow of income model, what is the role of financial intermediaries?
2. What is fiscal policy?
3. Discuss the market for labor in terms of stocks and flows.
4. Give three examples each of final and intermediate goods.
5. The basic idea of the circular flow of income model is that the economic and physical flows are opposite but equal. What ensures the equality of flows?
6. Visit **www.bea.doc.gov** to see the latest estimates of the gross domestic product by the Bureau of Economic Analysis of the Department of Commerce. What are the estimates for the latest quarter in both nominal and real terms? What is the index year of the real estimates? What is the current value of the price index used in calculating the real estimates?

7. What is the impact of home schooling on the estimation of GDP?

8. The box to the right shows the "market basket" of a typical student at Moo U. Use this information to create a price index in which 2000 is the index year. That is, if the index in 2000 is 100, what is value of the index in 2001?

Item	Units Consumed	Price per unit 2000	Price per unit 2001
Soda	10	$0.70	$0.75
Burgers	5	$1.45	$1.65
Pizza	4	$5.75	$6.25

9. Why does GDP per capita underestimate the well-being of the poor in the poorest countries?

10. What are the earnings and expenditures of households, firms, and governments called?

Fiscal Policy

*O*ur view of the macroeconomic system is now nearly complete. We have explored the financial system and the circular flow of income. We have analyzed monetary policy and learned that by adjusting the rate of monetary growth the Federal Reserve Board can influence the three goals of macroeconomic policy: full employment, stable prices, and economic growth. As we shall see in this chapter, it is also possible to influence these policy objectives through fiscal policy. Briefly stated, fiscal policy deals with purposeful attempts by the federal government to influence the macroeconomy through changes in its taxing and spending patterns. Because of the importance of governments in the circular flow of income, changes in the earnings (taxes) or expenditures (spending) of this sector can significantly influence the performance of the entire macroeconomy. Seemingly small changes in fiscal policy can cause relatively large changes in the direction of the nation's economy.[1]

When it comes to fiscal policy, there is typically less than general agreement among economists concerning appropriate macroeconomic policies for any given situation. In fact, belligerent disagreement is not uncommon. The reason for the disagreement is that different economists have different perspectives about how the economy works and the relative importance of different aspects of the economy. Most economists a generation or two ago would be classified as belonging to the "classical" school of macroeconomic thought. Today most economists are trained in the Keynesian school based on the theories introduced by John Maynard Keynes in the post-World War I era. But not all economists today are Keynesians. A small minority of "radical" and "institutional" economists reject the Keynesian approach as being too far removed from the political or institutional framework within which an economy operates. Yet others adhere to the "rational expectations" school, which argues that the expected impact of fiscal policy is already anticipated in sophisticated markets, hence the impact of any change in fiscal policy is negated. In spite of the many different "flavors" of macroeconomics today, it is safe to say that for the past 50 years, the Keynesian approach has been preeminent in most academic programs and has implicitly, and often unwittingly, been the foundation for most political programs dealing with the macroeconomy.

DEBT AND DEFICITS

Governments, as a large part of our economy, are important economic agents whether by purposeful policy or simply by their large size. It was pointed out earlier that in terms of contributions to the gross domestic product, state and local

---

[1] A basic topic in any intermediate or advanced course in macroeconomics is the "multiplier effect". The essence of this basic premise of macroeconomics is that a dollar's worth of government spending will result in several dollars of additional economic activity. The concept and action are very similar to the money multiplier associated with monetary policy.

governments were larger than the federal government. This can be very deceptive because most federal spending is not for final goods and services but instead for transfer payments and interest payments. Transfer payments refer to federal spending in which funds are transferred from the federal government to households, firms, or other governments. These funds are then spent by the recipients, thus adding to the GDP. A common example of a transfer payment is Social Security. In this case, funds are transferred from the federal government to households. While the federal government does not actually *spend* the money in the GDP sense of spending on final goods and services, it does create the ability of households to spend. When we look at the total flow of dollars through governments rather than spending in the strict GDP sense, we find that the federal government is about twice as large as all state and local governments combined. Moreover, about one-fourth of all expenditures by state and local governments are funded by transfers from the federal government. Hence, in terms of total economic impact, the actions of the federal government far outweigh those of state and local governments. For the remainder of this chapter, "spending" will refer to total spending including transfers, and "government" will refer to the federal government.

Surplus when government receipts exceed government expenditures during a fiscal year.

Over time the government taxes and it spends in accordance with needs and obligations as approved by Congress. During any given year,[2] if the amount of revenue (taxes, and so on) exceeds the amount of spending, then the government is said to have run a **surplus.** In fiscal 1998 the federal government (with much fanfare by the president) had a surplus of about $70 billion. This was the first surplus since 1969. Surpluses continued until the September 11, 2001, terrorist attacks generated additional spending at the same time President Bush's tax cuts kicked in. As a result, the federal government was spending more than it earned, thereby running a **deficit.** The amount of the deficit in any given year is simply the difference between federal revenues and federal expenses.

Deficit when government receipts are less than government expenditures during a fiscal year.

In 1992, the year of the largest deficit ever, the federal government collected "only" $1,091 billion while it spent $1,382 billion. The deficit was $290 billion, or more than $1,000 for every American citizen. How, you might ask, can the government spend more than it earns? The answer is that the government does it exactly the same way consumers do it—by borrowing the difference. Consumers load up credit card balances or secure a mortgage to purchase a new home. In both of these cases consumers borrow to finance current spending beyond current earnings. In the case of the federal government, this borrowing takes the form of selling bonds. Each week the U.S. Treasury sells billions of dollars worth of bonds to finance the government's voracious appetite for spending. As the Treasury sells these bonds, the amount of indebtedness of the federal government increases. The total amount of this indebtedness is known as the "**federal debt.**"

Federal debt total amount of money borrowed by the federal government to finance deficits.

As previously shown, in 1992 the federal government spent $290 billion more than it collected in revenues. This "extra" spending was paid for by increasing the debt by $290 billion during the 1992 fiscal year. So the *debt* at a point in time is simply the accumulation of previous *deficits*.

Debt ceilings legislative limits on the amount of the federal debt.

From time to time Congress, which must approve all federal spending, will impose a limit on the amount of borrowing the Treasury can amass. These limits, known as **debt ceilings,** are usually increased shortly before the Treasury runs out of borrowing authority. Changes in the debt ceiling are usually accompanied by

---

[2] The fiscal or accounting year for the federal government is October 1 through September 30.

substantial (if not substantive) oratory about the need for fiscal restraint and the like. In late 1995 a defiant Congress refused to increase the debt ceiling, causing a partial shutdown of the federal government.

The process of government spending and borrowing has serious implications for the macroeconomy. As the largest borrower on bond markets, the government can influence interest rates, and we have already seen the powerful influence of interest rates on the macroeconomy. Government spending, a significant component in the circular flow of income, can significantly influence the macroeconomy by adding to or taking from the aggregate level of expenditures.

Our basic objective in this chapter is to provide the reader with an appreciation of what fiscal policy is and how changes in fiscal policy can affect each of us in our daily economic lives. Fiscal policy is interlaced with political dogma, and it is thus difficult to separate politics from economics in matters of fiscal policy. In fact, throughout the nineteenth century this branch of economics was known as "political economy." In this chapter we seek to develop a *conceptual* (rather than theoretical) understanding of macroeconomics from the point of view of both the classical and Keynesian schools of thought. In an appendix we do this by tracing the development of fiscal policy during the past fifty years.

The Classical School

Say's Law

Throughout the nineteenth century and the first third of the twentieth century, macroeconomic policy was viewed as a relatively trivial matter. The classical economists embraced a general principle known as **Say's law of markets.** Simply stated, Say's law stipulates that "supply creates its own demand." That is, the production process generates factor payments, which constitute the means for payment for the goods and services produced. Say's law is an affirmation of the idea that the circular flow of income is a closed system that is usually in equilibrium.

Say's law of markets supply creates its own demand, or the circular flow creates its own equilibrium.

Moreover, according to Say's law of markets, the closed circular flow of income contained a self-correcting mechanism that would automatically stabilize the system, should it temporarily fall into disequilibrium. The entire economy was viewed as being analogous to a single market with production on the supply side and consumption on the demand side. If at any point in time there is excess production of aggregate goods relative to the quantity demanded at existing price levels, then prices must fall in order to clear all markets. As prices fall, the ability to acquire goods with the given money supply increases until such time as the excess production is removed from the economy. As shown in Figure 8–1, aggregate supply and aggregate demand interact to determine a **price level** for all goods.[3] In Figure 8–1, price level P_e is the natural or equilibrium price level for the economy. Any other price level will result in either excess production or deficient production relative to the purchasing power or demand within the economy. For instance, at price level P_1 the quantity supplied exceeds the quantity demanded such that a surplus of magnitude $Q_s - Q_d$ appears. This surplus production would encourage

Price level the general level of prices in an economy as measured by a price index. An increase in the price level is inflation; a decrease is deflation.

---

[3] A price level in the macroeconomic system is analogous to a price in a market for a single good. An increase in price levels is called inflation, and a decrease is known as deflation.

FIGURE 8–1
Classical view of the
macroeconomy.

producers to reduce prices, which would cause some of the very marginal producers to cease production, resulting in a decline in output from Q_s to Q_e. As prices
decline, the quantity of goods that can be purchased with a given level of income
increases. This is shown as an increase in the quantity demanded from Q_d to Q_e. At
price P_e the combined effect of the increased quantity demanded and the decreased
quantity supplied is sufficient to eliminate the surplus that had existed at P_1, and
a stable equilibrium is once again established.

The reduction in the quantity supplied is accomplished by driving some marginal producers out of business. Marginal businesses are those that were just barely
able to earn a profit at price level P_1, but find it impossible to do so at P_e. As these
businesses fold, the demand for labor shifts inward, resulting in unemployment at
existing wage rates. The classical view of the labor market was that of a relatively
fixed supply of labor such that any demand shifts would cause changes in wages
to maintain full employment. Thus, any unemployment in the economy was
viewed as a short-run disequilibrium situation reflecting a natural adjustment
back to a full-employment equilibrium.

Classical Macroeconomic Policy

The bare bones of the classical view of the macroeconomy should now be clear.
Price level adjustments will automatically correct any disequilibrium between aggregate production and aggregate consumption. Given this classical perspective,
what are the appropriate macroeconomic policies a government should pursue to
achieve its eco-political objectives? The classical writers argued that since the economy is self-correcting, the appropriate government policy is to leave the economy
alone and let it take care of itself. Should the economy fall into disequilibrium because of some shock to the system, the best thing to do is not to interfere with the
price level adjustment mechanism that will bring the economy back to equilibrium. This policy of nonintervention of the government in the economy is known
as **laissez-faire** policy.

Laissez-faire
macroeconomic policy
that the government
should do nothing.
Nonintervention on the
part of government.

Any unemployment, inflation, recession, or other unpleasant and politically
unpopular consequences of the adjustment process were viewed as part of the essential purging of the forces that created the disequilibrium, and as such they
could not be and should not be ameliorated. To do so would only prolong the self-
correcting process. The classical premise that government nonintervention is the

best policy is particularly apparent in the monetary area. The classical writers felt that efforts to regulate the economy through monetary policy would result in price level changes rather than changes in output levels. So, from the classical perspective, fiscal policy is considered to be unnecessary and monetary policy is dangerous at best. The political admonitions of the classical macroeconomists are consistent with the Jeffersonian concept that the "government which governs least governs best".

All of this was to change abruptly during the 1930s.

THE KEYNESIAN REVOLUTION

A revolution involves rapid and substantial change. By these criteria, the change in macroeconomic thought stimulated by the work of John Maynard Keynes between the two world wars was most certainly a revolution. Within a decade the attitude of most economists toward macroeconomic policy changed from support of Say's law and all of its political implications, to support of the views of Keynes. In retrospect, we can see that the force of this revolution was partly due to the power of Keynes' arguments and partly due to the failure of the economy to automatically correct itself during the Great Depression of the 1930s. In the next few pages we will analyze the failure of the classical system during this turbulent period of our history before turning to the contributions of Keynes.

The Great Depression

While the initial causes of the Great Depression were several, we will focus on the "savings gap" because of its role in sustaining the depression. To do this, we need to return to our model of the circular flow of income. As we saw at the end of the previous chapter, savings by households are converted into investments by business firms through financial intermediaries. This process accomplishes two important goals. First, it sustains the circular flow of income at a given level, thereby maintaining full employment. Second, the additional investment financed by savings ensures future economic growth through the construction of new plant and equipment. But what happens when the financial intermediaries are not able to play the important role of recycling savings into investment? The economic machine is thrown into reverse, and we get the opposite of economic growth—a downward spiral in the economy. This is exactly what happened in the Great Depression.

Earlier we talked about the trauma caused by the financial failure of many banks, particularly rural banks, during the early 1930s. As savers saw banks, insurance companies, and other financial institutions collapse around them, they did what was prudent under the circumstances. They withdrew their deposits and began to save by **hoarding.** Since prices were falling during this period and financial intermediaries could not offer unquestioned security, there was a strong incentive to save by placing money in a cookie jar, stuffing it under the mattress, or burying it in the backyard. Today, these practices seem a bit ridiculous, but in the 1930s it was prudent (because of reduced risks) to "save" by hoarding cash.

Hoarding savings that are not put into financial intermediaries, but instead are held by households as cash.

We have in this instance a classic example of the fallacy of composition. While it was prudent for the individual to hoard, the collective impact on the economy of everyone hoarding is nothing short of an all-out disaster. The effect of hoarding on the macroeconomy can be seen in Figure 8–2. As with those before, this figure should be read from left to right, with the height of each column measuring the gross domestic product. Earnings received by households in 1931 are used for

FIGURE 8–2 A savings gap leads to economic depression.

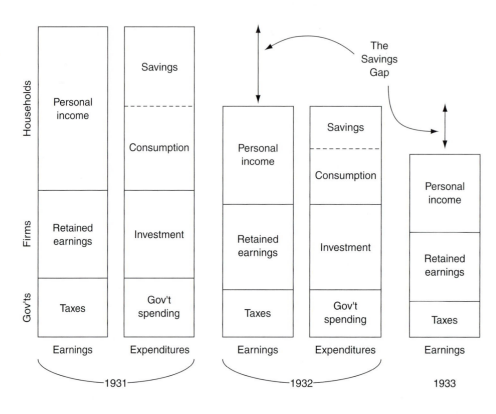

Savings gap that portion of household earnings that is neither spent nor saved through financial intermediaries.

expenditures and some saving. If this saving is in the form of hoarding, it does not enter the earnings stream for 1932, creating a **savings gap.** The money that is hoarded is not recycled into investment by financial intermediaries but, instead, is lost from the economy. Consequently, earnings and expenditures of each sector in 1932 are less than in 1931. The same pattern is repeated in 1932: what "saving" there is by households is in the form of hoarding, which is lost from the economy in 1933. So long as the hoarding continues, a vicious downward spiral ensues in which each year's GDP is less than in the previous year by the amount of the savings gap. This endless downward spiral will continue as the economy declines without any solution in sight. And as the GDP declines, unemployment increases and the human cost of the savings gap becomes very real.

At this point, it is worthwhile to compare Figure 8–1 and Figure 8–2. In the first, which depicts Say's law of markets, we see an economy that is automatically self-correcting. In the situation shown in Figure 8–2, where a savings gap is created by hoarding rather than by saving through financial intermediaries, there is not a self-correcting mechanism. Instead, the economy only worsens each year. Obviously, Say's law is not always true. The contribution of Keynes was to show why the economy in the 1930s was not automatically returning to a healthier state and to suggest what should be done to correct an economy caught in a seemingly endless, downward vortex.

The Keynesian Contribution

John Maynard Keynes was an outstanding British economist who played a leading role in European and world monetary affairs through both world wars. But his greatest contribution was the publication in 1936 of *The General Theory of Employment, In-*

terest and Money. In this work he argued that a modern industrial economy is not necessarily self-correcting, and therefore, Say's law of markets is not a solid foundation on which to build the structure of macroeconomic policy. While his *General Theory* is quite complex, several of Keynes' main arguments can be easily comprehended.

On the monetary side, Keynes argued that the classical theory of money was deficient because it considered only the supply of money without giving due consideration to the demand for money. In the classical theory of money it is implicitly assumed that the only use or demand for money is for transactions. But if there are other uses for money beyond transactions, then the strong link between the money supply and the price level will be broken. Keynes argued that there was also a **"speculative demand" for money** that must be taken into consideration. If the general price level is declining (deflation), there will be a demand to hold money rather than spend it in the hope that the money will be able to purchase more next year than it could this year.[4] This speculative demand would, of course, lead to hoarding by households and cause the savings gap we saw in Figure 8–2. Because of the existence of a speculative demand for money, the mechanical link between the money supply and prices predicted by the classical school becomes less certain.

A second attack that Keynes made on the implicit assumptions of Say's law concerned the flexibility of prices—particularly wage rates. Say's law stipulates that the price level will adjust to clear the aggregate market. This adjustment process implies that during periods of surplus production, product prices should decline. As product prices decline, factor prices should also decline. But with the advent of large corporations and large labor unions in modern industrial economies, we find an institutional framework in which prices are downward inflexible. Even in bad times union workers will argue for higher wages, but they will never accept lower wages. If wages are downward inflexible, then obviously the price of products that labor produces will also be downward inflexible. In an institutional framework in which prices go up with relative ease but down only with great difficulty, the self-correcting mechanism of Say's law is destroyed. Thus, Keynes argued that the unemployment problems in the U.S. economy would not eventually and automatically correct themselves.

The impact of **downward inflexible prices** on Say's law of markets is illustrated in Figure 8–3. Here we see an initial equilibrium at price level P_0 and production level Q_0. For some reason, such as the stock market crash of 1929, the aggregate demand curve shifts inward to D_1. Say's law would hold that the price level should fall to P_1. But if the price level is downward inflexible, there will be a market surplus of Q_1Q_0 at price level P_0. The aggregate supply curve shows the quantity that producers are *willing* to produce at price level P_0, but if consumers are willing to purchase only Q_1 units, producers will be forced to cut production to Q_1, which is less than the quantity they are willing to produce (Q_0). This cut in production, an undesired cut, will cause unemployment in the labor market, which

Speculative demand for money Keynes' argument that at times households hold cash for speculative purposes rather than for transactions, creating a disequilibrium in the circular flow of income.

Downward Inflexible prices Keynes' argument that because of institutional constraints, the classical assumption of flexible prices that would either rise or fall to achieve equilibrium was not valid.

---

[4] Since the last deflation in the United States was in 1955, it is sometimes difficult for students today to appreciate the speculative demand for money. Suppose your grandfather had $1,000 to save in 1930. He had three alternatives: (a) put the money in a savings account in a rural bank, (b) buy prime farmland at $50/acre, or (c) hoard the $1,000. The return on the first alternative was quite low in 1930—maybe 2 or 3 percent, *and* the risk of losing everything in a bank failure was great because deposits were not insured. The second alternative of buying 20 acres of land with the money seems sound enough, unless land prices decline. And decline they did! By 1933 our hypothetical land had declined to only $25/acre. Therefore, if your grandfather was smart, he hoarded his savings in 1930 and bought 40 acres of land in 1933. Of the three alternatives, only hoarding has a high return with low risk. As a consequence, there was a demand for money to be held in speculative balances.

FIGURE 8–3 Effect of downward inflexible prices.

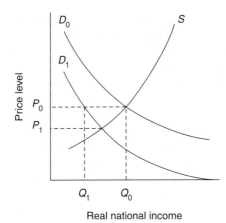

FIGURE 8–4 Keynesian aggregate supply curve.

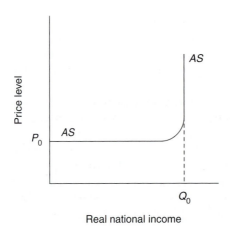

will cause yet another shift of the aggregate demand curve to the left. This will cause even more unemployment, and the vicious downward spiral continues.

From this argument it followed that the traditional aggregate supply function that is always upward sloping (as shown in Figure 8–3) is incorrect. Since downward inflexible prices would drive the output level in Figure 8–3 to Q_1, the actual supply function would be a horizontal line at price P_0. Following this line of logic, Keynes argued that the correct form of the aggregate supply curve is similar to that shown in Figure 8–4. At some price level, P_0, the aggregate supply function becomes horizontal, meaning that shifts of aggregate demand to the left would result in decreasing output (and hence declining employment) without creating the disequilibrium present in the classical model. In Figure 8–1, any decrease (an inward/downward shift) in aggregate demand results in disequilibrium,[5] which eventually brings about the self-correcting changes in price levels. In the Keynesian model in Figure 8–4, it is possible to have equilibrium between aggregate supply and aggregate demand at less than full employment. And it is possible for output to decline (unemployment to increase) without creating any

---

[5] Disequilibrium meaning that the aggregate quantity demanded is no longer equal to the aggregate quantity supplied at the prevailing price level.

disequilibria. For the classical economists, equilibrium and full employment were synonymous. For Keynes, equilibrium was possible at any employment level.

In Keynes' view, what was happening in the 1930s was that the savings gap was causing the aggregate demand curve to continually shift inward along the perfectly horizontal aggregate supply curve, resulting in a downward spiral of output with no self-correcting mechanism, because each demand shift resulted in a new equilibrium situation with lower output, lower employment, and stable price levels. Given the aggregate supply curve shown in Figure 8–4, the policy perscription is clear: stimulate aggregate demand such that the aggregate demand curve shifts outward along the horizontal portion of the aggregate supply curve. One way to shift that aggregate demand curve outward is through an increase in government spending, *ceteris paribus.* So long as the aggregate supply curve remains horizontal, the economy can be stimulated (greater output, more employment) without causing the price level to increase (i.e., inflation).

Keynes argued that if there is a speculative demand for money, or if the prices of some important factors of production are downward inflexible, then the economy will not automatically self-correct as the classical economists had always postulated. This evaluation of the economic situation then confronting most of the industrial economies during the 1930s won rapid endorsement from many economists. However, there was less agreement concerning the economic policy recommendations and political implications of Keynes' analysis. An examination of these implications is now in order.

As we have seen, the first element of Keynes' work was to show that the economy was not necessarily self-correcting. The second was to demonstrate that the central government could use its taxing and spending powers to stimulate an economy that is caught in a vicious downward spiral. The third element of Keynes' work borders on social philosophy more than economics. He and his followers argued that since the central government could regulate the economy, it was the correct and proper role of the government to intervene directly in the economy in an effort to bring about the simultaneous achievement of full employment, stable prices, and economic growth. This last assertion was in complete and direct conflict with the laissez-faire policy approach taken by the classical economists preceding Keynes' work. As a result, it ignited a substantial debate concerning the proper role of government in regulating the economy that continues to this day. Rather than get involved in what is essentially a question of political philosophy, we will turn our direction to the second element of Keynes' work and see how the government can influence or regulate the economy through fiscal policy.

Fiscal Policy in the 1930s

In the Keynesian model, a depression is caused by insufficient aggregate expenditures or demand. This was shown in Figure 8–2, where the expenditures in each year decreased as a result of the savings gap. Keynes argued that when aggregate spending within the private sectors of the economy is inadequate to sustain the circular flow of income, it is incumbent upon government to increase its own spending to make up for it. That is, if aggregate private demand is not sufficient to absorb the aggregate full-employment supply at the existing (and downward inflexible) price level, then government spending should be increased in order to bring the

FIGURE 8–5 Use of deficit spending to close savings gap.

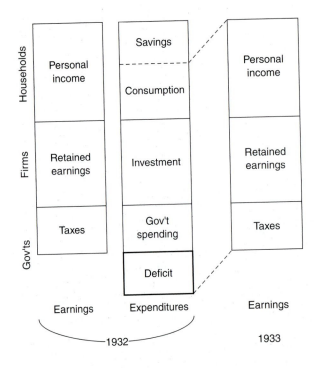

aggregate quantity demanded and full-employment quantity supplied into balance, thereby ensuring that full employment is maintained.

The process of closing the savings gap with additional government spending is illustrated in Figure 8–5 (which is similar to Figure 8–2). In this example, a portion of the earnings in 1932 are "saved" by hoarding. Without financial intermediation these earnings will leave the circular flow of the economy. To compensate for this loss of spending in the private sectors, government will increase its expenditures in 1932, running a budget deficit equal in size to the savings gap. The government, as a dissaver, injects the deficit expenditures into the economy in order to offset the leakage from the economy caused by hoarding in the household sector. As a result of the government **deficit spending,** the total earnings received in 1933 are the same as in 1932: a depression has been avoided. The cost of avoiding this depression is an increase in the deficit of the federal government, but given a political choice between a depression or a deficit, there is usually no contest.

The savings gap in Figure 8–5 could also be closed through a tax cut, with government spending remaining constant.[6] A tax cut would increase the deficit of the government to the level necessary to offset the savings gap without causing the size of government spending to increase. In both cases, the argument is the same: government dissaving resulting in a government deficit is necessary to offset a savings gap or deficient spending in the private sector.

In retrospect, the "make work" projects that President Franklin Roosevelt embraced as a last resort to support the unemployed workers of the era were good macroeconomic policies. The projects were financed with government deficits that

Deficit spending
policy of purposeful government deficits to compensate for insufficient aggregate demand in other sectors of the economy.

_____

[6] This proposition would be true only if households actually spent the proceeds from the tax cut. If they put the reduced taxes in the cookie jar, there would be no fiscal impact.

filled the substantial savings gap that had developed. The banking reform measures introduced during the famous first 100 days of the Roosevelt administration also did much to reduce the disintermediation associated with the savings gap.[7] Had Roosevelt continued with President Herbert Hoover's policies of avoiding deficits at all costs, the depression certainly would have been longer and deeper than it was.

The use of government deficits to ensure an adequate level of aggregate demand during periods of economic stagnation was the basic prescription that evolved from Keynes' work. The other side of the coin was also of importance to Keynes but not of immediate relevance. During periods when the aggregate demands of the private sector are greater than the quantity supplied at existing price levels, inflationary pressures develop. The extreme version of this situation is illustrated in Figure 8–4 with the vertical portion of the Keynesian aggregate supply curve. In this case, the full employment of all resources would be capable of producing at output level Q_0. Any increases (i.e., upward shifts) of aggregate demand will not increase output but will result in inflation as the price level increases.

In this case, the appropriate role of government fiscal policy is to cut spending (reducing aggregate demand), or increase taxes (take some of the spending power out of the private sector), or both. In each case, the government would run a surplus to offset excessive spending in the private sector. It was argued that a Keynesian fiscal policy would have a sound financial basis over time since government surpluses created during periods of excess aggregate demand would balance off any deficits that may be incurred during periods of stagnation. Keynes would never have endorsed the continuous federal deficits that we have seen during most of the post-World War II era.[8]

So while the classical authors argued that unemployment and inflation were merely part of the adjustment process back to an equilibrium situation, Keynes argued that it was possible to have a macroeconomic equilibrium and at the same time have either unemployment or inflation. That is, the automatic adjustment process that is inherent to markets is not necessarily present in the macroeconomy as the classical writers had maintained. The policy challenge, therefore, was to keep aggregate demand within that curved portion of the Keynesian aggregate supply curve where employment is high and inflation is low.

SUMMARY

Budget deficits (surpluses) are the amount by which the spending of the federal government exceeds (is exceeded by) federal receipts during a fiscal year. Deficits add to the federal debt, which is the total amount of federal borrowing outstanding at a point in time. Congress imposes debt ceilings in an effort to control the total amount of federal debt.

---

[7] "Disintermediation" refers to the failure to use financial intermediaries to convert savings into investment. Hoarding or the speculative demand for money is a form of disintermediation.

[8] To Keynes the idea of occasional surpluses offsetting occasional deficits was all part of the natural order. Unfortunately, he did not anticipate the fact that deficits (stimulus) are politically attractive while surpluses (restraint) are political suicide. Politicians, who are usually more interested in their own well-being than in other lofty goals, have a natural incentive to embrace deficits and shun surpluses.

The classical view of the macroeconomy was that it was very similar to a market and that adjustments of the price level would eventually drive the economy to an equilibrium. Say's law of markets held that supply creates its own demand—that the circular flow of income perpetuates itself. The policy prescription of the classical school was laissez-faire, or do nothing.

The combined impact of the Great Depression and the publication of Keynes' *General Theory* dramatically changed economists' view of the macroeconomy. Keynes argued that the classical theory was invalid because of the speculative demand for money and the institutionalized downward inflexibility of prices. Unlike the classical theorists, he argued that it was possible to have a less than full-employment equilibrium.

Keynes argued that the federal government can and should use its economic power to regulate the macroeconomy. In the case of a depression the federal government should run a deficit of sufficient magnitude to offset the savings gap created by speculative hoarding.

KEY TERMS

Debt ceilings

Deficit

Deficit spending

Downward inflexible prices

Federal debt

Hoarding

Laissez-faire

Price level

Savings gap

Say's law of markets

Speculative demand for money

Surplus

PROBLEMS AND DISCUSSION QUESTIONS

1. Draw an aggregate supply curve as viewed by the classical school of economics, making sure to properly label the axes. Clearly label this curve with a "C." Now draw an aggregate supply curve as viewed by the Keynesian school. Clearly label it with a "K."

2. Assume that the federal debt on December 31, 2000, was $490 billion. The 2001 (calendar year) budget deficit was $115 billion. What is the federal debt on December 31, 2001?

3. Compare and contrast the macroeconomic policy recommendations of the classical school and the Keynesian school.

4. During the Great Depression what created the "savings gap"?

5. What is "stagflation," and when did it strike the American economy?

6. What is the basic premise of the monetary school of macroeconomic thought?

7. Keynes argued that the classical view of the macroeconomy was not always valid. Why? (Give two reasons.)

APPENDIX

POST-WORLD WAR II MONETARY AND FISCAL POLICY

The conceptual framework for monetary and fiscal policy have been laid out in the preceding chapters. Within the institutional framework of the United States, the responsibility for conducting monetary policy falls upon the Federal Reserve Board of Governors. As an agency that is independent of both the President and Congress, the Fed has tremendous latitude to establish monetary policy and the ability to implement it quickly. Fiscal policy, however, requires action by both houses of Congress and approval by the President. The process is ponderous, as a result, the problem that was to be addressed has often solved itself by the time a policy becomes reality.

In this appendix we review the economic history of the United States in the post-World War II era. This is the period of time when government accepted responsibility for regulating the economy through the purposeful manipulation of fiscal and monetary policy. In this historical review we will discover that conducting economic policy is not quite as easy as the preceding chapters have made it appear.

Post-World War II Economic Policy

Within the Keynesian framework, fiscal policy may be either the accelerator or the brake of the macroeconomic system depending on the requirements of the moment. Within this system, the level of government spending is not as important as whether the government sector is in a surplus or deficit position, for surpluses slow down the economy and deficits stimulate it. Note that the same political trade-offs we have seen before exist within the Keynesian model. During periods of stagnation when unemployment is high, the government should be stimulative by running deficits. As the economy is stimulated, inflationary pressures may develop. Therefore, the political price of improving the employment picture is a potential deterioration of price stability.

From the 1940s through the 1960s

The Second World War caused massive deficit spending that more than killed off the last signs of the depression. After the war the concern was on the other side of the Keynesian aggregate supply curve—avoiding inflation from an economy that was overheated. During the war inflation had been avoided by the use of price controls—something the public was willing to accept during the war but unwilling to accept once peace was declared.

Faced with the end of the war and aware of the Keynesian revolution that was sweeping macroeconomic thought, President Harry Truman proposed the Full Employment Act of 1946, which created the **Council of Economic Advisors** as a permanent part of the President's staff and embraced the Keynesian notion of managing

Council of Economic Advisors established in 1946 as part of the White House staff. Its creation signaled that management of fiscal policy was now the responsibility of the President.

151

the economy through deliberate fiscal policy. With the passage of this act, the role of the presidency was greatly expanded to include management of the macroeconomy.

Keynesian fiscal policy was highly successful during the 20-year period from the early 1950s to the early 1970s. Whenever the economy was not operating in the desired manner, slight adjustments in federal tax or spending policies were sufficient to clear up the problem. The existence of the unpleasant alternatives—inflation if there is too much stimulus or unemployment if there is not enough—was generally accepted as macroeconomic reality. The idea that the economy could be managed within a free enterprise system gained wide acceptance during this period—a development that caused no end of grief for the more conservative politicians who continued to consider Keynesian macroeconomics little more than untested economic theory with thoroughly repugnant political implications concerning the intrusive role of government.

By 1972, the Keynesian approach to fiscal policy was absolutely dominant in Congress, in the White House, and to some extent even in the Federal Reserve System. The reason for this dominance was the close correspondence between predicted performance of the economy and actual performance. In short, the theories of Keynes seemed to be working. Inflation was low, employment was high, and the economy was growing rapidly with only minor fits of an occasional recession.

The postwar period until 1972 was a time of unprecedented economic prosperity for the United States. As Paul Krugman points out, the living standard of the average American doubled over this period and labor productivity (output per worker) was growing at an annual rate of 2.8 percent compared with a prewar rate of 1.8 percent.[9]

Unfortunately, the 1970s ruined the order and tranquility economists had grown to enjoy.

Stagflation in the 1970s

Keynesian macroeconomic policies pulled the economy out of the depression, through World War II, and into two and a half decades of substantial economic growth with fairly low levels of unemployment and inflation. The Keynesian prescriptions seemed to be working. Economists could control the economy like a trucker controls a semi. But then came the 1970s and a new series of challenges for economic policy makers.

During the decades of the 1950s and 1960s the U.S. economy behaved exactly as predicted. Economists carefully plotted the course of the economy and consistently found that employment and inflation seemed to be moving along the curved portion of the Keynesian supply curve as illustrated in Figure 8–6. It was clear that the aggregate demand curve had been moving back and forth along the Keynesian aggregate supply curve. Periods of slightly lower employment also had lower inflation (points on the lower left of the curve). And higher employment was usually associated with higher inflation (points on the upper right of the curve). While very attractive from a political point of view, zero unemployment and zero inflation (points on the lower right of the graph) were not simultaneously possible. There was a trade-off between inflation and unemployment that was very predictable.

---

[9] Krugman, Paul. *Peddling Prosperity: Economic Sense and Nonsense in the Age of Diminished Expectations.* W.W. Norton, 1994, p. 57.

FIGURE 8–7
Economic performance—1970s

Price level

AS

The 1970s

AS

Real national income

FIGURE 8–6
Economic performance—1950s and 1960s

Price level

AS

AS

Real national income

In the 1970s (at least after 1972), things begin to change in strange ways that economists could not explain. As economists pored over the tea leaves of economic data, a strange pattern emerged with higher rates of inflation than in the previous decades *and* higher rates of unemployment. The simultaneous existence of high rates of unemployment and inflation in the 1970s frustrated the Nixon, Ford, and Carter administrations with rather dire political consequences. The old trade-off between inflation and unemployment just wasn't responding the way it was supposed to based on previous experience. The quandary faced by the macroeconomic policy makers in the 1970s became known as "**stagflation**"—the combination of economic stagnation and inflation.

The phenomenon of stagflation is illustrated in Figure 8–7 with observed high rates of inflation and low rates of output (i.e., high unemployment). Within the Keynesian framework there was no way to explain what was happening to the economy in the 1970s. This, of course, led to a lot of serious reexamination of macroeconomic theory. The only possible explanation of what was happening in the "real world" was that the aggregate supply curve must have shifted upward. In Figure 8–7 imagine another aggregate supply curve parallel to the one drawn but passing through the observed points for the 1970s. Shifts of aggregate demand alone could not explain the behavior of the economy during this period.

Keynes had postulated that the aggregate supply curve was fairly benign and not subject to adjustment by economic policies. All of the focus of Keynes was upon fiscal policy affecting aggregate demand. If fiscal policy doesn't shift aggregate supply, then what must have caused the observed shift? Several possible structural adjustments have been suggested as responsible for the aggregate supply shift:

- The changing nature of the labor force during the 1970s may have changed the way the unemployment-inflation trade-off behaves. Two major shifts occurred in the labor force during this period: a substantial increase in the number of working women, and vastly improved employment opportunities for racial minorities. As a consequence, the labor force in the 1970s was structurally quite different from that which existed in the late 1950s and 1960s.[10] It has been suggested that these structural changes

Stagflation
economic stagnation (high unemployment) occurring simultaneously with high inflation.

[10] For a pop culture verification of this change, compare the female roles in TV programs of the 1950s ("Ozzie and Harriet," "I Love Lucy," and "Leave It to Beaver") with those of the 1980s and 1990s ("Murphy Brown," "Ally McBeal," and "Oprah").

produced a labor force that is less productive and that has a higher level of frictional unemployment (i.e., worker turnover) than in previous decades.[11] If this is the case, then any given level of inflation would logically be associated with higher unemployment rates and the aggregate supply curve would shift upward.

- A changing pattern of investment in plant and equipment may also have shifted the aggregate supply curve. Before the early 1970s, most new investment was for additional plant and equipment that brought additional jobs into the economy and produced additional goods and services. Following the creation of the Environmental Protection Agency in 1970, concern for environmental protection resulted in a significant portion of all new investment going for pollution control equipment. While such investments have significantly cleaned up the environment, they do not result in an expansion of the production capacity of the economy.

- The dramatic increases in energy prices during the 1970s created a number of economic dislocations. The importance of energy to the total economy suggests that radical price changes in energy inevitably led to substantial adjustments throughout the economy. Higher rates of inflation for a given level of employment can easily be explained or justified by the changes in energy prices in the 1970s.[12]

- In the early 1970s the U.S. dollar was devalued and allowed to "float" against other currencies. The convertibility of the dollar into gold was also suspended. These changes in the international monetary system made it impossible for the United States to continue to export its inflation, as many of our trading partners had accused us of doing in the 1960s. We don't need to deal with the complexities of the international monetary system at this time, but changes in that system certainly changed our ability to deal with inflation.

The combined effect of these four basic structural changes during the early 1970s may well have caused the aggregate supply curve to shift upward, thereby establishing a new level of trade-offs between inflation and unemployment with both higher unemployment and higher rates of inflation.[13]

Policy makers in the early 1970s were not certain what was happening to the economy. All they could see was that stagflation had become a problem. President Richard Nixon, with his demand-oriented policy tools, was faced with a choice of trying to fight inflation by restricting aggregate demand or fighting unemployment by stimulating aggregate demand. Initially, he chose to fight inflation, and the consequence was the recession of 1974–1975. To get out of the recession Presidents Nixon

---

[11] Gilder, George, *Wealth and Poverty.* New York: Basic Books, 1981, p. 16.

[12] For today's students the energy crises of the 1970s are ancient history, and the economic shocks felt then are not fully appreciated. In 1973 the price of gasoline quadrupled almost overnight. So, to understand the shock, imagine what your behavior would be like today if you suddenly awoke to $5 per gallon for gasoline and electric utility bills two or three times their current level. That's what it was like in 1973 and again in 1979.

[13] There were also significant political events during this period of time. The United States was winding up its involvement in the unpopular Vietnam War by "declaring victory" and quitting. President Lyndon Johnson had been hounded out of office when it became apparent that he had lied to the American public. Later, Watergate was swirling around the presidency of Mr. Nixon, who resigned rather than face possible impeachment. To a significant degree, Americans had lost faith in their government and the presidency in particular.

and Ford were forced to pursue stimulative fiscal and monetary policies that only served to reignite the fires of inflation that President Carter did little to stamp out.

The Wild Ride of the 1980s

By the late 1970s, some economists began to argue that the almost exclusive pre-occupation of Keynesian economists with the aggregate demand side of the economy had caused them to lose sight of the other side of the market. Sure, they argued, the Great Depression of the 1930s was caused by a lack of aggregate demand and cured by Keynesian deficit spending; but that doesn't mean it is safe to assume that the supply side of the economy will automatically take care of itself if aggregate demand is appropriately regulated through fiscal policies.[14]

This new approach to macroeconomics that emphasized the role of aggregate supply quickly became known as **supply side economics.** The election of President Ronald Reagan in 1980 provided the supply siders with an opportunity to put into practice policies that were consistent with their view of the macroeconomic reality. Their primary policy objective was to shift the aggregate supply curve outward/ downward in order to encourage more production and lower prices. The specific policies proposed to achieve this objective included substantial reductions in tax rates, increased tax incentives for additional investment by business firms, elimination of many government regulations, and incentives for increased private savings by households. Within 2 years the Reagan package with each of these policies had been approved by Congress.

As the 1970s drew to a close and it was clear that the most severe economic problem was double-digit inflation, President Jimmy Carter brought Paul Volker into the chairmanship of the Federal Reserve Board. Mr. Volker, as president of the New York Fed branch, had been very vocal about the failures of fiscal policy to solve the inflation problem, which he viewed as being primarily a monetary problem. Mr. Volker arrived in Washington in October 1979, and within a week he had charted the monetary course that would dominate the decades of the 1980s and 1990s.

Since the end of World War II, the main objective of the Fed had been to provide enough liquidity (i.e., money) in the banking system to keep interest rates low enough to promote economic growth and full employment. Mr. Volker and other **monetarists** felt that this approach had allowed the money supply to grow so rapidly that inflation was the obvious, inevitable result. The monetarists felt that the Fed should attempt to regulate the rate of growth of the money supply and let the interest rate go to whatever level the market dictated. In essence, the Volker-led Fed went from a policy of regulating the price of money to one of regulating the quantity of money.

Imagine the scene at the beginning of the 1980s in Washington. The economic policy environment was undergoing a complete change. After 30 years of relatively stable economic institutions in Washington (regardless of the party in power), there were three new actors all arriving at the same time. First, there was President Reagan, who was telling the American people that he was going to cut taxes in or-

Supply side economics   a school of economic thought emerging in the early 1980s that emphasized policies to shift the aggregate supply curve rather than the aggregate demand curve as suggested by the Keynesians.

Monetarists   school of economic thought that emphasizes monetary policy and the role of the growth of the money supply in macroeconomic policy.

---

[14] Agriculture has been an interesting exception to this generalization. Since the New Deal most macroeconomic policies dealing with agriculture have focused on the supply side of the industry rather than the demand side.

der to balance the budget.[15] Second, there were the supply siders, who said it was time to abandon the Keynesian tools that had worked so well for the past 30 years. And finally, an activist monetarist in the form of Paul Volker was at the Fed, rapidly changing the Fed's policy and asserting the primacy of monetary policy over fiscal policy. It *was* a time of change.

In retrospect it is easy to see that these three new forces provided a volatile mixture that was a train wreck waiting to happen. And happen it did! As indicated earlier, the legislative agenda of the supply siders was approved by Congress, including President Reagan's tax rate cuts. At the same time the Volker Fed slashed the rate of growth of the money supply in an effort to restrain inflation. The result was a strange contradiction—a very stimulative fiscal policy (tax cuts) and a very tight monetary policy (low money expansion). The economy was very much like a semi-truck booming down the interstate with the right foot pushing the accelerator to the floor while the left foot slammed on the brakes. As any trucker knows, this is a surefire way to burn up the brakes, or the engine, or both.

This strange mixture of policies and priorities led to four distinguishing economic events of the 1980s: a massive recession, enormous federal deficits, the collapse of the savings and loan industry, and substantial trade deficits.

Recession

Recession period of time during which the GDP declines. A long, severe recession is called a depression.

In the early 1980s the Fed (the brakes), having complete autonomy, vowed that it would do whatever was necessary with monetary policy to overcome the inflation that was gripping the nation. And it did what it said it would do, sending the nation into the deepest, longest **recession** since the depression of the 1930s. As a result of tight money, interest rates soared into previously unknown heights with short-term rates approaching 20 percent and home mortgage rates in the 15 percent range. Prospective home buyers didn't buy, prospective car buyers didn't buy, and prospective vacationers didn't travel to Florida. As a result, the carpenter, the fender installer, and the Mickey Mouse impersonator all found themselves unemployed. In 1982 and 1983 the unemployment rate hung around 10 percent. Farm bankruptcies reached levels not seen since the 1930s. Farm assets (mostly land value) fell from $982 billion in 1981 to $724 billion in 1986. The real GDP fell by 2.2 percent in 1982—the largest decline in one year since the 1930s.

The Reagan/Volker depression was for real. And the policy worked! By the end of the Reagan administration, inflation had moderated, employment was back up, and the economy was buzzing along as it had in the 1950s and 1960s. Volker and the monetarists had replaced the Keynesians as the economic miracle workers. But there were storm clouds brewing.

Deficits

While the early 1980s were a pretty rough scene, economically speaking, the later 1980s became known as the "feel good" era of economic prosperity. Unfortu-

---

[15] While this was one of President Ronald Reagan's favorite lines, most economists were skeptical at best. The argument Reagan's advisers made was that a reduction in tax rates would stimulate the economy so strongly that tax receipts would actually increase as more income was taxed at a lower rate. For example, if the economy currently generated $100 of income that was taxed at 30 percent, the tax receipts would be $30. Reagan argued that lowering the tax rate to 20 percent would cause the economy to grow rapidly to a $200 income, and tax receipts would then be $40. Bingo—lower rates = higher receipts. History proved him wrong on this one.

nately, much of that prosperity was paid for with massive deficit spending by the Reagan administration. In spite of the rhetoric of budget balancing, the Reagan administration pursued a very stimulative fiscal policy with massive budget deficits. In 1962 the federal government had its first $100 billion budget. In 1982 it had its first $100 billion deficit. And the deficit didn't fall below that level again until 1997.

In 1980 the publicly held national debt[16] was $712 billion. By 1992, at the end of the Reagan/Bush (Sr.) era, it had more than quadrupled to $3,000 billion (or $3 trillion). Fiscal stimulus of this magnitude had not hit the economy since World War II, and the results were predictable—prosperity. While many wailed about the massive deficits, most enjoyed the "feel good" prosperity that comes from running up the balance on your charge card. "Buy now, pay later" was the order of the day.

With governments, as with individuals, the amount of debt is best measured in terms of the income available to support that debt. For instance, no bank would be concerned if Bill Gates[17] borrowed $1 million because he can probably pay it off with little difficulty. However, most college professors would be laughed out of a bank if a loan of $1 million were requested.

Figure 8–8 tells an interesting and a worrisome story. In 1940, as the country was coming out of the depression, the national debt was about 50 percent of the gross domestic product. With the demands of the Second World War, the ratio of debt to GDP soared to nearly 110 percent. But after the war ended, the country started paying the debt off in a relative sense. Even though the amount of debt increased throughout the postwar period, the economy was growing faster than the debt such that the debt/GDP ratio steadily fell to a low of about 25 percent—considered to be a reasonable debt load by most economists.

Then in the 1980s the debt started increasing more rapidly than the economic base that supported that debt. By the mid-1990s, the debt/GDP ratio was up to about 50 percent. So our debt, in terms of our capacity to finance that debt, doubled in the 1980–1992 period. A combination of tax increases and budget restraint during the Clinton administration produced budget surpluses that brought this critical indicator back down to about 33 percent.

Savings and Loan Debacle

The deregulation of the savings and loan industry in the early 1980s allowed many S&Ls to engage in highly risky endeavors that eventually led to widespread bankruptcies in the industry. By the time the smoke had cleared, Uncle Sam was left with a $550 billion bill to bail out failed savings associations. By the 1990s, the financial industry had pretty well shaken out all of the overly risky S&Ls, and the industry today appears to be in a fairly healthy condition. The question remains, nonetheless, of whether it could happen again or if a similar fate could hit the recently deregulated banks. While there has been some minor re-regulation since the deregulation, the conditions that allowed the debacle to happen are still pretty much in place.

---

[16] Slightly less than half of the national debt is unfunded liabilities of the Treasury to branches of the federal government. Most of this is unfunded liabilities to the Social Security Administration. The publicly held debt is that portion of the debt for which the Treasury has actually sold bonds.

[17] Bill Gates, founder and chief executive of Microsoft® Corporation, is thought to be the richest person on earth with a personal worth of around $60 billion (give or take a few billion).

FIGURE 8–8 Federal debt as a percentage of GDP.

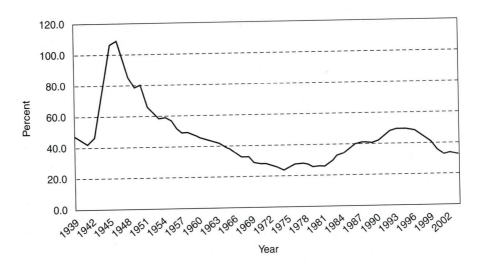

Foreign Debt

As nations trade with one another, they frequently lend to and borrow from one another in order to cover imbalances in trade patterns. In the post-World War II era the United States extended massive credits to the countries of Europe to help them rebuild. By 1985 the United States was by far the largest creditor nation in the world. Since that time the United States has been on a massive borrowing spree (in part to cover the national debt) to the point where today we are the world's largest debtor nation with a total external debt of more than $1,800 billion.

As the nation continues to run persistent trade deficits, there is little prospect that we are going to slow the growth of this external debt. The greatest danger that the debt carries is that some of our trading partners may refuse to extend us even more credit, thereby putting the United States in a position of having to stop the foreign buying spree, which would result in a lower level of living for American consumers.

Through the 1990s

In the 1980s we experienced many adverse economic situations. Nonetheless, at the end of the decade things were in pretty good shape economically speaking. Inflation was a thing of the past, employment levels were relatively high, the economy was growing slowly, and monetarism seemed to be working under the guidance of a strong chairman of the Federal Reserve Board, Alan Greenspan. Compared with the economic rancor at the beginning of the decade, the end of the 1980s was a pussycat.

Nonetheless, in the early 1990s it was difficult to shake off the "borrow and spend" legacy of the 1980s. Steady, persistent budget deficits required ever more borrowing by the federal government. The same thing was happening in the foreign sector, where we continued to pile up foreign debt. Once again, the policy was one of "borrow and spend."

The late 1990s were characterized by low inflation, low unemployment, and rapid economic growth. The growing economy generated additional tax revenue, and a frugal Congress (with help from the end of the cold war) kept federal spending down. As a result, the persistent deficits of the 1980s were eliminated and the federal debt as a percentage of GDP once again declined. Reduced federal borrowing and the elimination of deficit stimulus allowed the Fed to ease interest rates to the lowest levels seen in decades. So through the 1990s we saw a slow, smooth transition from fiscal stimulus to monetary stimulus with very positive consequences.

President Bill Clinton and the Republican Congress both claim credit for creating a budgetary surplus, and both are probably partially correct. Most economists give the lion's share of the credit to the steady policies of the Federal Reserve Board under the leadership of Chairman Alan Greenspan.

The New Millennium

Early in his term of office, President George W. Bush received the tax cuts from Congress that he wanted. The Fed, fearing fiscal stimulus, slowly pushed interest rates up to avoid the possibility of a return of inflation. The monetary restraint worked predictably, and by late 2001 the economy was slowing into a mild recession. The terrorist attacks of September 11, 2001, were an additional blow to the economy. In an attempt to revive the economy the Fed lowered interest rates an unprecedented seven times in 2001 to an equally unprecedented low target federal funds rate of 1.75 percent.

SUMMARY

The combination of President Franklin Roosevelt's domestic policies and the Second World War gave the economy sufficient stimulus to end the Great Depression. The 1950s and 1960s were a period of Keynesian bliss. It seemed as though the macroeconomy could be easily controlled as long as there were a sufficient number of Keynesian economists in the government. The 1970s ended the smug complacency as stagflation (high unemployment and high inflation) savaged the macroeconomy. Traditional fiscal policy seemed to be unable to control it.

In October 1979 a monetarist, Paul Volker, took over as chairman of the Board of Governors of the Federal Reserve. He argued that to control inflation the quantity of money in the economy must be controlled. The short-run impacts of this monetary policy were high interest rates and a severe recession in the early 1980s. The long-run impact was the death of rampant inflation. The late 1980s were characterized by stimulative fiscal policy (large federal deficits) and tight monetary policy (high interest rates).

The 1990s saw fiscal policy become neutral as massive federal deficits gave way to small surpluses. This allowed monetary policy to loosen, resulting in an unprecedented peacetime economic boom with relatively stable prices and low interest rates.

The bliss of the 1990s began to fade in the 2000s. A promised tax cut was made, but increasingly tight monetary policy and the terrorist attacks of September 11, 2001, sent the economy into a mild recession. The Fed reacted by aggressively cutting interest rates.

KEY TERMS

Council of Economic Advisors   Monetarists
Stagflation   Recession
Supply side economics

International Trade

*A*dam Smith, the first modern economist, argued that the basis of economic activity was a "certain propensity in human nature . . . to truck, barter, and exchange one thing for another."[1] Throughout the history of the Western Hemisphere, trade has been important to the economic system. Remains of the pre-Columbian Indians in the American Southwest indicate that trade had been well established with other Indian groups residing as far away as the Pacific coast of Mexico. Columbus was in search of an improved trade route to the riches of the Indies when he bumped into a stubborn land mass that he repeatedly attempted to circumnavigate. The first colonists in Jamestown arrived with the hope they would be able to export precious metals and gems, but alas, the eastern seaboard offered no riches until the new settlers learned from the Indians how to smoke the leaves from a certain "noxious weed"—tobacco. This weed created the basis for trade between the colonies and Europe. Today trade, including the trade of several different weeds, is of vital importance to our economy and to our agriculture. In recent years, nearly one-half of U.S. cropland has been used to produce commodities for export. Certainly our study of the macroeconomy and its relationship with the agricultural sector would not be complete without an understanding of the causes and consequences of international trade.

CHANGING U.S. TRADE PATTERNS

During the past generation, the pattern of U.S. trade with other countries has changed in two significant ways. We have opened our economy to a greater amount of trade and at the same time we have become a debtor nation. Both of these changes are illustrated in Figure 9–1.

Role of Trade in the U.S. Economy

The period between the two world wars was a time characterized by very intransigent isolationist sentiments by a majority of the U.S. population. These feelings—a consequence of the massive waves of immigration around the turn of the century and the ultimate entanglement of the United States in World War I, which many Americans considered to be a "European war"—manifested themselves politically in ever higher trade barriers in an effort to make each country self-sufficient and independent. Most economists agree that one of the primary contributing causes

---

[1] Adam Smith was a Scottish philosopher who published *The Wealth of Nations* in 1776. This is generally considered to be the first book published in the field of economics.

| | Trade as a Percentage of Gross Domestic Product | | |
Year	U.S. Exports	U.S. Imports	Trade Balance ($ Billions)
1950	4.5	3.9	1.4
1960	4.9	4.4	5.4
1970	5.6	5.5	2.8
1980	10.3	10.8	−23.4
1990	10.0	11.3	−115.8
2000	7.2	12.2	−493.1

FIGURE 9–1
Importance of international trade to the U.S. economy: historical perspective.

of the Great Depression was the reduction in world trade associated with high **tariffs** (import taxes) and "beggar thy neighbor" economic policies.

Tariff a tax on imports imposed by the importing country. Tariffs are usually applied to discourage the importation of a particular item or imports in general.

While the general mood of the public after the Second World War was more internationalist (rather than isolationist), the economy was still fundamentally isolationist. This is illustrated in Figure 9–1 which shows the value of U.S. trade as a percentage of gross domestic product (GDP). This is a measure of what proportion of U.S. domestic resources were used to produce goods for sale to foreigners. The percentage of GDP accounted for in imports is a measure of what proportion of our total domestic consumption was purchased from foreigners. As shown in Figure 9–1, in 1950 imports and exports each accounted for about 4 percent of total economic activity. This pattern was little changed until the decade of the 1970s, when our economy finally opened up with the amount of trade relative to total economic activity almost doubling in one short decade. While this has represented a vast opening for the U.S. economy, our international trade is still relatively small when compared with that of most other industrialized nations.

The reasons for this explosion in world trade are many. First, a number of international treaties brought about fundamental changes in the trading relations among nations, with trade barriers falling rapidly. The economic consequences of isolationism were replaced with the trade and prosperity of internationalism. Second, the globe was rapidly shrinking. Jet travel and global telecommunications greatly facilitated international trade and the means to finance it.[2] Finally, both Japan and Europe had fully recovered from the effects of the Second World War and had become active traders in the world economy. In the 1950s "Made in Japan" was synonymous with "junk." Today U.S. consumers pay a premium for the opportunity to drive a Japanese car or listen to a Japanese boombox.

From Creditor to Debtor

The numbers in the last column of Figure 9–1 reveal a rather dark side of the current U.S. economy. If during a period of time Joan earns $20,000 and spends $18,000 with the remainder going into a savings account, then Joan has become a **creditor**—one

Creditor one to whom others owe money.

[2] In 1969 one author was a graduate student at Purdue University in West Lafayette, Indiana. At that time, Lafayette being something of a backward place, it was not yet possible to telephone his parents in Albuquerque, New Mexico, using direct dial. Each call required the intervention of an operator and at least 25 tin cans strung together. Later that year he temporarily moved to Santiago, Chile, where it was possible to direct dial from his apartment to Albuquerque! The other author couldn't call Durham, Oklahoma, using direct dial until 1975. In 1995 AT&T announced that with the addition of North Korea it was now possible to direct dial to every country in the world—even "far away" Cuba.

Debtor   one who owes money to others.

to whom others (the bank in this case) owe money. If, by comparison, Sam earns $20,000 and spends $25,000 by borrowing from the bank to buy that set of wheels he "just had to have," then he has become a **debtor**—one who owes money to others. In general it is "good" to be a creditor and "bad" to be a debtor—particularly a debtor year after year with the accumulating effects of repeated indebtedness. The yin and yang of being a creditor or debtor boils down to a decision of whether you would rather drive a flashy new set of wheels that the bank owns or an old junker that you own. Debt allows us to consume beyond our means, and for many of us that is a temptation that is hard to refuse.

Countries also may be either creditors or debtors depending on the collective behavior of the citizens of the country. From the First World War until 1985 the United States was a creditor nation, but since 1985 we have become a debtor nation. In fact, the United States is currently the world's largest debtor nation with a total debt to other countries in excess of $2.2 trillion. The cause of this phenomenon can be seen in Figure 9–1. In 1950, 1960, and 1970 the United States exported more than it imported; that is, it had a positive **trade balance.** How did other countries buy more from us than we bought from them? Simple, they borrowed from the United States to allow them to consume more than they earned. As other countries borrowed from the United States, we became a creditor country. During most of the twentieth century the United States was a net creditor such that by 1983 the accumulated foreign credits of the United States exceeded $160 billion—the largest of any nation. But by 1986 the United States was $300 billion in debt to other nations. What happened?

Trade balance   value of a country's exports minus imports.

As shown in Figure 9–1, in 1980 and beyond the United States purchased more from foreigners than they bought from us. How did we finance those purchases? Simple, we borrowed from other countries so that it was possible for the United States to spend more than it earned. Currently we are borrowing at a rate of more than one-half billion dollars a day. And since the United States has been running annual trade deficits since 1982, the cumulative effect has grown to a total **external deficit** in excess of $2.2 trillion at the end of 2000. In 2002 the external deficit of the United States was growing at a rate of about $1 billion per day.

External deficit amount borrowed from outside the United States to finance net imports.

To be a debtor nation is not inherently "bad" or "good," but several aspects of the recent movement of the United States from the world's largest creditor nation to the world's largest debtor nation are worrisome. The United States became a debtor nation for all the wrong reasons: we borrowed to consume rather than to invest. And the foreign investment that was attracted to our markets is the kind of investment that increases financial volatility rather than adding to our productive capacity. One of the major economic challenges of the new century is to extricate the United States from this situation without causing major, irreparable harm.

The Importance of World Trade to U.S. Agriculture

International markets are vital to American agricultural producers, and to American consumers. If international trade were to cease, American producers would find that approximately 60 percent of the market for wheat, rice, and soybeans—and one quarter of the market for corn—had disappeared. Consumers would find the shelves bare when they looked for coffee, chocolate, bananas, spices, or tea.

The size and importance of agriculture within the total trade picture are demonstrated in Figure 9–2. As shown in the first column of data, the value of agri-

| U.S. Exports* | | | |
Year	Agricultural	Nonagricultural	Total	Percent Agricultural
1950	2,873	7,269	10,142	28
1960	4,832	15,543	29,375	24
1970	7,259	35,331	42,590	17
1980	41,256	175,336	216,592	19
1990	39,363	335,830	375,193	10
2000	51,580	660,707	712,287	7

| U.S. Imports* | | | |
Year	Agricultural	Nonagricultural	Total	Percent Agricultural
1950	3,987	4,756	8,743	46
1960	3,824	11,190	15,014	25
1970	5,770	33,986	39,756	15
1980	17,366	222,577	239,943	7
1990	22,770	468,205	490,975	5
2000	38,991	1,166,348	1,205,339	3

| U.S. Trade Balance* | | |
Year	Agricultural	Nonagricultural	Total
1950	−1,114	+2,513	+1,399
1960	+1,008	+4,353	+5,361
1970	+1,489	+1,345	+2,834
1980	+23,890	−47,241	−23,351
1990	+16,593	−132,375	−115,782
2000	+12,589	−505,641	−493,052

*Millions of dollars.

Source: USDA, **www.ers.usda.gov/data/fatus/DATA**

FIGURE 9–2 Value of U.S. foreign trade and trade balance, summary for years 1950–2000.

cultural exports rose dramatically in the decade of the 1970s to more than $41 billion in 1980. At the same time, nonagricultural exports were increasing at approximately the same rate, such that the proportion of total exports originating in agriculture remained fairly constant at just under one-fifth. Things changed dramatically in the 1980s. Once again total exports almost doubled during the decade, but agricultural exports were basically unchanged. As a result, the share of exports from agriculture fell from one-fifth of the total to one-tenth. That trend continued in the 1990s with agricultural exports falling to only 7 percent of total exports.

However, agricultural imports (center panel of Figure 9–2) have not increased as rapidly as exports and have fallen rapidly as a proportion of total imports. As a result of the shifting trade patterns, the agricultural sector produced a sizable trade balance (exports minus imports) of nearly $24 and $17 billion in 1980 and 1990, respectively (bottom panel of Figure 9–2). This compares with a small deficit in the agricultural trade balance in 1950. The shift of the agricultural sector from a position of deficit to one of sustained surpluses has been one of the more significant structural changes in American agriculture during the post-World War II years.

	2000 Exports*	Percentage of Agricultural Exports	Exports as a Percentage of Farm Cash Receipts
All commodities	$57,245	100.0%	28.3%
Animal products	7,952	13.9	8.6
Grains	11,147	19.5	29.8
Food grains	5,166	9.0	50.0
Wheat	4,234	7.4	49.2
Rice	932	1.6	53.9
Feed grains	5,981	10.4	22.1
Corn	5,172	9.0	21.2
Other feed grains	809	1.4	30.0
Oilseeds and products	8,326	14.5	41.7
Cotton	2,709	4.7	44.1
Tobacco	1,553	2.7	51.1
Fruits	4,235	7.4	36.2
All other	21,323	37.2	68.4

*Millions of dollars.

Source: Foreign Agricultural Trade of the United States, USDA, Calendar, 1997 Supplement, and Agricultural Statistics, 1998, USDA. Note: Exports as a percentage of farm cash receipts will overestimate the impact of exports on a particular commodity the extent that export values include shipment costs and processing performed prior to export.

FIGURE 9–3   U.S. agricultural exports: value by commodity and share of cash receipts.

Food grains   those grains that are usually consumed by humans as food. The primary food grains are wheat and rice.

Feed grains   those grains that are usually used as livestock feed. All feed grains are used for human consumption (oats for oatmeal, rye for rye flour, and barley for beer), but they are generally considered to be inferior to food grains for human consumption. The most common feed grain is corn (field corn, not the sweet corn that you find in the store). Others include rye, oats, barley, millet, and sorghum (also called milo).

As shown in Figure 9–3, total U.S. agricultural exports exceeded $52 billion in 2000. This was approximately 27 percent of farm cash receipts for the year. Since many agricultural exports include beyond farm processing, this percentage overestimates the role of agricultural exports in farm income, but it does provide a good measure of the approximate magnitude of exports relative to production.

Approximately one-half of all cash receipts of grain farmers can be traced to the export market. It is estimated that about 2 out of every 5 acres of cropland in the United States are used to produce crops for export. This is equal to all the cropland east of the Mississippi River with Texas thrown in for good measure. About 9 percent of total agricultural export value comes from the two **food grains**—wheat and rice. For both of these commodities, exports account for about 60 percent of total farm level sales. The other two important agricultural exports in terms of sales value are **feed grains** (primarily corn) and **oilseeds** (primarily soybeans). Together they account for approximately one-fourth of agricultural exports today, but several decades ago they accounted for nearly one-half of export value. Clearly, foreign competition has severely cut into the export markets for corn and soybeans—our two main midwestern crops.

Sophisticated farmers realize that the market price they receive for their crop depends just as much on world markets as on the vagaries of weather. American wheat farmers became gleefully aware of the importance of foreign markets in the early 1970s when successive bad harvests in the former Soviet Union caused the Russians to become heavy buyers of American wheat. The increased foreign demand in 1973 and 1974 caused the average price received by wheat farmers to increase from $1.76 per bushel in 1972 to $4.09 in 1974. Corn and soybean prices also rose dramatically. As a result, in 1973 the per capita disposable (after-tax) income of the farm population surpassed that of the non-farm population for the first time in many, many years. As is always the case, the "boom" of the mid-1970s was followed by the "bust" of the early 1980s when thousands of American farmers were driven into bankruptcy—partially because of weak export markets. The message to the American farmer is clear: your destiny is partially in your own hands, and partially in the hands of our trading partners.

The 1990s experienced another boom–bust cycle partially driven by the vagaries of the export market. The combination of two bad harvests in 1993 and 1994 and a vibrant export market drove corn prices up to nearly $5.00 per bushel in 1995. Many predicted an extended period of prosperity for the American farmer driven by the exponential growth of export markets. Alas, as always the euphoria of the boom was followed by the inevitable bust, and by the late 1990s the price of corn was back to about $2.00 per bushel and exports were stagnant in the $50 billion per year range.

THE IMPORTANCE OF U.S. EXPORTS IN WORLD TRADE

The data in Figures 9–4 through 9–7 describe the patterns of world production and trade of grains and soybeans during the 2000-2001 crop year.[3] Several broad observations deserve attention before considering the wheat, rice, feed grains, and soybean markets individually:

- Of the nearly 1,900 million metric tons of grain produced in the world in 2000-2001, roughly one-half was food grains (wheat or rice) and the other half was feed grains. Wheat currently accounts for about three-fifths of food grain production and is increasing as a proportion of the total. Corn is the most important feed grain.

- Grain traded on international markets as a percentage of total production is greatest for wheat. About 22 percent of all wheat produced was exported from the producing country, compared with 14 percent for feed grains and only 7 percent for rice. This latter figure emphasizes the fact that most rice is consumed near the location of its production.[4]

- The United States is easily the world's largest grain exporting nation. The United States was the country of origin (for 47 percent) of all feed grains, 23 percent of all wheat, and 11 percent of all rice that entered world markets in 2000-2001. The United States (accounted for 32 percent of total world grain exports even though it accounted for only 19 percent) of world production.

- The importance of continued U.S. agricultural exports to the world food situation is awesome. For every 20 tons of grain consumed outside the United States, approximately 1 ton came from U.S. exports. That is, for the average non-U.S. resident, imports from the United States provide grain for 17 days of consumption per year. If rice is eliminated from the data, the dependence of the rest of the world on U.S. agricultural exports is even more striking.

Oilseeds those crops that are generally crushed under high pressure and heat to produce vegetable oil and meal. The meal is usually used for livestock feed, and the oil is used in a variety of food products such as margarine, mayonnaise, and cooking oil. The primary oilseed is soybeans. Others include sunflower, rapeseed, cottonseed, peanuts, olive, and flaxseed.

---

[3] A crop year begins with the harvest, hence the crop year includes the September through November harvest in the Northern Hemisphere and the January through April harvest in the Southern Hemisphere.

[4] An exception was the prerevolutionary coast in the Charleston, South Carolina, area. In the 1650–1870 era large rice plantations were created on the estuary rivers with most of the rice exported to England. For a wonderful history of this region and time read Edward Ball's *Slaves in the Family,* Farrar, Straus and Giroux, 1998.

FIGURE 9–4 World
wheat: Production,
trade, and use,
2000–2001.

Country	Production	Exports	Imports	Domestic Use[1]
	(Millions of metric tons)			
World	583	127	126	589
U.S.	61	29	2	36
Total non-U.S.	522	98	123	553
Major Exporters				
EU-15[2]	105	39	27	92
Canada	27	17		8
Australia	24	16		7
Argentina	16	12		4
Major Importers				
N. Africa[3]	10		18	29
Brazil	2		7	10
FSU-12[4]	63	5	5	63

Note: Detail in figure might not match total due to rounding.
[1]Domestic use equals production minus exports plus imports and changes in stocks (not shown).
[2]Fifteen members of the European Community; includes trade among members of the EC.
[3]Algeria, Egypt, Libya, Morocco, and Tunisia.
[4]Former Soviet Union, not Florida State University; includes trade among former members of FSU.
Source: USDA, *World Agricultural Supply and Demand Estimates,* #383.

Wheat

The vital statistics of the world market for wheat are shown in Figure 9–4. By far, the largest importers of wheat are the countries of North Africa. These are markets for our wheat that hardly existed three decades ago because wheat is not indigenous to the region. Strong market development efforts have created a market for wheat where none existed previously. The former Soviet Union (FSU) is both the world's largest producer and a major importer of wheat. China used to be a major importer of wheat, but with the recent reforms it has become self-sufficient.[5] Pakistan and India used to be substantial importers of wheat, but the development of improved varieties has made these countries self-sufficient in recent years.

The United States is the largest exporter of wheat with 22 percent of the world market. Most of the trade shown for the EU-15 is intra-Europe trade rather than exports to countries outside the region. Other significant exporters include Canada, Argentina, and Australia. Each exports a larger proportion of their domestic production than the United States does. Since wheat exports are such an important part of these countries' agricultural economies, they are fierce competitors on the world market.

Mainland China and the FSU were the largest importers of wheat in the early 1990s. Historically they have also been the most variable importers. Their year-to-year fluctuation in imports is the result of two factors: the fragile, tenuous, and often fickle environment in which wheat is grown (particularly in the FSU), and political instability. This high degree of production variability causes import requirements to be highly variable which in turn causes market demand for wheat in the United States to be highly variable.

---

[5] In northern China wheat (usually in the form of noodles) is the staple of the diet, while in southern China rice is the staple.

Country	Production	Exports	Imports	Domestic Use
		(Millions of metric tons)		
World	857	120	116	878
U.S.	273	56	3	216
Total non-U.S.	584	64	113	663
Major Exporters				
Argentina	20	11	—	8
Canada	24	4	3	25
Australia	11	5	—	5
Major Importers				
Japan	0	—	20	20
EU-15	108	24	17	103
Mexico	24	—	11	36
S. Korea	0	—	9	9

FIGURE 9–5 World feed grains: Production, trade, and use, 2000–2001.

Note: Detail in figure might not match totals due to rounding.
Source: USDA, World Agricultural Supply and Demand Estimates, #383.

The data on domestic use (which is equal to consumption plus inventory adjustments) illustrate differences between the consumption patterns in the United States and other areas. For example, note that the FSU consumes[6] almost two times as much wheat as the United States even though its population is only 20 percent larger than that of the United States. This means that the average per capita consumption of wheat in the FSU is almost two times as great as in the United States. Part of this is accounted for by the use of wheat as a livestock feed grain in the FSU (very little wheat is fed in the United States), but most of the difference is an indication that wheat is more important in the Russian diet than in the United States. The same pattern can also be observed in Europe, but to a lesser degree.

Feed Grains

Production and trade patterns for the feed grains are detailed in Figure 9–5. The United States is the undisputed, dominant producer with output levels more than twice that of any other country or region. The United States is also dominant in world export markets, exporting nearly as much as the rest of the world combined. Major export markets are Japan and western Europe (EU-15).

Feed grain exports to Europe and Japan are used primarily for livestock feed. Since meat consumption is closely tied to income levels, it is those countries with high per capita incomes that constitute the primary markets for our feed grain exports. A second important segment of the export market includes many of the smaller low-income countries. In these countries, most of the demand for feed grains is for food rather than feed—tortillas in Mexico and so forth. Since these grains are usually considered to be inferior to wheat and rice as food grains, they usually sell at a price well below that of the food grains. Consequently, low-income countries import feed grains primarily for domestic food consumption.

---

[6] Henceforth it will be assumed that domestic use is equal to consumption.

FIGURE 9–6 World
rice: Production, trade,
and use, 2000–2001.

Country	Production	Exports	Imports	Domestic Use
	(Millions of metric tons)			
World	397	26	22	403
U.S.	6	3	—	4
Total non-U.S.	391	23	22	399
China	131	2		134
Major Exporters				
Thailand	17	8		9
Vietnam	20	4		17
Major Importers				
Indonesia	32		1	36

Source: USDA, *World Agricultural Supply and Demand Estimates*, #383.

The United States consumes far more feed grain (both total and per capita) than any other country. Most consumption is in the form of livestock feed or processed foods (corn syrup, cornflakes, and beer, for example). Per capita consumption in western Europe is slightly less than in the United States, but in the FSU it is only about one-fourth of the U.S. level. The economic hardships associated with the dissolution of the former Soviet Union have caused a significant deterioration in the quality of the average diet in the FSU. As a consequence, there has been a clear shift in import patterns away from feed grains (for meat) toward food grains—from the hamburger to the bun.

Rice

As shown in Figure 9–6, the world market for rice is quite a bit different from that of the other grains. First of all, the United States is a rather insignificant producer with 1.5 percent of the world total. Mainland China produces slightly less than one-third of the world's rice, yet it exports only an insignificant amount. India is the second largest producer. As in the case of wheat, India used to be a net importer of rice prior to the introduction of high-yielding varieties and the production technologies required to grow these varieties. Today India is self-sufficient in rice.

World trade in rice is relatively small compared with the other grains. About half of all exports are accounted for by Thailand, Vietnam, and the United States. As an exporter, the United States is an interesting case. With only 1.5 percent of the world's rice production, the United States accounts for 11 percent of all world exports. Most U.S. rice exports are to Middle Eastern and African countries. Within the last decade Vietnam has moved from being a rice importer to its current status as the second largest exporting nation.

Obviously, rice consumption in the United States is minor compared with that in many Asian countries. The population of mainland China is roughly four times that of the United States. This means that if the average Chinese consumed as much rice as the average American, total Chinese consumption would be 12 million tons ($4 \times 3 = 12$). However, actual consumption in China is about 11 times this amount. This means that the average Chinese consumes at least 11 times as much rice as an average American. Since about two-fifths of the domestic consumption of rice in the

Country	Production	Exports	Imports	Domestic Use
	(Millions of metric tons)			
World	175	54	56	173
U.S.	75	27	—	49
Total non-U.S.	100	28	56	124
Major Exporters				
Brazil	39	16	1	25
Argentina	28	7		18
Major Importers				
EU-15	1	1	19	19
Japan	0		5	5
China	15		13	27

FIGURE 9–7 World soybeans: Production, trade, and use, 2000–2001.

Note: Detail in figure might not match totals due to rounding.
Source: USDA, *World Agricultural Supply and Demand Estimates*, #383.

United States is by food processors,[7] the amount of rice consumed as food by the average Chinese is certainly more like 15 times that of the average American.

Soybeans

Soybeans are the major oilseed produced in the world today. Virtually all soybeans are crushed to create two **joint products**—soybean oil and soybean meal. The oil is used in a variety of foods such as margarine, potato chips, and cooking oil. The meal is used almost exclusively as a protein source in animal feeds. A minor use of meal is in food products such as soyburgers. Because of its favorable nutritional characteristics, many expect to see a rapid expansion of soymeal in food products—particularly with the introduction of **nutriceuticals.**

As shown in Figure 9–7, the United States produces almost half of the world's soybeans and accounts for one-half of all exports. Several decades ago the United States dominated about 90 percent of the world export market, but rapid expansion by Brazil and Argentina has reduced our dominance in the world export market.

The major importers of soybeans are western Europe and Japan, where relatively high per capita incomes support significant animal industries that require the high protein that soybeans provide. Since soybean consumption and trade are closely tied to per capita incomes, this promises to be a dynamic market for U.S. agriculture in the foreseeable future.

AGRICULTURAL IMPORTS OF THE UNITED STATES

For the most part, imports of agricultural commodities into the United States are not as important to the agricultural sector as export markets. In a typical year, a little less than one-fourth of all U.S. agricultural imports are commodities that are not produced in the United States, and, therefore, do not compete with domestic production. An interesting example of a **noncompetitive import** is coffee.[8] In 1980

Joint products
when two or more products are produced by a single production process, the resulting products are called joint products.

Nutriceuticals
engineered foods that have specific health effects, such as a margarine that contains compounds that have been shown to reduce cholesterol levels in consumers.

Noncompetitive import imports of agricultural commodities that are not produced in the United States, such as bananas.

---

[7] About one-fifth of domestic rice consumption is for beer (Budweiser is a classic example), and another fifth is for processed foods such as Rice Krispies and soups.
[8] Technically, coffee should not be considered as noncompetitive because there is some minor coffee production in our most southern state—Hawaii.

almost one-fourth of all agricultural imports in terms of value were coffee imports. But because of changing consumer attitudes about caffeine, coffee accounted for only about 7 percent of the $39 billion of agricultural imports in 2000. Other tropical products such as cocoa, bananas, silk, rubber, tea, and spices make up most of the rest of the noncompetitive imports.

Competitive imports
imports of items that are commercially produced in the United States, such as wine.

Competitive imports accounted for $31.2 billion in 2000. The major categories of these imports in 2000 were animal products[9] ($8.3 billion); fruits, nuts, and vegetables ($8.2 billion); wine and beer ($4.8 billion); and sugar ($1.6 billion). American producers of these products feel that imports displace domestic production and cause domestic prices to decline. But in most cases, imports are very small relative to domestic production, and they frequently are not directly competitive. For example, many wine experts would argue that French wines do not compete with California wines because they are not in the same class. Needless to say, such an assertion would bring a speedy rebuttal from California wine producers. For some other products, the imports are clearly competitive in one sense but not in a seasonal sense. For instance, Chilean table grapes have become a major agricultural import during the December–February Southern Hemisphere harvest season. Not too many U.S. table grape producers can legitimately complain about foreign competition in these months.

Since competitive imports do displace some domestic production, it is common for domestic producers to seek a political remedy to what is essentially an economic problem. The cattle industry has been successful in getting Congress to establish meat import quotas to limit the amount of red meat that can be imported. The orange juice industry has been equally successful in creating tariff barriers to avoid massive imports from Brazil. Sugar, oilseeds, dairy, and all the other affected sectors have mobilized political support to reduce, limit, or prevent the importation of commodities that are perceived to destroy domestic markets. Whether imports of agricultural products should be limited, and how to implement any restrictions that may be approved, are basically policy issues. Let's turn now to see why trade in these commodities occurs and then explore the world of trade policy.

WHY DO NATIONS TRADE?

Why do nations trade? This question should really be rephrased as, Why do people trade? Simply stated, people trade because they feel they can gain as a consequence. We trade because by doing so we are able to obtain goods that have been produced more **efficiently** by someone else. Most people take their car to a mechanic when repairs are needed. While we hate to pay for "old Betsy's" repairs, we realize that it is cheaper for the mechanic to do it than for each of us to learn to be a mechanic and to acquire the tools and equipment that are necessary to do the job properly. However, many drivers change the oil in their cars themselves since this is a task that requires little time to learn and few tools to perform.

Efficiency a general economic concept used in a variety of situations measuring output per unit of input. The higher the ratio, the more efficient the process.

When trade is possible and competition is present, every resource will be employed in that pursuit for which it is relatively efficient. In most instances the mechanic buys his tools from a factory that can produce tools more efficiently than he

---

[9] Much of the imported meat is not really competitive. Examples include mutton from New Zealand, corned beef from Brazil, and Danish hams. Also included are hides, tallow, and frog's legs: where they came from and where they went are anybody's guess.

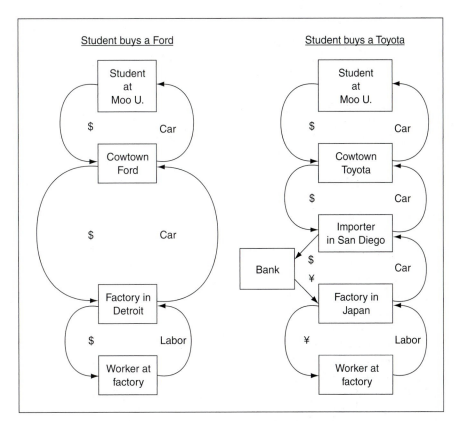

FIGURE 9–8 The difference between domestic and international trade.

could. The relationship is symbiotic. The mechanic buys tools from the factory, and the factory worker gets his car fixed at the mechanic's garage. Each realizes that the other is more capable of doing his own job. By trading their services, they are both better off.

Nations don't trade, but people in different nations do. When a student at Moo U. buys a new car, it makes little difference to her whether that car is a Toyota or a Ford, as long as she gets the better car at the better price.[10] The only essential economic difference between a Ford and a Toyota is that the workers who assembled the Ford insist on being paid in dollars, while the workers who assembled the Toyota expect to be paid in yen. In either case, the student feels she will benefit by trading her dollars for a car. The transactions involved in the purchase of a Ford and a Toyota are illustrated in Figure 9–8. Since students at Moo U. and the Ford factory both use the same currency, there are no complications if the student elects to buy a Ford. But Moo U. and Toyota's factory are in different countries with different currencies. So if the student should decide to purchase a Toyota, not only is a car exchanged but the currency paid by the student is also exchanged at a bank so that Toyota can pay its workers in Japan with the yen they prefer. This latter complication is what makes international trade unique.

---

[10] In the discussion that follows it is assumed that Toyotas are made in Japan and that Fords are made in the United States. In reality, many "Fords" are made outside the United States (including Japan), and many "Toyotas" are made in Kentucky. For this discussion, think of Toyota and Ford as foreign and domestic.

Thus, it is people who trade, not countries. When trade involves different currencies, we frequently say that countries are trading since each currency is unique to its own country. Rather than saying dollars are being traded for yen, we say that the United States trades with Japan.

The Basis for Trade

Trade occurs because of interregional or international differences in production efficiencies and therefore in the costs of production. These differences may be due to natural resource endowments, technological advantages, or differences in resource productivities. It is important to realize that the same economic forces that cause Minnesota consumers to buy citrus from Florida producers also cause Manitoba consumers to buy citrus from Florida producers. Quite simply, Florida citrus producers are more efficient than potential citrus producers in either Minnesota or Manitoba.

At the same time, Florida consumers buy pancakes, bread, and sticky buns made with wheat from Minnesota. While some Florida farmers grow a little bit of wheat, it is relatively cheaper to produce wheat during the 1 week of summer in Minnesota because the opportunity cost of doing so is lower than in Florida. The bottom line is that in general, a country will import those goods that it produces (or could produce) at relatively high opportunity cost and exports those goods it produces at relatively low opportunity cost.

Commodities
undifferentiated goods in which one producer's product is indistinguishable from another's. Examples are iron ore, field corn, and iceberg lettuce.

Wheat and oranges are examples of **commodities**—undifferentiated[11] products that are traded almost exclusively on the basis of price. Lower cost producers are able to dominate the market. Think of how ludicrous it would be to drive into Minnesota and see a billboard that says "Take pride in Minnesota: Eat only Minnesota oranges." Which would the consumer prefer, Minnesota oranges at $10/pound or Florida oranges at $1/pound? Since the consumer perceives no difference between the products of the two states, she is going to buy from the lower cost producer. So, the pattern of trade in commodities is based primarily on costs of production.[12]

Products   goods that are differentiated: one producer's output is distinguishable from another's. Most products carry a brand name—Heinz ketchup, for instance.

Goods that are differentiated are called **products.** Most products are sold under a brand name to identify one producer's product as being different from another's. While the trade in products is also driven by relative costs of production, there are additional forces that determine the flow of trade. Products are differentiated to cater to the unique tastes and preferences of individual consumers. When consumers buy a product, the purchase decision is usually made on the basis of value—a balance between the perceived satisfaction of using the product and the price of the product. And since different people have different perceptions, they behave differently. As a result, you can buy French wines in California and Porsches in Detroit. One does not buy French wine or Porsche cars because they are the least expensive product available. Instead, the consumer *perceives* their value to be greater than some less costly alternatives. Another important perception that drives consumption is what Thorstein Veblen called "conspicuous consumption."[13] That

---

[11] Undifferentiated means that there is little or no difference between one unit and another. Wheat is wheat, flour is flour, and oranges are oranges. While there are different types or varieties (white versus rye flour, navel versus valencia oranges), there is little difference between one mill's flour and another's, or one grove's navel oranges and another's.

[12] Costs of transportation will also be important, but for the moment these costs will be ignored.

[13] Veblen, Thorstein, *The Theory of the Leisure Class,* Macmillan, 1899.

is, we consume certain goods in the hopes that others will observe our consumption and perceive of us in a certain fashion. The host who serves guests only French wines seeks an image more than a bargain. Because perceptions and tastes vary widely across national boundaries, it is not uncommon to find a Frenchman driving a U.S.-made car and an American driving a French-made car.

So, while the trade in commodities is usually unidirectional, flowing from the country with lower relative costs to the country with higher relative costs, the flow of products is multidirectional, driven by the variety of tastes and preferences. In the case of products it is value (a perception of the individual consumer) rather than costs that dictate the flow of trade.

Excess Supply/Demand

The forces that determine the magnitude and direction of international trade can be examined using the basic tools of supply and demand developed earlier. In our earlier analyses we used supply and demand in a "closed" economy, that is, one in which there is neither international trade nor the possibility of trade. Now we will expand on that model within the context of an "open" economy in which trade beyond the domestic economy is possible.

The case of an open economy is illustrated in Figure 9–9. If no trade were allowed, the interaction of supply and demand would result in a domestic price of $20/unit with the quantity demanded = quantity supplied = 50 units. At prices below the domestic equilibrium price of $20 a domestic shortage develops. If trade is allowed, this domestic "shortage" could be filled with imports from other countries. For example, at a price of $10 per unit the quantity domestic consumers want to consume is 75 units, and the amount domestic producers are willing to produce is 25 units. From a domestic point of view this would appear as a shortage of 50 units, but from an international trade perspective, this appears as an import demand for 50 units at a price of $10 per unit.

Likewise, at prices above the domestic equilibrium price there is an exportable surplus equal to the difference between the domestic quantity supplied (about 62 units at $25) and the domestic quantity demanded (about 38 units at $25). At prices greater than $25 the exportable surplus is even greater.

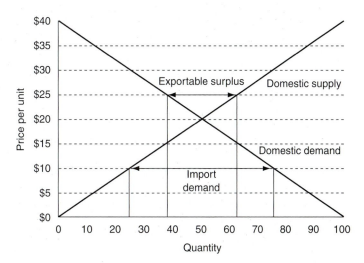

FIGURE 9–9 Trade opportunities in an open economy.

FIGURE 9–10
Derivation of import
demand and export
supply.

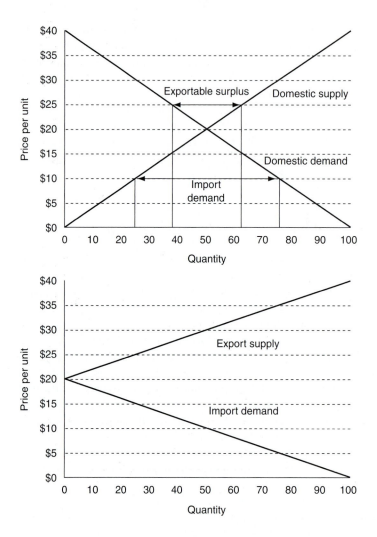

Import demand
quantities of goods
domestic consumers
are willing to import at
alternative prices,
ceteris paribus.

So at a price other than the domestic equilibrium price there is either an **import demand** or an **export supply** in an open economy. This is illustrated in Figure 9–10.

In this case, at the domestic equilibrium price of $20 the quantity demanded for imports is zero and the quantity supplied for export is zero. At a price of $40 per unit the quantity supplied for exports is equal to 100, and at a price of zero the quantity demanded of imports is 100.

A Simple Trade Model

Export supply
quantities of goods
domestic producers
are willing to export at
alternative prices,
ceteris paribus.

The concepts of import demand and export supply can be used to illustrate how cost differentials between two countries explain the flow of trade. To keep matters simple, assume a world of two countries, both of which produce and consume a single commodity—call it "stuff." Further assume that there are no transportation costs and no barriers to trade such as tariffs or taxes. Because of different resource endowments and resource productivities, one country is a lower cost producer of stuff while the other is a higher cost producer.

FIGURE 9–11 A two-country, one-commodity trade model.

The domestic supply and demand diagrams for both countries are shown in the right and left panels of Figure 9–11. Country A (left panel) is a relatively high cost producer of stuff, while Country B is a relatively low cost producer. Without trade between the two, a price of P_a would prevail in Country A and a price of P_b would prevail in Country B. The price differential between the two countries suggests that there is an incentive to trade. The center panel of Figure 9–11 shows the import demand of Country A (the high cost producer wants imports) and the export supply of Country B (which seeks markets for what it can produce at a low opportunity cost).

The import demand and export supply on the world market operate like any other supply–demand situation. The interaction of potential buyers and sellers determines an equilibrium price at which the market is cleared. This is shown as P_w. At this price the quantity that Country B is willing to export is equal to the quantity that Country A is willing to import and the world market clears. At this one unique price, the three line segments (quantity imported, quantity exported, and quantity traded) are of equal length showing that the international market clears with world quantity demanded = world quantity supplied.

Producers in Country B are happy because they are selling more stuff at higher prices than prevailed without trade. Likewise, consumers in Country A are delighted because they can now consume more stuff at a lower price. So, the impulse to trade internationally comes from differences in domestic prices that would prevail in the absence of trade. These differences arise because of different resource endowments and different resource productivities.

GAINS FROM TRADE

Trade, whether among regions or among nations, encourages resources to seek those employments where they are relatively efficient. From a global point of view, this reallocation of resources has the effect of increasing global production and hence global well-being. This improvement in global well-being is possible only so long as free trade is unobstructed by national or international intervention. Economists, usually a rather contentious group of individuals, universally agree on two basic propositions dealing with trade:

- Trade increases global well-being by causing resources to be used more efficiently.
- Trade increases the overall well-being of the citizens of each trading partner.

FIGURE 9–12 Output per unit labor.

	Wheat	Cloth
United States	10 bushels	6 yards
United Kingdom	5 bushels	10 yards

FIGURE 9–13 Impact of reallocating one unit of labor in each country.

	Wheat	Cloth
United States	+10 bushels	−6 yards
United Kingdom	−5 bushels	+10 yards
World	+5 bushels	+4 yards

That is, while there are individual winners and losers from trade, the aggregate gains of the winners will outweigh the losses of the losers.[14]

To illustrate the first point let's use a simple two-country, two-good model. Assume that the United States and the United Kingdom both produce wheat and cloth. The productivity of labor in both countries for both goods is shown in Figure 9–12. Clearly the United States is able to produce wheat more efficiently than the United Kingdom, while the latter is more efficient in the production of cloth. Therefore, if trade were allowed between the two countries, we would expect the United States to export wheat and the United Kingdom to export cloth.

To illustrate that trade and the resulting reallocation of resources would improve the global well-being, let's conduct the following exercise. Assume that each country has a fixed number of laborers involved in the production of each commodity. Now assume that each country reallocates just one unit of that labor into the production of the product that is produced more efficiently. What will happen to global production? The result is shown in Figure 9–13. In the United States when one unit of labor is withdrawn from the relatively inefficient cloth industry and reallocated to wheat production, we find that cloth production falls by 6 yards while wheat production increases by 10 bushels. In the United Kingdom, a similar reallocation in the other direction causes wheat production to fall by 5 bushels while cloth production increases by 10 yards.

What happens within each country is relatively unimportant. What is important is what has happened to production at the world level. As is clear in Figure 9–13, global production of both commodities has increased as a result of the kind of resource allocation that would occur as a result of trade. So unlike the situation in a closed economy where something must be forgone in order to increase output of something else, in an open economy the possibility of a "win-win" situation is a certainty. This is the reason that virtually all economists embrace free trade.

By now the astute reader is probably asking, "If free trade is such a good deal, why doesn't everybody embrace it?" The easy answer is that while trade will always make society *as a whole* better off, there will be winners and losers within the total society. To see this dichotomy, return to the trade example in Figure 9–13. Look at the impacts of this reallocation on producers and consumers in the United States. If trade is opened with the United Kingdom, then relatively cheap cloth will come into

---

[14] This is an appropriate time to revisit the zero-sum game fallacy discussed in Chapter 2.

FIGURE 9–14
Winners and losers in the United States with open markets.

the U.S. cloth market. American consumers will be happy because they are getting more cloth at a lower price. But U.S. cloth producers will be unhappy because they will be producing less cloth and receiving a lower price for what they do produce. Layoffs and idle resources in the U.S. cloth industry will be grave concerns for producers of cloth. If those resources can be reallocated easily, then there won't be too much grief over the reallocation, but in most cases it is very difficult to convert capital and labor from one employment to another.

In the wheat market, U.S. wheat producers will be delighted to export to the United Kingdom because it means that they are producing more wheat at higher prices than in the no-trade situation. However, American wheat consumers are unhappy because prices are higher than they were in the no-trade situation and a lesser quantity is available for domestic consumption.

So while trade is a win-win situation from the perspective of the society *as a whole* in both countries, it is a win-lose situation from the point of view of producers and consumers of each good within each country. The winners and losers in the United States from trade with the United Kingdom are summarized in Figure 9–14. The reactions to the prospect of trade are always the same: producers of goods being exported are happy, producers of goods being imported are unhappy, consumers of goods that are imported are happy, and consumers of goods that are being exported are unhappy.

While the U.S. consumer of wheat is made worse off by free trade with the United Kingdom, the pain is so small and spread across so many consumers that it is almost imperceptible. And even if the consumer notes that the price of a loaf of bread has gone up by a penny or two, the consumer is not driven to find a political remedy to this economic reality. However, the textile mill owners and workers who see their fortunes and jobs disappearing as cheap cloth from the United Kingdom enters the United States are going to be enraged. Usually this rage will manifest itself in a call for a political remedy to what is perceived as unfair foreign competition. The most common political solution to this problem is a restraint on trade. Free trade is great so long as you are not the one adversely affected by it.

RESTRAINTS TO TRADE

As shown in the previous section, free international (or interregional) trade will be beneficial, in the aggregate, to citizens in both of the trading countries. By shifting the production of each good to the country that is more efficient, the total output of both goods increases and the total amount of consumption in both of the countries increases. In theory, more consumers are made better off by trade than are made worse off. But in the real world, we often find that trade among nations is restricted by tariffs, quotas, or other barriers. A tariff is a tax imposed by the importing country that is levied at the point of entry. A quota is a quantitative limitation of the quantity of a good that may be imported per unit of time. Such restraints to trade are usually imposed by the importing country in order to protect entrenched domestic factors of production from foreign competition.

Tariffs

Ad valorem tariff a tariff that is calculated as a percentage of the value of the imported good.

Specific tariff a tariff that is a fixed amount per unit of the good, regardless of the value of the good.

A tariff is a tax or surcharge levied on an imported good. Tariffs may be either **"ad valorem,"** which means the tariff is computed at a fixed rate per dollar of imported value, or **"specific,"** which means the tariff amount is quoted as so many dollars per unit of the imported good. The main justification for imposing tariffs today is to reduce foreign competition in order to protect domestic producers. Tariffs are also a revenue source for the government imposing the tariff. Today tariffs are important tax sources in many smaller developing countries, but they are relatively insignificant, as a revenue source, in the United States.[15]

The impact of a tariff can be illustrated using the two-country, one-good model introduced earlier. The curves labeled export supply and import demand in Figure 9–15 illustrate the situation on the world market in the absence of a tariff. In this example, the world market clears at a price of $20 with 50 units being traded.[16] The quantity exported is just equal to the quantity imported, and the world market is cleared. The markets in each country also clear at the world price. In the exporting country, domestic production at a price of $20 is equal to the quantity consumed domestically plus exports. In the importing country, domestic consumption at a price of $20 is equal to the quantity produced domestically plus imports.

This trade will be viewed favorably by producers in the exporting country (higher prices, more output) and consumers in the importing country (lower prices, more consumption). Their gains will be offset by those groups that are affected adversely by the trade: consumers in the exporting country (higher prices, lower consumption) and producers in the importing country (lower prices, less production). It is this latter group that invariably argues most vociferously in favor of imposing tariffs to protect domestic jobs.

Assume that the importing country imposes a specific tariff of $10 per unit. The effect of the tariff is to shift upward the world market export supply curve *as viewed by the importing country.* This occurs because, from the viewpoint of consumers in the importing country, each unit offered for sale on the world market has increased in price by $10. The world market export supply curve *as viewed by the exporting country* is unaffected by the tariff since its producers are still willing to produce the same quantity at each and every price offered. In this example, the exporting country is still willing to export 50 units at $20 per unit. But when those 50 units arrive at the port of entry of the importing country, a $10 per unit tax will be added. Now the 50 units are valued at $30 per unit within the importing country. But at a price of $30 per unit, the quantity demanded by consumers in the importing country is zero, so a market disequilibrium occurs at the pretariff equilibrium price/quantity combination.

When the export supply curve (as perceived by the importing country) shifts upward, the intersection of the import demand and the export supply plus

---

[15] In the early days of the U.S. government, its two main sources of revenue were tariffs and profits from the Post Office.

[16] Transportation charges and other transaction costs continue to be ignored in this illustration.

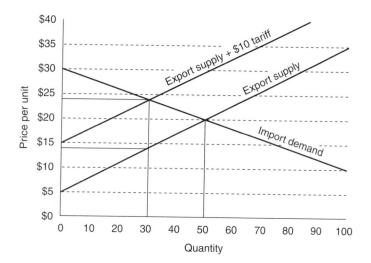

FIGURE 9–15 Impact of imposing a specific tariff of $10/unit.

tariff occurs at a higher price and lower volume than for the equilibrium without the tariff. After the tariff, consumers in the importing country will pay $24 per unit, and imports have been reduced to only 30 units. Because of the $4 increase in the internal price, domestic producers in the importing country increase production and consumers reduce the quantity demanded such that the internal market in the importing country is in equilibrium. The increase in domestic production and the reduction in the quantity of imports are the desired effects of the tariff.

With the $10 tariff and a $24 imported price, the producers in the exporting country must be receiving only $14 per unit. This is the price that corresponds to an export volume of 30 units on the world market export supply curve without the tariff, which is the relevant export supply curve for the exporting country. At a domestic price of $14 in the exporting country its internal market also clears, resulting from a combination of an increase in domestic consumption (because of a decline in the internal price) and a decrease in domestic production.

The net effect of the tariff is to cause a divergence between the market prices in the importing and exporting countries. With completely free trade, the price in the two markets was exactly the same at $20. The tariff allows trade to occur, but maintains the price differential between the two countries at a level equal to the amount of the tariff. If the tariff in this example had been $25 per unit or more, the effect of the tariff would be to completely discourage any trade because the tariff is greater than the price differential without trade.[17] At any tariff less than $25, there will be an incentive for some trade between the two countries.

An appropriate question to raise at this point is, Who pays the tariff? At first, it would seem reasonable to say consumers in the importing country pay the tariff since the $10 tariff is added to the world price by the importing country. This is an

---

[17] The no-trade domestic equilibrium price in the importing country is $30 per unit and is shown as the intersection of the import demand curve and the vertical axis. That is, without trade the domestic market is clearing at $30, and therefore the import demand is zero. At any price less than $30 there is a nonzero import demand. Likewise, in the exporting country the domestic equilibrium price is $5 per unit, and at any price above $5 there is an exportable supply. The difference between these two no-trade equilibria is $25.

FIGURE 9–16
Comparison of specific
and ad valorem tariffs.

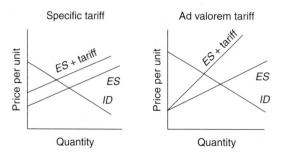

oversimplification, for trade restrictions affect both importers and exporters. Notice that the price the consumer in the importing country paid in Figure 9–15 was only $4 higher than the $20 price that would have prevailed with completely free trade. The other $6 of the tariff is "paid" by producers in the exporting country who, as a natural consequence of competition, lower their prices as they each fight to maintain their share of a smaller export market. That is, a tariff causes a reduction in total volume traded on world markets, causing a domestic surplus in the exporting country. In time, this surplus will result in a reduction of domestic production and a reduction in the export price as less efficient producers are driven out of business. Thus, the burden of a tariff is shared by consumers in the importing country and producers in the exporting country. The share that each will bear is dependent on the elasticity of the domestic supply and demand curves in each country.

The example in Figure 9–15 illustrates the impact of a specific tariff of $10 per unit on some good. The imposition of an ad valorem tariff would have similar effects. The only difference is that with an ad valorem tariff the shift in the export supply curve with tariff would be proportional rather than equidistant. The two cases are illustrated in Figure 9–16. The impact of a tariff in either case is similar, as is the distribution of the burdens between the two countries.

Quotas

Quota limitation on
the quantity of a good
that may be imported
per unit of time.

A **quota** is a restriction on the quantity of a good that is allowed to be imported during a given period of time. Like other trade restrictions, the purpose of a quota is to protect domestic resources from foreign competition. The most important quota from the point of view of American agriculture is a red meat import quota that is designed to protect American producers of beef, mutton, and pork from imports originating in countries with lower costs of production—particularly Australia and New Zealand.[18] The United States also has a very strong quota on sugar.[19]

Figure 9–17 shows how a quota on U.S. meat imports affects both Australia (the exporter) and the United States. Without any trade restrictions, the world price would be P_W and the quantity traded on world markets would be F. For political

---

[18] Meat imports are prohibited from those countries where hoof-and-mouth disease exists. This nontariff trade barrier (NTB in the State Department lingo) is for herd health maintenance, and it effectively prohibits imports from most of Latin America.

[19] The sugar quota is designed to protect domestic sugar producers in the United States. Because of the quota, raw sugar prices in the United States are about three times the world price. Makers of hard candy have reacted to the U.S. sugar quota in a rational manner—they have moved their plants to Mexico where they can buy cheap Mexican sugar for their candy. There are no trade restrictions on candy entering the United States so the sugar (in the form of candy) enters the United States freely.

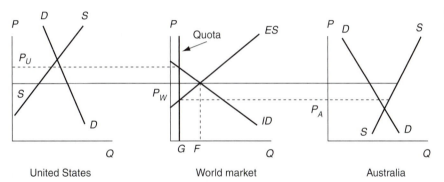

FIGURE 9–17 Impact of a quota.

reasons, F units of imported meat are considered to be excessive, so Congress passes a law establishing a quota and gives the Secretary of Agriculture authority to administer the program. After much evaluation, the secretary determines that imports should be limited to G units per year. With only G units being imported, the price that consumers are willing to pay for the imports in the United States will increase to P_U and the price that Australian producers will receive will fall to P_A.

The similarity of the quota and tariff should be clear. Both create a two-price market. Tariffs work through the price side of the world market, while quotas are implemented on the quantity side. In the case of a tariff, the difference between the export and import prices is the tariff itself. But in the case of a quota, who gets that price differential? In the absence of any other controls, the importer, who is fortunate enough to ship meat before the quota is filled, would receive a windfall profit equal to the difference in prices $(P_U - P_A)$ times the quantity imported (G). Since the windfall profit would be available to any importer that came in under the wire, there would be a wild rush to import until the quota is filled.

To avoid this problem, a quota is usually implemented through a system of import permits that are sold by the government to the highest bidder at a free auction. The highest bidding importers will be willing to pay $P_U - P_A$ for the import permits. In this manner, the windfall is returned to the government in the form of permit fees. Thus, for a quota, as was the case for tariffs, the government creates and collects the price differential associated with a trade restraint.

Restrict Domestic Demand

A third trade restraint policy is to introduce programs to restrict domestic demand for the imported product. Presumably, if domestic demand for the imported good can be restrained, then imports of the good will fall.

An example of a demand restricting policy is the so-called gas guzzler tax Congress imposed some years ago on cars that get low gas mileage. The idea is that by taxing low mileage cars, the consumer will be enticed to buy high mileage cars and will thereby consume less gasoline, and the United States will have to import less crude oil than would be the case without the tax. The economics of such a policy is illustrated in Figure 9–18, in which ID refers to the import demand before the tax is imposed. The United States is importing quantity Q_0 of crude oil at a price of Q_0. Imposing the gas guzzler tax causes an inward shift of the import demand curve to ID' as consumers want less gas at every price for gas. As a result of the inward shift of the import demand curve, the policy objective of reducing imports is achieved as the quantity imported falls to Q_1.

FIGURE 9–18
Restrict domestic
demand.

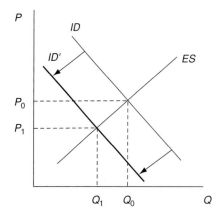

In addition to achieving the desired policy objective, a demand restriction policy also has the salubrious result that the price of imports falls from P_0 to P_1. So, unlike tariffs and quotas that result in higher domestic prices, a demand restriction results in lower domestic prices. With both the quantity of imports and the price of imports reduced, spending by domestic consumers is greatly reduced.

FOREIGN EXCHANGE MARKETS

Every physical trade generates an equal, but opposite, flow of money to pay for the goods. When a Japanese car is imported into the United States, dollars flow from the United States to Japan. Or when wheat is exported to Japan, yen are received in the United States as payment for the wheat. The American exporter really doesn't want the yen, nor does the Japanese auto exporter want dollars. Therefore, each of these exporters will take the **foreign exchange** they received to their respective banks for conversion into domestic currencies. The U.S. and the Japanese banks will then get together and swap the foreign exchange such that dollars return to the United States and yen return to Japan. The determination of the terms of trade for this swap is established in what is known as the **foreign exchange market.** This market is no different than the market for dog food in terms of how it operates. What is unique is that the commodity being traded is the currency of a country rather than Fido's reward for faithful guard duty and lots of naps.

An example of a foreign exchange market is shown in Figure 9–19. In this case, we are looking at the market for U.S. dollars in Japan. Dollars and dog food have a lot in common in Japan: both have recognized value, yet neither is readily accepted as a means of payment.[20] The demand for dollars in Japan comes from Japanese wheat importers who need dollars to purchase wheat from American exporters. This demand curve is downward sloping because as the yen price of the dollar declines, the yen price of American wheat also declines and more wheat will be demanded. For example, if wheat imported to Japan costs $3 per bushel and each dollar costs 150 yen, then the price of American wheat to the Japanese consumer is 450 yen. If the price of the dollar should fall to 100 yen/$, *ceteris paribus,*

Foreign exchange
currency of another
country. In Japan,
dollars are foreign
exchange.

**Foreign exchange
market**   market on
which foreign curren-
cies are traded.

---

[20] Take special note of how the axes are labeled in Figure 9–19. If we were to analyze the market for dog food in Japan, the vertical axis would measure the price as yen per pound of dog food, and the horizontal axis would measure quantity as pounds of dog food per unit of time. Instead of dog food, we are looking at the market for dollars in Japan. Hence, the vertical price axis measures yen per dollar—the price of a dollar in Japan.

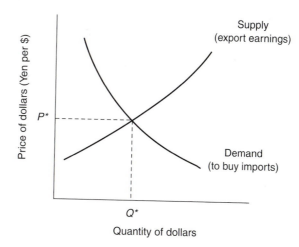

FIGURE 9-19 Market for U.S. dollars in Japan.

then the price of wheat to the consumer would decline to 300 yen and the quantity of wheat demanded would increase. With more wheat demanded at a constant dollar price for the wheat, more dollars will be demanded. Conversely, if the price of the dollar, measured in yen per dollar, increases, then fewer dollars will be demanded in Japan.

The supply of dollars in Japan is created by Americans making dollar payments for Japanese exports to the United States. It is upward sloping because when the price of the dollar measured in yen is low, it takes a large number of dollars to buy Japanese products. From the point of view of American consumers, imports from Japan are expensive, so trade volume is low and the inflow of dollars to Japan (the quantity supplied) is low. As the yen price of the dollar increases, Japanese goods become cheaper to American consumers and the quantity of dollars flowing into Japan will increase. For example, a pocket radio that costs 1,500 yen in Japan will sell for $15 in the United States (ignoring transportation costs) if the price of the dollar in Japan is 100 yen per dollar. If the price of the dollar in Japan were to increase to 150 yen per dollar, the same radio would now cost $10 in the United States. Since more radios would be demanded by American consumers at the lower dollar price, the quantity of dollars flowing to Japan would increase.[21]

As is the case in any market, the market for U.S. dollars in Japan will establish an equilibrium price (measured in yen per dollar) that will just balance the quantity of dollars demanded with the quantity supplied per unit of time. An equilibrium price in a foreign exchange market is called an **exchange rate.** The exchange rate for dollars in Tokyo (yen per dollar) depends on the quantity of dollars demanded and supplied at any given moment. There is also a market for yen in New York City that will determine the exchange rate for yen measured in dollars per yen. If, at a given moment, the dollar per yen price in New York is not a perfect reciprocal of the yen per dollar price in Tokyo, then dealers (called arbitragers) will simultaneously buy in the low-priced market and sell in the high-priced market.

Exchange rate
equilibrium price on a foreign exchange market.

---

[21] If American consumers were not very price responsive, it is possible that they would continue to purchase the same number of radios at the lower dollar price. If that were the case, then the total number of dollars supplied to Japan would decrease when the yen price of the dollar increased. While it is not common to find instances in which the supply of foreign exchange has a negatively sloped curve, the supply of U.S. dollars to petroleum exporting countries may well be an exception.

FIGURE 9–20 Supply shift in foreign exchange market.

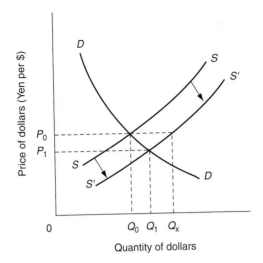

The buying activity in the low-priced market will drive the price up, and the selling activity in the high-priced market will drive the price down until an equilibrium exchange rate between markets is achieved. Since trading occurs continuously, foreign exchange markets are very dynamic with frequent, but usually small, changes in exchange rates from hour to hour as traders attempt to keep one step ahead of the developments affecting foreign exchange markets.

If Japan exports more to the United States than it imports from the United States, there will develop a surplus of dollars in Japan at the existing exchange rate. As this surplus of dollars grows, there will be pressure for the price of the dollar to fall. This is shown in Figure 9–20, which is similar to Figure 9–19 except there has been a change in some *ceteris paribus* condition that caused an outward shift in the supply of dollars in Japan.[22] Before the shift the equilibrium exchange rate was P_0. If the exchange rate remains at P_0 after the supply shifts outward to S', there will be a surplus of dollars in each time period equal to the distance of Q_0Q_x. If these surpluses continue to mount in Japanese banks, the yen price for dollars will eventually decline until a new equilibrium is reached at a price of P_1.

At the new equilibrium price of P_1 the quantity of dollars entering Japan in payment for Japanese exports has increased from Q_0 to Q_1. There are two forces at work here. If American consumers continued to buy the same number of cars at P_1 as they did at P_0, then the quantity of dollars supplied would be Q_x, because more dollars are required to buy the same quantity of yen to buy the car. From the American perspective the price of Japanese cars measured in dollars has gone up, so the number of cars sold will go down with a final result of Q_1 dollars entering the Japanese market at P_1.

At the new equilibrium exchange rate of P_1 the quantity of dollars demanded in Japan has also increased from Q_0 to Q_1. This occurs because from the point of view of the Japanese consumer, American imports are cheaper, since at P_1 the Japanese consumer has to pay fewer yen to purchase each dollar. Hence, goods for which the dollar price is constant will have lower yen prices in Japan than before, and a greater quantity of dollars will be demanded.

---

[22] This shift might have been caused by a change in consumers' preferences in the luxury car market away from Mercedes and Porsche to Lexus and Infiniti models.

In the previous example, the **depreciation** of the dollar from P_0 to P_1 has the dual effect of discouraging Japanese exports to the United States and encouraging Japanese imports from the United States. The interaction of these two pressures will establish a new equilibrium between the quantity of dollars demanded and supplied in the Japanese market at a lower exchange rate. Therefore, over time exchange rate adjustments will ensure that the value of exports and imports of any given country is maintained in approximate balance. In other words, exchange rate adjustments will eventually correct a persistent trade imbalance.

Adjustments of exchange rates because of trade imbalances are not instantaneous because it takes time for market pressures to build up to the point where exchange rates change and because governments frequently intervene in foreign exchange markets in an effort to maintain exchange rates above equilibrium rates in order to encourage exports and discourage imports. For example, in Figure 9–20, the internal politics of Japan would prefer to maintain P_0 after the shift to S', since at this exchange rate exports (i.e., domestic employment) are higher than would be the case at P_1. And at P_0 imports (i.e., foreign competition) are lower than they would be at P_1. The only problem with maintaining the exchange rate at P_0 is that the government must intervene to absorb Q_0Q_x dollars per unit of time. A policy to maintain exchange rates at artificially high levels is called "**overvaluation**" of the currency. In Figure 9–20 the dollar is overvalued at price P_0. That is, the number of yen necessary to purchase a dollar is greater than what the market would indicate its price should be. The dollar is overvalued or priced too high in light of the existing supply and demand situation.

Overvaluation of the dollar was a very serious problem in the late 1960s and early 1970s. For a number of reasons the dollar was seriously overvalued relative to the currencies of most of the United States' major industrial trading partners. The overvaluation of the dollar discouraged exports from the United States and encouraged imports into the United States, causing a persistent trade imbalance. This trade imbalance led to the massive accumulation of dollars by our trading partners. Prior to 1971, a policy of relatively fixed exchange rates was in existence, so the exchange rates between the United States and other currencies did not adjust to clear the foreign exchange markets that had become clogged with excessive dollars. Finally, in 1971 and again in 1973, President Richard Nixon moved to **devalue** the dollar relative to other currencies by allowing the price of the dollar to be freely determined on world foreign exchange markets. The effect of the devaluations was to reduce the cost of the dollar to foreigners (a move from P_0 to P_1 in Figure 9–20 represents a devaluation of the dollar) and to increase the dollar cost of imports into the United States. Within the United States both of these changes are viewed positively since they both serve to stimulate the domestic economy. Both of these changes are viewed negatively by our trading partners for just the opposite reasons.

The impact of the 1971 and 1973 devaluations of the U.S. dollar on relative prices in Japan and the United States is illustrated in Figure 9–21. As the dollar depreciated against the yen, the price of a dollar in Japan fell from 358 yen per dollar in 1969 to only 80 yen per dollar in 1994. Since 1994, the dollar has **appreciated** against the yen by more than 60 percent to a level around 130 yen/dollar. If the price of a bushel of wheat in the United States remained constant over this time at $3/bushel, then the cost to the Japanese consumer of American wheat (assuming free trade and no transportation costs) fell from 1,075 yen in 1969 to only 242 yen in 1994. Consequently, the quantity of wheat demanded by Japanese consumers has increased, resulting in increased exports for

Depreciation a decline in the value of a country's currency relative to the currency of another country.

Overvaluation effort to maintain the exchange rate of a currency at a level higher than the free market exchange rate.

Devalue a change in the official value of one currency relative to another or allowing market forces to decrease the exchange rate.

Appreciation an increase in the value of a country's currency relative to the currency of another country. If A appreciates relative to B, then B depreciates relative to A.

	Year					
	1969	1974	1979	1984	1994	2002
Exchange rates:						
$/yen	$0.0028	$0.0034	$0.0045	$0.0042	$0.0124	$0.0077
yen/$	¥358.38	¥291.53	¥221.24	¥237.46	¥80.63	¥130.00
Price of U.S. wheat						
$/bushel	$3.00	$3.00	$3.00	$3.00	$3.00	$3.00
yen/bushel	¥1,075	¥875	¥664	¥712	¥242	¥390
Price of Japanese car						
yen/car	¥1.32m	¥1.32m	¥1.32m	¥1.32m	¥1.32m	¥1.32m
$/car	$3,683	$4,528	$5,966	$5,559	$16,371	$10,154

FIGURE 9–21   Effect of dollar devaluations assuming constant internal prices.

the United States.[23] Since 1994, with the appreciation of the dollar the price of wheat has increased to 390 yen and the quantity of wheat that would be exported to Japan has declined.

However, the devaluation of the dollar caused the price of yen (measured in dollars per yen) to increase, thus driving up the dollar price of Japanese goods. If internal car prices in Japan had remained stable over the past 30 years at 1.32 million yen per car, then the cost to the American consumer would have increased from approximately $3,700 in 1969 to nearly $16,400 in 1994. As the dollar price of Japanese cars increases because of the depreciation of the dollar, American-made automobiles should be able to regain a competitive price advantage. For instance, in the 1960s one reason many Americans purchased Volkswagens was because they were cheaper than domestically produced automobiles. But as the dollar depreciated against the German mark, Volkswagens became relatively more expensive to the point where today the basic VW models sell at a substantial premium to comparable domestic automobiles. In fact, the price disadvantage of German-manufactured Volkswagens became so serious that VW was forced to open a production assembly plant in the United States to reduce the proportion of the total cost of the car that must be paid in German marks. Stated more bluntly, before the devaluations of the dollar, the dollar cost of German labor was well below that of American labor because the dollar price of the German mark was so low. But today, the dollar cost of German labor is greater than the dollar cost of U.S. labor. So Volkswagen, operating in its own self-interest, moved its production facilities to that country with the relatively cheap labor—the United States.

---

[23] This result is valid only in the theoretical, and necessarily limited, world of comparative statistics. Secondary effects of the primary change are often important. The increased demand for American wheat by Japanese consumers would certainly be translated into higher domestic (i.e., dollar) prices for wheat to the benefit of American wheat farmers. Changes in the wheat market also cause adjustments in other markets. As U.S. wheat became relatively less expensive than Japanese rice, an exportable surplus of Japanese rice developed. Action by the Japanese government to protect relatively high domestic rice prices enlarged this exportable surplus. Japanese rice subsequently became a strong competitor for U.S. rice in certain Asian markets—a fact that is from time to time forcibly called to the attention of at least one of the authors by domestic rice producers.

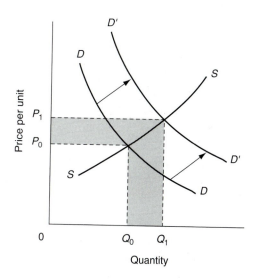

FIGURE 9–22 Effect of dollar devaluation on U.S. agricultural sector.

The devaluation of the dollar has been of particular importance to the agricultural sector of the U.S. economy because a significant portion—more than one-fourth in 2002—of all U.S. agricultural production is eventually exported. When the overvalued dollar was devalued, American agricultural exports became cheaper from the point of view of potential importers, even though the internal or domestic prices of U.S. agricultural products did not change. As shown in Figure 9–22, the devaluation of the dollar causes an outward shift in the total (domestic plus foreign) demand for agricultural commodities in the United States because there is an increase in the quantity demanded by foreigners at each and every dollar price. This occurs because, from the point of view of foreign importers, it is necessary to buy dollars first and then use these dollars to buy wheat or other agricultural exports. If the price of wheat remains the same but the price of the dollar falls, then the price of the wheat to the importer has fallen. Of course, the price of wheat in dollars will also increase because of the demand shift in the domestic market shown in Figure 9–22.

The effect of additional export demand on the American farm sector is to increase prices received by farmers (because of the demand shift) and to increase the quantity clearing the market. What more could farmers want? After a devaluation they will sell more at a higher dollar price. As a consequence, gross receipts of farmers increased from $P_0 \cdot Q_0$ to $P_1 \cdot Q_1$, an increase shown by the shaded area in Figure 9–22. It's no wonder that in 1973, following the second devaluation of the dollar, the per capita disposable income of the farm population surpassed that of the non-farm population for the first time in recent history. During the late 1970s and early 1980s this trend reversed itself, and the dollar strengthened against most other currencies. The appreciating, stronger dollar was one of the fundamental causes of the farm sector depression that hit in the early 1980s and carried through to the late 1980s. From 1985 to 1994 the dollar depreciated substantially against the Japanese yen and to a lesser extent against most other currencies, and farm income (measured in dollars) rose. Since 1994 the dollar has appreciated relative to the Canadian dollar (our largest trading partner in terms of export value) and the Japanese yen. For other currencies changes since 1994 have been relatively modest. As a result, expanding export markets have not driven agricultural income higher in the United States, and in some years export earnings have fallen substantially.

Trade Agreements

The trade history of the past century can be divided into two broad epochs, with the Second World War as a dividing line. The first half of the century saw increasing isolationism in the form of higher and higher trade barriers, and the second half saw trade liberalization with lower and lower trade barriers. The primary instrument of trade liberalization has been the General Agreement on Tariffs and Trade.

General Agreement on Tariffs and Trade

General Agreement on Tariffs and Trade (GATT) a multilateral trade agreement among most major countries that establishes the rules for fair trade and calls for the mutual reduction of trade barriers such as tariffs.

In 1947 representatives from many of the leading nations of the world completed a multilateral trade agreement known as the **General Agreement on Tariffs and Trade,** or **GATT.** This agreement established rules for fair trade among the signatories and called for mutual reductions in tariffs. Since then additional "rounds" of discussions have resulted in additional treaties liberalizing trade incrementally.

The latest round, which was completed in 1994, was known as the Uruguay Round. This round was very important for several reasons. First, trade in agriculture, services, and intellectual property were included in the agreement for the first time. Agricultural trade was, and continues to be, a very contentious issue. Second, the name of the organization was changed from GATT to the **World Trade Organization,** or **WTO.** The name change was primarily cosmetic. Third, trade dispute resolution was turned over to a panel of independent judges, who have the final say in trade disputes.

World Trade Organization (WTO) current version of GATT, which includes trade in agriculture, services, and intellectual property.

The next round of WTO negotiations were scheduled to begin with an agenda-setting meeting of world leaders in Seattle in 1999. Protestors, primarily opposed to globalization and its environmental impact, turned the Seattle meeting into a circus and no initial agreement on the agenda was reached. There was a second, equally disruptive attempt to establish an agenda in 2000. Finally, in the small Arab Gulf state of Qatar (which was closed to protestors), an agenda for the next round was agreed to in the fall of 2001. The last two rounds lasted 7 and 8 years, so it may be a while before a new agreement is signed.

North American Free Trade Agreement

North American Free Trade Agreement (NAFTA) agreement among Canada, the United States, and Mexico that will eventually lead to a free market in North America with no trade barriers.

In 1993 Canada, the United States, and Mexico signed the trilateral **North American Free Trade Agreement,** or **NAFTA.** Under the terms of this treaty, trade barriers among the three countries will be reduced over a period of 15 years until all barriers are eliminated. At that time, the three countries will become a free trade zone, and trade with Mexico or Canada should be no different than trade between North and South Dakota.

NAFTA was, and continues to be, hotly debated. As with any change in trade patterns there are sure to be some individual winners and losers. Corn and livestock producers in the United States view the Mexican market for their products as one with great promise. Fruit and vegetable producers in the United States view Mexican producers as low-cost competitors who do not have to match the labor and environmental standards of the United States. A recent evaluation of the impact of NAFTA in *Business Week* magazine concludes that "so far, NAFTA's record is a good one."[24]

---

[24] *Business Week,* July 9, 2001, p. 56.

Free Trade Area of the Americas

In the first major international policy initiative of his young presidency, President George W. Bush proposed the creation of a free trade area for all of the Americas with the exception of Cuba. The basic idea was to expand NAFTA to embrace all of the nations of Central and South America. Some have suggested that a first step in this process would be to include Chile in NAFTA. Since Brazil and Argentina are competitors with the United States in many agricultural export markets (particularly soybeans), it may be very difficult to develop a free trade area. But at least the proposal is on the table.

SUMMARY

International trade is becoming increasingly important for the American economy in general and for agriculture in particular. Although the agricultural sector consistently generates trade surpluses, the rest of the economy produces chronic trade deficits that have made the United States the largest debtor nation in the world.

The most important agricultural exports are wheat, corn, and soybeans. The United States is the world's largest exporter for each of these crops. It is estimated that about two-fifths of all cropland in the United States is used to produce crops that are eventually exported. About one-fourth of agricultural imports are non-competitive commodities like bananas, coffee, and spices. Many of the competitive imports are specialty products like cheeses and wines, where the commodity is competitive but the specific brand or product imported may be unique.

Free trade allows each country to specialize in the production of what its resources can produce relatively efficiently. This specialization allows more "stuff" to be produced globally than would be produced if there were no trade. Hence, trade is always net beneficial from a global perspective. However, there are both winners and losers as a result of trade. The losers are domestic producers who are not as efficient as foreign producers and see low-cost imports hurting their domestic market. Such producers frequently seek protection from foreign competition in the form of a tariff (import tax) or a quota (quantitative limit on imports). Both a tariff and a quota have the effect of driving up the price the importing consumer pays above what the exporting producer receives.

Markets for foreign exchange establish equilibrium prices for currency called exchange rates. Normal pressures of supply and demand cause exchange rates to vary. If the home currency commands fewer units of foreign currency, we say the home currency has depreciated. The depreciation of one currency can also be viewed as an appreciation of the other currency. Relative to the currencies of most of our major trading partners, the dollar has depreciated over the past 15 years.

The United States is part of two important trade agreements: one old and one new. The World Trade Organization (formerly the General Agreement on Tariffs and Trade) was created after World War II to establish fair trade rules and mutual agreements to lower tariffs. The most recent WTO agreement included agricultural products for the first time. The North American Free Trade Agreement (NAFTA) is a 1993 trilateral agreement with Canada and Mexico that will create a free trade zone among the three countries within 15 years.

KEY TERMS

Ad valorem tariff
Appreciation
Commodities
Competitive imports
Creditor
Debtor
Depreciation
Devalue
Efficiency
Exchange rate
Export supply
External deficit
Feed grains
Food grains
Foreign exchange

Foreign exchange market
General Agreement on Tariffs and Trade
Import demand
Joint products
Noncompetitive import
North American Free Trade Agreement
Nutriceuticals
Oilseeds
Overvaluation
Products
Quota
Specific tariff
Tariff
Trade balance
World Trade Organization

PROBLEMS AND DISCUSSION QUESTIONS

1. Shown below are the domestic supply and demand situations in two
   countries: Highland and Lowland. Accurately draw the appropriate export
   supply and import demand curves for the world market. Label the curves you
   have drawn, and identify the world price of the good if free trade is allowed.

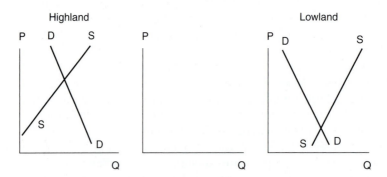

2. Based on the information in the table below, what is the domestic (i.e.,
   dollar) price of wheat in the United States in 1998 and 1999? (Assume no
   transport costs, tariffs, and so on).

	Peso Price of Wheat in Peru	Exchange Rate of Peruvian Peso ($/P)
1998	6.00	0.50
1999	6.50	0.60

3. The diagram to the right shows a free trade world market. On the diagram show the changes that would occur if the importing country imposed a tariff. On the diagram clearly identify the posttariff price paid by consumers in the importing country as P_c and the price received by producers in the exporting country as P_p. Show the posttariff quantity traded as Q_t.

4. The pound (£) and the mark (DM) are the currencies of England and Germany, respectively. On January 1, 1995, a German investor withdrew DM10,000 from his account and bought British pounds, which he then deposited in a London account that earns 7 percent per annum (simple interest, payable annually). On January 1, 1996, he withdrew all the pounds that had accumulated and converted them back to German marks. How many marks did he receive? The relevant exchange rates are:

| January 1, 1995 | DM 2.10/£ |
| January 1, 1996 | DM 2.30/£ |

Answer: _____

5. Discuss the following proposition: Textile mills used to generate thousands of jobs in the southeastern part of the United States, but import competition has caused most of the mills to shut down. Therefore, the U.S. government should impose high tariffs on textile imports.

6. The United States is the leading world exporter of which major agricultural crops?

7. What are the three major portions of the balance of payments, and what is the relationship among the three?

8. For the past 15 years the United States has had a deficit on the current account of the balance of payments. How is this deficit financed?

9. NAFTA is a process of creating free trade among the United States, Canada, and Mexico. In your state or province, what economic groups are the expected "winners" and "losers" from the prospect of this free trade?

APPENDIX

BALANCE OF PAYMENTS

It has been shown that each country (or region) engaged in trade will improve the aggregate well-being of its citizens as a result of free trade. Early economists tried to devise schemes to capture all the gains from trade for their countries. Such efforts ended in dismal failure because the gains from trade can be realized only when each country simultaneously exports and imports. In essence, exports are necessary to finance imports.

What is commonly called the **balance of payments** is a system of accounts in which all transactions of producers and consumers in one country with the producers and consumers of other countries are summarized. This system of accounts is called a "balance" because the bottom line is always zero. A very simple balance of payments is shown in Figure 9–23.

The balance of payments has three parts: the current account, the capital account, and official reserves. The current account shows trade in goods and services and transfers. In balance of payments accounting, exports are always treated as a positive entry (since money flows in) and imports as a negative entry. The balance on the current account shows the net trade position of the country.

What would happen if the United States exported more than it imported during some period of time? In this case, the export earnings would be more than adequate to pay for import needs, and a portion of the foreign exchange (i.e., foreign currency) earned from exports would accumulate in the United States. This accumulation is called a **surplus on the balance of payments.** A country that imports more than it exports is said to run a **deficit on its balance of payments.** The negative value of the current account balance in Figure 9–23 means the United States ran a deficit of $445 billion in 2000.

FIGURE 9–23
Simplified U.S. balance of payments, 2000 ($ billions).

Current account		
Exports of goods and services	+ 1,065	
Imports of goods and services	− 1,441	
Balance on goods and services		− 376
Net investment income	− 15	
Net unilateral transfers	− 54	
Balance on current account		− 445
Capital account		
U.S. assets abroad	− 581	
Foreign assets in U.S.	+ 987	
Balance on capital account		+ 406
Balance on current and capital accounts		− 39
Official reserves	+ 37	
Statistical discrepancy	+ 2	
Balance of payments		0

Source: Bureau of Economic Analysis, **www.bea.gov.**

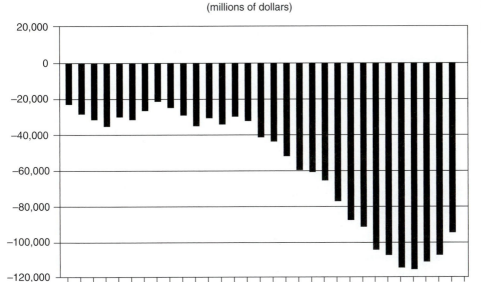

Balance on current account
(millions of dollars)

FIGURE 9–24
Bureau of economic
analysis data from the
balance of payments
accounts.
Source: Bureau of
Economic Analysis.

For a variety of reasons not the least of which is our unquenchable thirst for petroleum, the U.S. balance of payments has been consistently and massively negative—that is, in deficit—for nearly two decades. The recent trend is shown in Figure 9–24. A deficit is financed by either reducing our holdings of foreign currency (official reserves) in an amount equivalent to the deficit or increasing our indebtedness to other countries: As was pointed out earlier, we have taken the latter approach, becoming the largest debtor nation in the world. The massive borrowing necessary to pay for our trade deficit is shown in the balance on the capital account with net foreign assets in the United States (IOUs) sufficient to cover the trade deficit. So, at the present time, a current account deficit is being financed by a capital account surplus.

The deficit that the United States has run on its balance of payments since 1982 means that dollar payments by U.S. consumers to foreign producers have been much greater than receipts of American producers from foreign consumers.

Put quite simply, dollars flowed out of the United States faster than they were flowing back in. As shown in Figure 9–24, our current account deficits have become chronic and seem to be getting bigger. Each quarter in which we have a deficit means that the amount of our international debt is increased. To date, none of our trading partners have suggested that we have reached our credit limit, so the spending continues unabated.

KEY TERMS

Balance of payments
Deficit on balance of payments
Surplus on balance of payments

10 *Agricultural Policy*

*A*gricultural policy may be viewed as a two-stage process. The first stage is a discussion of what ought to be. This is the process of identifying the goals of the policy-making process. The second stage is an examination of how to use the powers of governments and markets to achieve the objectives identified. Most discussions about what ought to be naturally occur within the political process and are a reflection of the perceived problems of the time. The Boston Tea Party, the whiskey rebellion, and John Brown's raid of the Harpers Ferry arsenal are examples of these national discussions moving beyond mere words. The transcontinental railroad and the numerous homestead acts are examples of implemented agricultural policies using the power of government to achieve a national objective. The Civil War was fought over an agricultural policy issue: Should a system of agricultural production based on human slavery be allowed to continue?[1]

There are two reasons agricultural policy issues are so potent. First, policy issues inherently deal with what ought to be rather than what is. The framers of the Constitution were divided between the interests of the merchants from Massachusetts (John Adams) and the planters from Virginia (Thomas Jefferson). Their visions of the proper role of government in economic policy varied from the federalists to the antifederalists. Those visions have not changed greatly over the course of more than two centuries.

The second reason that agricultural policy issues are so important is that agriculture and the food industry are important in our economy. Until very recently, food expenditures were the largest single item in the typical American family's budget.[2] As a result, food issues are very much a "gut" issue.

In our more recent history we have seen the policy pendulum swing in the federalists' direction starting with the New Deal and culminating with the declaration of a "war on poverty" during the first half of the 1960s. The different programs that were inaugurated in this era were variously hailed by some as the first really significant progress in modern social legislation, and by others as the first significant American step toward socialism.

In the 1980s the policy pendulum started swinging in the antifederalists' direction as the "Reagan revolution" promised to get big government off the backs

---

[1] The Civil War played a role in two of the most important agricultural policies in our country's history. The southern states opposed a federal role in agriculture, and with one-half of the Senate seats they blocked all such efforts for several decades. In 1862, with most of the southern states out of the Union, an agrarian president from the western state of Illinois pushed through Congress a bill establishing the U.S. Department of Agriculture and the Morrill Act providing for the establishment of land grant universities in each state to teach the "agricultural and mechanical arts."

[2] In the early 1990s health care expenses as a percentage of total consumer spending exceeded food expenses. The primary reason is that the real price of food continues to fall while the real price of health care continues to rise. Health care today is about 14 percent of the family budget, while food is down to about 12 percent.

of farmers. Calls for ending "welfare for farmers" and restoring agriculture to a market economy have heralded a decided shift of public opinion about what ought to be. This pendulum passed its nadir with the passage of the 1996 farm bill by the first Congress since 1927 in which the Republican Party controlled both houses.

THE PERFECT FOOD SYSTEM

Discussions of **agricultural or food policy** deal with what ought to be. One's perception of this depends greatly upon individual circumstances. The tomato farmer in south Florida, the cattle rancher on the high plains of Texas, and the consumer in Fairbanks, Alaska, probably have very different perspectives about "what ought to be" in American agriculture. The point is that the perception of the food producer may not necessarily be consistent with that of the food consumer. And among producers there is frequently disagreement about "what ought to be." The Illinois corn farmer seeks high corn prices, while Tyson Foods and all other feeders of livestock seek low corn prices.

Nonetheless, some general outlines of "what ought to be" can be identified. While agreement on such issues is never unanimous, there is, nonetheless, a general consensus about what our food system should do for us. The ideal food system should do the following:

- Provide adequate food for all
- Provide cheap food
- Provide reliable food over time
- Provide safe food
- Provide a reasonable way of life for the farmer

In this chapter we are going to look at some of the unique problems of agriculture in the United States that make it difficult to achieve the above objectives and then turn to some of the policies implemented by government in an effort to make the food system behave the way we want it too.

THE NATURE OF AGRICULTURAL PROBLEMS

No problem is greater for U.S. agriculture than the tendency to **overproduce.** Our capacity to produce is growing much faster than our capacity to consume or export. As one observer put it: "Our ability to produce is growing more rapidly than our waistlines." What drives our ability to produce is the relentless improvement of technology. What results is a need for a difficult, if not impossible, **resource adjustment** process.

Adoption of a new technology (such as a higher yielding crop variety) will lower the cost per unit of output, resulting in additional profits for the early adopters. But as more and more producers adopt the new variety, the increase in the total output of that product will cause prices to fall.[3] This would suggest that in a free market environment production should be reduced. But the problem arises of what to do with resources such as land or labor that are displaced. If the land is diverted to another crop, then the problem has been transferred, but it still exists.

Agricultural or food policy purposeful government action in the agricultural and food sectors designed to produce results consistent with a societal belief about what "ought to be."

Overproduction the most fundamental problem facing U.S. agriculture. Our ability to produce and expand production far exceeds our capacity to consume and expand consumption.

Resource adjustment the free market flow of production resources from activities with low economic returns into those uses providing the highest return to each resource.

[3] Notice the fallacy of composition here. What is good for the individual (the early adopter) is not necessarily good for all farmers.

The fact that many agricultural resources can be adjusted out of agricultural uses only at great expense and agonizing pain is at the heart of the overproduction issue.

New technology (farm machinery, for example) frequently requires that a farm unit be enlarged in order to take advantage of the potential cost reduction. If farm businesses must grow in size to survive the new technology, there must necessarily be fewer farm businesses. If there are fewer farms, there must necessarily be fewer farmers. If there are fewer farmers, what is to be done with the people who have been displaced?[4] This leads directly to the question of the "family farm." What has become and what is to become of the family farm? Will advances in technology expand the economically efficient size of the farm unit beyond the ability of a family to supply the majority of the labor and management? Will the advance in technology likely expand farm investment needs beyond the ability of the farm family to acquire control of enough capital to give them a majority interest in the business? Are technological advances in the agribusiness sector likely to change the marketing pattern such that the family farm will become extinct? Should public action be taken to discourage (or render uneconomic) the continuing growth in average farm size?[5]

The Economic Environment of Agricultural Policy Issues

Given the arguments found throughout this text and the economic literature that free markets are an inherently efficient and effective means of allocation, one might conclude that the best of all possible worlds would be one in which unbridled capitalism prevented all barriers to trade among individuals, regions, and nations. But one of the necessary conditions of the perfect competition model is that resources are perfectly mobile; and as we have seen, a lot of the resources involved in agriculture are not the least bit mobile.

The agricultural sector is a victim of the capacity to overproduce with little chance of the necessary resource adjustment occurring. The simple line diagram in Figure 10–1 of the market forces of supply and demand can be used to illustrate the consequences of this problem in a grossly oversimplified fashion.

Several things are obvious about the demand for food in the United States. First, the demand is not growing rapidly because the population itself is not growing rapidly and most of us have little unmet demand. In fact, many of us would do better to eat a little less. Second, the demand for food is inelastic: it is not very price responsive. That is, if food prices fall, how do consumers respond? The answer is not much at all. This characteristic of the food market means that the demand curve for food is almost a vertical line as shown in Figure 10–1.

Rapid increases in technology and production efficiency have caused the food supply curve to shift outward over time. As supply shifts outward across the nearly vertical demand curve, the result, as shown in Figure 10–1, is a fall in food

---

[4] The magnitude of this resource reallocation should not be underestimated. In 1930, 30.5 million Americans lived on 6.3 million farms. In 1990, 4.6 million people lived on 2.0 million farms. In 1930, 1 out of 4 Americans lived on a farm. In 1990, it was 1 out of 55.

[5] France currently has laws on the books that make the consolidation of small farms difficult if not impossible.

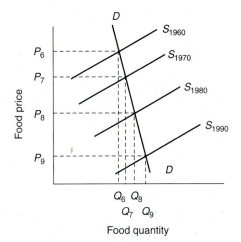

FIGURE 10–1 Macro-market for food over time.

prices with very little increase in the equilibrium quantity produced.[6] As a result, farm incomes would fall over time if left to the vagaries of a totally free market, and it would be impossible for farmers to earn a reasonable return for their labors. Hence the need for policies to prevent the adjustments suggested in Figure 10–1 from happening.

In a nutshell, the purpose of many agricultural policies is to prevent the achievement of the market equilibrium that would normally be expected to prevail. Thus, our "capitalistic" economic system is politically "corrupted" in the interests of compassion for those micro-units that could be disadvantaged by a completely free market system. That is, the weakness of the free market system as an allocative mechanism has been acknowledged and ameliorated through political action.

TYPES OF AGRICULTURAL POLICY

The types of agricultural policies that have been utilized in the United States can be broken into two general classes: developmental and price/income support. The developmental types of policies have been characterized by programs such as the Homestead Act, which was designed to extend production agriculture into previously unsettled areas; the Morrill Act, which created the Land Grant College system to meet the research needs of the farm sector and to extend knowledge gained through research to farmers; and the Federal Farm Loan Act, which was passed to provide for improved farm mortgage credit and was later expanded into the cooperative Farm Credit System to meet a broader range of farm credit needs.

Price and income support types of agricultural policy issues are probably more familiar to most Americans since these are the issues that receive the greatest public attention. Interestingly, much of the need for farm price and income support policies flows from the success of various developmental policies.

---

[6] Figure 10–1 should be viewed as a gross oversimplification of what *would* have happened over the past 40 years if there had not been any farm support programs. For simplification it is assumed that demand has not changed over the time period shown. In reality, demand has also shifted outward over time, but the demand shifts are quite small compared with the technology induced supply shifts.

Developmental Agricultural Policies

Developmental agricultural policies
policies designed to improve the infrastructure of the food system.

The primary **developmental agricultural policies** during recent decades have included the following:

- The continuing agricultural research and extension effort financed by the federal and state government sectors
- Various lending programs such as those administered by the Farm Service Agency
- The development of water retention structures to retain water from snow melt and heavy rainfall in the moisture deficit areas of the West
- The various resource protection efforts such as soil and water conservation, clean water programs, and environmental protection
- The use of export markets as an outlet for U.S. farm products to improve the U.S. balance of payments while creating markets for our production surplus

These efforts have not always been totally compatible with each other. For example, pesticide bans thwart output expansion—and as a result farmers have gotten a very mixed set of signals. The various developmental agricultural policies have not always enjoyed a constant degree of emphasis. For example, research programs have waxed and waned with the changes of interest on the part of various administrations. In the rough-and-tumble world of politics, what "ought to be" is a moving target.

In general, developmental agricultural policies are designed to assist the individual farmer, or the consumer, or the environment. The reality is that most developmental agricultural policies in the final analysis contribute to a worsening of the fundamental overproduction problem.

Agricultural Price and/or Income Support Policies

The micro-macro "trap" illustrated in Figure 10–1 has nagged at American agriculture for the past 150 years. At the micro level, it is in the farmer's self-interest to adopt new, cost-cutting technologies. But at the macro level, the consequence of the new technologies is overproduction and lower farm prices. Lower farm prices result in lower farm incomes, depriving the farmer of a reasonable way of life. Recall that a reasonable return to farming was one of the objectives identified in the ideal food system. One way to avoid the trap is for government to support farm prices and/or incomes at a socially acceptable level.

Agricultural price and income support policies   policies designed to increase agricultural prices and/or agricultural incomes above the level that would prevail in the absence of the policy.

As indicated previously, the **agricultural price and income support policy** pendulum has gone through some historic swings from free markets to strong government intervention. The critical date that marks the reversal of the swing and the beginning of a new era is 1933.

Prior to 1933

From colonial days to 1933, American agriculture operated in a classical free market environment. Farm prices were determined by the shifting patterns of supply and demand. Then, as now, long-run supply adjustment was a major problem. As a result, agriculture went through some long swings of feast and famine.

Up until the 1850s America's agricultural production was not sufficient to feed its population. Exports of tobacco and cotton were used to finance imports of sugar and grains. The western frontier was Kentucky and Ohio. The small amount of agricultural produce that was shipped from the western frontier to the population centers on the East Coast flowed down the Ohio and Mississippi rivers and then by ocean from New Orleans to New York and Philadelphia. Much of the grain shipped along this route was first converted into whiskey to make storage and transportation more efficient.

The second half of the nineteenth century witnessed the first of three great supply shifts in American agriculture. This supply shift, as illustrated in Figure 10–1, was the result of a rapid expansion of the land base supporting agriculture. Over this period, the midwest and the Great Plains moved from frontier status to being fully populated. The history of this region during this period of time is a thrilling saga. As always, several factors converged to create this vast expansion of agricultural production and our first extended bout of overproduction and falling prices. Railroads provided transportation links to population centers in the East that had not previously existed. Barbed wire made it possible to fence what had previously been open range. The demise of the buffalo and the Plains Indians made the region a less inhospitable place. And finally, massive immigrations of European farmers came directly to the new lands without even disembarking on the East Coast. Farm prices, high after Civil War shortages, fell continuously until the turn of the century.

The period from 1900 to 1920 is frequently called the "golden age" of American agriculture. With the closing of the frontier on the Plains, the relentless supply surge ended. Industrialization, urbanization, and immigration fueled the demand for agricultural products, and prices rose to a level that provided most farmers with a return sufficient to support a family. The outbreak of war in Europe in 1914 further increased the demand for U.S. agriculture to replace production lost in Europe. Unfortunately, the end of World War I quickly extinguished the golden age.

After World War I a second, massive supply expansion put U.S. agriculture into a long, difficult recession that was destined to last for the next two decades. Several forces were at play. First, after the end of the war European farming returned to normal, and within a year the fantastic export markets that American agriculture had enjoyed disappeared. This caused an inward shift of the demand curve. Second, with the men away fighting the war and with farm prices high, the country was pushed into the mechanical era—an era in which the tractor replaced the draft animal. This substitution of machine for muscle had two effects. First, farm yields increased dramatically as plowing and tilling improved. Second, a portion of the food supply was no longer needed to support the draft animals. The combined effect of these two forces rapidly pushed the food supply curve outward.

With the demand curve shifting inward and the supply curve shifting outward, the free market trap illustrated in Figure 10–1 accelerated. Throughout the 1920s farm prices and incomes decreased, and along with them land prices fell. The decline in land values contributed to the demise of the rural banking system and the Great Depression. By the early 1930s, to be on the farm was to be in poverty. Good farmers were going broke, and poor farmers had already gone broke. The typical American farm had neither electricity nor running water. The average farm family income was one-sixth that of non-farm families.

Given this situation, newly elected President Franklin Roosevelt promised to help farmers during the "first 100 days" of his New Deal. His basic philosophical approach was that if free markets couldn't support farmers, then the federal government should.

A "New Deal" for Agriculture

In 1933 Congress passed the Agricultural Adjustment Act (AAA). The ultimate objective of this legislation, and similar legislation that has followed ever since, was to increase farm income. There are basically two ways in which farm incomes can be improved: direct cash payments to farmers, or indirect support by increasing the prices farmers receive for their crops. Since 1933, both approaches have been used through a complex and confusing system of measures to assure farmers of specific crops an "adequate" price for their product and cash payments if prices were not "high enough."

Price Supports

Price supports any policy designed to maintain market prices at a level above the price that would prevail in a free market.

There are three approaches to **price supports** that are designed to maintain farm prices at a level deemed to be sufficient to provide farmers with an adequate income. In all three cases the basic premise is that free markets, if left to themselves, fail to provide the farmer with prices high enough to provide the farmer with an adequate income. Given this failure of markets, the government must intervene to increase prices above the level that would otherwise prevail.

Price floor a government-guaranteed minimum price. The government buys "surplus" production at this price to ensure that the market price does not fall below the floor.

Price Floor   The effect of a **price floor** program is illustrated in Figure 10–2. *DD* and *SS* are the market demand and supply curves. In the absence of any governmental intervention, the price prevailing in the market would be P_0 and the quantity traded in equilibrium is Q_0. But price P_0 is below the price floor established in the farm bill, so the government supports a higher price at P_s. Basically the government says that if the market price falls to P_s, it will buy as much of the commodity as necessary to maintain the price at that level. At price P_s the quantity demanded by consumers is Q_d and the quantity producers are willing to produce

FIGURE 10–2   Effect of a price floor.

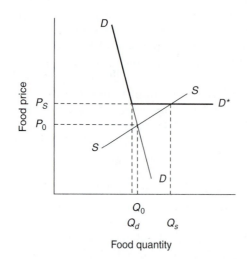

Food quantity

is Q_s. Since consumers will take only Q_d off the market, the government must buy the difference equal to the distance Q_dQ_s.

By setting the price floor at P_s, the government has effectively changed the demand curve from DD to DD^* shown by the heavy line in Figure 10–2. The cost of the program is equal to the units purchased by the government times the price per unit.

Since 1933 most grains, cereals, oilseeds, and cotton have had price floor programs with the government buying the surplus at the established price floor. Operationally, the price floor was established through a "loan program" (see Marketing Assistance Loans below). During periods of low farm prices (i.e., overproduction), the government incurred high demands on the budget and experienced the embarrassment of owning huge stockpiles of agricultural commodities.

Notice the perverse effects of a price floor. Because of overproduction, market prices are deemed by the government to be too low. As shown in Figure 10–2, a price floor to support prices actually encourages producers to expand production, which increases the overproduction and drives prices even lower. By imposing a price floor program the government gets caught in a downward cycle from which there is no exit.

Marketing Assistance Loans   The "**loan program**" has been a part of every farm bill from 1933 to the present with few minor changes. This program essentially establishes a minimum price, the **loan rate,** that the farmer will receive even if the market price falls below the minimum price. All producers of wheat, feed grains, rice, oilseeds and cotton are eligible to participate in the loan program. The government assumes the responsibility, if necessary, of paying farmers this minimum price.

At harvest time, participants in the loan program may, at their option, secure a **nonrecourse loan** from the Commodity Credit Corporation (CCC) in the amount of the loan rate times the number of bushels put into storage. This provides the farmer with much needed cash at harvest time without forcing the farmer to actually sell the crop at a time when prices are usually quite low. Hence, the loan provides the farmer with "marketing assistance."

Later in the year when the farmer decides to sell the crop one of two things can happen:

1. If the market price is greater than the loan rate, the farmer repays the loan to the CCC with interest and sells the commodity at the market price.
2. If the market price is less than the loan rate, the farmer defaults on the nonrecourse loan[7] and sells the commodity at the market price. Since the farmer did not receive the minimum price from the market, the government makes a loan deficiency payment to the farmer in the amount of the difference between the loan rate and the market price.

Loan rates, set at levels specified in the farm bill, are designed to provide an interim source of cash flow to assist farmers in orderly marketing and to maintain a minimum price guarantee to the farmer. The loan rate becomes the minimum price for the farmer because the government will compensate farmers if the market price is less than the loan rate.

Loan program
USDA program that provides a farmer with a loan against his or her crop at harvest. If the farmer sells the crop at a market price below the loan rate, the loan is forgiven and the farmer receives a payment equal to the difference between the loan rate and the market price.

Loan rate   the amount that is lent to the farmer under the loan program for each bushel put into storage. Loan rates are currently set by the 2002 farm bill.

Nonrecourse loan
a loan on which the borrower has the right to default with no adverse consequences.

---

[7] A "nonrecourse" loan is a special type of loan provided by the CCC that gives the borrower the right to default on the loan without any adverse implications on credit ratings and the like.

Price Support Via Loans to and Purchases from Processors   Support of farm prices through loans to and purchases from processors is provided for those products for which high degrees of perishability make purchases by the government in the open market infeasible. Loans to or purchases from processors are typically consummated on the condition that farmers are paid at least the specified minimum support price. The largest volume of activity in this general price support category of programs is in the milk price support program. Cane sugar prices are also supported through this vehicle.

Marketing Quota Programs   Today tobacco is the only commodity with a price support system built around a system of mandatory marketing quotas. In years past, a similar program existed for peanuts but that program eventually self-destructed. Both tobacco and peanuts are grown primarily in the southeastern part of the country, traditionally by small, low-income farmers. Price supports through a quota system were viewed as a means to solve this social problem.

The operation of the tobacco marketing quota system is pretty straightforward and smacks of central planning. Each year someone in the bowels of the U.S. Department of Agriculture estimates how much tobacco will be needed in the coming year. Next, it is determined how many acres will be needed to produce this amount. Then the government gives **acreage allotments** proportionately to historic producers of tobacco. It is illegal to produce tobacco without an allotment, so the government artificially restricts production, which has the desired effect of driving prices for tobacco up.

Allotment holders are also given a **production quota.** This is the maximum amount of tobacco that can be sold from the allotted acres. Should a tobacco farmer exceed his production quota, the excess must be sold for export at the world price, which is substantially below the protected domestic price.

To implement a marketing quota program, there must be an absolute ban on the importation of tobacco, because otherwise cheap foreign tobacco would flood the domestic market and drive tobacco prices down. Such import restrictions are prohibited by the World Trade Organization agreement, which is what led to the demise of the peanut marketing quota program. Tobacco will probably suffer a similar fate in the near future.

Income Support   In the 1950s **income supports** were added to the existing system of price supports for many commodities.[8] While each subsequent farm bill has added its own unique features to the income support program, the basic essence of it has not changed. The farm bill or the Secretary of Agriculture determines **target prices** for each covered commodity. The intent is that the target price is high enough to cover the costs of production of an efficient farmer.

If the annual average price of a commodity is less than the target price, then the government sends a check to the farmer in the amount of the difference between the target price and the average market price multiplied by the number of bushels the farmer produced. These direct cash payments to farmers are known as "**deficiency payments**" because they compensate the farmer for the failure of the market to provide farmers with adequate prices. Income support through defi-

---

Acreage allotments government permission to produce a given acreage of a product for domestic consumption. By restricting acreage, and hence production, the government assures holders of the allotments of high prices for their production.

Production quota a quantitative limit on the amount of product that can be sold from an allotment.

Income supports any government program designed to provide farmers with higher incomes than they would receive otherwise.

Target prices set annually by the farm bill or the secretary of agriculture based on estimated total cost of production.

Deficiency payment if average market prices are less than the target price, a cash payment is made to farmers to make up the difference.

---

[8] Income supports were a feature of every farm bill since the 1950s until 1996. In the 1996 farm bill, income supports were eliminated with much political fanfare about ending "welfare" for farmers. After a few years of low farm prices, income supports were reinstated in the 2002 farm bill.

ciency payments is a countercyclical policy. That is, when market prices are low, deficiency payments are high, and vice versa.

Prior to the 1996 farm bill, farmers who wished to receive deficiency payments had to sign an annual contract with the USDA specifying which crops the farmer was eligible to produce under the program. In this way, the USDA was able to control how much of each crop was produced. Farmers contended that the USDA was "telling them what to produce." In addition, farmers had to "**set aside**" or not use a portion of their land. This restriction was, of course, an effort to address the problem of excess production capacity. Both of these production controls were much despised by most farmers. Non-farm critics accused the government of "paying farmers not to produce." In the 1996 farm bill, both of these production controls were eliminated.

Set-aside land that a farmer had to take out of production in order to qualify for price and income support.

The 1996 Farm Bill

Amid much fanfare, Congress passed a farm bill in 1996 designed to remedy many of the faults of the crazy quilt of price and income support programs. The 1996 farm bill made three significant changes:

- Set asides and all other production controls were eliminated. Farmers were free to plant whatever they wanted to plant and to plant it on 100 percent of their acreage.
- The system of countercyclical deficiency payments was terminated and it was replaced by a system of direct cash payments (checks in the mail) that were totally decoupled (i.e., unrelated) from market prices and production. Farmers got a check just because they were farmers.
- The bill eliminated price support programs for producers of wool, mohair, and honey.

    This new system worked well initially because market prices were high, but by 1999 when prices began to fall due to the old nemesis of overproduction, it became obvious that the direct cash payments were not enough to keep many farmers afloat. Congress started throwing emergency payments at farmers that seemed to increase in amount each year. By 2002 it was clear that Congress did not have the political will to leave farmers to the vagaries of a free market.

2002 Farm Bill

In 2002 Congress passed a new, 6-year farm bill. The primary features of the 2002 bill included the following:

- The bill retained the direct income payment feature of the 1996 bill.
- The bill reinstated the countercyclical deficiency payment program.
- The bill continued with no set-aside nor production controls.
- The bill reinstated price support programs for producers of wool, mohair, and honey. In addition, producers of pulse crops (small chickpeas, lentils, and dry peas) were added.

This farm bill signaled the end of any pretense of getting U.S. agriculture off the government dole. It is estimated that under the provisions of the 2002 farm bill payments to farmers will increase by about 70 percent from where they were under the 1996 farm bill. The political will to "get government out of agriculture" is clearly lacking.

As we continue to encourage farmers to produce more without any form of production restrictions, the micro-macro trap confronting agriculture will continue. The self-interest of the micro unit (the farmer) only worsens the problems for all farmers (the macro). The prospects for continued overproduction and the subsequent low prices are not very encouraging.

SUMMARY

Agricultural policy deals with purposeful or deliberate government actions that are designed to bring about results that are consistent with a societal concept of what ought to be. Developmental agricultural policies are those actions that seek to improve the infrastructure that supports the food industry. Agricultural price and income support policies seek to maintain prices and incomes at higher levels than a free market will provide.

With the exception of a few periods, the primary problem facing U.S. agriculture for the past 150 years has been the capacity to overproduce. During periods of overproduction, market prices of food fall dramatically as markets try to clear themselves. Low farm prices result in low farm incomes that drives farmers into poverty and eventually force some out of agriculture. Unfortunately, when farmers are driven out of agriculture, someone else picks up the land and continues producing. The inability to push resources out of agriculture is a resource adjustment problem that negates the automatic adjustments that occur in other industries when there is an overproduction problem.

Because of agriculture's overproduction problem and lack of resource adjustments during periods of low prices, various agricultural price and income policies have attempted to support agricultural prices and incomes at higher levels than can be achieved by free markets.

The first agricultural price support policy was implemented as part of President Franklin Roosevelt's New Deal in 1933. His basic philosophy was that if free markets would not provide farmers with a decent living, then government should. Price supports were implemented with a loan program in which the government bought surplus production from the farmers at a price known as the loan rate. Later an income support feature was added in which the government sent a check to the farmer at the end of the year if market prices for the product were less than a target price. These payments were known as deficiency payments. In order to participate in these programs farmers had to sign an annual contract with the government promising to plant specific crops and to take a portion of land out of production. These production controls imposed by the government were detested by the farmers, who wanted the flexibility to plant whatever they wanted.

In 1996 the policy tide turned away from production controls and towards free markets. Under the farm bill of 1996, participating farmers received a cash payment each year regardless of what they planted and regardless of whether farm prices were high or low. In the latter part of the 1990s the bottom fell out of most farm prices, and farmers started calling for more income support. The 1996 farm bill was supposed to transition American farmers to a free market, but by the turn of the century government support of farmers had actually increased. By 2002 the 1996 farm bill was universally considered a failure.

The 2002 farm bill retained the production flexibility and income payments of the 1996 act and added deficiency payments once again. Absent any production controls and given the resource adjustment problem, the probability of continued, substantial overproduction is quite high. The hopes that a substantial expansion of exports would absorb the surpluses have all but vanished.

KEY TERMS

Acreage allotments
Agricultural or food policy
Agricultural price and income
  support policies
Deficiency payment
Developmental agricultural policies
Income supports
Loan program
Loan rate

Nonrecourse loan
Overproduction
Price floor
Price supports
Production quota
Resource adjustment
Set-aside
Target prices

PROBLEMS AND DISCUSSION QUESTIONS

1. Our federal government has substantial and expensive price and income support policies for agriculture but none for copper, cement, or automobiles. What are the unique characteristics of agriculture that merit this special attention?

2. What were the supply and demand shifts that drove U.S. agriculture into the recession of the 1920s?

3. The deficiency payment program is a countercyclical program. Explain.

4. The problem of overproduction in U.S. agriculture has been described as a micro-macro trap and as an illustration of the fallacy of composition. Explain both.

5. What are the price and income support components of the 2002 farm bill?

6. What are the fundamental differences between the farm bills of 1996 and 2002?

7. What aspects of the 1933–1995 programs did farmers most detest?

8. One way to support farm prices is to induce an artificial shortage with a marketing quota policy. Explain how a marketing quota policy operates.

9. One of the interesting aspects of studying agricultural policy is that there is always some new topic being considered. One branch of the U.S. Department of Agriculture, the Economic Research Service (ERS), is charged with evaluating alternative policies affecting agriculture, the environment, and food. On their Web page the ERS maintains Briefing Rooms with brief studies on the latest issues coming before them. See what issues are current at **http://www.ers.usda.gov/whatsnew/issues/**.

The Firm as a Production Unit

Microeconomics the branch of economics that deals with the economic behavior of individual units—either producers or consumers.

Microeconomics deals with the behavior of the individual economic unit. Each of those units is engaged in either production or consumption. In this chapter the behavior of the production unit is examined. The economic model developed invokes a number of rather critical assumptions, not the least of which is that the producing unit—a firm—produces under conditions of perfect competition. Once the model of the perfectly competitive firm is thoroughly understood, it will be possible to modify that assumption and examine the behavior of a firm operating under conditions of imperfect competition in a later chapter.

PERFECTLY COMPETITIVE MARKETS

A model of a perfectly competitive market is the easiest market model to understand and it serves as a good beginning point to the understanding of other markets that don't have all of the attributes of perfect competition. These latter markets are lumped together in what is called imperfect competition.

The essential key to perfectly competitive markets is that there are a large number of buyers (consumer demand) and a large number of sellers (producer supply), each of whom is so small relative to the total market that their individual actions will not affect the market. When these conditions and a few other conditions that will be mentioned later are met, we have perfect competition. In perfect competition, both buyers and sellers recognize that price is something beyond their control such that each potential participant in the market can only make a "take it or leave it" decision at the price dictated by the market.

Does perfect competition really exist in any market? Consider agriculture, one of the most frequently cited examples of perfect competition, and specifically the market for iceberg lettuce. There are a large number of buyers and a large number of sellers, and price adjusts over time to clear the market. Examples of imperfect competition abound. The market for military aircraft is one in which there are few buyers and few sellers. The market for live cattle is one with many sellers but only four major buyers. The automobile industry is one with a few sellers and many buyers.

In this chapter and the next we will examine the behavior of the firm under the conditions of perfect competition. Later we will examine firm behavior under conditions of imperfect competition.

THE PERFECTLY COMPETITIVE FIRM

The basic theory of a perfectly competitive firm assumes that the firm is so small relative to the market that actions by the firm do not affect the market. This model closely approximates the typical family farm, so it is quite useful for understanding management decisions faced by most farmers and other small businesses. There are ample examples of perfectly competitive firms in the non-farm sector also. Most barber shops, beauty salons, not-so-beautiful saloons, Chinese restaurants, and shoe repair shops are examples of firms that operate under the conditions of nearly perfect competition.

Objective of the Perfectly Competitive Firm

In basic microeconomics it is always assumed that the perfectly competitive firm makes management decisions with the sole objective of maximizing **economic profit.** While it seems intuitively comfortable to assume that a firm seeks to maximize profit, there are several nuances that deserve further attention.

The first of these is the concept of economic profit. For most of us, profit is simply the difference between the receipts of a firm and its expenses. This is what economists call "**accounting profit**" since this is the concept of profit that is typically reported by an accountant. This is a very limited concept of profit because the only costs that are considered are those for which payment is actually made. Accounting profit can be misleading because it may omit some very important costs of production. This is illustrated in Figure 11–1. Here we have two farms that are similar in every respect except that Farm A makes cash payment for some items for which Farm B makes no cash payment. As a result, the accounting profits of Farm B greatly exceed those of Farm A.

Notice that the accountant entered a zero for labor on Farm B's account since no cash payment for labor was made. Does this imply that the *value* of the farmer's labor is zero? Of course not! That labor is quite valuable, even if a cash payment for its use is not made. This is where the economist and the accountant part company. The economist measures *value,* not payment, in the computation of economic profit. For those productive services for which a cash payment is not made, the economist estimates their value using the concept of **opportunity cost.** Opportunity cost is an estimate of how much payment a resource would receive if that resource were employed in another activity for which payment would be made. That is, how much of an earning opportunity is given up by using the resource in its current employment. The economist uses this estimate of value in the computation of the economic profits of a firm.

Economic profit the difference between all revenues or receipts of the firm and the value of all inputs used by the firm, whether paid or not.

Accounting profit the difference between all revenues or receipts of the firm and all expenses paid.

Opportunity cost a measure of how much of an earning opportunity is forgone by using a resource in its current employment. Used by economists to establish an economic value for those resources that do not have an expressed market value.

	Farm A	Farm B
	(Big city lawyer who rents land, hires all machinery services, and hires all labor)	(Family farmer who owns land, owns equipment, and uses only own labor)
Revenue (400 acres of wheat; 30 bu/acre @ $5/bu)	$60,000	$60,000
(−) Operating expenses	30,000	30,000
(−) Land rent ($30/acre)	12,000	0
(−) Machinery ($20/acre)	8,000	0
(−) Hired labor ($5/acre)	2,000	0
(=) Accounting profit	8,000	30,000

FIGURE 11–1 Hypothetical accounting profits for two firms.

To compute the economic profit of Farm B in Figure 11–1, it would be necessary to include the opportunity cost of the farmer's land, labor, and machinery. The opportunity cost of the land would be equal to what the farmer would be paid for the land if he rented it out rather than farming it. The opportunity cost of the farmer's labor is equal to what the farmer could earn if he were employed in the highest paying alternative employment. The opportunity cost of the farmer's machinery is what he would have to pay to acquire the same services on a custom hire basis.[1] Since each of these three opportunity costs would be roughly equal to the payments made for the factor services by Farm A, the economic profits of the two farms would be similar even though their accounting profits are greatly different. The important point to remember is that economic profit includes the *value* of all factors of production regardless of whether they are actually paid or not. Hereafter, the term "profit" will always refer to economic profit.

A second concern with the assumption that the perfectly competitive firm maximizes profit is that other objectives of the firm are ignored. Other objectives of the firm might include expansion of farm assets, risk minimization, maintaining a way of life, size maximization, and avoidance of debt. Extensive research has been conducted by agricultural economists in an effort to determine to what extent farmers are profit maximizers, and to identify other objectives of American farm managers. The evidence indicates that most farmers behave as if they were attempting to maximize profits even if the farmer states it is not his or her objective to maximize profits. Since the object of our economic study is to understand behavior of the firm and since firms behave as if they were attempting to maximize economic profit, the assumption that this is the objective of the firm is a sound assumption.

Conditions of Perfect Competition

Atomistic each economic unit is so small relative to the total market that actions by that unit will not affect the market.

The most important characteristic of the perfectly competitive firm is that it is **atomistic.** That is, the perfectly competitive firm is so small relative to the market that any action by the firm will not have a noticeable effect on the market. By this definition, the typical family farm in the corn belt is certainly perfectly competitive, for if that farmer decided to halt production or destroy the crop, the impact on the market for corn would be imperceptible. However, Ocean Spray, the processor of about 80 percent of the U.S. cranberry crop, is hardly a perfectly competitive firm. This does not mean that Ocean Spray is not a very competitive company, just that it is a company that does not fit the perfectly competitive model of a firm.

Homogeneous products that are alike such that the output of one competitor cannot be distinguished from that of another competitor.

Another condition of perfect competition is that each firm in the market produces a **homogeneous** product. That is, each producer's output cannot be distinguished from that of another producer. This is certainly the case in production agriculture where there is no perceptible difference between No. 2 corn produced by farmer X in Iowa and farmer Y in Indiana.

A third strong assumption about the perfectly competitive firm is that resources (i.e., factors of production such as labor, capital, and land) are free to move in and out of production. That is, if a farmer decides she wants to be a computer technician instead of a farmer, she could do it without any costs involved. Obvi-

---

[1] "Custom hire" refers to the common practice of one farmer (without machinery) hiring another farmer (with machinery) to perform plowing, planting, and harvesting work on a fixed rate basis.

ously this is a limiting assumption for the farm firm where, in reality, a lot of resources are "locked in" to the farming operation and could not be easily transferred out of agriculture. This is the same resource adjustment problem that was noted in the previous chapter.

A fourth assumption of perfect competition is that all market participants share the same knowledge about the market (buyers and sellers both know what is going on in related markets, and so on). In 2001 three American economists[2] received the Nobel Prize for Economic Science for their work on the behavior of markets where there is imperfect information. For example, one of them studied the market for used cars and found that sellers had more information than buyers. This knowledge advantage gave the seller market power over the buyer.

Behavior of the Perfectly Competitive Firm

Because of its inconsequential size and its inability to distinguish or differentiate its product from that of its competitors, the perfectly competitive firm is a **price taker,** not a **price maker.** Again, a typical family farm is a good illustration of this point. The typical farmer is told what the prices are for the inputs he purchases and is told what price he can receive at any given time for his product. The only decision the farmer makes is whether to accept the given price or not. Glory be to the soybean farmer who proudly tells the operator of a grain elevator that he is going to demand $5.50 per bushel for his crop, when the market price is $5.25. The farmer will quickly discover that nobody will purchase his crop at $5.50. Moreover, until he accepts the market price, the farmer will never be able to sell his crop. Truly, the farmer is a price taker. Then who makes prices? As you learned earlier, markets make prices and perfectly competitive firms take prices.

Once again, the difference between the perfectly competitive firm and Ocean Spray should be clear. Ocean Spray sets the price at which it sells frozen concentrated cranberry juice to food wholesalers rather than being dictated to by the market. Nonetheless, Ocean Spray is at the mercy of the market, for if it sets the price too high, consumers will not buy Ocean Spray, and if consumers don't buy it, then wholesalers won't buy it, and they will lose the market. So Ocean Spray sets the price for its products within a competitive market system. As such, Ocean Spray is a price maker rather than a price taker. Wouldn't it be a fine day for the American farmer if he or she had that kind of market power?

Price taker potential buyers and potential sellers in a perfectly competitive market who face a "take it or leave it" decision at the prevailing market price.

Price maker market in which the individual producer or consumer is able to establish price.

PRODUCTION

Economic activity involves a continuous interaction between producers and consumers. Producers, each of which is called a firm, are involved in production. **Production** is a process in which factors of production (also called inputs or resources) are combined to produce an output (also called a product). Many of the inputs involved in a particular production process will be intermediate goods that are a result of previous production processes.

Production process of converting inputs (factors, resources) into outputs (products); converting costs into revenues.

[2] George A. Akerlof from the University of California at Berkeley, A. Michael Spence from Stanford, and Joseph E. Stiglitz from Columbia.

On a typical farm in the United States there are numerous production activities taking place simultaneously. A farmer may be involved in the simultaneous production of soybeans, corn, and fat cattle. Each of these production activities constitutes an **enterprise** of the firm. In our initial analysis of the firm, we will evaluate the simple case of a one-enterprise firm. In an appendix to the next chapter the question of which enterprises a multiproduct firm should pursue will be addressed.

Enterprise a single production activity.

Fixed and Variable Inputs

Inputs are very important in the production process. The manager must decide which inputs to use, how much of each to use, and how to combine them in the most efficient manner to produce the output desired. To simplify our analysis, we will deal with two kinds of inputs: fixed and variable. **Fixed inputs** are those for which the use rate does not change as the level of output changes. In most instances, land is a fixed input in agriculture. The farmer must determine how to combine fertilizer and other variable inputs with a fixed or predetermined quantity of land. **Variable inputs** are those inputs that affect the level of output and change with it. Since the manager of a perfectly competitive firm is a price taker, the amount of the variable input used per unit of the fixed factor is the only variable the manager can control. Hence, the essence of management is understanding the economics of determining the profit-maximizing quantity of the variable input to use.

Fixed inputs inputs whose use rate does not change as the output level changes. Property taxes are a fixed input: they are the same whether a restaurant serves 1 customer or 100.

Variable inputs inputs whose use rate changes as the output level changes.

Length of Run

Production processes are also classified according to the "length of run" or time period being considered. The "**short run**" is a time period that is short enough such that some factors of production are considered by the manager to be fixed. There is no predetermined amount of time that constitutes the short run since it depends greatly on the product being produced. For example, for a typical grain farmer, the short run would be one crop year since the amount of land being farmed cannot be adjusted once the year begins. For a radish producer in south Florida, the short run is 29 days because that is the length of time a crop will tie-up or "fix" the land resource. However, the short run for a citrus producer would be at least 4 years since that is the amount of time it takes to bring a newly established grove into production.

In the short run the task of the manager is to determine which variable resources should be combined with the fixed resources in order to maximize the profits of the enterprise. In the **long run** when all resources are variable, management must evaluate investment alternatives such as whether the firm should purchase more land or more equipment. For the time being, we will concentrate exclusively on production decisions in the short run because as John Maynard Keynes once said: "In the long-run, we're all dead." That is, if the manger can't make good short-run decisions, there is little need to be concerned about managerial ability in the long-run.[3]

Short run period of time short enough that some inputs are considered by the manager to be fixed inputs.

Long run period of time in which all inputs are considered variable inputs by the manager.

---

[3] Long-run decision making is covered in Chapter 20, "Investment Analysis."

Returns to Scale

In the long run all factors of production are variable. Suppose the manager of a particular production process increased the quantity of each input used by 50 percent. What would happen to output? If output also increased by 50 percent, then we would say that the firm exhibits **constant returns to scale** (or size). If output increased more or less than 50 percent, we would say the firm has **increasing or decreasing returns to scale,** respectively.

If increasing returns to scale exist in a particular production process, then we would logically expect to see larger firms driving the smaller ones out of business since the larger firms could produce more output per bundle of inputs than the smaller firms. In economics, the ratio of output per unit of input is called **efficiency,** so industries (collections of firms) that have production processes with increasing returns to scale would likely have a few large, efficient firms rather than many smaller, less efficient ones. If returns to scale are constant, then large firms and small firms are equally efficient and could be expected to happily coexist.

Economic studies have found that with the exception of very small farms, U.S. agriculture is characterized by constant returns to scale. This explains two phenomena that can be observed. First, it explains the apparently peaceful coexistence of quite large and relatively modest farms in the United States without any stampede to "corporate farming" or "industrialization" as so many in the popular press have predicted. And second, we can understand the demise of the small farm as a self-sustaining economic unit. Very small farms, as farm units, are simply not viable in today's economic climate because of the increasing returns to scale for bigger units.

The Production Function

Returns to scale measures the impact of a proportional change in all inputs. In the short run, farm managers are not able to increase all inputs in like proportions because one or more of the inputs are fixed. A simple and straightforward question such as "How much fertilizer per acre should I apply?" deals with **variable proportions.** In this case, the proportions between fertilizer (a variable input) and land (a fixed input) change as additional fertilizer is applied to the fixed quantity of land. If land and fertilizer are being used to produce corn, then we would expect to see both the corn/land and corn/fertilizer proportions change as additional quantities of fertilizer/land are used. It is these proportions that constitute the heart of the short-run microeconomics of the firm, so we need to examine them closely.

A **production function** is a relationship between units of a variable input and units of output. It is a technical, or physical, relationship that is determined by the particular technology being used in the production process. It is important to emphasize that economics does not determine the nature of the production function. To the contrary, the nature of the production function determines economics.

To begin our analysis of the firm, we will use the simplest production function possible in which there is a single variable input used in combination with one or more fixed inputs to produce a single product. This simple model is usually called the "factor-product" model because there is one variable factor producing one product. In appendices to the next chapter you can explore more complicated models with multiple inputs and/or multiple outputs.

Constant returns to scale as all inputs are increased by a given proportion, output increases by the same proportion.

Increasing returns to scale as all inputs are increased by a given proportion, output increases by a greater proportion.

Decreasing returns to scale as all inputs are increased by a given proportion, output increases by a lesser proportion.

Efficiency a lower general economic concept used in a variety of situations measuring output per unit of input. The higher the ratio, the more efficient the process.

Variable proportions in the short run as additional units of the variable input are used, the ratio or proportion of variable to fixed inputs changes.

Production function in the short run, relationship between units of the variable input and units of output, where units of the variable input and output are both measured per unit of the fixed input.

FIGURE 11–2 A hypothetical production function—schedule.

Input Fertilizer/Land (lb/Acre)	Output Corn/Land (bu/Acre)
0	0
50	10
100	30
150	60
200	85
250	100
300	110
350	117
400	121
450	123
500	124
550	122
600	115

In the factor-product model, the production function describes the relationship between a single product and a single variable input that is used in combination with any number of other inputs that are fixed or predetermined. To simplify matters, assume that we have a production function in which fertilizer is the variable input, land represents all fixed inputs, and corn is the product. Then the production function would describe the relationship between the quantity of fertilizer per acre used and the amount of corn per acre produced. That is, the production function describes the relationship between two proportions: fertilizer/acre and corn/acre.[4]

The Total Product

Common sense tells us a good deal about the nature of this particular relationship. With low levels of fertilizer/acre, we would expect low levels of corn/acre. As the fertilizer/acre ratio is increased, we would expect the corn/acre ratio to increase as well. The direct relationship between fertilizer/acre and corn/acre will continue until eventually a point is reached at which additional units of fertilizer/acre will begin to burn the crop and corn/acre will decrease.

As with any relationship, the nature of the production relationship may be expressed in a variety of manners. We have just expressed the fertilizer-corn relationship verbally. It may also be expressed in the form of a schedule, graph, or formula. A hypothetical fertilizer-corn production function is shown in the form of a schedule in Figure 11–2. A graph of the same production function is shown in Figure 11–3. The curve shown in Figure 11–3 is labeled "*TP*," which stands for **Total Product**—the name given to this input-output relationship. It is a "total" relationship because it describes the total amount of corn/acre produced from different

Total product
relationship between variable input and output.

---

[4] A note to the reader: "fertilizer/acre" is read as "fertilizer per acre" to emphasize that we are dealing with a variable proportion of fertilizer to land. Land represents the fixed factor of production in our examples. All examples will be on a "per acre" basis.

FIGURE 11–3   A hypothetical production function—graph.

combinations of fertilizer/acre. Later we will convert this physical relationship to an economic relationship.

Figures 11–2 and 11–3 illustrate identical relationships. As fertilizer/acre increases, output/acre initially increases at an increasing rate, then it increases at a decreasing rate, and finally it reaches a maximum value beyond which it decreases. This is the pattern followed by a normal, or typical, production function.

DIMINISHING MARGINAL PRODUCT

The previous discussion touches on one of the most important concepts in economics—marginality. In the language of economics, "marginal" refers to additional. In the case of a production function, when we speak about **marginal products,** we are talking about the additional production associated with a unit increase in the variable input. That is, marginal product answers the following question that a producer must ask: "If I add one more unit of the variable input to my bundle of fixed inputs, how much more output will I receive?" Or using our earlier example: "If I add one more pound of fertilizer/acre, by how much would my corn/acre increase?" That additional output is known as the marginal product.

Marginal product measures the rate of change of the total product.[5] As previously mentioned, at low levels of the variable input use, output increases at an increasing rate. This is referred to as **increasing marginal returns.** Beyond some level of variable input use, output increases at a decreasing rate. This is called **decreasing marginal returns.** Then eventually output reaches a maximum and begins to decrease. This is known as **negative marginal returns.** The relationship between total product and marginal product is illustrated in Figure 11–4.

Marginal product additional output (product) associated with a unit increase of the variable input.

Increasing marginal returns   as additional units of the variable input are used, output increases at an increasing rate.

Decreasing marginal returns   as additional units of the variable input are used, output increases at a decreasing rate.

Negative marginal returns   as additional units of the variable input are used, output decreases.

---

[5] The concept of marginal returns can be easily illustrated using the language of calculus. In calculus, the first derivative of a function measures the rate of change of that function. Think of a production function as $Q=f(V\mid F)$ where Q is output, V is a variable input, and F is a fixed input. The rate of change of Q at any level of V is measured by $\delta Q/\delta V$ (since F is a constant and the first derivative of a constant is zero, F falls out of the first derivative).

FIGURE 11–4
Relationship between
total product and
marginal product.

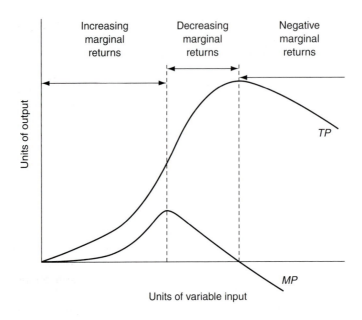

Remember that a production function is a technical, not an economic, relationship. That this technical relationship must have decreasing returns gives rise to an important point. There are very few "laws" in economics, but one of the rare exceptions is the **law of diminishing marginal product,** or the law of variable proportions as it is sometimes called. This law may be stated in the following manner:

Law of diminishing marginal product   as equal increments of the variable input are added to the fixed inputs, there will inevitably occur a decrease in the rate of increase of the total product.

> *Assuming that technology and all inputs except one remain constant, as equal increments of the variable input are added to the fixed inputs, there will inevitably occur a decrease in the rate of increase of the total product.*

Stated differently, for every simple factor-product production function, there must be a point of diminishing marginal product beyond which the rate of increase of the total product decreases.[6]

To illustrate this point, consider the case of a serving counter at a fast-food emporium (we will not deign to call it a "restaurant"). The fixed resources are the physical facilities, and the variable resource is the number of counter workers employed. The product may be measured in the number of customers served per hour. There can be little doubt that if one worker can serve x customers, two workers could serve more than $2x$ customers because each of the two workers would be able to specialize, thereby performing each task more efficiently. This would be a case of increasing marginal returns. A third worker would most likely increase the total product even more dramatically. But, according to the law of diminishing marginal returns, there will come a point beyond which additional workers will not cause the total product to increase at an increasing rate, but instead to increase at a decreasing rate. To rapidly conclude that there must, in fact, be a point of diminishing marginal productivity, consider what a fast-food emporium would look like with 20 people behind the counter! Moreover, at some point, the marginal

---

[6] Mathematically, the point of diminishing marginal returns is the inflection point of the production function. At this point the second derivative of the production function is equal to zero.

product of an additional worker would become negative as the workers bumped hopelessly into one another rather than serving the customers.

The production function is the foundation for the economics of the perfectly competitive firm in the short run. It is a technical relationship dictated by the technology that relates input use to output capacity. In the next chapter we will take this technical relationship and convert it into an economic relationship between costs (inputs) and revenues (outputs) of the firm.

SUMMARY

Perfect competition is an economic model used to describe the behavior of the firm as a production unit. The firm buys inputs (land, labor, and capital) and converts them into products (corn, wheat) that the firm sells. The difference between the costs of inputs and the revenue of products is the profit of the firm. In the perfectly competitive model the objective of the firm is assumed to be that of profit maximization.

The perfectly competitive model is founded on four essential assumptions. First, the firm is assumed to be so small relative to the total market that the actions of a single firm will not affect the market. That is, if one corn farmer in Illinois decides to plant soybeans rather than corn, what is the impact of this decision on the national markets for corn and soybeans? None! Because small firms can't affect markets, they are price takers: they are at the mercy of the market for price determination. Second, perfectly competitive firms produce homogeneous products: each producer's product is the same as that of other producers. Third, resources are free to move into or out of different productive uses in search of the highest return possible. Fourth, all participants in the market have access to the same information with no single participant able to take advantage of superior information at the expense of other participants.

Inputs may be classified as either fixed or variable. Fixed inputs are those that are available to the firm manager in a given amount for the production period. Variable inputs are those inputs over which the manager has control. It is the use rate of the variable factors that the manager can adjust in an effort to maximize profits.

The short run is a period of time in which the manager considers some factors of production to be fixed. In the long run, all inputs are variable and the manager can consider changing the size or scale of the operation. Critical profit-maximizing decisions are usually short-run decisions.

In the short run a production function shows the amount of output the firm can produce at different use rates of the variable input applied to a given quantity of the fixed input. A fertilizer response function is an example of a production function. Varying quantities of fertilizer per unit of land will produce varying quantities of output per unit of land. A production function is called a total product curve because it shows the total amount of product that can be obtained from the given fixed input.

As the amount of the variable input is increased, *ceteris paribus*, the amount of output will increase at an increasing rate, then increase at a decreasing rate, and finally decrease. The rate of change of output per unit of the variable input is called the marginal product. A fundamental concept in economics is the "law" of diminishing marginal product. This law stipulates that every production function will eventually exhibit a diminishing marginal product; that is, output will increase at a decreasing rate as units of the variable input are added to the fixed inputs.

KEY TERMS

Accounting profit

Atomistic

Constant returns to scale

Decreasing marginal returns

Decreasing returns to scale

Economic profit

Efficiency

Enterprise

Fixed inputs

Homogeneous

Increasing marginal returns

Increasing returns to scale

Law of diminishing marginal product

Long run

Marginal product

Microeconomics

Negative marginal returns

Opportunity cost

Price maker

Price taker

Production

Production function

Short run

Total product

Variable inputs

Variable proportions

PROBLEMS AND DISCUSSION QUESTIONS

[handwritten margin notes: Producers small Price takers Resources mobile Homogeneous product Dairy Hats Grain]

1. Clearly distinguish between economic profits and accounting profits.

2. What are the three strong assumptions upon which the model of a perfectly competitive firm rests?

3. Give four examples of local businesses that operate in near-perfect competition. *[handwritten: Barbershop, Chinese Restaurants, Lawn services, taverns]*

4. The manager of a perfectly competitive firm is a price taker for both the prices paid for inputs and prices received for products. He or she has no control over prices. What does the firm manager control and adjust in an effort to maximize profits?

5. Give examples of inputs of the typical farmer that would be considered fixed inputs for one production cycle. Also, give examples of variable inputs.

6. Using the production function below, what is the variable input range for which there are:

   a. Increasing marginal returns?

   b. Decreasing marginal returns?

   c. Negative marginal returns?

Units of Variable Input	Units of Output
0	0
1	10
2	25
3	50
4	65
5	75
6	80
7	82
8	80
9	75

7. Based on the same production function, what is the marginal product of the sixth unit of the variable input?

MATHEMATICAL APPENDIX

T he basic elements of a production function can be summarized using the language of mathematics. The production function describes a relationship between units of output (Q) and units of a variable input (V) used in combination with a bundle of fixed inputs (F). So,

$$Q = f(V \mid F)$$

The marginal product (MP) of this production function is the rate of change of output as the variable input changes, which is the first derivative of the total product curve with respect to the variable input:

$$MP = \frac{\delta Q}{\delta V}$$

As an illustration, take a very simple production function that exhibits only decreasing marginal returns and negative marginal returns—a simple quadratic function:

$$Q = 20V - 2V^2 \mid F$$

Some values for this equation are shown in Figure 11–5 and the function is graphed in Figure 11–6. As can be seen in Figure 11–6 this production function initially exhibits output increasing at a decreasing rate, reaching a maximum value at 5 units of the variable input, and thereafter decreasing.

The marginal product of this production function is

$$\frac{\delta Q}{\delta V} = 20 - 4V$$

Variable Input	Output
1	18
2	32
3	42
4	48
5	50
6	48
7	42

FIGURE 11–5
Production function—schedule.

FIGURE 11–6
Production function—
graph.

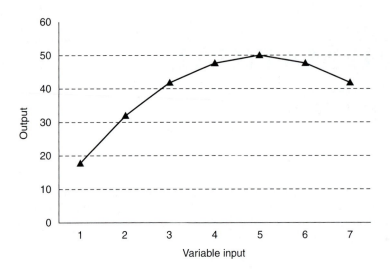

This can be solved to find the marginal product at any level of the variable input (V). For instance, at 3 units of the variable input, the marginal product would be 8 units. As can be seen in the schedules in Figure 11–5, the marginal product (change in output) between 2 and 3 units of V is 10, and between 3 and 4 it is 6; so, it stands to reason that the marginal product at 3 is 8.

In calculus one learns that the extrema of a function are found at those points at which the first derivative is equal to zero. Translated into economics, this means that the maximum value of the total product (Q) will occur when the marginal product (MP) is equal to zero. Doing that,

$$20 - 4V = 0$$

$$V = 5$$

we find that the maximum total product occurs at a variable input level of 5 units, which can be confirmed by glancing at Figure 11–5. At 5 units of the variable product, the total product is

$$Q = 20 \cdot 5 - 2 \cdot 5^2$$
$$Q = 50$$

Again, this result can be confirmed by looking at Figure 11–5 or 11–6.

Finally, the second derivative of the total product with respect to the variable input will determine whether marginal returns are increasing or decreasing. In our example

$$\frac{\delta^2 Q}{\delta V^2} = \frac{\delta MP}{\delta V} = -2$$

Since the second derivative is negative for all values of V, we know that the marginal returns for this production function are always decreasing.

Costs and Optimal Output Levels

We now come to the heart of the microeconomics of the firm: profit maximization. In this chapter we will examine the short-run, managerial rules for maximizing the profit of a perfectly competitive firm. As in the last chapter we will examine the simple factor-product model in which it is assumed the firm has only one variable input that is used in combination with a bundle of other inputs whose quantity is fixed in the short run. These inputs, variable and fixed, are used to produce a single output in a perfectly competitive market.[1]

Before embarking on this journey, it will be useful to reflect on those items that are **exogenous** to the firm and those that are **endogenous.** Exogenous factors are those factors that are beyond the control of the manager. The manager must be knowledgeable about exogenous factors, but the manager cannot control these factors. In fact, to some extent these factors control the manager. Endogenous factors are those things that the manager can control—decisions that the manager must make.

In the short run the production function, reflecting the technology being used in the production process, is given or fixed. In the short run the production function is exogenous. Assume the manager of the firm faces a typical production function that has regions of increasing, decreasing, and negative marginal returns. No manager would be caught dead producing where the marginal returns are negative, because in this range it would be possible to increase output (and hence revenues) by using fewer units of the variable input (reducing costs). Likewise, the manager would not produce where marginal returns are increasing because the manager would clearly add inputs so long as output is expanding at an expanding rate. So by process of elimination we know that the manager is going to be facing that portion of the production function in which output is increasing at a decreasing rate.

Within this relevant segment of the production function there is a one-to-one relationship between input and output. That is, for each level of variable input use there is one and only one level of output. So, by the manager's choice of how many units of the variable input to use, the level of output is uniquely determined. The choice of the input-output level is endogenous to the firm manager.

Finally, prices are exogenous to the firm. In perfect competition, prices are determined by the market and accepted by the manager. This is true for both the price of the product and the price of the variable input. Fixed costs are predetermined and thus exogenous to the manager.

Exogenous external to the firm; beyond the control of the manager of the firm.

Endogenous internal to the firm; may be controlled by the firm manager.

---

[1] In appendixes to this chapter the factor-product model is expanded to the factor-factor-product model and the factor-product-product model.

OPTIMAL OUTPUT LEVEL

Since about the only thing the firm's manager can control is output, the question that the manager must ask is, What is the profit-maximizing level of output of the firm? As we examine the economics of profit maximization, there are several things that should be kept in mind:

- Profit is the difference between revenues from selling products and costs of buying inputs.
- The only way the firm can increase revenue is by increasing production.
- The only way the firm can increase production is by increasing variable input use.
- Increased variable input use will cause an increase in costs.
- So, the only way to increase revenue is to increase costs.
- If revenue increases more than costs increase, then profit is increasing, and vice versa.

Think of the firm as having two sides—a cost side and a revenue side. The interplay between the two determines profit. We are going to look at the cost side first and then turn to the revenue side of the firm.

Costs of the Firm

As in the case of the production function, our cost curve analysis will be a short-run analysis in which there is assumed to be one product (corn) and one variable factor of production (fertilizer) that is used in combination with a bundle of fixed factors (land).

Total Cost

Total cost all costs of producing a given level of output. The sum of fixed and variable costs.

The **total cost** (*TC*) of producing a given level of output is equal to the sum of the **total variable costs** (*TVC*) and the **total fixed costs** (*TFC*). As the output level changes, the total variable costs change but, by definition, the total fixed costs do not.

Total variable cost all costs associated with the variable input at a given level of output.

To derive these cost curves, let's return to our original production function in which the quantity of corn produced was a function of the amount of fertilizer applied, *ceteris paribus*. In that construct, units of the variable input were measured on the horizontal axis and units of the product were listed on the vertical axis. Since we now want to focus on the relationship between output levels and input costs, we simply flip the production function over to transpose the axes. The result is shown in Figure 12–1.[2]

Total fixed cost all costs associated with the bundle of fixed factors. Fixed costs do not change as the level of output changes.

The units on the vertical axis are converted from physical units to economic units by simply multiplying pounds of fertilizer times the price of fertilizer. Since Figure 12–1 shows the relationship between levels of output (per acre of land) and the costs associated with the variable factor of production, we call this the total variable cost (*TVC*) curve.

---

[2] For a quick demonstration of this transformation, draw a production function on a clean piece of paper. Make sure to label your axes. Then pick the paper up and look at the production function from the back of the paper with the axes in the usual orientation. What you see should look like Figure 12–1.

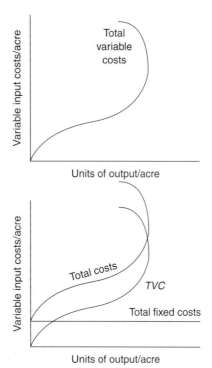

FIGURE 12–1 Total variable costs.

FIGURE 12–2 Total costs of production.

A total fixed cost (*TFC*) curve is about as exciting as watching a chess game on TV. By definition, fixed costs don't change with changes in the output level. Therefore, the total fixed cost curve is simply a horizontal line as shown in Figure 12–2. Note that the fixed costs are at the same level for all output levels including zero. In our fertilizer-corn example, a farmer's property tax is a good example of a fixed cost. The amount of property tax owed is the same whether the farmer produces zero or 200 bushels to the acre.

Since the total cost (*TC*) of different levels of output is equal to the sum of the total fixed cost and the total variable cost, we can add them together graphically as shown in Figure 12–2. The total cost curve in Figure 12–2 illustrates clearly why production in the segment of negative marginal returns of the production function is irrational. Note that it is possible to produce many output levels at either of two cost levels. Obviously it would be irrational to produce at the higher cost in the portion of the total cost curve with negative marginal returns.

A similar kind of presentation in schedule form is given in Figure 12–3, which is based on the fertilizer-corn production function introduced in the previous chapter, with the assumption of fixed costs per acre of $80 and a fertilizer price of $0.12/pound. Note that all the data in Figure 12–3 relate to the cost side of the firm. Later we will deal with the revenue side.

Average or per Unit Cost

The three *total* cost curves show costs per unit of the *fixed input*—land in our example. That is, the total cost curve shows costs per acre. The *average* cost curves show costs *per unit of output*—bushels of corn in our example.

FIGURE 12–3 Total costs of production—schedule.

Units of Input (lb/acre)	Units of Output (bu/acre)	Total Variable Costs ($/acre)	Total Fixed Costs ($/acre)	Total Costs ($/acre)
0	0	$0	$80	$80
50	10	6	80	86
100	30	12	80	92
150	60	18	80	98
200	85	24	80	104
250	100	30	80	110
300	110	36	80	116
350	117	42	80	122
400	121	48	80	128
450	123	54	80	134
500	124	60	80	140
550	122	66	80	146
600	115	72	80	152

Note: Above schedule is based on the following prices:
  Land (fixed input) @ $80/acre
  Fertilizer (variable input) @ $0.12/lb

As in the case of the total costs, there are three varieties of average costs: variable, fixed, and total. In each case, the average cost is equal to the level of total cost divided by units of output. The algebraic expression of the three average cost curves is

Average fixed cost
fixed costs per unit of output.

$$AVC = \frac{TVC}{TP} \qquad AFC = \frac{TFC}{TP} \qquad ATC = \frac{TC}{TP}$$

Average variable cost
variable costs per unit of output.

where TP = total product or output. Notice that the terms "output" and "total product" are being used interchangeably. These three cost relationships are shown in a schedule in Figure 12–4 and as graphs in Figure 12–5.[3]

Average total cost
total costs per unit of output.

Several observations about the structure of the three average cost curves need to be made. First, notice that the **average fixed cost** declines so long as output is expanding. This phenomenon is commonly referred to as "spreading the overhead." Both the **average variable cost** and **average total cost** curves have a "U" shape. The two curves are similarly shaped, with the vertical distance between them being the average fixed cost. As output expands, the average fixed cost decreases so that the average variable cost and average total cost curves grow closer together as output increases.

Economic efficiency
output per dollar of input cost. A decrease in costs per unit is an increase in economic efficiency.

Earlier efficiency was defined as the output/input ratio. **Economic efficiency** is measured in Figure 12–5 as costs per unit—the lower the cost per unit, the higher the economic efficiency. In fact, the fundamental economic problem that the manager

---

[3] As shown earlier, total cost curves "double back" on themselves in the negative marginal returns segment. Other strange things with cost curves also happen in this irrational range of production. For clarity, this segment has been omitted in all the cost curves drawn in the remainder of this chapter. This is really not important because the economics of this range deals with the economics of irrational behavior, and most students find the economics of rational behavior to be challenging enough.

Units of Variable Input (lb/acre)	Units of Output (*TP*) (bu/acre)	Average Variable Costs ($/bu)	Average Fixed Costs ($/bu)	Average Total Costs ($/bu)
0	0	——	——	——
50	10	$0.60	$8.00	$8.60
100	30	0.40	2.67	3.07
150	60	0.30	1.33	1.63
200	85	0.28	0.94	1.22
250	100	0.30	0.80	1.10
300	110	0.33	0.73	1.05
350	117	0.36	0.68	1.04
400	121	0.40	0.66	1.06
450	123	0.44	0.65	1.09
500	124	0.48	0.65	1.13
550	122	0.54	0.66	1.20
600	115	0.63	0.70	1.32

FIGURE 12–4
Average costs of production—schedule.

Note: Above schedule is based on the following prices:
   Land (fixed input) @ $80/acre
   Fertilizer (variable input) @ $0.12/lb
   Average costs are not defined for TP = 0

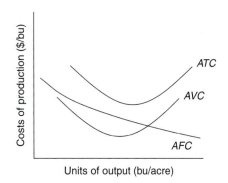

FIGURE 12–5
Average costs of production—graph.

must solve can be seen in Figure 12–5. The economic efficiency of the fixed factor at different levels of output is shown by the average fixed cost curve. Efficiency of the fixed factor increases as output increases over the entire range of output choices.[4]

The economic efficiency of the variable factor is shown by the average variable cost curve. At low output levels it too increases as output increases, but eventually average variable cost reaches a minimum point and then efficiency of the variable factor begins decreasing; that is, variable cost per unit of output increases. When the economic efficiency of both the fixed and the variable input is increasing, there are no choices to be made: expand production because the efficiency of both inputs is increased. But once the average variable cost reaches its minimum value and starts increasing, there is a trade-off to expanding production. If the manager expands production beyond the minimum average variable cost, the economic efficiency of

---

[4] Decreasing average fixed cost equals increasing economic efficiency of the fixed factor.

FIGURE 12–6
Marginal costs of
production—graph.

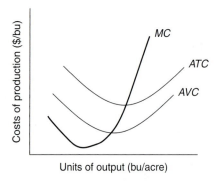

the fixed factor increases while the efficiency of the variable factor decreases. As output expands, the manager must deal with the benefits of increased efficiency of the fixed input versus the costs of decreased efficiency of the variable input.

The minimum point on the average variable cost curve is where the economic trade-off begins. Any output level lower than that at which the minimum average variable cost occurs would be irrational. Output levels greater than the one associated with the minimum average variable cost are known as the **rational range of production.**

Rational range of production   the rational firm will always produce at output levels for which the average variable cost is increasing and for which the marginal returns are not negative.

Marginal Cost

Marginal cost   the additional cost of producing one additional unit of output.

The concept of marginality is central to all microeconomic theory. Earlier the concept of marginal product was introduced. There is an analogous concept in the cost realm—**marginal cost.** Marginal cost is the additional cost associated with producing one additional unit of output. It is the rate of change of the total cost with respect to the output level. Over any output range, marginal cost is calculated as

$$MC = \frac{\Delta TC}{\Delta TP} = \frac{\Delta TVC}{\Delta TP}$$

where ΔTP is a change in output levels over which a change in costs is measured. A graph and a schedule with marginal cost are shown in Figures 12–6 and 12–7. In Figure 12–6 the average fixed cost curve has been omitted for clarity.

In Figure 12–7 the marginal cost is shown midway between any two production levels. This is done to indicate that this is the marginal cost between the two levels of output. For instance, the marginal cost of the additional 20 bushels of corn between output levels of 10 and 30 is $0.30 per additional bushel ($6.00/20 = $0.30).

Two aspects of the relationship between the average and marginal costs in Figure 12–6 need to be noted. First, note that the marginal cost is equal to the average variable cost and average total cost at their minimum points.[5] Second, since rational

---

[5] The logic of this is straightforward. If the marginal is less than the average, then the average is falling. If the marginal is greater than the average, then the average is increasing. Hence, the minimum point of the average is where the two are equal to one another. Think of it this way: imagine what the average weight is of all the brothers in the Alpha Gamma Rho house at Moo U. Now add one more brother—a Sumo wrestler from Japan. This additional or marginal brother is well above the average, so when he is added, the average goes up. Now add a jockey: the marginal is less than the average, and the average goes down.

Units of Input (lb/acre)	Units of Output (bu/acre)	Total Variable Costs ($/bu)	Marginal Costs ($/bu)
0	0	$0	
			$0.60
50	10	6	
			0.30
100	30	12	
			0.20
150	60	18	
			0.24
200	85	24	
			0.40
250	100	30	
			0.60
300	110	36	
			0.86
350	117	42	
			1.50
400	121	48	
			3.00
450	123	54	
			6.00
500	124	60	
			−3.00
550	122	66	
			−0.86
600	115	72	

FIGURE 12–7
Marginal costs of production—schedule.

production occurs at some output level greater than the output level at the minimum average variable cost, we can say that in the rational range of production marginal cost is always increasing as output increases. As we shall see in the next section, marginal cost is the key to the profit-maximizing behavior of the firm manager.

Revenue

The competitive firm should always be viewed as an interaction between inputs and outputs in a physical sense or costs and revenues in an economic sense. Throughout the rational range of production, constant (per unit) increases in output or revenues are matched by increasing marginal costs associated with the variable input.

Total Revenue

The **total revenue** of a simple factor-product firm is simply the value of sales, which is equal to the price per unit sold (a constant) times the number of units sold. As before, *total* revenue refers to revenue per unit of the fixed factor. In our fertilizer/land example, total revenue would be revenue per unit of land or revenue per acre. Because the product price is constant, the total revenue curve in Figure 12–8 is a straight line, the slope of which is equal to the price per unit of the product.

Total revenue total receipts from the sale of the output or product. Total revenue is equal to price of the product times number of units sold.

FIGURE 12–8   Total
revenue.

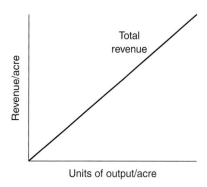

Average and Marginal Revenue

While total revenue refers to revenue per unit of the fixed factor, average and marginal revenue refer to revenues per unit of output. Since the price of the product is a constant, both average revenue and marginal revenue are equal to the price of the product. This simple assertion deserves a bit of reflection. First, with regards to the **average revenue,** we can define average revenue as total revenue per unit of output:

$$AR = \frac{TR}{TP}$$

Average revenue
revenue per unit of
output; equal to the
price of the product in
perfect competition.

Using "P_p" for the per unit price of the product, then

$$AR = \frac{TP \cdot P_p}{TP}$$

or

$$AR = P_p$$

Marginal revenue
additional revenue
associated with one
additional unit of
output; equal to the
price of the product in
perfect competition.

In the case of **marginal revenue,** the equality between marginal revenue and price of the product can be seen if we return to the fundamental concept of marginality. Marginal revenue is the additional revenue associated with one additional unit of output. Suppose rutabagas (because of their highly prized taste) are selling for $5 per pound. If farmer Polopolus sells one more pound of rutabagas, by how much does his revenue increase? Obviously, by $5. It doesn't matter whether his sales went from 5 to 6 pounds or from 500 to 501 pounds; the additional revenue associated with each additional unit sold is $5. So, marginal revenue is equal to the price of the product.

Since both marginal revenue and average revenue are equal to the price of the product at all output levels, they are also equal to one another. Average and marginal revenue are graphed in Figure 12–9.

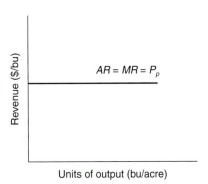

FIGURE 12–9
Average and marginal revenue.

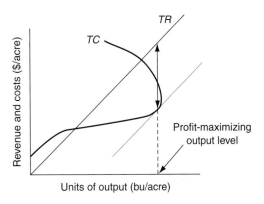

FIGURE 12–10 Profit maximization using total revenue and total cost—graph.

Profit Maximization

Assuming that profit maximization is the sole objective of the firm, how must the firm manager adjust the output level so as to maximize profit?[6] For the perfectly competitive firm, the price per unit at which the firm can sell its output is determined exogenously by the market. The manager has absolutely no control over the product price. The market offers the manager a price on a take it or leave it basis (much the same as a grocery store offers you a head of lettuce on a take it or leave it basis).

There are four equally valid approaches to finding the profit-maximizing output level. Profits can be determined from either the total cost/revenue information or the marginal cost/revenue information. Both sets of information can be presented in a schedule or in a graph. In the following discussion we will look at each of the four possible combinations.

Graphs Using TR and TC

Profit is the difference between revenues and costs. Finding that output level that will maximize the difference is the objective of the firm manager. As shown in Figure 12–10, the vertical difference between the total revenue line and the total

---

[6] In the simple factor-product model, the only way the manager can adjust output is by adjusting the use of the variable input. Therefore, the profit-maximizing output level is the same thing as the profit-maximizing input level viewed from a different perspective.

FIGURE 12–11 Profit maximization using *TR* and *TC*—schedule.

Units of Input (lb/acre)	Total Variable Costs ($/acre)	Total Fixed Costs ($/acre)	Total Costs ($/acre)	Total Revenue ($/acre)	Profit ($/acre)
0	$0	$80	$80	$0	−$80.00
50	6	80	86	25.00	−61.00
100	12	80	92	75.00	−17.00
150	18	80	98	150.00	52.00
200	24	80	104	212.50	108.50
250	30	80	110	250.00	140.00
300	36	80	116	275.00	159.00
350	42	80	122	292.50	170.50
400	48	80	128	302.50	174.50
450	54	80	134	307.50	173.50
500	60	80	140	310.00	170.00
550	66	80	146	305.00	159.00
600	72	80	152	287.50	135.50

Note: Above schedule is based on the following prices:

Input (fertilizer) @ $0.12/lb

Output (corn) @ $2.50/bu

cost curve is the amount of profit. The point of profit maximization (the maximum vertical difference between the two curves) is located at the point of tangency between the *TC* curve and a line drawn parallel to the *TR* curve. This is shown in Figure 12–10 with a narrow line tangent to the *TC* curve. The output level at the point of tangency is the profit-maximizing level of output. The amount of profit is the vertical distance shown by the arrow between the two curves.

Schedules Using TR and TC

Profit-maximizing behavior is easy to identify when working with schedules such as in Figure 12–11. Clearly, the greatest profit of $174.50 per acre is earned by using 400 pounds of fertilizer. To use either more or less than 400 pounds/acre would be to forego some possible profits. The schedule can be used to illustrate two important points.

First, notice that between 0 and 500 pounds/acre of fertilizer there is a direct relationship between total costs and total revenues. As additional units of the input are applied, output increases. As a result, both total costs and total revenues increase. Since both are increasing, it is not the increase that is critical; it is the rate of increase that is important. The rate of increase is measured by marginal cost and marginal revenue. As those rates of increase change, the firm's profits will change.

Second, look at the role of fixed costs in profit-maximizing behavior. Suppose that the fixed costs of the firm increased from $80/acre to $85/acre. What changes would occur to the data in Figure 12–11? Each item in the total fixed cost column would increase by $5. As a consequence, each item in the total cost column would increase by $5. There would be no changes in the total revenue column, and as a consequence, each entry in the profit column would fall by $5.

FIGURE 12–12 Profit maximization—marginal graph.

Now the profit-maximizing firm would earn only $169.50 of profits, but it would earn those profits by continuing to use the same amount of the variable input and producing the same level of output. So the bottom line is that an increase (decrease) in fixed costs:

- Does not affect the profit-maximizing output level
- Will cause the level of profits to decrease (increase)

Graphs Using MR and MC

Marginal cost is the additional cost associated with one additional unit of output. Marginal revenue is the additional revenue associated with one additional unit of output. The profit-maximizing firm should continue to expand production within the rational range of production so long as additions to revenue (marginal revenue) are greater than additions to costs (marginal costs). Since marginal costs increase and marginal revenue is constant, there will eventually be a point at which additions to cost become greater than additions to revenue. At that point, profits begin to fall. Therefore, the point at which marginal revenue is equal to marginal costs is the point of maximum profits. Graphically it is shown as point *a* on Figure 12–12, which combines the cost side of the firm with the revenue side of the firm.

Schedules Using MR and MC

While it is easy to visually identify the point of profit maximization on a set of marginal cost and marginal revenue curves such as those in Figure 12–12, the economics of profit maximization is better illustrated with a set of schedules such as in Figure 12–13. Let's walk through the economics of profit maximization in Figure 12–13 using a step-by-step approach. The first step is to begin examining the economics of expanding output within the rational range of production by looking at the relationship between additional costs and additional revenues for each possible output expansion. Suppose the firm is at an output level of 110 bushels/acre. Should it expand production to 117 bushels/acre? If it does, the marginal (or additional) costs of each of the additional 7 units would be $0.86/bushel. The additional revenue for each of the 7 units would be $2.50/bushel. Therefore an expansion of output to 117 bushels/acre would cause the firm's profit to increase by $1.64 for

FIGURE 12–13 Profit maximization—marginal schedule.

Units of Variable Input (lb/acre)	Units of Output (bu/acre)	Total Variable Costs ($/bu)	Marginal Costs ($/bu)	Marginal Revenues ($/bu)
0	0	$0		
			$0.60	$2.50
50	10	6		
			0.30	2.50
100	30	12		
			0.20	2.50
150	60	18		
			0.24	2.50
200	85	24		
			0.40	2.50
250	100	30		
			0.60	2.50
300	110	36		
			0.86	2.50
350	117	42		
			1.50	2.50
400	121	48		
			3.00	2.50
450	123	54		
			6.00	2.50
500	124	60		
			−3.00	2.50
550	122	66		
			−0.86	2.50
600	115	72		

Note: Above schedule is based on the following prices:
  Corn (output) @ $2.50/bu
  Fertilizer (variable input) @ $0.12/lb

each of the 7 additional bushels produced. So, 117 bushels/acre is preferred to 110 bushels/acre.

Next, examine the economics of moving from 117 bushels/acre to 121 bushels/acre. The additional cost of each of those 4 bushels would be $1.50/bushel, while the additional revenue would be $2.50/bushel. By expanding output to 121 bushels/acre, the firm is able to add $1.00/bushel of profit on 4 bushels to the level of profit that would be earned at 117 bushels/acre. We don't know what the amount of profits is at an output level of 117 bushels/acre, but we do know that the choice the manager of the firm faces is either taking that amount by producing 117 bushels/acre or taking that amount plus $4.00 by producing 121 bushels/acre. Obviously, the profit-maximizing manager would prefer the latter alternative.

Continue the process of examining the economics of expanding production by looking at the next possible expansion of output to 123 bushels/acre. The marginal cost of each of the 2 additional bushels is $3.00/bushel, while the marginal revenue is only $2.50/bushel. In this case, the firm would lose $0.50/bushel on each of the 2 additional bushels, bringing total profit down by $1.00 from where it was at an output level of 121 bushels/acre.

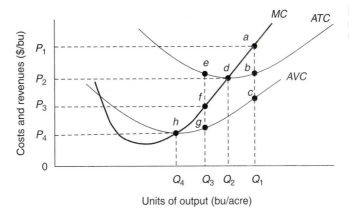

FIGURE 12–14 Profit maximization and loss minimization.

Profits of the firm are maximized at an output level of 121 bushels/acre. Imagine a producer who is at an output level of 121 bushels/acre. The manager reasons that he can change his cost-revenue relationship by either expanding or reducing the output level. If the output level is reduced to 117 bushels/acre, profit falls by $4.00. If output is expanded to 123 bushels/acre, profit falls by $1.00. Since profit falls from a movement in either direction from the output level of 121 bushels/acre, that must be the profit-maximizing level of output.[7] In fact, in this example 121 bushels/acre would be the profit-maximizing output level for any product price in the range between $1.50/bushel and $3.00/bushel.

Behavior of the Profit-Maximizing or Loss-Minimizing Firm

Cost curves allow a thorough examination of the economics of the profit-maximizing firm. In Figure 12–14, if the price of the product is P_1, then the profit-maximizing firm would adjust output to Q_1. The vertical distance aQ_1 measures the revenue per unit of output (average revenue). Vertical distance bQ_1 is the average total cost of producing Q_1 units. Vertical distance bc, being the difference between average total costs and average variable costs, is the average fixed cost of producing Q_1 units. Since the distance ab is the difference between per unit revenues and per unit costs, ab measures the average or per unit profit of producing Q_1 units of output. The vertical distance ab multiplied by the horizontal distance Q_1 is the total amount of profit earned by the firm. This would be equal to the size of a rectangle with corners at P_1, a, b, and a horizontal line from b intersecting the vertical axis.

---

[7] This process of finding the point of profit maximization can be illustrated with the help of a mountain climber. One might ask, How does a mountain climber know that she has reached the peak of a mountain? It's simple. If movement in any direction is downward, then where she is standing must be the top of the mountain. This is the same process used to find profit maximization on the schedules: find that point at which either an expansion or a reduction of output will result in a decrease in profit, and that must be the maximum point.

The astute student may realize that a mountain climber may have reached only a local maximum and that by descending from a small peak of 12,000 feet of altitude she can begin the ascent of the true 14,000-foot peak. The difference between local and global maximum points is a serious problem in advanced mathematical economics. In all the examples at the introductory level, all of these possibilities have been quietly assumed away. If you are greatly bothered by these assumptions, you may have a future in mathematical economics.

Break-even point
product price for
which the economic
profits of the firm are
zero.

Break-Even Point   Notice what would happen to average profits if the product price increased from P_1 to a higher price. Since the MC curve is rising more rapidly than the ATC curve, increases in the price of the product would lead to increases in the average profit per unit. Likewise, at prices below P_1 the average profit per unit produced becomes smaller and smaller until, at a price of P_2 and an output level of Q_2, the average profit per unit becomes zero. Point d at which economic profits fall to zero is known as the **break-even point.** At any price greater than P_2, the firm will earn economic profits. At any price less than P_2, economic profits will be negative (i.e., there will be economic losses).

Now let's look at the economics of losing money and answer the question, Why does the cattlerancher who claims to be losing $50 per head continue to produce cattle? Let's suppose the price of the product (over which the producer has no control) falls to P_3. At a market price of P_3 there is no way the firm can earn an economic profit, so the firm manager shifts from an objective of profit maximization to one of loss minimization in the short run. Our profit-maximizing criterion of marginal revenue equals marginal costs suggests that the firm manager should adjust output level to Q_3. This criterion is also valid for loss minimization. What are the economics of producing Q_3 units? The revenue per unit is equal to the vertical distance fQ_3 (or P_3), while the total cost per unit is equal to vertical distance eQ_3. Thus, there is a loss per unit equal to the vertical distance ef. The average variable cost per unit is vertical distance gQ_3, which is slightly less than the average revenue per unit. So, the firm is able to cover all variable costs (gQ_3) and have a little left over (distance gf) to contribute to fixed costs. At output level Q_3 the firm can't cover all fixed costs, but it can at least cover part of its fixed costs.

What is the alternative to producing at output level Q_3? Since the firm can't change the price of the product, producing either more or less than Q_3 units would cause the loss to be even greater than at output level Q_3. The only other alternative is to produce nothing. If the firm produced nothing, it would still have to pay the fixed costs. So, the choice is between (a) producing nothing and paying all fixed costs, or (b) producing at Q_3 units and covering a part of fixed costs. Given a choice between losing a little or losing a lot, the decision to lose a little looks pretty good even though the manager would rather be given a chance to earn a profit rather than minimizing a loss.

Shutdown point
product price for
which the firm would
cease production;
equal to the minimum
average variable cost.

ShutDown Point   The firm will minimize its loss by producing at output levels between Q and Q at prices between P_4 and P_2. Should the price of the product fall below the minimum average variable cost, then the firm is better off to produce nothing and the amount of the loss will be equal to the fixed costs. As a consequence, point h at output level Q_4 is known as the "shutdown" point. At any price less than P_4 in Figure 12–14, the firm would not be able to cover all of its variable costs, and it also couldn't cover any of the fixed costs. In such a situation, it is better to produce nothing at all in the short run, accept a loss equal to the fixed costs, and wait for market prices to go back up.

SUMMARY

The firm is a production unit that converts inputs into outputs. There are costs associated with the inputs and revenues associated with the outputs. The objective of the firm is to maximize profits—the difference between those revenues and costs. The costs of the firm are divided into fixed costs, which do not change as the level of output changes, and variable costs, which do change as output changes.

The simplest model of the firm is the factor-product model in which it is assumed that the firm uses one variable input in combination with a bundle of fixed inputs to produce one product. This is a short-run model of a firm in a perfectly competitive market. The only thing the firm manager can control is the amount of the variable input used and hence the quantity of product produced. All other factors, including the prices of inputs and output, are exogenous or beyond the control of the firm manager.

Within the rational range of production there is a one-to-one relationship between the amount of the variable input used and the amount of product produced. Within this range the economic efficiency of the fixed factors increases while the economic efficiency of the variable factor decreases.

The total costs of the firm may be divided into total variable costs and total fixed costs. Total costs are measured per unit of the fixed factor. Average costs (total, variable, and fixed) are measured per unit of output. Marginal cost is the additional cost associated with one additional unit of output.

The total revenue of the firm is equal to quantity of the product produced times the price per unit (which is a constant). Total revenue refers to revenue per unit of the fixed factor. Average revenue is the revenue per unit of output and is equal to the constant product price. Marginal revenue is the additional revenue associated with one additional unit of output and is also equal to the price of the product.

In order to maximize profits the manager of a factor-product firm should adjust the use of the variable input to that level at which the marginal cost is equal to the marginal revenue. The manager of the firm adjusts input use (and hence output) whenever the price of the product (i.e., the marginal revenue) changes.

At product prices above the minimum average total cost the firm will earn economic profits. The minimum average total cost is called the break-even point, because at product prices below this point the firm will have negative economic profits or losses. At product prices between the break-even point and the minimum average variable cost or shutdown point, the firm manager will engage in loss minimization by continuing to adjust variable input use to that point at which marginal revenue is equal to marginal cost. At product prices below the shutdown point the firm will cease production and limit losses to the amount of the fixed costs.

KEY TERMS

Average fixed cost	Marginal cost
Average revenue	Marginal revenue
Average total cost	Rational range of production
Average variable cost	Shutdown point
Break-even point	Total cost
Economic efficiency	Total fixed cost
Endogenous	Total revenue
Exogenous	Total variable cost

Problems and Discussion Questions

1. The following questions refer to the production function in the following table. For all questions, the price of the input is $11 and the price of the product (or output) is $4. Fixed costs are $30.

Units of Input	Units of Output
1	10
2	25
3	45
4	60
5	70
6	77
7	82
8	85
9	86
10	84
11	80

  a. What is the value of the following at 8 units of the variable input?

  *TP*_____

  *AVC*_____

  *TVC*_____

  b. The profit-maximizing firm would use _____ units of the variable input.

  c. The marginal cost of the fifth unit of the variable input is _____.

  d. If the firm used 10 units of the variable input, profits would be $_____.

  e. If the variable input were free, the firm would produce _____ units.

2. Fill in the blanks in the table below. Carry all calculations to two decimals. The price of the variable input is $3.00/unit, and the price of the product is $6.00/unit.

Units of Variable Input	Units of Output	Total Fixed Cost	Total Variable Cost	Total Cost	Marginal Cost
4	35	$40.00	_____	_____	
					_____
5	42	_____	_____	_____	

3. "Total" means amount per unit of _____, "average" means amount per unit of _____, and "marginal" means amount per unit of _____.

4. What are the assumptions made in the simple factor-product model?

5. What is the objective of the firm manager, and what is the criterion for determining the output level in each of the following cases:

  a. The price of the product is less than the shutdown price?

  b. The price of the product is greater than the shutdown price but less than the break-even price?

  c. The price of the product is greater than the break-even price?

APPENDIX 1

MATHEMATICAL APPROACH

Notational Conventions

Let

V = number of units of the variable factor being used

F = fixed factors of production

Q = output level corresponding to a certain level of variable input

P_v = price per unit of the variable input (a constant)

P_q = price per unit of the product (a constant)

Π = profit of the firm (revenues − costs)

then the production function is of the form

$$Q = f(V|F)$$

Total, Average, and Marginal

Total always refers to *per unit of the fixed factor.*
Average always refers to *per unit of output.*
Marginal always refers to *rate of change per unit change of output.*

Relationships

Costs are divided into those costs associated with the variable and the fixed factors. The sum of the two is total cost.

	Total	Average	Marginal
Revenue	*TR*	*AR*	*MR*
Cost (variable)	*TVC*	*AVC*	*MC*
Cost (fixed)	*TFC*	*AFC*	zero
Cost (total)	*TC*	*ATC*	*MC*

$$TR = P_q \cdot Q$$

$$AR = \frac{TR}{Q} = P_q$$

$$MR = \frac{\Delta TR}{\Delta Q} = P_q$$

$$TVC = P_v \cdot V$$

$$AVC = \frac{TVC}{Q}$$

$$MC = \frac{\Delta TVC}{\Delta Q}$$

$$TFC = \text{a constant}$$

$$AFC = \frac{TFC}{Q}$$

$$ATC = AVC + AFC$$

$$ATC = \frac{TC}{Q}$$

$$MC = \frac{\Delta TC}{\Delta Q} = \frac{\Delta TVC}{\Delta Q}$$

Profit Maximization

Profit is total revenues minus total costs:

$$\Pi = TR - TVC - TFC$$

that is:

$$\Pi = P_q \cdot Q - P_v \cdot V - TFC$$

To find profit-maximizing output level, differentiate profit function with respect to output and set the result equal to zero.

$$\frac{\delta \Pi}{\delta Q} = P_q \frac{\delta Q}{\delta Q} - P_v \frac{\delta V}{\delta Q} = 0$$

eliminating

$$\frac{\delta \Pi}{\delta Q} = P_q - P_v \frac{\delta V}{\delta Q}$$

setting equal to zero to find maximum profit

$$0 = P_q - P_v \frac{\delta V}{\delta Q}$$

or

$$P_q = P_v \frac{\delta V}{\delta Q}$$

$P_v \dfrac{\delta V}{\delta Q}$ is the rate of change of costs with respect to output, or marginal cost, so

$$P_q = MC$$

and, by definition

$$P_q = MR$$

Hence, profit maximization occurs when

$$MR = MC$$

APPENDIX 2

FACTOR-FACTOR MODEL

We have developed the factor-product model and used it to determine the profit-maximizing level of output. This is one of the decisions that the firm manager must make. But the world is usually more complex than the factor-product model would suggest. In many cases managers face situations in which there are multiple factors of production and/or multiple possible products to produce.

First, let's take up the situation of multiple factors of production. We will assume there are two variable factors of production, labor and capital, that can be used in combination with a bundle of fixed factors to produce a given product. This model is usually called the **factor-factor model** to emphasize the fact that the model has two variable factors rather than just one. Rather than asking what combination of capital and labor would maximize profit, we simplify the model by asking a simpler question: For a given level of output, what is the input combination that will minimize costs and hence maximize profits for that output level? Mathematically, this is known as **constrained optimization** because you constrain one variable (output in this case) and solve for the cost-minimizing combination of the other two. The solution is a **local optimization** because it applies only to the one level of output specified.

Suppose the product is 3 miles of ditch to be dug. We do our research and find there are at least three capital-labor combinations that can be used to dig this ditch. In Figure 12–15, point A illustrates a capital-intensive alternative: this would be a backhoe with one laborer to manipulate it. Point C is the labor-intensive alternative of perhaps 30 laborers with capital limited to one shovel per man. Point B is some intermediate alternative.

Which is the best alternative? Well, it's going to depend on the prices of labor and capital. In the United States, where capital is relatively inexpensive and labor is expensive, alternative A is probably the least costly way to dig the ditch. But in India, where labor is very cheap, alternative C may well be the least costly way of

---

Factor-factor model model of a firm with two variable factors of production used in producing a single product.

Constrained optimization simplifying an optimization problem by holding one or more variables constant (constrained) and finding the optimal levels of the remaining variables.

Local optimization a constrained optimal is valid only at the level at which the constrained variables are fixed. It is an optimization for a subset of the entire problem.

FIGURE 12–15
Factor-factor combinations to produce one level of output.

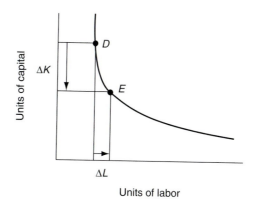

FIGURE 12–16
Isoproduct curve.

digging the ditch. So once again, economics is the study of trade-offs, and those trade-offs are driven by relative prices.

Figure 12–16 shows a more generalized set of alternatives, where so many alternative technologies have been evaluated that the curve linking them together has become a smooth line. Each point on this curve shows a capital-labor combination that is capable of producing one given level of output or product. Therefore, this curve is called an **isoproduct curve.**[8] Since output is the same at each point on this curve, revenue is also the same at each point on the curve. Therefore, local profit maximization is found by cost minimization.

Local Cost Minimization

Since fixed costs are fixed, cost minimization requires the minimization of the total variable costs associated with capital and labor. Using K and L as the quantities of capital and labor and P_k and P_l as prices of capital and labor, then total variable cost is

$$TVC = KP_k + LP_l$$

As you move along the isoproduct curve in Figure 12–16, TVC changes but total revenue does not. The question becomes one of finding the capital-labor combination for which TVC is minimized. Think about a movement from point D to point E. The costs associated with capital are going to decrease[9] by an amount equal to

$$\Delta K \cdot P_k$$

and the costs associated with labor are going to increase by

$$\Delta L \cdot P_l$$

Now it stands to reason that if the magnitude of the decrease in capital costs is greater than the increase in labor costs, then the move from D to E is a good move. Conversely, if the decrease in capital costs is less than the increase in labor costs, then the move from D to E is not a good move and we should be moving in

Isoproduct curve a curve showing combinations of two variable inputs that may be used to produce a single level of output.

---

[8] The iso- prefix means equal, so an isoproduct curve is an equal product curve.
[9] We know that a movement from D to E will result in a decrease of capital costs because from D to E the sign of ΔK is negative. Recall that the Δ (Delta) symbol means "change in."

the other direction. Therefore, when we get to the point at which the magnitude of the decrease in capital costs is just equal to the magnitude of the increase in labor costs, we will have found the point of total variable cost minimization.[10] So, at cost minimization

$$|\Delta L \cdot P_l| = |\Delta K \cdot P_k|$$

Rearranging this requirement for cost minimization gives

$$\frac{\Delta K}{\Delta L} = \frac{P_l}{P_k} \tag{12–1}$$

Constant Output

We have stipulated that points D and E in Figure 12–16 both represent the same level of output. Therefore, the contribution to output given up by the decrease in capital use must be compensated by the increase in output associated with the increased labor use. In both cases, the contribution to output is equal to the number of units of capital or labor times the respective marginal products. For a movement from D to E to be on an isoproduct curve requires that the magnitudes of the increase and the decrease of output be the same:

$$|\Delta L \cdot MP_l| = |\Delta K \cdot MP_k|$$

where MP_l and MP_k refer to the marginal products of labor and capital, respectively. Rearranging the terms in this gives

$$\frac{\Delta K}{\Delta L} = \frac{MP_l}{MP_k} \tag{12–2}$$

Local Profit Maximization

The right-hand sides of Equations 12–1 and 12–2 are both equal to $\Delta K / \Delta L$ and, therefore, must be equal to one another:

$$\frac{P_l}{P_k} = \frac{MP_l}{MP_k} \tag{12–3}$$

Rearranging terms in this expression gives the constrained or local profit-maximizing condition:

$$\frac{MP_l}{P_l} = \frac{MP_k}{P_k} \tag{12–4}$$

---

[10] Note that it is the magnitude of the changes that are equal. One is a decrease and the other is an increase; hence the signs are different, which explains the absolute value symbols shown.

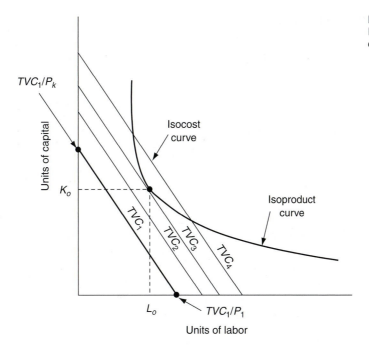

FIGURE 12–17
Isoproduct and isocost curves.

Here we have the economically meaningful condition for profit maximization in the factor-factor model. The marginal contribution to output per dollar of input cost must be the same for both labor and capital. That is, if the price of labor is \$2/unit and the price of capital is \$4/unit, then in order to minimize costs the marginal product of capital should be twice that of labor such that the additional output per dollar of each variable input is the same.

For the sake of argument, look at a situation where the conditions of Equation 12–4 are not met. At the prices given previously, assume the marginal product of labor is 5 units of output and the marginal product of capital is 15 units of output. In this case, the marginal product per dollar of labor is 2.5, and the marginal product per dollar of capital is 3.0. In this case it is clear that the manager would increase capital use and reduce labor use. Only when the marginal products per dollar of both capital and labor are equal is there no further opportunity to decrease costs while keeping output constant.

Graphical Solution

The same solution to the factor-factor model can be shown graphically. In Figure 12–17 a single isoproduct curve is shown. Recall that each point on this line represents a given level of total revenue and that the problem is to find the cost-minimizing combination of capital and labor. At any point on this curve, the slope of the curve is the ratio of the rise over the run of a line drawn tangent to the isoproduct curve:

$$\frac{\Delta K}{\Delta L} \qquad\qquad (12\text{--}5)$$

Marginal rate of factor substitution rate at which one variable input must be substituted for the other variable input in order to keep output constant.

Diminishing marginal rate of factor substitution as more and more units of one variable input are used, the quantity of the other input that would have to be substituted for it to keep production constant falls.

Isocost line a graphical line showing the various combinations of two variable inputs that have the same total variable cost.

This ratio is known as the **marginal rate of factor substitution** because it shows that rate at which one factor must be substituted for the other in order to maintain a constant output level. Notice that as one moves along the isoproduct curve from upper left to lower right, the marginal rate of factor substitution declines. This is known as **diminishing marginal rate of factor substitution.** Because of the diminishing marginal rate of factor substitution, the isoproduct curve in Figure 12–17 takes the shape of being convex to the origin.

Now we need to introduce information about costs on our graph. Suppose the firm spends TVC_1 on labor and capital. If all of that were spent on capital only, then TVC_1/P_k units of capital could be purchased. In this case no labor would be purchased, so the input combination would lie on the capital axis as shown by the dot on Figure 12–17. If all input spending were for labor alone, then the input combination would lie on the labor axis. All other combinations of capital and labor that could be acquired with an outlay of TVC_1 lie on a straight line between these two points. This straight line is known as the **isocost line** because each point on the line represents the same amount of total variable cost to the firm.

As shown in Figure 12–17, no input combination that can be acquired with an outlay equal to TVC_1 is capable of producing the level of output on the isoproduct curve. If the total amount of spending on variable inputs were increased, the isocost line would shift outward as it would be possible to buy either more capital or more labor or both. The new isocost line (TVC_2) will be parallel to TVC_1 because the proportions of increase for capital and labor are the same.

Since they are parallel to one another, the slopes of both TVC_1 and TVC_2 are the same. As always, the slope of a line is equal to its rise over its run, so the slope of either isocost line is

$$\frac{TVC/P_k}{TVC/P_l} = \frac{P_l}{P_k} \qquad (12\text{–}6)$$

So the slope of an isocost line is determined by the ratio of the prices of the two variable inputs.

Any number of isocost lines can be drawn on Figure 12–17 representing different levels of total variable cost. Since our objective is to minimize total variable costs needed to produce the amount of product specified by the isoproduct curve, we will select TVC_3 because this is the least costly combination of capital and labor that is capable of producing the level of output for the given isoproduct curve. We know this is the least costly alternative because TVC_3 is the isocost line closest to the origin that just touches the isoproduct curve. It would be possible to produce the quantity of output indicated by the isoproduct curve using TVC_4, but this would be more costly than TVC_3. So the cost-minimizing firm would select that isocost line that is just tangent to the isoproduct curve. At this point of tangency the firm would use K_o units of capital and L_o units of labor. At this point of tangency, the slope of the isoproduct curve (i.e., the marginal rate of factor substitution) is equal to the slope of the isocost line. At this point of tangency, the rate at which labor substitutes for capital in production (isoproduct) is equal to the rate at which labor substitutes for capital in the market (isocost). Combining Equation 12–5 with 12–6 gives

$$\frac{\Delta K_o}{\Delta L_o} = \frac{P_l}{P_k}$$

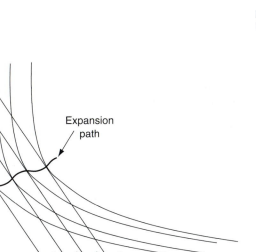

FIGURE 12–18
Expansion path.

Expansion
path

Units of capital

TVC_1 TVC_2 TVC_3 TVC_4

Units of labor

Substituting from Equation 12–2 gives

$$\frac{MP_l}{MP_k} = \frac{P_l}{P_k}$$

or, rearranging:

$$\frac{MP_l}{P_l} = \frac{MP_k}{P_k}$$

This is the same result we got in Equation 12–4 indicating that the marginal product per dollar of input should be the same for both of the inputs. If this were not the case, it would be possible to decrease total variable costs by rearranging inputs.

The factor-factor results presented here for a two-factor, one-product model can be generalized to a multifactor situation:

$$\frac{MP_i}{P_i} = \frac{MP_j}{P_j} = \frac{MP_n}{P_n} \tag{12–7}$$

for all i, j, and n.

Expansion Path

The solution to the factor-factor model above is a local solution for a given level of output. If the level of output were to change, the cost-minimizing input combination would also change. In Figure 12–18 we have drawn several isoproduct curves and the isocost curves that are tangent to them. Since the isocost lines are all drawn for a given set of variable input prices, they are all parallel to one another.

Expansion path
locus of points of local optimal factor-factor combinations for multiple isoproduct curves.

The locus of all of the cost-minimizing points is called the **expansion path,** because as the firm expands production, it would move from one cost-minimizing point to another. Each point on the expansion path is a point of local cost minimization for the given level of output. At each point on the expansion path the local cost-minimizing condition in Equation 12–7 is met.

The relevant question then becomes, Which of the many points on the expansion path provides a global profit maximization? We learned in the factor-product model that the profit-maximizing output level was at the point where the marginal cost of producing the last unit is equal to its marginal revenue, or price of the product in perfect competition.

Profit maximization along the expansion path will occur at that output level of product Q for which

$$MC_l = MC_k = MR_q$$

Meeting the local cost-minimization criteria of Equation 12–7 ensures that the two marginal costs are equal to one another at each point on the expansion path, so the trick is to move along the expansion path until the point is reached where the marginal costs of each variable input are equal to the marginal revenue. Expansion of this result to a multiple variable factor situation is straightforward:

$$MC_i = MC_j = \cdots = MC_n = MR_q$$

for all n variable inputs.

KEY TERMS

Constrained optimization
Diminishing marginal rate
    of factor substitution
Expansion path
Factor-factor model

Isocost line
Isoproduct curve
Local optimization
Marginal rate of factor substitution

APPENDIX 3

PRODUCT-PRODUCT MODEL

We come now to the final generalization of the factor-product model. In the simple one-factor, one-product model we found that the firm could maximize profit by adjusting output to that point at which the marginal cost of additional input is equal to the marginal revenue of additional output. Then we showed that in the case of multiple variable inputs, the firm should adjust the use of each input such that the marginal cost of each input is equal to the marginal revenue of the product. Now we turn to the case of a firm with multiple products.

The **product-product model** examines the case of a firm with two products that are produced using a given bundle of fixed and variable inputs. As before, this is a local or constrained optimization problem because the analysis assumes that the quantity of inputs is predetermined, and as a consequence, total costs are predetermined. Profit maximization therefore becomes a question of local revenue maximization.

Product-product model   model of the firm in which the firm produces two products using a given bundle of fixed and variable inputs.

Local Revenue Maximization

Assume a firm with a set of resources that can be used to produce either of two products: canned peaches or fresh peaches. Since total costs are fixed, the firm seeks to maximize total revenue, which is given by

$$TR = C \cdot P_c + F \cdot P_f$$

where:

TR = total revenue

C = units of canned peaches produced

F = units of fresh peaches produced

P_c = price per unit of canned peaches

P_f = price per unit of fresh peaches

Because of limited resources, any effort to increase canned production will come at the expense of reducing fresh production. If this were not the case, the firm would obviously increase the production of both. That is, the only relevant economic question is how to adjust production of the two products when there is an economic trade-off. Assume the firm is currently producing half and half. The firm manager asks if the firm should produce more fresh peaches. To answer this question the manager calculates the additional revenue (MR_f) associated with more fresh production as

$$MR_f = \Delta F \cdot P_f$$

and the loss of revenue associated with less canned production is

$$-MR_c = -\Delta C \cdot P_c$$

where ΔC is negative and hence MR_c is negative.

If the magnitude of the additional revenue (MR_f) is greater than the magnitude of the loss of revenue from canned production (MR_c), then it makes economic sense to make the adjustment. If $MR_f < |MR_c|$, then the manager should be considering an expansion of canned rather than fresh.

As more and more fresh is substituted for canned, we would expect the marginal revenue from fresh to decline because of the diminishing marginal productivity of the inputs used in the production of fresh, and we would expect the magnitude of the marginal revenue of canned to increase for the same reason. As the magnitudes of the two marginal revenues change, we should finally arrive at a point at which the two magnitudes are equal. At this point there is no remaining reallocation of production that can increase revenue, so this point must be the point of revenue maximization. That is, in order to maximize revenue, the firm should adjust production of the two goods to the point at which

$$|MR_f| = |MR_c|$$

To do otherwise would suggest that the firm is not reaching a constrained optimum, because a reallocation of the available inputs will increase revenue whenever the two marginal revenues are not equal.

Graphical Solution

This same principle of equi-marginal constrained revenue maximization can be illustrated graphically. Figure 12–19 shows the different combinations of fresh and canned peaches that can be produced with a given resource allocation. The concave to the origin shape of this curve suggests that as more and more canned peaches are produced, a greater and greater quantity of fresh must be given up to free up the resources needed to produce one more unit of canned. This changing substitution rate is a consequence of the diminishing marginal productivity of available resources. As more canned peaches are produced, the marginal productivity of resources used for canned falls, and as fewer fresh peaches are produced, the marginal productivity of resources used for fresh increases.

Production possibilities curve   a curve showing different combinations of two products that can be produced using a given bundle of fixed and variable inputs.

The curve in Figure 12–19 is called a **production possibilities curve,** and it is based on the predetermined bundle of inputs. Changing the size of the input bundle would produce a different production possibilities curve. Given the input constraint, the local optimization problem is to find the combination of the two products that will maximize revenue.

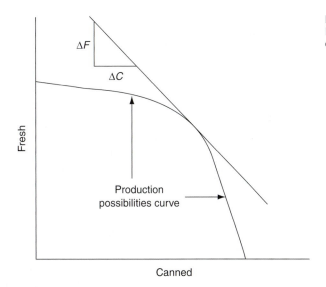

FIGURE 12–19
Production possibilities
curve.

The slope of the production possibilities curve at any point on the curve is equal to the slope of a tangent to the curve at that point. The slope of the tangent is equal to the rise over the run or

$$\frac{\Delta F}{\Delta C}$$

This is called the **marginal rate of product substitution.** To find the point of local revenue maximization, we need to have some information about revenues.

Figure 12–20 shows different combinations of the two goods that are capable of generating a given amount of total revenue. For a given amount of total revenue (TR_1), if only fresh were produced, it would take TR_1/P_f units of fresh output to produce TR_1. The output combination of all fresh and no canned is marked with a dot on the vertical axis. Likewise if only canned were produced, it would take TR_1/P_c units of canned production to generate TR_1. This output combination is marked with a dot on the horizontal axis. Output combinations on the straight line between the dots also generate TR_1. This line is called an **isorevenue line.**

The slope of the isorevenue line TR_1 is equal to its rise over the run, which is given by

$$\frac{TR_1/P_f}{TR_1/P_c} = \frac{P_c}{P_f} \tag{12–8}$$

Numerous isorevenue lines can be drawn representing different levels of total revenue. Since the slope of these lines is equal to the ratio of product prices, they will all be parallel to one another for a given set of product prices. The greater the total revenue on an isorevenue line, the farther the line is from the origin. So revenue maximization seeks that isorevenue line that is farthest from the origin within the limits of the resource constraint.

Revenue maximization will be found at the point of tangency between the production possibility curve and the highest isorevenue line drawn to that point of

Marginal rate of product substitution rate at which one product can be substituted for another in the production process using a given bundle of fixed and variable inputs.

Isorevenue line a line showing the different combinations of two products that will produce a given total revenue.

FIGURE 12–20
Isorevenue lines.

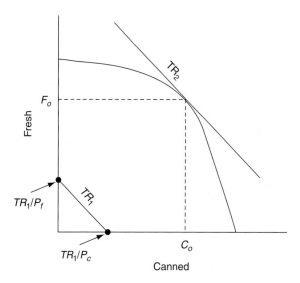

tangency. At output combination F_o and C_o, the firm will maximize revenue. At this point, the slope of the isorevenue curve is equal to the marginal rate of product substitution. That is, at this point, the rate of substitution in production is equal to the rate of substitution in the market. Since the two slopes are equal at this point, we can combine Equations 12–8 and 12–9 to yield the revenue-maximizing condition:

$$\frac{\Delta F_o}{\Delta C_o} = \frac{P_c}{P_f}$$

Cross multiplying gives

$$\Delta F_o \cdot P_f = \Delta C_o \cdot P_c$$

where a change in physical output times the price of the product is by definition the marginal revenue associated with the change in production so

$$MR_f = MR_c = \cdots = MC_n$$

This is the same result obtained previously.

Generalization

The results of the product-product model can be generalized for a multiproduct firm. Local revenue maximization from a given bundle of resources will be found where

$$MR_i = MR_j = \cdots = MR_n$$

for all i, j, and n.

　　　　Alternate sets of constrained input bundles would produce alternate production possibilities curves, and a local optimum could be identified for each. A line through these local optimums would generate an expansion path in output space similar to that in Figure 12–18 for input space.

A global or unconstrained optimum along this expansion path would occur at that point at which the marginal revenues of each product are equal to the marginal cost of the production possibilities curve:

$$MR_i = MR_j = \ldots = MR_n = MC$$

for all n products of the firm.

The results of the factor-factor model can be combined with the above result to provide the profit-maximizing rule for a multifactor, multiproduct firm:

$$MR_i = MR_j = \ldots = MR_n = MC_p = MC_q = \ldots = MC_n$$

for all n products and r inputs.

KEY TERMS

Isorevenue line

Marginal rate of product substitution

Production possibilities curve

Product-product model

Firm Supply and the Market

*T*he basic microeconomic theory of the perfectly competitive firm has been developed in the last two chapters. In the short run, the profit-maximizing firm manager adjusts input levels (and hence output) to that point at which additions to cost are equal to additions to revenue; that is, marginal cost is equal to marginal revenue. Changes in those factors external to the firm (such as the price of the product) will cause the firm manager to react by changing the input/output level. Failure to adjust internally to changes caused externally result in suboptimal performance of the firm. Let's face it, the college town restaurant manager who has the same crew on the Thursday of spring break as the Saturday of a home football game is a manager who is throwing a lot of money into an empty hole. The job of the manager is to make endogenous adjustments to exogenous changes.

In our perfectly competitive model one of the fundamental assumptions is that the firm is so small relative to the market that no actions by the individual firm can affect the market. However, if prices exogenous to the individual firm change, then we would expect all firms within the market to adjust independently to the new situation. As all firms within an **industry** change, the market itself will change. That is, individual firm managers, each acting in their own self-interest, will collectively bring about changes in the market. It is this relationship between the individual firm and the industry to which this chapter is addressed.

Industry a collection of firms producing the same or similar products.

FIRM SUPPLY

Supply curve of the firm quantities of a good the firm is willing to produce at alternative prices for the good, *ceteris paribus*. It is equal to the marginal cost curve of the firm beyond the shutdown point.

The cost curves of the individual firm can be used to derive the **supply curve of the firm.** Recall that supply is a relationship between prices of a product and the quantities the firm is willing to produce at alternative prices, *ceteris paribus*.

Figure 13–1 shows a typical set of cost curves for a firm. These curves, as is the case for all cost curves, are drawn assuming that all other factors remain constant and are drawn for a short-run time period in which some factors of production are fixed. At alternative prices, the firm adjusts output such that the marginal revenue (i.e., the price of the product) is equal to the marginal cost in order to maximize profit or minimize loss. Several price-output combinations are listed on the schedule below the chart. Each combination indicates how many units the firm is willing to produce at each alternative price. Therefore, this schedule is a supply schedule. Now, if these points on the supply schedule were plotted on the axes above, they would graph a supply curve. That curve would be superimposed on the marginal cost curve at any price greater than the shutdown price. In fact, the supply curve of the firm is the marginal cost curve above the shutdown price.

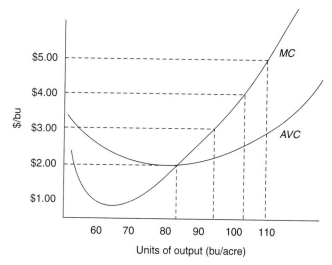

FIGURE 13–1
Derivation of the firm's
supply curve.

Price per unit	$1.00	$2.00	$3.00	$4.00	$5.00
Units produced	0	83	94	103	109

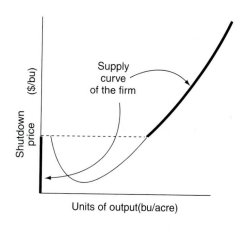

FIGURE 13–2 Supply
curve of the firm.

As we saw previously, for any price less than the minimum average variable cost, the quantity supplied would be zero. A typical firm supply curve is shown in Figure 13–2. Note that the supply function is discontinuous at the shutdown price.

MARKET SUPPLY

A **market supply curve** is simply the horizontal summation of all the firm supply curves in the market. Anything that affects the typical firm's supply function would therefore affect the market supply. Why changes in input prices and technology are market supply shifters should now be obvious. Anything that affects the marginal cost curve of the individual firm in the industry thus affects the market supply curve of the industry.

In addition, the market supply curve will shift as individual firms enter or leave the industry. If additional firms enter the industry, the supply curve will shift outward as there is more product produced at each alternative price. Conversely,

Market supply curve
the summation of the
firm supply curves for
all the firms in the
industry.

as firms leave the industry, *ceteris paribus,* the market supply curve will shift inward. As we will see in a moment, the entry and exit of firms in a perfectly competitive industry is a driving force behind Adam Smith's "invisible hand."

> **CAUTION:** *A change in the price of fertilizer (or any other input) will shift the firm's supply curve of corn. A change in the technology of producing corn, such as precision agriculture or genetically modified seeds, will shift the firm's supply curve of corn. An increase or decrease in the number of corn producers will shift the market supply of corn. But, a change in the price of corn will* not *shift the supply of corn. A change in the price of corn will cause a movement along the supply curve but not a shift of the supply relationship itself. Likewise, a change in the demand for corn will* not *cause a shift in the supply of corn, but it may lead to an eventual market adjustment that does entail a supply shift.*

It is appropriate at this time to briefly review the ground that has been covered. Our final destination was a short-run market supply curve. It is simply the summation of individual firm supply curves. The firm supply curve is the marginal cost curve above the break-even price. The marginal cost curve is derived from the total cost curve. The total cost curve is derived from the production function. So, ultimately the market supply curve is determined by the noneconomic, technical relationship between inputs and outputs we know as the production function.

DYNAMIC RELATIONSHIP BETWEEN THE FIRM AND THE MARKET

Static an economic analysis at a point in time.

Dynamic an economic analysis over a period of time analyzing the adjustment process.

The analyses to this point have been **static;** that is, it has been assumed that there is some externally determined price and that the firm must adjust to this price. In reality, we know that prices of agricultural commodities are continually changing over time. In examining the relationship between the firm and the market over time we can begin to appreciate the **dynamics** of Adam Smith's "invisible hand."

Figure 13–3 illustrates the long-run, stable equilibrium relationship between a typical firm in an industry and the market of that industry. A stable equilibrium means there are no market forces pushing for adjustments in the market. A shift in either market demand or market supply caused by a change in some *ceteris paribus* condition would lead to a disequilibirum situation, forcing firms to adjust to the new situation in the search for a return to equilibrium.

The interaction of supply and demand in the market for the entire industry leads to a market equilibrium price of P^* and an equilibrium quantity traded of Q^*. P^* and Q^* are equilibrium values because the quantity demanded is equal to the quantity supplied; therefore, the market is cleared. The individual firm in the industry, being a price taker and a maximizer of economic profits, adjusts output to q^* such that the marginal cost of producing q^* is equal to the marginal revenue received, or P^*. For the marginal firm (the highest cost producer in the industry), the market equilibrium price, P^*, is equal to the shutdown point or the minimum average total cost. Since at this point the average revenue (P^*) is equal to the average

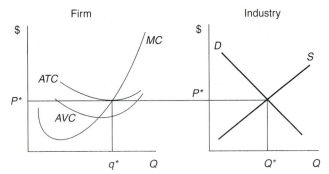

FIGURE 13–3 Long-run, stable equilibrium.

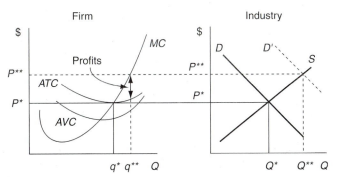

FIGURE 13–4 Demand shift causes short-run economic profits.

total cost, the economic profits of this marginal firm are zero.[1] The relationship between the firm and the industry shown in Figure 13–3 is a long-run equilibrium situation because there are no pressures on the firm or in the industry to change. Since the marginal firm is earning zero economic profits, there are no incentives for other firms to enter the industry, nor are there pressures for this marginal firm to leave the industry. This equilibrium situation will remain stable until such time as some exogenous change requires market, and hence firm level, adjustments. These exogenous forces could be a change in any of the market supply or demand shifters (i.e., the *ceteris paribus* conditions).

If, as a result of a change in one of the *ceteris paribus* conditions, the demand in the market should shift upward to D' as shown in Figure 13–4, then the market clearing price would increase from P^* to P^{**}.[2] In the short run, as the market price increases, existing firms react by increasing production to q^{**} such that the quantity traded on the market increases to Q^{**}. At price P^{**} the typical firm in the industry is earning pure economic profits at output level q^{**}. In the longer run the existence of these economic profits attracts additional firms to the industry. As more firms enter the industry, the industry supply curve (being the summation of a now larger number of firm supply curves) shifts out to S' as shown in Figure 13–5.

---

[1] Remember that when economic profits are zero, all factors of production are earning their opportunity costs. This includes the services of management.

[2] The dynamics of this price adjustment are important. Before the demand shift there is an equilibrium at P^*. When demand shifts to D', there is a disequilibrium at P^* as the quantity demanded far exceeds what producers are willing to produce at P^*. This results in a shortage at P^* which causes potential buyers to bid up the price of the product to P^{**} for a new market equilibrium with Q^{**} units traded.

FIGURE 13–5
Economic profits attract
new firms into industry.

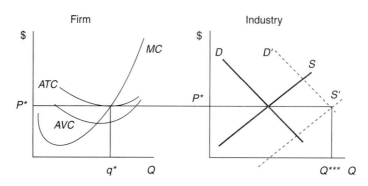

Eventually the industry supply curve shifts outward enough to bring the market price back to the long-run equilibrium price of *P**. At this new long-run equilibrium, the quantity produced by the typical firm falls back to *q** and the market clearing quantity expands to *Q**** because there are now more firms in the industry. This illustrates the automatic, self-correcting nature of markets that Adam Smith attributed to the force of an invisible hand.

The dynamics illustrated in Figures 13–3 through 13–5 show the relationship between the market and one firm in that market. Since the economic profits of the firm shown are zero, this is what is known as the "**marginal firm**" or the highest cost firm remaining in this industry. There are many firms in a market, each with its own unique production function and therefore unique **cost structure.** Some of the other firms in this industry may be more efficient than the firm shown. These more efficient firms would have cost structures lower than for the firm shown and therefore would earn economic profits at a market price of *P**. So the firm shown is the least efficient firm in the industry that is just willing to come in at zero economic profits.

So, short-run prices above the break-even price of the marginal firm attract firms into the industry and eventually drive the long-run price back to equilibrium. A similar sequence of events will occur at prices below the shutdown point. If the short-run market price should fall below the shutdown price, firms would leave the industry. As firms leave the industry, the market supply curve shifts inward, thus causing the price to increase back up to the shutdown point of the remaining marginal firm.

At prices between the break-even point and the shutdown point the adjustment process is the same but much slower. As we have already seen, at prices in this range the loss-minimizing firm will continue to operate in the short run although the firm has negative profits. Eventually, if prices in this range persist, the firm will cease production and leave the industry. This will shift the industry supply curve inward and drive the market equilibrium price up. This process will continue until the market price reaches the break-even point and another long-run, stable equilibrium is established.

The primary difference between adjustments below the shutdown point and above it is in the speed of adjustment. At prices below shutdown the adjustment is quite rapid. At prices above it the adjustment is much slower as marginal firms hang on in the hopes of eventual price improvements. But as even the once mighty Pan Am Airlines discovered, you can't fly at a loss forever.

Marginal firm   a firm in an industry with the highest cost structure and hence the most likely firm to leave the industry if prices fall.

Cost structure   the relative importance of fixed and variable costs in the total costs of the firm.

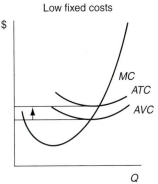

COST STRUCTURE AND PRICE VARIABILITY

Different firms in different industries have different cost structures in terms of how important fixed costs are in the total cost structure. Two different firms, one with high fixed costs and the other with low fixed costs, are illustrated in Figure 13–6. Airlines, auto manufacturers, and citrus groves are examples of firms with very high fixed costs relative to the variable costs. For these firms, the price range between the break-even point and the shutdown point is great. Therefore, a fall in the price can easily push a firm with high fixed costs below the break-even point and into negative profits, but it takes a massive price reduction to push the firm into going out of production at the shutdown point.

USAir is an example of a company that has had negative profits for a number of years but continues to fly because the market price is between its break-even point and its shutdown point. For USAir to continue to fly is rational behavior in the short run. So, for the time being USAir continues to fly in the hope that competition will ease and allow prices to increase, or that variable costs (such as fuel) will fall.

Unfortunately for the airline industry, most of their costs are highly fixed. For example, a new jumbo jet runs about $125 million with spare parts. If USAir borrowed the money for a new plane at 10 percent, it would have an interest expense of $12.5 million per year, or about $34,000 per day per plane. So USAir can stand to lose as much as $34,000 per day per plane and still continue to fly in the short run.

Of course, USAir can't survive as a company if it suffers losses forever. Eventually the company will run out of assets in the long run and be forced into bankruptcy. That is exactly what happened to Eastern Airlines and Pan Am.

By comparison, a cattle feedlot is an example of a firm with very few fixed costs (land) and very high variable costs (feed). As a consequence, very small movements of cattle prices will result in either short-run economic profits or a shutdown (i.e., the feedlot operator leaves the feedlot vacant) until prices recover.

Agriculture has abundant examples of firms with different cost structures—some with high fixed costs and some with very low fixed costs. Examples of firms with high fixed costs would be a cow-calf operator, orchards, and forestry. Low fixed costs are found in the broiler industry, high value vegetable production, and feedlots.

One of the basic assumptions of a perfectly competitive market is that firms are free to enter or exit the industry. As we have seen, at market prices above the break-even point the firm will earn economic profits. This will attract additional firms to the industry, shifting the market supply curve outward and causing the price to fall back to the break-even point. At market prices below the shutdown point firms will leave the industry, thereby causing the market supply curve to shift upward resulting in higher prices. That is, at market prices above break-even and below shutdown, speedy adjustments by firms in the industry are expected.

As a result, we expect to see market prices vary within the upper and lower limits imposed by the break-even and shutdown points as illustrated in Figure 13–6. The implication of this is that for firms in high fixed cost industries, tremendous price variation is a fact of life and firms are slow to enter or leave the industry. For firms in low fixed cost industries, relatively small price variation is expected over time but a lot of firms enter and leave as the adjustment process takes place.

In this respect, compare the cow-calf operator (high fixed costs in land and cow herd) and the feedlot operator (most costs variable in the form of feed). In the past 20 years we have seen feeder cattle prices[3] vary from as low as $15/cwt to as high as $115/cwt, but most cow-calf producers just hang in there for the ride. By comparison, it is not at all uncommon to see all or part of a feedlot standing idle because the price of fat cattle[4] has fallen by just a few dollars per hundredweight. Because of the low fixed costs, the feedlot operator can exit and enter the business at a very low cost. As a result, fat cattle prices over the past 20 years have varied far less than feeder cattle prices. So, the cost structure of the typical firm in an industry will determine the extent of price variability in that industry.

SUMMARY

The supply curve of an individual firm within an industry is equal to the marginal cost curve of the firm at prices above the shutdown point. At prices below the shutdown point the quantity the firm will produce is zero.

The market supply curve is the horizontal summation of all the firm supply curves in the industry. Therefore, any change in *ceteris paribus* conditions that shifts the firm's supply curve will also shift the market supply curve. Moreover, the market supply curve can be shifted if firms enter or leave the industry.

In a long-run, stable equilibrium situation, the economic profits of the marginal, highest cost firm are zero. There is no incentive for existing firms in the industry to exit nor is there incentive for additional firms to enter. A short-run disequilibrium is created whenever a change in one of the *ceteris paribus* conditions causes a shift in market supply or demand.

The dynamic relationship between the firm and the market may be illustrated with an outward shift of the market demand curve. The market price will increase, which will cause each firm to move along its firm supply curve, producing more at the higher price. Now the marginal firm is earning economic profits, which sends a signal to investors to enter this industry. As additional firms enter the industry, the market supply curve will shift outward, causing the market price to fall. This dynamic adjustment will continue until the market price falls to that point at which the marginal firm is earning economic profits of zero.

---

[3] This is the price paid to the cow-calf operator for the cattle he or she has weaned and raised to about 500 pounds.

[4] This is the price paid to feedlot operators for the cattle they have fattened to about 1,100 pounds for slaughter.

At prices above the break-even price or below the shutdown point market adjustment occurs rapidly as firms enter or leave the industry. However, at prices between the shutdown price and the break-even price the adjustment process is very slow, because firms stay in the industry and continue to produce as they attempt to minimize losses.

For industries with high fixed costs, the price variation from shutdown to breakeven is large. As a consequence, prices can fluctuate over this wide range with no short-run adjustments by firms in the industry. In such industries, wide price swings are common. By comparison, industries with low fixed costs require only small price changes to bring about short-run adjustment.

KEY TERMS

Cost structure
Dynamic
Industry
Marginal firm

Market supply curve
Static
Supply curve of the firm

PROBLEMS AND DISCUSSION QUESTIONS

1. What changes would cause the market supply curve to shift but not shift individual firm supply curves?
2. Explain why a firm will not produce at prices below the shutdown point.
3. At prices above the shutdown point, what criterion does the firm manager use to identify the output level that will maximize profits or minimize losses?
4. Trace the lineage between the production function and the market supply curve.
5. Assume the market for tomatoes is in a long-run, stable equilibrium. Trace the dynamic adjustments that would occur in this market as a result of an inward shift of the market supply curve.
6. What distinguishes the "marginal" firm from all other firms in an industry?
7. Explain why adjustment is slow when the market price falls to a range below the break-even point and above the shutdown point.
8. Discuss the implications of cost structure on market price variability.

14 Imperfect Competition and Government Regulation

*I*n the previous chapter we examined the behavior of the profit-maximizing firm in a perfectly competitive market. A skeptic might question the utility of the economic theory of the perfectly competitive firm because there are very few instances in which producers and consumers interact under the conditions of perfect competition. Nonetheless, a vast number of industries behave as if they are perfectly competitive. Nonetheless, many firms do not operate under conditions of the perfectly competitive model. In this chapter we will examine the economics of less than perfectly competitive firms—hence the term "imperfect competition."

In reality, most markets are less than perfectly competitive. In fact, in most markets for consumer goods, the assumption that the producer is so small relative to the market that the producer has no control over prices is not a valid assumption. Certainly Campbell's has some pricing power in the soup market, and Kellogg's has pricing power in the breakfast cereal market. Should that power become excessive, government regulations might be necessary to protect the consumer from predatory business practices.

MARKET STRUCTURE

Market structure the number of firms in an industry and the relationship among them.

Economists use the term **market structure** to refer to the number of firms in an industry and the relationship among them. The opposite end of the spectrum from perfect competition is pure monopoly, in which there is only one firm in the industry. In between these two extremes lie many firms in many markets. Two kinds of structure in between the extremes will be examined in this chapter: monopolistic competition and oligopoly. In studying these market structures you will learn about the markets you, the consumer, frequently trade in.

Market structure also refers to the relative ease with which additional firms may enter the industry. In a monopoly structure, there is one firm and entry of other firms is blocked completely. In an oligopoly structure, there are a few firms and entry is difficult. In a monopolistic competition structure, there are few or many firms with virtually no barriers to entry.

Conduct behavior of the profit-maximizing firm manager. Conduct is determined by structure.

One of the canons of economics is that the market structure in which a firm finds itself determines the **conduct** and performance of the firm. That is, firms in different market structures behave differently as the managers of the firm seek to maximize profit to the firm.

PERFECT COMPETITION

Structure

Before dealing with imperfect competition it would be worthwhile to review the conditions necessary for the existence of perfect competition:

- There are so many producers and consumers that the individual producer or consumer is insignificant in relation to the total market.
- The product is homogeneous.
- There are no artificial limitations on entry to or exit from the market.

In the economic sense, perfect competition simply refers to a market structure in which the individual unit provides such a minute portion of the total market supply (or demand) that the actions of the individual cannot influence the market price of the product sold (or bought).

The second condition of homogeneity of the product is concerned with the uniformity of the product bought and sold. One bushel of wheat, for example, is pretty much like another bushel of wheat. One chicken is pretty much like another. One choice grade 1,000-pound slaughter steer is very much like another. In other words, when we are concerned with homogeneity, a product cannot be identified as to source or destination once it gets into the marketplace.

The third condition of no artificial limitations on entry to or exit from the market is concerned largely with the freedom of choice on the parts of both producers and consumers, and with the mobility of resources and products. Prices are assumed to be free to move in response to changes in market supply and market demand. Resources are free to move into those alternative employments that pay the highest returns to the resources. Goods and services are free to move to those consumers and into those areas that are willing to pay the highest prices.

Conduct

What kind of conduct by firm management can we expect in a perfectly competitive structure? We've already seen that under conditions of perfect competition the firm's marginal cost curve defines the firm's supply curve. We've seen how the demand curve faced by the firm appears as a horizontal line at the market price level. This line defines the marginal and average revenue curves as well as the demand function faced by the individual firm in Figure 14–1. Note that the quantity axis for the market is measured in much larger units than the quantity axis for the firm. Thus, the individual firm provides only an infinitesimally small part of the market supply. Firm managers maximize profits by adjusting output such that marginal costs and marginal revenue are equal.

In the world of perfect competition, we have said that resources are free to move into those industries in which returns are the greatest. What does this mean in the case of economic profits? If average total costs (including the opportunity costs for all resources used) are less than average revenue per unit of a particular product, as at price P_1 in Figure 14–1, in what direction would resources be

FIGURE 14–1
Relationship between a
perfectly competitive
firm and the market.

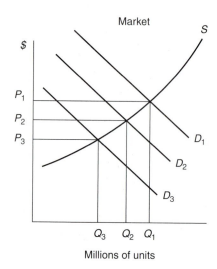

expected to flow? Obviously, since the returns in this business are greater than
"normal"—that is, since resources are earning returns above their opportunity
costs—resource owners could be expected to attempt to cut themselves in for a
piece of the action. As a result, resources would be expected to flow into the industry where economic profits are being realized. As resources come into the production of the good in question, the market supply curve for that product would shift
to the right, and the price would be reduced, shifting downward the demand curve
faced by each individual firm, causing the economic profits to ultimately disappear.

The existence of the perfectly competitive markets is rare in the real world
outside of basic commodity markets. However, the perfectly competitive market
model provides us with a very convenient standard for comparing the impacts of
various types of market structure. Further, we do have certain important segments
of our economy, notably farming, in which the real world situation *approaches* the
perfectly competitive model.

PURE MONOPOLY

Structure

Monopoly market
structure in which
there is only one firm
in the industry, there
are no close substi-
tutes, and entry into
the industry is
blocked.

Now, using our perfectly competitive standard for comparison, let's examine a
market structure at the other extreme: pure **monopoly.** The conditions necessary
for the existence of pure monopoly include:

- There is one and only one seller of a given product in a given market. The
  market demand function is the demand function faced by that individual
  firm. The firm and the market are one and the same.
- There are no close substitute goods for the product. If there were, then the
  firm would lose its monopoly power.
- Entry of other firms into the market for this product is blocked.

Like perfect competition, the incidence of pure monopoly is rare in the real world.
One example of pure monopoly is the American postal system so far as first class
mail is concerned. However, the emergence of delivery services such as Federal Ex-

press, United Parcel Service, and e-mail has created close substitutes that have reduced this monopoly power. Many public utility systems approach the purely monopolistic case, at least in a local sense. For example, most communities will grant a franchise to a single seller of electricity and another to a single seller of natural gas. Electricity and natural gas will substitute for one another to some degree, so while the monopolistic character of these examples is not "pure," it unquestionably approaches purity at least in a locational sense.[1] With nearly 95 percent of the market for operating systems for personal computers, Microsoft® is considered by many to be a monopoly firm, and it has been accused in federal court of behaving like a monopoly. Other examples abound.

Barriers to Entry

A necessary condition for a monopoly to exist is that barriers prevent other firms from entering the industry. If other firms could enter, then obviously the monopolist would be subjected to competition from the other firms, as the U.S. Postal Service is now subjected to substantial competition in most fields. In fact, the only monopoly power the USPS retains is the right to use your physical mailbox, and the value of that monopoly power is diminishing as e-mailboxes and door-to-door deliveries replace the quaint thing with a little flag on the side.

The most common barrier to entry is a **patent.** Patents are rights granted inventors to the exclusive use of their invention for a period of time, currently 20 years in the United States. The logic of patents is straightforward: an inventor of a product should have the exclusive right to earn the returns to the invention without others stealing the idea and duplicating it. The economic consequence of patents is to create a 20-year monopoly. Patents are very common in the pharmaceutical industry. Many of the new genetically modified agricultural seeds are being patented.

Another effective barrier to entry is a company secret. The Coca-Cola Co. has never revealed its recipe—one of the most sacred of industrial secrets in the United States. Software and chip designers frequently keep their designs secret, realizing that 20 years of patent protection is meaningless in the computer business.

A third barrier to entry may be the size of the market to be served. It may be so small that the existence of another firm would drive prices so low that both firms would be forced into bankruptcy. This barrier to entry probably has more effect on agriculture than any other. In many farming communities, for example, farmers are forced to patronize a particular feed or fertilizer dealer because the local market cannot support more than one such business. The nearest alternative source of these products is distant enough that the transportation cost prohibits an effective transfer of this patronage. Another example may be found in the case of a physician or a hospital in a sparsely populated area. By the time a patient could get to an alternative source of medical care, those services may no longer be required.

Finally, in many cases governments sanction monopolies. These monopolies fall into three categories. First, the government can grant trade associations the power to create monopolies in their products. A most visible example of this is

Patent rights granted inventors to the exclusive use of their invention for a period of time, currently 20 years in the United States.

---

[1] But this too is about to change. Recent federal legislation has effectively forced a separation of electric power generation from power distribution. In the future, a monopolist will continue to bring the power to your meter, but you will be free to buy that power from any power generator. Large power users such as industrial plants are already benefiting greatly as they are able to negotiate with alternative power providers to find the most attractive price. The monopoly of the local power generator has been broken.

Major League Baseball, where the owners' association has been given the power to control the number and location of teams. Second, government can grant a franchise or concession to a firm and allow it to operate as a monopolist. For instance, all hotels, stores, and eating establishments in Yellowstone Park are operated by a division of a company called Amfac Parks and Resorts. This is an exclusive franchise granted by the National Park Service. In many cities franchises create local monopolies in garbage collection, school buses, and cable TV. Third, in many cases, particularly in the utilities, one firm can operate more cheaply that two or three could in competition. Imagine having three or four water companies competing to bring water to your house. There would be four sets of water mains, four companies digging up the street, and so forth. In these kinds of cases, called natural monopolies, governments grant monopoly rights to a single firm. Natural monopolies will be discussed further later.

Conduct of the Monopoly Firm

Let's compare the analytical concepts of pure monopoly with their counterparts under the conditions of perfect competition. For purposes of simplicity, let's assume that our friend the monopolist buys his resources in a purely competitive market. Since the basic difference in monopoly and pure competition lies in the manner in which the product is sold, we can treat the monopolist's cost curves as if they were derived in exactly the same manner as the cost curves for the purely competitive firm.

Since the monopolist is the only seller of the product, the demand curve faced by the firm is the market demand curve. Thus, the only way the monopolist can expand sales during any given time interval is to lower the price at which the product is sold. The market demand curve is the firm's average revenue curve. For any level of output, it shows what price the firm can command, and that price is the average revenue per unit sold at that level of output. So unlike the perfectly competitive firm, which faces a perfectly horizontal average revenue curve, the monopolist faces a downward-sloping average revenue function.

The downward-sloping average revenue curve creates a marginal revenue curve that is also downward sloping. The marginal revenue curve always lies below the average revenue curve and is more steeply sloped than the average revenue curve. The derivation of two points on a marginal revenue curve is illustrated in Figure 14–2. Three points on the demand curve are identified, and the total rev-

FIGURE 14–2
Monopoly: Average and marginal revenue.

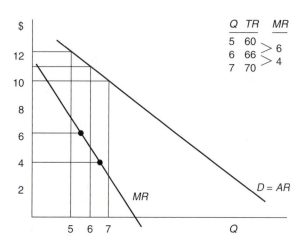

Q	TR	MR
5	60	6
6	66	4
7	70	

enue generated at each of the three output levels is noted. The marginal revenue between total revenues may then be calculated. These points are plotted on the graph showing the expected result: The marginal revenue curve falls below the average revenue curve (i.e., the demand curve) and is more steeply sloped.

The profit-maximizing behavior of the monopolist is identical with that of the profit-maximizing manager of a perfectly competitive firm: expand production so long as additions to revenue are greater than additions to cost. When the point is reached at which additions to revenue are equal to additions to cost, the point of profit maximization has been reached. That is, the firm will maximize profit by adjusting output to that point at which marginal revenue equals marginal cost. Regardless of market structure, profit maximization always requires $MR = MC$.

Once the profit-maximizing level of output has been determined, the manager of the monopoly must determine a price. Unlike the competitive firm, the monopolist is a price maker. However, he or she is a price maker within the constraints imposed by the market. In fact, the monopolist makes the price according to what the market will bear as dictated by market demand. In Figure 14–3, the profit-maximizing output is Q_o where $MR = MC$. The manager would set the price at P_o, because at this price Q_o units will trade. If the manager set a price lower than P_o, the firm would forego some profit. At a price higher than P_o, consumers would not purchase Q_o units. So P_o is the profit-maximizing price to set.

In Figure 14–3, the average revenue per unit of output (P_o) is substantially greater than the average total cost per unit of output (C_t), the difference being pure economic profit. The total revenue is $P_o \cdot Q_o$ or all of the shaded areas on Figure 14–3. Total variable costs are shaded diagonally, and total fixed costs are shaded horizontally. The difference between total revenue and total cost is the profit of the monopoly firm, shaded vertically.

We come now to the fundamental difference between the monopoly firm and the perfectly competitive firm. In competition, if the typical firm is earning economic profits, that will send out a signal to resource owners to shift their resources into that industry, and eventually the industry will return to a long-run equilibrium situation with zero economic profits. The profits earned by the monopolist send out the same signals, but resource owners find that entry into the industry is blocked by one or more of the barriers to entry discussed earlier. As a consequence of the barriers to entry, the monopolist firm is able to earn economic profits in the long run as there is no chance for market adjustment.

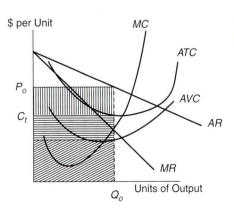

FIGURE 14–3 Output and pricing for a monopoly firm.

It is the promise of those economic profits under the protection of the patent system that drives pharmaceutical companies to invest millions in research in an effort to develop new products. For the 20 years of patent protection, the firm is a monopolist. At the end of the patent period, other companies introduce generic versions, and the price of the drug falls dramatically as a new long-run equilibrium is established. The presence of those monopoly profits also sends out a signal to other firms to develop products that have a similar use but are chemically different, which can also be patented. As a result, we have any number of distinct yet similar antibiotics on the market today, many of which are still under patent.

Unprofitable Monopolies

Monopolistic firms are *not* necessarily always profitable. Examples of this may be found in abundance in the rural areas of the United States. In the case where a single grocery store remains in a community, if the building were to burn down, the business would often cease to exist since the returns that can be generated are so limited that an investment in a new building would be unlikely to pay for itself.

This situation is illustrated in Figure 14–4. As before, the loss-minimizing firm adjusts output to that point at which marginal cost is equal to marginal revenue and the price (P) is the average revenue at that level of output. In this example, the monopolist is making some contribution to her fixed costs but is not

FIGURE 14–4
Monopolies aren't always profitable.

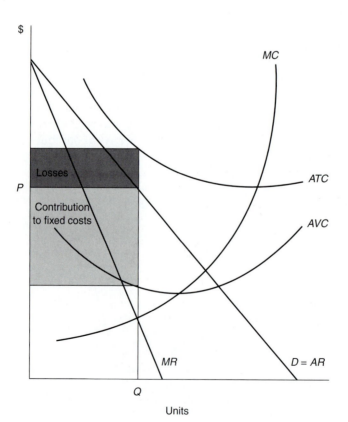

completely covering the expense necessary to provide for replacing all the capital equipment used in her business. If some contribution to overhead is possible, she will continue to do business until she has depleted (or used up) the investment in fixed equipment. Once it becomes necessary to replace the building (for example, in the case of a rural grocery store), the business will cease to operate.

Not all unprofitable monopolies are small rural monopolies. Amtrak has a virtual monopoly on passenger rail travel in the United States, but it has never had a profitable year. The once powerful Penn Central Railroad went bankrupt in 1970 because the opening of the Pennsylvania Turnpike provided an alternative transportation route across Pennsylvania. For many years Western Union had a monopoly in the market for nearly instantaneous communication. The first nail in its coffin was the telephone, and the last was the advent of the fax machine.

Performance

What, then, are the effects of monopoly? Is monopoly necessarily *bad?* If the market is of the nature where some competition could feasibly exist, consumers will pay a higher price under monopoly conditions than they would pay under conditions of competition. There are no economic profits under most competitive situations once enough time has elapsed to permit economic adjustment to occur. But the economic profits extracted by the monopolist will continue to be ripped out of the consumer's hide in the long run—there being no opportunity for market adjustment. Thus, the effects of monopoly in a market that is large enough to support competition are:

- Higher prices
- Reduced availability of product
- A transfer of wealth from consumers to the monopolist through the economic profits above and beyond the opportunity cost of all resources.

If, however, the monopoly is of the locational type as a result of a limited size market, consumers are very likely to be in a more favorable position under monopoly. In the case of the rural feed store that has a local monopoly, local consumers will grudgingly pay monopoly profits to the local store so long as its prices are less than the transportation cost of going to a distant, competitive market. "Natural" monopolies are always preferred to any form of competition—more on that will be discussed later.

MONOPOLISTIC COMPETITION

We've discussed the two extremes of market structure—perfect competition and pure monopoly—and some of the circumstances surrounding the existence of these two types of markets. We have recognized that these two types of market structure rarely exist in the purest form in the real world, but certain industries do in fact approach perfect competition, and in a locational sense we often encounter what amounts to pure monopoly. Between these two extremes lies a broad area that includes many industries. The two main economic paradigms used to describe the structure and conduct of these industries are **monopolistic competition** and oligopoly.

Monopolistic competition market structure in which there are many firms selling differentiated products.

Structure

Monopolistic competition is a form of imperfect competition that is very common in a number of markets for consumer goods from shampoo to bread. Monopolistic competition is characterized by many firms selling **differentiated products.** Entry by additional firms is easy.

Product differentiation is the endless quest of the monopolistically competi-tive firm. Differentiation is the effort to produce a unique product in what might otherwise be a homogeneous product market. If products degenerate into a ho-mogeneous mass, then monopolistic competition degenerates into perfect compe-tition and low profits. In order to differentiate its product and earn some monopoly profits, the monopolistically competitive firm is continually striving for more and stronger differentiated products by introducing "new and improved" versions of existing products or new products altogether.

There are several ways monopolistically competitive firms can differenti-ate their products:

- *Brand name.* Put an exotic-sounding French name on a bottle of shampoo, and you can sell it for a dollar or two more than the Kmart house brand.

- *Minor ingredients.* Just plain shampoo is a competitive market for what some consumers see as a commodity. But put a nickel's worth of egg or beer or special fragrance in the shampoo, and you have a differentiated product you can sell for a dollar more.

- *Product features.* Many consumers are very environmentally conscious. To tap this segment of the total shampoo market, put "biodegradable" in big letters across the front of your shampoo bottle and sell it for a buck more than the same stuff without the label. If your stuff is biodegradable, the implication (whether true or false) must be that the other stuff isn't.

- *Packaging.* Marketing experts know that beer drinkers are a diverse bunch. There's "six-pack Joe" and the little old lady who likes to have a few sips before her afternoon nap. Nonetheless, almost all beer is marketed in the familiar 12-ounce bottle or can.[2] Given the diversity of beer consumers, beer makers have tried (mostly unsuccessfully) to grab market share by selling beer in different size packages. For many years a small brewery in Golden, Colorado, sold beer in 7-ounce cans at about the same price as the 12-ounce brew. Other brewers have tried 16-ounce and 1-liter cans with little success. One imported German brew comes in a 5-liter can! Look at the diversity of packaging in the soft drink market compared with the beer market.

- *Market Segments.* Another strategy in product differentiation is to identify unique segments of a market and produce slightly different products for each segment. For instance, breakfast cereal makers produce sugar-coated brands for kids, vitamin-enhanced brands for health-conscious consumers, and high-fiber products for the elderly. Why? Simple—if you can spray 2-cents worth of sugar on your cornflakes and sell them to kids for a quarter more, why not?

---

[2] When Canada went metric several decades ago, the familiar 12-ounce bottle of beer was replaced with a 356-milliliter bottle. Now that's a nice round number that just happens to be equal to . . . yup, you guessed it.

If the monopolistically competitive firm is successful in its efforts at product differentiation, then the firm holds a quasi-monopoly position in that differentiated product and it can earn monopoly profits so long as that quasi-monopoly position is held. Once competitors are able to match the differentiated product, the monopoly disappears and competition prevails—hence the term "monopolistic competition."

Proctor & Gamble is one of the leading producers of consumer goods and one of the best in playing the monopolistic competition game. Among its well-known brand lines is Crest toothpaste. In the 1950s it was common for most folks (and particularly kids) to visit the dentist regularly to have a coat of ill-tasting fluoride applied to their teeth. Research had shown that such applications on a regular basis greatly reduced the incidence of cavities. P&G researchers (working with university researchers) came up with a differentiated product plan. Instead of the dentist putting fluoride on your teeth every 6 months, why not put the fluoride in toothpaste so that you would fluoride your teeth with each brushing? After several years of research the product was ready for launch, but before launching the new product P&G asked for and received an endorsement from the American Dental Association of this new product.

In 1955 this new product with its one important differentiating characteristic was launched. A massive advertising campaign accompanied the new product with the critical tag line: "The only toothpaste endorsed by the American Dental Association." The image that Crest, rather than fluoride (an ingredient in Crest), was endorsed by the ADA stuck for many years, and Crest was able to charge monopoly level prices[3] well above its competitors even after they added fluoride and received the blessing of the ADA for their fluoridated products.

Recently Proctor & Gamble introduced Crest Gum Care toothpaste. This product is designed for "reducing gingivitis[4] and fighting cavities." Initial prices are about twice that of normal toothpaste. Right now P&G is a monopolist in this market (protected by U.S. patent #5,004,597), and will behave like a monopolist—charging whatever price the market will bear.

Conduct of the Monopolistically Competitive Firm

The economic dynamics of a firm in monopolistic competition are illustrated in Figures 14–5, 14–6, and 14–7. Initially when a firm introduces a differentiated product, it holds a short-run monopoly in that product. This is shown in Figure 14–5, which is similar to Figure 14–3 for the monopoly firm. The firm faces a downward-sloping demand curve, which is seen by the firm as the average revenue curve. Knowing that the firm will maximize its profits if $MC = MR$, the firm, a price maker, will adjust the market price to P_2 such that Q^* units are traded. At Q^* units traded $MC = MR$, so the firm is maximizing its profits. At Q^* units of output the average total costs of producing the product is P_1 and the monopoly profits per unit produced is $P_2 - P_1$.

In the short run the firm will retain this monopoly position and earn monopoly profits. But unlike the monopolist, the monopolistically competitive firm has competitors, and the firm is unable to block entry of those competitors into the

---

[3] While the price was higher than ordinary toothpaste, it replaced the not too cheap visits to the dentist for fluoride treatments, so many consumers were happy to pay more for toothpaste and less for dentists.

[4] Gum disease.

FIGURE 14–5
Monopolistic
competition in the
short run.

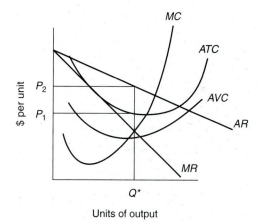

FIGURE 14–6
Monopolistic
competition in the
intermediate run.

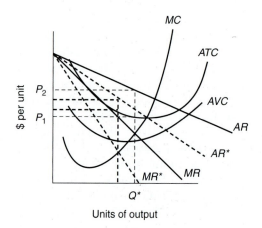

FIGURE 14–7
Monopolistic
competition in the
long run.

differentiated market. As competitors for the differentiated product enter the market in the intermediate run, the share of the market for the initial firm shrinks. The firm sees this as a downward rotation of the average revenue and marginal revenue curves shown as dashed lines in Figure 14–6. The shifting revenue curves reduce the profit-maximizing quantity to produce, which in turn causes the firm to reduce its profit-maximizing product price. As a result of these adjustments, profit per unit falls to the distance between the two heavy dashed lines in Figure 14–6.[5]

This process will continue over time until a long-run equilibrium such as that shown in Figure 14–7 is reached. The firm has lost its monopoly power and is sharing the market with competitors. Output of the firm has fallen to Q^{**}, and the price the firm must charge to maintain $MR = MC$ is P_3, which is also equal to the average total cost, so economic profits are zero. The firm is a competitor in the market for its formally differentiated product, and the time for a "new and improved" version of the product has arrived.

Performance

Monopolistic competition has its opponents and its proponents. The opponents point out that in the long-run equilibrium situation the profit-maximizing firm is not producing at minimum average total costs, that expensive market promotion costs are inevitable, and that firms earn monopoly profits at the expense of consumers in the short run. Proponents argue that consumers benefit from monopolistic competition because firms are driven to develop ever better products in an effort to gain market advantage. There is no such drive in the commodity businesses faced by perfectly competitive firms.

The drive to develop differentiated products and to introduce new products inevitably leads the monopolistically competitive firm into product advertising and other forms of promotion. It is estimated that there are about 5,000 new food products introduced each year. Trying to get the consumer's attention is no small task. A quick look at any of the food-oriented magazines usually found at the checkout counter of supermarkets will vividly illustrate the dynamics of the process. The ads scream out that our "new" barbecue sauce has habanero peppers[6] in it or our "new" diapers have improved elastic bands to prevent leaking. Never mind that they also cut off all blood flow to the lower extremities.

Product advertising sometimes is designed to acquaint the consumer with a new, differentiated product. Other times it is designed to reinforce an existing brand. It is barren landscape indeed that doesn't have a Coca-Cola logo on it somewhere. Or what is Umm, Umm Good? Or whose blimps are going to be at every major sporting event? If you know, then this brand-reinforcing advertising is doing its job.

A final kind of advertising that is important in agriculture is what is known as generic advertising. Generic ads are for a commodity rather than a brand of that commodity. These ads are usually financed by a tax on the producers of the food

---

[5] In the language of marketing, this process is one of "losing market share" and the product is becoming "mature."

[6] It is not important that most consumers don't know what habanero peppers are, so long as they know that their current barbecue sauce doesn't have them and your product does. Your product is different: that's all that matters.

commodity. The Florida Sunshine Tree reminds you to drink your orange juice and to be certain it is genuine Florida juice and not that of some other dubious origin. Notice that it matters not what brand of juice you buy; just buy it.[7] Other generic ad campaigns include the successful "other white meat" campaign and the much-maligned milk mustache marketing promotion. Again, if you know what "the other white meat" is, then the generic advertising is effective.

OLIGOPOLY

Structure

Oligopoly market structure with few firms that are highly interdependent.

The other form of imperfect competition that we as consumers confront is the **oligopoly** type of market structure. Examples of oligopolistic market structure include the retail gasoline and airline industries. Under conditions of oligopoly, there are but a few sellers of a good. The conditions necessary for the presence of oligopoly include:

- A market size that is saturated by existing firms in the market. Entry of a new firm or expansion of an existing firm would imply loss of market share of other existing firms. Thus, action taken by any individual market participant is likely to provoke retaliation on the part of the others.
- Every market participant recognizes that potential retaliation must be considered in decisions regarding price, output, sales promotion, and so forth.
- A product that is basically homogeneous but is subject to minor product differentiation through techniques such as location, advertising, spice blends, additional services, or frequent flyer programs. (What real difference is there between Exxon and Texaco or between Delta and United?)

Conduct

The decisions as to pricing and output by each oligopolistic firm will have a definite impact on the volume of sales and profits realized by all other firms in the industry. Thus, any time one oligopolistic firm changes its pattern of operations, it is a pretty good bet that the competing oligopolists who share that market are going to retaliate. It is this interdependence of firms in the industry that is the distinguishing characteristic of the oligopoly market structure.

A classic example of oligopoly is provided by the retail gasoline industry. Almost every community has at least two service stations that are affiliated with different oil companies. If one should attempt to increase its volume of sales by cutting the price of gasoline by a few cents per gallon, what happens? We all know from experience (pleasant experience, unless you happen to own a filling station) that a full-scale price war may well be in the making. Price wars, a form of competitive retaliation, are characteristic of oligopolistic industries.

---

[7] Notice that this message is consistent with the desires of who is paying for the ads—the grove owners. A grove owner doesn't care which processor buys his or her fruit. The only thing the grove owner cares about is that the price of oranges is high because of robust demand for juice.

In perfect competition producers and consumers are passive price takers. Not so in the case of oligopoly. The chieftains of oligopolistic firms spend lots of time looking over their shoulder to see what their competitor is doing and plotting how to react to any changes that occur. Oligopolies live in a world of action and reaction—action and retaliation. It is a highly visceral form of competition.

Managers in an oligopolistic industry are apt to be very, very cautious about reducing prices. They must consider the impact that their actions will have on their rivals and the retaliatory measures that those rivals may adopt. Rather than competing on the basis of price, firms operating under oligopolistic conditions are more likely to rely on advertising and devices such as special services, frequent flyer programs, or trading stamps, since the reaction to these techniques is generally less immediate and less disastrous than the reaction to a price reduction.[8]

In a long-run equilibrium situation, each competing oligopolist will have a market share that all participants in the market perceive to be "normal". Prices tend to be uniform among the firms in the market, and prices are very "sticky"—that is, not prone to change. At that "normal" volume of sales, if the oligopolist firm increases its price, its customers desert it—fleeing to its rivals who are charging lower prices. If it lowers its price, its rivals respond to this action with price reductions of their own, and all the competing oligopolists simply pick up their "normal" share of the increased volume sold in the total market.

Game Theory

Perhaps the best way to understand the behavior of an oligopolistic firm manager is through the use of game theory.[9] Game theory emphasizes firm behavior in an interdependent, noncooperative environment of action and reaction. Each action is viewed as having a payoff (profit) that depends not only on what action the firm takes but also on the reaction of the competitors.

To keep things simple, let's assume we have an industry with two firms selling grain on the world market—Cargill and Archer, Daniels, Midland (ADM). Each firm must make a pricing decision—whether to price the grain it offers for sale at a high price or at a low price. Based on past experience, the managers know what happens to profits in each of the four pricing possibilities shown in Figure 14–8.

If Cargill opts for a high price and ADM matches its high price, then they both earn 14 and the total profit between them is 28—the highest total profit possible. But if Cargill opts for the high price, ADM can improve its lot from 14 to 18 by selecting a low price and buying market share away from Cargill. In this case Cargill's reaction is clear: it can earn either 6 with high prices or 8 by matching the low price of ADM, so they both end up with low prices and total profits of 16.

Clearly, it is in their joint interest that both select high prices, and they both know that. But how far do you trust your competitor to work in your joint interests rather than in his or her individual self-interest? If either foregoes high prices,

---

[8] All of which enhances the tendency of oligopolies to offer homogeneous products. When one airline started a frequent flyer program, all the other airlines retaliated by creating their own programs.

[9] In 1994 the Nobel prize for economic sciences was awarded to John C. Harsanyi, John F. Nash, Jr. (the subject of the film *A Beautiful Mind*), and Reinhard Selten for their pioneering analysis of equilibria in the theory of noncooperative games.

FIGURE 14–8 Payoff
matrix for two
interdependent
oligopoly firms.

Cargill's Price	ADM's Price	Cargill's Profit	ADM's Profit
High	High	14	14
Low	High	18	6
High	Low	6	18
Low	Low	8	8

the other will also and they are equally worse off. When one firm in the industry lowers its price, the others will retaliate by lowering theirs to protect their market share. Price reductions are always matched; however, price increases may or may not be.

This illustrates another characteristic of oligopoly market structure—the existence of price leaders. On any given day, American, United and Continental airlines all charge the same fare on the very competitive New York to Los Angeles route. One day the price leader, American, announces a 5 percent increase in its fares on that route. How do United and Continental react? They both realize that if they go along with American, they will be 5 percent better off with constant market shares. Suppose United goes along and increases its fares by 5 percent. Now Continental is in the catbird seat. It must weigh the advantage of a 5 percent fare increase against an expected increase in market share if it doesn't go along. After much thought, Continental decides a 10 percent increase in market share at existing prices is better than a 5 percent fare increase at existing market shares. What must United and American do now? Each realizes that it stands to lose market share to Continental. Reacting to Continental's move, they both will have to announce that they have rescinded the 5 percent fare increase immediately. This kind of interdependent action-reaction pricing goes on daily on hundreds of airline routes and at thousands of gas stations.

GOVERNMENT REGULATION

The game theory illustration shows that competition among oligopolists inevitably leads both companies to accept low prices and hence low profits. This less-than-desirable result (from the perspective of the oligopolists) became very obvious to the robber barons of the late nineteenth century. The industrial revolution led to the development of large corporations. The titans of these industries quickly learned that competition was not in their best interest and that profit could be increased if they cooperated with one another. There were basically two approaches to avoiding competition, illustrated by the railroads and Standard Oil.

Railroads

The rail bosses learned early on that competition was not in the best interest of either party, so they simply engaged in collusion to divide the market into geographic districts with the understanding that no one would invade another's territory. That made each a local monopolist in the designated area, able to earn monopoly profits because entry was blocked by the secret agreement. These agreements among owners of independent railroads became known as **trusts.** They were very effective at creating a number of rail millionaires who depended on the power of the trust to maintain their local monopolies.

Trusts noncompete agreements among oligopoly firms.

Standard Oil

John D. Rockefeller was facing the same problem in the oligopolistic petroleum industry about the same time. His approach was a little different. If another firm attempted to compete with Standard Oil, Rockefeller would simply merge the competitor into Standard Oil and thus regain control of pricing. Over time, Rockefeller merged with most of the competition, turning Standard Oil into a near monopoly in the petroleum business. The basic philosophy here is that it is better to merge and cooperate than to compete.

Antitrust

By the late 1880's it was clear that the public interest was not being served by the railroad trusts and other monopolists. Particularly disadvantaged were the farmers streaming into the Great Plains, who were totally dependent on the railroads to ship their crops to the markets in the East. Agrarian unrest finally led to the passage of the Interstate Commerce Act regulating railroads in 1887. This act required railroads to publish and post freight rates, and it created the Interstate Commerce Commission to regulate those rates to be certain they were "reasonable and just." Three years later the Sherman Anti-Trust Act made mergers that create monopolies illegal and prohibited practices that result in a restraint of trade. These acts and subsequent legislation are known collectively as **antitrust** legislation.

Antitrust laws prohibiting business behavior that threatens competition, such as price-fixing, collusion, and anticompetitive mergers.

Today, these laws are still on the books. They prohibit price fixing, collusion, and other anticompetitive activity. Proposed mergers that might restrain competition must be approved by the Federal Trade Commission—a regulatory branch of the federal government. So, while it would be in their collective best interest for Cargill and ADM in Figure 14–8 to get together and agree on high prices, it would, under current antitrust law, be illegal to do so.[10]

Natural Monopolies

We saw earlier that some monopolies are in the best interest of the public. We call these **natural monopolies.** They usually occur in industries with very high fixed costs such that if two or more firms divided the market among themselves, the cost to the consumer would be higher than if a monopoly provided the service. From an economic perspective, a natural monopoly is a firm operating on the downward-sloping portion of the average total cost curve. Examples of natural monopolies include the utilities (gas, water, sewer, electricity, garbage, cable, phone, and so on), mass transit, airports, and the like.

Natural monopolies high fixed-cost industries in which the costs of a monopoly firm are lower than would be the costs of several competitive firms.

In the case of a natural monopoly the best public policy is to grant a franchise to the monopoly firm giving that firm exclusive rights to provide the service as a monopolist. In return, the franchisee is limited to charging consumers no more

---

[10] In 1996 ADM was found guilty of price fixing with its competitors on two specialty products. The company was fined nearly $200 million—the largest antitrust settlement to that time.

than its average total costs of production (including normal profits). State and local governments usually have regulatory commissions that are responsible for making certain the franchised monopoly provides the required service and that the prices charged are reasonable. In this way, consumers get the advantages of the natural monopoly without paying for monopoly profits.[11]

Marketing Orders in Agriculture

In 1937 Congress passed legislation that allows the secretary of agriculture to create marketing orders to regulate processors or handlers (e.g., packers) of highly perishable agricultural commodities. The marketing orders were created because farmers of perishable commodities (fruits, vegetables and milk) felt that processors or handlers of their products were taking advantage of farmers who had little market power.

Marketing orders are requested by a vote of farmers and imposed on the processors or handlers. The orders basically require the processors to collude on behalf of the farmers and exempts them from antitrust when they do so. This, of course, is detrimental to the consumer of products that are processed under marketing orders. The most common elements of marketing orders are uniform grades and standards and flow control mechanisms.

Marketing orders in agriculture are very controversial. In any other industry, such behavior would fall under antitrust scrutiny. In the last couple of decades, the number of marketing orders has been declining as secretaries of agriculture have canceled orders considered to be no longer necessary for "orderly" marketing. Nonetheless, virtually all milk processed in the United States is processed under the directives of a marketing order assuring both farmer and consumer of high milk prices.

SUMMARY

Market structure refers to the number of firms in an industry and relationship among them. The only market structure that has been examined to this point is perfect competition. In this chapter some of the restrictive assumptions of the perfectly competitive model will be relaxed in the examination of three additional market structures. In each case we will find that the market structure determines the conduct of the typical firm in the industry.

Monopoly is a market structure in which there is only one firm in the industry. In order for a monopoly to exist there must be no close substitutes for the product and there must be barriers to the entry of additional firms to the industry. The most common form of barrier to entry is a patent on the product.

The cost structure of a monopoly is identical to that of a perfectly competitive firm. The revenue side of the firm is very different, however. Since the demand curve of the market is the demand curve of the firm, the firm faces a downward-sloping demand curve such that if the monopoly firm changes its level of output, the price that it can command in the market will change. The market demand curve is the firm's average revenue curve. The marginal revenue is also downward sloping and lies below and to the left of the average revenue curve.

---

[11] To see this system in operation, ask yourself what you would do if the phone company increased your local service by $5 a month. Answer—no change because demand is very inelastic. Well, don't you think the phone company knows this? If they were not a regulated monopoly, can you imagine what they would charge? Awesome.

As with any other profit-maximizing/loss-minimizing firm, the monopolist adjusts output to that level at which marginal revenue is equal to marginal cost. At that level of output the average revenue (demand) curve shows the price that can be charged. In most cases the monopoly firm will earn economic profits beyond average total cost, but being a monopoly does not guarantee economic profits. The unique characteristic of a monopoly is that because of the barriers to entry, the firm can earn economic profits in the long run as well as the short run.

In most cases, monopolies result in higher prices and lower quantities traded than would be the case in competition. However, there are two situations in which monopolies can be justified. Local monopolies are those that exist in markets so small that having more than one firm is not economically viable. Many rural farm towns can support only one feed store, so that store becomes a local monopoly. A second type of acceptable monopoly is called a natural monopoly. These exist in industries with high fixed costs such that the monopoly firm produces in the downward-sloping portion of the average total cost curve. In this case, if the market were split in two, both firms would have higher costs than the monopolist. Natural monopolies are usually found in the utilities such as electric, gas, and water. In the case of a natural monopoly, the appropriate public policy is to grant the monopoly firm a franchise and then regulate the price charged to the customers.

Monopolistic competition is a market structure that is very common in many consumer goods. As its name implies, this is a structure with some characteristics of monopoly and some characteristics of competition. In the short run the firm behaves as a monopolist, and in the long run the firm behaves as a competitor. There are typically a few to many firms in the industry, and entry is easy. The key and distinguishing characteristic of this market structure is product differentiation. The firm seeks to differentiate its product by adding features that competitors' products do not have. At the time a new feature differentiating the product is introduced, the firm has a monopoly on that product feature. As competitors match the feature, the short-run monopoly position is lost.

Features that are frequently used to differentiate include brand names, minor ingredients, packaging, and products designed for a segment of a market. A product as mundane as laundry detergent is subject to product differentiation. Almost every year the market leader comes out with a "new and improved" product. Then it is up to competitors to match the improvements and recapture market share. If the differentiating feature can be patented, then the firm has the prospect of a longer-term monopoly position. Competitors will then have to trump the patent with an even better product—a practice that is common in the pharmaceutical business.

As with a monopolist, in the short run the firm is the market and the firm adjusts output to equate marginal revenue and marginal cost. Price is the average revenue at this output level. As other firms enter the market, the monopolist loses market share and the average revenue curve shifts downward reducing the amount of economic profits earned. This process continues until there are enough firms in the market to drive the price down to the average total cost of each firm such that there are zero economic profits. In the terminology of marketing, the product has matured.

In the short run the firm is a monopolist and is able to charge monopoly prices that generate economic profits to the firm. Long-run competition drives prices down to the average total cost, and economic profits disappear. While consumers pay more in the short run, they are continuously provided with more and more product features. An inevitable consequence of this market structure is advertising.

A third form of imperfect competition is called oligopoly. In an oligopolistic market structure there are few firms, but those firms are able to saturate the market. The product is fairly homogeneous (in spite of great efforts to differentiate it). The distinguishing characteristic of oligopoly market structure is that the firms are interdependent. A classic example of an industry characterized by oligopoly is the airline industry. If one airline lowers its price on a route, other airlines will react by making similar price reductions. If one airline increases the price on a route, others might match the increase or not. If they don't match the increase, then the airline initiating the increase will rescind it or face the prospect of losing market share.

One approach to evaluating the behavior of firms in an oligopoly is game theory. This is a mathematical technique that can be used to explain the rational behavior of interdependent firms. In most cases, the independent behavior of oligopoly firms is not consistent with the collective best interest of all firms. As a result, the potential returns to collusion, price fixing, and other noncompetitive behaviors among oligopoly firms are substantial.

Since economic returns to noncompetitive behavior can be very substantial, a network of federal laws known as antitrust laws has evolved to protect the consumer from noncompetitive behaviors. Practices that are prohibited include collusion, price fixing, lowering prices to run competitors out of business, and mergers to eliminate competition.

A form of government-sponsored imperfect competition that is unique to agriculture is called marketing orders. Marketing orders are government directives imposed on the processors of perishable commodities that require the processor to behave in the best interest of the producer (the farmer) rather than the self-interest of the processor. The net effect of marketing orders is to create cartels, which ultimately result in higher prices to consumers and higher returns for producers than would exist in a competitive realm. In recent years several marketing orders have been eliminated.

KEY TERMS

Antitrust	Monopoly
Conduct	Natural monopolies
Differentiated products	Oligopoly
Market structure	Patent
Monopolistic competition	Trusts

PROBLEMS AND DISCUSSION QUESTIONS

1. Suppose a monopolist correctly adjusts output to that level at which marginal cost is equal to marginal revenue. What would happen if:
   a. The firm priced the product at a price below the average revenue?
   b. The firm priced the product at a price above the average revenue?
2. Explain why average and marginal revenue are the same for a perfectly competitive firm but different for a monopoly firm.
3. In the past the U.S. Post Office had a virtual monopoly in the market for sending and receiving packages. Today it still has a monopoly on your

mailbox: no one else can legally use it. What happened to the package delivery monopoly?

4. Blocking the entry of other firms and/or substitute goods is essential for maintaining a monopoly. What are some of the business strategies used to do this blocking?

5. A natural monopoly produces in the downward-sloping segment of the average total cost curve. Draw the cost and revenue curves for a profit-maximizing firm that exhibits this characteristic.

6. What is a firm in monopolistic competition driven to do in an effort to gain a short-run monopoly position?

7. Describe the dynamics that move a monopolistically competitive firm from short-run monopolist to long-run competitor.

8. What do we mean by market share, and why is it so important to the monopolistically competitive firm?

9. What are the distinguishing characteristics of an oligopoly market structure?

10. The payoff matrix below shows the amount of profits each firm (A and B) earns as each determines whether or not to advertise.

		Firm A	
		No Ads	Ads
Firm B	No Ads	A = 10 B = 10	A = 13 B = 5
	Ads	A = 3 B = 14	A = 8 B = 8

a. Which strategy has the highest total payoff?
b. If A advertises, what will B do to retaliate?
c. If B advertises, what will A do to retaliate?
d. What is the final equilibrium of this game where neither firm has any incentive to change strategy?

The Theory of Consumer Behavior

*T*he laws of supply and demand are to a large degree the forces that cause our economy to operate. We have discussed the concept of supply and the factors underlying this concept in some detail. But production and supply of any good are meaningless unless that good is ultimately to be utilized in the satisfaction of some of the needs and wants of humanity. So we move from production and supply to consumption and demand—the theory of consumer behavior.

Production theory is based on the analysis of a production function—a real, tangible relationship between inputs and outputs. Using that production function we were able to derive optimizing behaviors for the firm manager. Consumption theory is based on the behavior of the individual consumer as that consumer seeks to optimize his or her self-interest. It deals with how the consumer behaves in an effort to maximize the benefits from consumption and how the consumer evaluates those benefits. This is neither tangible nor real because we can't make interpersonal comparisons between consumers and we can't quantitatively measure satisfaction. So our treatment of the consumer as an optimizing unit will be more subjective and abstract than was the case for the producer. Nonetheless, the theory is quite robust in describing consumer behavior.

THE LAW OF DEMAND

We saw in an earlier chapter that demand refers to the quantities of a good consumers are willing to consume at alternative prices, *ceteris paribus*. Demand is determined for a given time and a given place. The law of demand simply states that as the price of a good increases, *ceteris paribus,* the quantity of the good consumers are willing to consume will decrease. This doesn't imply that every consumer in every market will react according to the law of demand, but that in the aggregate of many consumers there will be an inverse relationship between quantities and prices. Rest assured that if the price of gas goes up by a dime a gallon, a millionaire is not going to buy less gas, but there are enough of us who will change our behavior to have a market impact.[1]

REAL INCOME AND SUBSTITUTION EFFECTS

The "law" of demand is, like much of economics, common sense made difficult. It is easy to assert that as the price of hamburger goes up, *ceteris paribus* (i.e., the price of

---

[1] The demand for some goods may violate the law of demand by exhibiting upward, sloping demand curves. Such goods are known as Giffin goods after a nineteenth-century writer who suggested their existence. For instance, a perfume retailer may find that by increasing the price of one perfume, *ceteris paribus,* sales actually increase because consumers assume that in being more expensive it is better and therefore buy more of it. So, some "snob" or super-premium goods may be Giffin goods.

chicken, pork, and fish remaining constant), the quantity of hamburger consumers are willing to consume will go down. There are two reasons we expect the law of demand to be valid. They are known as the **substitution effect** and the **real income effect.**

To see how each of these two effects leads to a downward-sloping demand curve, let's create a mythical consumer, a poorly nourished college student named Phred, who has a budget of $150/week. Suppose initially that Phred buys 25 pounds of hamburger a week at $2.00 per pound, or total spending on hamburger of $50. The other $100 is spent on 100 units of stuff[2] that costs $1.00 per unit.

Substitution Effect

Now suppose the price of hamburger doubles to $4.00 per pound, *ceteris paribus.* While this initially looks like an increase in the price of hamburger, we can see that it also looks like the price of stuff, relative to hamburger, just got cheaper. So how does Phred react? He increases his purchases of the relatively cheap stuff (which includes chicken) and decreases his purchases of hamburger. He may reduce his consumption of hamburger to 10 pounds, or $40, and increase his purchases of stuff to $110. He has substituted stuff for hamburger as the price of hamburger went up. Notice the two effects of the substitution effect: consumption of hamburger went down (law of demand) and the consumption of stuff went up (substitution effect).

Real Income Effect

When the price of hamburger goes up to $4 per pound, Phred finds (or phinds) that he can no longer buy 25 pounds of hamburger a week and 100 units of stuff a week on his budget of $150. The increase in the price of beef has reduced the amount of goods that Phred is able to buy with his $150. His purchasing power or real income has fallen. To compensate for the loss of his purchasing power he must buy less of both hamburger and stuff. If he reduces his consumption of both goods proportionately, he would buy 18.75 pounds of hamburger per week and 75 units of stuff. His hamburger budget would increase to $75/week ($4.00 · 18.75), and his stuff budget would fall from $100 to $75. Spending $75 on each commodity would keep him within his total budget of $150. Notice the impact of the real income effect: as the price of hamburger goes up, *ceteris paribus,* the quantity of hamburger consumed goes down (law of demand) and the quantity of stuff consumed also goes down (real income effect).

Taken together, the substitution and real income effects both suggest that as the price of hamburger goes up, the quantity demanded of hamburger goes down. Both effects confirm the law of demand. The impact of an increase in the price of hamburger on the consumption of stuff is indeterminate, depending on the relative strengths of the two effects. If the substitution effect is stronger, then consumption of stuff will increase; but, if the real income effect is stronger, then consumption of stuff will fall.

MARKET DEMAND AND INDIVIDUAL DEMAND

We saw earlier that supply originates at the level of the firm. Market supply is the aggregation of all the supply curves of firms in the market. Adding more firms to

Substitution effect
as the price of good *A* increases, *ceteris paribus*, the relative price of good *B* decreases and the consumer substitutes *B* for *A* in consumption.

Real income effect
as the price of good *A* increases, *ceteris paribus*, the real income, or purchasing power, of the consumer falls and as a result less of both good *A* and *B* are consumed.

---

[2] This is a technical term economists use to refer to all other goods and services, such as a little salad to go along with 25 pounds of hamburger a week.

the industry has the effect of shifting the market supply curve outward. In a similar manner, demand originates with the behavior of the individual consumer. Those individual demand curves are added up to generate market demand. The addition of more consumers to the market will have the effect of shifting the market demand curve outward.

Therefore, in order to understand the forces that drive market demand it is important that we understand how the typical consumer behaves—how the individual demand curve is shaped. To do this we will introduce the utility theory of consumer behavior.[3] Realizing that different consumers behave differently, we will analyze the behavior of a typical consumer to develop an understanding of the economics of consumer behavior.

UTILITY ANALYSIS

Consumers buy stuff because they want to (hamburgers), have to (gasoline), ought to (cod liver oil) or out of habit (cigarettes). Regardless of the motivation, the consumer receives satisfaction through consumption. Economists refer to the satisfaction gained from consumption as **utility.** Utility is created by the consumption of goods and services.

Unfortunately, utility cannot be measured in an objective fashion. Despite years of dedicated research and development our utilometer is still not functioning. Nonetheless, we can say a good deal about the utility associated with consumption. But first, let's investigate a few assumptions about our utility model.

Utility the satisfaction created by the consumption of goods and services.

Assumptions about the Utility Model

As with any economic model, the utility model of consumer behavior is founded on several important assumptions. Before getting into the model itself, it is best to make those assumptions explicit.

Opportunity Costs and Price

The consumer will purchase a product so long as the utility created by its consumption is greater than the opportunity cost of consuming it. Most of the opportunity cost of consuming a good is the price of the good itself. Price is a measure of the consumption foregone of other goods when the purchase is made. But there are also other acquisition costs over and above price that should be included in the decision matrix. For instance, there may be transactions costs such as waiting in line (time is money) or tax implications. There may be travel or locational costs involved. For instance, you wouldn't drive 10 miles across town to get a good deal on a gallon of milk, but you might do so to get a good deal on a new car.

---

[3] There are two classic approaches to developing the theory of consumer behavior. What is presented in this chapter is the utility approach. An appendix to this chapter presents the indifference curve approach. Most instructors use either one approach or the other, but not both. If you want to use the indifference curve approach, skip to the appendix after reading the assumptions that follow and then omit the rest of the section on Utility Analysis. Rejoin this chapter at The Market Demand Function near the end of the chapter.

The key point is that the opportunity cost of consuming a good may well be more than the price of the good. With that in mind, in the remainder of this chapter we are going to talk about the prices of goods as a shorthand for the opportunity cost of goods.

Rational Behavior

We are going to assume that consumers behave in a rational fashion. There are really three fundamental assumptions concerning rationality. First, consumers will consume a good only if the utility of consuming it is greater than the disutility (price) of acquiring it. That is, consumers won't buy things that don't provide them with a net utility gain. If the consumption of a good creates a disutility, then the consumer would not buy it at any price. For vegetarian consumers, the consumption of any meat would create a disutility, so no meat is purchased at any price. For meat eaters, meat will be purchased so long as the utility of eating the meat is greater than the disutility of having to pay for it.

Second, we assume that more is better than less. More stuff is a constant desire regardless of how much stuff we have.[4]

Third, our wants are unlimited. The hungry person wants food. The overfed person wants a new car. The person with a new car wants an exotic vacation. Bill Gates wanted a new house that cost $35 million to build. Our wants exceed our means, so we must chose among our wants. Choice is what economics is all about.

Preferences

It is assumed that the consumer is able to evaluate the utility gained from the consumption of alternative goods and is able to establish a system of **preferences** between any two goods at any time. In practice this assumption means that a consumer can walk into the local Mickey-D, look at the menu board, and decide what he or she wants. We are basically assuming that the consumer is not clueless.

Preferences the ability of the consumer to identify which of two goods will produce a greater amount of utility in consumption.

Budget Constraint

It is assumed that our typical consumer is constrained in his or her purchasing decisions by a limited budget. For most of us this is a far too realistic assumption[5]

---

[4] There are two exceptions to this statement: (1) when Mother Teresa died, her worldly possessions included one sweater and her eyeglasses (she wanted nothing more); (2) most goods have a positive price—that is, we pay to acquire them. A few goods (garbage being the most obvious) have a negative price—that is, we pay someone to take it away from us. The economic behavior of unusual people and of ordinary people with unusual goods is great stuff for rump sessions with graduate students, but it detracts from the current discussion about ordinary people and ordinary goods.

[5] As always there may be an exception or two. President John Kennedy never carried money with him. He just took what he wanted and left it to others to figure out how to pay for it. President George Bush (the first), while campaigning in 1992, wanted to provide a photo-op to show he was just a good ol' boy. He went to a small town department store to buy his own socks—just like the rest of us do. Well after 12 years in the White House as vice president and president, Mr. Bush totally blew the photo-op by going wild over the scanner at the checkout: he had never seen one. So much for George, the common man. These few exceptions aside, the assumption of a budget constraint is valid for the ordinary consumer.

Purchasing and Consuming

The bumper sticker that proclaims "born to shop" suggests that some folks gain utility from the act of purchasing that is separate from that of actually consuming what is purchased. For most, the act of shopping for food creates a disutility—one that supermarkets work hard at minimizing. But for many, shopping for clothing is fun—a utility creator that is independent of the actual consumption of the final purchase. For our purposes we consolidate these separate utilities into a single utility that we call consumption.

Objective of the Consumer

We assume that the consumer is a utility maximizer, given the limited budget available. The set of consumption choices of the individual will depend on the tastes and preferences of the individual. Each of us has our own unique set of tastes and preferences and therefore will have our own unique pattern of consumption choices. While each of us will come to a different conclusion, each of us arrives there with the same objective—utility maximization.

Total and Marginal Utility

Util a hypothetical or imaginary unit of utility.

As previously indicated, the objective of the consumer is to consume that combination of goods that will provide the consumer with the greatest amount of utility possible, given a budget constraint. Our task then is to develop behavior rules that will indicate how the consumer achieves this goal. To simplify matters, we assume that utility can be measured in units called **utils.** And, while the consumer may not know how many utils of satisfaction are obtained from a given good, the consumer is able to identify which of two goods will provide the greater number of utils.

To begin, let's look at the utility associated with the consumption of a single good—gatorburgers. This is a good that is highly prized by college students throughout the southeastern part of the United States and by others during spring break. Ignoring (for the moment) the disutility of obtaining gatorburgers, let's look at the utility created by a typical consumer, Tina, consuming this treat. As shown in Figure 15–1, as Tina consumes more and more gatorburgers, the total amount of utility she obtains from them increases at a decreasing rate, reaches a maximum, and then declines after four gatorburgers when she gets into the overdose range.

FIGURE 15–1 Total utility and marginal utility from consuming gatorburgers— schedule.

Gatorburgers/Day	Total Utility/Day	Marginal Utility/Day
0	0	
		10
1	10	
		7
2	17	
		4
3	21	
		2
4	23	
		−2
5	21	

To maximize her utility Tina should consume four gatorburgers, but remember that we have not yet considered the opportunity cost of buying the gatorburgers. The third column of Figure 15–1 shows Tina's marginal utility obtained by consuming gatorburgers. As expected, the marginal or additional utility associated with the consumption of the first gatorburger is greater than that of the second, which is greater than that of the third, and so on. This reflects the natural tendency towards satiation in consumption.

This leads us to one of the fundamental tenets in the theory of consumer behavior—the **law of diminishing marginal utility:** as additional units of one good are consumed, *ceteris paribus,* the marginal or additional utility obtained from each additional unit of that good will decrease.

The left panel of Figure 15–2 graphs the total utility per day Tina gains by consuming gatorburgers. Total utility is maximized at four gatorburgers, and then it begins to decrease, indicating that the marginal utility is negative as shown in the right panel of Figure 15–2. As expected, marginal utility falls steadily and then finally becomes negative when the total utility is at its maximum level.

In a case where the consumer consumes only one good, utility-optimizing behavior is rather simple. If the price of gatorburgers is $4 each and the budget is $30, then the consumer would consume four gatorburgers to maximize utility. But if the budget were $15, the consumer would consume only three gatorburgers because consumption is limited by the budget constraint.

Now let's move to a more relevant example in which the consumer consumes two goods and must select between them in order to maximize utility. Figure 15–3 shows the relevant information to solve this problem. The first three columns of Figure 15–3 are a repeat of Figure 15–1. The fourth column is the amount of marginal utility per dollar that each additional unit of gatorburgers will generate based on a price of $4 per gatorburger. With these numbers, we can analyze how much utility, or "bang for the buck", Tina gets from each dollar spent. Her objective is to get the greatest amount of utility possible within her limited budget.

Law of diminishing marginal utility as additional units of one good are consumed, *ceteris paribus*, the marginal utility obtained from each additional unit of that good will decrease.

 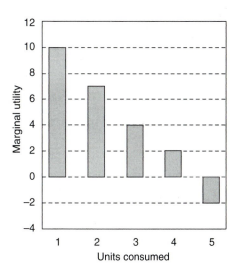

FIGURE 15–2 Total utility and marginal utility from consuming gatorburgers—graph.

	Gatorburgers Price = $4/Unit				Gator Gulps Price = $5/Unit		
Gatorburgers	Total Utility	Marginal Utility	MU_b/P_b	Gator Gulps	Total Utility	Marginal Utility	MU_g/P_g
0	0			0	0		
		10	2.50			20	4.00
1	10			1	20		
		7	1.75			15	3.00
2	17			2	35		
		4	1.00			10	2.00
3	21			3	45		
		2	0.50			5	1.00
4	23			4	50		
		−2	−0.50			2	0.40
5	21			5	52		

FIGURE 15–3 Consumption of gatorburgers and Gator Gulps.

FIGURE 15–4 Utility maximization within a budget constraint.

Alternatives	Choice	Marginal Utility	Total Utility	Budget Remaining
1st Gator Gulp 1st gatorburger	1st Gator Gulp	20	20	$22
2nd Gator Gulp 1st gatorburger	2nd Gator Gulp	15	35	$17
3rd Gator Gulp 1st gatorburger	1st gatorburger	10	45	$13
3rd Gator Gulp 2nd gatorburger	3rd Gator Gulp	10	55	$8
4th Gator Gulp 2nd gatorburger	2nd gatorburger	7	62	$4
4th Gator Gulp 3rd gatorburger	3rd gatorburger	4	66	$0

The right half of Figure 15–3 shows similar information for Gator Gulps, a highly prized sports drink that Tina likes to down while eating gatorburgers. If the prices of gatorburgers and Gator Gulps are $4 and $5 each, respectively, and Tina's budget is $27, how would she maximize the total utility she derives from her limited budget?

Assume she is consuming nothing. Then the choices before her are to buy either the first gatorburger or the first Gator Gulp. Since the marginal utility per dollar of the first Gator Gulp is greater than for the first gatorburger, she can make the greatest addition to her total utility by selecting a Gator Gulp. That uses up $5 of her budget, so she still has $22 left as shown in Figure 15–4.

Now, what are the choices facing Tina? As shown in Figure 15–4, she can take either the first unit of gatorburgers or the second unit of Gator Gulps. Since the second Gator Gulp produces more marginal utility per dollar, she will take that. This reduces her budget by another $5, so she has $17 left.

As shown in Figure 15–4, the process continues until the choice is between a third gatorburger or a fourth Gator Gulp. Both choices contribute 1 util per dollar to the total utility Tina receives. But she has only \$4 left, so she buys the gator-burger giving her a total utility of 66 utils. Her budget is totally expended.

Now let's generalize the results using subscripts b and g for burgers and Gulps. The behavior rule is very simple:

When $MU_b/P_b > MU_g/P_g$ reallocate consumption giving up Gator Gulps and adding gatorburgers

When $MU_b/P_b < MU_g/P_g$ reallocate consumption giving up gatorburgers and adding Gator Gulps

thus:

When $MU_b/P_b = MU_g/P_g$ no further reallocation can increase total utility. Utility is maximized.

This result can be generalized to a multigood general rule for utility optimization:

$$\frac{MU_1}{P_1} = \frac{MU_2}{P_2} = \cdots = \frac{MU_i}{P_i}$$

for all i goods consumed. That is, the marginal contribution to total utility per dollar of expenditure must be the same for all goods. If it were not, then some sort of reallocation is possible that would result in an increase in total utility. This is known as the **equi-marginal principle of optimization.**

Deriving the Demand Curve

The law of demand posits that there is an inverse relationship between price of the product and the quantity demanded of that product, *ceteris paribus*. We can use the equi-marginal utility optimization principle to demonstrate the law of demand. Let's see what happens if the price of Gator Gulps changes, *ceteris paribus*. Suppose the price of Gator Gulps falls from \$5/unit to \$4/unit. The impact of this price change is shown in Figure 15–5 which is identical to Figure 15–3

Equi-marginal principle of optimization in order to optimize utility given a limited budget, the consumer will adjust the consumption pattern such that the marginal utility per dollar of expenditure for each good is the same.

Gatorburgers Price = \$4/Unit				Gator Gulps Price = \$4/Unit			
Gatorburgers	Total Utility	Marginal Utility	MU_b/P_b	Gator Gulps	Total Utility	Marginal Utility	MU_g/P_g
0	0			0	0		
		10	2.50			20	5.00
1	10			1	20		
		7	1.75			15	3.75
2	17			2	35		
		4	1.00			10	2.50
3	21			3	45		
		2	0.50			5	1.25
4	23			4	50		
		−2	−0.50			2	0.50
5	21			5	52		

FIGURE 15–5 Consumption of gatorburgers and Gator Gulps after a price change.

FIGURE 15–6 Tina's demand for Gator Gulps.

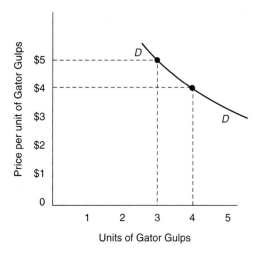

with the exception of the last column, which reflects the change in the price of Gator Gulps. As the price of Gator Gulps falls, the marginal utility per dollar of expenditure on Gator Gulps increases.

Using the data in Figure 15–5, work through the process of utility maximization as was done in Figure 15–4. You should find that Tina will consume four units of Gator Gulps and three units of gatorburgers. So as the price of Gator Gulps fell, the quantity consumed increased as shown in Figure 15–6. In this example we have found two points on the demand curve for Gator Gulps. Repeating the process would lead to additional points on the curve.

This example is a good illustration of the real income effect. The decline in the price of Gator Gulp allowed Tina to consume one more unit of Gator Gulps than before and still have $3 left over. So a decrease in the price of Gator Gulps increased the real income of Tina, allowing her to consume more from her $27 budget. Note that in this example there was no substitution effect.

THE MARKET DEMAND FUNCTION

We've seen how consumers behave in their efforts to achieve the maximum level of utility possible within the limits of their income constraint. In the process of maximizing utility, individual demand curves can be specified. The market demand schedule can be derived by simply adding the quantities of product that each consumer is willing to purchase at each specified level of price. Thus, as in the case of supply, the market demand is simply the horizontal summation of all the demand curves for all the individuals who are buying in a given market at a given time.

Several characteristics of the market demand schedule should be specified at this point. First of all, in the case of market demand there are more *ceteris paribus* conditions than for individuals. The factors of income, prices for alternative products, and tastes and preferences are defined to be constant within each of the individual demand curves. But the market curve includes some additional factors that must be held constant. Other *ceteris paribus* conditions that are important in market demand include:

- Size of the population
- Demographic composition of the population
- Distribution of income

- The general price level
- International trade patterns

Changes in any of these factors would change the market demand, resulting in a shift of the market demand curve even though individual demands remain unchanged.

SUMMARY

The law of demand states that as the price of a good increases, *ceteris paribus,* the quantity demanded of that good will fall. The law of demand is justified by the substitution effect and the real income effect. The substitution effect says that as the price of beef goes up, *ceteris paribus,* consumers will buy more chicken and substitute it for beef such that beef consumption falls. The real income effect posits that as the price of beef goes up, *ceteris paribus,* the quantity of beef that can be purchased on a fixed budget will fall. Both effects validate the law of demand.

Consumption creates utility. We assume that the consumer seeks to maximize total utility given a limited budget. The law of diminishing marginal utility states that as additional units of a good are consumed, *ceteris paribus,* the marginal or additional utility associated with each additional unit will decrease. In order to maximize utility from consumption, the consumer should consume each good to that point at which the marginal utility per dollar of expenditure is the same for all goods.

By changing the price of one good, *ceteris paribus,* a schedule of individual demand can be developed showing the quantities of the good the consumer will consume at alternative prices of the good. Individual demand curves can be aggregated to produce market demand. Any changes in the *ceteris paribus* conditions will result in a shift of individual, and hence market, demand. Other factors that may shift market demand were noted.

KEY TERMS

Equi-marginal principle of optimization   Substitution effect
Law of diminishing marginal utility   Util
Preferences   Utility
Real income effect

PROBLEMS AND DISCUSSION QUESTIONS

1. The table below shows the total utility a consumer gets from consuming two goods—*A* and *B.*

	Total Utility	
Units	A	B
0	0	0
1	30	42
2	50	70
3	60	85
4	65	94
5	67	98

Assume that the price of good *A* is $5 per unit and the price of good *B* is $10 per unit.

a. For a budget of $55 how many units of each good would the consumer consume?

b. If the budget were to increase by $10, how many units of each good would the consumer consume?

2. Is the law of diminishing marginal utility valid for a true chocolate fanatic?

3. Suppose the price of rutabagas falls, *ceteris paribus.* Describe the impact the substitution effect and the real income effect would have on the quantity demanded of rutabagas.

4. Frequently the opportunity cost of acquiring a good is more than the price of the good. Why?

5. Weird Harold, being devoid of an economics education, declares that he is going to maximize his marginal utility. What consumption pattern would achieve this objective?

6. Assume Sam is a rational consumer. Nonetheless, Sam's entire food budget of $40/week is used only for burgers and soda. Burgers cost $0.69 each, and soda is $0.75 per can. His marginal utility from burgers is 234 utils, and his marginal utility from soda is 175 utils. What should Sam do to increase his total utility?

7. One day Sue ordered two hot dogs and three orders of fries at the local diner (Sue is an unusually hearty eater). The next day she ordered three hot dogs and two orders of fries. Assuming that her rather voracious tastes and preferences did not change from day to day, what must have happened?

8. Prices at convenience stores are consistently higher than at supermarkets. Why don't they go out of business?

APPENDIX

INDIFFERENCE CURVE ANALYSIS

An alternative approach to developing the theory of consumer behavior is known as indifference curve analysis. Through the use of indifference curves we can develop behavioral rules for utility maximization given a budget restraint. In addition, with indifference curves we can examine in detail the impact of changing some of the *ceteris paribus* conditions defining consumer demand.

We have defined utility to be the satisfaction that consumers derive from the consumption or possession of goods. Utility can also be derived from services such as medical care, dental care, or police protection since these services also fulfill human wants and needs. The idea behind the entire concept of demand is that every rational consumer selects that combination of goods and services that will permit him or her to maximize utility within the limits imposed by his or her budget. This idea of maximum consumer utility implies that consumers know the relative amounts of utility they individually can derive from the consumption of all the items available to them.

Let's suppose that there are only two items available in our economy—food, representing the necessities of life, and clothing, representing the luxury items. We know that we can derive satisfaction from the consumption of each of these goods.

Imagine that satisfaction or utility gained from consuming these two goods is a three-dimensional hill as shown in Figure 15–7. Since this hill shows the level of utility associated with the consumption of the two goods, it is called a **utility surface.** As we move up that hill, we achieve progressively higher and higher levels of utility as measured on the vertical axis. If, however, we walk around the hill, we are merely staying on the *same* level of satisfaction (in exactly the same sense that a terrace on a hillside field maintains a given level of elevation). Thus, each line or terrace going around the hill defines some constant level of utility. The various combinations of food and clothing that will give us that particular level of utility are defined by the line around the utility surface. Therefore, we are indifferent as to where we are on that line because our level of utility is unchanged.

Now let's imagine that we are in an airplane looking straight down at the utility hill. All we see are the lines or the terraces that define the various levels of satisfaction as shown in Figure 15–8. This type of illustration is the same as a military contour map or a topographic map: the lines indicate the elevation or level of utility. This type of diagram is known as a **utility map.** As we move away from the origin toward the northeast on the utility map, we are going up the hill to higher and higher terraces, thereby increasing the level of the consumer's total utility.

The lines defining the levels of utility are known as **indifference curves,** since we are indifferent as to where we are along any single curve. There are several characteristics of indifference curves that should be specified. First of all, indifference curves slope downward and to the right. Second, because of diminishing

Utility surface a three-dimensional representation of the utility gained by consuming two goods simultaneously.

Utility map contour lines of a utility surface.

Indifference curves lines on a utility map indicating alternative combinations of two goods that will generate a constant level of utility in their consumption.

289

FIGURE 15–7　The utility surface.

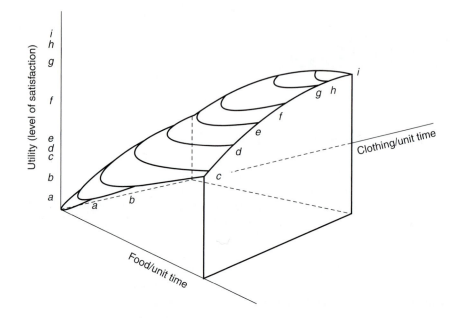

FIGURE 15–8　The utility map or indifference map of the utility surface.

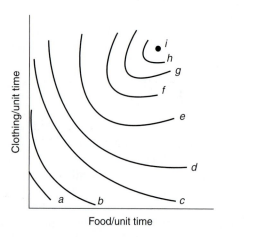

marginal utility[6] they are convex to the origin with the "bow" of the curve pointing toward the origin or corner of the diagram. Third, they cannot intersect.[7]

　　The curves slope downward and to the right because in order for a consumer to give up some of one commodity and still remain on the same level of satisfaction, the consumer must be compensated with additional units of another product. Figure 15–9 illustrates the principle of diminishing marginal rates of substitution. As successive units of one product are lost, it will take progressively more and more of the substitute commodity to adequately compensate for the loss of satisfaction. When the consumer has lots of food and not much cloth-

---

[6] As additional units of one good are consumed, *ceteris paribus*, the marginal utility obtained from each additional unit of that good will decrease.

[7] By this point, you should have identified indifference curves as being closely analogous to the isoproduct curves or isoquants in the appendix to Chapter 12. Indifference curves and isoproduct curves have exactly the same characteristics for exactly the same reasons.

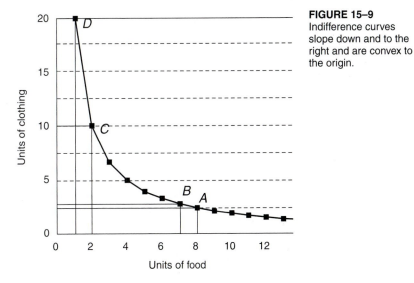

FIGURE 15–9
Indifference curves slope down and to the right and are convex to the origin.

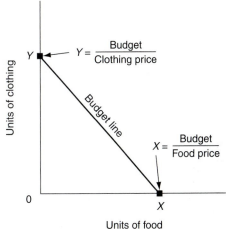

FIGURE 15–10
Construction of the budget line using the consumer's budget and the prices of the alternative commodities.

ing, it doesn't take much clothing to compensate for the loss of one unit of food (as from point A to point B). Conversely, when the consumer has lots of clothes and little food, he or she will gladly trade lots of clothes to get one more unit of food. The consumer at point D has only one unit of food and a strong hunger. In this case, the consumer is willing to give up 10 units or half of his clothes to get the second unit of food.

We now have our two-product model, and we have identified the utility that these products can yield from the indifference map of the utility surface. We also know the rates at which those products will substitute for one another in maintaining any given level of satisfaction. All we need to determine the quantities of food and clothing that our sample consumer will buy is information concerning the prices of those commodities and the consumer's income or budget for those items. If the consumer should spend all of his budget on food, there is some maximum amount of food that can be bought. To find it we divide his budget by the price for food. If he buys no clothing and spends all of his budget on food, he can buy X units of food in Figure 15–10.

FIGURE 15–11
Budgetary limit on the
utility surface.

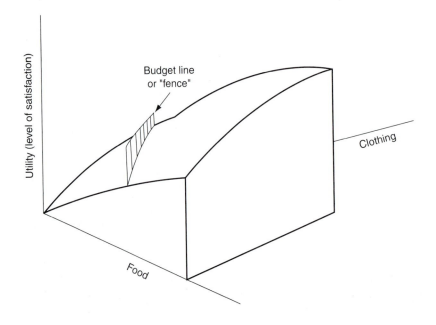

Likewise, if all of the budget is spent on clothing, the consumer can buy *Y* units of clothing. A straight line connecting these two points shows all combinations of food and clothing purchases that can be made with the consumer's budget. The constraint imposed by the budget will permit the consumer to purchase any combination of food and clothing that falls on or below this **budget line.** The consumer's objective is to maximize total utility within the limits imposed by this budget line. Therefore, he or she is going to attempt the highest possible level of satisfaction that this budget permits.

In a very real sense, a consumer's budget line does the same thing to the utility surface that a fence does to livestock on a hillside pasture (Figure 15–11). No matter how badly consumers might wish to graze the tender grasses available at higher elevations, they are prevented from doing so by the unpleasant fact that there is a budget fence between them and their unlimited wants.

Budget line
combinations of two goods the consumer is able to purchase given a budget constraint.

Utility Maximization

Now, let's combine the indifference map (wants and desires) with the budget line (ability), as shown in Figure 15–12. The objective of our analysis is to determine what combination of items the consumer is going to select for consumption, given income, the prices of the items, and a map of the consumer's tastes and preferences.

First, let's ask a question. Which level of satisfaction is our consumer, Anne, going to select? Obviously, she is going to get the greatest amount of satisfaction her income (i.e., budget) will permit. Any point on or below her budget line constraint is attainable, but we have already said that we are going to assume that Anne is rational. Therefore she will not select a combination of goods such as *A*, which is below her budgetary constraint, since she can increase satisfaction by moving out to the budget limit. She will not select combination *E* on U_1 since she will have a higher level of utility at any of the combinations *B* or *D* because they are on U_2, with a higher total utility. Since combination *C* is on U_3 that just touches (or is tangent to) the budget line,

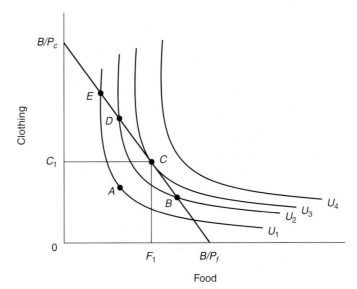

FIGURE 15–12 Utility optimization for a given budget.

this is the highest possible level of utility that Anne can achieve, given her income constraint and the product prices. Combination C is the point at which the rational consumer will choose to operate, consuming C_1 units of clothing and F_1 units of food.

At point C the slope of the budget line is equal to the slope of the indifference curve. This means that the rate at which food and clothing substitute for one another in consumption (slope of the indifference curve) is the same as the rate at which they substitute for one another in the market (slope of the budget line).

Mathematical Illustration

The slope of the indifference curve at any point on that curve is the marginal rate of substitution, which would be equal to the rise over the run or the rate of change of clothing per unit change in food. So,

$$\text{Slope of the indifference curve} = \frac{\Delta C}{\Delta F} \qquad (15\text{–}1)$$

Every point on an indifference curve represents the same amount of total utility. So movement along an indifference curve suggests that the additional utility of one good will be exactly equal to the decrease in the utility of the other. Ignoring signs, that is

$$\Delta C \bullet MU_c = \Delta F \bullet MU_f \qquad (15\text{–}2)$$

Rearranging Equation 15–2 gives

$$\frac{\Delta C}{\Delta F} = \frac{MU_f}{MU_c} \qquad (15\text{–}3)$$

Since the right-hand term of Equation 15–1 is equal to the left-hand term of Equation 15–3, we find that

$$\text{Slope of the indifference curve} = \frac{MU_f}{MU_c} \qquad (15\text{–}4)$$

The slope of the budget line is the rise over the run, so if B is the amount of the budget, then

$$\text{Slope of the budget line} = \frac{B/P_c}{B/P_f} = \frac{P_f}{P_c} \qquad (15\text{–}5)$$

Since at the optimizing point C in Figure 15–12 the slope of the indifference curve is equal to the slope of the budget at the point of tangency, we can combine the right-hand sides of Equations 15–4 and 15–5 to get the optimizing criterion:

$$\frac{MU_f}{MU_c} = \frac{P_f}{P_c} \qquad (15\text{–}6)$$

Rearranging the terms of Equation 15–6 gives the utility-maximizing behavior criterion:

$$\frac{MU_f}{P_f} = \frac{MU_c}{P_c} \qquad (15\text{–}7)$$

Here we again have the equi-marginal principle that utility optimization is achieved when the marginal utilities per dollar of the two goods are equal. If there were not, some rearranging of the consumption pattern would allow for additional utility to be obtained.

The Impact of Changes in *Ceteris Paribus* Conditions

Demand is a relationship between prices and quantities assuming everything else remains constant. In reality, these conditions are in a continuous state of flux. We merely assume them to be constant (or we hold them constant) so that we can sort out the effects of various types of changes. The *ceteris paribus* conditions do change over time, and when they change, they cause changes in the demand schedule. In the case of an individual consumer's demand curve, the *ceteris paribus* conditions include income, prices for substitute and complementary goods, and the preference pattern of the individual consumer.

Change in the Budget

The impact of a change in the budget, *ceteris paribus*, is illustrated in Figure 15–13. This figure shows the same consumer that we considered in Figure 15–12 who maximized utility given the budget constraint by adjusting the consumption of food and clothing to F_1 and C_1. Now what would happen if the budget of the consumer increased from B to B^*, *ceteris paribus*?

Since the slope of the budget line is equal to a ratio of the prices for food and clothing and since these prices are held constant, the shift of the budget line will be

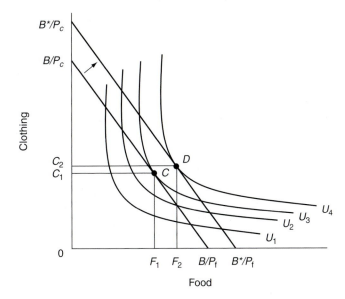

FIGURE 15–13
Impact of an increase in the budget.

a parallel shift. In the example in Figure 15–13, we are looking at an increase of the budget, which means the amount of food and/or clothing that can be purchased has increased. As the budget grows from B to B^*, the endpoints of the budget line move out to B^*/P_f and B^*/P_c.

For this particular consumer, the higher budget line results in increased consumption of both food and clothing to F_2 and C_2. And the consumer has increased total utility from U_3 to U_4.

While in the normal case one would expect an increase in the budget to result in increased consumption of both goods, it does not necessarily have to be so. To see this, in your mind's eye drag the indifference curve U_4 downward such that point D slides down the budget line. With just a little slide, C_2 would quickly be less than C_1. An example of something like this would be a consumer who consumes beans and meat. With an increase in the budget, the consumer is able to increase meat consumption, which allows a reduction in bean consumption.

Change in the Price of a Good

A second *ceteris paribus* condition that might change is the price of either of the two goods. This is illustrated in Figure 15–14, where we have an increase in the price of clothing, *ceteris paribus*. The budget and the price of food do not change, so the endpoint of the budget line on the food axis does not change.

An increase in the price of clothing to P_{c2} with the budget remaining constant will cause the endpoint of the budget line on the clothing axis to be closer to the origin. With the budget given, the maximum quantity of clothing that can be purchased is reduced by the price increase. This causes a downward rotation of the budget line (shown by the arrow) around a pivot point on the food axis.

In the case illustrated in Figure 15–14, the impact of the increased price of clothing is to consume less clothing at C_2 (law of demand) and less food at F_2 (income effect). In addition, the total utility of the consumer falls from U_3 to U_2.

The impact of the clothing price change on food consumption is indeterminate because of the trade-off between the income effect and the substitution effect. The magnitude of the two effects can be seen in the following manner. Draw a budget line

FIGURE 15–14
Impact of an increase
in the price of clothing.

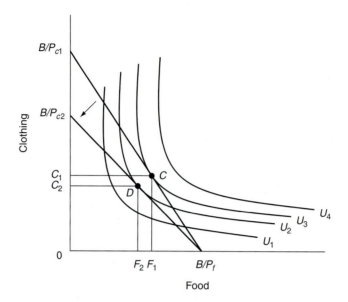

tangent to U_2 that is parallel to the prior budget line. The change in food consumption from F_1 to the point of tangency is the total income effect. Then slide this imaginary budget line along U_2 until you get to point D on the line. The change in food consumption as you slide along U_2 is a measure of the substitution effect.

Change in Consumer's Tastes and Preferences

A final *ceteris paribus* condition that might change would be the tastes and preferences of the consumer. Any such changes would result in a different set of indifference curves for the consumer. Such changes can occur rapidly or slowly over time. An impending hurricane in Florida can produce a phenomenon many Americans have never experienced—bare shelves at the supermarket. A slower, longer change is the move away from coffee consumption and the corresponding increase in soft drink consumption. The average American now consumes more ounces of soft drinks per day than coffee and water combined.

Such changes in tastes and preferences result in shifts of the indifference map with no change in the budget line. Figure 15–15 illustrates the coffee–soft drink example. We know that tastes and preferences have changed and that as a result consumption has changed, but we are unable to determine if the utility level U_{1960} is greater than or less than U_{2000}.

Substitutes and Complements

Substitutes goods which may be replaced, one for the other, in consumption. An increase in the consumption of one substitute good (Coke) will result in a decrease of the other (Pepsi).

We know that the tremendous range of commodities available in our society gives the consumer a wide range of consumption alternatives. If beef becomes too expensive, the consumer has the option of shifting to pork. If both beef and pork are too expensive, the consumer can meet protein needs with poultry, fish, cheese, or vegetable sources such as dry beans. For any particular consumer, these products all possess varying degrees of substitutability.

The relationships between commodities can be classified into two broad categories. Products such as beef, pork, poultry, fish, cheese, and dry beans are generally considered to be **substitutes.** Quantities of any of these products can to a

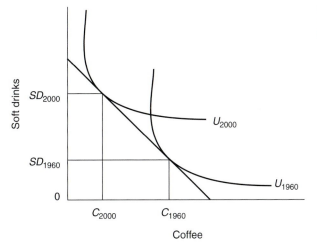

FIGURE 15–15
Impact of a change in tastes and preferences.

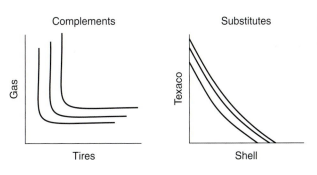

FIGURE 15–16
Indifference curves for complementary and substitute goods.

large degree replace quantities of another. The rate of substitution may not be—and probably is not—a one-to-one relationship. But if you eat pork chops for dinner, you aren't likely to be eating roast beef as well. Thus, an increase in the consumption of pork will likely be associated with a decrease in the consumption of the substitute products, other things being equal.

The counterpart of substitute commodities is that group of items that are complementary in nature. Shoes and shoe laces, gasoline and tires, or ham and eggs are examples of commodities that tend to be **complements.** Complementary types of products tend to be consumed together. Thus, an increase in the use of one complementary item would most likely be associated with an increase in the use of the other.

The shape (or degree of convexity) exhibited by the indifference curves indicates the type of relationship that exists between products. As shown in Figure 15–16 products that are almost perfectly substitutable—two brands of gasoline, for example—will be associated with an indifference map that shows the curves to be nearly straight. If the indifference curve had a 45-degree slope, then the loss of one unit of one brand of gasoline could be fully compensated by one unit of the other brand at any point on the curve. Strong complements (two products that must be consumed in exact proportions) would be shown on an indifference map whose curves have an extreme degree of convexity. The amount of gasoline consumed largely determines the amount of tires consumed.

Substitute and complementary goods behave very differently in light of relative price changes. In Figure 15–17 we repeat the same indifference curves we had in Figure 15–16, but we have added two budget lines to each set of indifference curves. Both of the steeply sloped budget lines have the same slope and both of the flatter budget lines have the same slope. Unlike previous examples of price

Complements
goods that are typically consumed together. An increase in the consumption of one complementary good (gasoline) will result in an increase of the other good (tires).

FIGURE 15–17
Impact of price
changes on
complementary and
substitute goods.

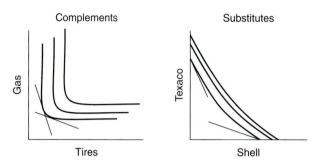

changes, in this illustration we have allowed the budget to adjust after the price change in order to maintain the amount of total utility. That is, we have moved along a single indifference curve as prices changed.

In the case of close substitutes, a small change in relative prices pushed the consumer from a position of consuming Shell only to consuming Texaco only. So small changes in prices bring about substantial substitution and significant consumption adjustments. In the case of complements, the same change in relative prices brings about very little change in the consumption pattern. In the case of complements there is little substitutability, so most of the impact of a price change in either commodity would show up as an income effect rather than a substitution effect. If the price of either good goes up, *ceteris paribus*, the consumption of both goes down.

Derivation of the Individual Demand Curve

Our indifference curve analysis can be used to derive the demand curve of the individual consumer. The process of doing this is illustrated in Figure 15–18. Here we have a consumer, Sam, who is making consumption choices between pizza and Pepsi (both measured in servings). Three budget lines have been drawn for Sam. Each budget line shown reflects a budget of $5.00 and a price of Pepsi of $0.50 per serving. Therefore, each budget line crosses the Pepsi axis at 10 units.

Each of the three budget lines are drawn for different prices of pizza. The lower budget line shows that Sam is able to buy 2.5 units of pizza if only pizza is purchased with a budget of $5.00 and a pizza price of $2.00 per serving. At this price for pizza, Sam will actually consume 1.5 servings of pizza to maximize his utility from pizza and pepsi.

The middle budget line intersects the pizza axis at 5 units, so for the $5.00 budget this budget line must represent the case of pizza being $1.00 per serving. When pizza is $1.00 per unit, Sam consumes 3.2 units of pizza.

The upper budget line intersects the pizza axis at 10 units (trust us), so for the $5.00 budget this must be the budget line for pizza at $0.50 per serving. So, at a budget of $5.00 and the price of pizza and Pepsi being $0.50 each, Sam will consume 5.8 units of pizza.

The information contained in each of the three budget lines on Figure 15–18 is summarized in Figure 15–19. The budget for each line was $5.00, and the price of Pepsi was $0.50 for each. The price of pizza was $2.00, $1.00, and $0.50 for the three budget lines. The quantity of pizza that Sam is willing to consume varies inversely with the price of pizza, confirming once again the law of demand.

The two right columns of Figure 15–19 show the quantity of pizza Sam is willing to consume at alternative prices for pizza. The two left columns show that other factors remained constant, i.e., *ceteris paribus*. Therefore, what we have in Figure 15–19

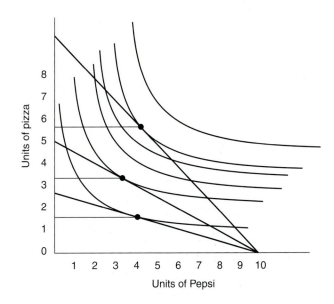

FIGURE 15–18
Derivation of the individual demand curve.

Budget	Price of Pepsi	Price of Pizza	Pizza Consumed
$5.00	$0.50	$2.00	1.5
5.00	0.50	1.00	3.2
5.00	0.50	0.50	5.8

FIGURE 15–19
Sam's actual consumption pattern.

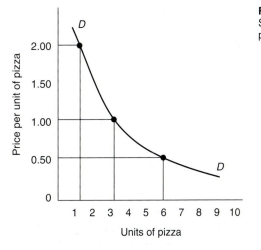

FIGURE 15–20
Sam's demand for pizza.

is the quantity of pizza Sam is willing to consume at alternative prices for pizza, *ceteris paribus*. We have Sam's demand for pizza.

The information from the table in Figure 15–19 is plotted on Figure 15–20 for the three budget lines in Figure 15–18. A curve drawn through these points is Sam's demand curve for pizza, *ceteris paribus*.

The indifference curve approach to deriving demand emphasizes the importance of the *ceteris paribus* conditions. If either the budget or the price of Pepsi were to change, the endpoints of the budget lines in Figure 15–18 would change and the quantity of pizza that Sam would consume at each price of pizza would also change. A change in tastes and preferences would result in a change in the indifference curves and a change in Sam's consumption behavior. These three factors—income or budget, prices of other goods, and tastes and preferences—are the three main shifters of individual demand.

SUMMARY

A utility surface is a three-dimensional representation showing the total utility derived from consuming two goods. Contour lines drawn on this surface and dropped onto a two-dimensional diagram with the two goods on the axes are called a utility map. The individual curves are called indifference curves because at every point along the curve the amount of utility is the same. The further an indifference curve is from the origin, the higher the level of utility. The slope of a tangent at any point along an indifference curve shows the marginal rate of substitution of one good for the other at that point.

A budget line shows the combinations of the two goods that the consumer is able to buy given a limited budget. The budget line is a constraint. To maximize utility given this constraint the consumer seeks that highest (furthest from the origin) indifference curve that is just tangent to the budget line. This point of tangency defines the quantity of each good to be consumed in order to maximize utility. At this point of tangency the rate of substitution in consumption is equal to the rate of substitution in the market.

Indifference curves can be used to illustrate the impact on the consumer of a change in budget, a change in the price of either good, and a change in tastes and preferences. The impact of price changes of the two goods depends on whether the goods are substitutes in consumption or complements. Indifference curves can also be used to derive the demand curve of the individual consumer.

KEY TERMS

Budget line	Substitutes
Complements	Utility map
Indifference curves	Utility surface

PROBLEMS AND DISCUSSION QUESTIONS

1. Draw a set of axes with the quantities of two goods, *A* and *B*, measured on the axes. Draw a typical budget line. Now show how this budget line would change for each of the following changes in the *ceteris paribus* conditions:
   - An increase in the price of *A*, *ceteris paribus*
   - A decrease in the price of *A*, *ceteris paribus*
   - An increase in the price of *B*, *ceteris paribus*
   - A decrease in the price of *B*, *ceteris paribus*
   - An increase in income, *ceteris paribus*
   - A decrease in income, *ceteris paribus*
   - A 10 percent decrease in the price of both *A* and *B*, *ceteris paribus*.

2. Indifference curves never intersect. Why?
3. Use a set of indifference curves to derive the demand for a good.

The Concept of Elasticity

We know that the price system will merely whisper about a change in the availability of one good while it will positively scream about a change in the availability of another. On the other side of this coin, consumers will accept an increase in the price of one product without too much reaction; but an increase in the price of another good will be met with stubborn resistance and a refusal to purchase.

We also know that a strong price increase for some commodities will induce large numbers of producers to increase production and will further interest other people in becoming producers of that commodity. Yet there are other products that will absorb a price increase with little reaction on the part of producers. A third situation is that an increase in consumer income will be associated with a reduction in the use of one commodity, an increase in the use of another, and no change in the use of a third.

A measure of the sensitivity of consumers and producers to changes in prices and incomes is known as **elasticity.** Elasticity always deals with the sensitivity of the quantity demanded or quantity supplied to changes in some other factor. Thus, the elasticity of demand with respect to price would be concerned with the change in the quantity demanded of a good in response to a change in the price of that good.

An understanding of the elasticity concept indicates to managers how to make adjustments in response to some of the changes that affect their businesses. Through the use of elasticity estimates, managers can anticipate the probable direction of the market impact of various sorts of changes. Further, elasticity can help them to predict the degree of the impact. For example, if the borders of the United States were opened to unlimited imports of beef, and if Australia and New Zealand could ship enough product to increase the beef available in U.S. markets by 3 percent, the elasticity of demand for beef could be used to anticipate by how much the beef price would be expected to fall.

The number and complexity of elasticities are almost limitless. We are going to focus on four fundamental elasticities—demand, supply, cross-price and income. Each can be used to characterize any given market. Let's see how.

ELASTICITY OF DEMAND

We define the **elasticity of demand** as the *responsiveness* of the quantity demanded to a change in the price of the product. As one moves along a given demand curve, how quickly does quantity respond to changes in price? The degree of responsiveness is measured by an **elasticity coefficient.** Elasticity coefficients are frequently called "elasticities." At the most fundamental level, we can define the elasticity of demand coefficient, ϵ, to be:

Elasticity a measure of how responsive the quantity demanded by consumers or the quantity supplied by producers is to a change in the equilibrium price.

Elasticity of demand a measure of the sensitivity of quantity demanded to changes in the price of the product.

Elasticity coefficient a quantitative measure of the degree of responsiveness for a product in a market. Equal to the rate of change of quantity demanded (or supplied) divided by the rate of change of the other variable such as price of the product, and so forth.

$$\epsilon = \frac{\text{rate of change of quantity demanded}}{\text{rate of change of price}}$$

If the rate of change of the quantity demanded is greater than the rate of change in price, then we say that the demand relationship is **elastic.** Conversely, if the rate of change of quantity is less than the rate of change of price, then the relationship is said to be **inelastic.** That is, if the demand for a good is elastic, then we know that consumers are very responsive to price changes.

It should be clear by now that elasticity and elasticity coefficients have a lot to do with rates of change. How that rate of change is measured therefore becomes a matter of central concern. As you move along a demand curve, both price and quantity are changing simultaneously. The rate of change in each can be measured between two discrete points on a demand curve or at a single point on the demand curve. The first approach is called **arc elasticity** because we measure elasticity over an arc of the demand curve; the latter approach is called **point elasticity** because elasticity is measured at a finite point on the demand curve. Since measurement of point elasticities requires some elementary calculus, we will concentrate only on arc elasticities. Conceptually, a point elasticity is simply an arc elasticity measured over an infinitely small arc.

Elastic describes a demand relationship in which the rate of change of quantity demanded is greater than the rate of change of price.

Inelastic describes a demand relationship in which the rate of change of quantity demanded is less than the rate of change of price.

Arc elasticity the measurement of the elasticity of demand coefficient between two points on a demand curve.

Arc Elasticity

We can measure the elasticity of demand by dividing the rate of change in the quantity demanded by the rate of change in price for a small segment or arc along a given demand curve. Algebraically, the relationship may be expressed as[1]

Point elasticity the measurement of the elasticity of demand coefficient at a single finite point on the demand curve.

$$\epsilon = \frac{\Delta Q/Q}{\Delta P/P} \tag{16-1}$$

where:

ϵ is the demand elasticity coefficient

Q is the quantity purchased

P is the price of the product

The mathematical symbol Δ (delta) means "change in." The algebraic formulation is shown geometrically in Figure 16–1. The change from point A to point B along the demand curve is the arc over which we measure the elasticity coefficient. The change from Q_1 to Q_2 represents ΔQ in our formula, and the change from P_1 to P_2 represents ΔP. If our initial situation is at point A, and if the values of Q_1, Q_2, P_1, and P_2 are as shown below,

Point A	Point B
$Q_1 = 20$	$Q_2 = 25$
$P_1 = \$8.00$	$P_2 = \$7.50$

then our calculation of the elasticity of demand with respect to price for moving from point A to point B would be

---

[1] This chapter includes a number of algebraic equations. For ease of reference the equations are numbered consecutively in parentheses to the right of the equation.

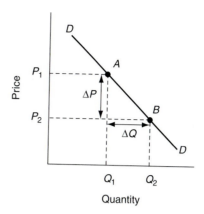

FIGURE 16–1 Arc elasticity of demand.

$$\epsilon = \frac{(Q_1 - Q_2)/Q_1}{(P_1 - P_2)/P_1} = \frac{(20 - 25)/20}{(8.00 - 7.50)/8.00} =$$

$$\frac{-5/20}{0.50/8} = \frac{-5}{20} \cdot \frac{8}{0.5} = \frac{-40}{10} = -4.0 \tag{16–2}$$

If however, we were to calculate the elasticity for moving from point B to point A, the estimate would be:

$$\epsilon = \frac{(Q_2 - Q_1)/Q_2}{(P_2 - P_1)/P_2} = \frac{(25 - 20)/25}{(7.50 - 8.00)/7.50} = \tag{16–3}$$

$$\frac{5/25}{-0.50/7.50} = \frac{5}{25} \cdot \frac{7.50}{-0.5} = \frac{37.50}{-12.5} = -3.0$$

Obviously, there is something amiss when we get two different estimates of the elasticity coefficient measured over the same arc. The key to our difficulty lies in the fact that our rates of change are different depending on the point we select as our initial situation. This shows that our calculation of the elasticity for the arc between A and B is merely an approximation. The greater the size of the arc between A and B, the greater the difference between our two estimates and the less confidence that may be attached to either. Therefore, it is imperative that the arc be small if the resulting estimate of the elasticity coefficient is to have any degree of reliability.

We can modify our basic elasticity formula to eliminate the discrepancy that arises from selecting either of the two endpoints of the arc $A-B$ as the initial situation. This modification is accomplished by using the midpoints of Q_1 and Q_2, and of P_1 and P_2, in the calculation of the rates of change, such that

$$\epsilon = \frac{\dfrac{Q_1 - Q_2}{(Q_1 + Q_2)/2}}{\dfrac{P_1 - P_2}{(P_1 + P_2)/2}} = \frac{\dfrac{Q_1 - Q_2}{Q_1 + Q_2}}{\dfrac{P_1 - P_2}{P_1 + P_2}} \tag{16–4}$$

Thus, our calculation for our example would be:

$$\epsilon = \frac{\dfrac{20 - 25}{20 + 25}}{\dfrac{8.00 - 7.50}{8.00 + 7.50}} = \frac{\dfrac{-5}{45}}{\dfrac{0.50}{15.50}} = \frac{-5}{45} \cdot \frac{15.50}{0.50} = \tag{16-5}$$

$$= \frac{-77.50}{22.50} = -3.44$$

The modified formula gives us an approximation of the elasticity within the arc from A to B in Figure 16–1. This represents an average of sorts of the two estimates that result from equations 16–2 and 16–3. Further, using the midpoints eliminates the problem of the discrepancy that arises from using either endpoint in equation 16–1: no matter which end of the arc is selected as the initial situation, the resulting estimate of the elasticity coefficient is the same.

It should be pointed out that both the numerator and the denominator in the elasticity formula represent rates of change. Thus, the elasticity coefficient itself is a pure number, with no dimensions. The algebraic sign of the elasticity estimate tells nothing more than the direction of the relationship. In our example, the sign is negative because the slope of the demand function in Figure 16–1 is negative. That is, within the arc between points A and B, if price is increased by 1 percent, we would expect the quantity consumed to decline by approximately 3.44 percent. Since a 1 percent change in price is associated with more than 1 percent change in quantity taken, demand is relatively elastic with respect to price within that arc.

As shown in Figure 16–2, if the value of the demand elasticity coefficient is between zero and − 1, then demand is inelastic. If the value is less than − 1, it is elastic. If the elasticity coefficient should be exactly equal to − 1, elasticity is said to be unitary. That is, a 1 percent change in price will be associated with exactly 1 percent change in the quantity consumed. The value of the demand elasticity coefficient can range between zero and minus infinity on any given demand curve, changing in magnitude as you move along a given demand curve.

Demand curves will often exhibit all three ranges of elasticity (elastic, inelastic, and unitary) within a single curve. This is always true in situations where the demand curve is a straight line. Straight line demand curves are elastic with respect to price at relatively high prices and inelastic at relatively low prices, as shown in Figure 16–3. This suggests that as the price of a product falls, sales will increase to some saturation point at which consumers are virtually "filled up" on the product. When this is the case, further price cuts will not induce buyers to increase purchases at a rate as high as the rate at which the price has been cut (i.e., demand becomes inelastic). Conversely, when prices are already high, further price increases will induce buyers to either seek

FIGURE 16–2
Demand elasticity
ranges.

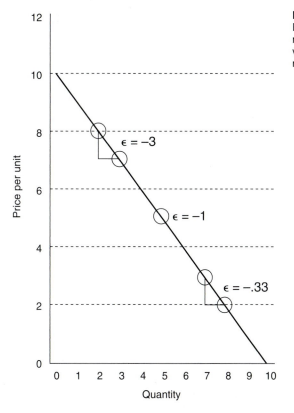

FIGURE 16–3
Elasticity measurements at various points on a market demand curve.

out substitute goods or to do without the product, causing the reduction in sales to be relatively greater than the increase in price (in this case, demand is elastic).

Since both the elastic and inelastic ranges can occur within a single demand curve, it is obvious that as consumers pass from the elastic into the inelastic range, they must pass through some point (or range) of unitary elasticity. For a straight line demand curve like Figure 16–3, this will always occur at the midpoint on the quantity axis between the origin and where the demand curve hits the horizontal axis.

Some Special Cases

There is one special case and two extreme cases of the elasticity of demand that should be mentioned. The two extremes are shown in Figure 16–4. These are the cases in which the elasticity coefficient is equal to zero (or **perfectly inelastic**) at all points on the function, and in which the elasticity coefficient is infinite (or **perfectly elastic**) at all points of the function. When demand is perfectly inelastic, the same quantity will be demanded no matter what the price happens to be—that is, the demand function is perfectly vertical. This sort of demand function is largely theoretical, but the demand for an item that normally represents a small part of the total budget and is an absolute necessity, such as table salt, will approach this situation. The demand for insulin is also very inelastic.

The perfectly elastic demand function is one you have already seen. This is the situation that is faced by the individual firm operating under conditions in which the manager cannot affect the price received, no matter how much is sold. That is, the market will absorb any quantity offered at the prevailing price. Since

Perfectly inelastic   a demand relationship in which any change of price brings about no quantity demanded adjustment.

Perfectly elastic   a demand relationship in which any change of quantity demanded brings about no price adjustment.

FIGURE 16–4
Demand functions—
perfectly elastic and
perfectly inelastic.

this situation approximates the conditions under which most farmers sell their products, the perfectly elastic demand function is an important concept in agricultural economics.

The special case of a demand curve that is unitarily elastic throughout its range is rare. However, there are occasional examples of empirical demand curves for commodities that approach a unitarily elastic situation. A demand curve that has an elasticity of 1 at all points on the function is a rectangular hyperbola.

Elasticity of Demand Related to Total Revenue

The elasticity of demand for a good and the total revenues of a firm producing that good are very much interrelated. Think about a movement along a demand curve from left to right. That movement will result in an increase in quantity consumed and a decrease in the price per unit. Since the total revenue of the firm is equal to price times quantity, what happens to total revenue depends on whether quantity increases at a faster rate than price decreases. Since the demand elasticity coefficient is a measure of the relative rate of change of quantity to price, the coefficient tells us what will happen to total revenue as price and quantity change.

A demand schedule, along with the total revenue generated by the various levels of sales, is shown in Figure 16–5. Price reductions in the elastic range of the demand curve are associated with increases in the total revenue. Price reductions in the inelastic range are associated with reductions total revenue. When elasticity is unitary, total revenue is at its maximum. This may be shown graphically as in Figure 16–6. Remember that elasticity is unitary at the midpoint of the relevant range along the quantity axis. Thus, that portion of a straight line demand curve which lies to the left of the midpoint is elastic with respect to price. The portion to the right of this point is inelastic. At this midpoint, demand is unitarily elastic. Another way of stating these relationships is illustrated in Figure 16–6. If the change in total revenue that is associated with a one-unit change in sales (that is, the marginal revenue) is positive, demand is elastic with regard to price. If marginal revenue is negative, demand is inelastic. If marginal revenue is zero, demand is unitary.

Factors Affecting Demand Elasticity

We have seen that demand functions may include all three ranges of elasticity. While that is a nice theoretical construct, in reality the relevant portion of the demand curve that reflects current market conditions will usually be either elastic or inelastic depending on the nature of the good in question. What are the characteristics of goods

Price per Unit	Quantity Sold	Elasticity Coefficient		Classification	Total Revenue	Change in Total Revenue		Revenue Trend
$10.00	1				$10.00			
		>	−6.33	Elastic		>	+$8.00	Increasing
9.00	2				18.00			
		>	−3.56	Elastic		>	+$6.00	Increasing
8.00	3				24.00			
		>	−2.00	Elastic		>	+$4.00	Increasing
7.00	4				28.00			
		>	−1.44	Elastic		>	+$2.00	Increasing
6.00	5				30.00			
		>	−1.00	Unitary		>	$0.00	No Change
5.00	6				30.00			
		>	−0.69	Inelastic		>	−$2.00	Decreasing
4.00	7				28.00			
		>	−0.47	Inelastic		>	−$4.00	Decreasing
3.00	8				24.00			
		>	−0.29	Inelastic		>	−$6.00	Decreasing
2.00	9				18.00			
		>	−0.16	Inelastic		>	−$8.00	Decreasing
1.00	10				10.00			

FIGURE 16–5   Relationship between elasticity and total revenue.

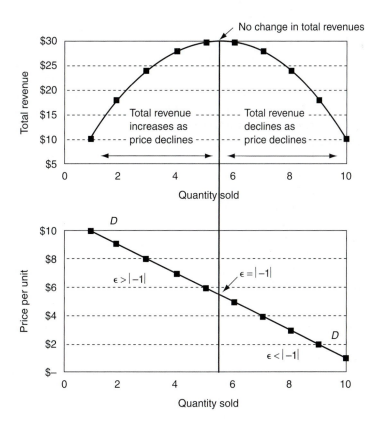

FIGURE 16–6
Relationship among total revenue, demand, and elasticity.

that determine whether demand is elastic or inelastic? In general, the price elasticity of demand for any product will be more elastic as the number of substitutes is greater. Demand elasticity will normally be more elastic if expenditure on this product represents a large item in the consumer's total budget. Finally, demand is likely to be more elastic for luxuries as opposed to necessities, since consumers can do very nicely without luxuries.

Let's discuss these determinants to see if they make sense logically. Can we think of an item that has no close substitutes? Salt was the example mentioned earlier. There are simply no good substitutes to which the consumer can turn if the price of salt goes from 69 cents to 79 cents per pound. Furthermore, a household's expenditure on salt is such a small part of a family's total budget that the total impact of this price increase is negligible. Finally, the product is looked upon as a necessity. Baking powder won't make those biscuits rise unless some salt is present. As we might expect, the elasticity of demand coefficient for salt is close to zero, indicating that demand for salt is very inelastic.

However, the demand for a Sony boom box might be expected to be relatively elastic. There are a good many substitutes available from Toshiba, General Electric, and Sanyo, not to mention FM radio and other forms of entertainment. The price of the Sony system is large in relation to the average consumer's budget, so a change in price will generally have a very significant impact on that budget. Further, to most families, a sound system is a luxury and therefore an optional item in their budgets. All of these factors make Sony boom box consumers relatively price sensitive.

There are numerous other factors that can affect demand elasticity. Consumers are creatures of habit. It is only over a period of time that they alter their customary patterns of consumption in response to price changes. Demand therefore tends to be more elastic as the length of time period in question is extended. Finally, the durability of some products will affect the elasticity of demand for them. Repairing older durable goods is very frequently a good substitute for buying a new model. Durability/reparability therefore tends to make demand more elastic than might otherwise be the case. Finally, culture and tradition can affect demand elasticity. For example, in late November the demand for turkey by many Americans becomes highly inelastic due to the Thanksgiving tradition. In the other 51 weeks of the year the demand for turkey may be quite elastic as there are numerous substitues for the noble bird.

PRICE DISCRIMINATION

Price discrimination revenue-maximizing behavior of a firm that faces two different markets with two different elasticities for its single product. The price discriminator charges a high price to the inelastic market and a low price to the elastic market, thereby increasing revenues in both markets above what would be earned with a single price.

The last two sections have discussed the relationship between demand elasticity and the total revenue of a firm producing a product, and the characteristics of goods that make the demand for them elastic or inelastic. We can bring these two threads together to explain a real-world phenomenon that we all observe, but few understand.

When a firm produces a product that is sold in two different markets with different demand elasticities, the firm can probably increase revenues by engaging in **price discrimination,** that is, charging different prices in the two different markets. An example of price discrimination in the food industry is a vegetable packer that can sell in either the fresh market (inelastic demand) or the frozen market (elastic demand). Another example is the producer of tomato sauce that can be sold either as a branded product (inelastic demand) or as a generic (elastic demand).

The example we will use here to illustrate price discrimination is airline tickets. Airlines produce one product—flying seats; but, they sell to two different markets. These two markets are the business traveler and the leisure traveler. These two markets have vastly different demand elasticities. For the business traveler, a flight is a necessity rather than a luxury, there are no close substitutes, and the traveler usually isn't paying for it from personal funds so who cares what the ticket costs. All of these factors make the demand of business travelers very inelastic.

By comparison, the demand of leisure travelers is very elastic. The leisure traveler is very price sensitive because this traveler is paying for the ticket with his or her own funds. Leisure travel is a luxury rather than a necessity, and, there are substitutes. If the price of an airline ticket from Cleveland to Orlando is $600, then a family of four will quite likely drive to Disney World rather than fly. All of these factors give rise to a very elastic demand for airlines by leisure travelers.

So, airlines produce one product and sell it in two markets—one with an inelastic demand and the other with an elastic demand. Now think about the cost side of the airline: what is the marginal cost of serving one more customer? The costs of the plane, the crew, the ground infrastructure, and the fuel are the same whether there are 130 or 131 customers on board. On most flights, the marginal cost of a customer is the cost of a can of soda and a bag of peanuts. If an airline can sell an available seat at more than the marginal cost, then the airline is adding to its profit.

The objective of the airline is to extract as much revenue from each flight as possible since the costs of each flight are pretty much fixed costs. How to do this? For the inelastic part of the market, our theory tells us that the firm can increase revenues by increasing prices. So airlines charge high prices to business travelers. For the elastic part of the market, the firm can increase revenue by reducing prices and thereby expanding volume. If the airline charged all flyers the same fare, revenue would be less than what they can earn by socking it to the business flyer and giving a price break to the leisure flyer.

The remaining issue then is how to segregate the two markets. That is, how do you keep the guy in the three-piece suit from putting on a loud sport shirt and posing as a tourist sitting in the cheap seats? Two simple devices are used. To get the cheap seats you have to have a Saturday night stay-over. Most leisure travel naturally includes a Saturday stay-over but most business travelers loath a Saturday night on the road. Second, require a 14-day advance purchase. The leisure traveler is usually planning for travel 2 or 3 months in advance, whereas the business traveler usually doesn't know where he or she will be next week. So, by imposing these two restrictions on leisure fares, the airlines are able to effectively segment the ticket buying public into the two market segments with different pricing systems.

To the typical traveler, the pricing of airline tickets appears to be chaotic. But to the economist familiar with the price discrimination model, it is a very rational attempt by the airlines to maximize the total revenue earned on each flight. Again, the key to price discrimination is that there must be two markets for one product with vastly different demand elasticities. In the inelastic market push low volume and high prices, and in the elastic market push high volume and low prices.

CROSS-PRICE ELASTICITY

The elasticity of demand with respect to price describes the price-quantity relationship as one moves along a given demand curve. Another group of elasticities measures changes in the demand curve itself when one of the *ceteris paribus* conditions

Cross-price elasticity
a measure of the
sensitivity of quantity
demanded to changes
in the price of another
product, usually a
substitute or comple-
mentary good.

changes. One of these estimates is the **cross-price elasticity,** which measures the adjustment that consumers make in their consumption of one product in response to a change in the price of another. Another way of saying this is that cross-price elasticity measures the extent to which the demands for various commodities are related.

Cross-price elasticity is calculated in very much the same fashion as demand elasticity. Only a slight alteration in the basic elasticity formula is required. If we are interested in what happens to the consumption of beef as the price of pork is changed, for example, we simply divide the rate of change in the quantity of beef purchased by the rate of change in pork price. In terms of our basic elasticity formula, this would be:

$$\epsilon_c = \frac{\Delta Q_B / Q_B}{\Delta P_P / P_P} \tag{16-6}$$

where:

ϵ_c is the cross-price elasticity coefficient

Q_B is the quantity of one good purchased (beef in this example)

P_p is the price of another good (pork in this example)

which may be modified to eliminate the problem of discrepancy by using midpoints (equation 16–7).

$$\epsilon_c = \frac{\dfrac{Q_{1B} - Q_{2B}}{Q_{1B} + Q_{2B}}}{\dfrac{P_{1P} - P_{2P}}{P_{1P} + P_{2P}}} \tag{16-7}$$

Substitutes   two
goods with a positive
cross-price elasticity.

The relationship with which we are most concerned when using cross-price elasticity coefficients is the degree of substitutability or complementarity between the two commodities. When two commodities are **substitutes** for each other, the algebraic sign of the cross-price elasticity coefficient between them will be positive. That is, if the price of one increases, the quantity of the other commodity purchased will also increase. Beef and pork, for example, tend to be substitutes. As the price of pork rises, *ceteris paribus,* consumers respond by reducing consumption of pork and substituting beef in an effort to maximize their satisfaction within the limitations of their budgets.

Complements   two
goods with a negative
cross-price elasticity.

Commodities that are **complementary** to each other have negative cross-price elasticity coefficients. Dress shirts and neckties serve as an illustration. An increase in the price of dress shirts, *ceteris paribus,* would cut dress shirt consumption and hopefully the consumption of neckties (which are useless and archaic articles of apparel to begin with). The change in the price of dress shirts is accompanied by a change in quantity of neckties consumed, with the change in necktie consumption being opposite in direction to the change in shirt price. Therefore, the cross-price elasticity coefficient will be negative.

It should be recognized that the cross-price elasticity between the price of one product and the consumption of another may be quite different when the direction is reversed. For example, Brandow found the cross-price elasticity coefficient for lamb with respect to the price of beef to be 0.62, but the cross-price elasticity coefficient for beef with respect to the price of lamb was only 0.04.[2] This may be interpreted to mean that beef may be substituted for lamb rather readily, but that lamb is in no way a satisfactory substitute for beef.

INCOME ELASTICITY

A second *ceteris paribus* condition that, if allowed to change, will cause a shift in the demand curve is that of consumer income. Here again, we have an elasticity measure that will indicate the degree of sensitivity that consumers show in response to changes in income. An **income elasticity** coefficient shows the manner in which consumers alter their purchases of any good as a result of changes in income. With slight alterations, our basic arc elasticity formula can be used to define income elasticity:

$$\epsilon_I = \frac{\Delta Q/Q}{\Delta I/I} \qquad (16\text{--}8)$$

Income elasticity a measure of the sensitivity of quantity demanded to changes in consumers' income.

where:

ϵ_I is the income elasticity coefficient

Q is the quantity purchased

I is income

which may be modified into the standard arc, midpoint formula:

$$\epsilon_I = \frac{\dfrac{Q_1 - Q_2}{Q_1 + Q_2}}{\dfrac{I_1 - I_2}{I_1 + I_2}} \qquad (16\text{--}9)$$

This formula simply relates the rate of change in the quantity of some good that is purchased to the rate of change in consumer income.

Normally, we expect the algebraic sign of the income elasticity coefficient to be positive. That is, as a consumer has more purchasing power, his consumption of the good in question will increase. Such goods are called **normal goods.** However, there are a limited number of goods—lard, for example—that will exhibit negative income elasticities.[3] As consumers' incomes rise, they will tend to reduce their consumption of these **inferior goods;** that is, if they can afford to substitute vegetable shortening for hog lard, they will do so.

If the income elasticity of demand for a particular good is zero, the demand for that good is not affected by changes in income. This would normally be the case for items such as salt and other condiments that are an insignificant part of the budget. If the income elasticity of demand for a good is greater than 1, it means that an increasing proportion of the consumer's income is spent on the good as his or her income increases. Examples of such goods are protein sources among the

Normal goods goods with a positive income elasticity.

Inferior goods goods with a negative income elasticity.

---

[2] G. E. Brandow, *Interrelations Among Demand for Farm Products and Implications for Control of Market Supply,* Pennsylvania Agricultural Experiment Station Bulletin 680, 1961.
[3] Brandow found in 1961 that of twenty-four food products, only lard exhibited a negative income elasticity. George and King analyzed the demand for 48 food products in 1971 and again found lard to be the only one exhibiting a negative income elasticity coefficient.

poor in developing countries. Numerous studies have found the income elasticity of demand for milk among the poor to be well above 1. Most goods have an income elasticity of less than 1, meaning that the proportion of income spent on the good falls as the consumer becomes richer. Most foods in developed countries fall into this classification.

ELASTICITY OF SUPPLY

Elasticity of supply
a measure of the sensitivity of quantity supplied to changes in the price of the product.

The idea of **elasticity of supply** is almost identical with the concept of elasticity of demand. The formula for measurement is identical, but whereas the algebraic sign of the elasticity of demand coefficient is normally negative, that of the elasticity of supply coefficient is generally positive. That is, since the quantity supplied increases as price increases, the supply function slopes upward to the right, with a positive slope—hence the positive elasticity of supply coefficient with respect to price.

As with demand, supply is considered to be inelastic when the elasticity coefficient is less than 1 and elastic when it is greater than 1. By far, the most important factor in determining supply elasticity is time. The longer the time period considered, and the more time there is for production adjustments, the more elastic the supply.

In the very short run (frequently called the market period), the quantity of the good on the market is fixed and no amount of price change is going to bring more product forward. Therefore, market period supply is very inelastic. In the short run, existing firms can adjust output as prices vary. So in the short run there is some price-quantity reaction among existing firms, and therefore there is some elasticity in supply. In the long-run, additional firms can enter or leave the industry bringing about substantial quantity adjustments for small price changes. In the long run supply is quite elastic.

For annual crops such as corn, wheat, and soybeans, once the harvest is completed, the relevant supply curve for the remainder of the marketing year is very inelastic. In that case, prices of these goods are almost entirely demand determined. Price variations from year to year are determined by both demand and supply, but within a single year most price changes are driven by demand shifts.

SUMMARY

Elasticity is a measure of the responsiveness of changes in one economic variable to changes in another economic variable. An elasticity coefficient measures the ratio of the rates of change of the two variables.

An elasticity of demand coefficient measures the ratio of the rate of change of the quantity demanded relative to the rate of change of the price of the product. Because the demand relationship is inverse, the demand elasticity coefficient is always a negative number. If the value of the coefficient is between zero and -1, demand is said to be inelastic; that is, quantity demanded changes at a slower rate than price. If the value of the coefficient is less than -1, then demand is said to be elastic; quantity is more responsive than price.

When demand is elastic, there is an inverse relationship between changes in price and changes in total revenue of the firm. However, for inelastic demand, the relationship is direct: higher prices result in higher total revenue (or higher consumption expenses).

The degree of elasticity in demand depends on three basic factors. Demand will tend to be more inelastic for goods that have few substitutes, for goods that are necessities, and for goods that are relatively unimportant in the family budget. Salt and insulin are examples of goods with highly inelastic demand.

A firm that faces two markets for its product that have different demand elasticities can increase total revenues by segregating the two markets and charging a high price in the inelastic segment and a low price in the elastic segment. This practice is known as price discrimination. Examples of price discrimination include fresh/processed vegetables, business/leisure air travel and fluid/solid dairy products.

A cross-price elasticity coefficient measures the rate of change of the quantity demanded of one good with respect to the rate of change of the price of another good. If the sign of the cross-price coefficient is positive, then the two goods are substitutes for one another. If the coefficient is negative, the two goods are complements.

An income elasticity coefficient measures the rate of change of the quantity demanded with respect to the rate of change of income. For most goods, the sign of the income elasticity coefficient is positive, indicating that as income increases, consumption increases. These are called normal goods. For some goods, known as inferior goods, the sign of the coefficient is negative.

The elasticity of supply is similar to the elasticity of demand except that the sign of the coefficient is always positive. It measures the rate of change of the quantity supplied with respect to the rate of change of the price of the good. Elasticity of supply coefficients that are less than 1 are inelastic, while those greater than 1 are elastic. The elasticity of supply depends, more than anything else, on the time period being considered. The shorter the time period, the more inelastic the supply, because there is no time for production adjustments.

KEY TERMS

Arc elasticity
Complements
Cross-price elasticity
Elastic
Elasticity
Elasticity coefficient
Elasticity of demand
Elasticity of supply
Income elasticity

Inelastic
Inferior goods
Normal goods
Perfectly elastic
Perfectly inelastic
Point elasticity
Price discrimination
Substitutes

PROBLEMS AND DISCUSSION QUESTIONS

1. It was pointed out that the income elasticity for milk among the poor in developing countries is greater than 1.0. Interpret this by explaining what would happen if a poor person in such a country received one more dollar of income.

2. What would you suppose is value of the cross-price elasticity coefficient of the demand for ground beef with respect to the price of latex wall paint? Why?

3. The demand for veterinary services in general is very inelastic, but the demand for the services of a specific vet is very elastic. Explain why.

4. Duck Airlines charges all passengers the same $400 fare on one of its routes. The average flight carries 60 people in a plane with a capacity of 100. One-third of the flyers are business travelers, and two-thirds are leisure travelers. A bright, young economist tells the airline that it should engage in price discrimination. She estimates that if it increases the business fares by 10 percent, it will lose 5 percent of the business flyers, and if it reduces leisure fares by 10 percent, it will increase leisure traffic by 20 percent. Calculate the total revenue of Duck under its current one-price plan and under the price discrimination plan.

5. Calculate the arc elasticity of demand coefficient between point *A* and point *B* for the demand relationship to the right. Over this range, is demand elastic or inelastic?

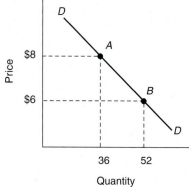

6. The income elasticity of turnips is + 0.7. If consumers' incomes were to increase by 10 percent, what would be the percentage increase in the quantity of turnips consumed?

7. Think about the markets for two goods. Both the supply and demand of good *A* is very inelastic. Both the supply and demand of good *B* is very elastic.

   a. Compare the potential for price variability in the two markets.

   b. Which of these two is most likely to be the market for food?

8. The elasticity of demand coefficient for milk is about − 0.25, while that of beef and chicken is about − 1.0. What does this suggest about milk compared with the meats?

9. The university drama department has determined that the elasticity of demand for its productions is − 0.70. If the drama department wanted to increase its total revenue, what should it do?

10. As the price of maple syrup increased from $6 per pint to $7 per pint, production increased from 250 pints to 300 pints. What is the arc elasticity of supply over this range? Is supply elastic or inelastic over this range?

Food Marketing: From Stable to Table

The food marketing system in the United States is something to behold. On a cold winter day in Minnesota, Igmar punches through a snow drift on the way to the supermarket in search of a head of iceberg lettuce. And there in the warm glow of the supermarket she finds a head of lettuce waiting for her. How did that lettuce know she was coming? On a hot, humid day in Miami, the radiator of Juan's car boils over as he arrives at the supermarket in search of a head of iceberg lettuce. And there in the cool, air-conditioned comfort of the supermarket he finds a head of iceberg lettuce waiting for him. How did that lettuce know he was coming?

Just think about the millions of food items that are purchased every day at the 300,000 retail food stores and 600,000 eating and drinking establishments that dot the nation, and then think about how many times in your own experience you have walked into a supermarket or restaurant and have not been able to find an item that you desire. You may not like the price, but almost always the item will be there when you want it, where you want it, and in the form you want it. Milk in large containers, milk in small containers, milk with no fat, milk with 2 percent fat, milk with chocolate added, canned milk, and powdered milk: they are all there awaiting your selection.

A typical large, modern supermarket has about 40,000 UPCs (universal product codes, or bar codes) on its shelf. Spaghetti for dinner tonight? Do I want a large package or a small package? Imported or domestic? Green or white? Which of four different brands? Think of the choices you have and the richness this brings to our lives. And each of those choices is available to you every day of the year.

This marvelous system that ties the consumer and the farmer together is usually referred to as the food marketing system, and the study of that system is called "food marketing." The complexity of producing, distributing, and selling millions of food products a day is mind-boggling. The process of controlling, simplifying, and routinizing this system is what food marketing is all about.

FOOD MARKETING DEFINED

Food marketing obviously deals with food—what we eat. When we think of food, we naturally think of the farmer or rancher. But our vision should not be so narrow. We should also think about the oysterman, the fisherman, and the crabber. And don't forget the importers who bring us coffee, tea, spices, bananas, and chocolate. And finally, some of what we eat comes from industrial plants such as salt, vitamin and mineral supplements, and yeast. All of these players are part of the food production system.

The food marketing system refers to all the activities and services that occur between the producers/providers of food and the consumers of food. Food marketing

Food marketing all the activities and services that occur between the producers/providers of food and foodstuffs and the consumer. Food marketing creates utility for the consumer.

deals with how the product of a wheat farmer in Kansas, an underground salt mine in New York, and a manufacturer of fungi in St. Louis eventually ends up as your hamburger bun at a fast-food outlet in California. A customer at the Burger Barn would derive little or no utility from a serving of wheat, salt, and yeast, but the customer receives great utility from a hamburger bun and is gleefully willing to pay for that utility.

There is another marketing system that is important for agriculture and that is the input or **farm service marketing** system that sells purchased inputs such as fertilizers and chemicals to farmers. While nowhere near as large in terms of dollar volume as the food marketing system, the farm service marketing system is equally critical in achieving the ultimate goal of getting food to the consumer.

Firms engaged in farm service marketing, agricultural production, and food marketing are known collectively as **agribusiness.** The study of the management, marketing, and finance of agribusiness firms has become a specialized field at many colleges of agriculture. The agribusiness sector accounts for more than one out of five jobs in the American economy.

FOOD MARKETING CREATES UTILITY

Food marketing can be thought of as a production process just like the farmer or rancher is a production process. The farmer buys inputs and combines them in some unique fashion to produce an output. In a similar fashion, food marketing firms buy inputs at one price, enhance those inputs in one manner or another, which adds utility to the inputs, and then sell the output at a higher price reflecting the additional utility. So in a very real sense, food marketing is about creating or producing utility.

The Four Utilities of Food Marketing

Food marketing produces utility—utility for which the ultimate consumer is willing to pay. The four utilities that are produced are time, place, form, and possession. Let's look at each through the eyes of a consumer at the Burger Barn in California.

Time

The Kansas wheat farmer harvests all of his wheat in the month of June, but the consumer at the Burger Barn wants a hamburger bun in April. Since buns have a shelf life of no more than a week or so, someone somewhere must have stored the flour the bun was made of or, more likely, stored the wheat the flour was made of. The agribusiness firm that stored the wheat or the flour created a **time utility,** allowing production and consumption to occur at different points of time. Since storage is not a free good, the consumer will ultimately pay for the time utility that is created.

Place

The wheat is produced in Kansas and the Burger Barn is in California. Either the wheat has to go to California, or the customer has to go to Kansas. Given those choices, the California customer is more than willing to pay someone to create **place utility** for her. Moving the product to the consumer creates place utility and adds to the value of the good as perceived by the consumer.

Farm service marketing   all the activities and services that are brought to the farmer, rancher, or producer in the form of purchased inputs.

Agribusiness   firms engaged in farm service marketing, agricultural production, food processing, food distribution, and consumption.

Time utility   utility created by storage activities.

Place utility   utility created by the transportation function.

Form

The Kansas farmer has wheat and the California consumer wants a bun to wrap around the burger. Before it reaches the consumer, the wheat must be converted into flour by some agribusiness firm, and the flour must be converted into a bun by another: agribusiness firm. These conversions or production processes create **form utility**: they change the form of the product into something that the consumer wants. In doing so, they add utility to the product—additional utility that the consumer is willing to pay for.

Form utility utility created by the processing function.

Possession

A bun sitting on the Burger Barn shelf provides the consumer with very little utility and may even create a little disutility associated with the yearning for a burger. Clearly, the possession of the bun on the shelf belongs to the Burger Barn, and the consumer can't (or at least shouldn't) eat it. When the marketing system changes the possession of that bun (along with its burger) to our consumer, her utility immediately increases. It was the expected increase of **possession utility** that encouraged her to exchange some green slips of paper for the right to claim possession. Chomp. Yummm. Burp. Ahhhh. Utility has been created.

Possession utility utility created through exchange in the marketing system.

Why do Food Marketing Firms Produce Utility?

Why does the grain elevator operator store wheat from June until April? Why does the truck driver carry wheat from Kansas to California? Simple: They both hope that their customers (other agribusiness or food marketing firms) will pay more for the utility added than it cost them to produce that utility. The difference is profit. So, it is the profit motive that drives the marketing system.

The search for profits in the creation or production of time, place, form, and possession utilities is a continuous, dynamic process that is part of what makes food marketing such an exciting area. How does the trucker loading up with wheat in Kansas know whether to go to California, Oregon, or Rhode Island? Whichever region is willing to pay the most for the utility he creates is the region that will get the wheat. If Oregon has abundant quantities of wheat and flour while California is scraping the bottom of the barrel, then the value of the utility created in California will be greater and the willingness to pay the trucker to create that utility will be greater.

The dynamic price system and the profit motive are like a giant, integrated information system that continually sends out signals about what is needed where and in what form by whom. That is, information about the demand for time, place, form, and possession utilities is conveyed by the dynamic price system. And it is an information system with a good memory: it remembers to send fewer buns to the Burger Barn during spring break and more on the weekends of home football games.

Choices

The food marketing system and the competition within that system create choices for the consumer. Choice is one of the foundations of economics: without choice there is no need to allocate those scarce resources. Having choices allows consumers to express their preferences in the marketplace—maximizing utility from a given budget or minimizing the cost of obtaining a given level of utility.

A dynamic, vibrant food marketing system provides consumers with abundant choices. The food marketing firm that can give the potential customer what he wants (form), when he wants it (time), where he wants it (place), and at the lowest price (possession) is the firm that will make the sale and prosper. Reflect on this by asking—"Why have Wal-Mart and McDonald's been two of the most successful companies in the past 30 years?"

APPROACHES TO THE STUDY OF FOOD MARKETING

Food marketing is a very complex system with literally millions of interactions that must, from the perspective of an astronaut, look like a colony of ants after the anthill has been disturbed. What appears to the observer as chaos is really an integrated system in which everybody is motivated by self-interest. As we try to understand this system, we can identify four different approaches that have been taken in studying the apparent chaos.

Functional

Functional approach study of marketing systems emphasizing how each particular activity, like transportation, is accomplished.

In the **functional approach** to the study of the food marketing system, the complexity of the system is divided into specific tasks that must be performed and each task is studied independently. We have already been introduced to several functions or tasks. Transportation and storage are two of the more important functions that can be analyzed. Others will be covered later in this chapter.

Institutional

Institutional approach study of marketing systems emphasizing the role of different participants, such as commodity brokers, in the marketing chain and the role of governmental agencies.

The **institutional approach** to the study of food marketing emphasizes the role of different participants in the food marketing chain and their relationships to one another. The institutional approach also examines the role of governmental and regulatory agencies in the food marketing system.

Market Levels

Market level approach study of marketing systems that views the system as a series of stages or levels through which the food passes. Marketing may be thought of as a chain in which food passes from link to link. The market level approach emphasizes the study of each link independent of the other links.

The **market level approach** to food marketing analysis follows food through the marketing system as it moves from stage to stage. This is akin to studying each link of a chain to evaluate its contribution to the chain. The analysis looks at the different steps in the process and evaluates the contributions to the creation of utility at each of these steps. We will look at several examples later in this chapter.

Commodity

Commodity approach the study of all aspects of the marketing system for a single commodity.

A final approach to food marketing analysis is the **commodity approach** in which the entire marketing chain of a single product is examined. All aspects, functional and institutional, of the marketing of a specific commodity are studied in an integrated fashion. One of the most studied commodities is dairy. Most colleges of agriculture will have at least one professor who is a dairy marketing specialist and studies dairy market functions and institutions as they affect both producers and consumers in that particular state.

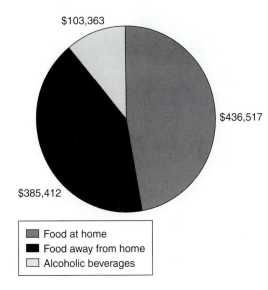

FIGURE 17–1 Total food expenditures, U.S., 2000 (millions of dollars).

$103,363

$436,517

$385,412

■ Food at home
■ Food away from home
□ Alcoholic beverages

THE FOOD BILL

American consumers spent $925 billion on food in 2000.[1] This **food bill** works out to almost $3,280 per person in the United States. As shown in Figure 17–1, about 11 percent of total food expenditures are for alcoholic beverages. All would agree that alcoholic beverages are agricultural products since these products are nothing more than fermented grains, but most would also agree that alcoholic beverages are not "food" in the traditional sense. In all subsequent discussions these products are eliminated from consideration.

Food bill value of total expenditures on food in any given year.

With the elimination of alcoholic beverages, total 2000 food expenditures in the United States amounted to approximately $822 billion, or about $2,913 per person. This represented only 10.2 percent of disposable (i.e., after tax) personal income. In 1980 this number stood at 13.4 percent, and food was the largest single expense item in the family budget. Since then food's share of the family's budget has continued to fall, and the share of health care has increased and now exceeds the share for food.

Away from Home Share

As can be seen in Figure 17–2, about 47 percent of our total food expenditures are for food consumed **away from home.** The USDA estimates that about one-third of all food quantity (as opposed to expenditures) is consumed away from home. Of all meals eaten away from home approximately one in six is eaten in a car or other vehicle.

Away from home expenditures on food that is not prepared at an individual's residence.

Figure 17–3 illustrates what has been one of the most persistent trends in food expenditures for the past 50 years: the steady increase in the percentage of food

---

[1] All data in this section were provided by the Economic Research Service of the U.S. Department of Agriculture. The data may be accessed at **www.ers.usda.gov/Briefing/CPIFood AndExpenditures/index.htm.**

FIGURE 17–2 Food expenditures at home and away, 2000.

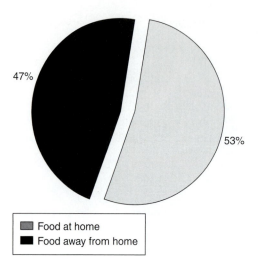

Legend:
- Food at home
- Food away from home

47%

53%

FIGURE 17–3 Food away from home as a percentage of total.

expenditures for food eaten away from home.[2] Since 1960, the percentage away from home has increased by about 7 to 8 percentage points each decade.

THE FOOD MARKETING BILL

As we saw earlier, the food marketing system produces utility or value by changing some characteristic of a product as it moves from the farm to the consumer. Each of these productive activities has a cost that must ultimately be paid for by the consumer. The sum of all of these costs is called the **food marketing bill.**

Food marketing bill
that portion of the food bill that is created by the marketing system. The food bill minus farm value.

Size and Composition

As shown in Figure 17–4, of the total $822 billion of food expenditures in 2000 about $160 billion is for food products that are not from domestic farms. A large portion

[2] The anomaly in Figure 17–3 for 1945 is due to the number of meals eaten away from home in fox holes or on military bases. By 1950 the men and women were home and things had returned to normal.

Total food expenditures = $821.9

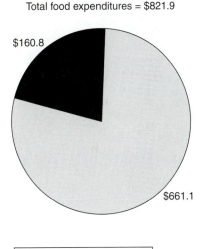

$160.8

$661.1

☐ Domestic farm foods
■ Imported and non-farm

FIGURE 17–4
Expenditures for food,
2000 (billions of
dollars).

Total domestic farm food = $661.1

$123.3

$537.8

■ Domestic farm value
☐ Marketing bill

FIGURE 17–5 Farm
value of domestic food
expenditures, 2000
(billions of dollars).

of these expenditures are for imports and non-farm foods such as salt. The remaining $661 billion is the portion of total food expenditures for domestic farm food.

When the consumer checks out at the supermarket and pays $100 for several bags of food, what is that consumer buying? Basically, two things are being purchased: the farm value of the agricultural commodity and the food marketing services that have been added to the value of the food as it moved through the marketing chain. As shown in Figure 17–5, the vast majority of what the consumer purchases is marketing services as opposed to farm value. Of the total $564 billion spent on domestic farm food in 2000, only $123 billion or 19 percent was for the agricultural product itself. More than four times as much was spent

FIGURE 17–6
Components of the
food marketing bill,
2000 (billions of
dollars).

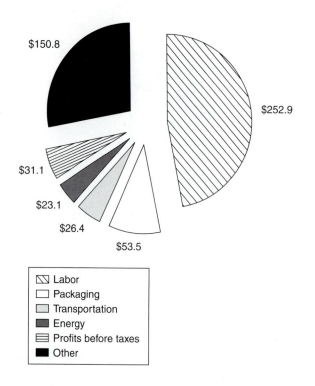

$150.8

$252.9

$31.1

$23.1

$26.4

$53.5

◫	Labor
▢	Packaging
▨	Transportation
▩	Energy
▤	Profits before taxes
■	Other

on marketing services—those additional utilities that were added to your food products.

The component parts of the food marketing bill for domestic farm food are broken out in Figure 17–6. Of the total marketing bill of $538 billion, almost half of it is for labor. This labor includes everything from the driver of the truck to the butcher to the cashier at the supermarket. Each of these people enhances the utility of what you buy, and you, the consumer, ultimately pay for that additional utility.

The other half of the food marketing bill is a collection of various different expenses, the largest of which is packaging—a necessary utility that is usually added by the processor. The "other" category includes expenses such as advertising, depreciation, interest, rent, repairs, and taxes. No one of these items exceeds $30 billion.

By Commodity

Farm share value of
farm production as a
percentage of the retail
price of food.

We have seen that the marketing bill for domestic farm food is 81 percent of the total retail price and that the **farm share** is 19 percent. Over time, as shown in Figure 17–7, the marketing bill has grown much faster than the farm share. This reflects an increasing demand for convenience foods, further processed foods, and food away from home. As is frequently the case, an average can hide the tremendous variation that exists within the data for which the average is calculated.

Figure 17–8 shows the farm share for several different food products. The highest farm share (i.e., lowest marketing bill) is for beef and eggs. That is, the amount of utility added to the farm product is quite low for beef and eggs. The reasons the marketing bill for eggs is low are rather obvious. The time utility added is minimal: layers (the hens that produce eggs) and people get along quite well with a typical layer

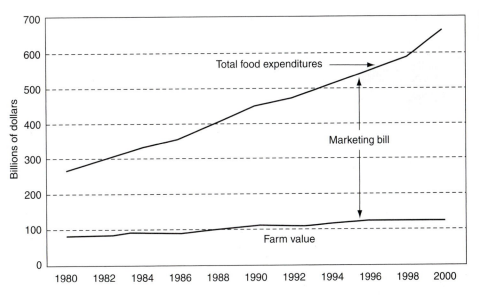

FIGURE 17–7 Food expenditures, 1980–2000.

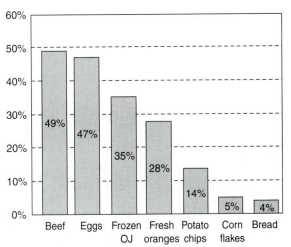

FIGURE 17–8 Farm value share of retail food prices, 1999.

producing slightly less than one egg a day and the typical consumer eating about one egg a day. There is virtually no seasonality with regard to either production or consumption (Easter being an exception) and, therefore, little need for storage.

There is also little place utility created in the egg business. Since layers produce in hen houses that can be built in any climate, it is much easier to take the layers to the customer than to ship the eggs to the customer. As a consequence, there is typically very little transportation cost for eggs.

The form utility is also minimal in the case of eggs. The eggs are washed, graded, and packed, but what the consumer gets is pretty much what the hen laid. Finally, the possession utility is also minimal. In most cases the supermarket buys eggs directly from the farmer/packer and the consumer buys them from the supermarket, so there are only two changes of possession. By comparison, many products will go through five to seven changes of possession before the consumer owns the product. Each change of possession entails costs, and it is the consumer who ultimately pays those costs.

The farm value share for beef is also quite high. There is little time utility created as both production and consumption show no marked seasonality. Usually a substantial amount of transportation is required, but most of it is done by low-cost rail. While the form change is substantial from the animal on the hoof to the steak in the display case, that form change is completed in highly efficient packing plants at relatively low costs.

The difference between the farm share of frozen concentrated orange juice (FCOJ) and fresh oranges is quite interesting. The basic difference here is the cost of marketing a nonperishable commodity (FCOJ) versus a perishable one (fresh oranges). Since fresh oranges cannot be stored for any appreciable length of time, they must get to the market as quickly as possible. This means shipping by refrigerated truck, which is, next to air cargo, the most expensive mode of transportation. So while there is little form utility in fresh oranges, there is substantial place utility created. Since most fresh oranges come from California and since most consumers are in the eastern part of the country, the amount of shipping is substantial.[3]

By comparison, FCOJ goes through substantial changes in form, converting it into a storable, nonperishable commodity that eliminates problems of seasonality and lowers the cost of transportation. As a result, the marketing bill for FCOJ is substantially below that of fresh oranges.

At the bottom of the list of farm share are bread and cornflakes. The 4 percent shown for bread is 3 percent for wheat and 1 percent for other agricultural products such as lard, salt and sugar.

The case of cornflakes is an almost perfect counterpoint to the case of eggs. There is a tremendous seasonality to the production of corn and virtually none in consumption. Therefore, storage becomes a very important cost element. Place utility is also high because every Kellogg cornflake sold in the United States is produced in Battle Creek, Michigan. The form utility change is also substantial. The corn is ground into a slush and then baked, which requires a high energy cost. Finally the possession utility is fairly substantial. At a minimum, there are six possession changes between the corn farmer and the cornflake consumer, and a few more are quite likely in most cases. Since each change of possession has a cost associated with it, these costs get added on to the retail price of the cornflakes.

Farm Service Marketing Bill

Up to now we have looked at the food marketing bill, which covers the marketing costs between the farmer and the consumer. But the farmer is also a buyer of inputs that are marketed to the farmer. The farmer essentially passes these marketing costs on to the consumer as part of the 19 percent of farm value in the retail food cost. Of these costs, it is estimated that 12 percent are for inputs purchased by farmers and the other 7 percent is value added by the farmer.

If this is the case, then when you buy $100 of food at retail, you are actually buying $12 of farmer-bought marketing costs and $81 of postfarmer marketing costs for a total of $93 of marketing costs. So the value added by

---

[3] About 10 percent of Florida's orange crop goes into the fresh market. The other 90 percent goes into FCOJ. By comparison, only about 10 percent of the California crop goes into juice. At certain times of the year it is difficult to find fresh Florida oranges in Florida supermarkets, but there are always ample quantities of California fruit.

marketing in your food bill is about 13 times as large as the value added by the farmer. If you want to find the money in the food business, look to marketing, not farming.

FOOD MARKET LEVELS

The study of food market levels examines the different middlemen that a typical product will move through. Some foods will move through many different levels, while others will take a more direct approach. In some instances the roles of several different middlemen may be combined into a single firm or activity.

Assemblers

The first postharvest activity is **assembly,** in which a small quantity of output from a large number of producers is brought together in large enough volume to enter into the processing chain. The cattle drive of times since gone is an example of the assembly process. Two contemporary examples of assembly will suffice.

The local **grain elevator** in grain producing regions is a classic example of the assembly process.[4] Most grain that leaves the farm leaves in a farm truck. The truck carries the grain to the elevator where it is purchased by the elevator operator. The farmer's truckload of grain is added to hundreds of other truckloads in the elevator's storage compartments. As small loads are assembled into larger loads, the production of a number of farmers is commingled in the elevator's storage compartments. When the elevator's storage is about full, the elevator operator will look for a buyer of the grain. It will be sold by the railcar load—a fairly standard unit of commerce among the big grain handlers. So the grain elevator buys grain by the truckload and sells it by the carload—assembly.

Another example is in the marketing of fresh vegetables. The first market level for most fresh vegetables is the local broker. Local brokers buy numerous small shipments from local farmers, combine them into truckload lots, and arrange for shipping. So the local broker buys by the box and sells by the truckload.

Commodity Processors

Commodity processors are firms that buy raw agricultural commodities such as corn or wheat and process them into ingredients for retail food products. Most consumers have never heard of companies such as Archer Daniels Midland, Cargill, CPC International, or ConAgra, yet they eat food processed by them every day. These are the companies that buy soybeans by trainload (yes, trainload, not carload), crush the beans into soybean oil and soybean meal, and then ship the oil by

Assembly the collection of small amounts of product from many farmers to create a large enough amount of product for efficient shipment.

Grain elevator a grain storage facility that buys grain from farmers by the truckload and sells it to processors by the railcar load.

Commodity processors companies that buy raw agricultural commodities (such as soybeans) and process them into food product ingredients.

---

[4] For those not familiar with grain elevators, they are the tall, usually circular structures found adjacent to railroad tracks in grain farming regions. Frequently several of these large silos will be joined together in a long bank of adjoined cylinders. They are called grain elevators because when grain is put into them, it is carried to the top of the silo by an elevator and put on the top of the rest of the grain in storage. When grain is taken out, it flows out of the bottom of the structure by gravity feed or by an auger.

the carload to manufacturers of margarine and mayonnaise. These are the companies that buy wheat by the trainload and produce flour for sale to the bakeries. These are the companies that buy corn by the trainload to make high fructose corn sweetener that is sold to soft drink bottlers by the tanker carload.

Food Processors

Food processors
companies that buy ingredients and/or raw agricultural commodities and process them into retail products.

Food processors are manufacturers of final food products. They have names we all know like Campbell's, Heinz, Kellogg's, and Quaker Oats. These firms buy both raw agricultural products from assemblers and processed ingredients from commodity processors and convert them into finished food products ready for the shelf.

Distributors

Distributors
wholesales and others who buy large lots of food from processors and distribute it to many retailers in smaller lots.

Distributors are the mirror image of assemblers. They buy from the food processor by the carload and sell to many retailers by the carton. Most distributors are traditional wholesalers who earn their keep by buying large lots and selling small lots.

The importance of food wholesalers is diminishing. Today most wholesalers serve independent supermarkets and small chains of convenience stores. Most supermarket chains do their own wholesaling, which is one reason the large chains can usually underprice the independents, there being one fewer possession change.

In some cases of foods with short shelf lives, the processor is also the distributor. This is done so the processor can be certain that no product past its time will be on the retail shelf. If you try brand X hamburger buns and find that two days later they look like a science fair project on the properties of molds, you probably won't buy that brand again. To avoid this, brand X sends its own distributor into the retail outlet to pull the stale and stock the fresh. Hang around the back of a supermarket one day and you will quickly learn which processors are also distributors: bread, potato chips, beer, soft drinks, and some cookies. In these cases the distribution system is the same for independents, chain supermarkets, and convenience stores.

Retailers

Retailers the supermarket and other vendors from whom the public buys food.

At the last level in the food chain we find the **retailer** from whom the customer buys the food product. This is the part of the marketing chain that is best known to most of us. It is a fiercely competitive business in which stores attempt to attract customers on the basis of convenience and price. Here are a few trends in the food retail business:

1. From having virtually no presence in the food retailing business in 1990, Wal-Mart has grown to be the second largest food retailer in the United States through the expansion of its superstore concept. For those who have not had the experience, a superstore is a full-sized Wal-Mart discount store plus a full-sized supermarket all under one roof.

2. There is rapid consolidation in the industry as big fish gobble up little fish to get even bigger. Recently Kroger (the largest food retailer) bought up the Fred Meyer chain of supermarkets, and Albertson's (the third largest) bought American Stores. The consolidation trend has international dimensions too. Ahold, a Dutch food retailer, recently bought Giant stores in the greater Washington, D.C., area; and A&P is now owned by a German retailer.

3. Larger stores with more nonfood boutiques are all the rage in supermarket land. Pharmacies, banks, flower shops, photo processing labs, and even restaurants are appearing inside of supermarkets—anything to snag a customer.

4. Some supermarkets are putting in play areas and day care to entertain the kids while mom or dad shops.

5. Further prepared foods are available from the deli, which you can pick up and pop in the microwave when you get home.[5]

6. And finally, in a throwback to the old days, many supermarkets now offer home delivery. The "shopper" can fax or e-mail an order, and the store will pull the items and deliver at the appointed time for a small service charge. For a two-worker family this can be very attractive. A few companies have tried the e-commerce route where a customer orders from a catalog on the Internet and in several days the order is delivered by a delivery service, or in some communities delivery is available the same day by the e-company itself.[6] During the recession of 2001 most of the food e-tailing ventures joined the dot.com meltdown and went out of business.

Vertical Integration

One of the most notable trends in food marketing is **vertical integration.** This refers to the combination of two or more marketing levels into a single firm. Then the coordination between the levels is accomplished by management directive rather than through markets sending price signals. An example of vertical coordination is a chain of popular drive-through convenience stores in the Miami area called The Milk Store. About all they sell are dairy products from their own processing plant that gets its raw milk from its own dairy farm. So everything from the cow to the milk on the shelf is under a single management structure.

In a more typical situation, the dairy farmer sells raw milk to a processor. Then the processor sells milk to the convenience store. By vertically integrating, The Milk Store is able to eliminate these two changes of possession and the costs associated with those exchanges.

> **Vertical integration** the combination of different businesses at different stages of the production/marketing sequence under a single management.

Industrialization

Another trend in the food marketing business has been given the name of **industrialization.** Basically this refers to the use of modern industrial concepts of production routinization, procurement through strategic alliances, coordination, and contracting in the food marketing system.

For example, when McDonald's decided to get into the salad business, it determined the best thing to do was outsource the job because it really didn't know anything about salads and fresh vegetable markets. The company knew and understood burgers, but not salads. So McDonald's found one salad maker that agreed to produce all salads needed in the United States under a rigid contract specifying salad content, packaging, freshness, and the like. This is what is known

> **Industrialization** the use of modern industrial concepts of production routinization, procurement through strategic alliances, coordination, and contracting in the food marketing system.

---

[5] A colleague never goes to restaurants when traveling by car: he buys all of his meals at supermarket delis and eats them in the comfort of his motel room.

[6] If you want to see the new world of a virtual supermarket, try **www.peapod.com** on the Internet.

as a strategic alliance in which the two companies rely heavily on each other and agree to share information with each other. Instead of competition there is cooperation in recognition of their interdependence. The salad maker in turn contracts with lettuce producers to provide a steady flow of lettuce. With contracts, a prior agreement replaces the role of the market as a controlling force. Management control replaces market control.

MARKET FUNCTIONS

Another way to analyze markets is to study how the various functional activities are performed. What is the mode of transportation? Who stores the grain, the assembler or the processor? These are the kinds of questions that get asked in the functional approach.

Primary Functions

We have already introduced the four primary functions of creating time, place, form, and possession utility. These four utilities are created by the transportation system, the storage system, the processing system, and the exchange system. But these are not the only four functions in a marketing system. The other functions are called the facilitating functions.

Facilitating Functions

Grades and standards the sorting of diverse products into uniform groups based on attributes such as quality and size.

Markets operate more efficiently if buyers and sellers can agree on a price without a physical examination of the product. To facilitate this there must be a system of **grades and standards** that both buyers and sellers agree on. In some cases it is the federal government that creates grades and standards, and in other cases the industry will impose grades and standards upon itself.

In the case of tomatoes, for instance, there are federal standards with regards to quality and size. Quality is listed as U.S. #1, #2 or #3. A combination grade is also used such as 85 percent U.S. #1 where 85 percent of the pack must meet U.S. #1 standards. Size is referred to as extra large, large, and so forth. Thus, a broker in Chicago can talk with a broker in Florida and get a price quote for Florida mature green, U.S. #1 large and know exactly what he will get without ever examining it. He can check with three or four Florida brokers to see who has the best price for U.S. #1 large, knowing that he is comparing tomatoes with tomatoes. For tomatoes, the size of the box is not part of the federal grades and standards, but it is part of the industry standards for the Federal Marketing Order 966 for tomatoes. The Chicago broker does not have to ask each Florida seller the size of the box because Florida mature green tomatoes must be packed in 25-pound containers.

A second facilitating function is financing. The creation of the time utility implies storage costs, but it also implies a financial cost for the time value of money for whoever has ownership of the commodity while it is in storage. So financing the ownership of a commodity during the marketing period of that commodity becomes a part of the marketing cost that the consumer must eventually pay.

A third facilitating function is risk bearing. During the marketing process there are two significant risks that the owner of the commodity/product faces. There is a physical risk that the commodity/product may be destroyed in a fire or accident. And there is the price risk that between the time the good is bought and sold, its price may have changed.

Physical risk is pretty easy to deal with because a well-established insurance system is in place to deal with these risks. Insurance is simply paying someone else to assume a risk you are not willing to take. In the marketing system insurance against physical loss is very common.

Price risk is another matter. This is a risk that most insurance companies won't touch. Large, sophisticated firms in the food marketing system use a system called hedging on futures markets to control price risk. Hedging does not eliminate price risk, nor does it fully insure against price losses, but hedging does allow the food marketing firm to shift most of this risk elsewhere. In the next chapter we will examine hedging and futures markets more fully.

A final facilitating function is market information. For markets to work efficiently and effectively, both buyers and sellers need full information about prevailing prices and quantities of goods that are moving at those prices. The only thing worse than no information is misinformation, so it is very important that market information be created by a disinterested party. Most market information in the food marketing system is created by the federal government and reported over information services of private providers. The creation and dissemination of this information to anyone who wants it establishes the proverbial "level playing field" because everybody has similar information.[7]

> **Physical risk** the risk that a product in the marketing system will be accidentally destroyed.

> **Price risk** the risk that while a product is moving through the marketing chain its market value may change.

MARKETING MARGINS

We have seen that marketing creates utility and that the consumer ultimately pays for the utility created. The value of a good that the consumer purchases is equal to the value of that good when it leaves the farm plus the value that is added by the marketing system. The difference between the value or price of a good at the retail level and at the farm level is known as the **marketing margin.** So the marketing margin is the amount of value created by the marketing system.

> **Marketing margin** the difference between the prices of a product at any two points in the marketing chain. The marketing margin is equal to the marketing costs between those two points.

Derived Demand

As we saw in an earlier chapter, demand originates at the level of the final consumer. The consumer by his or her actions determines how many units of a good will be demanded at alternative prices for the commodity. The law of demand stipulates that as the price of the good goes up, *ceteris paribus*, the quantity demanded will go down. The summation of individual demands at each price results in market demand.

---

[7] In 2001 three American economists, George A. Akerlof, A. Michael Spence, and Joseph E. Stiglitz, won the Nobel prize in economic sciences for the work they had done concerning the operation of markets in which there is "asymmetric information" (i.e., when buyer and seller do not have the same information). The example that was used in one of the landmark studies in this field was the market for used cars where the dealer has more knowledge than the potential buyer. This may be why used car dealers are so universally scorned.

FIGURE 17–9
Derived farm level
demand.

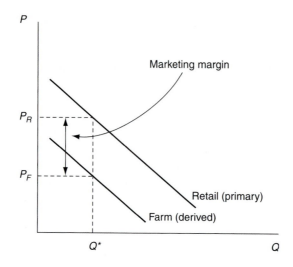

Market demand is expressed at the retail level where consumers make their purchases. For this reason, retail level market demand is called primary demand. What about demand at the farm level? It is passed down to the farmer through the marketing chain. For any given quantity demanded, such as Q^* in Figure 17–9, the retail price minus the marketing margin will give the farm level price, which is a point on the **derived farm level demand** curve.

Derived farm level demand   the primary retail level demand minus the marketing margin.

If, as shown in Figure 17–9, we assume the marketing margin is constant for all output levels, then the farm level demand is parallel to the retail level demand but shifted down by the amount of the marketing margin.[8] The farm level demand is called a derived demand since it is based on, or derived from, the primary demand at the retail level. Shifts in the primary demand, *ceteris paribus*, will result in shifts in the derived farm level demand. Changes in the marketing margin will shift the derived farm level demand but not change the primary retail demand.

Derived Supply

A similar derivation can be made on the supply side of the market. There is, however, one important difference: the primary supply originates at the level of the producer or farmer based on the costs of production. From this primary supply, the marketing margin is added on to obtain the **derived retail level supply.**

Derived retail level supply   the primary farm level supply plus the marketing margin.

As shown in Figure 17–10, for any given quantity supplied such as Q^*, the farm level price is determined from the primary supply curve, and the retail level price is equal to the farm level price plus the marketing margin. Repeating this process for all possible quantities supplied traces out the derived retail level supply curve. Again assuming a constant marketing margin at all output levels, the derived retail level supply curve is parallel to and above the primary farm level supply.

---

[8] The parallel shift from retail to farm in Figure 17–9 suggests that the marketing margin is the same at all output levels. The assumption of a constant marketing margin is, in most cases, unrealistic. Marketing, like other production processes, normally exhibits diminishing marginal productivity, which translates into increasing marginal costs. The assumption of a constant marketing margin in no way detracts from the basic economic principles being discussed, and it makes the entire presentation much simpler.

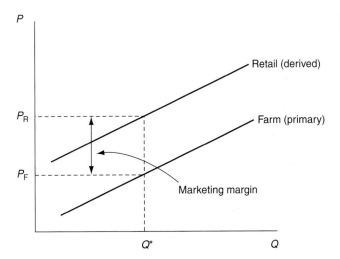

FIGURE 17–10
Derived retail level
supply.

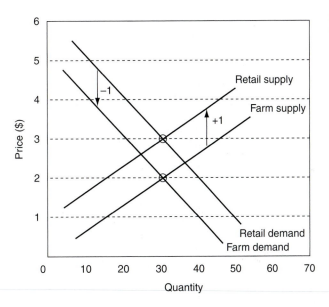

FIGURE 17–11   Multi-
level equilibrium.

Market Equilibrium

The farm and retail level supply and demand can now be combined into a single
analysis as in Figure 17–11. Here we have an example with a constant marketing
margin of $1. The primary retail level demand is used to derive the farm level de-
mand by subtracting $1 from the retail price at all output levels. The primary farm
level supply is used to derive the retail level supply by adding $1 to the farm level
price at each output level.

There is a retail level market equilibrium at 30 units with a retail price of $3 per
unit. There is a farm level market equilibrium also at 30 units but at a farm level price
of $2 per unit. The difference between the equilibrium retail price and the equilib-
rium farm price is $1, which is equal to the marketing margin. Since the market clear-
ing quantity at both levels is the same, this is an overall, stable equilibrium situation.

FIGURE 17–12
Primary demand shift.

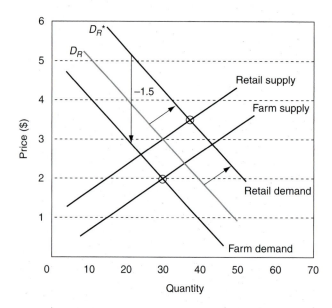

Dynamic Adjustment

The situation shown in Figure 17–11 is a long-run equilibrium situation. Now let's see what happens if a change in a *ceteris paribus* condition upsets this equilibrium. Suppose there is a change in consumers' tastes and preferences that causes an outward shift of the primary demand curve from D_R to D^*_R, as shown in Figure 17–12.

At the retail level the outward shift of demand results in a new retail equilibrium quantity of 37 units trading at about $3.50 per unit. At the farm level in the short run, farmers continue to produce 30 units, selling them at $2.00 per unit. Clearly this is a short-run disequilibrium situation because the quantity being produced at the farm level is less than the quantity being taken at the retail level. Two things are happening here: (1) inventories are being drawn down as consumption exceeds production, and (2) the marketing margin has grown to $1.50 even though marketing costs remain at $1.00. The middlemen are earning pure economic profits of $0.50 per unit traded.

With profits available and inventories declining, the middlemen will bid up the prices they are willing to pay farmers, causing an upward shift of the farm level derived demand curve from D_F to D^*_F. As shown in Figure 17–13, this process will continue until such time as the drain on inventories is stopped by shifting the derived farm level demand up to the point where farmers are willingly producing the same 37 units consumers are now consuming. At this new equilibrium, the farm level price is $2.50 and the economic profits of the middlemen are back to zero. A global equilibrium has been restored.

Gains from Marketing Efficiency

In the 1870s grain moved from the Great Plains farmer to the East Coast consumer in grain sacks. Each time the mode of transportation changed from the farmer's wagon to the train bound to Chicago to the barge bound for New York City, the transfer was made on a human back. This was a very inefficient method for transferring grain, but

FIGURE 17–13
Adjustment to a
primary demand shift.

it was the only one available. Grain was moved and traded one sack at a time. Then some genius came up with a revolutionary idea that resulted in the development of grain elevators that allowed grain to flow in a continuous stream like a liquid.

The development of the grain elevator eliminated the need for expensive sacks and eliminated the backbreaking labor of off-loading and reloading individual sacks. This greatly reduced the marketing costs associated with grain handling. When the costs of providing a certain market function are reduced, we say that **marketing efficiency** has increased.

Now let's look at the impact of increased marketing efficiency. As a tangible, more recent example let's examine the impact of the development of the interstate highway system on the marketing of fresh vegetables. Since most fresh vegetables are shipped by refrigerated truck, anything that reduces transport costs increases the efficiency of the marketing system. Who stands to gain from increased efficiency of the marketing system?

Figure 17–14 illustrates the impact of a more efficient (less costly) marketing system. The primary supply and demand in the diagram are the same as in Figure 17–11, which was drawn with a marketing margin of $1.00 per unit. The derived farm level demand and retail level supply associated with a $1.00 marketing margin are shown as faded dashed lines in Figure 17–14. The prior equilibria at 30 units and prices of $2.00 at the farm level and $3.00 at the retail level are shown as faded circles. Figure 17–14 is drawn with a more efficient marketing system that has reduced the marketing margin to $0.50 per unit. The change in marketing efficiency, *ceteris paribus*, will have no impact on the primary supply and demand but will shift both the derived farm level demand and the derived retail level supply, shown as solid lines. The new equilibria at both market levels are indicated with solid circles.

At the new equilibria, 33 units are being traded at a farm level price of $2.20 and a retail price of $2.70. The difference between the two prices, $0.50, is the marketing margin. Now let's look at the impact of the interstate highway system on farmers. Compared with the old marketing system, farmers are selling more product at higher prices: they are better off. How about consumers? They are consuming more at lower prices: they are better off. So who benefits from increased marketing efficiency? Both consumers and producers are better off.

Marketing efficiency
a measure of the costs of performing marketing tasks. The lower the costs, *ceteris paribus*, the greater the efficiency.

FIGURE 17–14
Increased marketing
efficiency.

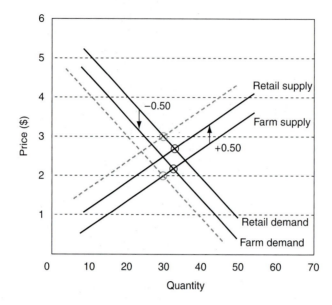

So investments that result in a more efficient marketing system—like the interstate highway system, improved market information, and containerized freight—result in a true win-win situation in which everybody is better off. A few jobs among the middlemen in the marketing system may be lost, but that is a small price to pay for efficient marketing.

Elasticity by Market Level

We have seen that our concept of market equilibrium takes on a new and more complex meaning when we begin to examine the different market levels that exist for any given product. Equilibrium may well exist at the retail level at the same time disequilibrium reigns at the farm level. Inventory adjustments along the marketing chain will eventually return the entire marketing system back to a global equilibrium.

Elasticities by market level in any given market for any given commodity, the elasticities of supply and demand will always be more inelastic at the farm level than at the retail level.

The concept of elasticity also becomes more complex when we look at different market levels. When we look at market **elasticities by market level,** we find that what previously was a straightforward concept becomes a multidimensional concept with very interesting consequences. Because the marketing margin drives a price wedge between retail prices and farm prices, we find that the elasticity of demand (and supply) at the retail level is different from the farm level.

Consider the situation in Figure 17–15. Here we have a retail level demand curve and a derived farm level demand curve. The marketing margin is $30. Using the mid-point conventions, calculate the arc elasticity between 5 and 15 units of output. As shown, the absolute value of the retail level elasticity is greater than the farm level because the midpoint prices are different ($55 versus $25). Because the farm level elasticity coefficient is numerically smaller (i.e., closer to zero) than the retail level coefficient, we conclude that demand at the farm level is more inelastic than at the retail level.

The meaning of this finding can be seen in Figure 17–15. Consider what it takes to bring about a quantity change from 5 to 15 units. At the retail level an 18 percent (10/55 as a percentage) change in price was needed to bring about the

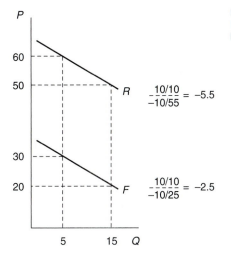

FIGURE 17–15
Elasticity by market level.

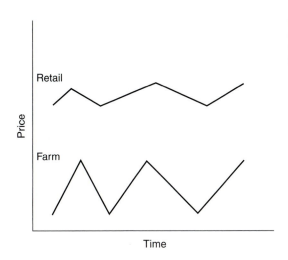

FIGURE 17–16
Implications of different elasticities at different market levels.

quantity change. By comparison, at the farm level a 40 percent change in price was necessary to bring about the same quantity change. Small price adjustments at the retail level produce much larger price adjustments at the farm level.

As shown in Figure 17–16 small price variations at the retail level become very substantial price variations at the farm level. This explains why the supermarket shopper may notice that hamburger was down by $0.20 per pound and then see an evening news story about ranchers losing $50 a head on their herds.

The same is also true for the elasticity of supply: it is more inelastic at the farm level than at the retail level. The combination of relatively inelastic supply and demand at the farm level compared with the retail level ensures the kind of price variability shown in Figure 17–16. And the greater the marketing margin, the more removed farm level prices are from retail prices. In 1999, an $0.89 retail loaf of bread contained slightly less than $0.04 of wheat. If the price of wheat were to double, the cost of the loaf of bread would increase to $0.93. A 100 percent increase in wheat prices would lead to a 4.5 percent change in retail bread prices. Thus, it is easy to see why farmers moan and groan (or whoop it up) while retail consumers hardly notice a change.

FOOD MARKET REGULATIONS

When consumer surveys are conducted, one concern that comes through repeatedly is food safety. From *E-coli* to mad cow disease, consumers are very worried about the safety of the food they eat. This is hardly a new phenomenon. Public interest in meat inspection was galvanized by the publication of Upton Sinclair's *The Jungle* in 1906, which described the conditions in Chicago packing houses (see box).

The public uproar following the publication of *The Jungle* led Congress in 1906 to pass the Meat Inspection Act and the Pure Food and Drug Act. Together, these acts gave the U.S. Department of Agriculture the responsibility for ensuring food safety. Since those seminal acts, there has been general agreement, reinforced with repeated legislative acts, that the federal government has a responsibility to ensure the safety of our food. As one observer pointed out, this is one of the few areas in which there seems to be broad public support for more government rather than less.

> *"There would be meat stored in great piles in rooms; and the water from leaky roofs would drip over it, and thousands of rats would race about on it. It was too dark in the storage places to see well, but a man could run his hand over these piles of meat and sweep up handfuls of the dried dung of rats. These rats were nuisances, and the packers would put poisoned bread out for them; they would die, and then rats, bread and meat would go into the [sausage] hoppers together." (Upton Sinclair,* The Jungle, *New York: Doubleday, Page & Co., 1906)*

Today most food processing is subject to some sort of inspection by a federal agency. The standards and procedures change over time, but the basic idea that food processors and providers should be inspected periodically is well established.

In 1962 another blockbuster book was published: Rachel Carson's *Silent Spring* (see box). In it she argued that as a result of the increasing use of insecticides (primarily DDT), we were slowly poisoning our ecosystem and, as the poisons moved up the food chain, we were slowly poisoning ourselves. It was a moving book whose message was made even more poignant by the death of Ms. Carson in 1964: the cause of death was cancer.

> *"There was a strange stillness. The birds, for example—where had they gone? Many people spoke of them, puzzled and disturbed. The feeding stations in the backyards were deserted. The few birds seen anywhere were moribund; they trembled violently and could not fly. It was a spring without voices. On the mornings that had once throbbed with the dawn chorus of robins, catbirds, doves, jays, wrens, and scores of other bird voices there was now no sound; only silence lay over the fields and woods and marsh."* [*Excerpt from* Silent Spring *by Rachel Carson. Copyright (c) 1962 by Rachel L. Carson, renewed 1990 by Roger Christie. Reprinted by permission of Houghton Mifflin Co. All rights reserved.*]

As a result of the issues raised in *Silent Spring,* Congress created the Environmental Protection Agency (EPA) and passed the Federal Insecticide, Fungicide and Rodenticide Act (FIFRA) in 1972. FIFRA gave the EPA the power to regulate the chemicals that farmers use on their crops based on the toxicity of those chemicals. Since then there has been an ongoing conflict between consumers, farmers, and the chemical companies. Consumers have zero tolerance and want to be assured that they will not be exposed to any known carcinogens even though many foods, such as peanut butter, have minute quantities of known carcinogens in them naturally. Farmers want access to the most effective chemicals possible and freedom from the oppressive rules and regulations of the EPA. Chemical companies complain that they must spend millions of dollars to get a chemical registered with the EPA for an approved use.

The most recent manifestation of federal regulation of chemical use in food crops is the 1996 Food Quality Protection Act (FQPA). At the time of its passage the FQPA was generally praised by all parties as a reasonable compromise.

SUMMARY

Food marketing refers to all the activities that occur between the producer (farmer, rancher, and so on) and the consumer of our food. Farm service marketing refers to the provision of inputs to producers. Firms engaged in marketing activities are known collectively as agribusinesses.

Marketing creates utility. The most important utilities created are time, place, form, and possession. Additional functional utilities are grades and standards, financing, risk bearing, and information. The creation of these utilities involve costs that become a part of the value of an item as it moves through the marketing chain.

There are several ways to approach the study of marketing: functional, institutional, market level, and commodity. Each approach has strengths and weaknesses.

The food bill refers to total expenditures on food by final consumers. The food bill as a percentage of disposable family income has steadily declined over the years and is currently about 10.2 percent. Almost half of the total food bill is for food prepared away from the home. The marketing bill is that portion of the food bill that pays for marketing costs rather than for agricultural commodities. Currently the marketing bill is 81 percent of the food bill, and it is increasing over time. About half of the marketing bill is for labor expenses. The marketing bill varies substantially among food products depending on how much utility has been added in the marketing process.

Five marketing levels can be identified: assembling, commodity processing, food processing, distributing, and retailing. Important trends in the food marketing system include consolidation among retailers, vertical integration of market levels, and the industrialization of food products.

A marketing margin is the difference in the value of a commodity at different marketing levels. Demand originates at the level of the consumer, while supply originates at the level of the producer. Subtracting the marketing margin from consumer demand gives farm level demand. Adding the marketing margin to farm supply gives retail supply. Market equilibrium and adjustment occur at both the farm level and the retail level.

Increasing marketing efficiency—that is, lowering marketing costs—is a win-win situation in which both producers and consumers are made better off.

Both supply and demand are more inelastic at the farm level than at the retail level. As a consequence, larger price adjustments are necessary at the farm level than at the retail level to bring about a given quantity adjustment.

Food safety is a major consumer concern. The first federal food marketing regulations went into effect in the early 1900s. Most aspects of food processing and marketing have been tightly regulated by state and federal requirements since then. It was not until the early 1970s that food producers were made subject to federal regulations.

KEY TERMS

Agribusiness
Assembly
Away from home
Commodity approach
Commodity processors
Derived farm level demand
Derived retail level supply
Distributors
Elasticities by market level
Farm service marketing
Farm share
Food bill
Food marketing
Food marketing bill
Food processors
Form utility

Functional approach
Grades and standards
Grain elevator
Industrialization
Institutional approach
Market level approach
Marketing efficiency
Marketing margin
Physical risk
Place utility
Possession utility
Price risk
Retailers
Time utility
Vertical integration

PROBLEMS AND DISCUSSION QUESTIONS

1. A good way to discover the new trends in the food retailing business is through a trade publication called *Progressive Grocer.* This monthly publication designed to be read by store managers features a "Store of the Month" in each issue. Stop by the library and read about this month's cutting edge store.

2. The consumer deals with only one marketing system, but the farmer/rancher/producer must deal with two marketing systems. Explain.

3. Identify the marketing utilities you purchase when you buy a bag of potato chips.

4. Companies involved in food marketing are often derisively called "middlemen". In almost every society there is a belief that the "middleman gets all the profit."

   a. Why do people believe this?

   b. Get on the internet, and go to the financial information available on most portals to get sales and profit (called earnings or net earnings) for Kroger, the largest food retailer in the United States. Kroger's stock symbol is KR. For the latest quarter or latest year calculate Kroger's profit as a percentage of sales. (On **yahoo.com,** you would click on "Yahoo! Finance" on the homepage, then enter KR in the "get quotes" box, and then click on "profile" when the stock price of KR is returned. That will take you to a page of information about Kroger and financial results of Kroger. In Yahoo, sales and earnings are both reported on a per share basis, so you would calculate the profit ratio using these figures.)

   c. If the middleman gets all the profit, why don't we hear 10-year-olds saying they want to be a middleman when they grow up?

5. As shown in Figure 17–7 the marketing bill has consistently grown over the past 50 years. What are some of the factors that have led to this growth?

6. Give some examples of vertical integration in the food marketing system.

7. The diagram to the right shows the primary supply and demand curves for a firm. Using a constant marketing margin, draw the derived demand and derived supply curves and show where the market clears at both the retail and farm levels.

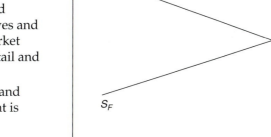

8. The retail level demand function for eggplant is

$$Q = 100 - 3P$$

Where Q = quantity demanded and P = price. There is a 30-cent marketing margin, so the farm level demand is

$$Q = 70 - 3P$$

Calculate the arc elasticity of demand between 10 and 15 units at the retail and farm levels. For which is demand more inelastic?

Futures Markets

Cash markets
markets in which delivery is expected immediately upon payment.

*I*n ordinary markets, frequently called **cash markets,** the buyer and seller mutually agree on a price. Then cash and the goods are exchanged, and the transaction is completed. Supermarkets, drugstores, a farmer buying fence repair materials, and cattle auctions are examples of cash markets. Farmers, operating in conditions of near perfect competition, are subject to the vagaries of extreme price variation in cash markets for both their purchases and their sales. For instance, a feedlot operator is a major buyer of corn, feeder cattle, and soybean meal, and a seller of fat cattle. At the time a feedlot operator puts a load of cattle into the lot, she can pretty well identify all the costs of feeding the cattle to slaughter, but the revenue side is hard to manage because the sale of the animals is still 6 months off and almost anything can happen to cattle prices over a 6-month period. In order to assist farmers in dealing with the extreme price risks they face, an alternative to cash markets, called **futures markets,** has evolved for agricultural commodities.

Futures markets
markets in which price is agreed upon now and delivery is specified for a future point in time.

Long ago, futures markets existed only for agricultural commodities, but over time futures markets have evolved for a variety of commodities such as lumber, gold, copper, and crude oil. More recently futures markets have been developed for a variety of financial instruments such as Treasury bonds, foreign exchange, and stock market indexes. While the basic concepts and operations in all futures markets are essentially alike, this chapter will concentrate only on agricultural futures markets.

FORWARD PRICING

Risk management
the managerial responsibility for maintaining the risk exposure of the firm at acceptable levels.

Faced with the price risks inherent in agriculture, many farmers have sought a means of shifting price risk to someone else such that the farmer can earn his keep as a producer rather than as a price speculator. It doesn't take many experiences of toiling for a year for a crop only to find cash prices are less than costs of production to convince farmers that **risk management** is important.

Forward price an agreement today on the price that will be paid for the delivery of a commodity at some future date.

In an effort to attract business and to make a buck, some enterprising grain buyers started offering farmers a **forward price** for their expected crop.[1] That is, at planting time the eventual buyer of the crop and the farmer would agree on a price to be received at harvest time. If cash prices are low at harvest time, then the farmer will be pleased he used forward pricing, and if the cash price is high at harvest time, the buyer will be pleased he used forward pricing. Basically a forward price shifts

---

[1] In the examples that follow in this section the use of forward pricing of a typical farmer's output is reviewed. Farmers may also use forward pricing to minimize price risk of purchased inputs.

the risk of price changes from the producer to the buyer and assures the farmer of a price that will cover the costs of production with a reasonable rate of return.[2]

Today forward pricing is fairly common in the midwest where local grain buyers will provide their customers with forward prices for corn, wheat, soybeans, and the like. The forward prices are offered as a service to the buyer's customers in an effort to lock up the farmer's business. Since, like the farmer, the grain buyer really doesn't want to accept the price risk, he will usually shift that risk to someone else through the use of futures markets. In such cases, the grain buyer is nothing more than a service bureau for futures markets for those farmers who lack either the sophistication or the will to use futures markets directly.

Forward pricing has evolved in some cases to **contract farming.** In contract farming, the farmer signs a contract (frequently multiyear) with the buyer before planting, stipulating exactly what will be produced, how it will be produced, and what price will be paid for the product. For example, anyone who has ever tried to cook okra knows that different varieties of okra cook differently. That variation is something that large commercial processors like Campbell Soup won't tolerate. To provide product uniformity, Campbell Soup contracts for its okra with farmers in south Georgia. The contracts specify the exact variety to be grown, what and when pesticides may be applied, and a variety of other stipulations. The price that will be paid is set in the contract along with penalties for delivering okra that doesn't meet contract specifications. In essence the farmer becomes a piece-rate employee of Campbell Soup. By producing on a contract, the farmer eliminates the price risk that is inherent in producing okra for the cash market.

The crucial point here is that a farmer today is not only a production manager but a risk manager as well. There are two kinds of risk inherent in agriculture—physical risk of losing the crop and price risk associated with buying or selling at unfavorable prices. Physical risk is something common to home owners, boat owners, and farmers. This risk is typically managed with casualty insurance covering the possibility of physical loss of the home, boat, or crop. Physical risk management through the use of insurance is usually considered to be very prudent management. In essence, the risk of physical loss is shifted from the owner of the property to the insurance company.

The techniques for managing the other kind of risk—the risk of price variability—are less well known than insurance because most home owners and boat owners don't face the same kind of price variability that farmers face. Both forward pricing and contract farming are techniques for managing price variability risk. Both are techniques for shifting price variability risk from the farmer to another party—the potential buyer in the case of forward pricing or the processor in the case of contract farming. A third price risk management technique that is available to the farmer (and to processors, handlers, and so forth) is the use of futures markets. As in the case of insurance, futures markets bring together parties seeking to avoid risk and parties willing to accept risk.

Contract farming
farmers producing to the specifications of a contract with the buyer, rather than relying on the dictates of the market.

---

[2] The use of forward prices does not automatically assure the farmer of a profit, but presumably a farmer would not accept a forward price that did not at least cover the expected costs of production. Also, while forward prices do eliminate most price risks, they do nothing about physical risks including weather risks.

FUTURES MARKETS

Futures contract a standardized contract created by and traded on a futures exchange that calls on one party to make delivery of a specified good on a specified date and the other party to accept delivery of the same good on the same date at a price that is agreed upon now.

Futures exchange a commercial market-place designed to create and trade futures contracts. Also called futures markets.

Speculator a trader on a futures exchange who attempts to buy low and sell high with no intention of ever taking or having physical possession of the commodity.

Hedger a trader on a futures exchange who uses futures contracts to significantly reduce the price risk inherent in cash markets.

Pit the location on the floor of a futures exchange where a specific commodity is traded.

A **futures contract** is a standardized contract that is traded on a **futures exchange** that created the contract. Traders buy and sell futures contracts with either of two intentions. The **speculator** is an individual who hopes to profit by accepting the risks associated with price variations. In the case of physical risk, the fire insurance company is a speculator that bets your house won't burn down. A **hedger** is an individual who wants to be rid of price risk. The transfer of price risk from hedger to speculator creates a market for futures contracts. These basic notions are explored below.

Exchanges

Futures contracts are created by and traded on commodity exchanges. These are commercial companies that have been created (under some government regulation) to facilitate the shifting of price risk from hedger to speculator through the purchase and sale of standardized contracts. When traders buy or sell a futures contract on an exchange, the exchange itself gets a share of the commission on the trade. These commissions are used to finance the operation of the exchange.

The exchanges are marketplaces for futures contracts. In fact, since the exchange both creates and trades the contracts, the exchange is the only marketplace for a given contract. Most large brokerage houses (Merrill Lynch, and so on) will have representatives who are authorized to trade on an exchange. These are the folks you have seen in film and on TV who stand around a circular **pit** and shout wildly at one another while waving their arms. These representatives, called floor traders, buy and sell contracts when orders from the broker's clients come in. For instance, suppose a floor trader gets a call from the home office saying a client wants to buy a contract at a certain price. The floor trader will run to the appropriate pit and shout out his offer to buy in the hope of finding someone with an equal desire to sell. By voice and hand signals the offer is transmitted to all others in the pit. If a trade is completed, both parties (i.e., both floor traders) make note of the agreement and report the results of the trade back to their home offices.

The trading floor of a typical exchange will contain several pits where the actual trades occur. Each pit is assigned a specific commodity, which is traded at that pit only. So at a typical exchange there may be a corn pit and a soybean pit. The pits are a series of circular stairs that lead to the bottom of the pit. By standing on a specific stair of the pit the trader indicates the maturity[3] of the contract he desires to trade. So all the chaos we frequently see on TV has a purpose. The physical location of the floor trader indicates exactly what he[4] desires to trade, and the direction of the palm of the hand indicates whether he wants to buy or sell the specific contract. Fingers are used to indicate the specific price and the number of contracts he is currently offering.

---

[3] Maturities will be discussed in the next section.

[4] The use of the masculine in this case is almost justified. Although a handful of women have become floor traders, the rough-and-tumble of floor trading continues to be almost exclusively masculine. Commodity exchanges are a lot like college football in this respect.

While there are many exchanges in the United States and abroad, the "biggies" for U.S. agricultural commodities are the Chicago Board of Trade (CBT) and the Chicago Mercantile Exchange (CME).[5] Each of these exchanges trade futures contracts in those commodities that are indigenous to midwestern agriculture. The CBT concentrates on grains and oilseeds, while the CME deals with livestock futures.

It is important to emphasize that what is traded on exchanges are futures contracts, not commodities. These contracts are promises to do something in the future. These contracts, like any other contract, are legally binding promises. If you fail to fulfill your promise, you are liable to be sued. These promises pertain to the exchange of a particular commodity at a future point in time. The commodity is not traded on the exchanges. What is traded are promises to exchange a commodity in the future. Futures markets are trading places for promises, not commodities.

Futures Contracts

A futures contract is a standardized contract created by the exchange on which it is traded. It is standardized because the exchange specifies all terms of the contract except price. All contracts for a given commodity and a given maturity date will be the same, except for the price. The contract is a promise either to make delivery of a commodity to the exchange or to accept delivery of a commodity from the exchange. When a trader **sells a contract,** that trader is making a contractual commitment to *make delivery* of a specified commodity to the exchange's warehouse at a specified time. The price that the trader will receive upon delivery of the commodity is determined at the time the contract is established on the floor of the exchange. That is, the interaction between buyer and seller on the floor of the exchange determines what price will be received upon delivery. When a trader **buys a contract,** that trader is making a contractual commitment to *accept delivery* of a specified commodity at the exchange's warehouse at a specified time. The specified time at which the exchange of the commodity is to occur is called the **maturity** of the contract. The maturity date is the contractual make delivery/accept delivery date.

> **Sell a contract** the seller of a futures contract agrees to make delivery of a specified commodity on a specified future date at a price agreed upon today.

> **Buy a contract** the buyer of a futures contract agrees to accept delivery of a specified commodity on a specified future date at a price agreed upon today.

> **Maturity** the date at which time a futures contract specifies the commodity is to be physically exchanged between the buyer and seller of the contract.

Opening a Contract

Before getting lost in the complexity of specific contracts, let's take a look at the relationship between buyer, seller, and the exchange. The buyer wants to accept delivery of a commodity at some future point in time at a price agreed upon now. The seller wants to make delivery of a commodity at some future point in time at a price agreed upon now. The exchange brings the two together and lets them decide on a mutually agreeable price. Once a price is agreed on, the exchange then enters into a separate contract with each of the two parties. The exchange agrees to accept delivery from the seller and to make delivery to the buyer. Hence, the exchange is in

---

[5] A recent issue of *The Wall Street Journal* included price quotes from the CBT and CME as well as the following: Coffee, Sugar & Cocoa Exchange, New York; COMEX, New York; New York Cotton Exchange; Deutsche Terminboerse; International Petroleum Exchange; Kansas City Board of Trade; London International Financial Futures Exchange; Marche a Terme International De France; Montreal Exchange; MidAmerica Commodity Exchange; Minneapolis Grain Exchange; New York Mercantile Exchange; Singapore International Monetary Exchange; Sydney Futures Exchange; Toronto Futures Exchange; and the Winnipeg Commodity Exchange.

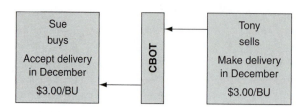

a neutral position having no net obligation in the commodity. The buyer never knows who the seller is, and vice versa, because each sees the contract as being between themselves and the exchange.

When this pair of contracts is created,[6] the exchange is said to **open** another contract. The number of pairs of contracts open at any point in time is called the **open interest.** The size of the open interest for a given commodity is reported daily in the financial sections of many newspapers.

Figure 18–1 illustrates how Sue and Tony can open a contract. Sue, in Atlanta, calls her broker in January and indicates she wants to buy a contract for December delivery of corn. At about the same time, Tony in New York calls his broker and says he wants to sell a contract for December delivery of corn. For the time being, don't worry about *why* they want to take these positions. The floor traders for Sue and Tony are able to agree on a price of $3.00 per bushel. At the time a price is agreed upon, the Chicago Board of Trade creates a pair of contracts. With Sue, the CBT agrees to make a delivery to her and she has agreed to accept delivery. With Tony, the CBT agrees to accept delivery in December and he promises to make delivery. The CBT is in a neutral position because it has promised to accept delivery and make delivery on the same day.

Standardized Contracts

The pair of contracts created are exact mirror images of each other such that there is no chance for a misunderstanding when the delivery time arrives.[7] Since both buyer and seller have contracted with the exchange rather than with each other, any litigation will be between the individual and the exchange. Along with a lot of other minutia, a typical contract to make delivery includes the following items:

- *Commodity.* Exactly what is to be delivered.
- *Quantity.* Exactly how much is to be delivered.
- *Quality.* What the quality specifications are and what the penalties are if the specifications are not met.
- *Delivery date.* At what specific date in the future the delivery is to be made.
- *Delivery location.* Where the delivery must be made. Usually there are several alternative delivery locations.

At any given time, an exchange will typically trade contracts for six to eight different maturity dates for each commodity that stretch out over the next year or two. The specific dates traded are usually related to the seasonality (if any) of the

Open a contract
when a potential buyer and potential seller of a futures contract agree upon a price for future delivery, a contract is created between each party and the futures exchange. To create this contract is to open a contract.

Open interest
number of contracts that have been opened by a futures exchange and that have not yet been closed.

---

[6] The exchange will only deal in pairs of contracts so that its net position is always neutral.

[7] The remainder of this section is written from the "make delivery" perspective. To see the mirror image simply replace the words "make delivery" with "accept delivery."

commodity. For instance, delivery dates on the corn contract are March, May, July, September, and December. The December corn contract usually gets the most scrutiny because it is the first postharvest contract. As one delivery date reaches maturity, trading of that delivery date ends and a new delivery date is opened for trading by the exchange.

The one thing that is not stipulated in the standardized contract is the price at which the make delivery/accept delivery transaction will occur. This price is determined on the floor of the exchange for each pair of contracts. That's what all of the shouting is about. Different pairs of contracts will have different prices based on the ebb and flow of prices on the exchange floor. In general, as cash prices increase, futures prices increase. This point will be discussed further a little later.

Delivery or Closing a Contract

When a buyer and seller agree on a contract price, a new pair of contracts is opened by the exchange. The exchange may create as many contracts as the market will bear. There are two ways the holder of a contract may **close** or extinguish the contract: make delivery/accept delivery of the commodity as specified in the contract, or buy/sell an offsetting (i.e., opposite) contract.

Close a contract to remove or complete the contractual obligations of an open contract.

It is important to remember that what is being traded is not the commodity itself but a contract to make delivery or accept delivery of the commodity in the future. People frequently ask, How can you sell something you don't have? What the seller is selling is a promise—not a commodity. To understand this concept, let's look at an academic analogy. A corrupt professor[8] could easily "sell" the promise to award "buyers" a final grade of A in a particular course. The contract would be made at the beginning of the term, but the actual delivery of the terms of the contract would not be made until the end of the semester.[9] Those students doing poorly during the semester would want the professor to deliver according to the terms of the contract, but those students who are legitimately earning a grade of A in the course would prefer to buy back the contract since they would receive an A anyway. The analogy holds for futures contracts.

The holder of a futures contract may actually make delivery (the seller of a contract) or accept delivery (the buyer of a contract) of the physical commodity as specified in the contract. But because the actual delivery must be made according to all the terms of the contract, most traders find physical delivery to be very inconvenient. In fact, only 2 percent of all open contracts typically result in actual delivery.

The other 98 percent of all open contracts are closed by taking an offsetting position in the same commodity for the same delivery month prior to maturity of the contract. Since all contracts are between the individual and the exchange, the trader wishing to close a position does not have to trade with the same individual with whom the position was opened. And since the exchange only deals with pairs of contracts, it always has a net zero position in the commodity being traded. Suppose a trader opened a position by selling a contract and later wants to close that position by buying a contract. What happens, you may ask, if you can't find someone willing to sell when you want to buy? This is where the natural dynamics of

---

[8] Clearly an oxymoron.
[9] A professor who submitted final grades at the beginning of the semester would probably fall under the scrutiny of an astute registrar.

FIGURE 18–2 Sue and Jim open a contract in June.

FIGURE 18–3 Sue has closed her position.

markets come into play. If you want to buy, rest assured there will be someone, somewhere who will be willing to sell *at a price*. Let's illustrate the closing of a position with an example.

The process of closing a position is illustrated in Figure 18–2. Recall that Sue had opened a position with Tony in January with Sue on the buying side. Now in June, Sue again calls her broker and says she would like to sell a contract for December delivery of corn. At about the same time, Jim in Seattle calls his broker and says he would like to buy a contract for December delivery. The floor traders for Sue and Jim receive the orders and negotiate a deal at the prevailing price of $3.50 per bushel. As before, the Chicago Board of Trade creates a pair of contracts, one between the CBT and the buyer, and the other between the CBT and the seller.

For an instant, Sue has two contracts with the CBT: one as a buyer and one as a seller. The CBT sees that she no longer has an open position with it, and her position is closed as shown in Figure 18–3. Sue no longer has any obligations to the CBT. The CBT now has one pair of contracts outstanding—one with Tony as a seller, and the other with Jim as the buyer. The net position of the CBT is still neutral.

Now we can start to deal with the question of *why* Sue did what she did. Note on Figure 18–2 that in January Sue bought a contract at $3.00/bushel and in June she sold a contract for $3.50/bushel. Sue gets to keep the $0.50/bushel difference between the buy and sell prices. And since the contract was for 5,000 bushels of corn, she gets a cool $2,500. As with most markets, if you can consistently buy low and sell high, you are going to make some money. Sue was astute (or lucky) and earned a profit on her trade as a result.

Arbitrage

Arbitrage has been around for as long as man has exchanged goods. Arbitrage simply means the buying and selling of a good in two different markets to take advantage of price differences between the markets. The arbitrager buys commodities in a cheap market and sells them in a high market, pocketing the difference. For example, in the days after hurricane Andrew demolished the south side of Miami, there were a number of enterprising arbitragers who drove to Ft. Lauderdale and bought ice at convenience stores at the usual $1.00/bag price and then drove it to Miami where they could sell it for $3.00/bag. This is a classic example of simple arbitrage.

Arbitrage is at work in grain markets also. If cash corn (i.e., corn for immediate delivery) is $3.00/bushel in western Iowa and $2.50/bushel in Peoria, Illinois, and the shipping cost from Peoria to Iowa is $0.30/bushel, then anyone with a truck can figure out what to do. Buy corn in Peoria for $2.50, truck it to Iowa, and sell it for $3.00 and pocket $0.20 per bushel in profit from the trade. This is an example of **spatial arbitrage.** Notice the effect of the action of the arbitragers. By increasing the buying in the Peoria market, they will tend to drive the price up in Peoria, and by bringing additional grain into the Iowa market, they will tend to drive prices down there. Once the two prices return to a "normal" spread of $0.30 (reflecting the shipping costs), then the arbitragers will cease to operate.

Another kind of arbitrage with particular application to futures markets is **temporal arbitrage.** When prices at two points in time differ by more than the storage cost, the arbitragers can profit by buying at the cheap point in time and selling at the expensive point in time. If futures prices today are significantly higher than today's cash price plus the storage costs to maturity, then arbitragers can earn a profit by buying cash grain today and selling a futures contract today—buying cheap and selling dear.[10]

Notice that the arbitrager takes very little risk since a single commodity is simultaneously bought and sold in two different markets separated by either space or time. The economic role of the arbitrager is extremely important because the arbitrager, operating in his or her own self-interest, keeps prices in spatially or temporally separated markets efficient. That is, the arbitragers will force price differences in different markets to the smallest difference possible—a difference that reflects the true cost differences between the two markets.

Arbitrage the practice of simultaneously buying and selling of a single prodct on two different markets to profit from the price differential between the two markets.

Spatial arbitrage arbitrage in which the two markets traded are in different physical locations.

Temporal arbitrage arbitrage in which the two markets traded are separated by time.

Futures Contract Prices

Now is the appropriate time to ask, What determines the price of futures contracts? Why was the contract Sue bought in January priced at $3.00/bushel and the one she sold in June at $3.50/bushel? As shown in Figure 18–4, for a storable commodity like corn the price of a futures contract at any point in time will approximate the current cash price of the commodity plus the storage cost of the commodity until maturity of the contract. The logic behind this statement is rather straightforward. If the January price of a futures contract were significantly above the current cash price plus storage costs, then arbitragers would buy the commodity, store it, and then deliver in December. That is, arbitrage will ensure the

---

[10] This chapter deals only with storable commodities. The economics of futures contracts for nonstorable commodities is a little more complex.

FIGURE 18–4
Determination of
futures contract prices.

Cash Price in January

Plus

Storage Costs between January and December

Equals

Price in January of a Futures Contract with a December Delivery Date

close approximation to the pricing pattern shown in Figure 18–4. If the cost of storage is $0.02 per bushel per month, then the 11-month storage cost from mid-January to mid-December would be $0.22/bushel. Thus, the current cash price in January (when Sue bought her contract) must have been about $2.78/bushel.

Since the price of a futures contract is equal to the current cash price (which varies considerably from day to day) plus the storage costs (which do not vary on a daily basis but do decrease as the storage time decreases), it follows that prices of futures contracts and cash prices change in a tandem or parallel fashion. That is, if cash prices increase, then it follows that futures contract prices will also increase.

Basis of Futures Contracts

A very important concept in futures markets is the concept of *basis*. The basis of any futures contract is simply the difference between the current price of a contract and the current cash price of a commodity. In the case of corn contracts the basis will be equal to the storage costs if futures markets are operating efficiently.[11] And since storage costs are highly stable and predictable, the basis is also predictable. This leads to a very important rule for futures markets: for a storable commodity, as a futures contract moves nearer to maturity, the basis of the contract will fall, reaching close to zero at maturity. The relationship between cash and futures contract prices is illustrated in Figure 18–5. The two important things to note in Figure 18–5 are that:

- Futures contract prices and cash prices move in tandem.
- As a contract moves towards maturity, the basis moves towards zero.

The predictability of these two characteristics is the foundation upon which hedging is based. Their importance will become obvious in the examples that follow.

---

[11] Most research on the efficiency of futures markets suggests that they are efficient where efficiency is a measure of how close futures prices are to the model shown in Figure 18–5. For some commodities that are not storable and/or that are not traded heavily, there is an increased risk that the basis may not behave in a predictable or efficient manner.

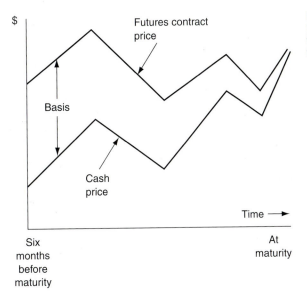

FIGURE 18–5
Behavior of cash and futures prices over time.

Speculators

As indicated earlier, futures markets bring together those individuals who want to avoid price risk, called hedgers, and those who are willing to accept price risk, called speculators. A speculator is an individual who embraces risk and hopes to profit thereby. The speculator is to price risk what the insurance company is to physical risk.[12] The speculator buys or sells a futures contract not because he wants to make or accept delivery of a commodity but because he expects the price of the futures contract to either go up or go down. If the speculator thinks the price of a futures contract is going to go down,[13] then the speculator would sell a futures contract today in the hope of being able to buy it back in several months at a lower price. The difference between the sell price and the buy price would be profit for the speculator. However, if the speculator thinks the price of the commodity (and hence the price of a futures contract) is going to go up, then he would buy a futures contract now in the hope of selling it for a profit at a later point in time.

If the expectations of the speculator with regard to the direction of price change turn out to be incorrect, then the speculator suffers losses instead of profits. The speculator accepts the risks inherent in price variability in the hope of making a profit from that variability.

Let's take a look at a common speculative strategy to illustrate the behavior of the speculator. Ruth is a successful neurosurgeon in Atlanta who has more money than she knows what to do with. But as human nature would have it, she

---

[12] Lloyd's of London is best known as an insurer of cargo ships. What it does is sell annual loss policies on 100 ships for $1 million per policy in the hope that only one ship worth $75 million goes down during the year. In that case, Lloyd's has earned a cool $25 million for the year. However, if two go down, Lloyd's is out $50 million (minus the interest earned on the policy premiums prior to paying for the losses).

[13] Remember that what would make the price of a futures contract go down is a decrease in the price of the underlying commodity.

wants more. She calls her broker, and he suggests she look at FCOJ futures contracts as part of her investment portfolio. A prudent investor, she does some homework and learns that FCOJ is frozen concentrated orange juice and that FCOJ
futures contracts are traded on the New York Cotton Exchange. Each contract calls
for the exchange of 15,000 pounds of what are known as "solids" in the FCOJ business.[14] Ruth was an intern in the Orlando area, and she recalls that during the 1980s
the Florida citrus industry was hit with three substantial freezes.[15] In her further
research she finds that following each of the three freezes the cash price of FCOJ
(and hence the futures contract price of FCOJ) jumped by an average of 50 percent.

With this knowledge in hand she adopts the following strategy: each year on
December 1 she buys 10 FCOJ futures contracts with a March delivery date and
then prays for a freeze in Florida. If a freeze hits, she sells for a 50 percent profit following the freeze. If no freeze hits, she sells in mid-February to close her position.
If no freeze hits, the price may have gone up or down by 10 percent—a risk she is
willing to accept.

Notice that in this example the speculator buys a position with no intention
whatsoever of taking actual delivery of the commodity. The last thing in the world
a neurosurgeon wants sitting in her office is 150,000 pounds of FCOJ slowly thaw-
ing! The speculator is in the market solely in search of making a profit as a result
of price variability.

Hedgers

While speculators are the risk takers in futures markets, the hedger is a risk averter.
The hedger comes into futures markets to "buy insurance" to protect against the risk
of price variations. Just how this is done will be illustrated later with two examples:
what is important at this point is to realize *why* the hedger is using futures markets.

One of the distinguishing, inherent characteristics of agriculture is a high degree of price variability. An example of this is illustrated in Figure 18–6, which
shows March (harvest time) prices for Valencia (the most common variety) oranges
in Florida. In 1990 producers had a windfall with prices above $13.00/box only to
be followed 3 years later with prices below $2.00/box.[16] Over this period of time
there was no substantial change in the costs of production, which are about
$4.00/box, so producers went from pure economic profits in 1990 to substantial
economic losses in 1993. Because the citrus industry is characterized by very high
fixed costs relative to the variable costs, producers continued to produce in 1993,
accepting a price of $1.80/box as being better than nothing. At least their variable
costs of production were covered.

How can producers avoid, or at least reduce, the violent kinds of price
swings illustrated in Figure 18–6? As indicated previously, a producer can use forward prices or contracts with processors or purchasing cooperatives, or the pro-

[14] Roughly speaking, 1 pound of solids will produce 1 gallon of orange juice, so one FCOJ
contract is for 15,000 gallons of juice or 300,000 6-ounce servings.

[15] Most citrus in Florida is harvested in the Thanksgiving to Easter period. Most freezes occur
in the mid-December to mid-February period. If the temperature in a grove falls to 28° F or below for
a period of more than 4 hours, the fruit on a citrus tree will freeze and the fruit becomes worthless.
Longer/deeper freezes will destroy not only the fruit but also the tree itself.

[16] A box of Florida oranges is defined as 90 pounds. While yields vary from year to year, one
box will typically yield about 6 pounds of solids or approximately 6 gallons of juice.

Year	March Price
1989	$6.05
1990	13.15
1991	8.40
1992	6.10
1993	1.80
1994	3.95
1995	4.10
1996	5.15
1997	4.20
1998	4.00
1999	8.90
2000	5.55
2001	4.10

FIGURE 18–6 Florida Valencia orange prices.

Prices are on-tree price per box for fresh use. Source: Citrus Summary, 2000–2001 *(and prior issues), Florida Agricultural Statistics Service.*

ducer can enter futures markets directly. A Florida producer may look at the data in Figure 18–6 and note that the 5-year average price from 1997–2001 has been $5.35/box. If the producer knows his production costs are $4.00/box, he would probably be very happy to accept a 5-year production contract with a packer at a fixed price of $5.35/box. This would assure the producer of a return on his investment of $1.35/box over the next 5 years with absolutely no risk of price variability to the producer. In effect, the producer would shift the price risk to the packer who made the contract. From the perspective of the producer, contracts totally eliminate price risk, assuming that the producer had a good lawyer draw up the contract with no loopholes for the packer to crawl through if the market price should fall to $2.00/box.

Hedging Example: A Citrus Producer

The use of futures contracts by the producer cannot eliminate risk to the extent that production contracts can, but futures contracts can be used to avoid most price risks. Let's look at an example of how an orange grove owner, Sam, can use futures markets to substantially reduce the price risk he faces. Suppose it is March. Sam has just finished a harvest and is looking forward to the next year. He logs onto the Internet and notes that the closing price yesterday on a FCOJ futures contract that matures next January (when he will begin the harvest) is quoted at $0.80 per pound solids. He uses a rule of thumb of 6 pounds of solids per box, which means the futures contract is trading at approximately $4.80 per box. Knowing his production costs are approximately $4.00/box, Sam would be perfectly happy if he could receive $4.80/box for his crop next year. The problem is that he is still 9 months away from harvest, and anything could happen to prices between March and January.[17]

---

[17] A bumper crop in Brazil (where the harvest is from June to August) could drive prices down or a freeze in December could drive them up.

Opening the Hedge   In March Sam could hedge or lock in a price of $0.80 per pound solids by *selling* January futures contracts equal to the amount of his expected production.[18] Remember that by "selling" futures contracts he is not really selling anything in the normal sense. Instead, on this March day he is making a commitment to make delivery of FCOJ in January in accord with the terms of the FCOJ contract at the agreed on price of $0.80 per pound solids. By selling contracts in March Sam has assured himself a price of $0.80/pound solids regardless of what the market price turns out to be in January. This is an important part of hedging: once the hedge is **"set" or "opened"**, the hedger is protected from any future variation be it good or bad. The effect of the hedge is to lock in the agreed upon price at the time the futures contracts were opened.

It is important that both the motivation and the operation of the hedge be understood. Sam set his hedge in March to "lock in" a price for his fruit in January of about $4.80/box. He wanted to avoid the risk of the price of fruit falling between March and January. He set the hedge in March by putting himself in a position where he would make opposite trades in January in the two markets—cash and futures. By selling a futures contract in March, he put himself in a position where he would be buying a futures contract in January to close his futures position at the same time he is selling his fruit in the cash market. Since cash and futures prices move in tandem, any losses in one market in January will be covered by gains in the other.

Notice that by selling contracts in March for the delivery of FCOJ in January, Sam is selling something he never intends to have or to be able to actually deliver. He is a grove owner who expects to have fruit in January to deliver to the processor to be made into FCOJ. There being no futures contract on fruit, he trades the FCOJ contract because he knows that the price of fruit and that of FCOJ move in tandem because they are simply at different stages in the food marketing chain. He is certain that if fruit prices fall, FCOJ prices and the price of an FCOJ futures contract will also fall. The success of a hedge depends on these three prices moving in tandem.

Once the hedge is set, Sam can relax. He has "insured" himself against any potential future price variation. While his neighbors are frantically calling produce brokers and carefully following the daily trend of FCOJ and fruit prices, Sam fishes a little and sees his blood pressure fall significantly. Also, he assures his daughter that they will be able to afford her first year at Moo U. because he already knows he is going to be making about $0.80 per box of profit above his costs.

If the price of FCOJ futures contracts in March were $0.67/pound (equivalent to $4.00/box), then Sam would not want to set the hedge because he would be locking in a price at his cost of production.[19] In this case it would be better to remain unhedged ("go naked" in the interesting lingo of futures markets) until such time as futures prices rose above the costs of production or until harvest. Clearly, deciding when to set the hedge is the most difficult part of the hedging strategy. As with all marketing decisions timing is critically important. A hedger who initially sells a contract obviously wants to sell at the highest price possible. Unfortunately, we only know what that is in beautiful hindsight. There are many advanced techniques to help producers decide when to set a hedge, but they are beyond the scope of this chapter.

Set or open a hedge the creation of a hedged position today by buying or selling a futures contract on a commodity that you plan to buy or sell on cash markets in the future.

---

[18] Sam usually averages about 350 boxes/acre or 2,100 pounds of solids per acre. One FCOJ contract is for 15,000 pounds of solids or the production of about 7.15 acres of Sam's groves.

[19] Unless Sam had reason to believe that $4.00 was going to be the best price possible during the season.

Closing the Hedge   In the previous example, Sam hedged by selling a futures contract in March to make delivery of FCOJ in January. Very few futures contracts ever result in actual delivery. In most cases, hedged positions are **closed** out before actual delivery is scheduled. The advantage of closing out the position rather than delivering is primarily a matter of convenience. Sam has oranges, but the contract calls for the delivery of FCOJ. Sam's groves are in Frostproof, and delivery under the contract must be made in Orlando. Sam will harvest from December through March, but the contract calls for all delivery in January. For these and other reasons, Sam will choose to close out his futures contract position and sell his fruit on the cash market.

Using the previous example, let's look at what happens if Sam closes out his futures position in January and sells his fruit on the cash market. In March Sam set the hedge by selling futures contracts at $0.80/pound. In January he *buys* a futures contract to close his open position in the futures market and *sells* his fruit on the cash market. What is the price at which he is able to buy futures contracts to close his position? What is the price at which he can sell his oranges on the cash market? It really doesn't matter. This is illustrated with the examples in Figures 18–7 and 18–8.

Let's look at Figure 18–7 first. In this example it is assumed that the cash price of FCOJ in January is $0.60/pound. Sam sold a futures contract in March for $0.80/pound that he now buys back at $0.60/pound in January. How do we know the price of a contract will be $0.60/pound? Because as the contract nears maturity, the basis (i.e., storage costs) falls to zero and the contract price is equal to the current cash price.[20] Thus, Sam gains $0.20/pound on the futures contract. But he is able to sell his fruit for only the FCOJ equivalent of $0.60/pound,[21] so his total proceeds from gains in the futures market and sales in the cash market are $0.80/pound—the price he "locked in" when he set the hedge in March.

In Figure 18–8 a January cash price for FCOJ of $1.00/pound is assumed. In this case, Sam buys back the futures contract at a price of $1.00/pound in January netting a loss of $0.20/pound on the futures transactions. He then sells his fruit at the going cash price of $6.00/box, equivalent to $1.00/pound for FCOJ, for a total net receipt of $0.80/pound from the two markets. Again, the total receipts in January are exactly equal to the price established by the hedge in March.

As these two examples illustrate, what happens in the cash market after the hedge is placed really doesn't matter to the hedged producer. The net returns from the futures and cash markets will always be equal to the price at which the hedge was placed so long as the actual basis behaves as expected.[22] In one example, Sam was better off because he hedged than he would have been if he had relied strictly on cash markets. In the other example, he was worse off. When placing a hedge there is no way of knowing whether the hedge will make the producer better off or

Close a hedge   to cancel the contractual obligations made when a hedge was opened by buying or selling an offsetting position in futures markets. The closing of a hedge is usually associated with some action in the cash market for the commodity.

---

[20] In reality, the basis will never fall all the way to zero because there will always be costs associated with the physical delivery. For clarity, this small difference is assumed away. Also ignored are the costs of brokers' commissions and the like.

[21] Or $3.60/box using the 6 pounds per box rule of thumb.

[22] The possibility that the basis won't behave as expected is known as "basis risk." The user of futures contracts exchanges price risk for basis risk. Because of effective arbitrage between cash and futures markets, the risk associated with basis is typically much smaller than that associated with prices. The amount of basis risk varies substantially from commodity to commodity. In general, storable commodities have less basis risk than nonstorable commodities. If the basis ever gets out of line from what is expected, arbitragers will come into the market and drive the basis back to a normal level.

FIGURE 18–7 Hedge without physical delivery assuming January cash price of $0.60/lb.

	Futures Market	Cash Market
In March →	Sell futures contract for January delivery @ $0.80/lb	
In January →	Buy futures contract for January delivery @ $0.60/lb	Sell fruit at $0.60/lb
Net Gains/Losses →	$0.20/lb	$0.60/lb

FIGURE 18–8 Hedge without physical delivery assuming January cash price of $1.00/lb.

	Futures Market	Cash Market
In March →	Sell futures contract for January delivery @ $0.80/lb	
In January →	Buy futures contract for January delivery @ $1.00/lb	Sell fruit at $1.00/lb
Net Gains/Losses →	–$0.20/lb	$1.00/lb

worse off than he would have been without a hedge. In this case, Sam enjoyed the comfort of knowing that by placing the hedge in March he had a profit already locked in for the forthcoming harvest. He preferred a sure profit at $0.80/pound (on an FCOJ price basis) rather than the possibility of a large profit at $1.00/pound or a loss at $0.60/pound. By hedging in March Sam was able to shift the risks associated with price variation to someone else on the futures markets.[23]

Hedging Example: A Cattle Feeder

The cattle feeder is in the business of fattening cattle for slaughter. The business essentially involves three steps:

- Buy a lot of 500-pound animals (called "feeder cattle") to place on feed.
- Over a 6-month period buy corn to feed the cattle.
- At the end of 6 months sell the animals at 1,100 pounds (called "fat cattle").

If the cattle feeder is able to sell the animals for more than the costs in the first two steps, then he will earn a profit. The trick, of course, is that the price in the first step is the only price that is known at the time the cattle are placed on feed. If, over the course of 6 months, corn prices rise and fat cattle prices fall, then the feedlot operator will be in a situation where a lot of money is being lost on each animal.

Suppose Doak is a feedlot operator who is trying to decide whether to place a lot of feeder cattle on feed. The feeder cattle will cost him $70/cwt (or $0.70/pound).[24] With a feed conversion rate of 8 pounds of corn for 1 pound of

---

[23] That "someone else" may be a speculator or a large purchaser of FCOJ (such as Coca-Cola) that wants to hedge against the possibility of FCOJ prices going up too much.

[24] Cwt is an abbreviation for hundredweight or 100 pounds. The "c" in cwt is from the Latin word for hundred, which is also the root of "cents" in a dollar and "century."

(+)Sale of fat cattle		
1,100 lb @ $75/cwt	$825	
(−)Cost of feeder cattle		
500 lb @ $70/cwt	350	
(−)Cost of corn		
85 bu @ $2.20/bu	187	
(=)Gross returns per animal	288	
(−)Other costs	200	
(=)Net profit per animal	$ 88	

FIGURE 18–9
Feedlot arithmetic at $2.20/bu for corn and $75/cwt for fat cattle.

(+)Sale of fat cattle		
1,100 lb @ $60/cwt	$660	
(−)Cost of feeder cattle		
500 lb @ $70/cwt	350	
(−)Cost of corn		
85 bu @ $2.40/bu	204	
(=)Gross returns per animal	106	
(−)Other costs	200	
(=)Net profit per animal	−$ 94	

FIGURE 18–10
Feedlot arithmetic at $2.40/bu for corn and $60/cwt for fat cattle.

gain, he can expect to purchase 4,800 pounds or approximately 85 bushels per animal. He plans to buy the feeder cattle in December and sell the fat cattle in June. His noncorn costs of production are $200/animal.[25]

Doak checks the futures prices for corn and fat cattle and finds that a March futures contract for corn is $2.20/bushel and the June contract for fat cattle is $75/cwt.[26] At these prices Doak does a little cowboy arithmetic shown in Figure 18–9 and finds that he can earn a profit of $88 per animal at these prices.

If he can be certain of the prices for corn and fat cattle, then Doak can be certain of a profit per animal of $88. As in the example before, he can "lock in" the corn and fat cattle prices in December by hedging his positions in both markets at the same time as he buys the feeder steers.[27] The reason Doak would want to hedge his positions is that he fears that corn may increase in price, or that fat cattle prices might fall, or worse yet both. As an illustration of the sensitivity of feedlot profits to price variability, Figure 18–10 shows the same arithmetic at $2.40/bushel for corn and $60/cwt for fat cattle, resulting in a loss of $94 per animal fed. Price changes of this magnitude are not uncommon, so Doak certainly wants to hedge both his future costs and his future returns.

---

[25] While corn is the main ingredient in the ration fed to the cattle, there is also some protein supplement and roughage included. In addition, there are the fixed costs of the buildings and equipment.

[26] For the sake of simplicity a March corn contract is being used as a proxy for corn purchases. Obviously Doak will have to buy corn throughout the 6 months, and more sophisticated strategies can be used to spread the risk over the full feeding period.

[27] Note that Doak now has "basis risk" in two different markets, so he certainly is not without risk, but the magnitude of the risk is greatly reduced.

	Futures Market	Cash Market
In December →	1. Sell futures contract for June delivery of fat cattle @ $75/cwt	Buy feeder cattle @ $70/cwt
	2. Buy futures contract for March delivery of corn @ $2.20/bu	
In March →	Sell futures contract for March delivery of corn @ $2.40/bu	Buy corn @ $2.40/bu
In June→	Buy futures contract for June delivery of fat cattle @ $60/cwt	Sell fat cattle @ $60/cwt

Figure 18–11 shows what Doak would do to fully hedge his operation. In December he buys the feeder cattle on the cash market and hedges his future costs and returns. Since he will be buying corn in the cash market in March, he hedges his position by buying March futures contracts in December. The March corn contract has a price of $2.20, so he can hedge the expected purchase and lock in a price of $2.20/bushel. Likewise, he will be selling fat cattle on the cash market in June, so he sells a futures contract at $75/cwt.

As March rolls around, Doak finds that his worst fears have been realized: corn prices have risen to $2.40/bushel. Poor Doak: he has no choice but to pay the market price for corn of $2.40/bushel. But the good news is that he can sell his futures contract to close out his corn position at a profit of $0.20/bushel. So, the cost of the corn plus the profit in the futures markets gives him a net cost for corn of $2.20/bushel—exactly the price he had established when he placed the hedge.

By June Doak is convinced the markets are against him as fat cattle have fallen to $60/cwt. He sells his animals at that price and then buys back his futures position. He had sold this futures contract in December for $75/cwt and now is able to buy it back at only $60/cwt for a nice profit of $15/cwt. Between the cash and the futures markets the net price received for the fat cattle is $75/cwt.[28]

By hedging the prices at which he would have to buy and sell Doak was able to take the profits that the markets were giving him in December and proceed to produce with little fear of price variability. This strategy, with a lot of variations and complications, is used by most feedlot operators today. And if at any particular time the futures prices don't provide a margin of profit that the operator is comfortable with, he will simply leave the feedlot vacant until either feeder prices come down or fat cattle prices go up.

A FINAL WORD

Risk is inherent in agriculture. Weather risk undoubtedly explains why farmers attend places of worship more frequently than the population in general. An alternative approach is to use crop insurance, which is widely available but little used.

---

[28] In this simple illustration it is assumed that the basis goes to zero (it usually won't) and that there are no commissions or other expenses of hedging (there always are).

Most farmers do insure their property and carry insurance against any liabilities that might arise.[29] Forward pricing and futures markets can be used by farmers as a form of "insurance" against the risks of price variability.

Exchanges on which futures contracts are traded bring together those who wish to accept price risk and those who wish to avoid it. The risk acceptors or speculators are willing to accept risk in the hope of high returns on relatively small investments. While the opportunity for reward to the speculator is great, so too is the opportunity for loss.[30] The risk avoiders, or hedgers, seek to establish a price today at which a transaction in the future will occur. To the hedger a bird in the hand is worth two in the bush.

While hedging is a very conservative, risk averse strategy, it is also a strategy that requires a significant amount of managerial oversight. The two most difficult parts of hedging management are knowing when to set the hedge and the willingness to stick with a hedge even when it moves against you.

Knowing when (or even if) to set the hedge is difficult. In hindsight most hedges are not set at the most opportune time, but few of us can use hindsight to view the future. What is important is to realize that a producer who uses hedging is at least making an informed, purposeful judgment in setting prices rather than simply accepting whatever the market dictates at the time of purchase or sale. Which strategy is better: judgment calls or taking whatever the market will give you? For a good manager, judgment is obviously the better choice. In this case good management requires a lot of homework, knowledge of previous price and basis patterns, and a good knowledge of the forces driving prices in the current market. Sam, the citrus producer, should be just as interested in rainfall and freezes in Sao Paulo as he is in his own grove in Frostproof for he realizes that the market price for his oranges next spring will be strongly influenced by the crop this summer in Brazil.

Sticking with a hedge can sometimes be very difficult. Let's go back to our example of Sam the citrus producer. In March he set a hedge at $0.80/pound by selling futures contracts. Suppose during the summer it is revealed that the Brazilian crop was much smaller than expected. This would drive world prices of FCOJ up, which would also drive up the price of the futures contracts Sam sold in March. Rising prices work against Sam in two ways. First, as the price of the contract increases, he is suffering paper losses on his contracts that he will have to buy back at a higher price than he sold them. Second, he has locked in a price of $0.80/pound but now faces the prospect of a significantly higher cash price than what he initially locked in with his March trade. As prices increase during August and September based on the news from Brazil, Sam may be tempted to remove the hedge, take

---

[29] In some midwestern states a farmer can be sued by a motorist for damages caused to an automobile that runs into livestock on a highway.

[30] Speculators on futures contracts should live by the same rules as gamblers in Vegas: (1) if you don't know what you are doing, don't do it; and (2) if you don't have it to lose, don't bet it. In fact, futures markets are more dangerous than Vegas. In Vegas, if you wager a dollar, the most you can lose is that dollar. In futures markets, if you gamble one dollar, you may lose five or ten dollars. This is because most speculators buy and sell contracts on "margin." This means that the buyer/seller of a contract does not have to put up the full value of the contract when it is opened, but instead just a portion of the value of the contract. For instance, in the 1970s there was a futures contract for Mexican pesos. The number of pesos in the contract was worth about $150,000, but the speculator was only required to pay a margin of $5,000. If the value of the contract went from $150,000 to $155,000, then the speculator who bought at $150,000 would have a 100 percent rate of return on the initial $5,000 investment. Unfortunately, one day the Mexican government devalued the peso, and the value of the contract fell by approximately $65,000 overnight. So the speculator who had gambled only $5,000 actually lost $65,000. Those who had bought this contract received a "margin call" from their brokers asking for an additional $60,000, now!

some losses in the futures market, and hope that the price will continue to increase. The temptation to lift the hedge is great. However, it is important to recognize that to lift the hedge is to move from a conservative position of being risk averse to a very aggressive position of being a price risk speculator. While in many circumstances lifting a hedge prematurely may be good management, it is important that the manager realize that by doing so the firm is moving from a hedged position to a speculative position. In a practical sense, if Sam was happy with $0.80 in March, why wouldn't he be just as happy with $0.80 in August? Usually the best advice for a hedger is to "set it and forget it."

Summary

Cash markets are markets in which immediate delivery is made after buyer and seller agree on a price. Futures markets are markets in which buyer and seller agree on a price now for the future delivery of a commodity.

There are three common methods of setting the price today for delivery in the future. The first is forward pricing, in which the future buyer and future seller agree on a price that will be paid upon delivery to the buyer. The second is contracting, where the farmer signs a production contract specifying what will be produced and how it will be produced and binding the farmer to sell to the buyer at a specified price regardless of market conditions. The third approach is to use futures contracts.

A futures contract is a standardized contract for future delivery in which the quantity and quality of the commodity to be delivered in the future are specified, the date of delivery is specified, and the location of delivery is specified. The only thing that is not standardized is the price to be paid at delivery. Futures contracts are created by and traded on futures exchanges. The exchange is an intermediary between the buyer and seller. The buyer promises to accept delivery from the exchange, while the seller promises to make delivery to the exchange. The price to be paid at delivery in the future is established today by the mutual agreement of the brokers of the buyer and the seller on the trading floor of the exchange. If they agree on a price, then a contract is opened. Each party now has a contractual obligation to the exchange.

There are two ways a futures contract can be closed. First, delivery of the commodity in the contract can be made/accepted according to the terms of the contract. Second, the holder of an open position in a futures contract can take an opposite position to offset the open position. That is, someone who bought a futures contract several months ago can sell the same futures contract today and thus cancel the delivery obligation. Most futures contracts are eventually offset in this fashion.

Arbitrage is the simultaneous purchase and sale of the same good in two different markets. The markets may be separated by time or space. An arbitrager seeks immediate profit by buying in the cheap market and selling in the expensive market. By their actions arbitragers drive up the price in the cheap market and drive down the price in the expensive market until there is no longer any profit to be made from arbitrage. Their actions keep price differences in the separated markets rational. Their actions in futures markets assure a predictable linkage between current cash prices and futures contract prices.

For a storable commodity, the price of a futures contract should be equal to the cash price of the commodity plus the costs of storing the commodity to maturity. If this is not the case, then there is a profit potential for arbitragers. For nonstorable commodities expectations and holding costs are prime links between cash prices and futures contract prices.

At any point in time, basis is the difference between the price of a futures contract and the cash price. In general, basis is predictable and stable over time. As cash prices go up and down, basis remains fairly constant. Over time as a futures contract nears maturity, the amount of basis will decrease. At maturity basis will reflect only delivery costs. It is the predictability of basis that makes hedging a viable strategy to avoid price risk.

Speculators are individuals who buy and sell futures contracts in the hope of being able to close their position at a profit. Speculators tend to trade on the basis of market information (such as weather information) and price trends or movements. A speculator neither owns nor intends to own the commodity in the futures contract.

Hedgers are individuals who come into futures markets with the objective of greatly reducing price risk over time. A hedger either owns or intends to own the physical commodity upon which the futures contract is based. By using a hedge, the hedger can "lock-in" today's futures contract price as the net price to be paid/received at some time in the future when the hedger buys/sells the physical commodity. The key to a hedge is to put the hedger opposite positions in two markets—cash and futures—at some point in the future by setting or creating the hedge today. A hedge is part of a price risk management strategy. Hedging is widely used by major agribusiness firms.

KEY TERMS

Arbitrage
Buy a contract
Cash markets
Close a contract
Close a hedge
Contract farming
Forward price
Futures contract
Futures exchange
Futures markets
Hedger

Maturity
Open a contract
Open interest
Pit
Risk management
Sell a contract
Set or open a hedge
Spatial arbitrage
Speculator
Temporal arbitrage

PROBLEMS AND DISCUSSION QUESTIONS

1. Processors of FCOJ face price risks that the price of oranges may go up because of a freeze or a bad crop. In a table similar to Figure 18–7 show the steps a processor would go through to hedge this risk.

2. Clearly distinguish between the objectives of the speculator and the hedger. Which is more likely to closely follow prices of futures contracts after a position has been opened?

3. If you want to learn more about futures markets and/or futures contracts, the two Chicago exchanges have excellent webpages. Visit **www.cbt.com** for the Chicago Board of Trade or **www.cme.com** for the Chicago Mercantile Exchange.

4. One of the important things that makes futures markets work is the use of arbitrage by speculators. For wheat contracts within a single crop year the

difference in prices for different maturity dates is equal to the carrying (i.e., storage) costs. A speculator knows that the usual carrying cost of wheat is about $0.02/bushel/month plus a $0.02/bushel placement fee. Therefore, one would expect the December wheat contract to be priced at the September contract plus $0.08. At present (in June), both contracts are trading at the exact same price, $3.75/bushel. This presents an opportunity for temporal (i.e., across time) arbitrage.

a. What two trades would the speculator make in June on the September and December wheat futures contracts to take advantage of arbitrage?

b. What is the effect of these trades (and those of similar speculators) on the prices of the two contracts?

c. Assume that by August the usual $0.08 spread between the September and December contracts has returned. If the price of the September contract has fallen to $3.50/bushel and the speculator closes out both positions, what has he or she gained?

d. Assume that by August the usual $0.08 spread between the September and December contracts has returned. If the price of the September contract has risen to $3.90/bushel and the speculator closes out both positions, what has he or she gained? Note that in this example, the speculator is speculating not on the price of wheat but on the price differential between the two different delivery months. Thus, the speculator makes markets efficient.

5. In order to hedge effectively, the hedger must have knowledge about expected basis. Traders and brokers have tables that show what a typical basis is in any given month for a particular contract. Sam is a soybean farmer. In October he will harvest 5,000 bushels of soybeans (one contract). Based on past experience he expects the basis on the December contract to be $− 0.08 in October. That is, a December futures contract will trade in October for $0.08 more than the cash price in October.

In January (a slow time for soybean farmers) Sam notes that a December contract is trading at $7.80/bushel. Sam figures his cost of production and returns to land to be $6.80/bushel. So, in January he hedges his crop. Show below how the hedge will work under two alternative October cash prices assuming an October basis of $− 0.08. (Remember: basis = cash − futures.)

October cash price is $6.30/bushel

	Cash Market	Futures Market
In January		_____
In October	_____	_____
Net profit or loss	_____	_____
Net proceeds from both markets	_____	

October cash price is $9.30/bushel

	Cash Market	Futures Market
In January		_____
In October	_____	_____
Net profit or loss	_____	_____
Net proceeds from both markets	_____	

Farm Service Sector

*I*n an earlier chapter we studied food marketing from the farm to the consumer. We mentioned a second critical marketing system that provides inputs to the farmer, rancher, or grower called the farm service sector. This chapter will hit some of the high points of this sector of the U.S. economy and point out some of the unique characteristics of the farm service sector.

PURCHASED INPUTS

Farmers, like any other producer, buy lots of stuff. They combine this stuff with a little bit of land, labor, sunshine, and rain to produce food. Some of the major categories of purchases are illustrated in Figure 19–1. In 2000 farmers bought nearly $25 billion of livestock feed. Most of that feed was purchased from some sort of feed dealer, but as we look at the dealers in agriculture, we find that there are a variety of different dealers using different marketing channels to deliver the feed, seed, and other inputs farmers buy. The following discussion of alternative farm

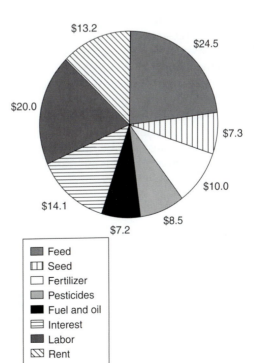

FIGURE 19–1 Major purchases in the Farm Service Sector (2000, billions of dollars).

service marketing structures will include an in-depth look at an institution that is almost unique to agriculture—the cooperative corporation.

Direct Sales

In some instances farmers buy goods and services directly from the producer of those goods and services. For instance, most banking services are purchased directly from the local bank. At least one national manufacturer of livestock feed maintains a national sales force that sells directly to the farmer. This company's feed is not available at any retail outlet: the only way to purchase this feed is directly from the company. Direct sales are also common in many specialty areas such as vegetable seeds, irrigation systems, and special purpose equipment. Direct sales foster and require a close working relationship between the farmer and the company representative. The ability to develop and maintain a company-owned sales force is usually a factor limiting the growth of direct sales firms.

Franchise Agents

Franchise agents
agents authorized by a manufacturer to sell the products of the manufacturer. Usually the agents are given an exclusive territory such that they become local monopolies.

The use of **franchise agents** is a very common marketing structure in the farm service sector. Examples include the local John Deere equipment dealer and the Purina feed dealer. In this marketing system the producer of farm inputs signs a marketing agreement with a local merchant to become the local representative of the producer. Usually the franchise is a locally exclusive franchise meaning that the company will not allow any other merchant in the area to market its products. As a result, most farm communities will have one John Deere dealer, but never two. The franchise agent thus becomes a local monopoly of the company's merchandise. In this system, what competition exists at the local level is between agents of different manufacturers rather than between different agents of a given manufacturer.

In the franchise marketing system, the primary marketing efforts of the manufacturer (Deere, Purina, and so on) are directed towards the franchise agent rather than to the farmer. The agent becomes the local representative of the manufacturer such that the reputation for reliability and service of the manufacturer rests on the reliability and service of the franchise agent. If the franchise agent does not meet the standards of the manufacturer, then the agent loses the franchise.

The franchise agent system of marketing is very common in the non-farm sector also. The owners of fast (and not so fast) food restaurants are usually franchise agents. Soft drink and beer distributors are local monopolies created by a franchise. National chains of motels are franchised, which explains why you may find a Best Western at every interchange on the interstate, but you will never find two of them at a single interchange.

General Store

Lots of farm inputs—particularly feed, seed, insecticides, and pesticides—are sold by farm community general stores. These stores typically buy materials from a variety of vendors to offer their farmer/customers both full service and selection. Such stores are usually locally owned and operated. In many cases, they will more readily extend credit than other input dealers because of their local roots. Frequently, general stores will become franchise agents for a particular item and run the rest of the store parallel to the franchise. Manufacturers of some inputs, such as chemicals, will wholesale their products to any retailer, so while there may be only one dealer of Deere equipment in a community, there may well be three or four dealers of DuPont chemicals.

Cooperatives

Processors and farm service suppliers often have local monopoly power in a farm community and use that power to extract monopoly profits from the hapless farmers. One counter strategy has been for farmers themselves to join together in a cooperative association to go into the processing or farm service business. Since these businesses are owned by the farmers, they serve the interests of the farmers.

For instance, it is very common for cotton farmers in a region to band together to create a local cotton ginning business that becomes the buyer of the farmers' raw cotton. The cooperative business will gin the cotton and sell the lint and seeds on behalf of the farmer-owners.

What is a Cooperative?

In order to discuss agricultural cooperation, we must define some terms. First of all, just what is a **cooperative?** In the simplest of terms, a cooperative is an organizational method for doing business. Various forms of business organizations are compared in Figure 19–2. Legally, a cooperative is a special type of corporation. There are two major differences between a cooperative corporation and an ordinary corporation:

- The cooperative is designed to do business primarily with its **member-patrons** rather than with the public at large.
- The earnings (i.e., profits) of a cooperative are distributed to the members on the basis of **patronage**[1] rather than on the basis of stock ownership.

An agricultural cooperative is a form of business organization set up by a group of individuals in the agricultural industry for the purpose of performing a service for themselves. The service they perform cooperatively may be one that was formerly purchased from some other organization, or it may be one that the members of the cooperative formerly did without. The cooperative association is voluntarily owned and controlled by its member-patrons. Almost any group of individuals, agencies, or businesses that have a common need for some service in agriculture can combine into a cooperative corporation. By combining into a cooperative, farmers gain bargaining power collectively that they would not have individually.

A cooperative exists for the purpose of giving greater economic returns to the members of the organization than could otherwise be achieved. Cooperatives are often spoken of as "nonprofit" organizations. Nothing could be further from the truth. Cooperatives seek to maximize profits, just as any noncooperative business seeks to maximize profits. As with any other business, the cooperative seeks to maximize profits by adjusting output to that level at which the marginal costs of production are equal to the marginal revenue earned. The difference is that the

Cooperative a form of business organization in which the company is owned by the farmers it serves.

Member-patrons farmers who own a cooperative are called members of the cooperative, and farmers who do business with the cooperative are called patrons.

Patronage the amount of business a member does with the cooperative.

---

[1] Patronage refers to the amount of business the co-op member does with the co-op. The more a farmer buys from or sells to the co-op, the greater that amount of profits that will be returned to the farmer. The profits of an ordinary corporation, by comparison, are distributed on the basis of ownership.

Type of Business Organization

Question	Single Proprietorship	Partnership	Limited Partnership	Ordinary Corporation	Cooperative Corporation
Who owns the business?	The proprietor	The partners	The partners	The stockholders	The members who buy stock as they do business with the firm
How is the business managed?	By proprietor	By partners	By a manager hired by the partners	By management hired by board of directors	By management hired by board of directors
With whom does the firm do business?	The general pubic	The general public	The general public	The general public	The member-patrons
What is the extent of the owner's personal liability for unpaid debts of the firm?	Total	Total (both partners are liable for all debts)	Limited to partner's share of ownership	None	None
How are earnings (profits) distributed?	To proprietor	To partners according to the partnership agreement	To partners according to the partnership agreement	To stockholders on the basis of share of ownership	To members on basis of patronage
What taxes are paid?	Property tax plus personal income tax on proprietor's earnings	Property tax plus personal income tax on partner's earnings	Property tax plus personal income tax on partner's earnings	Property tax plus corporate income tax on corporate earnings. Stockholders pay personal income tax on dividends distributed from after-tax earnings.	Property tax plus corporate income tax on earnings not refunded on patronage basis. Member-patrons pay personal income tax on patronage refunds.

FIGURE 19–2   Comparison of alternative types of business organization.

profits of a cooperative are distributed to the member-patrons on the basis of patronage rather than to owners on the basis of ownership as is the case in an ordinary corporation.

Marketing coopera-tive   a cooperative that processes and distributes farmers' products. Ocean Spray is a marketing cooperative owned by cranberry producers.

Types of Cooperatives

There are three basic types of cooperative associations. Probably the most familiar is the **marketing cooperative,** whose function is to improve the efficiency of the marketing of farm products. Some of the brand name items that may be found in any grocery store are processed, packaged, and marketed by cooperatives. These include Sunkist oranges, Welch's grape juice, Ocean Spray cranberry products, Sunmaid raisins, and Sunsweet prunes.

A second type of cooperative is the **purchasing cooperative** designed to take advantage of the bulk lot discounts offered by many manufacturers, and otherwise minimize the cost of procuring materials used in the member-patrons' businesses. Most purchasing cooperatives are regional in nature. Examples include Farmland Industries in the Midwest and Gold Kist in the Southeast. Most purchasing co-ops provide services identical with those of a general store, but with a higher level of buying power than a local general store can muster.

A third type of cooperative is the **service cooperative,** which provides some service to its members at minimal cost. Examples of service cooperatives include rural electric cooperatives, the nationwide Farm Credit System, and the insurance companies operated by organizations such as the Farmer's Union and Farm Bureau.

Economic Integration

Frequently, a single cooperative association may operate in all three areas. A cooperative grain elevator that serves as a marketing agency will often mix and sell fertilizer to its members and may also provide a service such as hail insurance or fertilizer application. This type of economic integration is very common among agricultural cooperatives.

When we speak of **economic integration,** we mean the tying together of two or more economic activities under some sort of unified control. Economic integration may be thought of as a fusion or coordination of business units. There are two main types of economic integration: horizontal and vertical. The terms "horizontal" and "vertical" are used to convey the characteristics of the type of business coordination.

Horizontal integration refers to the general grouping of similar business units under one administrative control. These businesses will be performing the same production or marketing functions at exactly the same point in the marketing sequence. Retail food chains represent an example of horizontal integration. In a retail food chain, there is a collection of stores brought under one management, each of which is performing exactly the same function.

A second example of horizontal integration is provided by an organization such as Continental Grain Company, in which many individual grain elevators have been consolidated under one management. The federation of local grain marketing cooperatives into a regional grain marketing organization provides still a third example of horizontal integration. The main point to remember about horizontal integration is that a single management gains control over a series of firms performing similar activities at the same level in the production or marketing sequence.

Vertical integration refers to the knitting together of two or more stages of the production and/or marketing sequence under a single managerial control. It occurs when a firm combines activities that are unlike but sequentially related to those that it currently performs. An example of vertical integration is provided by the oil industry, where refiners frequently own their own retail outlets. A second example is the food retailer that processes its own dairy or meat products.

When farmers band together in a cooperative association for the purpose of marketing their products, purchasing, or performing some other service for themselves, we have an example of both horizontal and vertical integration. The act of banding together in an association represents horizontal integration, and the farm producers going into the related but unlike activity of marketing, purchasing, or service represents vertical integration.

Purchasing cooperative a cooperative that buys farm inputs in bulk and sells them to individual members at the lowest cost possible.

Service cooperative a cooperative that provides some service to its members such as electrical power or financial services.

Economic integration the combination of two or more related economic activities under the control of a single management.

Horizontal integration the combination of similar businesses under a single management.

Vertical integration the combination of different businesses at different stages of the production/marketing sequence under a single management.

This idea of farmers banding together in cooperative associations for the purpose of achieving **market power** through horizontal and vertical integration is the basis behind the farm cooperative movement. But because of the extreme economic competition present in the agricultural industry, the market power that could be achieved by the local cooperative associations working independently was negligible. That is, the agricultural industry was so big that even the individual cooperative marketing associations operated essentially as pure competitors.

This provided an incentive and an opportunity for still further horizontal integration among local cooperatives. While a single co-op could not afford a massive research program, for example, an association of cooperatives could make this investment. While a single association did not have enough volume to invest in an installation to process certain by-products, an association of cooperatives could benefit from such an action. As a result, a number of federations of cooperative associations have been formed. These expansions of horizontal integration permitted the expansion of vertical integration into such areas as export marketing and political lobbying.

INSURANCE

Agriculture, a biological process, is an inherently risky business. The management of this risk is one of the primary responsibilities of the farm manager. Most farmers, like most urban home owners, carry property and liability insurance on the farm. But the farmer is exposed to two other risks:

- **Production risk** that the crop may fail or the livestock may die
- **Price risk** that the bottom may fall out of the market leaving the farmer with a negative economic profit

Insurance is one alternative for managing these risks.

Crop Insurance

In one form or another crop insurance has been available to farmers for a number of years. In crop insurance, the farmer pays a premium to insure against crop losses. If a loss occurs, the farmer is compensated for the value of the loss.

Most efforts to provide crop insurance through private companies and/or the federal government have been unsuccessful for several reasons. The biggest problem is that any effort to price the premiums at a level that is actuarially sound results in premiums that are so high that only high-risk farmers will buy the coverage. A second problem is that when there are losses, those losses tend to be catastrophic and widespread, which overwhelms the reserves of the insurance company. A third problem is that when there are catastrophic losses, the federal government has provided disaster relief payments to the farmers adversely affected. Farmers reason, Why buy insurance if the government will give me disaster relief?

In 1995 Congress declared that the government was going to get out of the disaster relief business forever. Congress reasoned that if farmers were given a strong incentive to buy insurance, there would be no need for disaster relief. To make insurance affordable, Congress approved funding to allow the U.S. Department of Agriculture to serve as a reinsurance agency for commercial insurance companies. Under this scheme, the USDA basically insures the insurance companies so that they will not be wiped out by a catastrophic loss. Three years later Congress, unable to break its old habits, approved $3.5 billion of disaster relief for farmers. The president vetoed the bill, sending it back to Congress saying that he wanted a bill for $7.0 billion. Congress obliged, and the president signed it. So much for "forever."

The one insurance product that has been successful is hail insurance. The problems with broad crop insurance don't apply to limited hail insurance. First, there are no high-risk or low-risk farmers—hail is pretty much a random event. Second, while hail can easily ruin three or four farmers' crops, losses are never widespread enough to generate catastrophic losses that would threaten the financial health of the insurers. Third, because hail damage is limited to small areas, there is no political support for federal disaster relief, and farmers expect none. A number of private companies offer hail insurance.

Income Insurance

Crop insurance covers only production risk. Recently some pilot programs have tested insurance that covers both production and price risk. These policies identify an amount of gross receipts a producer is expected to receive from a crop. If the receipts from the crop don't meet the insured amount because of either crop losses or low prices, then the farmer is compensated up to the insured amount. While income insurance is still in an experimental stage, there is little likelihood that it will be successful so long as Congress continues to pass out disaster relief on a regular basis.

CREDIT

As shown in Figure 19–1, farmers spent $14.1 billion in 2000 on interest payments—nearly twice as much as they spent on fuel and oil. The total amount of debt (i.e., borrowing) by farms in the United States in 2000 was $184 billion, or about 15 percent of total assets. These figures really underestimate the importance of credit to farmers because they are the December 31 balance sheet figures, which excludes a lot of borrowing during the year that is repaid at harvest time.

Types of Credit

The credit needs of farmers are very unique and varied. Those needs can be categorized into long term, intermediate term, and short term. The long-term credit needs of farmers are almost exclusively for the purchase of land. The amount to be borrowed is usually quite large, and the expected repayment period is quite long. Unlike some other farm credit needs, these loans are secured by the ultimate **collateral**—the land itself. Absent a complete collapse in land prices, there can be no safer collateral from the perspective of the lender.

Medium-term credit is used to purchase machinery and equipment, buildings and structures, and livestock herds. As with land, the collateral on these loans is usually pretty good.

Short-term credit is very common in crop agriculture. The cost of getting a crop in the ground can easily run $200,000 for a modest-sized farm. Since most farmers don't have this kind of money sitting around, they must borrow to cover

Collateral the pledge of real property that a loan will be paid off. If the borrower defaults on a loan, the lender takes possession of the collateral and sells it to recover the defaulted loan.

Production loan   a
loan from a commer-
cial bank to a farmer
to finance the variable
or operating costs of
producing a crop.
Typically the loan is
repaid at harvest.

their planting costs. Such loans are called **production loans.** Most production loans are extended with the understanding that they are to be repaid at harvest time. Since the only collateral for production loans is the crop itself, these loans entail a substantial element of risk on the part of the lender.

Sources of Credit

Agricultural credit, because of its unique characteristics, is a very specialized part of our overall credit system. Most agricultural lenders specialize in credit to agriculture only, and most that don't specialize won't consider making an agricultural loan. As with any loan, the lender should understand the business of the borrower and know the borrower. As a result several unique credit sources have evolved to serve the needs of the agricultural borrower.

Farm Credit System

The Farm Credit System (FCS) is a financial cooperative that is owned by the member-borrowers of the cooperative. As with other cooperative organizations, the FCS exists to serve its members. In this case the service is to meet the financial needs of the members. As with other cooperatives, each FCS association seeks to maximize profit and return those profits to the members on the basis of patronage.

The FCS is a vertically and horizontally integrated system. Local farmer-borrowers own the local cooperative. Local cooperatives in a particular region of the country collectively own a regional bank that serves as a source of funds for the local co-ops. The seven regional banks collectively own the FCS Funding Corporation (which is also a cooperative). The Funding Corporation sells bonds on behalf of the entire system on the New York bond market. By integrating the several regional banks into one Funding Corporation, market power is increased, which means the Funding Corporation is able to sell bonds at a more attractive price than any of the seven banks could do on their own. In fact, the FCS Funding Corporation is the second largest issuer of bonds on the New York market—second only to the U.S. Treasury.

Proceeds from the sale of bonds in New York is distributed to the seven regional banks, which then distribute the funds to the local associations. Because of this vertical integration, local associations are able to acquire funds at a much lower cost than would be the case if each local association tried to raise funds on its own. Once again vertical integration within a cooperative structure provides efficiencies that would not otherwise be available.

Local FCS cooperatives make long-, medium-, and short-term loans to local farmers. That is their only business. Each co-op elects a board of directors from among its membership. The board directs the lending practices of the staff and usually retains the right to review any large loan request. Since the board is composed of local farmers, they likely know the loan applicant personally and they are able to evaluate the feasibility of the project for which the loan is requested. As a result, the possibility of making a poor loan is greatly reduced.[2] In addition, each board member realizes that a poor decision on a loan is going to reduce his or her pa-

---

[2] The board of one North Carolina association approved a $5 million loan to a well-known local farmer only to discover that for many years he had concealed his gambling addiction. He blew the entire $5 million in one trip to Las Vegas.

tronage refund at the end of the year. Because the system is self-policing, loan losses in the FCS are very low compared with other lenders. Low loan losses translate into lower interest rates and higher patronage refunds for the member-borrowers.

Farm Service Agency

Another unique, specialized source of agricultural credit is the Farm Service Agency (FSA). This federal agency is a branch of the U.S. Department of Agriculture. The role of the FSA is to be an agricultural lender of last resort. In fact, to be eligible to borrow from the FSA, a borrower must have been turned down by another credit source.

The FSA has two types of clientele. The first is young farmers who have neither the collateral nor the experience to have an established credit record. The other is farmers who are struggling to survive financially in agriculture. Frequently these farmers have experienced some bad luck in the form of crop losses, low prices, or family tragedies that makes it impossible to continue farming without some financial support. Because the FSA lends to these high-risk individuals, their loan losses are well beyond what would be accepted in the commercial sector.

Credit from the FSA is both subsidized and supervised. Loans from the FSA are subsidized by the USDA to lower the interest rate that must be paid. It is hoped that this will help the borrowers become financially independent. When a borrower applies for credit from the FSA, a business plan must be submitted. If the loan is approved, the credit officer will supervise that loan to be certain the business plan is being implemented and to assist with the financial management of the farm.[3]

Insurance Companies

One of the basic tenets of financial management is that financial intermediaries should match the timing of their assets to that of their liabilities. That is, a firm should not sell three-year notes to raise cash to make 30-year mortgage loans. The liabilities of insurance companies, particularly life insurance companies, are usually (the insured hopes) long-term. Therefore, insurance companies look for long-term assets with collateral that will retain its value over the long haul. Agricultural mortgages fit this need perfectly, so many insurance companies have subsidiaries that are in the business of making loans on agricultural land. These loans are usually quite large, which cuts down the transactions costs from other alternatives such as residential home mortgages.

Commercial Banks

Within the banking business there is a group of banks known as **rural banks.** These are banks that primarily serve agriculture. Most rural banks are locally owned and locally operated, serving farmers in the community. Traditionally rural banks were a source for intermediate- and short-term credit, avoiding long-term mortgage credit. Rural banks are a primary source of production loans to finance a crop. As a result, the welfare of the bank usually depends on the welfare of the local farmers.

Rural banks banks that primarily serve local farmers and ranchers.

---

[3] Some farmers take exception to federal employees snooping around their farm. A student intern working with the FSA had a loaded pistol pointed at his head as he was invited to leave the premises. He left.

Farmer Mac   a federal agency that buys mortgages from rural banks and resells them on financial markets to investors.

Farmer Mac   In the 1980s Congress established the Federal Agricultural Mortgage Corporation (popularly known as **Farmer Mac**) to encourage rural banks to become active in the long-term agricultural mortgage market. Under this program, a rural bank that originates an agricultural mortgage can sell 90 percent of the mortgage to Farmer Mac, which then bundles many of these mortgages into packages that are sold to the public as investments. In this way, most of the capital for long-term agricultural credit comes from Farmer Mac rather than from the rural bank. In addition, the rural bank gets to keep the loan origination fees (usually called points) so that the bank gets paid for lending out someone else's money. Farmer Mac has been very successful in getting rural banks into the market for agricultural mortgages.

Individuals

A significant source of agricultural credit is from individuals. Much of this represents loans between generations of a family. A common strategy is for a farmer ready to retire to sell the farm to a son or daughter who wants to continue farming. Rather than making the young farmer borrow the money commercially, the retiring farmer lends the money by signing over the farm in exchange for an agreed upon schedule of payments. This strategy does two important things in terms of intergenerational planning. First, since the son or daughter becomes owner of the land, the land will not be part of older generation's estate and will not be subject to estate taxes, which can be very costly for farmers. Second, the retiring farmer is assured of a reliable annual income as the loan is paid off.

FARM LABOR

Labor is one of the farmer's larger purchased inputs. While many farms are self-sufficient with family labor, the trend is toward more and more purchased labor. In 2000 farmers spent $20.0 billion on hired labor, and tenant farmers paid non-operator landlords $13.2 billion in rent, which is in essence a payment for the use of the landowner's land in exchange for the tenant's labor.

Tenant Labor

Tenants   farm operators who do not own the land they use.

Tenants are farm operators who do not own their land. They rent the land from the landowner. Approximately 10 percent of U.S. farms are tenant operated. The managerial responsibilities of owner and operator (or landlord and renter) are negotiated between the two parties.

There are two common types of rental agreements. In a cash rent agreement a specific amount of rent is agreed upon between the two parties. In a share agreement the landowner claims a share of the crop. Frequently in a share agreement the owner will also share in some of the input expenses. In a share rent agreement, what the owner will earn in any given year depends on the success of the tenant's farming and market prices for the crop.

Labor Contractors

An increasing proportion of the hired labor on U.S. farms is provided by labor contractors. These intermediaries are very common in the fruit and vegetable sectors where a substantial quantity of seasonal, usually migrant, labor is required. The farmer signs a contract with the contractor to provide a certain quantity of labor at a certain time. The contractor then performs a number of tasks that the farmer really does not want to mess with.

The contractor will hire the labor, transport the labor, certify that the labor is legally entitled to work in the United States, and ensure that all labor laws (such as child labor and sanitation services) are satisfied. By using a labor contractor the farmer is able to avoid many hassles and shift the legal liability for labor law and immigration compliance onto the contractor. It is the ability to shift legal liability that makes working with labor contractors so attractive to the farmer needing seasonal labor.

Custom Hire

Custom hire refers to the practice of hiring labor and equipment to perform some task on the farm. The most common form of custom hire is to hire someone with a combine to harvest the crop. In some cases this may be a neighbor who happens to own a combine who will do custom work for farmers who don't. In other cases it may be a small firm with multiple combines that hires drivers and hires out their services. This latter alternative is very common in the wheat belt of the Great Plains. Since the wheat harvest starts in the southern end of the belt in Texas in May and continues through August in the northern part of the wheat belt, custom combine companies just follow the harvest north like a circus troupe.

Consultants

Farmers are, of necessity, jacks of all trades. But increasingly, they are relying on expert consultants to help them out. Farmers have used legal and financial consultants for many years, but now there are evolving three additional types of consultants who respond to the needs of farmers in an increasingly complex regulatory environment, and to the needs of the bottom line.

"Scouts" are professional consultants who will periodically walk a farmer's fields in search of pests or diseases. If a problem is discovered, then a specific plan of action is recommended. The use of scouts replaces the "spray everything" approach to pest management, which is good for the environment and reduces the farmer's cost of production.[4]

Waste management consultants help farmers determine how to handle manure from livestock operations within the guidelines of increasingly strict environmental protection laws. Advice is given on crops to produce and application rates on those crops. From the farmer's perspective, the use of a waste management consultant shifts the liability for environmental compliance from the farmer to the consultant.

Crop advisers are consultants who work with farmers providing agronomic advice such as seed selection, fertilizer rates, and the new field of precision farming. Precision farming refers to adjusting application rates of fertilizers and other chemicals to the specific needs of the spot in the field where the application is being made. The combined use of yield-sensing equipment and global positioning

---

[4] To meet the demand for scouting consultants, the University of Florida has become the first university to offer a Doctor of Plant Medicine degree. It is similar to a Doctor of Veterinary Medicine degree in that it is a medical practice degree rather than a research degree. Candidates for the DPM take a heavy dose of entomology and plant pathology courses to learn about pests and diseases. In addition, they also take pesticide application and environmental regulation courses.

technologies allows crop advisers to produce very detailed maps of each field down to the square meter and to adjust application equipment on the fly in accord with the computer-generated maps. As an indicator of the importance of crop advisers, the Certified Crop Advisers industry group now has 12,000 members.

SUMMARY

The farm service sector refers to that group of agribusinesses that provide inputs and services to agricultural producers. Distribution channels include direct sales, franchise agents, and general stores.

Cooperatives are a form of business organization that is unique to agriculture in the United States. Cooperatives are agribusiness corporations that are farmer owned. They provide inputs, services, processing, and/or marketing to the farmers who own the business. Cooperative corporations differ from ordinary corporations in that most of their business is conducted with the owner-members of the cooperative and profits are distributed on the basis of patronage rather than ownership.

Agricultural cooperatives provide vivid examples of economic integration where multiple economic activities are brought under a single management. Horizontal integration refers to bringing similar activities under a single management such as supermarket chains. Vertical integration refers to the coordination of several links of the marketing chain into a single management structure. Many supermarket chains have their own dairy processing plants: this is an example of vertical integration.

While most farmers carry property and liability insurance, few use crop insurance, despite efforts of the USDA to encourage farmers to do so. The one exception is hail insurance because the premiums are quite low. Some initial efforts are being made to introduce income insurance that would protect against crop losses and price risks.

Agricultural producers have rather unusual credit needs. As a result, a group of financial service organizations has evolved to meet the needs of agriculture. The three main players are the Farm Credit System, a cooperative; the Farm Service Agency, a government agency; and rural commercial banks. Some insurance companies are active in the farm mortgage business.

Tenants are those farm operators who do not own the land they farm. Rents are paid either on a cash basis or on a share basis. Among fruit and vegetable producers there is a growing trend toward the use of labor contractors who provide all labor services and accept legal liabilities associated with labor on a contract basis. Many farmers use custom hire services to provide specific services such as harvesting. Consultants are becoming increasingly important in many aspects of agriculture.

KEY TERMS

Collateral	Patronage
Cooperative	Price risk
Economic integration	Production loan
Farmer Mac	Production risk
Franchise agents	Purchasing cooperative
Horizontal integration	Rural banks
Market power	Service cooperative
Marketing cooperative	Tenants
Member-patrons	Vertical integration

PROBLEMS AND DISCUSSION QUESTIONS

1. Farmland Industries and Gold Kist were mentioned as two of the giant integrated cooperatives. You can learn more about these interesting agribusinesses at their websites: **www.farmland.com** and **www.goldkist.com**.

2. What is a local monopoly? Why are they common in the farm service sector? Look around your community to see if you can identify any farm service local monopolies.

3. Compare and contrast an ordinary corporation and a cooperative corporation.

4. What are the strengths and weaknesses of a franchise agent distribution system?

5. Give three examples of agribusiness firms that are horizontally integrated. Do the same for vertically integrated firms.

6. What are the reasons crop insurance is not widely used by farmers?

7. The Farm Credit System is both vertically and horizontally integrated. Explain.

8. Why have rural banks gotten back into the agricultural mortgage market?

CHAPTER
20 *Investment Analysis*

*T*o this point, our analysis of the economic behavior of the firm has been limited to the short-run time period in which the firm manager adjusts variable input levels in an effort to maximize profits. Now we are going to take a longer-run view and examine the economics of making long-run decisions about whether or not to invest in assets that were considered fixed inputs in our previous analyses.

Questions faced by the farm manager such as "Should I buy more land?" or "Should I expand my cow herd?" are investment questions. There are two important differences between these types of questions and those that have been considered in preceding chapters.

- *Lumpiness.* Investments usually involve the purchase of assets for which the marginal analysis approach is not appropriate because it is not possible to buy or use a marginal unit. While it is quite easy to evaluate fertilizer application rates with marginal analysis, it is impossible for the typical farm to evaluate adding one-tenth of a combine[1] or adding one acre of land. Combines come in all-or-nothing packages, and land is usually sold in rather large blocks. For lumpy assets like these, the marginal approach is neither practical nor appropriate.

- *Time.* In our previous analyses, we looked exclusively at the short run or a single production period for the typical farm firm. Decisions regarding investments in fixed assets are by definition decisions that involve multiple production periods. A farmer pondering the question of whether or not to buy a new combine certainly will not analyze the contribution of the combine to a single production period. Instead he will look at the economics of the combine over the expected life of the combine.

As in previous cases, the basic economics associated with any input use decision revolves around the relationship between costs and returns. The firm is assumed to be profit maximizing—seeking to purchase those assets for which the difference between expected returns and expected costs is the greatest. Because of lumpiness, we cannot evaluate costs and returns on the margin; instead, we must evaluate the investment as a whole. And because of the time considerations the simple difference between total costs and total returns is not an appropriate profit-maximizing criterion. Instead we must look at the present value of the expected costs and the present value of the expected returns.

---

[1] A combine is a large mechanical device used for harvesting many crops such as wheat, soybeans, and corn. These machines cut down the entire plant and thresh it by separating the wheat from the chaff, or the corn from the ear. Because these machines do both tasks, their early brethren were known as combination machines, or combines.

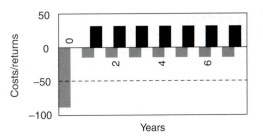

FIGURE 20–1
Investment in a
combine.

A final, important distinction between our short-run analyses and the long-run analyses discussed in this chapter is tax management. In the short run most expenditures and revenues are treated by federal income taxes as receipts and expenditures in the current tax year. In the long run, assets are depreciated over a period of years, and hence the tax implications of investment alternatives become very important. For the remainder of this chapter these tax implications will be ignored.

TYPICAL LIFE OF AN INVESTMENT

No two investments in assets are alike, but most share the same basic characteristics. They involve a substantial expenditure at the time of purchase, some smaller costs during each production period, and some returns during each production period. This is illustrated in Figure 20–1 which shows the estimated costs and returns over the 7-year life of a combine.[2] In time period zero (i.e., today) the farmer would buy the machine for $90,000. Estimated annual operating costs are $10,000, and estimated annual returns are $30,000. Returns are calculated using the concept of opportunity cost: if the farmer did not buy the combine, then he would have to pay a custom operator $30,000 to harvest his crop for him.

Another example of an investment was illustrated in the preface of this text. That is, the investment that you—the college student—are making in yourself. For four or more years you incur the costs of your investment—both direct costs for tuition and the like and opportunity costs of income forgone by attending the university rather than flipping hamburgers at Mickey D's. The returns to this investment in yourself come in the form of incrementally higher earnings as a college graduate compared with those of a nongraduate.

ECONOMIC PROFITABILITY OF AN INVESTMENT

As with any economic analysis, the profitability of an investment is based on a comparison of the returns and costs of the investment. The simple summation of costs and returns over the lifetime of an investment is not appropriate because some of the costs occur now and some of the returns occur in the future. Because

---

[2] For the purposes of simplicity Figure 20–1 assumes there is no salvage value of the combine at the end of its 7-year life. If there were some remaining value of the asset at the end of its productive life, that would be added to the expected returns in the last year of the analysis.

Time value of money because of the opportunity cost, money received today has a greater value than money received in the future.

Present value the value today of a payment to be made in the future.

of the **time value of money,** one dollar today is worth more than one dollar at some future time period. In order to account for the time value of money in investment analyses, all future costs and returns are converted to their present values so that a meaningful comparison can be made.

Present Value

The **present value** of any future economic flow is equal to that future flow minus the opportunity cost of waiting for that flow.

Opportunity Cost of Money

Ask yourself, Would you rather receive $100 today or $100 5 years from now? The answer to that question is pretty easy: I'll take the $100 today, thank you. Why? There are three basic reasons that you prefer $100 today. First, current consumption has more value to us than future consumption because waiting for consumption has a cost associated with the wait. Second, if I got the $100 today, I could put it in the bank and in 5 years I would have substantially more than $100 as a result of the interest earned. Finally, there is the risk that inflation may reduce the purchasing power of the $100 several years from now.

Let's phrase the previous question in a slightly different way: How much would you be willing to pay today for a promise to deliver $100 5 years from now? That is, what is your opportunity cost of waiting to receive the $100? The relationship between **future value** and present value is the opportunity cost of waiting to receive the money. Different consumers will have different opportunity costs, but for all the opportunity cost is greater than zero. The fundamental relationship is

Future value the amount of a payment to be made in a future time period.

$$\text{Present value} = \text{future value} - \text{opportunity cost}$$

For example, suppose Ann is willing to pay $70 for the pledge to receive $100 in 5 years. Ann is saying that the opportunity cost of waiting is worth $30 to her. For her that is the time value of money. Since Ann is indifferent between $70 today and $100 in the future, we say that for Ann $70 is the present value of $100 5 years from now.

Discount Rate

The opportunity cost associated with future returns or costs is frequently expressed as an annual percentage rate rather than in dollars as was previously done. This percentage rate of opportunity cost is known as the **discount rate.** Ann's opportunity cost of $30 is the equivalent of a discount rate of 7.39 percent.[3] That is, Ann discounts the future value of something to the present at an annual rate of 7.39 percent. At this rate of discount, the present value of $100 a year from now is $92.61, or 7.39 percent less than the future value.

Discount rate the time value of money expressed as a percentage rate.

Compounding

Compounding the process of finding a future value, given a present value.

In order to understand the relationship between present value and future value let's begin with an example that is familiar to most—**compound** interest rates. Sup-

---

[3] Don't worry for now about how this was calculated.

pose $100 is placed in a bank account that promises to pay 10 percent compounded annually. At the end of the first year the amount in the account is $110, consisting of $100 of the original deposit plus $10 of interest. At the end of the second year there would be $121 in the account consisting of

Original deposit	$100
Interest on $100 in first year	10
Subtotal, end of first year	110
Interest on $110 in second year	11
Total, end of second year	$121

Mathematically the amount at the end of the second year is

$$100 \cdot (1 + 0.10) \cdot (1 + 0.10) = 121$$

or

$$100 \cdot (1 + 0.10)^2 = 121$$

This can be generalized as

$$F = P \cdot (1 + i)^n$$

where:

F = future value

P = present value

i = interest rate per time period

n = number of time periods between the present and the future

This is the general equation for compounding that is used to find the future value of some amount in the present.

Discounting

Discounting is the process of running the compounding machine in reverse. Discounting is used to determine the present value today of some future value. Take the above equation and solve for P, and you have the general rule for discounting:

$$P = \frac{F}{(1 + i)^n}$$

Discounting the process of finding a present value, given a future value.

where i is the appropriate discount rate. In the earlier example of $100 to be received 5 years from now, where the discount rate was 7.39 percent, the discounting formula would be

$$P = \frac{100}{(1 + 0.0739)^5} = \frac{100}{1.428} = 70.01$$

	Discount Rate per Time Period						
Number of Time Periods	3%	5%	7%	9%	11%	13%	15%
1	0.970874	0.952381	0.934579	0.917431	0.900901	0.884956	0.839565
2	0.942596	0.907029	0.873439	0.841680	0.811622	0.783147	0.756144
3	0.915142	0.863838	0.816298	0.772183	0.731191	0.693050	0.657516
4	0.888487	0.822702	0.762895	0.708425	0.658731	0.613319	0.571753
5	0.862609	0.783526	0.712986	0.649931	0.593451	0.542760	0.497177
6	0.837484	0.746215	0.666342	0.596267	0.534641	0.480319	0.432328
7	0.813092	0.710681	0.622750	0.547034	0.481658	0.425061	0.375937
8	0.789409	0.676839	0.582009	0.501866	0.433926	0.376160	0.323902
9	0.766417	0.644609	0.543934	0.460428	0.390925	0.332885	0.284262
10	0.744094	0.613913	0.508349	0.422411	0.352184	0.294588	0.247185
15	0.641862	0.481017	0.362466	0.274538	0.209004	0.159891	0.122894
20	0.553676	0.376889	0.258419	0.178431	0.124034	0.086782	0.061100
25	0.477606	0.295303	0.184249	0.115968	0.073608	0.047102	0.030378
30	0.411987	0.231377	0.131367	0.075371	0.043683	0.025565	0.015103
35	0.355383	0.181290	0.093663	0.048986	0.025924	0.013876	0.007509
40	0.306557	0.142046	0.066780	0.031838	0.015384	0.007531	0.003733
45	0.264439	0.111297	0.047613	0.020692	0.009130	0.004088	0.001856
50	0.228107	0.087204	0.033948	0.013449	0.005418	0.002219	0.000923

FIGURE 20–2   Discount factors: Value today of $1.00 to be received in the future.

Aside from a one-penny rounding error we have determined that the present value today of $100 to be received 5 years from now is $70 at a discount rate of 7.39 percent. If a discount rate of 9 percent were used, then

$$P = \frac{100}{(1 + 0.09)^5} = \frac{100}{1.539} = 64.99$$

Notice what is at work here: as the discount rate increased, the present value of $100 in the future decreased. This illustrates the basic principle that the discount rate and present value are inversely related.

Discounting a Single Payment   The formula presented above can be used to find the present value today of a single payment or cost in the future. The calculations can be done using any calculator that handles exponentials or any personal computer spreadsheet. An alternative approach is to use special financial tables that are published in a variety of finance books. Figure 20–2 shows the **discount factors** for several different discount rates and several different time periods.

Discount factor   the ratio of present value to future value.

Each discount factor shown in Figure 20–2 indicates how much $1.00 to be received in any particular year is worth today. For instance, the discount factor for 5 years at 9 percent is 0.649931. Multiply this times $100 to find that the present value of $100 to be received 5 years from now is $64.99—the same result obtained earlier.

Discount Rate per Time Period

Number of Time Periods	3%	5%	7%	9%	11%	13%	15%
1	0.970874	0.952381	0.934579	0.917431	0.900901	0.884956	0.869565
2	1.913470	1.859410	1.808018	1.759111	1.712513	1.668102	1.625709
3	2.828611	2.723248	2.624316	2.531295	2.443715	2.361153	2.283225
4	3.717098	3.545951	3.387211	3.239720	3.102446	2.974471	2.854978
5	4.579707	4.329477	4.100197	3.889651	3.695897	3.517231	3.352155
6	5.417191	5.075692	4.766540	4.485919	4.230538	3.997550	3.784483
7	6.230283	5.786373	5.389289	5.032953	4.712196	4.422610	4.160420
8	7.019692	6.463213	5.971299	5.534819	5.146123	4.798770	4.487322
9	7.786109	7.107822	6.515232	5.995247	5.537048	5.131655	4.771584
10	8.530203	7.721735	7.023582	6.417658	5.889232	5.426243	5.018769
15	11.937935	10.379658	9.107914	8.060688	7.190870	6.462379	5.847370
20	14.877475	12.462210	10.594014	9.128546	7.963328	7.024752	6.529331
25	17.413148	14.093945	11.653583	9.822580	8.421745	7.329985	6.464149
30	19.600441	15.372451	12.409041	10.273654	8.693793	7.495653	6.565980
35	21.487220	16.374194	12.947672	10.566821	8.855240	7.585572	6.616607
40	23.114772	17.159086	13.331709	10.757360	8.951051	7.634376	6.641778
45	24.518713	17.774070	13.605522	10.881197	9.007910	7.660864	6.654293
50	25.729764	18.255925	13.800746	10.961683	9.041653	7.675242	6.660515

FIGURE 20–3 Annuity factors: Value today of $1.00 to be received each year in the future.

Discounting a Stream of Payments Frequently, as in the previous example of a combine, the costs and/or returns from an investment will be a financial stream over several years or production periods. In the combine example, operating costs were estimated to be $10,000 per year for each of the next 7 years. The total present value of this stream at a discount rate of 9 percent is calculated as

$$P = \frac{10{,}000}{(1 + 0.09)^1} + \frac{10{,}000}{(1 + 0.09)^2} + \cdots + \frac{10{,}000}{(1 + 0.09)^7}$$

Calculating this with a calculator is something of a chore. Fortunately, there is an easy way out. Take a look at Figure 20–3, the present value of an **annuity factor.** This is simply the summation of the discount factors over the number of years shown.

To solve the above problem, find the annuity factor for 7 years at a 9 percent discount factor, which is 5.032953. Multiply it by $10,000, and the present value of $10,000 paid in each of 7 years is $50,329.53. Using the same annuity factor, the present value of the annual returns to the combine investment of $30,000 per year is $150,988.59.

Annuity factor the sum of discount factors over a period of time.

Discounting an Infinite Stream of Payments In the unique case of land itself, the benefits from the investment may be thought of as infinite because, unlike machinery and equipment, land does not wear out so long as it is well managed. A quick look at the discount and annuity columns of Figure 20–2 illustrates that as we get out to 50 years into the future, the discount factor is pretty small and the annuity factor is therefore increasing at a very small rate. In fact, the annuity factor for 9 percent in 50 years is 10.962. For 100 years it is 11.109, and for 1,000 it is 11.111. If carried to infinity, the annuity factor is 11.111, which happens to be the reciprocal of 0.09. That is, in the case of an infinite stream,

$$P = \frac{F}{i}$$

In the case of a parcel of land that can be rented out at $50/acre, the present value of that infinite stream of rents at a 9 percent discount rate is

$$P = \frac{50}{0.09} = 555.56$$

This, of course, assumes that the real rental rate for that infinite time period remains at $50/acre.

Net Present Value

Net present value
difference between the present value of all returns and the present value of all costs associated with an investment.

Net present value (NPV) is the difference between the present value of all returns from an investment and the present value of all costs of that investment. This is the "bottom line" of an investment analysis. Let's return to the example of the combine illustrated in Figure 20–1. The present value of the $90,000 initial investment is $90,000 because there is no opportunity cost for immediate spending. Using a 9 percent discount rate, the net present value of the combine is

PV total returns	$ 150,988.59	
PV initial investment		$ −90,000.00
PV operating costs		$ −50,329.53
PV total costs	$−140,329.53	
Net present value	$ 10,659.06	

Since the net present value in this case is positive, it means that the investor would find this investment to be profitable. If the net present value had turned out to be negative (costs greater than returns), then it would be an investment to avoid.

Internal Rate of Return

Internal rate of return
that discount rate that will drive the net present value of an investment to zero.

An alternative evaluation criterion to the net present value is the **internal rate of return** (IRR). In the previous combine example, the investment was analyzed using a discount rate of 9 percent. If the discount rate were increased to 12 percent, what would happen to the economics of this investment? Well, since most of the costs are not discounted at all, a higher discount rate would reduce returns more than costs. If a 12 percent rate is used, the NPV of the combine falls from $10,659.06 to a mere $1,275.14. At a 15 percent discount rate, the NPV of the combine is − $6,791.60. The point is that by increasing the discount rate the NPV of the investment falls. This is because costs are up front and returns tend to be further out in the future.

Clearly, somewhere between a discount rate of 12 percent and 15 percent there is a single discount rate for which the NPV of the combine would be exactly zero. The discount rate that drives the NPV of an investment to zero is called the internal rate of return. The higher the IRR, the more profitable a potential investment.

With an ordinary calculator, the only way to calculate IRR is by trial and error—a long and trying experience. Fortunately, spreadsheets for personal computers and high-power financial calculators have made the calculation of the IRR a piece of cake. Using such a spreadsheet, we find that the IRR for the combine is 12.446 percent. If the investor is able to borrow funds at a rate less than 12.446 percent, then this potential investment is profitable. If two potential investments are being compared, then the one with the higher IRR is generally preferred. One disadvantage of using IRR to evaluate investments is that it gives you no estimate of the magnitude of the net returns from the investment.

EVALUATING ALTERNATIVES

Evaluating investment alternatives is an art rather than a science. So long as the estimated net present value is greater than zero (or the internal rate of return is greater than the cost of funds), then the investment is viable. In addition to ranking alternatives by the amount of NPV, there are several other factors to take into consideration.

- *Return on Investment.* Assume there are two alternative investments, each of which has an NPV of $4,000. The first requires an investment of $40,000, and the second requires an initial investment of $20,000. Which is preferred? Clearly the second alternative provides a better rate of return on investment than the first.

- *Economic Life.* Again, assume two investment alternatives, each of which has an NPV of $4,000. The first has a useful economic life of 8 years, and the second has an economic life of 4 years. Which is preferred? Clearly the second, because the investor is able to earn the NPV in a shorter time period. By choosing the second alternative twice, the investor would be able to earn $8,000 in 8 years, or double what the first alternative would earn in 8 years.

- *Risk.* Once again, if faced with two otherwise similar investments, the investor would prefer the one with a lower degree of estimated risk. Unfortunately, risk is one of those things that is very difficult to measure. Nonetheless, questions to be asked include, How proven is the technology? How certain are the estimated costs/returns? and What are the factors that could fundamentally change the investment?

There are numerous other considerations that the investor must also consider. What are the opportunity costs of the investor? What financing is available? What are the tax implications? And the list goes on and on. In any case, the first step is to push that old pencil around to determine NPV or IRR.

SUMMARY

Marginal analysis is an appropriate decision-making criterion for variable factors of production in the short run. In long-run analyses, decision making requires investment analysis. Long-run decision making usually involves assets that are expensive, lumpy, and that have extended lifetimes.

An investment usually entails a substantial up-front expenditure to purchase the asset, and then over the life of an asset there is a stream of costs and returns in each year of the asset's useful life. At the end of the useful life there may be a salvage value.

In order to compare a dollar spent today with a dollar to be earned 10 years from now, we must adjust for the time value of money by discounting all future costs and returns to the present. The difference between the present value of all returns and the present value of all costs is called the net present value (NPV). If the NPV of an investment is positive, then the investment is viable.

An alternative criterion for evaluating investments is the internal rate of return (IRR). The IRR is that discount rate that will drive the NPV of an investment to zero. If the IRR of an investment is greater than the cost of funds, then the investment is viable.

Other factors to consider when making long-run investment decisions are the rate of return on the investment, the expected life of the asset, the risk involved, the impact of poor estimates of costs and returns, and the tax implications.

KEY TERMS

Annuity factor

Compounding

Discount factor

Discount rate

Discounting

Future value

Internal rate of return

Net present value

Present value

Time value of money

PROBLEMS AND DISCUSSION QUESTIONS

1. Suppose a new pump costs $600. It has a useful life of 5 years. In each of those 5 years the operating costs of the pump are $50, and the returns to the pump are $200. Put this information into a spreadsheet and:

   a. Find the NPV using a 7 percent discount rate.

   b. Find the NPV using a 10 percent discount rate.

   c. Find what happens to NPV when the discount rate increases.

   d. Find the IRR.

2. What is the present value of $200 to be received 10 years from now using a 7 percent discount rate?

3. What is the value 10 years from now of $200 deposited in an account earning 12 percent interest?

4. What is the present value of a stream of $200 payments received in each of the next 10 years using a 7 percent discount rate?

5. As the discount rate increases, the present value of the returns falls more rapidly than the present value of the costs. Why?

Environmental Policy and Market Failure

*I*n the second chapter of this text it was pointed out that each society must de-cide what kind of allocation system it will use to perform the decision making necessary for an economy to function. The authors, laying their hearts on the line, indicated that they are unabashed proponents of capitalism and the price system of allocation using free markets. Throughout this text we have crowed about how markets work. Now it is time to eat a little crow and talk about situations in which markets fail to produce socially optimal results—**market failure.** One of the clear-est cases of market failure is in the broad spectrum of issues associated with the natural environment.

Market failure when free markets do not produce results that are consistent with the desires of society.

ADVANTAGES OF MARKETS

The reason most economists endorse the price allocation system is that the price system is inherently efficient and it provides total individual liberty. Before dis-cussing what happens when markets fail, let's spend a little time reviewing what happens when markets succeed.

Coordination

One of the primary roles of any allocation system is to coordinate producers and consumers to their mutual satisfaction. In a free market system the coordinating force is price. In a system in which millions of consumers' desires are combined and communicated to thousands of producers, price has been shown to be a very effective, impersonal, and efficient coordination mechanism.

In the United States about 95 percent of all the iceberg lettuce is produced in a single county in the southern part of California. Several years ago heavy rains and floods in this part of California all but wiped out the lettuce crop. How did the "in-visible hand" respond? How did producers tell consumers "We just had a flood and there isn't as much lettuce as there usually is"? Simple! The price of lettuce shot up to an unprecedented price of $1.99 per head. Many a shopper decided that at that price they could forgo lettuce for a few weeks. This is an example of how the price system provides the all-important coordination of production and consumption.

Prices Driven to Minimum Cost

A second advantage of free markets is that prices for the consumer will be driven to the minimum average total cost such that the consumer gets the product at the low-est price possible and the producer produces in the most efficient manner possible.

This efficiency means that the available resources of the society produce as much "stuff" as possible. Since we all want "mo' stuff," this tendency of markets to allocate resources efficiently is socially desirable.

Disequilibria Are Self-Correcting

A third advantage of markets is that they are self-correcting if a disequilibrium should occur. Shifts in either supply or demand create a market disequilibrium at the prevailing price. That is, at the former price the quantity demanded is no longer equal to the quantity supplied—a disequilibrium situation. When this happens, a market—as if driven by an "invisible hand"—automatically adjusts to a new equilibrium price.

No Coercion

Finally, a free market provides both producers and consumers with complete, total freedom of action. The consumer is sovereign, buying what she desires and not buying what she does not desire. Likewise, the producer produces what he wants to produce. On both sides of the market there is an absence of coercion by any form of government or other coercive power. Life, liberty, and the pursuit of happiness are thereby maximized.

Types of Market Failure

Markets, while efficient in most cases, do not always provide socially optimal results. For example, the dairy farmer has a problem with manure disposal. The most efficient, that is, cheapest, solution to the problem is to dump the manure into the creek that runs through the farm. Most would probably agree that this solution would not be socially optimal—that is, it would not generate the greatest good for the greatest number in our society.[1] While the farmer is better off because the manure is eliminated as cheaply as possible, society as a whole is worse off because the creek and the river into which it flows become polluted. In this case there is a divergence between the **private** interests of the farmer and the **social** interests of all members of society.

> **Private** refers to the costs, benefits, or self-interest of the individuals involved in some economic activity.

> **Social** refers to the costs, benefits, or interests of all members of society affected by an economic activity.

Education is another example of market failure. If we went to a free market approach for elementary education, there would undoubtedly be some children who, because of low-income parents or other circumstances, would be excluded from consumption, which is another free market result that most of us would agree is not socially optimal.

These two quick examples illustrate that markets sometimes fail to produce socially optimal results. While the causes of market failure are usually fairly clear, the policies to deal with such failure are much more obscure. In the sections that

---

[1] What is "socially optimal" is difficult to define. Probably this notion of the greatest good for the greatest number is as close as we can get. Within our democratic form of government we vest the responsibility for determining what is socially optimal in our elected officials. Whether they accurately reflect what is socially optimal or not is the basis for a branch of economics known as the theory of public choice.

follow we will examine three types of goods for which market failure is common. These are goods with poorly defined property rights, public goods, and common property goods. In these three cases it is the nature of the good itself that leads to market failure. We will then turn to the case in which market failure is a result of a difference between the private and social valuations of a good. Finally, we look at market failures caused by information disparaties between the buyer and the seller.

Poorly Defined Property Rights

For markets to operate efficiently, the property or ownership rights to the resource being allocated must be clearly defined. In those cases where such rights are uncertain or unclear, market failure will frequently occur.

Property Rights in a Market

Property rights refer to the legal control or ownership of a good. In normal market transactions those rights are clearly defined. If you enter a grocery store to buy a gallon of milk, it is clear who owns the milk. The store owns it until such time as you swap something you own (like money) for the milk. At that time, the store becomes the owner of the money and you become the owner of the milk. The store even gives you a receipt as proof of your ownership. In this example, the rights are so clear as to be almost trivial. Such is the case for most goods traded on markets. For bigger ticket items like a car or boat we use a system of titles to clearly define property rights and the exchange thereof.

> **Property rights** legal control or ownership of a good.

Problems arise when property rights are not so clearly defined. For example, who holds property rights to groundwater?[2] In some parts of the United States, whoever owns the surface land owns the right to extract as much water as he or she can from a well drilled on that land. Therefore, a farmer can pump thousands of gallons from his well even though he is drawing down the water table of each of his neighbors.

This became a serious problem in the Tampa-St. Petersburg, Florida, area in the 1960s. Tampa had pumped so much water from under the city that saltwater started seeping into the void left from the heavy pumping. Since the good people of Tampa didn't want to drink saltwater, the city fathers bought a few farms about 30 miles inland. On these farms the City of Tampa built enormous wells and pumped water like crazy to ship to Tampa. Within a few years, the city had drawn the water table down so much that saltwater began intruding into those wells. This, of course, enraged neighboring farmers, who used the groundwater for irrigation. They learned in a hurry that strawberries don't grow very well when fed a diet of saltwater irrigation.

Since the property rights to the underground water were not clearly defined, a free market allocation was not a socially optimal solution. To correct this problem the Florida legislature in 1972 created water management districts with the authority, among other things, to issue consumptive use permits for groundwater. In essence the property rights for the groundwater became clearly defined through

---

[2] Groundwater refers to water underground that can be pumped up. Groundwater moves from place to place and, like an underground lake, can be exhausted by too much pumping.

the rights granted by the use permits. By limiting the number of use permits granted, the water management folks try to avoid the problems of excessive pumping by any one or two users in a given area.

Air: An Example of Poorly Defined Property Rights

A good example of a situation in which we have moved from a system of poorly defined rights to well-defined rights is the case of air in an airport. While the matter of who owns what rights to air may not be too relevant to a farmer in Kansas,[3] there are certainly a lot of folks in Los Angeles for whom air has become a very important economic good.

Anyway, back to the airport. In days gone by, it was assumed (by custom) that smokers held the property rights to all the air in the airport. That is, smokers could smoke anywhere they wanted: all the air was theirs to pollute. Under this system, the nonsmoker had no property rights to smoke-free air. Since the rights to air were not clearly defined, the smokers took it all.

Finally, in the 1980s a revolution of sorts took place in most airports. The airport authorities began to clearly identify the property rights of nonsmokers by designating portions of the airport as a nonsmoking section. A few simple signs had the effect of conferring on nonsmokers the rights they had been denied under the old system in which there were no clearly defined rights.

The clear assignment of property rights for air in airports is a more socially desirable solution than was achieved under a system of poorly defined rights. What is the basis for this judgment? The designation of nonsmoking areas did not make anyone worse off since smokers could still smoke in designated smoking areas; and it made a lot of nonsmokers better off. By definition, social welfare or well-being of the totality of society was increased.

Coase Theorem

The matter of property rights and market failure is a fairly recent topic in economic literature. One of the leaders in the field is a professor at the University of Chicago named Ronald Coase. He has both an economics degree and a law degree, so he can blend the two traditions together. In 1991 he won the Nobel prize for economic science based on his work that led to what is now known as the **Coase Theorem:**

Coase theorem
identifies the conditions under which a successful economic transaction will occur.

If: 1. Property rights are clearly defined, and
           2. Both parties to a transaction stand to gain from the transaction, and
           3. Transaction costs are low,

Then: The transaction will occur.

This theorem appears to be rather simple at first blush, but the contribution was certainly great enough to get a Nobel prize, so something of value must be there. Prior to Coase's work, economists had assumed that if item #2 above was

---

[3] A revered former colleague of the authors frequently argued that the average wind speed in Kansas is zero. Half the time it blows 50 mph from north to south, and the other half of the time it blows 50 mph from south to north. Hence, the average is zero.

met, there would be a transaction. What Coase showed was that items #1 and #3 were also necessary for a successful transaction.

Returning to the airport example, in the old days not only were rights poorly defined but the potential costs of claiming those rights were substantial— particularly if the smoker you were attempting to claim rights from was a 250-pound former linebacker. The simple posting of signs designating smoking and nonsmoking sections of an airport both defined the property rights and reduced the transaction cost. The transaction, (that is, clean air for nonsmokers), was thus completed.

Policy Implications

The policy implications of the Coase theorem are clear. Where market failure is observed, make certain that property rights are assigned in a clear fashion and be certain the transaction costs of completing the transaction are minimized. How to accomplish these two items will vary from situation to situation in which market failure is observed.

Public Goods

The price of wheat at any point in time is relatively easy to determine. Wheat is traded freely on a number of markets, all of which are interconnected by dealers who always stand ready to buy at a relatively low price in one market in order to sell at a relatively higher price in another market. Wheat and most other agricultural commodities are called **market goods** because their prices are determined in a market through the interaction of supply and demand. But there are many goods and services for which no market exists. For example, there is a supply, a demand, and a price for fire protection services, but there is no market in which the price and quantity traded of fire protection are determined. In the absence of a market for this service, the price/quantity decisions are made in an administrative manner by political bodies. Consequently, **nonmarket goods** are frequently called **public goods.**

Characteristics of Public Goods

Public goods share two characteristics that distinguish them from ordinary market goods:

- Consumption of public goods is **nonrival.** The consumption of most goods is **rival.** That is, if I consume a lobster, that means that you can't consume it. We are rivals in consumption of lobster. For nonrival goods, the consumption of the good by one person in no way diminishes the ability of another person to also consume the product. If I watch Big Bird on "Sesame Street," that in no way diminishes your ability to "consume" the same show.
- Consumption of public goods is **nonexcludable.** This means that everybody can consume the product whether they paid for it or not. The local Public Broadcasting System radio station claims that only one of 13 listeners actually pays (i.e., contributes to) the station. Likewise, most college students don't pay taxes in their local community but still use the "services" of the local constabulary.

Market goods those goods for which viable markets exist.

Nonmarket goods those goods, such as police protection, for which no market exists.

Public goods same thing as nonmarket goods: no market for the good exists.

Nonrival consumption of the good by one person does not preclude consumption by a second person.

Rival consumption by one person precludes consumption by a second person because the first person used up the good.

Nonexcludable everyone can consume the good whether they pay for it or not.

Examples of public goods include national defense, police protection, national parks, local recreational parks, and the air traffic control system. The main difference between these public goods and the more common market goods is that there is no direct linkage between the satisfaction derived from the good or service and payment made for that service. For market goods a direct link exists: if no payment for a hamburger is made, there will be no satisfaction from consuming a hamburger. But for nonmarket goods the ability to relate payment to consumption disappears. For example, if your house has never caught on fire, you have derived no satisfaction from the existence of the fire department, even though you must pay for it each year. However, if speedy action by the fire department saves a home owner thousands of dollars by preventing the spread of a minor fire, there is no increase in the cost of fire protection services for the home owner next year (although he may feel compelled to buy a few tickets to the firemen's ball).

Public Goods and Problems with Free Riders

Free rider someone who consumes a public good without paying for it.

In the days of the Sheriff of Nottingham, all who entered the town paid a tax to the sheriff upon entering. Today as you drive into Nottingham, or any other community, you expect to find a local law enforcement agency ready to serve you (particularly if you drive in at a high rate of speed) even though you have not paid for that service. You are what is known as a **free rider**—an individual who consumes a public good without paying for it.[4] Since consumption of public goods is nonexcludable, free riders will always be a problem. Public television is a clear example of this problem.

Policy Implications

Since there is no direct linkage between satisfaction received and payment made for public goods, and because of the free rider problem, the market is not an appropriate allocative mechanism. That is, the market is not able to accurately reflect the aggregate preferences of consumers. In the absence of any market expression of consumer preferences for these goods, allocative decisions must be made through a command or political system. For a small rural town, the political decision regarding the level of fire protection is close to being a market decision. All the townspeople assemble to evaluate the costs of alternative fire protection systems and then vote to tax themselves the amount necessary to support such a system. In a more urbanized environment it is impossible to assemble all the townspeople, so a system of elected representatives is vested with the authority of reflecting the preferences of the populace. The proper role of the economist in dealing with public goods is to evaluate the costs and returns of alternatives that should be examined by the appropriate political entities such that the decisions of the body politic are consistent with the aggregate preferences

---

[4] The term "free rider" originally referred to the practice in the early West where neighbors had a common fence between their pastures and would share the duty of "riding" the fence to be certain it was sound. A neighbor who refused to share in the riding, making his neighbor do it all, became known as a "free rider."

of society. Of course, if the decisions are not consistent with the preferences of a majority of the consumers of nonmarket goods, then the remedy is to "vote the rascals out."

Common Property Goods

You have already been introduced to a common property good in the earlier example of groundwater in the Tampa, Florida, area. **Common property** refers to goods that, like the common pastures of early England, have no clear ownership or property rights.

Common property goods for which property rights are poorly defined and for which consumption is rival.

Common Property Goods Defined

There are two distinguishing characteristics of common property resources:

- Property rights to the goods are poorly defined or nonexistent.
- Consumption is rival.

Examples of common property resources include groundwater, fisheries, tribal pasture land, and highways.

The problem with common property resources is that individuals have incentives to extract or use up the good as quickly as possible before a potential consumption rival shows up. This tendency is clearly illustrated by the remark that the other guy is "driving like he owned the road."

Shrimp Harvesting—An Example

Fisheries, forestry, and mining are all extraction industries where a harvest today affects what will be available to be harvested in the future. Fishing, however, is different in that the property rights to harvest are not as clearly defined as they are in the case of forestry and mining. The shrimp industry is an example of a common property good for which markets fail to provide a biologically optimal harvest rate.

Maximum Sustainable Yield   **Maximum sustainable yield** (MSY) is a biological concept referring to the highest annual harvest rate of a renewable resource that is possible over an infinite time period. That is, what is the maximum extraction rate that will not diminish the stock so severely that future extraction rates will fall?

Maximum sustainable yield   a biological concept identifying the largest annual harvest of a renewable resource that will allow the population to be sustained at a specified level.

Based on scientific research biologists can determine the MSY of a shrimp fishery. The problem with common property resources is illustrated in Figure 21–1. The demand curve is derived from the demand of shrimp consumers. The supply is the marginal cost curve of shrimpers. If a free market is used to determine the annual harvest rate, shrimpers will extract Q_0 units in order to maximize their profits and the price will be P_0. Unfortunately, the biologists have determined that the MSY is less than Q_0, so we have a clear case of market failure. In this case, the short-run self-interest of the shrimpers differs from the long-run interest of society.

FIGURE 21–1 Shrimp harvesting.

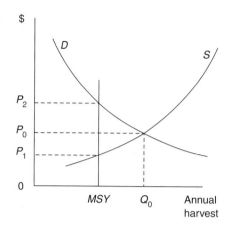

Use of Nonmarket Restrictions   Given the situation illustrated in Figure 21–1, some form of market intervention is necessary to ensure that the amount of shrimp harvested is no more than the MSY. This can be accomplished in either of two ways:

- The government could impose a tax on each ton of shrimp harvested. The amount of the tax would have to be large enough to push the supply curve up to that point where the MSY and demand lines cross. The market price of shrimp would be P_2, and the tax would be the vertical distance P_1P_2. The after-tax receipts of the shrimpers would be P_1.

- The government could ration the harvest to no more than MSY by issuing permits or auctioning the right to harvest shrimp. If the permits were auctioned, shrimpers would be willing to pay up to P_1P_2 for the permits. Consumers would pay P_2 for shrimp, and the net proceeds of the shrimpers would be P_1. If the permits were issued at no cost to the shrimpers, then the shrimpers would have a smaller harvest than in a free market but receive a higher price of P_2. This is clearly the preferred option from the point of view of the producers.[5]

The effect of either option is the same from the perspective of the consumer. Fewer shrimp will be available *this* year, and the price will be higher than what would occur without government intervention. However, the long-run or sustainable quantity available to the consumer will be greater because the stock is not being exploited beyond its sustainable level.

Policy Alternatives

There are basically three ways government can intervene in the markets for common property goods in an effort to provide socially optimal allocations. First, the property rights can be clearly identified, thereby converting common property into private property to be allocated by markets. Second, a tax can be imposed on extracting or using the common resource. As the cost of using the resource increases, use will fall to some socially or biologically desirable level. Third, some system of permits or licenses can be imposed to limit the use of the resource. The use of permits also implies a more clearly defined system of property rights.

---

[5] The impact of a harvest restriction on the receipts of shrimpers would depend on the elasticity of demand of shrimp consumers.

EXTERNALITIES CAUSE MARKET FAILURE

The economic system of the United States is composed of more than 10 million producing units such as farms, service enterprises, professional enterprises, and the like, and hundreds of millions of consuming units. The producing and consuming units are repeatedly linked together by literally billions of economic transactions that occur every day. For the most part, the activities of these millions of independent economic factors are coordinated by transactions in markets where the primary driving force of each unit is self-interest. In most instances, the self-interest of one individual does not affect the self-interest of other individuals. Within the modern supermarket, hundreds of shoppers are simultaneously attempting to maximize their welfare out of individual self-interest. A college student seeks to purchase pickles at the lowest possible price. Her action as a typical shopper for pickles will not in any way improve or damage the **welfare** of other shoppers. For the most part, the welfare of each shopper is completely independent of the actions of all other shoppers. Only infrequently is there a conflict between the welfare of one shopper and that of another. For instance, it is in the first shopper's best self-interest to squeeze each loaf of bread to find that loaf which appears to be the freshest. But all of this squeezing is not in the best interests of the second shopper, who is left with only presqueezed loaves from which to select. In this case, the welfare of one consumer is dependent on the actions of another consumer.

> **Welfare** the well-being or self-interest of an individual.

The classic Hollywood scene of a small group of shipwrecked survivors huddled together in a lifeboat is an example of a situation in which individual welfares become very highly interdependent. In fact, this interdependence as it conflicts with self-interest is the heady stuff that has supported many Hollywood scripts.

Fortunately, the college student shopping for her favorite dill pickles is not subjected daily to such drama as she makes her way through the economic maze. A supermarket is an example of an economic environment in which conflicts of interest rarely occur even though thousands of economic decisions are made during a day. Unfortunately, the case of production agriculture is less tranquil. Production decisions by the farmer that lead to his profit maximization are frequently in conflict with the best interests of neighboring farmers, consumers, recreationists, and the environment. A single application of pesticide to control a particularly nasty bug problem could bring the wrath of all four groups: neighboring farmers whose bees were killed, consumers who fear pesticide residue in the food they eat, recreationists who bemoan the loss of wildlife for hunting as predators of the pest also die, and environmentalists who fear the impact of the spraying on the quality of water running off the previously buggy field. The poor farmer seemingly can't do anything that is in his own self-interest without having someone complain.

Externalities Defined

The impacts of economic activity on those not immediately involved in the economic activity are called **externalities.** Innocent bystanders frequently have very legitimate concerns about the impact of someone else's activity on their own welfare. For instance, a student who, out of self-interest, cuts an article out of a journal in the library creates an externality for all subsequent students who wish to read the article. The economics of trying to balance off two legitimate but contradictory self-interests is what externalities are all about. Most analyses of externalities include two parts: an estimation of the costs and benefits of the economic activity to

> **Externalities** the economic or welfare impacts of an economic transaction on those not involved in the transaction.

the entire society, and an evaluation of the policy alternatives available to encourage private individuals to conduct their economic transactions in a socially desirable manner. Both of these issues will be explored in the following paragraphs.

Private and Social Costs/Benefits

The economic evaluation of externalities is part of a branch of economics known as "welfare analysis." This is not the analysis of "welfare" in the sense of a government program but in the sense of "well-being" of individuals in society and of those individuals in the aggregate.

Welfare analysis uses the familiar structure of a supply-demand diagram in a slightly different manner. The diagram and the axes are the same—quantities of a resource or good measured on the horizontal axis and the price per unit measured on the vertical axis. What is different is that instead of supply and demand, we talk about costs and benefits of an economic activity. Since the supply curve is nothing more than a marginal cost curve and a demand curve is nothing more than a marginal utility curve, the leap from supply-demand to cost-benefit is not a particularly long one. In fact most of the distance is in words rather than in concepts, as will be illustrated shortly.

The significant conceptual contribution of welfare analysis is the distinction between private costs/benefits and social costs/benefits. Private costs/benefits of an economic activity refer to the values of that activity paid/received by the individuals engaged in the activity. In most cases, most costs and benefits of an economic activity are captured by the individuals engaged in that activity, as in the case of a pickle shopper.

Social costs/benefits refer to the private costs/benefits of any economic activity plus any externalities associated with that activity. In those cases were externalities are significant, the divergence between private and social costs/benefits becomes the focus of the analysis. A couple of examples will illustrate the impacts of externalities and the tools of welfare analysis.

Pesticide Use—An Example of Externalities

The use of pesticides by a farmer is an example of an economic activity that has significant externalities on the cost side as illustrated in Figure 21–2. The marginal private benefit (or demand) is downward sloping, indicating that as more pesticide is

FIGURE 21–2
Pesticide use.

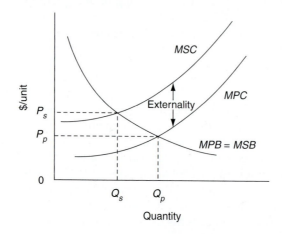

used, the additional benefit of each additional unit decreases. The marginal private benefit to the farmer of using pesticides is equal to the demand for pesticides in production. That is, the marginal private benefits captured by the farmer are equal to the value of the additional output obtained from each additional unit of pesticide use. In Figure 21–2 the marginal social benefits (*MSB*) are equal to the marginal private benefits (*MPB*), indicating that there are no externalities on the benefit side.

The marginal private cost of pesticide use is drawn as an upward-sloping curve, suggesting that as pesticide application increases, the cost per application increases. What is critical is that the marginal social cost (*MSC*) is greater than the marginal private cost (*MPC*) at every quantity reflecting the externalities associated with pesticide use. The effect of these externalities is to shift the *MSC* curve above the *MPC* curve with the vertical distance between them being the amount of the externality.

If left to the vagaries of the market, the farmer would use pesticides in the amount of Q_p (in Figure 21–2) where the marginal *private* cost is equal to the marginal *private* benefit. To use either more or less than this amount would be suboptimal from the perspective of the self-interest of the farmer. However, society wants the farmer to restrict pesticide use to a social optimum at quantity Q_s, where marginal *social* cost is equal to marginal *social* benefit.

The market failure is now clear. The result that a free market will generate is not consistent with the result society wants. Markets alone will fail to provide a socially optimal allocation of pesticide use.

A socially optimal level of pesticide use can be achieved by imposing a tax on pesticides that will increase the marginal private cost of using pesticides. That is, by imposing a tax equal to the amount of the externality, the private costs of pesticides would increase to the level shown as *MSC* on Figure 21–2. With such a tax imposed, the farmer's self-interest would encourage him to use Q_s units of pesticide. In this case, the use of a tax shifted the private costs of pesticides such that the market solution and the social optimum solution are one and the same. By using a tax, the market failure can be avoided and all the advantages of free market allocation are retained.

An alternative, and somewhat less friendly approach, would be to issue government regulations restricting the amount of pesticide use. Some sort of compliance enforcement would be required in this case. In general, when given the choice between markets and mandates, most folks prefer markets.

Higher Education—Another Example of Externalities

Higher education provides a second example of externalities. In this case, the externalities are to be found on the benefit side where the social benefits of higher education exceed the private benefits that the students capture. This is illustrated in Figure 21–3. The marginal private benefits of higher education are those benefits captured by the graduates in the form of higher salaries than for similar nongraduates.[6]

There are externalities society captures as a result of education. In the first place the typical graduate will pay more taxes and demand fewer social services than the nongraduate. Also, a better educated person is less likely to turn to crime and should

---

[6] Higher education is frequently thought of as an investment in human capital. The salary differential between graduates and nongraduates is a return to the initial investment. Some argue that higher education is also partially a consumer good that is purchased for the immediate utility it creates. In this analysis we will assume that the consumption value of education is zero. For most college students this is a very questionable assumption, but one that makes the economic point being made easier to comprehend.

FIGURE 21–3
College Education.

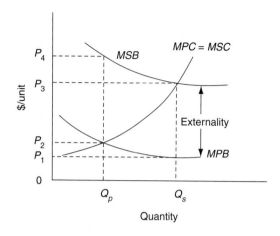

be a better informed voter.[7] Because of these and other externalities, the marginal social benefits of higher education far exceed the marginal private benefits. While there may be some exceptions, we assume the private and social costs to be the same.

If the student were required to pay the full costs of education, as is the case at some private schools, then the market clearing number of students would be Q_p. The cost of education for each student in the strictly private system would be P_2. But to view higher education within a strictly private framework is deceptive. As shown in Figure 21–3, from a societal point of view there is a market disequilibrium at enrollment level Q_p. At this level, society is gaining benefits of P_4 but the costs are only P_2. Obviously, at this level of enrollment society is underinvesting in higher education even though the private sector is investing at a level of private optimization. Social welfare will be optimized at an enrollment of Q_s, where marginal social benefits and marginal social costs are equalized. At this level of "production," the cost of education is P_3, but the marginal student is willing to pay only P_1. So, in order to entice Q_s students into higher education, the state must pay a subsidy for higher education in the amount of P_3P_1. In this manner, the total costs of educating Q_s students (P_3) are divided between the private costs to the students (P_1) and the social costs in the form of a government subsidy (P_1P_3).

Figure 21–3 illustrates the current situation in higher education in the United States, where we have a mixture of private colleges and public universities. The public sector has $Q_s - Q_p$ students in its universities, each of whom pays a price of P_1 even though the cost of providing that education is P_3. The difference is the state supported subsidy. The private sector serves Q_p students. But the cost to the private sector of producing the education has risen to the market clearing level of P_3. To see this, think about the market for college professors. If there were only private colleges and universities, there would be far fewer students and college professors would have to compete with one another for the few jobs available. Therefore, professors' salaries would be far lower than they are when the public sector is involved. That is, by getting into the education business the public sector has bid up the cost of providing that education from P_2 to P_3. The increased costs

---

[7] This is why Thomas Jefferson was such a strong supporter of public higher education. As president he asked Congress to approve the creation of a national university. After he failed to gain approval from Congress for a national university, he returned to Virginia to found the University of Virginia.

are the same for the private sector as for the public sector. Thus, those students seeking an education in the private schools end up paying the full cost of that education, which is P_3.

So in the case of higher education, as in all other cases where there are externalities, there is valid justification for government intervention in the private market such that the private market will adjust to a socially optimal output level. In most instances, the adjustment process from the private optimal to the social optimal will imply that the individual welfare of some members of society will be reduced[8] such that the collective welfare of all members of society can be increased.

Optimal Level of Pollution

One of the clearest examples of market failure resulting from externalities is pollution. A valid question is, How much pollution do you want? The usual response is "none." Stop and think about this response for a moment. Do you really want a world of zero pollution? How would you cook? Giant solar concentrators perhaps. How would you travel? Bicycle? Nope, making the steel for the bicycle produces pollution. Rollerblades? Nope, making the plastic involves petrochemicals and that involves refineries and they generate pollution. So, in fact the answer is not "none" but instead "less." How much less? Let's see how the economist approaches this question.

The costs associated with pollution are many and varied. There are costs associated with cleaning everything from cars to windows, there are health costs associated with the increased incidence of illness, and there are aesthetic costs associated with sunsets missed or outdoor works of sculpture ruined. As with any costs, the marginal social costs of pollution increase as the amount of pollution increases. This is illustrated in Figure 21–4 where marginal social costs per unit of pollution are measured on the vertical axis and the amount of pollution is measured on the horizontal axis, ranging from zero pollution at the origin to 100 percent at the end of the horizontal axis. Following the usual canons of economics, as the amount of pollution is increased, *ceteris paribus*, the marginal social costs of each additional unit of pollution increases. The social costs of the last marginal unit of additional pollution will be very high.[9] Obviously the marginal social costs of the last and next to last units of pollution are so great that this pollution must be avoided. Likewise, the costs of the first and second units of pollution (close to the origin) are so low that they are probably acceptable. The trick is to find the middle ground.

In order to reduce pollution, society must spend money on **pollution abatement** or control. As with other economic goods, the marginal social cost of pollution abatement increases as the amount of abatement increases. This is illustrated in Figure 21–5, which is similar to Figure 21–4 except that units of pollution abatement are measured on the horizontal axis. The first two or three units of abatement (that is, pollution control) come at a very low marginal social cost, while the last few units of abatement have such high social costs as to be of little practical relevance. Once again, no abatement is not enough and total abatement is too much.

Pollution abatement
the control or
reduction of pollution.

---

[8] In Figure 21–3 the "losers" are those individuals who would have attended private universities if there were only a private system. They have seen the cost of their education bid up from P_2 to P_3.

[9] The radioactive cloud that swept over Europe following the meltdown of a nuclear power plant *at Chernobyl,* Ukraine in 1986 might be an example of this extremely costly last marginal unit of pollution.

FIGURE 21–4 Social costs of pollution.

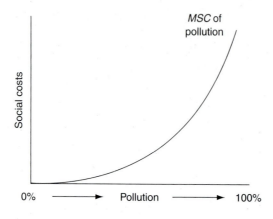

FIGURE 21–5 Social costs of abatement.

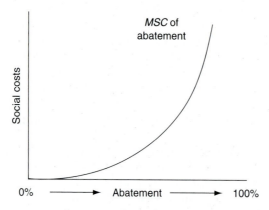

FIGURE 21–6 Social costs of pollution and abatement.

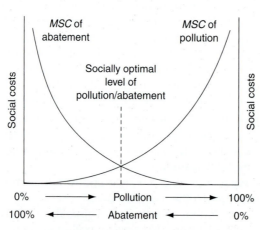

To find the "right" amount of pollution (and abatement) we need to combine the information in Figures 21–4 and 21–5. The result is shown in Figure 21–6 where Figure 21–5 has been flipped over and superimposed on Figure 21–4. This is possible since one more unit of abatement is equal to one less unit of pollution. Therefore, we can use a common horizontal axis on which pollution increases as abatement decreases (or reading from right to left, as abatement increases pollution decreases). Since the two curves in Figure 21–6 measure the marginal social costs of pollution and abatement, the socially optimal amount of pollution and abatement will occur at the point where marginal social costs of adding an addi-

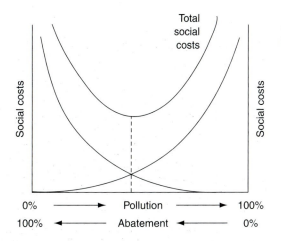

FIGURE 21–7 Total social costs of pollution/abatement.

tional unit of abatement are just equal to the marginal social costs of an additional unit of pollution. Abatement beyond the social optimum would have higher marginal social costs than the marginal social benefits gained from reduced pollution.

To abate either more or less than that, the amount shown as socially optimal in Figure 21–6 would imply higher total social costs. This can be seen in Figure 21–7. Here the total social costs of pollution plus abatement are shown. At zero abatement, the total social costs are very high because there is a lot of pollution. The first few units of abatement have low social costs but eliminate pollution with very high social costs. As a result, the total cost falls rapidly as the first few units of abatement are added. The socially optimal amount of pollution (shown by a dotted line in Figure 21–7) is that amount for which the total of pollution costs plus abatement costs is minimized. To add abatement beyond this level would cause the cost of abatement to increase more than the reduced cost of pollution and the total social cost would increase.

Returning to the question at the beginning of this section—How much pollution do you want?—we find that the answer depends on the marginal social costs of pollution and the marginal social costs of pollution abatement. The cynic might look at Figure 21–7 and say, "Nice diagram, but how do you measure that in the real world?" It is to the measurement issue that we now turn.

Benefit-Cost Analyses

When markets fail to provide socially optimal solutions because of the existence of externalities, the economist can attempt to estimate the socially optimal price/quantity using the technique of **benefit-cost analysis.** A b/c analysis is basically a form of investment analysis in which all the private and social costs and benefits are measured in a consistent fashion. As with investment analysis, all future costs and benefits must be reduced to the present value using an appropriate discount rate.

The trick to b/c analysis is to place a value on the externalities associated with the proposed economic activity. In many cases assigning these values is very difficult because there are no well-defined markets in which these values are established. This is where economics and art become very close, for it is certainly a subjective art to determine the best way of valuing an externality.

For example, suppose a proposed pollution abatement project is estimated to save 100 lives per year from reduced cancer. What is the value of 100 lives? The answer, of course, depends greatly on who the 100 folks are. If my mother is one of

Benefit-cost analysis
an economic analysis of an investment or policy alternative in which estimated total social benefits are compared with estimated total social costs.

the 100, then the value of the lives is quite great. But if they are all commuters in Los Angeles, then the value may not be so great. Obviously, this is something that is very subjective. The creative economist (and most are very creative—particularly around April 15) would look for a market in which people are putting a value on their own life. It could be done with interviews or a contact panel, but a better way is to let markets operate. Each of us answers the question "What am I worth?" when we buy life insurance. To find the value of 100 lives saved, simply determine the average insurance coverage for people in that population and multiply that by 100.

Once the economist has identified all externalities, has placed a value on all costs and benefits, and has converted all costs and benefits to present value, then simply divide the total benefit by the total cost to determine the benefit/cost ratio. If the ratio is greater than one, then the social benefits are greater than the social costs and the investment is feasible. If it is less than one, the activity is not viable from a societal point of view. A private b/c ratio can also be computed and compared with the social b/c ratio to highlight the divergence between private and social interests caused by externalities.

A marginal approach to solving the optimal pollution problem is possible using multiple benefit-cost analyses for alternative levels of abatement. If benefit-cost analyses were completed for abatement levels of 10 percent through 90 percent in increments of 10 percent what we would find is that the b/c ratio for the first 10 percent of abatement would be quite high and the b/c ratio for the last 10 percent would be quite low. Somewhere in between 10 percent abatement and 90 percent abatement, the b/c ratio would cross over from being greater than 1.0 to being less than 1.0. This would be the point of socially optimal abatement/pollution.

Benefit-cost analyses are frequently used (and in many cases mandated by enabling legislation) to evaluate policy alternatives proposed to correct market failure. We turn now to look at some of the innovative ways beyond simple taxes and subsidies that have been used to correct for market failures caused by externalities.

Policy Alternatives

If the welfare of society is best served by applying less pesticide than what the farmer wants to apply, then how is that application rate to be enforced? We have already seen that farmers left to their own self-interests in a freely competitive market will apply more pesticide than is socially optimal. Therefore, we have a case where a freely competitive market will not generate a socially optimal level of pesticide use. Society, through its democratic processes, can resolve this dilemma in either of five manners:

- Allow the free market to operate, with those sectors affected by the externalities paying the costs of those externalities.
- Allow the free market to operate, with the government using moral suasion in an effort to affect markets.
- Allow the free market to operate, with those sectors affected by the externalities being reimbursed by society for the additional costs.
- Allow the free market to operate, with those sectors creating the externalities being forced to pay for the additional social costs created by their private decisions.
- Have the government intervene in the market to force private decisions to conform to the broader interests of society.

The choice of approach is strictly a political decision. The role of the econo-mist in this political framework is twofold. First, the economist can estimate the magnitude and distribution of the costs and benefits of alternative courses of ac-tion; and second, the economist can evaluate the impact of each approach and identify appropriate means to achieve it.

The serious questions of environmental concern raised in the past two decades have been addressed with a combination of each of the five policy alter-natives previously indicated. Examples of each of the five will demonstrate how economic externalities have been handled in a world of political reality. In all but the first case, governmental intervention into the private, competitive market is necessary to resolve the differences between private and social benefits and costs.

Nonintervention

A policy of nonintervention in which those who bear the costs of externalities are forced to pay for them characterized environmental policy in the United States prior to the late 1960s and continues to characterize most of our policies today with regard to pollution on the high seas. If an oil spill from a Mexican drilling platform in the Gulf of Mexico spoils the shrimp harvest and tourist business along the Texas shore of the gulf, who pays the costs of that pollution to the shrimpers and the tourist industry? Under current international agreements (or lack thereof), exter-nalities are typically absorbed by the innocent bystanders that happen to be ad-versely affected by what happens in international waters. Therefore, the costs of a poor shrimp harvest caused by a Mexican oil spill are paid for by the Texas shrimp industry.[10] Likewise, it is the owners of motels, restaurants, and other tourist at-tractions that bear the cost, in terms of lost revenue, from having a previously beau-tiful beach covered with black goo. A policy of nonintervention to correct for externalities in this example is fine for the Mexicans, terrible for the Texans, and so-cially unjust and unfair from the point of view of most of us.

Moral Suasion

An alternative approach is to allow markets to operate and let the costs of exter-nalities fall on those who are affected, but with efforts by the government or pro-ducers to change the behavior of individuals to be more socially acceptable. For instance, a beer can label includes the words "recyclable aluminum" while a root beer can label includes the words "Please recycle." The latter is a stronger state-ment that clearly appeals to your moral responsibilities as a good and just indi-vidual. How could you possibly throw away a can that politely asks you not to?

Sometimes moral suasion is a little more heavy handed. The label on the beer can also includes the following: "Government warning: (1) According to the sur-geon general, women should not drink alcoholic beverages during pregnancy be-cause of the risk of birth defects." This is a clear case of government using moral suasion to change private behavior (i.e., the mother's decision to drink or not). It is also a clear case of externalities where the mother, who drinks the beer, does not bear the external costs of that drink. Instead it is the child that bears the cost.

---

[10] The Texas shrimp industry could try to sue the Mexican oil company, but then the only winners would be the lawyers.

Society Compensates Recipients of Externalities

A serious externality of the coal mining business is that many workers in the mines contract what is commonly known as black lung disease—an accumulation of coal dust in the lungs that eventually impairs the normal pulmonary function. Some time ago, Congress passed legislation that provided for controls to reduce the dangers of contracting the disease and for compensation to those workers whose productive lifetime is shortened by the disease. This black lung program is an example of a policy in which those affected by the externality (coal miners) are reimbursed by society (the federal government) for the social costs of the externality.

Producers of Externality Pay Full Social Cost

A fourth alternative is to make the polluter pay the full social cost rather than just the private cost for any economic activity. The simple way to do this, shown in the previous pesticide example, is to place a tax on the activity that creates the externality. There are several alternative policy approaches that have been used in the field of pollution control to place the financial burden of the pollution on the producer of that pollution. Let's take a look at three approaches.

Emission Charges   The traditional approach is to tax the polluter the amount of externality. The biggest problem with emission charges is in knowing at what level to set the tax and in taxing differently situated producers at the same rate. Should a plant that spews acid rain over the Grand Canyon be taxed at the same rate as a producer that creates acid rain over the Gulf of Mexico?

Transferable Pollution Rights   One of the problems with pollution is that property rights to pollute are poorly defined. An alternative policy approach that is currently being used in the electric power industry is for the Environmental Protection Agency to create **transferable pollution rights** in the form of discharge permits. Each permit entitles the holder to discharge a given amount of a given pollutant per unit of time. The permits create clear property rights to pollute.

Initially the permits were auctioned off to buyers. Once all the permits were sold, a private market for permits emerged with any holder perfectly free to sell excess discharge capacity to another firm at a mutually agreeable price. Suppose a firm is constrained by permits held for carbon monoxide. The firm can either:

- Keep its current technology and buy more permits or
- Install new abatement equipment that will allow it to expand production within the limits of currently held permits.

Since permits and new pollution control equipment are almost perfect substitutes, it stands to reason that in time the price of permits will approach that of the equipment. Since the number of permits does not change, the total amount of pollution never increases. The beauty of this plan is that property rights are clear and the freedom of the market is used to guide producers toward a socially optimal solution.

The advent of transferable rights has resulted in some interesting economic behavior. Recently a large utility in New York exchanged rights for one pollutant with a utility in Arizona for another pollutant. Since the current value of the per-

Transferable pollution rights
pollution discharge permits for a specific quantity of discharge per unit of time. The permits may be transferred (i.e., sold) from one producer to another, but the total amount of discharge remains constant.

mits was far greater than the original cost of the permits, both firms earned "profits" in an accounting sense without any change in the amount of pollution rights held. Both firms agreed to donate these profits to charity.

A second interesting use of the permits has been a move by some environmental organizations to enter the market for permits and then hold them unused. In essence, if an environmental group wants to reduce pollution, it can buy the real thing on the open market.

Bubble Policies   A "bubble" policy is essentially a local pollution control policy. A small geographic area can decide to put a bubble over the region and not allow any more pollution to be generated under the bubble. Suppose Gary, Indiana, put a bubble over itself and declared that no more pollution could be generated under the bubble. If Fran wanted to open a dry cleaning shop in a new shopping center, she couldn't open her new store until such time as she reduced the pollution elsewhere in an amount equal to what she would add to the bubble.[11] Fran has two choices:

- She could buy an existing dry cleaning establishment in an older, run-down part of town and close it down, thus reducing pollution and allowing her to open her new store.
- Fran could find the owner of an old store with old, high-pollution equipment and offer to help pay the cost of putting in new equipment that would reduce the pollution from the old shop so she could open her new store.

If Fran is not able to reduce pollution elsewhere under the bubble, then she can't open her fancy new store.

A disadvantage of the bubble approach is that the biggest "winners" are the oldest, worst polluters before the bubble was put in place. So while the bubble policy works, it tends to reward the past "bad" guys at the expense of good ol' Fran.

Government Intervention

The final policy alternative is for the government to intervene directly in the private market in an effort to make the market achieve social aims. This can be done by altering either of the two dimensions of a market—price or quantity. If governmental intervention changes one, then the other will certainly follow. Intervention on the price side usually takes the form of a tax or subsidy to offset the externality, but in some cases direct price fixing by government regulators completely replaces the allocative role of the market. In the pesticide example a tax on inputs tends to increase the marginal costs of production, thereby reducing the equilibrium input and output levels. A subsidy for pesticide use would produce exactly the opposite result.

The other avenue for governmental intervention into a market is through the quantity side of the market. Examples include restrictions on the amount of pollution a car may produce and the quantity of mature trees that can be harvested in the Pacific Northwest. These are cases where the government forsakes the velvet glove of market persuasion and uses the ugly club of bureaucratic mandates.

---

[11] Dry cleaners, particularly older ones, are very heavy polluters.

INFORMATION ASYMMETRIES

Asymmetric knowledge   when the buyer and seller do not have the same information about a market or good.

A final cause of market failure is what has become known in the literature as **asymmetric knowledge.** One of the assumptions about perfectly competitive markets is that both the buyer and the seller have the same information about a transaction. If either party to a transaction possesses more information than the other party, then we say the knowledge is asymmetric, or unequal. Recent studies, for which the Nobel prize in economic science was awarded in 2001, have shown that asymmetric knowledge leads to inefficient markets or market failure. Two examples will illustrate what happens when there is asymmetric knowledge.

Used Cars

Suppose Juan buys a brand new car for $25,000. After one week he decides he does not like the blue color and he really wants a red vehicle. So, even though the car only has 500 miles on the odometer, Juan tries to sell the car. If the average life of a car is 150,000 miles, then Juan has used up just 1/300 of its life, or a little less than $100. Is there any chance Juan is going to be able to sell the car to someone else for $24,900? Of course not. It will probably bring no more than $22,000 even though it was worth $25,000 just 500 miles ago. Why? The answer to this question is what won George A. Akerlof a Nobel prize.[12]

The answer, of course, lies in asymmetric information about the car. Juan knows that the car is perfectly fine, but what does the buyer know about the car? Absolutely nothing—and that is the source of the market failure. Absent any knowledge about the car, the buyer would speculate about the motives of Juan in selling the car. Did Juan buy it and discover that it is a lemon? Has it been wrecked and repaired? Has it been driven 15,000 miles and had the odometer turned back? As a result of these concerns, potential buyers will pay no more than $22,000 for Juan's car despite his protestations that the car is perfectly fine. Moreover, if the potential buyer were to consider a knowledge-based price of around $24,900, the buyer would say for $100 more he could get a new one without the lingering doubts.

Baseball's Free Agents

The labor market for baseball players is a most interesting market. For the first 6 years a player is in Major League Baseball, the player is essentially owned by his team. After 6 years the player may declare himself a free agent and sell his talent to the highest bidder. An interesting study[13] found that among free agent pitchers, those who changed teams spent an average of 28 days per season on the disabled list while those who do not switch teams spent only 5 days disabled. Why the astonishing disparity?

The answer, of course, lies in asymmetric information about the pitchers. After 6 years on a team prior to free agency, the team becomes quite knowledgeable about pitchers and who is more or less prone to injuries. For a pitcher who has few injuries, the original team is willing to match competitive bids of other teams to keep the guy on the team. For those pitchers that are injury prone, the original team is willing to let them go without much of a struggle.

---

[12] Akerlof, George A, "The Market for 'Lemons': Quality Uncertainty and the Market Mechanism," *Quarterly Journal of Economics,* August 1970, pp. 488–500.

[13] Lehn, Kenneth, "Information Asymmetries in Baseball's Free Agent Market," *Economic Inquiry,* Vol. 22, January 1984, pp. 37–44.

In this example, the seller (the original team) has far more knowledge than the buyer. This asymmetric information leads to the interesting result that injury-prone pitchers get traded more than injury-averse pitchers. Again, this market failure is caused by asymmetric information. The similarity between free agent pitchers and used car lemons in the previous example should be clear.

PROBLEMS IN DEALING WITH MARKET FAILURE

When markets fail, there is a difference between a market-determined allocation pattern and that which is socially optimal. In such cases intervention in the market by government can be justified. However, this does not mean that in all cases of market failure government intervention is appropriate. In fact, in some situations government intervention may take a bad situation and make it worse. Let's take a look at some of the limitations of government intervention to correct market failures.

Information Failure

Appropriate government intervention to correct market failure requires accurate information about the market failure itself and about what is socially optimal. If information is inadequate or incorrect, then intervention may be worse than the market failure itself.

For example, the federal government intervened on behalf of the spotted owl by prohibiting the cutting of large tracts of timber in the Pacific Northwest. The cutting of the timber would have destroyed the habitat of the owl and led to its eventual demise as a species. The implications of this government intervention in the market for timber are twofold:

- The spotted owl *may* continue as a distinct species.
- The price of lumber *did* go up.

The question is whether this intervention was socially optimal. When given a choice between maybe saving the owl or definitely paying several hundred dollars more for a house, we may find that a lot of home buyers don't give a hoot about owls.

Economic Efficiency Considerations

It is appropriate to consider the economic efficiency of government intervention in cases of market failure. The usual criterion for evaluating economic efficiency is the ratio between the value of the benefits from correcting market failure and the costs of so doing.

Direct Cost of Government Intervention

The direct costs of government intervention include the cost of government itself and the costs on the firms subjected to the intervention. In most cases, government intervention in a market implies regulation and that implies inspectors, rule makers, and lawyers within government. All of this is not without costs to the taxpayers. Regulatory activities have certainly been one of the more rapidly growing roles of government during the past few decades. The cost of running the government thus becomes a part of the social costs of government intervention.

The other direct costs of intervention are borne by the firms being regulated. In the first place, intervention may increase the costs of production of the firms. Second, there is the cost of compliance to the regulated firm.[14] Finally, the productivity of the firm may be reduced as a result of intervention.

Indirect Cost of Government Intervention

While it is extremely difficult to measure, there can be little doubt that government interventions and the regulations that may result are a drag on the economy in general. The extent to which the entrepreneurial spirit is squelched and innovation stifled is an indirect economic cost of government intervention that is shared by all.

Equity Considerations

Equity   the distributional impacts of a policy between the rich and the poor, between Americans and foreigners, and so forth.

Equity refers to the distributional implications of governmental intervention: Who are the winners and who are the losers? While most interventions to correct market failure are not designed explicitly to modify or affect the distribution of income, most of them do have some implications for equity.

Domestic

Policies of intervention to correct for market failures can have equity implications for both producers and consumers. On the consumer side, there is little doubt that two of the government's biggest interventions (in terms of dollars) are Social Security and Medicare, both of which tend to redistribute money from the workers to the elderly. Programs like the school lunch program redistribute from the wealthy to the poor.

Among producers, most government interventions are probably more costly to the small firm than the large. Large firms typically have specialists within the corporate structure who can interpret and implement regulations fairly efficiently. In the typical, small single proprietorship firm, these costs can be substantial, and the relative costs associated with inadvertent violation are probably greater than for a large firm. For instance, the U.S. Department of Agriculture is in the process of changing the way meat is inspected from visual inspection to bacterial inspection in a laboratory. Since the new procedures will better protect the wholesomeness of our meat supply, it is probably an efficient, effective intervention. However, for the small meat packer the costs of establishing and maintaining the required laboratory are going to be disproportionately higher than for large packers that already have labs and scientists.

International

Finally, what are the distributional implications of government intervention within a global context? Our international trade theory suggests that production will move to those countries that can produce relatively efficiently. As government interventions restrict the relative efficiency of producers in one country, it may cause production to shift to another. For example, there is little question that if left to its own devices, the steel industry is a heavy polluter of our atmosphere. In order to reduce that pollution in the United States the government has intervened.

---

[14] In today's litigious society an important part of compliance costs can be legal expenses.

Consequently, the cost of producing steel in the United States has increased dramatically (and pollution has fallen equally dramatically). But now we are in a position where it is less costly to mine the iron ore and coal in the United States, ship it to Korea to be made into steel in factories that are very efficient and that pollute like crazy, and then ship it back to the United States.

So, in essence, the implication of our pollution control measures in the United States has been to shift the steel industry away from the United States to those countries that are willing to pollute themselves more than we are willing to pollute ourselves. If a clean environment is our primary concern, then the pollution control measures have been effective. If it is American jobs and industrial strength or global pollution that is our primary concern, then the government intervention has been a disaster.

Environmental equity was one of the main concerns of environmentalists when the North American Free Trade Agreement (NAFTA) between Mexico, Canada, and the United States was being negotiated. Much of the concern centered around a group of factories located on the south side of the Mexico-U.S. border that engage in pollution generating activities that would not be allowed in the United States. While some say that if the Mexicans want to pollute their own environment, then let them, others view the environment in a global perspective and say that pollution anywhere damages the environment globally.

The bottom line is that government intervention to correct market failures can have the effect of shifting production from the United States to another country. In such cases, the intervention, rather than helping correct market failures, has the effect of increasing total pollution at the global level.

SUMMARY

In most cases, free competitive markets are efficient allocation systems. However, in some situations free markets will not produce results that are optimal from the point of view of society. These situations are called market failure. In cases of market failure it is appropriate for government to become involved, ensuring that the ultimate allocation meets the interests of the society.

One cause of market failure is poorly defined property rights. If ownership rights to a good are not well defined, then the ability of a market to allocate that good is hampered. Market failure also occurs in the allocation of public goods—those goods for which no markets exist. A common problem with public goods is free riders or users of the public good who do not pay their fair share of the costs of the good. Finally, common property goods frequently suffer market failure. Some system of quotas or permits may be used to allocate common property goods.

The private costs and returns of an economic transaction are those that are captured by the two parties to the transaction. Social costs and returns include any additional costs and returns captured by third parties. If there is a difference between social and private, then externalities exist. The presence of externalities usually results in market failure. In such cases taxes and subsidies may be used to encourage the private parties to behave in a socially desirable manner.

A social optimum is achieved when the marginal social cost of an activity is equal to the marginal social benefit of that activity. An example is pollution. An optimal amount of pollution is that amount at which the marginal social costs of pollution are equal to the marginal social cost of pollution abatement. At this point the total social costs of pollution plus abatement are minimized.

A benefit-cost analysis is a systematic accounting of all the private and social costs and returns associated with some economic activity. The identification and measurement of all externalities are the hard part of benefit-cost analyses.

Asymmetric information can also lead to market failure. This occurs when either the buyer or seller has more information about the product or market than the other side of a transaction.

Efforts to use the power of government to correct market failure are not without potential problems. It is not uncommon for government to operate with less than full information concerning the market failure. And governments do have real costs that must be compared with the benefits received from government intervention. Finally, government intervention usually has some equity implications associated with any redistribution effect.

KEY TERMS

Asymmetric information	Nonmarket goods
Benefit-cost analysis	Nonrival
Coase theorem	Pollution abatement
Common property	Private
Equity	Property rights
Externalities	Public goods
Free rider	Rival
Market failure	Social
Market goods	Transferable pollution rights
Maximum sustainable yield	Welfare
Nonexcludable	

PROBLEMS AND DISCUSSION QUESTIONS

1. Explain what market failure is, and identify four types of goods for which market failure is likely.
2. Give three additional examples of markets in which property rights are poorly defined.
3. The City of Springfield is considering the installation of downtown parking meters. Use the Coase theorem to discuss the steps that should be taken to make the program a success.
4. Identify three additional markets in which free riders are a significant problem.
5. Give further examples of goods that are rival and nonrival in consumption.
6. Discuss the following proposition: Pollution, like garbage, is a good with a negative price.
7. The mayor of Springfield justifies a proposed city bus system by pointing out that it has a benefit-cost ratio of 3 to 2. What does this mean?
8. There are numerous organizations dealing with environmental issues. Four that have stood the test of time are the Environmental Protection Agency (**www.epa.gov**), Resources for the Future (**www.rff.org**), the Environmental Working Group (**www.ewg.org**), and the Worldwatch Institute (**www.worldwatch.org**).

The Malthusian Dilemma

*F*or the past 200 years, the peoples of the world have faced the possibility of the human population exceeding the earth's capacity to feed it. To some, this is a scientific inevitability. To others, the fact that this has been an inevitability for 200 years suggests that it is not all that inevitable.[1] It is to the origins of this concern and its modern manifestations to which we now turn.

Two centuries ago the intellectual world was undergoing a revolution. In a variety of fields writers such as John Locke and Adam Smith wrote of the perfectibility of man. The general tenet was that in politics, economics, and all other endeavors man had the ability to improve his lot using the power of reason. On this side of the pond the search for material improvement in an age of reason inspired the framers of the Constitution. The phrase "in Order to form a more perfect Union" suggests that progress is possible and that such progress will be the result of man's efforts rather than of some divine phenomenon.

Within this "age of reason" and optimism came the generally pessimistic writings of **Thomas Malthus**—an English Calvinist minister who is primarily remembered for his *Essay on the Principles of Population,* first published in 1798. In this essay, and in subsequent revisions, Malthus argued that because of "human instinct," population growth would outpace the growth in the "means of subsistence" such that eventual famine was inevitable. In its simplest form the Malthusian doctrine holds that population increases at a geometric rate (2,4,8, 16 . . .) while food production increases at an arithmetic rate (2,3,4,5 . . .). Therefore, inevitably the population will outstrip the food supply and "misery and vice" will result. To avoid these unwelcome, inevitable consequences he called for "moral restraint" to reduce population growth. This pessimistic prognostication became known as the Malthusian dilemma.

The dilemma is still with us today. There is no shortage of neo-Malthusian scientists (and some pseudoscientists) warning us that man is stretching his environment beyond its limits.[2] Malthus's warning of "misery and vice" is replaced in the contemporary context with phrases like "sustainability" and "biodiversity." But the argument of an inevitable conflict between population growth and the finite resources of our earth remains. As Malthus put it: "Population was always pressing against food, and was always ready to start off at a faster rate than that at which the food was actually increasing."

Thomas Malthus an English Calvinist minister who is primarily remembered for his *Essay on the Principles of Population*, first published in 1798.

---

[1] One author is reminded of a popular saying in Brazil: "Brazil is the country of the future . . . and always will be."

[2] For many years a leading neo-Malthusian was Lester Brown. He created a think tank, Worldwatch Institute (**http://www.worldwatch.org/**), in Washington, D.C., to address the population issue. The publications of the institute are one of the best sources for literature in this field.

On the other side of this debate, the non-Malthusians argue that just as there has been no cataclysmic confrontation between man and food for the past 200 years, there will be no inevitable collision in the next 200 years. They argue that technological improvements and scientific advances will continue to expand our ability to produce more food using our available resources, and that population growth will continue to decline as the fruits of economic advancement are spread to all societies in our global community.

Let us now turn to a more thorough examination of these two worldviews: the neo-Malthusian and the non-Malthusian views.

THE NEO-MALTHUSIANS

The neo-Malthusians, and there are plenty of them, tend to emphasize the rapid increase in population that has occurred during recent years and the pressures that population growth puts not only on our food supply but also on the environment. In fact, most neo-Malthusians tend to emphasize the population pressure on the environment more than on the food system.

Since 1950 more people have been placed upon our small spaceship we call earth than in all time prior to 1950. Can our fragile planet handle the ever pressing needs of more and more mouths as they increase at a Malthusian geometric rate? As shown in Figure 22–1, the current population of earth is around 6.3 billion people with the expectation that the population will increase to about 9.5 billion within the next 50 years. For every two mouths today, there will be three by 2050—about the time most college students of traditional age will be slipping into retirement. The current population growth rate is about 9,000 additional mouths to feed per hour, resulting from about 15,000 births and 6,000 deaths per hour. This is the equivalent of creating a new city of 210,000 additional people every day. Just think about the farms, processing, and distribution required to feed a city of 210,000, and then think about adding that to our fragile globe every single day—endlessly. Under such pressure, something is bound to "snap" at some time.

FIGURE 22–1 World population projections to 2050. *Source:* U.S. Bureau of the Census, International Database.

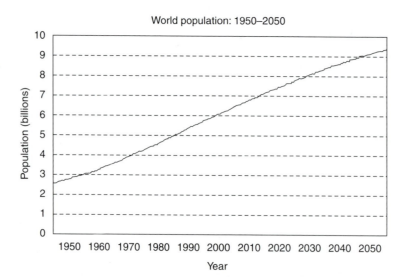

Moreover, the Neo-Malthusians point out, most of the population growth expected in the near future is in those countries that can least afford it. The reasons for this will be discussed shortly. By 2050 India, China, and Pakistan will be the three most populous countries in the world (in the order listed). About one-third of the world's population in 2050 will be in these three countries. The United States and Nigeria will round out the top five. Population in developed[3] countries is actually projected to fall between the present and 2050.

Unfortunately, food production is not keeping up with population growth. According to a recent report, grain production per capita peaked in 1984 at 342 kg/capita and had fallen to 317 kg/capita in 1998.[4] Part of the reason for this decline is that the ability to expand production through irrigation is near the limit of freshwater availability. As evidence of the finite limits of freshwater, the Worldwatch Institute points out that the "Yellow River, the northernmost of China's two major rivers, has run dry for a part of each year since 1985, with the dry period becoming progressively longer. In 1997, it failed to make it to the sea for 226 days."[5] This is a good illustration of the shift from the limits of food to the limits of the environment.

According to most neo-Malthusians, food and water are not the only limits to population growth. Other elements of our environment also have finite limits. Deforestation is blamed for many of the 11,000 deaths in Honduras and Nicaragua when hurricane Mitch dumped 2 feet of rain in 24 hours on denuded hillsides that turned into engulfing mudslides. Our fisheries are being depleted at a rapid rate; our cropland is turning into parking lots and golf courses; we are using more petroleum than we are finding; and to top it all off, there is a hole in the ozone layer.

In light of many disturbing trends, it is relatively easy to be pessimistic about what the future holds for planet earth. All will agree that current trends cannot be extended indefinitely. Something, somewhere is going to have to give. We turn now to the non-Malthusians, who see change and adjustment rather than continuity in the future. They, like Malthus, believe in the power of population control by man occurring before the gloom of population control by famine.

THE NON-MALTHUSIANS

The non-Malthusians argue that for more than two centuries the Malthusian inevitability has been propagated by alarmists who fear the end of the world as we know it. The non-Malthusians ask if the inevitable end is any more inevitable today than it was a century ago or two centuries ago?

At the most fundamental level the non-Malthusians argue that the planet and man are in a continuous state of adjustment to the reality of the times. These adjustments take a variety of forms: some are driven by economic forces, others by government policy, and yet others by the slow changes of culture over time. Let's look at examples of each of these forces.

The source of the protein we eat is grain. Some of that grain is eaten directly as food, while the rest is given to livestock as feed to create meat, eggs, and milk. Animals are inherently inefficient converters of vegetable protein into animal protein.

---

[3] Words used to compare the stage of development of a country are all value-laden. Some use the rich-poor dichotomy, while others use the traditional-developing-developed trichotomy.

[4] Lester R. Brown and associates, *Beyond Malthus: Sixteen Dimensions of the Population Problem*, Worldwatch Institute, Paper #143, 1998, p. 13.

[5] Brown, p. 16.

As a result, when we eat a pound of animal protein, we are really eating several pounds of grain protein. In India and other countries where food is not abundant, the economic system of price adjustment bids up the price of animal protein to a level that is so high that most people consume plant protein rather than animal protein. In this way, the available grain is consumed by humans rather than livestock.[6]

Government policy can be used to address the inevitability of a Malthusian crisis. The best example of this is China's "one child" policy that limits parents to one child only. Economic incentives are used to reward one-child families, and birth control/abortion is available to all at no cost. As a result, the population of China is expected to grow by only 21 percent by 2050, while that of India is projected to grow by 57 percent.

Finally, cultural changes occur that make obsolete the worst fears of the neo-Malthusians. The non-Malthusians point out that while the population of the world is increasing, it is increasing at a decreasing rate for reasons that will be developed in the next section. As shown in Figure 22–2 the rate of population growth is slowing and is expected to continue to slow well into the future. In the words of Malthus, the "moral restraint" of later marriage and smaller families is becoming the cultural norm, causing a slow decline in the rate of population growth to bring it in line with the growth of our food production.

In a wonderfully optimistic book, Dr. Don Paarlberg, a noted policy economist with Purdue University, writes that "the ancient enemy [of hunger] is in retreat. Coming into being is a world that will be well fed.... Ours is the first generation to dare to think in terms of food enough for all."[7] But he warns that the "Four Horsemen of the Apocalypse still ride. As we see the possibility of curbing one, Famine, two others appear as growing threats: War, in the form of nuclear holocaust, and Pestilence, a new deadly disease [AIDS] for which, as this is written, there is no known cure."[8]

Which worldview, the neo-Malthusian's or the non-Malthusian's, is correct? This takes us back to the "facts-beliefs-values" trilogy that is the foundation of all policy analysis. Because of different values, two prominent scientists can look at the same facts and have different beliefs about the future. All would agree that change is inevitable. Tomorrow won't look like today. Will that change be evolutionary or revolutionary? This is the basic question.

The Demographic Transition

Birthrate the number of births per thousand of population per year.

Death rate the number of deaths per thousand of population per year.

Demography is the study of populations and the dynamics of population growth and change. Economic demography therefore is the study of the impact of economic change on population change, and vice versa. One of the staples of economic demography is the demographic transition—an explanation of demographic change as it relates to economic change.

The rate of growth of the population in any country is based on two fundamental factors: the **birthrate** and the **death rate**. The greater the difference between the two, the faster the rate of growth of the population. Birthrates and death rates are

---

[6] In the United States we could easily support a population three or four times larger than the current one with no changes in food production. We would, however, have to get used to the idea of going to Wendy's for a soyburger rather than a hamburger.

[7] Don Paarlberg, *Toward a Well-Fed World*, Iowa State University Press, Ames, 1988, p. 260.

[8] Paarlberg, p. 254.

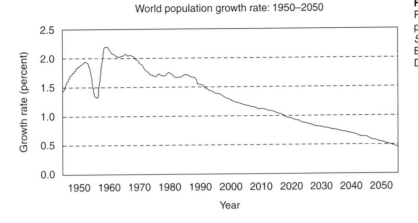

FIGURE 22–2
Population growth rate, projections to 2050. *Source:* U.S. Census Bureau, International Database.

usually expressed as a rate per thousand of the population. For instance, the current birthrate in the United States is about 14.8 per thousand, and the death rate is 8.8 per thousand. Thus, there is a **natural rate of population growth** (excluding migration) in the United States of 6.0 per thousand, or 0.6 percent. Birthrates are a cultural matter, while death rates depend primarily on the availability of food and health care.

To understand the **demographic transition,** we must divide the economic societies of the world into three categories: traditional, developing, and developed. These categories are based on the level of economic development or advancement of the country. Such rankings are subjective and inexact, but that does not distract from the explanatory powers of the demographic transition.

Natural rate of population growth the difference between the birthrate and the death rate. It is the biological rate at which the population is growing (excluding migration).

Demographic transition a model of population growth that emphasizes the relationship between economic growth and population growth.

Traditional

In traditional societies birthrates and death rates are both quite high. Most of the population is involved in subsistence agriculture or other activities outside of the small monetary economy of the country. For these individuals a large family is an asset that ensures ample labor to support the next generation. In addition there is usually neither awareness of nor availability of birth control devices. As a consequence birthrates are quite high.

Death rates are also quite high in traditional societies because of the poor availability of health care facilities and frequent famines. Many individuals, particularly the young and the old, are weakened by hunger, malnutrition, parasites, and disease, making them susceptible to death from the mildest of maladies. Of the 130 million babies born into the world this year, it is estimated that 8 million will never reach their first birthday.

Because both birthrates and death rates are high in traditional societies, the natural rate of increase in the population is fairly small. This is illustrated in Figure 22–3. Here, the birthrate and death rate are measured on the vertical axis, while the stage of development is measured along the horizontal axis. The difference between the birthrate and the death rate is the natural rate of population increase. In the traditional society high birthrates are checked by high death rates, and the natural rate of population increase is relatively small.

FIGURE 22–3 The demographic transition.

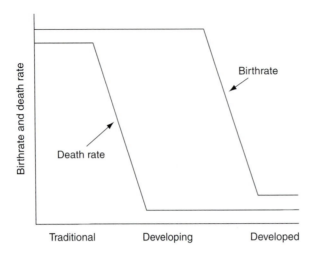

Developing

As an economic society moves from traditional to developing, the greatest initial pressure is on providing those services that prevent death. One universal instinct of man is survival: we seek to avoid the grim reaper as much as possible. Since the main causes of death are lack of food and health care, these are the first improvements people in developing countries desire. Improvement in both the quantity and quality of food is one of the earliest indicators of economic advancement. Likewise, early in the development process there is a distinct shift from folk medicine, usually administered by a shaman, to modern medicine stressing preventive measures such as immunizations and sanitation.

The impact of these changes on the death rate in developing societies is substantial and rapid. As shown in Figure 22–3 the death rate drops abruptly while the birthrate, largely determined by cultural factors, continues to be high. The result is that the first steps in the development process lead to high rates of natural population growth. A contemporary (and random) example of this is Bangladesh, with a birthrate of 30 and a death rate of 11. Notice that the death rate in Bangladesh is not greatly different from that of the United States, but the birthrate is still at a traditional level, resulting in a natural rate of increase of 19 per thousand, or 1.9 percent.

While the difference between a natural rate of increase for Bangladesh of 1.9 percent and 0.6 percent for the United States may not seem to be large, when those rates of growth are compounded over a period of time, the differences become quite pronounced. In 50 years, a population of 100 in Bangladesh will have grown to 256, while in the United States the same population will have grown to only 135.

So, in developing societies the demographic transition predicts a population explosion, which is exactly what we observe in countries such as India, Bangladesh, and Nigeria. It is almost as if economic development produces its own curse: just as the ability to provide improved nutrition and health care emerges, the population explosion overwhelms or checks those improvements.

Developed

In a developed society birthrates finally come down to match the low death rates. The changes are, of course, cultural, but those changes do have an economic explanation. For the traditional subsistence farmer, another child is viewed as a life-long asset by the parents. In traditional societies the size of the family labor pool determines the economic viability of the family. Not so in developed societies. Let us assure you, dear reader, that your parents considered you to be a liability (but, of course, a loved and cherished liability). We have seen estimates of the cost of a child in the United States from birth through college that run in the one-half-million-dollar range. When faced with this economic reality, the number of times parents want to roll those dice is usually two or three.

Of course there are all sorts of other things that contribute to lower birthrates in developed societies. Birth control is more available and is relatively inexpensive compared with the cost of another kid. Because of improved health care, the natural desire to have heirs and grandchildren no longer requires five or six kids to have one survive. In developed societies parents assume that a healthy baby will soon be a college graduate starting a family and giving grandma and grandpa something to do in their old age.

As shown in Figure 22–3, the natural rate of population increase in developed societies is quite low or even negative. Projections by the United Nations for population growth from 1998 to 2050 show the United States and the United Kingdom with small increases; while Russia, Japan, Germany, France, and Italy are projected to have population decreases. According to the demographic transition theory, most of the projected world population growth to 2050 is accounted for by those countries in the middle of the demographic transition.

Since most of the world's population is currently in the middle segment of the demographic transition, a critical question is, How long does it take to make the transition? Since the death rate change is driven by new technologies that can easily be borrowed from other societies, the change in the death rate is swift. But the change in the birthrate is a cultural change, and cultures are not easily shared across societies. Cultural change takes a lot of time and is measured in generations rather than years. Urbanization and education are highly correlated with family size. It has been our observation that our fellow college professors in Brazil have families that are about the same size as our colleagues in the United States. The difference, of course, is that there are a lot more professors (i.e., urbanized, educated people) in the United States than in Brazil, so the average family size in Brazil is greater than in the United States. Nonetheless, Brazil is moving through the transition with a birthrate down to 20 per thousand. South Korea is even further along the transition with a birthrate of 16 per thousand. In Spain, a country that is 99 percent Catholic, the birthrate is down to 10 per thousand.

Cultural change takes time as each generation reexamines its traditions through the changing prism of time. Family planning is a concerted effort to accelerate the process of cultural change. While some family planning efforts have had limited success, it is probably the forces of urbanization and education that will have the greatest impact on the speed of this cultural change.

One exception to the demographic transition deserves mention, and that is China. With approximately one-fifth of the world's population, China is clearly in the category of a developing nation and would be expected to have a rapidly growing natural population increase like that of Bangladesh (previously noted). To the contrary, China has adopted very strict laws limiting family size, and as a result, the birthrate and death rate in China are in essential balance. So rather than waiting for the slow cultural change associated with decreasing birthrates and paying the high costs associated with high rates of natural increase, China did with the rule of law what would have taken several generations to accomplish through cultural change.

FIGURE 22–4 World
land distribution.

	Millions of Hectares
World total	13,383
Nonagricultural	8,694
Agricultural	4,688
Grazing and pasture	3,212
Arable	1,476

LAND

Will Rogers once said, "Buy land—they aren't making any more of it." With the minor exception of the Dutch, his observation was correct. In times past, as the population grew, farmers moved to the frontier and opened new farmland. The pampas in Argentina and the Mato Grosso in Brazil have been opened up within the past 40 years. But land, particularly **arable land,** is finite on our earth. Most arable land is currently being farmed, so as the population grows, the amount of arable land per capita shrinks. The only way to feed more mouths is to increase the productivity per acre of available land. As discussed earlier, there is some indication that even productivity growth is not keeping up with population growth.

Arable land land that—because of its landform, climate, and soils—is suitable for the planting of crops.

As shown in Figure 22–4 the total amount of land on our earth is about 13.4 billion hectares[9], but only about one-third of it is suitable for agricultural use and only about one-third of that is arable—suitable for cropping. So we are left with 1.5 billion hectares of arable land to feed 6.3 billion mouths. Your individual share of land is exactly one-fourth of a hectare, or 0.62 acres. Most folks have difficulty thinking in terms of acres because they don't know how big one is. Here is an easy way to visualize an acre: it is a block of land that is 50 yards wide and 97 yards long. So a football field, goal line to the far 3 yard line, is an acre. Your share of that field, your 0.62 acre, would be the real estate between the goal line and the far 40 yard line. That's it. That is what feeds the average person on this earth.

By 2050, the world population is expected to be about 9.4 billion, which means (assuming we don't make any more arable land) each person will have to be fed from 0.39 acre, which is the distance from the goal line to the 38 yard line. So in the next 50 years or so, the amount of arable land available to you is roughly going to move from the far 40 yard line to the near one. You are going to have to live off one-third less land than you have today. To do that, your agricultural productivity (output per unit of land) is going to have to increase by 50 percent. That is the challenge facing us for the next 50 years.

SUMMARY

In 1798 Thomas Malthus wrote a small tract in which he argued that the population was growing at a rate faster than food production, and that the population growth would eventually be checked by starvation and famine—not a happy

---

[9] A hectare is the metric measure of surface area. A hectare contains 10,000 square meters or a square 100 meters on each side. An official soccer field is 100 m × 50 m, so two soccer fields equal one hectare. There are 2.47 acres in one hectare.

prospect. The notion that there are finite limits to growth has been around ever since and is usually associated with Malthus's name.

Today, neo-Malthusians concern themselves less with a finite food capacity and more with finite limits of the environment and natural resources. They argue that if current growth rates are sustained, we will soon hit the limits to growth for a number of resources.

Non-Malthusians counter that the neo-Malthusians have been saying the world is going to come to an end for 200 years and it still hasn't happened. They argue that change, adjustment, and technological improvements will keep moving the "limits" farther and farther out.

The demographic transition is a model that illustrates the relationship between demographic and economic development. Traditional societies and developed societies have relatively low rates of natural population increase because birthrates and death rates are more or less in balance. Developing countries usually have high rates of natural population increase because birthrates are high and death rates are low. Most of the projected population growth in the next 50 years will occur in the developing countries.

The amount of arable land per capita averages 0.62 acre. This is a plot the size of a football field from the goal line to the far 40 yard line. With the projected increase in the world population by 2050 your individual plot will shrink from the far 40 yard line to the near one.

KEY TERMS

Arable land	Demographic transition
Birthrate	Natural rate of population growth
Death rate	Thomas Malthus

PROBLEMS AND DISCUSSION QUESTIONS

1. Strange as it may seem, more than 200 years after Thomas Malthus wrote his famous *Essay*, there is an International Society of Malthus. You can learn more about Malthus and the neo-Malthusians on the ISM website: **www.igc.apc.org/desip/malthus/index.html**.

2. As indicated, one of the most responsible, consistent neo-Malthusians has been Dr. Lester Brown and his think tank, the Worldwatch Institute. They maintain a good website at **www.worldwatch.org** which includes summaries of the Institute's numerous studies. Another respected source is the Population Reference Bureau at **www.prb.org**.

3. Using an almanac or similar reference book, find the birthrates and death rates in countries that are characteristic of traditional, developing, and developed societies. Do these data confirm the demographic transition model?

CHAPTER
23
Economic Development and Food

*C*ountries are not rich and poor, although we frequently make statements such as "Dawgland is a poor country." What we really mean is that Dawgland is a country with a large number of very poor people. Every country has rich people, middle-class people, and poor people. The communist ideal of each person being no better off or no worse off than his neighbor just hasn't worked out. Even in Cuba, after an entire generation of the most strident communism, you still find elites (you don't see Fidel smoking cheap cigarettes) and you still find the poor.

Most west European countries are considered to be "rich" countries because a large proportion of the population is able to buy the three necessities of food, housing, and medical care[1] and still have money left over for vacations. In a global sense these folks are "rich." West European countries also have poor people in them, but the proportion of the poor is small. "Poor" countries frequently have several fabulously wealthy people in them, but they are few and far between.[2] Large proportions of the total population are poor in "poor" countries.

Between the "rich" and "poor" countries are the **developing countries**—those countries that are passing from being poor but are not yet rich. Of course, at any point in time most countries are developing in the sense that the economy is growing and the goods available to the ordinary citizen are improving. By "developing" countries we mean those countries that have started to move from an economy primarily based on subsistence agriculture to a mixed economy of industrial production, financial and other services, and natural resource industries.

There is probably no single statistic that differentiates the "poor" from the "developing" countries better than the percentage of the labor force in agriculture. For instance, Chad, a small "poor" country in west Africa, has 85 percent of its labor force in agriculture. Economic development is in its infancy in Chad. By comparison, Mexico—a prototype of a developing country—has 28 percent of its labor force in agriculture. Developed countries such as Germany, Japan, and the United States typically have 5 percent or less of the labor force on the farm. In this chapter we will explore the relationships between agriculture, food, and economic development. While each country is unique, it is possible to make some generalizations.

Developing countries those countries in the transition from an economy that is predominantly subsistence farming to a mixed economy of manufacturing, services, and commercial agriculture.

---

[1] No students, a car is not a necessity of the same magnitude. At least one student made it through all four years of a degree program without a car. Many adults in New York City have never owned a car, much less driven one.

[2] It was widely reported that at the time he finally died, former Philippines President Ferdinand Marcos had $30 million in the bank. While most of it was stolen from the Filipino people, he was wealthy nonetheless.

QUANTITY OF FOOD

As pointed out in the previous chapter, one of the universals among creatures is the struggle to survive. In the case of humans that involves a proper combination of air, water, food, and freedom from disease. While air and water of suitable quality are readily available to most, regardless of economic situation, food and medical services come at a price. As a result, the rich get what they want and the poor take what they can get. As one would suspect, the distribution of income and the distribution of food are very similar. We turn now to a topic of global importance that has probably never been experienced by most readers of this book—hunger.

For Want of Food

It is a sad but true fact that every day some members of the human race perish from this planet for want of food. Aside from the Malthusian argument presented in the previous chapter, there is the sober realization that day by day people are dying because of the lack of food and/or adequate and balanced nutrition. This death occurs in two forms—episodic and chronic.

Episodic

Episodic hunger is known as **famine**—one of the Four Horsemen of the Apocalypse. Famine refers to a one-time loss of food in some region or country that is caused by some external event. A famine is an abnormal event, and as such, it is usually newsworthy and highly visible. The most common causes of famine are droughts or floods that destroy one year's crop with a return to normal in the following year. Other causes of famine are wars that disrupt planting, locust swarms that clean the fields, and institutional chaos that sends farmers all the wrong signals.

Famine a one-time loss of food in some region or country that is caused by some external event.

A deadly combination of civil war and institutional chaos was responsible for the greatest famine of the past century—the Russian famine of 1919–1921. After the revolution in 1917 Lenin organized Soviet agriculture along the utopian communist model, and the peasants rebelled by planting only what they needed for their own consumption. At the same time the Red army and the White army engaged in a vicious 3-year civil war. It is estimated that more than 20 million perished as a result of the famine and the war. Lenin, realizing that a revolution without food was a losing proposition, proposed his "new economic plan" to return agriculture to more of a market-controlled system without state intervention. With this change, Soviet agriculture returned to normal levels of production for the remainder of the decade until Stalin began a program of collectivization.

Chronic

A chronic or continuing lack of food is known as **hunger** or undernourishment. Though not as visible as a famine, hunger kills far more people on a continuing basis because it never goes away. It is estimated that only 10 percent of hunger-related deaths are the result of famines. The rest are the result of chronic hunger. Hunger

Hunger a chronic or continuing lack of food and/or nutrients.

is the dual curse of not having a sufficient quantity of food and of not having an adequate nutritional balance. In areas of subsistence agriculture it is not at all uncommon to find diets that are deficient in a number of nutrients and micronutrients. For instance, a rice-based diet is deficient in iron and vitamin A—both of which can cause disease, blindness, and death. When hunger occurs, the incidence of disease increases and the likelihood of death becomes a reality. Add poor sanitation and inadequate medical services to the mix and the chances of becoming a statistic are quite high.[3]

A recent study by the Food & Agriculture Organization (FAO) of the United Nations estimated that there are 790 million undernourished people in developing countries.[4] Figure 23–1 identifies those countries in which hunger is prevalent. More than 500 million of the hungry are in Asia, with approximately 200 million in sub-Saharan Africa. This constitutes about 19 percent of the total population of the developing countries. So, about one out of five people in developing countries is undernourished.

Estimates of the number of people who die from hunger vary greatly, but something around 9 million per year is a consensus guess. This works out to about 24,000 people per day who die from hunger. The only good news is that the deaths per day are down from about 35,000 a decade ago, so progress is being made. Whatever the number, the magnitude of this human loss is enormous. And it goes on day after day with no prospect of eventually relenting. Hunger is a steady, quiet killer.

The specter of chronic hunger leads us to ask two key questions: Who is dying of hunger? and Why are they hungry?

Who Is Hungry?

The optimist would look at the figures presented above and say that of the 790 million who are hungry, only 9 million die annually. That is a death rate of only 1 percent of the hungry annually. Unfortunately, that optimism is ill-founded because certain segments of the hungry population are more prone to die of hunger than others.

Rural residents are far more likely to die from hunger than urban residents. The reasons for this are several. First, an urban hungry person probably has a better diet than a rural hungry person because the urban individual is eating processed foods that include essential micronutrients. Second, the urban resident has access to a distribution system that provides food throughout the year. The rural resident is subjected to more of a "feast or famine" life. Finally, albeit rudimentary, the urban resident probably has access to better medical care than the rural resident.

Death from hunger is definitely gender biased. A female is far more likely to die of hunger than a male. This is the result of cultural gender bias. In most cultures, if there is inadequate food for all members of the family, it is the females who will go hungry; and this is further complicated by the higher nutritional needs of women during the reproductive cycle.

---

[3] A recent study by the World Health Organization of the United Nations found that "about 50 percent of deaths among children under 5 are associated with malnutrition." Another study by CARE found that in developing countries 10 percent of children die before the age of 5.

[4] In addition, the FAO estimated 34 million malnourished in developed countries. Data are for 1995–1997 from *The State of Food Insecurity in the World, 1999,* **www.fao.org**.

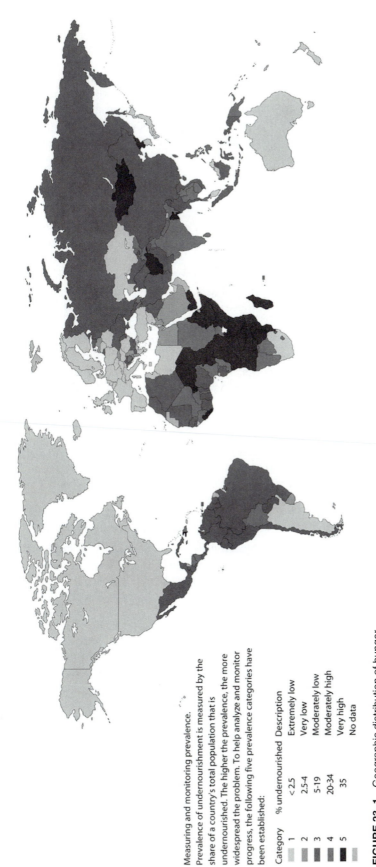

Measuring and monitoring prevalence.

Prevalence of undernourishment is measured by the share of a country's total population that is undernourished. The higher the prevalence, the more widespread the problem. To help analyze and monitor progress, the following five prevalence categories have been established:

Category	% undernourished	Description
1	< 2.5	Extremely low
2	2.5–4	Very low
3	5–19	Moderately low
4	20–34	Moderately high
5	35	Very high
		No data

FIGURE 23–1 Geographic distribution of hunger.
Source: Food and Agriculture Organization, United Nations, *The State of Food Insecurity in the World, 1999,* **http://www.fao.org/FOCUS/E/SOFI/under-e.htm.**

Finally, the young are far more likely to die than adults.[5] The young are more susceptible to diseases associated with hunger and have higher nutritional needs than adults. The grim truth is that if you make it through childhood, you are probably tough enough to last through adulthood. Life expectancy at birth in the United States is about 13 years longer than in India; yet life expectancy at age 20 is about the same in both countries. Unfortunately, the grim truth is that hunger and death stalk the young and vulnerable.[6]

Why Hunger?

As was noted in an earlier chapter, the United States, Japan, and western Europe have elaborate agricultural policy establishments designed to control the propensity to overproduce. In a global sense we have not yet reached the Malthusian inevitability of global food shortages. Food, in the aggregate, is abundant. Why then, in this abundance, is there hunger? There are basically two reasons there is hunger and death therefrom. Before discussing these it is important to identify what is *not* the problem. Those who see hunger as a lack of food miss the point. There is abundant food in the world. The **causes of hunger** must be found elsewhere.

Causes of hunger
poor distribution systems and lack of effective demand are the primary causes of hunger.

The first cause of hunger is to be found in the food distribution systems in many developing countries. For many subsistence farmers, there is essentially no distribution system—no roads, no storage, and no market access. When these farmers are not able to provide for themselves, there is no market system to fall back on.

ABUNDANT FOOD   *To state that food is abundant in light of obvious hunger throughout the world seems to be a contradiction, but it is not. According to the FAO, world food production in 1997 generated 2,782 calories per capita per day, 73.9 grams of protein per capita per day, and 71.7 grams of fat per capita per day. The minimum calories needed to support a working adult are in the 1,800 to 2,000 range. According to the Food and Nutrition Board of the National Academy of Sciences, the recommended dietary allowance of protein for an adult male is 63 grams and for an adult female, 50 grams. On a global basis there is ample food for the average person. Unfortunately many of the less fortunate are well below average.*

The second cause of hunger is the lack of effective demand. Quite simply, in order to acquire food from the distribution system one must have money. Subsistence farmers have little or no cash income and therefore little ability to command the food that does exist. In short, people are hungry not because there is no food but because they are poor.

The solution to hunger is not to be found in the production of more food. Instead the answer lies in improving the infrastructure of the distribution system to bring isolated farmers into the cash economy both as sellers of products and as buyers of food.

---

[5] According to the World Health Organization, 21 percent of all hunger-related deaths in 1995 were among those under 5 years of age.

[6] The grim reality was driven home to one of the authors as he traveled in a very poor rural part of Brazil. He noticed that in a small town the local undertaker's inventory had two adult-sized caskets and about 10 infant- through young-child-sized caskets. If you believe in markets. . . .

	Rate of Growth of Population	Rate of Growth of Income	Income Elasticity
Developed country	0.5%	3.0%	0.1
Developing country	3.5	3.0	1.0

FIGURE 23–2
Hypothetical growth rates of food consumption.

FOOD DEMAND DURING DEVELOPMENT

In the previous chapter we examined the demographic transition as the economic development process begins. As a society moves toward economic development, we expect to see a population surge with a high rate of natural increase. Because of this, developing countries must increase food production rapidly to at least maintain the amount of food available on a per capita basis.

Quantity

The demographic pressure on the food system in developing countries is not the only source of strain. With development come rapidly expanding incomes, which, combined with very high income elasticities, produce even higher rates of **growth in food demand.** Developed countries have very low income elasticities because most consumers already have more than enough to eat. If incomes rise, the consumer does not consume more food. However, in developing countries additional income is immediately converted into additional spending on food. Some studies have shown that the income elasticity for protein sources in developing countries exceeds 1.0. That is, a 10 percent increase in incomes would result in increased spending on protein sources in excess of 10 percent.

Figure 23–2 illustrates the difference between the rate of growth of food demand in a developed country and a developing country. The rate of growth in food demand is equal to the sum of the rate of change in the population and the rate of change of income times the income elasticity. In the developed country, the hypothetical rate of growth in the demand for food is less than 1 percent based on the assumptions given.[7] By comparison, the combination of high rates of population growth and high income elasticity gives the hypothetical developing country a rate of growth of food demand of 6.5 percent. At these hypothetical growth rates, food demand would increase by 17 percent over a 20-year period in the developed country and by 252 percent in the developing country. The impact of the development process on the agricultural sector should be obvious.

Growth in food demand   the rate of growth of food demand is equal to the rate of growth of the population plus the product of the rate of growth of per capita income times the income elasticity of demand for food.

Quality

Not only does the quantity of food demanded increase with the development process, but the quality of food increases dramatically as well. As incomes increase, consumers move away from traditional food sources such as beans, rice, and millet and toward protein sources such as meat, dairy products, and eggs. Most studies have shown that the income elasticities for these protein sources in developing

---

[7] In equation form we have $F = P + (I * E)$, where F = rate of growth of food demand, P = rate of growth of the population, I = rate of growth of income, and E = income elasticity. For the developed country, $F = 0.5 + (3.0 \cdot 0.1) = 0.8$ percent.

countries are well above 1.0, so even as total food demand is growing rapidly, the demand for these protein sources is growing even more rapidly.

Processing and Marketing

As development progresses and incomes rise, the typical diet moves away from beans, rice, and starches and toward meat, milk, and eggs. Take note of the marketing demands associated with these two sets of food products. Beans, rice, and starches require very little processing and can be easily stored for long periods of time. By comparison, meat and dairy products require substantial processing and must be refrigerated. In addition, as incomes increase, the quantity of marketing services included in food increases rapidly as the consumer shifts away from raw agricultural ingredients and toward food products that are already prepared. For example, most Mexicans today buy their tortillas from the store rather than making them at home.

So while food demand increases rapidly in developing countries, the **demand for food marketing services** increases even more rapidly making food marketing one of the engines of economic growth. One of the keys to facilitating and accelerating the development process is for government to provide the infrastructure that encourages the rapid expansion of food marketing. Some of the facilitative kinds of things governments can do are to provide good roads, good market information, and credible grades and standards. Previous attempts by governments to become directly involved in food distribution have generally been unsuccessful. Experience suggests that governments should support markets but not attempt to replace them.

Demand for food marketing services fastest growing segment of the food industry in a developing country as consumers shift their diet to animal protein sources and more prepared foods.

SUMMARY

Developing countries are those that are making a transition from an economy based primarily on subsistence farming or plantation agriculture to a mixed economy with vibrant manufacturing and service sectors.

It is estimated that about 790 million persons are undernourished in developing countries. This is about one-fifth of the population of developing countries. Of these, approximately 9 million die annually from hunger. Hunger may be episodic in the form of famines or chronic in the form of hunger and malnourishment. Most hunger is chronic.

Hunger, particularly chronic hunger, has very predictable demographic characteristics. Hunger is most prevalent among rural residents, women, and the young.

While hunger obviously results from a lack of food, it does not follow that simply producing more food will solve the problem. The world currently produces enough food to provide every person with an adequate diet. The causes of hunger are twofold: a lack of an adequate distribution system to connect the hungry with available foodstuffs, and a lack of effective demand among the poor with no cash income.

As economic development progresses and per capita incomes increase, three dramatic changes occur to the demand for food. First, the per capita quantity of food demanded increases at a rate well above the population growth rate because of the income elasticity effect. Second, the quality of food demanded shifts away from traditional beans, rice, and starches in favor of protein sources such as meat, milk, and eggs. Third, the demand for food marketing services increases at a rate that is even greater than the rate of growth of food demand as consumers want more services incorporated into the food products purchased.

KEY TERMS

Causes of hunger

Demand for food marketing services

Developing countries

Famine

Growth in food demand

Hunger

PROBLEMS AND DISCUSSION QUESTIONS

1. As discussed, one of the best indicators of the level of economic development of a country is the proportion of the population in agriculture. Using an almanac or other reference source, find the proportion of the population in agriculture and the per capita GDP for the following countries: Mozambique, China, India, Egypt, Mexico, and Spain. How well do the two indicators correlate? (*Note:* for "Netizens" you can find these data in *The World Factbook,* which is prepared by the CIA. Their web address is **www.odci.gov/cia/publications/factbook**.)

2. Two excellent sources of information on hunger and the plight of the disadvantaged are the World Health Organization (**www.who.org**) and the Food and Agriculture Organization (**www.fao.org**). Both are agencies of the United Nations, and both maintain excellent websites. For information on the latest famines, go to the Special Relief Operations link on the FAO home page.

3. For more information on hunger, its distribution, and its health effects, refer to *The State of Food Insecurity in the World, 1999* on the FAO website. Summaries are available on the Web, and the entire report can be downloaded.

4. It was pointed out that frequently the income elasticity for protein sources is greater than 1.0. Let's suppose it is 1.3 for milk: this means that if income goes up by 10 percent, expenditures on milk will increase by 13 percent. How can this be? What is going on here?

5. Calculate the rate of growth of food demand for the rich and poor countries in the table below.

	Population Growth Rate	Income Growth Rate	Income Elasticity
Rich	0.2%	4.3%	0.2
Poor	3.1	3.8	0.8

GLOSSARY

accounting profit   The difference between all revenues or receipts of the firm and all expenses paid.

acreage allotments   Government permission to produce a given acreage of a product for domestic consumption. By restricting acreage, and hence production, the government assures holders of the allotments of high prices for their production.

ad valorem tariff   A tariff that is calculated as a percentage of the value of the imported good.

aggregate demand   The total quantity of goods and services that will be purchased at alternative price levels.

aggregate supply   The total quantity of goods and services that will be produced at alternative price levels.

agribusiness   Firms engaged in farm service marketing, agricultural production, food processing, food distribution, and consumption.

agricultural economics   The social science that deals with the allocation of scarce resources among those competing alternative uses found in the production, processing, distribution, and consumption of food and fiber.

agricultural or food policy   Purposeful government action in the agricultural and food sectors designed to produce results consistent with a societal belief about what "ought to be."

agricultural price and income support policies   Policies designed to increase agricultural prices and/or agricultural incomes above the level that would prevail in the absence of the policy.

annuity factor   The sum of discount factors over a period of time.

antitrust   Laws prohibiting business behavior that threatens competition, such as price-fixing, collusion, and anticompetitive mergers.

appreciation   An increase in the value of a country's currency relative to the currency of another country. If A appreciates relative to B, then B depreciates relative to A.

arable land   Land that—because of its landform, climate, and soils—is suitable for the planting of crops.

arbitrage   The practice of simultaneously buying and selling a single product on two different markets to profit from the price differential between the two markets.

arc elasticity   The measurement of the elasticity of demand coefficient between two points on a demand curve.

ask   The lowest current offer to sell a stock, bond, or other financial instrument.

assemblers   Those firms that buy raw agricultural commodities directly from farmers (producers) in small quantities and sell to processors in larger quantities.

assembly   The collection of small amounts of product from many farmers to create a large enough amount of product for efficient shipment.

asymmetric knowledge   When the buyer and the seller do not have the same information about a market or good.

atomistic   Each economic unit is so small relative to the total market that actions by that unit will not affect the market.

average fixed cost   Fixed costs per unit of output.

average revenue   Revenue per unit of output; equal to the price of the product in perfect competition.

average total cost   Total costs per unit of output.

average variable cost   Variable costs per unit of output.

away from home   Expenditures on food that is not prepared at an individual's residence.

balance of payments   A system of accounts in which all transactions of producers and consumers in one country with the producers and consumers of other countries are summarized.

basic principle of the circular flow   For every physical flow there is an equal but opposite economic flow.

benefit-cost analysis   An economic analysis of an investment or policy alternative in which estimated total social benefits are compared with estimated total social costs.

bid   The highest current offer to buy a stock, bond, or other financial instrument.

bills   Very short-term bonds with maturities usually less than 1 year.

birthrate   The number of births per one thousand of population per year.

blue chips   Stocks of the biggest, most financially sound companies. These are companies that are expected to be around 10 years from now.

board of directors   A group of individuals elected by shareholders to manage a corporation on behalf of the shareholders. The board hires and fires the management of the company and makes broad policy decisions.

bond market   Market on which previously issued bonds are bought and sold.

bonds   Legal agreement between the lender and the borrower when business firms borrow from the public.

book value   The per share value of the corporation issuing the stock. That is, if the company were liquidated, what the per share value of the proceeds would be.

break-even point   Product price for which the economic profits of the firm are zero.

brokers   Individuals licensed to carry buy/sell orders of individuals to the different exchanges.

budget line   Combinations of two goods the consumer is able to purchase given a budget constraint.

buy a contract   The buyer of a futures contract agrees to accept delivery of a specified commodity on a specified future date at a price agreed upon today.

call   Redeem a bond prior to the maturity date specified on the face of the bond. Most bonds are callable at a premium over the face value.

cash markets   Markets in which delivery is expected immediately upon payment.

causes of hunger   Poor distribution systems and lack of effective demand are the primary causes of hunger.

central bank   A special bank created by the government to serve as a bank for commercial banks and for the national treasury.

ceteris paribus   A short-hand way of saying, "let one economic variable (the cause) change and see how another economic variable (the effect) changes, assuming that everything else remains unchanged.

charter   A legal document, similar to a constitution, that establishes a corporation and lays out the rules that will govern the corporation. Charters are submitted to and approved by the secretary of state in the state in which the corporation is legally established.

circular flow model   A macroeconomic model that emphasizes the continuous flow of goods and services through the production and consumption processes.

close a contract   To remove or complete the contractual obligations of an open contract.

close a hedge   To cancel the contractual obligations made when a hedge was opened by buying or selling an offsetting position in futures markets. The closing of a hedge is usually associated with some action in the cash market for the commodity.

closed-end funds   A mutual fund with a finite number of shares such that when one investor buys shares another must sell. Shares of the mutual fund basically trade like shares of stock in a corporation and may sell above or below the NAV of the fund.

Coase theorem   Theorem which identifies the conditions under which a successful economic transaction will occur.

collateral   The pledge of real property that a loan will be paid off. If the borrower defaults on a loan, the lender takes possession of the collateral and sells it to recover the defaulted loan.

command system   An allocative system in which economic choices are made by some central administrative unit.

commission   Service fee paid to brokers for each trade executed.

commodities   (1) Raw agricultural products that have not been processed. Wheat, cattle, and raw milk are examples; (2) undifferentiated goods in which one producer's product is indistinguishable from another's. Examples are iron ore, field corn, and iceberg lettuce.

commodity approach The study of all aspects of the marketing system for a single commodity.

commodity processors Companies that buy raw agricultural commodities (such as soybeans) and process them into food product ingredients.

common property Goods for which property rights are poorly defined and for which consumption is rival.

common stock A class of stock that gives shareholders full voting rights in the business of the corporation. Dividends on common stock are at the discretion of the board of directors. Usually the common shareholder is at the end of the line in terms of claimants for the earnings of the corporation, or for assets in the case of bankruptcy.

comparative statics A before-after comparison to determine the impact of some action.

competitive imports Imports of items that are commercially produced in the United States, such as wine.

complements (1) Goods that are typically consumed together. An increase in the consumption of one complementary good (gasoline) will result in an increase of the other good (tires); (2) two goods with a negative cross-price elasticity.

compounding The process of finding a future value, given a present value.

concentration The dominance of an industry by a few firms, usually measured by the percent of the total market owned by the largest four (or any other number) firms.

conduct Behavior of the profit-maximizing firm manager. Conduct is determined by structure.

constant returns to scale As all inputs are increased by a given proportion, output increases by the same proportion.

constrained optimization Simplifying an optimization problem by holding one or more variables constant (constrained) and finding the optimal levels of the remaining variables.

consumption Using up something that has been produced.

contract farming Farmers producing to the specifications of a contract with the buyer, rather than relying on the dictates of the market.

cooperative A form of business organization in which the company is owned by the farmers it serves.

corporation A legal entity that is formed to own and operate a business.

correlation and causation Correlation means that two variables are related to one another but not necessarily in a cause-effect manner. Causation means there is a cause-effect relation between the two variables. Causation implies correlation; correlation does not imply causation.

cost structure The relative importance of fixed and variable costs in the total costs of the firm.

Council of Economic Advisors Established in 1946 as part of the White House staff. Its creation signaled that management of fiscal policy was now the responsibility of the President.

coupon payment The annual interest payment promised by the bond issuer expressed in dollar amounts.

coupon rate The annual interest payment promised by the bond issuer expressed as a percentage of the face value. A bond with a 6 percent coupon rate promises to pay $60 per year.

creditor One to whom others owe money.

cross-price elasticity A measure of the sensitivity of quantity demanded to changes in the price of another product, usually a substitute or a complementary good.

current yield The coupon payment promised by a bond divided by the current market price of the bond expressed as a percentage.

day orders A limit order that is canceled at the end of the day if not executed.

death rate The number of deaths per thousand of population per year.

debt ceilings Legislative limits on the amount of the federal debt.

debtor One who owes money to others.

decreasing marginal returns As additional units of the variable input are used, output increases at a decreasing rate.

decreasing returns to scale As all inputs are increased by a given proportion, output increases by a lesser proportion.

deficiency payment If average market prices are less than the target price, a cash payment is made to farmers to make up the difference.

deficit   Status of the federal budget when government receipts are less than government expenditures during a fiscal year.

deficit on balance of payments   The value of a country's imports exceeds the value of its exports. A country with a deficit is losing foreign reserves.

deficit spending   Policy of purposeful government deficits to compensate for insufficient aggregate demand in other sectors of the economy.

demand   The quantities of a good that buyers are willing to purchase at a series of alternative prices, in a given market, during a given period of time, *ceteris paribus*.

demand curve   A two-dimensional graph illustrating a demand relationship.

demand deposits   Balances in checking accounts with commercial banks.

demand for food marketing services   Fastest growing segment of the food industry in a developing country as consumers shift their diet to animal protein sources and more prepared foods.

demand schedule   A schedule identifying specific price-quantity combinations that exist in a demand relationship.

demand/supply shift   A change in the demand/supply relationship caused by a change in one of the *ceteris paribus* conditions.

demographic transition   A model of population growth that emphasizes the relationship between economic growth and population growth.

depreciation   A decline in the value of a country's currency relative to the currency of another country.

derived farm level demand   The primary retail level demand minus the marketing margin.

derived retail level supply   The primary farm level supply plus the marketing margin.

devalue   A change in the official value of one currency relative to another or allowing market forces to decrease the exchange rate.

developing countries   Those countries in the transition from an economy that is predominately subsistence farming to a mixed economy of manufacturing, services, and commercial agriculture.

developmental agricultural policies   Policies designed to improve the infrastructure of the food system.

differentiated products   Products with unique characteristics that separate them from close substitutes.

dilution   Reducing the value of previously issued shares by issuing new shares. Assumes the value of the company does not grow as rapidly as the number of shares does.

diminishing marginal rate of factor substitution   As more and more units of one variable input are used, the quantity of the other input that would have to be substituted for it to keep production constant falls.

diminishing returns   As additional units of an economic variable are used, the additional impact of that variable will eventually increase at a decreasing rate.

discount factor   The ratio of present value to future value.

discount or below par   Bonds with a current market price below face value.

discount rate   (1) Interest rate charged when commercial banks borrow additional reserves from the Federal Reserve Bank; (2) the time value of money expressed as a percentage rate.

discounting   The process of finding a present value, given a future value.

distributors   Wholesalers and others who buy large lots of food from processors and distribute it to many retailers in smaller lots.

dividend   A distribution of the corporation's earnings to the owners of the corporation—the shareholders. Each share of stock receives the same dividend.

dividend yield   The amount of dividends paid per share during the past 12 months expressed as a percent of the current price of the stock.

Dow Jones Industrial Average   An index of the prices of 30 blue-chip stocks.

downward inflexible prices   Keynes's argument that because of institutional constraints, the classical assumption of flexible prices that would either rise or fall to achieve equilibrium was not valid.

dynamic   An economic analysis over a period of time analyzing the adjustment process.

earnings   Profits of the corporation. Earnings are usually reported on an earnings per share (EPS) basis. The higher the EPS of a stock, *ceteris paribus*, the higher the price of the stock.

economic efficiency   Output per dollar of input cost. A decrease in costs per unit is an increase in economic efficiency.

economic integration   The combination of two or more related economic activities under the control of a single management.

economic model   A conceptualization, based on assumptions, of how economic activity occurs.

economic profit   The difference between all revenues or receipts of the firm and the value of all inputs used by the firm, whether paid or not.

economic recession   Period of time when the real (i.e., inflation adjusted) economic growth is negative.

economics   The social science that deals with the allocation of scarce resources among an unlimited number of competing alternative uses.

efficiency   A general economic concept used in a variety of situations measuring output per unit of input. The higher the ratio, the more efficient the process.

elastic   A demand relationship in which the rate of change of quantity demanded is greater than the rate of change of price.

elasticities by market level   In any given market for any given commodity, the elasticities of supply and demand will always be more inelastic at the farm level than at the retail level.

elasticity   A measure of how responsive the quantity demanded by consumers or the quantity supplied by producers is to a change in prices, income, and other factors.

elasticity coefficient   A quantitative measure of the degree of responsiveness for a product in a market. Equal to the rate of change of quantity demanded (or supplied) divided by the rate of change of the other variable such as price of the product, and so forth.

elasticity of demand   A measure of the sensitivity of quantity demanded to changes in the price of the product.

elasticity of supply   A measure of the sensitivity of quantity supplied to changes in the price of the product.

endogenous   Internal to the firm; may be controlled by the firm manager.

enterprise   A single production activity.

equilibrium price   That price at which the quantity supplied in a market is equal to quantity demanded.

equi-marginal principle of optimization   In order to optimize utility given a limited budget, the consumer will adjust the consumption pattern such that the marginal utility per dollar of expenditure for each good is the same.

equity   The distributional impacts of a policy between the rich and the poor, between Americans and foreigners, and so forth.

excess reserves   Bank reserves in excess of the amount of required reserves.

exchange   Financial intermediaries that provide a physical marketplace where potential buyers and sellers of stock can meet. Each exchange "lists" or agrees to trade shares of specific companies. If a potential seller of shares of XYZ wanted to find potential buyers, the most likely place to look is at an exchange that lists XYZ. Corporations can have their shares listed on multiple exchanges.

exchange rate   Equilibrium price on a foreign exchange market.

exogenous   External to the firm; beyond the control of the manager of the firm.

expansion path   Locus of points of local optimal factor-factor combinations for multiple isoproduct curves.

export supply   Quantities of goods domestic producers are willing to export at alternative prices, *ceteris paribus*.

external deficit   Amount borrowed from outside the United States to finance net imports.

externalities   The economic or welfare impacts of an economic transaction on those not involved in the transaction.

face value   The amount borrowed when a bond is issued: always $1,000.

factor markets   Markets on which factors of production are traded.

factor-factor model   Model of a firm with two variable factors of production used in producing a single product.

factors of production   Goods, services and resources used in the production process to produce goods and services.

family of funds   Several different mutual funds with different investment objectives managed by a single manager.

famine   A one-time loss of food in some region or country that is caused by some external event.

farm Defined by the U.S. Department of Agriculture as any establishment that has (or should have had) at least $1,000 of sales of agricultural products during the year.

farm service sector Those firms that produce and distribute the goods and services that farmers (producers) buy as a part of their business activities.

farm service marketing All the activities and services that are brought to the farmer, rancher or producer in the form of purchased inputs.

farm share Value of farm production as a percentage of the retail price of food.

farm structure The study and analysis of farm characteristics such as the physical and economic size of farms, ownership of farms, and characteristics of the farm manager and his or her family.

Farmer Mac A federal agency that buys mortgages from rural banks and resells them on financial markets to investors.

federal debt Total amount of money borrowed by federal government to finance deficits.

federal funds rate Interest rate charged on an overnight loan of reserves between commercial banks.

Federal Open Market Committee Committee composed of all members of the Federal Reserve Board of Governors and five presidents of regional Federal Reserve Banks who meet periodically to establish the open market policy of the Fed.

Federal Reserve Board of Governors Seven-member committee that determines policies and procedures to be followed by the Federal Reserve Banks.

Federal Reserve System An independent federal agency of 12 regional Federal Reserve Banks that serve as banks for commercial banks.

feed grains Those grains that are usually used as livestock feed. All feed grains are used for human consumption (oats for oatmeal, rye for rye flour, and barley for beer) but they are generally considered to be inferior to food grains for human consumption. The most common feed grain is corn (field corn, not the sweet corn that you find in the store). Others include rye, oats, barley, millet, and sorghum (also called milo).

fiat A legal decree by government.

final goods Goods that are consumed or that become a part of the capital stock.

financial institutions Businesses that convert savings into investments. They buy and sell financial funds and in so doing create a market for funds. Also called "financial intermediaries".

financial intermediaries Those businesses that in one form or another are involved in the buying and selling of money.

fiscal policy The purposeful use of government taxing or spending authority in an effort to influence economic activity.

fixed inputs Inputs whose use rate does not change as the output level changes. Property taxes are a fixed input: they are the same whether a restaurant serves 1 customer or 100.

float Slang term for selling or issuing bonds.

flow Use of a factor of production during the production process.

food bill Value of total expenditures on food in any given year.

food grains Those grains that are usually consumed by humans as food. The primary food grains are wheat and rice.

food industry All firms, large and small, engaged in the production, processing, and/or distribution of food, fiber, and other agricultural products.

food marketing All the activities and services that occur between the producers/providers of food and foodstuffs and the consumer. Food marketing creates utility for the consumer.

food marketing bill That portion of the food bill that is created by the marketing system. The food bill minus farm value.

food processors Companies that buy ingredients and/or raw agricultural commodities and process them into retail products.

food products Food and agricultural commodities that have been processed into the form where they are ready for sale to the consumer.

food service That segment of the food industry that processes for and distributes to the away from home market for food.

food service distributors Those firms that distribute food products from food processors to away from home dining facilities.

foreign exchange Currency of another country. In Japan, dollars are foreign exchange.

foreign exchange market Market on which foreign currencies are traded.

form utility Utility created by the processing function.

forward price An agreement today on the price that will be paid for the delivery of a commodity at some future date.

fractional reserve system Commercial banking system in which the government requires banks to hold a portion of all deposits as reserves in the form of vault cash or deposits in the central bank.

franchise agents Agents authorized by a manufacturer to sell the products of the manufacturer. Usually the agents are given an exclusive territory such that they become local monopolies.

free rider Someone who consumes a public good without paying for it.

fully subscribed A new stock offering that is sold out.

functional approach Study of marketing systems emphasizing how each particular activity, like transportation, is accomplished.

fundamental analysts Stock market analysts who rely on tangible information about the company to estimate the value of the stock of the company.

future value The amount of a payment to be made in a future time period.

futures contract A standardized contract created by and traded on a futures exchange that calls on one party to make delivery of a specified good on a specified date and the other party to accept delivery of the same good on the same date at a price that is agreed upon now.

futures exchange A commercial marketplace designed to create and trade futures contracts. Also called futures markets.

futures markets Markets in which price is agreed upon now and delivery is specified for a future point in time.

General Agreement on Tariffs and Trade (GATT) A multilateral trade agreement among most major countries that establishes the rules for fair trade and calls for the mutual reduction of trade barriers such as tariffs.

globalization The expansion of firms across national boundaries.

good 'til canceled (GTC) A limit order that stands until it is either executed or canceled.

government expenditures Expenditures by the governments sector.

grades and standards The sorting of diverse products into uniform groups based on attributes such as quality and size.

grain elevator A grain storage facility that buys grain from farmers by the truckload and sells it to processors by the railcar load.

gross domestic product (GDP) Total expenditures on final goods and services during a period of time.

growth in food demand The rate of growth of food demand is equal to the rate of growth of the population plus the product of the rate of growth of per capita income times the income elasticity of demand for food.

growth stock Stock of a company with high expectations of future growth. These stocks are purchased in hopes of capital appreciation.

hedger A trader on a futures exchange who uses futures contracts to significantly reduce the price risk inherent in cash markets.

hoarding Savings that are not put into financial intermediaries, but instead are held by households as cash.

homogeneous Products that are alike such that the output of one competitor can not be distinguished from that of another competitor.

horizontal integration The combination of similar businesses under a single management.

hunger A chronic or continuing lack of food and/or nutrients.

hyperinflation A vicious inflationary environment in which prices of goods increase daily and there is panic buying of goods in an effort to avoid holding money.

import demand Quantities of goods domestic consumers are willing to import at alternative prices, *ceteris paribus*.

income elasticity A measure of the sensitivity of quantity demanded to changes in consumers' income.

income investors Investors who buy stocks that pay high dividends relative to the price of the stock.

income stock A stock for which the main attraction is the size and stability of its dividend.

income supports Any government program designed to provide farmers with higher incomes than they would receive otherwise.

increasing marginal returns As additional units of the variable input are used, output increases at an increasing rate.

increasing returns to scale   As all inputs are increased by a given proportion, output increases by a greater proportion.

index funds   Mutual funds that adjust the portfolio to mimic a market index such as the Standard & Poor's 500 in order to minimize the expense of an investment advisor.

indifference curves   Lines on a utility map indicating alternative combinations of two goods that will generate a constant level of utility in their consumption.

industrialization   The use of modern industrial concepts of production routinization, procurement through strategic alliances, coordination, and contracting in the food marketing system.

industry   A collection of firms producing the same or similar products.

inelastic   A demand relationship in which the rate of change of quantity demanded is less than the rate of change of price.

inferior goods   Goods with a negative income elasticity.

inflation   A decrease in the purchasing power of a currency.

initial public offering   A new stock offering by a corporation that has not previously offered stock to the public. No market price has been established for a company issuing an IPO.

institutional approach   Study of marketing systems emphasizing to role of different participants, such as commodity brokers, in the marketing chain and the role of governmental agencies.

interest rate   The price of money. Financial institutions buy money at one interest rate and sell it to potential borrowers at a higher interest rate, thereby earning a profit on the transaction.

intermediate goods   Goods that will be used in some further production process rather than being consumed.

internal rate of return   That discount rate that will drive the net present value of an investment to zero.

intrinsic value   The market value of the material from which money is made. Gold coins have intrinsic value while a common dime has little.

investment   (1) The purchase of plant and equipment by business firms; (2) expenditures by the business firms sector.

investor   Buyer of stock with a long-run objective of capital appreciation and/or dividends.

isocost line   A graphical line showing the various combinations of two variable inputs that have the same total variable cost.

isoproduct curve   A curve showing combinations of two variable inputs that may be used to produce a single level of output.

isorevenue line   A line showing the different combinations of two products that will produce a given total revenue.

joint products   When two or more products are produced by a single production process, the resulting products are called joint products.

junk bonds   Bonds issued by companies with extremely high levels of risk and/or bonds on which the issuer has ceased making coupon payments.

Keynesian policy   Fiscal policy, suggested by John Maynard Keynes, of using federal government budget surpluses and deficits to stabilize the macroeconomy during periods of disequilibrium.

laissez faire   Macroeconomic policy that the government should do nothing. Nonintervention on the part of government.

law of diminishing marginal product   As equal increments of the variable input are added to the fixed inputs, there will inevitably occur a decrease in the rate of increase of the total product.

law of diminishing marginal utility   As additional units of one good are consumed, *ceteris paribus,* the marginal utility obtained from each additional unit of that good will decrease.

lead underwriter   Usually no one underwriter wants to assume all of the risk of a new issue, so a consortium of underwriters is created to share the risks of a new issue. The lead underwriter creates the consortium and deals with the corporation on behalf of the other underwriters.

legal tender   A statement by the government that you must accept dollar currency to pay individual debts. Anyone not accepting dollars as a means of payment has no legal recourse to recover the unpaid debt.

limit order   Instruction to a broker to buy at no more than some specified price or to sell at no less than a specified price.

load or no-load funds Some mutual funds charge an initial sales commission when an investor buys shares. This commission is known as a front-end "load" and such funds are called "load funds". Mutual funds that do not charge any initial fee are called "no-load funds".

loan program USDA program that provides a farmer with a loan against his or her crop at harvest. If the farmer sells the crop at a market price below the loan rate, the loan is forgiven and the farmer keeps the amount of the loan.

loan rate The amount that is lent to the farmer under the loan program for each bushel put into storage. Loan rates are currently set by the 2002 farm bill.

loanable funds That portion of commercial bank deposits that do not have to be held as required reserves and can be loaned out.

local optimization A constrained optimal is valid only at the level at which the constrained variables are fixed. It is an optimization for a sub-set of the entire problem.

long run Period of time in which all inputs are considered variable inputs by the manager.

loose monetary policy Policy of accelerating the rate of growth of the money supply to stimulate the economy, causing faster economic growth and lower unemployment.

low-cap stocks Stocks with low market capitalization or market value as determined by the number of shares of the stock outstanding times the price per share.

M1 The narrowest measure of the money supply, includes currency, demand deposits and traveler's checks.

Malthus, Thomas An English Calvinist minister who is primarily remembered for his *Essay on the Principles of Population*, first published in 1798.

marginal An additional or an incremental unit of something.

marginal cost The additional cost of producing one additional unit of output.

marginal firm A firm in an industry with the highest cost structure and hence the most likely firm to leave the industry if prices fall.

marginal product Additional output (product) associated with a unit increase of the variable input.

marginal rate of factor substitution Rate at which one variable input must be substituted for the other variable input in order to keep output constant.

marginal rate of product substitution Rate at which one product can be substituted for another in the production process using a given bundle of fixed and variable inputs.

marginal revenue Additional revenue associated with one additional unit of output; equal to the price of the product in perfect competition.

market An interaction between potential buyers and potential sellers.

market failure When free markets do not produce results that are consistent with the desires of society.

market goods Those goods for which viable markets exist.

market level approach Study of marketing systems that views the system as a series of stages or levels through which the food passes. Marketing may be thought of as a chain in which food passes from link to link. The market level approach emphasizes the study of each link independent of the other links.

market order Instruction to a broker to buy or sell stock at the best price currently possible. That is, make the trade at whatever price is prevailing at the time.

market power The ability of a firm or a group of firms to control price and/or quantity traded in a market because of the dominance of the firm(s) in the market.

market rate of interest The prevailing risk- and term-adjusted interest rate at the present time. When bonds are issued they will be issued at a coupon rate equal to the market rate of interest at the time of issue. Over time the market rate of interest rises and falls as financial markets adjust.

market structure The number of firms in an industry and the relationship among them.

market supply curve The summation of the firm supply curves for all of the firms in the industry.

marketers sector That set of firms that distributes food products from processors to the final consumer when and where the consumer wants it. That consumer may be a retail shopper or someone eating at an away from home dining facility.

marketing The study of the creation of value that occurs as a good moves from producer to consumer.

marketing cooperative A cooperative that processes and distributes farmers' products. Ocean Spray is a marketing cooperative owned by cranberry producers.

marketing efficiency A measure of the costs of performing marketing tasks. The lower the costs, *ceteris paribus*, the greater the efficiency.

marketing margin The difference between the prices of a product at any two points in the marketing chain. The marketing margin is equal to the marketing costs between those two points.

maturity The date at which time a futures contract specifies the commodity is to be physically exchanged between the buyer and seller of the contract.

maturity date The date when a bond issuer promises to return the face value to the bondholder.

maximum sustainable yield A biological concept identifying the largest annual harvest of a renewable resource that will allow the population to be sustained at a specified level.

member-patrons Farmers who own a cooperative are called members of the cooperative and farmers who do business with the cooperative are called patrons.

microeconomics The branch of economics that deals with the economic behavior of individual units—either producers or consumers.

microeconomics of consumption The economics of the individual consumer making decisions about the allocation of the family budget.

microeconomics of production The economics of the individual producer or firm making management decisions.

monetarists School of economic thought that emphasizes monetary policy and the role of the growth of the money supply in macroeconomic policy.

monetary policy Deliberate changes in the rate of growth of the quantity of money in the economy in an effort to achieve macroeconomic objectives.

money Anything that is generally accepted and commonly used as a means of payment.

money market fund Mutual funds that invest exclusively in very short-term, near-cash in-

struments. The fund managers maintain the net asset value of the fund at $1.00 by varying the interest rate paid to investors. Checks can be written as a means of redeeming shares.

money supply Quantity of money in the economy at a given point in time.

monopolistic competition Market structure in which there are many firms selling differentiated products.

monopoly Market structure in which there is only one firm in the industry, there are no close substitutes, and entry into the industry is blocked.

mutual fund A professionally managed investment company that accepts funds from investors and invests those funds on behalf of the investors.

national income Total value of all factor payments during a period of time.

natural monopolies High fixed-cost industries in which the costs of a monopoly firm are lower than would be the costs of several competitive firms.

natural rate of population growth The difference between the birthrate and the death rate. It is the biological rate at which the population is growing (excluding migration).

near-money Financial assets not included in M1 that can be easily and quickly converted into cash.

negative marginal returns As additional units of the variable input are used, output decreases.

net asset value The current value of a mutual fund's portfolio divided by the number of shares of the mutual fund issued. NAV is the value of the assets held by the mutual fund per share of the fund.

net present value Difference between the present value of all returns and the present value of all costs associated with an investment.

"new" money Money that comes into the commercial banking system from outside the system that adds to the total amount of deposits in the system.

nominal prices Prices observed at any point in time measured in dollars of that time.

noncompetitive imports Imports of agricultural commodities that are not produced in the United States such as bananas.

nonexcludable Everyone can consume the good whether they pay for it or not.

nonmarket goods   Those goods, such as police protection, for which no market exists.

nonrecourse loan   A loan on which the borrower has the right to default with no adverse consequences.

nonrenewable resource   A factor of production that is available in a finite quantity, such as coal or petroleum.

nonrival   Consumption of the good by one person does not preclude consumption by a second person.

normal goods   Goods with a positive income elasticity.

North American Free Trade Agreement (NAFTA)   Agreement among Canada, the United States, and Mexico that will eventually lead to a free market in North America with no trade barriers.

notes   A class of bonds that is subordinate to some other debt instruments of the issuer, or is an intermediate-term bond.

nutriceuticals   Engineered foods that have specific health effects, such as a margarine that contains compounds that have been shown to reduce cholesterol levels in consumers.

objectives of macroeconomic policy   1) Stable prices, 2) full employment, 3) economic growth.

odd lots   Stock transactions involving less than 100 shares. The sale of 123 shares would involve one round lot and an odd lot of 23. Commission charges are higher for odd lots than for round lots.

oilseeds   Those crops that are generally crushed under high pressure and heat to produce vegetable oil and meal. The meal is usually used for livestock feed, and the oil is used in a variety of food products such as margarine, mayonnaise, and cooking oil. The primary oilseed is soybeans. Others include sunflower, rapeseed, cottonseed, peanuts, olive, and flaxseed.

oligopoly   Market structure with few firms that are highly interdependent.

open a contract   When a potential buyer and potential seller of a futures contract agree upon a price for future delivery, a contract is created between each party and the futures exchange. To create this contract is to open a contract.

open interest   Number of contracts that have been opened by a futures exchange and that have not yet been closed.

open market   The public, or open, market on which all kinds of bonds are traded.

open-end fund   A mutual fund that will issue additional shares of the fund whenever additional investment funds are received. The number of shares of the fund is unlimited.

opportunity cost   A measure of how much of an earning opportunity is foregone by using a resource in its current employment. Used by economists to establish an economic value for those resources that do not have an expressed market value.

overproduction   The most fundamental problem facing U.S. agriculture. Our ability to produce and expand production far exceeds our capacity of consume and expand consumption.

overvaluation   Effort to maintain the exchange rate of a currency at a level higher than the free market exchange rate.

patent   Rights granted to inventors to the exclusive use of their invention for a period of time, currently 20 years in the U.S.

patronage   The amount of business a member does with the cooperative.

penny stocks   Literally, stocks that can be purchased for just a few pennies. Most are either in bankruptcy proceedings or in highly speculative ventures.

perfect competition   A market in which there are so many buyers and so many sellers that no one of them can influence the market by his or her actions.

perfectly elastic   A demand relationship in which any change of quantity demanded brings about no price adjustment.

perfectly inelastic   A demand relationship in which any change of price brings about no quantity demanded adjustment.

personal consumption expenditures   Expenditures by the household sector.

personal income   Earnings in the household sector.

physical risk   The risk that a product in the marketing system will be accidentally destroyed.

pit   The location on the floor of a futures exchange where a specific commodity is traded.

place utility   Utility created by the transportation function.

point elasticity   The measurement of the elasticity of demand coefficient at a single finite point on the demand curve.

pollution abatement The control or reduction of pollution.

portfolio A listing of the items currently held by a mutual fund on behalf of the investors.

possession utility Utility created through exchange in the marketing system.

preferences The ability of the consumer to identify which of two goods will produce a greater amount of utility in consumption.

preferred stock A class of stock in which a fixed annual dividend is promised if the corporation has earnings from which to pay that dividend. All preferred dividends must be paid before any common dividends can be paid.

premium or above par Bonds with a current market price above face value.

present value The value today of a payment to be made in the future.

price discrimination Revenue-maximizing behavior of a firm that faces two different markets with two different elasticities for its single product. The price discriminator charges a high price to the inelastic market and a low price to the elastic market, thereby increasing revenues in both markets above what would be earned with a single price.

price floor A government-guaranteed minimum price. The government buys "surplus" production at this price to ensure that the market price does not fall below the floor.

price index An index number expressing the nominal cost of a market basket of goods at one point in time relative to the nominal cost of the same basket of goods at another point in time.

price level The general level of prices in an economy as measured by a price index. An increase in the price level is inflation; a decrease is deflation.

price maker Market in which the individual producer or consumer is able to establish price.

price of a bond The price at which a previously issued bond trades on the bond market. The price of a bond may be more than face value (above par) or less than face value (below par) depending on the forces of supply and demand for that particular bond.

price risk (1) The risk that while a product is moving through the marketing chain its market value may change; (2) the risk that by the time a crop is harvested or livestock is ready for sale, the market price will be less than production costs.

price supports Any policy designed to maintain market prices at a level above the price that would prevail in a free market.

price system An allocative system in which economic choices are based on prices.

price taker Potential buyers and potential sellers in a perfectly competitive market who face a "take it or leave it" decision at the prevailing market price.

price-earnings ratio The current price per share of a stock divided by the earnings (profits) per share during the past 12 months.

private Refers to the costs, benefits, or self-interest of the individuals involved in some economic activity.

processors sector Those firms that convert raw agricultural products into food products in the form that the consumer eventually buys.

producers sector Those firms engaged in the production of raw food, fiber, and other agricultural products.

product markets Markets on which final goods and services are traded.

production Process of converting inputs (factors, resources) into outputs (products); converting costs into revenues.

production function In the short run, relationship between units of the variable input and units of output, where units of the variable input and output are both measured per unit of the fixed input.

production loan A loan from a commercial bank to a farmer to finance the variable or operating costs of producing a crop. Typically the loan is repaid at harvest.

production possibilities curve A curve showing different combinations of two products that can be produced using a given bundle of fixed and variable inputs.

production quota A quantitative limit on the amount of product that can be sold from an allotment.

production risk The risk that crops will fail or livestock will die.

product-product model Model of the firm in which the firm produces two products using a given bundle of fixed and variable inputs.

products Goods that are differentiated; one producer's output is distinguishable from another's. Most products carry a brand name—Heinz catsup, for instance.

property rights Legal control or ownership of a good.

prospectus A document corporations must provide prospective buyers of the stock of the company. The prospectus gives a detailed account of the corporation's current financial and legal status, and discusses the intentions of the corporation with regards to the use of the funds raised by selling stock.

proxy battle A battle for the control of the board of directors. Each shareholder can vote his or her shares for either candidate by giving that candidate a proxy to vote the shares. Both candidates seek proxies from each shareholder.

public goods Same thing as nonmarket goods: no market for the good exists.

purchasing cooperative A cooperative that buys farm inputs in bulk and sells them to individual members at the lowest price possible.

purchasing power Value of money expressed in terms of units of goods that money can command.

quantity demanded How much of a good or service a buyer is willing to purchase at a single, specified price, in a given market, at a given time, *ceteris paribus.*

quantity supplied How much of a good or service a seller is willing to offer at a single, specified price, in a given market, at a given time, *ceteris paribus.*

quota Limitation on the quantity of a good that may be imported per unit of time.

rate of change The amount of change in one variable caused by or associated with a unit change in another variable.

rational range of production The rational firm will always produce at output levels for which the average variable cost is increasing and for which the marginal returns are not negative.

real income effect As the price of good *A* increases, *ceteris paribus,* the real income, or purchasing power, of the consumer falls and as a result less of both good *A* and *B* are consumed.

real price Price of a good adjusted for inflation.

recession Period of time during which the GDP declines. A long, severe recession is called a depression.

renewable resource A factor of production that can itself be produced, such as pulp for paper or human capital.

required reserves That portion of commercial bank deposits that the bank must hold in reserve (i.e., not loan out) against possible withdrawals.

resource adjustment The free market flow of production resources from activities with low economic returns into those uses providing the highest return to each resource.

retailers The supermarket and other vendors from whom the public buys food.

retained earnings Profits of a business firm that are retained by the firm rather than paid out to the owners of the firm. Retained earnings can be used by the firm to make additional investments in new plant and equipment.

risk management The managerial responsibility for maintaining the risk exposure of the firm at acceptable levels.

rival Consumption by one person precludes consumption by a second person because the first person used up the good.

round lots Stock transactions involving 100 shares or multiples of 100 shares of stock.

rural banks Banks that primarily serve local farmers and ranchers.

savings That part of income that is not used for consumption. Some saving is involuntary such as required payments into a retirement account.

savings gap That portion of household earnings that is neither spent nor saved through financial intermediaries.

Say's law of markets Supply creates it own demand, or the circular flow creates its own equilibrium.

secondary stocks Stocks of smaller, less financially certain companies. There is a higher degree of bankruptcy risk in secondary stocks than in blue chips.

Securities and Exchange Commission A federal regulatory agency that enforces laws to protect investors from fraud in the sale of stock by corporations and in the trading of stock by brokers and others.

sell a contract   The seller of a futures contract agrees to make delivery of a specified commodity on a specified future date at a price agreed upon today.

service cooperative   A cooperative that provides some service to its members such as electrical power or financial services.

set or open a hedge   The creation of a hedged position today by buying or selling a futures contract on a commodity that you plan to buy or sell on cash markets in the future.

set-aside   Land that a farmer had to take out of production in order to qualify for price and income support.

shares of stock   One share of stock means one unit of ownership of the corporation. If 4,000 shares of stock have been sold by the corporation to the public (i.e., individuals, pension funds, and the like), then the owner of one share owns one four-thousandth of the corporation. If the corporation issues (i.e., sells to the public) 1,000 additional shares, then the holder of one share owns one five-thousandth of the corporation. This is known as dilution. The terms "stock", "share" and "share of stock" are used interchangeably.

short run   Period of time short enough that some inputs are considered by the manager to be fixed inputs.

shutdown point   Product price for which the firm would cease production; equal to the minimum average variable cost.

slope   At any point on a curve, slope is equal to the ratio of rise (vertical change) to run (horizontal change); and it is equal to the rate of change of the relationship at that point.

social   Refers to the costs, benefits, or interests of all members of society affected by an economic activity.

spatial arbitrage   Arbitrage in which the two markets traded are in different physical locations.

specific tariff   A tariff that is a fixed amount per unit of the good, regardless of the value of the good.

speculative demand for money   Keynes's argument that at times households hold cash for speculative purposes rather than for transactions, creating a disequilibrium in the circular flow of income.

speculator   (1) A trader on a futures exchange who attempts to buy low and sell high with no intention of ever taking or having physical possession of the commodity; (2) buyer/seller of stock with short-run objectives of making a quick profit by buying low and selling high.

stagflation   Economic stagnation (high unemployment) occurring simultaneously with high inflation.

Standard & Poor's 500   An index of the prices of the 500 stocks with the highest market value.

static   An economic analysis at a point in time.

stock   (1) Amount of the factor of production available at a point in time; (2) claim of partial ownership of a business firm.

stock split   Action by the board of directors to give shareholders more shares for each share held. The purpose of a stock split is to reduce the price per share in the belief that many investors shun the stock of companies with high stock prices.

stop loss order   Instruction to a broker to sell a stock if the price of the stock falls below a specified level.

subordinate   A bond that has a lower priority than other (nonsubordinate) bonds in the distribution of proceeds in case of bankruptcy.

substitutes   (1) Goods which may be replaced, one for the other, in consumption. An increase in the consumption of one substitute good (Coke) will result in a decrease of the other (Pepsi); (2) two goods with a positive cross-price elasticity

substitution effect   As the price of good A increases, *ceteris paribus,* the relative price of good B decreases and the consumer substitutes B for A in consumption.

supply   The quantities of a good that sellers are willing to offer at a series of alternative prices, in a given market, during a given period of time, *ceteris paribus.*

supply curve   A two-dimensional graph illustrating a supply relationship.

supply curve of the firm   Quantities of a good the firm is willing to produce at alternative prices for the good, *ceteris paribus.* It is equal to the marginal cost curve of the firm beyond the shutdown point.

supply schedule A schedule identifying specific price-quantity combinations that exist in a supply relationship.

supply side economics A school of economic thought emerging in the early 1980s that emphasized policies to shift the aggregate supply curve rather than the aggregate demand curve as suggested by the Keynesians.

surplus When government receipts exceed government expenditures during a fiscal year.

surplus on balance of payments The value of a country's exports exceeds the value of its imports. A country with a surplus accumulates foreign reserves.

target prices Set annually by the farm bill or the secretary of agriculture based on estimated total cost of production.

tariff A tax on imports imposed by the importing country. Tariffs are usually applied to discourage the importation of a particular item or imports in general.

taxes Earnings in the governments sector.

technical analysts Market speculators who don't care about why a stock is moving up or down, just that it is moving.

temporal arbitrage Arbitrage in which the two markets traded are separated by time.

tenants Farm operators who do not own the land they use.

tight monetary policy A policy of slow growth of the money supply designed to restrain the economy and prevent or reduce inflation.

time deposits Account balances in savings accounts.

time utility Utility created by storage activities.

time value of money Because of the opportunity cost, money received today has a greater value than money received in the future.

tombstone An announcement in the newspaper that a corporation is selling shares of its stock to the public.

total cost All costs of producing a given level of output. The sum of fixed and variable costs.

total expense ratio All per-share expenses of a mutual fund's manager and advisor expressed as a percent of the NAV of the fund.

total fixed cost All costs associated with the bundle of fixed factors. Fixed costs do not change as the level of output changes.

total product Relationship between variable input and output.

total revenue Total receipts from the sale of the output or product. Total revenue is equal to the price of the product times number of units sold.

total variable cost All costs associated with the variable input at a given level of output.

trade balance Value of a country's exports minus imports.

transferable pollution rights Pollution discharge permits for a specific quantity of discharge per unit of time. The permits may be transferred (i.e., sold) from one producer to another, but the total amount of discharge remains constant.

trusts Noncompete agreements among oligopoly firms.

typology A system developed by the USDA that classifies farms based on economic size and characteristics of the farm operator.

underwriters Financial firms that buy newly issued stock from corporations in large lots (i.e., wholesale) and sell it to the public in smaller blocks (i.e., retail). The underwriters collect the difference between the wholesale price and the retail price. They also bear the risk that some of the stock may not sell at retail.

util A hypothetical or imaginary unit of utility.

utility The satisfaction created by the consumption of goods and services.

utility map Contour lines of a utility surface.

utility surface A three-dimensional representation of the utility gained by consuming two goods simultaneously.

value investors Investors who buy stock in companies that have share prices close to or below the book value of the company.

variable inputs Inputs whose use rate changes as the output level changes.

variable proportions In the short run as additional units of the variable input are used, the ratio or proportion of variable to fixed inputs changes.

vertical integration The combination of different businesses at different stages of the production/marketing sequence under a single management.

Wall Street A common reference to financial markets in general. Wall Street, in New York City, is the location of the New York Stock Exchange and many other major financial institutions.

wealth Total value of the stock of factors of production at a point in time.

welfare The well-being or self-interest of an individual.

World Trade Organization (WTO) Current version of GATT, which includes trade in agriculture, services and intellectual property.

INDEX